History of Psychology thro

Volume Two of *The History of Psychology through Symbols* continues a groundbreaking approach of using symbols to deepen the understanding of psychological history as well as the importance of how one lives, an emphasis on engagement with symbols and with specific exercises, called emancipatory opportunities, to apply the lessons of psychological history to daily life.

From the birth of modern psychology in the laboratory of Wilhelm Wundt, Volume Two discusses how the early theories of voluntarism, structuralism, evolution, and pragmatism influenced the modern development of psychology. The importance of making unconscious shadow forces in science conscious is explored through the impact of the eugenic movement, the controversies surrounding the development of psychological testing, and current research biases in psychology. Volume Two describes how clinical psychology emerged as a powerful profession in mental health care. The Four Forces of Psychology are explored through their natural and hermeneutic science influences. Psychoanalytic and Jungian analytical psychology comprise the first force, behaviorism the second force, humanistic-existential the third force, and transpersonal psychology the fourth force that includes a groundbreaking discussion of psychedelic history and research that could revolutionize mental health and drug and alcohol treatment. Rejecting that science transcends historical events, this volume provides a political, socioeconomic, and cultural context for modern psychology and all Four Forces of Psychology.

This book is ideal for those seeking a dynamic and engaging way of learning about or teaching the history of psychology and would also be of interest to students, practitioners, and scholars of science, philosophy, history and systems, religious studies, art, and mental health and drug and alcohol treatment, as well as those interested in applying the lessons of history to daily life.

James L. Broderick, PhD, ABPP, is Board Certified in Clinical Psychology and currently in private practice in Santa Barbara, California. He is the former Chair of the Clinical Psychology Program and current adjunct professor at Pacifica Graduate Institute, Carpinteria, California; he was formerly the director of Mental Health and Drug and Alcohol services in Shasta and Santa Barbara Counties in California. Website: newlifesb.com

"Jim Broderick's *The History of Psychology through Symbols* is a radically original and deeply thoughtful way of creatively reimagining a story that we tend to see as hum-drum and all-too-familiar."

Christine Downing, *author of* Mythopoetic Musings

"Long fascinated by the analysis of myth, symbol, and story-telling in understanding the human psyche, I approached *The History of Psychology through Symbols* by Jim Broderick with great interest. I was rewarded with an incredibly original, evocative, and encyclopedic yet highly readable work that employs the very medium he analyzes – the experience and meaning of symbols. Charting its political, historical, and socioeconomic evolution, Dr. Broderick invites the reader to explore the power of symbol from the earliest religions to modern psychology. It is with great pleasure that I recommend this book to all who share the enchantment of the symbol-producing brain."

John C. Robinson, **PhD, DMin**, *author*: Death of a Hero, Birth of the Soul; What Aging Men Want: The Odyssey as a Parable of Male Aging; Bedtime Stories for Elders: What Fairy Tales Can Teach Us About the New Aging

"Dr. Broderick's History of Psychology through Symbols does exactly what we would want from a history of psychology, it awakens our faith in the future. As a lover of history and teacher of the history of psychology, I have wanted a textbook that offers a rich description of psychological history but that is also inspirational and engaging, showing us (clinicians, educators, depth practitioners) opportunities to move into a shared, creative future.

His analysis integrates the history of individual experience within a cultural context that accounts for the emancipatory interests of genuine science while maintaining the creative energies necessary to help psychology find its own voice amongst other important disciplines. His writing style is fluid, compelling, and inviting all at the same time. This is truly a user-friendly approach to our shared history and is much needed. It is an encyclopedia without sounding like one."

Peter T Dunlap, PhD. Awakening our Faith in the Future: The Advent of Psychological Liberalism. Co-chair Clinical Psychology, Pacifica Graduate Institute.
Carpinteria, California

History of Psychology through Symbols

From Reflective Study to Active Engagement

Volume 2: Modern Development

James L. Broderick

NEW YORK AND LONDON

Designed cover image: © Getty
Illustrations by Danuta Bennett, PhD

First published 2024
by Routledge
605 Third Avenue, New York, NY 10158

and by Routledge
4 Park Square, Milton Park, Abingdon, Oxon, OX14 4RN

Routledge is an imprint of the Taylor & Francis Group, an informa business

© 2024 James L. Broderick

The right of James L. Broderick to be identified as author of this work has been asserted in accordance with sections 77 and 78 of the Copyright, Designs and Patents Act 1988.

All rights reserved. No part of this book may be reprinted or reproduced or utilised in any form or by any electronic, mechanical, or other means, now known or hereafter invented, including photocopying and recording, or in any information storage or retrieval system, without permission in writing from the publishers.

Trademark notice: Product or corporate names may be trademarks or registered trademarks, and are used only for identification and explanation without intent to infringe.

ISBN: 978-1-032-54335-2 (hbk)
ISBN: 978-1-032-53978-2 (pbk)
ISBN: 978-1-003-42473-4 (ebk)

DOI: 10.4324/9781003424734

Typeset in Times New Roman
by KnowledgeWorks Global Ltd.

To my wife, Janness Broderick, whose love has changed my life and whose support for this book was always unwavering. To my late cousin, Vickie Laboto, whose struggles with mental illness inspired my work as a psychologist and my call in the text for a radical reform of the mental health system. Finally, to my deceased parents, Jim and Kay Broderick, who provided the support to explore the world without fear and to my sister, Cheryl Tolin, who always supported following my dreams.

Contents

Acknowledgments   xi

1 Symbols of the Birth of Modern Psychology: Voluntarism, Functionalism,
the Darwinian Revolution, Eugenics, and Clinical Psychology   1

Introduction 1
  The Inspiration 1
  A Dynamic Broad-Based Profession 1
  Learning from History – A Warning 3
Modern Psychology 4
  Historical Analysis of the Birth of Modern Psychology 4
  Voluntarism 5
  Structuralism 8
  Functionalism 10
  Evolution 13
  Darwinian Revolution 15
  Eugenics 17
  Psychology and the Brain 21
  Birth of Objective Psychological Testing 23
  IQ Testing 26
  Birth of Projective Psychological Testing 30
  Birth of Clinical Psychology and the American Psychological Association 36
  Emancipatory Opportunities in the Birth of Psychology 42
Questions 1 44
Universal Meanings of Chapter Symbols 44
References 45

2 Symbols of Freudian and Relational Psychoanalysis:
The First Force in Psychology   49

Introduction 49
  The Four Forces of Psychology 49
  The First Force – Psychoanalysis 50
Freudian Psychoanalysis 50
  Historical Analysis 50
  Natural Science Influence 56

Hermeneutic Influence 61
Freudian Psychoanalytic Psychology 66
Emancipatory Opportunities in Freudian Psychoanalysis 76
Relational Psychoanalysis 78
Historical Analysis 78
Natural Science Influences 82
Hermeneutic Influences 86
Relational Psychoanalytic Psychology 88
Emancipatory Opportunities in Relational Psychoanalysis 97
Questions 2 100
Universal Meanings of the Chapter Symbols 100
References 101

3 The World of Symbol – Jungian Analytical Psychology: First Force in Psychology   105

Introduction 105
World of Symbol 105
Jung and Post-Jungians 106
The Historic Trip to Clark University 107
Post-Freudian and Jungian History 107
Jungian Analytical Psychology 109
Historical Analysis 109
Natural Science Interest 119
Hermeneutic Science Interest 127
Jungian Psychology 131
The Practice of Jungian Psychology 145
Emancipatory Opportunities in Jungian Psychology 154
Questions 3 155
Universal Meanings of the Chapter Symbols 156
References 156

4 Symbols of Behaviorism, Neobehaviorism, and Cognitive Behavioral Psychology: The Second Force in Psychology   161

Introduction 161
Three Generations of Behavioral Psychology 161
Behavioral Psychological Movement 163
Historical Analysis of the Behavioral Psychological Movement 163
Behaviorism 170
Natural Science Interest in Behaviorism 170
Hermeneutic Science Interest in Behaviorism 184
Behavioral Psychology 187
Emancipatory Opportunities in Behaviorism 189
Neobehaviorism 190
Natural Science Interest in Neobehaviorism 190

Contents ix

  Hermeneutic Science Interest in Neobehaviorism 195
  Neobehavioral Psychology 197
  Emancipatory Opportunities in Neobehaviorism 201
  Cognitive Behavioral Psychology 202
    Natural Science Interest in Cognitive Behavioral Psychology 202
    Hermeneutic Interest in Cognitive Behavioral Psychology 208
    Cognitive Behavioral Psychology 213
    Emancipatory Opportunities in Cognitive Behavioral Psychology 222
  Questions 4 223
  Universal Meanings of Chapter Symbols 223
  References 224

5 Symbols of Humanistic-Existential Psychology: The Third
  Force in Psychology   229

  Introduction 229
    Cultural Integration 230
  Humanistic-Existential Psychology 231
    Historical Analysis of Humanistic-Existential Psychology 231
    Natural Science Interest in Humanistic-Existential Psychology 240
    Hermeneutic Science Interest in Humanistic-Existential Psychology 246
    Humanistic-Existential Psychology 267
    *Emancipatory Opportunities in Humanistic-Existential
      Psychology 277*
  Questions 5 279
  Universal Meanings of Chapter Symbols 280
  References 281

6 Symbols of Transpersonal Psychology – A Return to the Axial
  Age and Beyond: The Fourth Force in Psychology   285

  Introduction 285
    The Transpersonal Renaissance and the Axial Age 285
    Criticism 286
    Transpersonal Psychology, Religion, and Spirituality 287
  Transpersonal Psychology 288
    Historical Analysis of Transpersonal Psychology 288
    Natural Science Interest in Transpersonal Psychology 294
    Hermeneutic Science Interest in Transpersonal Psychology 297
  Transpersonal Psychology: A Return to the Axial Age 308
    Greek Philosophy 308
    Zoroastrianism 310
    Hinduism 312
    Buddhism 317

x Contents

    Psychedelics and Transpersonal Psychology – Natural and Hermeneutic
      Science Integration 319
      The Psychedelic Renaissance – Paradigm Shift 319
      Unified Psychedelic Theory and the Psychedelics in the Axial Age 320
    The Major Psychedelics 322
      Psilocybin 323
      LSD-25 (Lysergic Acid Diethylamide) 324
      Mescaline (3,4,5-trimethoxyphenethylamine) 325
      MDMA (3,4-Methylenedioxymethamphetamine) 326
      DMT (N, N-2-Dimethyltryptamine) 326
      Ayahuasca 327
      5MeO-DMT (5-methoxy- N,N-Dimethyltryptamine) 328
    The Four Historic Psychedelic Periods 328
      The Four Historic Psychedelic Periods 328
      Psychotomimetic Period – Psychedelics and Psychosis 329
      Spiritual Emergency Counseling 329
      Psycholytic Period – Psychedelics and the Unconscious 330
      Underground Period – Psychedelics and Government Oversight 333
      Bioenergetic Analysis and Holotropic Breathwork 335
      Psychedelic Renaissance Period – Psychedelics and Clinical Efficacy 335
      Emancipatory Opportunities in Transpersonal Psychology 337
    Questions 6 340
    Universal Meanings of Chapter Symbols 340
    References 341

Index   348

Acknowledgments

I would like to take this opportunity to acknowledge and thank my wife, Janness Broderick, LCSW, for her ongoing support and love throughout the three-year writing process. I was also fortunate to find an incredible artist, Danuta Bennett, who embraced my vision and worked tirelessly to develop incredible artistic symbols that inspire an experience of history beyond my words. The Pacifica Graduate Institute, particularly mentors Allen Bishop and Christine Downing, who always supported my work as Chair and professor in the Clinical Psychology Program and to the students in my history and systems classes who encouraged the development of a more dynamic textbook. My writing editor, Barbara Brown, who gave me the confidence to write a book that was not only complex and detailed, but hopefully inspirational, visionary, and engaging. To my Santa Barbara "brothers" Michael Kramer and Wayne Hewitt, who provided love and support throughout the challenging times of writing a two-volume textbook. None of this would have been possible without the encouragement and patience of Adam Woods, the Editor at Routledge of Contextual and Historical Influences in Psychology (CHIP).

Figure 1.0

1 Symbols of the Birth of Modern Psychology

Voluntarism, Functionalism, the Darwinian Revolution, Eugenics, and Clinical Psychology

Introduction

The Inspiration

The Renaissance, the Scientific Revolution, and Enlightenment laid the foundation for the birth of psychology. Those movements inspired by the Greek scholars immortalized in the *School of Athens* fresco painted by Raphael. For centuries, philosophers and theologians had dominated the conversation about human behavior. They based their theories on philosophic principles or religious beliefs. Although a rebirth was occurring in science, something was still missing. Medicine took the body and religion took the soul to study. Psychology filled the void and took the *mind*, symbolized by its beginning in a laboratory. A new psychological science created to understand and change human behavior from the findings in the new experimental laboratories, research institutes, clinical treatment and psychological testing rooms.

A Dynamic Broad-Based Profession

The goal of this chapter is to provide the foundational theories and applied practices upon which modern psychology was built, beginning with the voluntarism of Wilhelm Wundt, the *structuralism* of Edward Titchener, the *functionalism* of William James, and the evolutionary theories of Darwin. These theories inspired psychologists to focus on the nature of *intelligence* to ask whether intelligence was inherited or determined by societal forces, which led to the ongoing *nature/nurture debate* in psychology. Beyond academic debates, psychologists began to measure intelligence by developing *psychological testing*; eventually, this became the *Intelligent Quotient* (I.Q.) score that remains the standard for the determination of intelligence.

On July 8, 1892, Granville Stanley Hall, professor of psychology and president of Clark University, invited 26 American psychologists to join the American Psychological Association. Although a rift developed between experimental and applied psychologists, there was agreement that the goal of psychology was to alleviate human suffering and social problems and have practical relevance to educators, businessmen, "asylum" superintendents, and counselors (Pickren & Rutherford, 2017). From that day in 1892, The American Psychological Association has grown from the 26 to over *130,000 members*.

2 *Symbols of the Birth of Modern Psychology*

Figure 1.1

Against initial resistance from some experimental psychologists, applied psychology, later clinical psychology, was born by the work of an original APA member, Lightner Witner, who first coined the term "clinical psychology" at the University of Pennsylvania. In 1896, Witner started the first university-based *psychological clinic*. To provide a more complete clinical picture beyond intelligence testing, by the 1940s, projective and personality testing emerged, especially the *Rorschach Test*, expanding testing repertoire to create a more comprehensive clinical assessment. By the late twentieth century, clinical psychology became a leading profession in health care, challenging psychiatry for preeminence, even procuring prescription privileges in a few states.

It has been said that history is written by the victors, this is also true in psychology. Although schooled and supportive of empirical and natural science methods, most of the great contributors who birthed the new psychological discipline believed if psychology was destined to emancipate humanity from ignorance and suffering, it would be necessary for psychology to develop a vision beyond the limitations of empiricism. This view started with Wilhelm Wundt, the father of modern psychology, who advocated for a *cultural psychology* and continued with William James, the father of American psychology, whose work inspired the development of *transpersonal psychology*.

Symbols of the Birth of Modern Psychology   3

Learning from History – A Warning

With all the progress and excitement about "the birth," there is also a warning and reminder that unconscious shadow forces are always present. This chapter will show how denial of shadow impacted the *Eugenics movement*, causing serious harm, especially to immigrants, and the mentally and developmentally disabled. Because of how an I.Q. score can impact the life of an individual, it is necessary to understand what history teaches about its misuse. This includes the controversial and disturbing *Bell Curve: Intelligence and Class Structure* research, which found that I.Q. determines who controls the power structure in American society.

Psychology has provided valuable psychological research that has addressed many major societal issues. For instance, the Stanley Milgram *Obedience to Authority* research, even with its ethical concerns, has shown that beyond Nazism, the dark unconscious shadow forces still exist in the human psyche. The *Dodo Bird Verdict* and the *Cyril Burt Affair* raise serious concerns about the shadows of researcher bias.

This chapter will explore how the good intentions of the early psychologists ignored an analysis of the shadow elements of their work personified by the famous Samuel Adams quote: "The road to hell is paved with good intentions."

Figure 1.2

Modern Psychology

Historical Analysis of the Birth of Modern Psychology

Political Systems

The birth of modern psychology occurred during the political ascendency of Darwinian and eugenic thought, which has often been applied to the role of government in the modern age. Since evolutionary theory has proven that nature evolved without human intervention, it made sense that the same could apply to political affairs. The dark shadow of *social Darwinism* emerged as a political force because of the belief that governments should model evolution and avoid interference and take *a laissez-faire* approach to governance. When Herbert Spencer, the esteemed English philosopher, who laid the foundation for social Darwinism, visited the United States in 1882, he was received as a hero. Andrew Carnegie, a leading industrialist, philanthropist of that time, and one of the richest men in American history, declared that evolution had now replaced institutional religion (Fuller, 2017).

Along with the eugenics movement, social Darwinism provided a perfect political model for capitalism and American individualism. The view supported by many psychologists throughout the early twentieth century was that the weak and vulnerable were inhibiting societal progress and that competition was not only natural; it was also an essential dynamic for the strong to persevere over the weak and disabled. *Every man for himself* was simply a natural part of the evolutionary process. The theory of social Darwinism and eugenics came to justify imperialism, colonialism, racism, and other shadow psychologies around the world because of the belief that some are naturally better fit to lead the world. The political remnants of social Darwinism and eugenics remain in political debates in American politics concerning the role of government in supporting social programs that help the most vulnerable and disabled.

Socioeconomic Systems

Most of early the leaders in the birth of modern psychology came from wealth and well-educated families. Francis Galton, Alfred Binet, and William James were independently wealthy. The father of Charles Darwin was a physician, and his mother came from a famous family known for the manufacture of Chinaware. In the family of Wilhelm Wundt, there were physicians, scientists, governmental officials, historians, and theologians, including two presidents of the University of Heidelberg. These pioneers were descendants of socioeconomic privilege and status that provided economic security and the ability to pursue their academic careers without significant financial concerns.

It is not surprising that early psychologists did not attend to socioeconomic issues, believing that their work was not based on values but facts. Since they lived in a financially secure world, there was no economic incentive to address or understand the impact of their theories on those with low income. In the name of eugenics, many questioned the value of social programs that might provide economic security. Social Darwinism allowed American capitalists to espouse the belief that class differences were natural and any reforms tampered with the natural economic order. To the psychologists who supported the eugenic movement, poverty was a sign of being unfit and wealth was a sign of evolutionary success, not greed or economic exploitation. For decades, the socioeconomic support systems for those with low income, disabilities, and older adults were dismal. It was not until the 1960s, after the decline of eugenics, that Medicare, Medicaid, and Great Society legislation passed Congress, which provided economic support to the most vulnerable in American society. However, America remains one of the only industrial nations in the world not to provide a comprehensive national healthcare system, which causes economic, social, and psychological distress on millions of American families.

Cultural Systems

The evolutionary theory of Darwin impacted all aspects of culture throughout the world, especially the cultural roles of men and women in society. Placing biology as the primary driver of evolution had a profound impact on the psychological and cultural relationships between the sexes. Darwin believed men were intellectually superior to women because throughout evolution men learned to use tools and weapons. Because of their biological nature, women had the primary responsibility for motherhood and the task to produce as many children as possible for the survival of the human race. In *The Sexes throughout Nature*, Antoinette Brown Blackwell (1875), an early female critic of Darwin and Spencer, wrote that their theories "defrauded womanhood" because their theories placed tremendous limitations on the role of women in society and negated any possibility for a healthy relationship between the sexes.

The subtitle of the *Origins of Species by Natural Selection* was *Or the Preservation of Favored Races in the Struggle for Life* (Darwin, 1859/2017). Although Darwin was a passionate opponent of slavery, he viewed the world through a white superiority perspective, ignoring the shadow elements of his racial theory. Darwin viewed the white race, especially the Europeans, as superior to the Black race. The so-called primitive people of the Third World provided the evolutionary proof to Darwin that primates were the foundation of human evolution. In the racial hierarchy, the Black race is inferior because they are more connected to their primate cousins than to the white civilized world.

Later in his career, Wilhelm Wundt advocated for a cultural psychology, a *volkerpsychologie*, loosely translated as *folk psychology* (Wundt, 1916/2016). His cultural psychology was rooted in the Enlightenment and, although mostly known for being the founder of experimental psychology, his views on culture have generally been neglected because folk psychology does not fit neatly into the current dominate empirical natural science paradigm. Wundt viewed cultural psychology as essential to understanding higher consciousness. In the tradition of *hermeneutics* interpretation to search for deeper meaning, Wundt provided a model for the psychological study of culture by incorporating historical analysis and natural observation in all aspects of culture, including language, the arts, mythology, religion, and ancient cultures (Wundt, 1916/2016).

Voluntarism

Wilhelm Wundt

Wilhelm Wundt (1832–1920) is considered the father of modern psychology, particularly experimental *psychology*. He was the first scientist of his day to separate psychology from philosophy and biology. In 1879, he founded the first department of psychology at the *University of Leipzig*. Wilhelm Wundt left an unparalleled impact on psychology. In 1991, writing in the *American Psychologist*, the leading journal of the American Psychological Association, American historians ranked Wundt as the first in "all-time eminence" in the history of psychology. William James and Sigmund Freud were ranked a distant second and third (Korn, Davis, & Davis, 1991).

Wundt would disagree with the great scientists of the Scientific Revolution and the Enlightenment, like Galileo and Kant, who believed psychology could never be a science. Over the objections of most scientists of his day, Wundt was a visionary who saw psychology as a special discipline. He rejected the British and French empiricist view of the mind and believed that consciousness and mental processes could be studied scientifically.

Voluntarism became the first school of thought in experimental psychology, a psychology based on immediate voluntary experience of will, choice, and purpose. Wundt believed the distinction between a *pure introspection*, unstructured observation, from an *experimental introspection*, which was structured, was the key to a psychological science. This was

6 Symbols of the Birth of Modern Psychology

not the St. Augustine introspection to find God or the Descartes introspection to find certain truth, or the *naïve introspection* of Kant who argued against the measurability of consciousness and criticized introspection as unstructured self-observation by independently thinking people. Wundt strongly disagreed that introspection could not be measured because a scientific psychology could develop a method to examine introspection *empirically*. This would be done by training individuals in self-observation under strict experimental control.

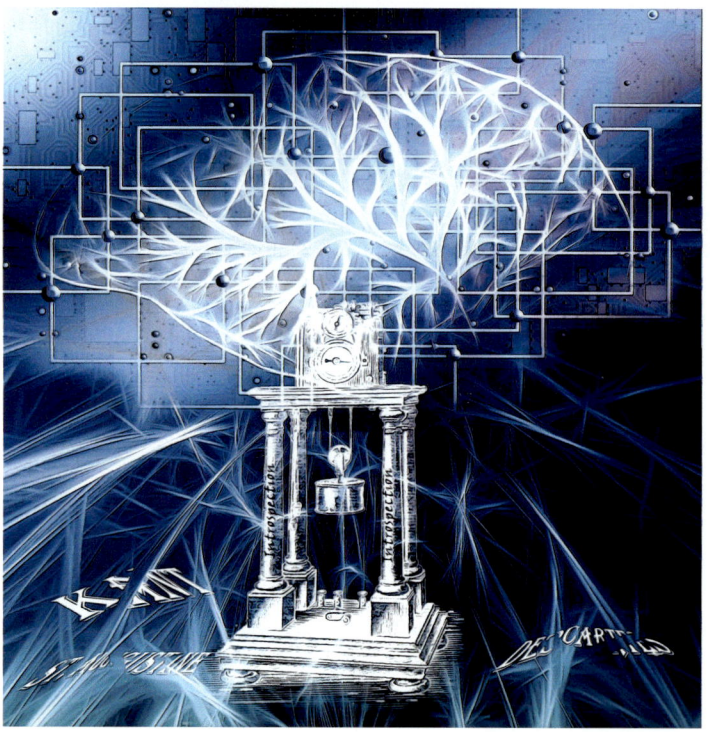

Figure 1.3

The *chronoscope* in a laboratory became the symbol of the birth of modern psychology. The first experiment was completed by a student trained using a chronoscope. This was a brass clock-like apparatus with a hanging weight and two dials to measure the reaction time of the student. The setup also consisted of a sounder and a metal stand with an elevated arm from which a ball would fall onto the platform and a telegrapher key for the student to press. This was wired together with five pieces of apparatus, the circuitry no more complicated than a present-day train set. Wundt; G. Stanley Hall, the founder of the APA; and *Max Friedrich*, a leading behaviorist, studied introspection by recording the time between the recognition of the ball hitting the platform and the student pressing the telegraph key (Bringman, Balance, William, et al, 1975).

> Although no one knows who made the ball drop or who hit the telegrapher key or who recorded the response time, modern psychology was born, unheralded, on a dark December day in 1879 in a shabby building in a laboratory at the University of Leipzig.

As the experiment was completed, Wundt viewed the long road from Thales to Kant to prove the existence of the mind had, with all its limitations, been proven. Mental processes could now be empirically measured through experimental processes which would make psychology a science. To many psychologists, the experimental psychology of Wundt freed psychology of metaphysics and philosophy. Critics argued that Wundt created a laboratory psychology without soul, without connection to the real world, a new discipline with no real interest in a psychology that could transform the world.

Wundt viewed the brain as being stimulated by sensations (Wundt, 1910). There was nothing in the mind that was not first in the senses, except the mind itself. Per the *Tridimensional Wundtian Theory of Feeling,* senses cause three types of feelings: pleasantness and unpleasantness, excitement and calm, and strain and relaxation. The mind processes sensations and feelings through the mental activities of *perception* and *apperception*. When the brain is stimulated by the senses, a perception occurs and the mind initially reacts passively without individual control. Because Wundt believed the mind was active and could only attend to one perception at a time, after perception, the mind became *apperceptive,* as in the Wundtian experiment, attending to what was under mental control. The Wundtian view of the perceptive and apperceptive elements of the mind led to the school of voluntarism, which would dominate early modern psychology.

Initially, Wundt believed in an unconscious. In *Why Did Wundt Abandon his Early Theory of the Unconscious,* Araujo (2012) explained that the reason was twofold: one psychological and one philosophical. Dissatisfied with the predominate view in anatomical physiology that sensations were immediately conscious, Wundt initially felt that there was an unconscious separation between sensation and perception. He abandoned this idea because he believed within the senses there was immediate unity and synthesis between sensation and perception, making an unconscious process irrelevant.

To abandon the unconscious in psychology, Wundt also turned to philosophy. He applied the philosophical critique of *ontology to* explain the limitations of *voluntarism* (Wundt, 1910). Ontological thought is the branch of philosophy that studies concepts of higher consciousness, such as existence, being, and becoming, which belong to metaphysics. Wundt believed thoughts in the mind do not exist in the physical world and therefore higher mental and intellectual functions could not be measured. This included concepts like the unconscious, soul, the existence of God, or any phenomenon not connected to the senses. He may have also abandoned the idea because psychology was striving to be recognized as a science and recognizing an unconscious mind would have been viewed as a form of metaphysics. The rejection of the unconscious by Wundt created early divisions between psychology and psychoanalysis.

Wundt would remain a strong advocate for psychology to remain rooted in philosophy. In *Psychology's Struggle for Existence* (Wundt, 1913/2013), Wundt summarized many of his beliefs, ranging from the strengths of the emerging experimental psychology movement to his view of the limitations of empirical science. Because his view of psychology was ultimately based in European rationalism, not American empiricism, he was concerned about the divorce between philosophy and psychology, which he believed would permanently damage both disciplines (Araujo, 2016). He was particularly concerned about this strict separation between psychology and philosophy in America and warned against Europeans following the American model of experimental psychology. He believed the American model lacked intellectual diversity by the rejection of its philosophical roots.

Although most of his fame resulted from developing experimental psychology, later in his career, he believed in a psychology beyond the laboratory, a volkerpsychologie, meaning a cultural psychology studied through historical analysis and naturalistic observation. (Wundt, 1916/2016). This passion came later in his career because it would have been very difficult during his time in history to advocate for scientific methods beyond experimental psychology because of his fight for the recognition of psychology as a science. However, after creating the new

8 Symbols of the Birth of Modern Psychology

discipline of psychology, Wundt would often criticize many of the ideas that made him famous (Wundt, 1916/2016). It remains difficult for traditional psychologists to reconcile how Wundt could discover both experimental psychology and advocate for volkerpsychologie. Which expanded psychology beyond empiricism toward the study of higher consciousness by analyzing and observing the cultural practices of religion, the arts, history, language, law, and mythology.

Structuralism

Edward Titchener

Edward Titchener (1867–1927) translated many of the works of Wundt into English and brought voluntarism to Cornell University in the United States, creating at the time the largest doctoral program in psychology. He was especially interested in the Wundtian concepts of introspective, apperception, and the structures of consciousness.

Figure 1.4

Titchener (1915/2018) attempted to classify the structures of consciousness by symbolically modeling chemistry. As the chemist breaks down chemicals to its component elements, like water into hydrogen and oxygen, Titchener believed that a similar process could occur by breaking down the structures of sensations and thoughts that compose the mind. Wundt wanted to explain consciousness while through structuralism, Titchener wanted to describe the structures of consciousness. He viewed the introspection of Wundt as inadequate, in need of much more structure. In response, Titchener developed intense training sessions on introspection with students, providing detailed manuals and many practicing drills. Without these trainings, Titchener worried there would be *stimulus error,* which would not adequately distinguish sensation from perception.

For instance, calling an object "an apple" was a stimulus error because it was a perception not a sensation response. He trained his students to report the sensation response through *systematic experimental introspection*, an educated and structured introspection. This process avoided phenomenological descriptions because Titchener believed attention was based on a contiguity of sensations, not singular voluntary responses. For instance, two sounds enhance music, and two colors enhance each other; structuralism advancing the concept of *associationism* in psychology. (Titchener, 1915/2018).

In trying to understand the structure of the mind, Titchener accounted for over 40,000 sensations, 30,000 related to vision and 12,000 to audition. Structuralism tried to study empirically what philosophers had tried to unsuccessfully explain for centuries. To totally focus on the physical, empirical world, Titchener exposed the great weakness of introspection that retrospective reports from memory were unreliable and susceptible to individual difference.

As initial psychological pioneers, Wundt and Titchener had solidified empiricism as the basic methodological orientation of psychology. They also left a deep shadow that would continue to plague modern psychology. For instance, Wundt and Titchener resisted the idea of an applied psychology. Although Wundt wanted psychology to expand by the inclusion of cultural studies, he rejected any ideas about psychology becoming an applied clinical profession.

Titchener was even more hostile. By creating an *Experimentalists* group at Cornell, he excluded anyone interested in applied psychology and resisted becoming a member of the new American Psychological Association because some of its members had interest in applied psychology. Although Titchener supported women at many levels, his Experimentalists group did not allow women membership because women were viewed as too emotional, not committed to higher learning, and not prone to swear or smoke.

At Cornell in 1894, Margaret Washburn became the first graduate student of Titchener and the first woman to be granted a doctoral degree in psychology. Cornell, an early leader in the women's movement, was also a leading university for women to attain doctoral degrees in psychology. In 1921, Margaret Washburn became the first woman and second president of the APA. She was one of the first women psychologists to study animal consciousness and behavior in a laboratory. She found that learning was incremental and occurred automatically, with no mediation and discovered principles of learning that applied equally to both human and animals.

Voluntarism and structuralism dominated psychology during its early years as a developing science. Structuralism died a quick death because it was simply too complex. Introspection was discredited because of its dependence on retrospective memory. Although encouraged by the results of laboratory experiments, there was increasing interest in psychology solving human problems that were being ignored in voluntarism and structuralism. The voluntarism

10 Symbols of the Birth of Modern Psychology

of Wundt would live on through functionalism, moving psychology from "what is" to "what for." As the Europeans explored expanding psychology in academic settings, in America, reacting to the teachings of Wundt and Titchener, a whole new way to view psychology was emerging.

Functionalism

The Pragmatism of William James

Upon his arrival in the United States, Wundtian psychology was broadened beyond the laboratory by William James (1842–1912). In *Principles of Psychology*, James (1890/2017) rejected the Wundtian psychology that viewed experience as separate sensations bound by associations. For James, experience flows like a river, a *stream of consciousness*. In this way, James channeled Heraclitan philosophy and the philosophy of an ever-changing world of you cannot step in the same river twice. Functionalism, a counter to voluntarism, symbolized a new psychology flowing from inside the confines of a laboratory to the outside world.

Functionalism is concerned about what consciousness does rather than what consciousness is; function is more important than content. Consciousness results when habit and instinct are not enough; something more needs to be done to adapt to the environment. James was an

Figure 1.5

empiricist; in fact, some believe he developed the first psychological laboratory and is the real founder of modern psychology or at least the father of American psychology. The empiricism of James is not Wundtian. He was a *radical empiricist* who maintained that every human experience is uniquely different. One experience is not superior to another, which made James critical of associationism, which he viewed as based on corpuscular and mental elements held together by repetition. If you give seven people one word of a sentence, no one will be able to know the complete meaning of the sentence. Every idea is uniquely owned; the mind is not an empty container filled by the agglomeration of associated experiences. A thought is not a thought, rather it is *my* thought. The experiences of the external world are uniquely selected, not universal experiences identical to everyone.

Our unique responses to the world result in the development of our individual personality, which consists of many selves. The *material self* is everything material in our lives, which includes our body, our family, and our property. The *social self* is how we are known to other people. The *spiritual self* is conscious of being connected to something greater than ourselves. These selves are integrated into the *empirical self*, which is our identity, and how we define ourselves. Considering his focus on *personality development*, James provided an early definition of *self-esteem,* which he defined as the ratio of things attempted to things achieved. He became one of the first psychologists to emphasize the importance of *self-esteem* for functioning effectively in the world.

James was amazed that Wundtian theory was so popular in psychology since nobody ever thinks or exists like in laboratory experiments. Since the laboratory became a powerful new symbol of a scientific psychology, James utilized the laboratory to expose the limitations of experimental methodologies. He called his critique *the psychologist's fallacy*. This is the fallacy that mental processes operate in the real world in the same manner as in a laboratory experiment. As an example, to understand memory, repeatedly giving a subject several words or materials to study and then testing their recall assumes that repetition is what creates memory. Even though James did not believe this is how people create memories in the real world, he did not advocate for the abandonment of the laboratory. He challenged psychologists to understand the limitations of the experimental method and develop laboratory methodologies that mirror how memory and other mental activity occurs in the real world.

James provided a value-neutral distinction between souls that are healthy and sick. The former soul views the world as basically good. The latter soul cannot overcome the melancholy, the depression, and the belief that the world is basically evil. *Conversion* is the key if one is to experience their own unique religious experience. To explain conversion, James utilizes the symbol of *mechanical equilibrium*. During a conversion, which is necessary for a true personal religious experience, there is incredible emotional excitement mixed with an equally emotional release of "letting go." This results in a *net force*, the secondary Newtonian *law of motion* of physics, which is the force and mass of an object being equal.

For James, healthy mindedness *religion* was the main contribution of America because religious views emanated from the *transcendentalism* of *Ralph Waldo Emerson, Walt Whitman,* and the *Christian science movement* of *Mary Baker Edy. Christian scientists* believe that truth comes from the Word of God and that Christ, the savior, atoned for the sins of world with love and provided humanity with the potential of reconciliation with their God, which meant sin and evil no longer exist and humanity is liberated.

12 *Symbols of the Birth of Modern Psychology*

Figure 1.6

James attempted to be a bridge between psychology and religion. James embraced the *New Thought Movement* based on the teachings of *Phineas Quimby* (1802–1866), a *Mesmerist* healer who preached that illness originated in the mind and was the result of an erroneous belief system. Any illness could be overcome with openness to the wisdom of God. During the early twentieth century, the *New Mind Movement* created the *Mind Cure*. This cure was the treatment preference for medical problems and total rejection of the godless medical profession. In *The Varieties of Religious Experience,* James (1902/2016) writes that *Mind Cure* treatment was based on a variety of important religious and philosophical sources that included the four Christian Gospels of transcendentalism, idealism, spiritualism, and Hinduism. What appealed most to James was the emotional appeal of Mind Cure because he viewed the treatment as inspirational, with the all-saving power and attitude of the healthy religious minded. The Mind Cure, unlike medicine, replaced the human anxieties of doubt and fear with the efficacy of hope, courage, and trust.

One of his most important theoretical contributions to psychology was his book, *Pragmatism* (James, 1902/2000); the work most often associated with the philosophy of pragmatism. James uses pragmatism to understand two different personality types in psychology. James defines two types of personalities, which has been a cause of historic tension and conflict within psychology. The *tenderminded personalities* are typically clinical psychologists; comfortable being emotional, irrational, idealistic, principle-oriented, idealistic, religious, and dogmatic. The *toughminded personalities* are typically research psychologists, who tend to be rational, fact-oriented, empiricist, irreligious, pessimistic, skeptical, and fatalistic. Pragmatism is the belief that all human knowledge and science should ultimately be judged on its practical value and usefulness because any other pursuit might be interesting and enlightening but will have little impact on overcoming ignorance and human suffering and improving the human condition.

The legacy of James is based on the hope that the emerging discipline of psychology would realize that the usefulness of this new profession was dependent on the success of both the tender and tough-minded psychologists because both have value and practical usefulness and need each other if psychology is to have the impact on the world that he envisioned.

Evolution

Herbert Spencer

William James tried to build many bridges in psychology. He expanded the empiricism of Wundt and attempted to again legitimize the study of philosophy and religion in psychology. He hoped that the different personalities in psychology could learn to live in harmony because he strongly advocated for an applied psychology, a psychology that was useful. But his greatest contribution may have been making psychology attractive to American culture by embracing Darwinian thought. For James, every stimulus in the brain had an adaptive response; every experience had some useful purpose for survival. In the spirit of Darwin, James emphasized *results, not method.* If an idea is not useful, it ultimately becomes insignificant; he possessed a critical-emancipatory attitude by wanting psychology to improve human existence.

With experimental psychologists under the thrall of a reductionistic and atomist science, James instead focused on the evolutionary function of consciousness.

In the evolution of the human species, consciousness is ever present with the intent to survive. The intent to survive is what causes consciousness. Sensations, cognitions, instinct, and habit, all the human physiological responses, were grounded in functional adaptations to the environment.

Evolution is rooted in Greek thought. The Greeks had a rudimentary understanding of evolution, especially the ideas developed by *Anaximander* (495 BCE–435 BCE), the great Greek philosopher and scientist who is credited with the map of the Black Sea. He hypothesized that life began in the sea. The first living creatures were born in moisture and enclosed in bark. As the sea evaporated around them, they learned to adapt and survive and become the humans of today. Although interested in what composed the natural world, the great Socratic philosophers did not develop an evolutionary theory. Plato held that there were pure Forms fixed forever. Aristotle observed in the *great chain of being* that each species was fixed and unchanged. The Greeks were more interested in a harmonic rather than an evolutionary view of the world, rather than a world that might be unfixed, evolving, and conflictual.

Even during the Scientific Revolution, there was little interest in evolution because Newtonian science viewed matter as dead and inert and had little interest in how matter evolved. Christian thought based in the biblical *Genesis* maintained that human beings were a divine creation and could only be changed by God. The concept of progress from the Enlightenment and other modern movements created the possibility to view humanity in different ways, opening the door to evolution. As European psychologists were embracing the experimental psychology of Wundt, American psychologists were embracing the pragmatism of James and the new theory of evolution, which provided a practical, less abstract, approach to human psychology.

Although generally rejected during his lifetime, *Jean Lamarck* (1744–1829), a French naturalist, was an early proponent of *biological evolution,* being the first to coin the modern term *biology,* which created the first theoretical framework for evolution. Lamarck believed that matter is alive, intelligent, and purposeful, constantly seeking perfection. Evolution occurs when an organism acquires new ways to adapt to the changing environment. Those that cannot develop new traits produce no offspring and become extinct. Lamarckism, or neo-Lamarckism, is the field of *genetic studies* that continues to exist as a *theory of inheritance of acquired characteristics*. The interest is in soft inheritance, the idea that an organism can pass on traits to its offspring that the parent acquired through use and disuse during their lifetime; or to state in simpler terms, evolution in the moment.

Figure 1.7

As Lamarck discovered that environmental changes were responsible for structural and evolutionary changes in plants and animals, *Herbert Spencer* (1820–1903) applied evolution to humans and the human mind. Spencer believed that matter starts out as an undifferentiated whole and through evolution a complex differentiation occurs. To explain the evolution of the human mind, in *Principles in Psychology*, Spencer (1855) combines Lamarckian thought with *associationism*. In understanding the principles of psychology, Spencer introduces the term *intelligence* that would inspire the study of *intelligence* by psychologists for generations.

Spencer wrote that the brain is what separates humans from other forms of life. The brain integrates experiences and makes associations that are passed on during the evolutionary process. Utilizing the term that will dominate evolutionary theory, survival of the fittest, Spencer (1855) hypothesized that the more intelligent brain makes stronger associations than the weaker brain. This leads to civilized societies dominated by brighter people and uncivilized societies dominated by the less intelligent. This is symbolized by the stronger fish eating the weaker fish, through the evolutionary chain. The concept of the survival of the fittest inspired the political philosophy of *social Darwinism,* which would flourish in the later part of the nineteenth century

Darwinian Revolution

Charles Darwin

Spencer would soon be eclipsed by *Darwinism* because *Charles Darwin* (1809–1882) was perceived more as a scientist and less as a political philosopher. Although controversial as to who is the real founder of evolutionary theory, Darwin stands above all the other theorists. Evolutionary theory revolutionized human psychology because it necessitated a new vision of what it meant to be human because evolution connected human beings not only to the natural world but to their animal ancestors.

Darwin was another ambivalent revolutionary. He began his life with the thought of becoming a minister. However, at 23 years of age, he became interested in studying insects. As an entomologist, Darwin traveled for five years (1831–1836) with Captain Robert Fitz Roy on the ship *Beagle* to Patagonia, Chile, Peru, and the Pacific Islands. Captain Fitz Roy, a devout Christian, wanted a natural scientist to refute evolutionary theory. Later, when Darwin became famous for his theory of evolution, Fitz Roy, despondent about the role he played in the Darwinian revolution, committed suicide. During the fourth year in the *Galapagos,* Darwin noticed that the same insects differed somewhat on each island. He concluded that during the evolutionary process, insects physically changed so they could penetrate the bark of a tree to find food. Some became long and thin and others short and sturdy. To his amazement, he discovered that the same species could make significant physical changes to adapt to their environment.

Darwin was influenced by the economist *Thomas Malthus* (1766–1834). Malthus challenged the Enlightenment view of progress that maintained that the abundance in food production would lead to a higher standard of living for all. In his book *An Essay on the Principle of Population* (Malthus, 1798/2008), Malthus argued that abundance causes populations to grow and lowers the standard of living. Population becomes controlled only after suffering famine and disease by the weaker lower classes.

It took over 20 years after his trip on the *Beagle* to write his epoch book on evolution, *On the Origin of Species by Means of Natural Selection* (Darwin, 1859/2017). Influenced by Malthus and encouraged by another great evolutionist, *Henry Wallace* (1823–1913), Darwin viewed *natural selection* as they key to evolution. By applying the importance of reproduction to evolution, Darwin turned to biology and away from political economics. The concept of natural selection was based on the idea that humans produce more children so that some will survive.

Darwin agreed with the concept of the survival of fittest, that some humans are better equipped to survive. However, his evolutionary theories of adaptation were not based on strength, aggression, or competitiveness. The Enlightenment argument about progress and societal perfection did not appear to be of much interest. For Darwin, evolution "just happens"; there is no specific purpose, no divine plan, nor ultimate meaning that seeks to be discovered or is hidden in nature.

After *On the Origin of Species by Means of Natural Selection* received critical scientific acclaim, Darwin (1871/2004) published *The Descent of Man in Relation to Sex*. This book was controversial and reviled by many, especially in the religious community because it was one thing to connect evolution to plants and animals. It was quite another to say that evolutionary theory also applied to humans. Expanding his theory of natural selection, Darwin added *sexual selection* as another key determinant in human evolution. Darwin defined sexual selection as the biological mechanism by which one chooses their mate for the best reproductive outcome. This reproductive drive creates intense competition between those of the same sex in their attempt to find the best mate that can assure future generational survival.

16 *Symbols of the Birth of Modern Psychology*

Even more controversial was when Darwin linked primates to their human ancestors. Darwin believed that human evolution began with primates and evolved into *Homo sapiens*, highly intelligent primates. As the only extant members of the subtribe hominid family, also known as the great apes, humans gradually developed the human traits of bipedalism, erect posture, language, and sexual selection with other evolving ape hominids. This evolutionary connection between humanity and the animal world was quickly rejected in Christian churches because of the belief that humans were superior and created by God; animals were inferior because God created animals to serve humanity.

If this was not enough for the world to digest, in his book, *The Expression of Emotions*, Darwin (1879/2009) went even further by connecting animal and human emotions. For Darwin, it is only by degrees that one can distinguish the emotional differences between animals and humans. Observing his son, William, he witnessed the remnants of animal emotions necessary for human survival. He recommended that parents attend to the emotional development of their children because of the human connection to their animal roots. Darwin viewed emotions as primarily biological, with cultural factors having a limited impact. He discovered *six primary emotional states*: happiness, sadness, fear, anger, surprise, and disgust. This was another proof for Darwin that humans evolved from the animal world since these were also the primary emotions of animals.

Figure 1.8

Darwin had a significant impact on the birth of modern psychology because his revolutionary ideas, like Copernicus and Newton, transformed human psychology and the way human beings viewed their psychological place in the world. Inspired by Darwin, psychology developed several evolutionary fields of study and began to study animal behavior and apply their findings to human behavior. His impact inspired an array of other psychological studies like psychobiology; behavioral genetics; and developmental, evolutionary, and comparative psychology.

Darwin seemed ambivalent about the future of humanity. In the *Descent of Man*, he viewed human morality from the standpoint of the social instincts of animals. In animals, he saw the heroic behavior of insects, the feelings of love between female apes and their children, and the bond of loyalty between dogs and their owners. He viewed cooperation and regard for others, not competition, as the most important legacy that the animal world left to the human world.

Darwin was also skeptical about the future of humanity after his experiences in a slave-holding colony of Brazil and his encounters with the *Yaghan peoples of Tierra del Fuego* (Yannielli, 2013). Inhumane conditions proved how quickly human beings can degenerate into barbarianism. Under the guise of a progressive civilization, human beings are capable of unimaginable cruelty. Approaching the once proud Yaghan people as wild animals in need of domestication of the slave holders provided an unsettling example of the closeness, a so-called civilized society to animal savagery and tribalism, another reminder of the unconscious shadow and *the road to hell is paved with good intentions*.

Charles Darwin and *Abraham Lincoln* were born on the same day, leaving a significant impact on humanity. They both tried to free humanity from the chains of slavery that degrade humanity. Even as flawed human beings, their efforts were revolutionary, although incomplete, Lincoln to end slavery and Darwin to bridge the gap between the human and natural world.

Eugenics

A Birth of Eugenics – Sir Francis Galton

> Why do we preserve the useless human beings? The abnormal prevent the development of the normal. This fact must be squarely faced. Why should society not dispose of the criminals and insane in a more economical manner?
>
> - Dr. Alexis Carrel (Whitaker, 2019, p. 66)

Nothing exemplifies the personification of the racist shadow in Darwinian thought more than the *theory of eugenics* espoused by *Dr. Alexis Carrel*, a member of the Rockefeller Institute for Medical Research who won a Nobel Prize in 1912. He used his scientific credentials to recommend that society dispose of criminals and the mentally ill in an "economical manner."

Sir Francis Galton (1822–1911) was a cousin of Darwin and was influenced by Darwin and his work on the *Origins of Species by Natural Selection or Preservation of the Favored Races in the Struggle for Life*. Galton developed one of the most destructive scientific theories in human history (Whitaker, 2019). His work, *Hereditary Genius: Inquiries into its Laws and Consequences* (Galton, 1869/2019), articulated the *theory of eugenics*. Eugenics was not only embraced by most of scientists of the day but was often used politically by the scientific community to systematically ostracize and often sterilize those perceived as the "misfits" of society and used later by Hitler to exterminate the Jews.

The Greek meaning of the word *eugenics* is "well bred." Galton advocated for *selective breeding* to strengthen society by encouraging bright people to mate and discouraging the mating of the less bright (Wright, 2001). He even went further by advocating public policies that would lead to the gradual extermination of the weaker members of society to avoid their debasement

18   Symbols of the Birth of Modern Psychology

of the genetic pool (Hunt, 1993). Galton believed that intelligence was inherited and, as an empiricist, he viewed intelligence as a matter of sensory acuity. The more acute the senses, the more intelligent the person. As an *extreme nativist,* he thought that sensory acuity was inherited by the highly intelligent, who, during evolution, triumphed over the less intelligent.

A Symbol of Eugenics – The Swastika

Figure 1.9

The swastika, rooted in major spiritual traditions and rich in universal symbolism, remains widely used in Hinduism, Buddhism, and Jainism. In Hinduism, it symbolizes the two forms of Brahman, the creator god, with arms pointing clockwise (卐), called a swastika, representing the sun, prosperity, good luck, and the evolution of the universe. The counterclockwise symbol is called *sauvastika*, symbolizing the involution of the universe, the night or tantric aspects of Kali. The four bent arms represent the four human aims of righteousness: right action; wealth and prosperity; love and worldly enjoyment; and moksha, spiritual liberation. Integrated, the swastika is symbolic of *sanatana dharma*, which is eternal order, the natural and eternal way to live. The swastika also represents the world wheel, where the eternal life keeps changing from one point to another, around a fixed center, which is God, superimposed in both directions of the swastika.

In Buddhism, the swastika symbolizes the auspicious footprints of the Buddha and marks the beginning of Buddhist texts symbolic of universal harmony, prosperity, plurality, good luck, abundance, dharma, fertility, long life, and eternity. In Jainism, the four arms placed clockwise symbolize the four possible places of rebirth, which include the animal or plant world, hell,

Symbols of the Birth of Modern Psychology 19

earth, or the spirit world. The crescent and the dots symbolize moksha, liberation from samsara, the cycle of birth, death, and rebirth. The Nazi symbol differs from the swastikas by its rotation at an angle of 45 degrees and the lack of dots. The swastika has become recognized in modern times more as a political than spiritual symbol.

As "scientists" explored the implications of the evolution revolution, science would again neglect the shadow by providing research findings in support of eugenics, which would have a horrific impact on the most vulnerable people in society. The so-called scientific theories of Galton and other eugenicists had an extremely negative affect on the treatment of the most vulnerable in the United States. From 1850 until 1919, asylums grew from 30,000 to 300,000.

The eugenics movement came to a climax when, in 1927, *Carrie Buck*, diagnosed as "feeble-minded," challenged a sterilization law in Virginia. Buck fought the diagnosis all the way to the Supreme Court. By a ruling of 8–1 the Supreme Court ruled that the state of Virginia had the right to *forcibly sterilize* a person they deemed unfit to procreate. Justice Oliver Wendell Holmes Jr. famously stated: "three generations of imbeciles are enough" (Cohen, 2016, p. 270). This was a major victory for the eugenics movement inspiring eugenic legislation throughout the United States. By 1945, over 45,000 individuals with mental illness were sterilized (Whitaker, 2019). Asylums were no longer places of compassionate treatment. They became warehouses for "defectives," determined by the powerful political and scientific agents of society.

There was no stronger proponent of implementing eugenics than *Adolph Hitler*. Hitler utilized the popular American and European theory to destroy any veneer of societal civility and

Figure 1.10

became the barbarian that Darwin feared. In *Mein Kampf: My Struggle,* Hitler (1925/1998) hailed eugenics, arguing that the destruction of the weak was more humane than their protection. In fact, destroying the weak would purify society for the strong and return the German race to its racially superior Aryan roots.

The swastika is the symbol not only of *Nazism* but of the *eugenics movement*. Hitler first "practiced" the effectiveness of the gas chambers on individuals with mental illness (Whitaker, 2019). In the early 1940s, over 40,000 individuals were murdered in the name of eugenics. The swastika also represented scientific racism; the eugenic theory of racial hygiene to cleanse society of races that are perceived to degrade the genetic fabric of a dominant racial culture. The swastika has become one of the most powerful symbols in human history, whether it was on the Greek monument to honor the Greek goddess Artemis or as a powerful Hindu spiritual symbol. Historically, it was a positive symbol, meaning good fortune and spiritual enlightenment. Hitler, in his hatred of communism, wanted a powerful counter symbol to the communist hammer and sickle. By politicizing the swastika, he forever reduced the swastika to its shadow side and made it a symbol of racial hatred, white supremacy, and diabolic philosophy. In the early twentieth century, because of renewed interest in the famous German archaeologist *Heinrich Schliemann* (1822–1890), the swastika exploded in popularity in Germany and throughout the world. Representing good fortune, it appeared as symbols on many American products, such as Coca-Cola, Boy Scout hats, and Girl Scout materials, and even on American military uniforms (Heller, 2000).

The power of the interface of myth with symbol was again exemplified by Schliemann's obsession with the *Iliad myth* of Homer and his unending quest for the city of Troy. Schliemann did not believe the epic poem was a myth and, after many unsuccessful attempts, in 1871, he allegedly discovered Troy during a dig in Turkey, which catapulted him to worldwide fame. From his travels to Tibet, Paraguay, and the Gold Coast of Africa, Schliemann would go on to discover the power of the swastika symbol everywhere throughout the world. Beyond his discovery of Troy, Schliemann would view the swastika as his most important discovery; a symbol that would be used to change human history (Heller, 2000).

Aryan was a term that was not initially associated with a race but with an Indo-European language group that German linguistic scholars began to link to German, Romance, and Sanskrit languages. In fact, the word swastika originated from the Sanskrit, meaning activity conducive to well-being. The swastika provided a needed symbol for German well-being and for a new identity because the German people were still suffering from their humiliating defeat in World War I. With the rising interest in evolution, eugenics, and racial hygiene, and through poor linguistic scholarship, an unfounded but popular theory emerged that claimed the German people were the descendants of the pure and undefiled mythical Aryan race. The German people were the superior, pure, master race now destined to racially cleanse the world by the military conquests of its powerful German army.

In 1933, *Joseph Goebbels*, the Nazi minister of propaganda, issued an edict to forever enshrine the swastika as a symbol of Nazism and white supremacy. The edict prevented unauthorized or commercial use of the swastika and emphasized that in the absence of Hitler, his personification was to be reflected in the symbol of the swastika (Heller, 2000). The swastika became an effective part of the Nazi propaganda machine and was to become a symbol for the inevitable victory of the German people to restore the superior Aryan race to a racially inferior world.

Alfred Rosenberg (1930/2017), a high-ranking and honored Nazi theorist, further expanded eugenic racist theory. He warned against the "proximity of the races," which could cause "spiritual and racial confusion." This was later echoed by the supporters of the African apartheid system and by American segregationists.

Intelligence and Eugenics

The concepts of intelligence and the development of *psychological testing* occurred during the emergence of eugenics. The positive contribution of Galton was his passion for measurement. Galton measured everything. He measured weather patterns, invented the weather map, measured fingerprints, the impact of prayer (found it ineffective), measured which countries had the most beautiful women, and measured boredom at scientific lectures. Nothing was beyond measurement for the "measurement scientist." He hoped that a psychological science would provide the mechanisms to strengthen the evolutionary process by utilizing psychological measurement (Galton, 1883/2015).

To prove that human traits such as morality and intelligence were inherited and not innate, he measured family lineage. This started a practice that would later be modeled by other eugenic theorists. Galton (1883/2015) found that the intellectually strong produced strong families and the intellectually challenged produced weak ones. This research led to his belief that eugenics was essential for the creation of a highly intelligent and "gifted society."

In 1915, *Thomas Morgan* (1886–1945), one of the great American Nobel Prize–winning evolutionary biologists, began an unsuccessful challenge to eugenics, but laid the foundation in genetic studies to refute the flawed eugenic theory. In his study, a red-eyed fruit fly hatched a white-eyed fruit fly, indicating that a genetic mutation can occur outside of inheritance (Kohler, 1994). The implication was that an intellectually gifted parent does not necessarily produce an intellectually gifted child. Morgan also criticized psychological theories that indicated the importance of personality traits. He believed that certain traits such as intelligence and criminality were totally subjective and not based on objective science and were open to societal abuse.

Galton discovered the statistical term of *regression to the mean* to support the concept that intelligence was inherited. The regression to mean proved to be one reason for the unraveling of eugenics because it showed that the genetic process was more complex because Galton used the regression to the mean with a similar biological sample, taller people. However, if taller people could produce smaller people and smaller people could produce taller people, then it might be possible that "normal" could produce the "abnormal" and the "abnormal" could produce the "normal." Further, could the elimination of smaller people jeopardize the evolutionary progress for the larger people and could the elimination of the less intelligent jeopardize the evolutionary progress of the highly intelligent?

Galton inspired one of the great controversies in history of psychology. *The nature-nurture* debate within psychology about whether intelligence is inherited and remains stable throughout a lifetime or is dependent on a nurturing and intellectually stimulating environment.

Psychology and the Brain

Phrenology

Galton also studied anthropometry, measuring the head size, arm span, height, and fingers of human beings. In an original effort to measure intelligence, he found that the brightest people had large heads. As the Greeks turned to nature for human knowledge, psychology turned to the head and the human brain to further human understanding. *Franz Gall* (1758–1828) created the first major *theory of brain functioning* that dominated the nineteenth century. Modeling natural science, the brain was now the seat of mental functioning as the stomach was the seat for digestion (Colbert, 1997).

22 Symbols of the Birth of Modern Psychology

Through the method of *cranioscopy,* Gall studied skull sizes and determined that the mind was a collection of independent faculties located within the brain and that personality was determined by the external shape of the skull. The idea that the brain was the center of human functioning was not new, since Plato viewed the brain as the seat of the soul. Medieval thinkers believed that various human faculties were in specific areas of the brain. Gall rejected what he considered those philosophical theories or any other metaphysical views of the brain. His empirical neuropsychological approach reduced the interface between mind and brain to pure physiology and to 27 fundamental brain functions (Colbert, 1997).

Bumps and uneven brain geography were caused by pressure rising from the brain. By studying the skull bumps of a human being, Gall would make assumptions about their character and personality traits from the location of the bumps on the skull. Among the bumps, he would assess memory, mechanical ability, ability to write poetry, and love of personal property. Most significantly, he would also make assumptions about a murder instinct.

A student of Gall, *Johann Spurzheim* (1776–1832) popularized the theory of bumps on the skull and coined the term *phrenology*, rooted in Greek, meaning "mind" or "knowledge" (Colbert, 1997). Gall preferred faculties of the brain rather than phrenology partly because he felt Spurzheim had stolen his ideas and partly because phrenology sounded more philosophical and less scientific. Phrenology symbolizes the entry of psychology into the study of psychobiology, the belief that the brain and mind are integrated physiological processes that determines human behavior.

Figure 1.11

Rejected in Europe, Spurzheim helped popularize phrenology in America. He made phrenology a *pop psychology* of its time and advocated for educational and criminal justice reform. Followers of phrenology opened offices where they would read the skull of people interested in learning more about their personality or what job they should seek or who they should marry. Some phrenologists became guidance counselors to strengthen willpower and improve morality. And some even utilized phrenology to discover the "faculty of veneration" that proved the existence of God (Colbert, 1997).

Birth of Objective Psychological Testing

James McKeen Cattell

Phrenology soon faded, but interest in the psychology of the brain and measurement of mental functioning was only beginning. *James McKeen Cattell* (1860–1944) studied under Wilhelm Wundt, G. Stanley Hall, and Galton. He was the first professor of psychology at the *University of Pennsylvania* and dean of American science. After becoming a trustee on the esteemed *Board of the Society for Science and the Public* (SSP), Cattell is credited with the recognition of psychology as a legitimate science in the United States. He was also editor and publisher of the journal *Science*, a peer-review journal of the *American Association for the Advancement of Science,* which remains one the most prestigious scientific journals in the world.

Under the influence of Wundt, Cattell became the first American psychologist to complete a *psychometric testing* doctoral dissertation. Influenced by Darwin, Cattell became interested in individual differences and the role of individual intelligence in the evolutionary process. He rejected the Galton view of a unitary intelligence in favor of a testing system that measured the unique individual characteristics that defined intelligence (Sokal, 1971). As a professor at the *University of Pennsylvania*, Cattell began to administer a battery of tests to university students. In 1891, he was first to coin the term *mental tests,* because of his belief that his mental tests measured intelligence. After his move to *Columbia University* and to predict the correlation between intelligence and academic success, his tests became compulsory for all admitted freshmen students.

Cattell became another advocate for eugenics. At one point, he offered his children a large sum of money if they married a professor or a highly educated academician (Sokal, 1971). He also suffered, losing his position at Columbia University because of his opposition to World War I. Besides his contributions to psychology and the development of the first stages of psychological testing, he is most remembered in academia for starting the practice of tenure, which was developed in reaction to his mistreatment. After Cattell, tenure was instituted in universities across America to protect academic freedom.

At the turn of the twentieth century in 1901, a moratorium on psychological testing began in America because *Clark Wissler* (1870–1947) used the *Pearson Correlation Coefficient* in his doctoral dissertation, which showed that Cattell was wrong because there was no statistical relationship between his mental tests and academic achievement (Guilford, 1967). Wissler was also a proponent of the *scientific racist movement*, continuing the early influence of eugenic thought of intelligence and psychological testing. He supported a hierarchical racial theory that viewed Nordic people higher on the racial hierarchy than African people (Shapiro, 1985).

A Multifaceted Approach to Intelligence – Alfred Binet

Now that the tests of Cattell appeared to have no practical value and Wissler left psychology for anthropology, *Alfred Binet* (1857–1911) emerged as the leading expert in the world on psychological testing. Being French, Binet took a totally different view of intelligence from his American counterparts (Wolf, 1973). In his understanding of intelligence, Binet was more in the rationalist than empiricist tradition. He rejected the Galton and Cattell overemphasis on sensory acuity. He believed they neglected the elements of higher mental functioning and minimized the differences between children and adults. Exposed to a much broader psychology in Europe, Binet studied with *Jean Charcot,* the famous French neurologist, who utilized hypnosis to "cure" hysteria and had a significant influence on Freud and the development of psychoanalysis. After Charcot was discredited in many of the scientific circles of his day, Binet turned to the study of intelligence by observing the cognitive development of his two daughters.

Responding to the Darwinian theory of evolutionary survival, Binet focused on psychological testing to improve the likelihood of a child surviving in the new industrial age. In 1903, the French government, which had recently mandated *universal education*, asked Binet to develop a test to separate "normal" students from the "deficient" to provide greater support to the learning disabled, especially the deaf and blind, instead of giving children a mental illness diagnosis and sending them to asylums (Wolf, 1973). In 1905, Binet and his colleague, *Theodore Simon,* responded to French authorities by creating the first comprehensive intelligence test, the *Binet-Simon Test,* which defined the intelligence of children by their *mental age*. The Binet-Simon Test expanded the concept of intelligence beyond mathematics and reading to include as equally important the cognitive skill sets of memory, imagery, attention comprehension, and judgment (Binet & Simon, 1916/2015).

Unlike American psychologists, Binet remained skeptical that any one test could truly quantify intelligence. He believed that intelligence was complex and not permanently fixed because children continue to learn by constantly incorporating new experiences. He recommended mental orthopedic *exercises* to improve the intelligence and behavior of children (Wolf, 1973). Binet also felt that measures of intelligence were not generalizable to the many challenges of life because the results were limited to children of similar cultural backgrounds and familial experiences. Unlike the *nativist eugenicists,* Binet found that most people function below their intellectual potential and that everyone possesses the potential for intellectual growth throughout their lifetime.

The *Binet-Simon Test* based intelligence on how a child at a specific age performed intellectually compared to the average intellectual performance of other children of the same chronological age (Binet & Simon, 1916/2015). Since the Binet-Simon Test lacked a standardized way to compare mental age scores across populations of children, *William Stern* (1871–1938), a German philosopher and psychologist, solved the problem by recommending a change in the mental age formula of the Binet-Simon Test and proposed dividing mental age by chronological age to create a *single statistical ratio* and coined the term *Intelligent Quotient* (I.Q.), which would forever provide a powerful symbol of intelligence (Stern, 1914/2018).

Immigration, Psychological Testing, and Family Genetics – Herbert Goddard

Henry Herbert Goddard (1866–1957) translated the Binet-Simon Test into English. Goddard accepted the Galton and Cattell views that intelligence was inherited (Zenderland, 1998). As a dedicated eugenicist, he advocated for some of the most draconian approaches to immigrants and the "feeble minded" (Goddard, 1919). Poor performance on psychological tests, especially by the "feeble-minded" and immigrants, was an indication to Goddard that there was a deterioration of native intelligence occurring throughout American society. In a similar way to Plato, he endorsed a philosopher king democracy, which meant being ruled by the most intelligent who would tell the less intelligent what they needed to do to be happy (Hunt, 1993).

In 1913, Goddard was asked to develop a testing program on Ellis Island to identify the "feeble-minded" immigrants who were not traveling first or second class, but steerage. Using translators instead of examiners who knew the language of the immigrants, he administered the Binet-Simon Test, and those deemed "mentally defective" were deported back to their home countries (Goddard, 1917). During this period in American history, deportation became another eugenic strategy to protect the "normal" from the "abnormal." Goddard found that between 1912 and 1913, 80 percent of immigrants that he tested were "feeble-minded." These were mostly Jews, Hungarians, Russians, and Italians (Gould, 1981; Hergenhahn, 2009). Although these findings were not specifically mentioned in the *Immigration Act of 1924*, the Act set quotas on the number of immigrants from those mentioned European countries (U.S. Department of State Office of the Historian, 1924) The Act also prevented immigration from all "yellow peril"

Asian countries. To the delight of the eugenics movement, the stated purpose of the Act was to "preserve the ideal of American homogeneity."

Figure 1.12

As the director of research at the *Vineland Training School for the Feeble-Minded Girls and Boys* in Vineland, New Jersey, Goddard developed the first known laboratory focus on intellectual disabilities. His research led to his infamous 1912 book on *The Kallikak Family: A Study in the Heredity of Feeble Mindedness* (Goddard, 1912). His finding substantiated his eugenic view that family genetics determines intelligence. The word *Kallikak* was chosen because the word connected two Greek words, beautiful and bad, because Goddard found that normal people produce good and beautiful children and the feeble-minded produce bad children.

His book explored the life of Deborah Kallikak, a so-called "feeble-minded" girl at the Training School. He followed her *genealogy* through the life of her grandfather, Martin Kallikak, a great revolutionary hero married to a beautiful Quaker woman. In a soap opera–like scenario, poor Martin is seduced by a bad feeble-minded barmaid, who had his child out of wedlock. Unlike the good Quaker wife who produced beautiful, healthy, and successful children, the barmaid produced bad, poor, insane, and "mentally retarded" children. The Kallikak Family became a powerful symbol of the supposed *genetic link* between good and bad families and provided another research finding for the eugenics movement in their support of sterilization and institutionalization of anyone deemed feeble-minded (Goddard, 1914). In his disdain for the so-called feeble-minded, Goddard is recognized as the psychologist who introduced the derogatory term of *moron* that has continued to stigmatize individuals with intellectual disabilities in modern times. Moron originated from the Greek, *moros*, meaning dull (Goddard, 1919). Moron is an I.Q. in the 51–70 range and used to describe a person on the Binet-Simon Test with a mental age in adulthood between 7 and 10 years.

To his credit, later in his life, Goddard addressed the shadow elements of his work, although many felt it was too late to reverse the damage he had done. He embraced the multidimensional view of intelligence of Binet (Hergenhahn, 2009) and rejected his previous advocacy for sterilization and institutionalization of the "feeble-minded." He became the first American psychologist to testify as an expert witness that the low intelligence of defendants should limit their criminal culpability. Goddard was a strong advocate for the development of clinical psychology and for the use of testing by psychologists in hospitals, the legal system, and in the military. He helped write the first law in the United States that mandated that all public schools provide special education to the blind, deaf, and the intellectually disabled (Wolf, 1973).

IQ Testing

I.Q. Formula Standardized – Lewis Terman

By World War I, the Binet-Simon Test was widely used throughout the world. Being a shrewd businessman, *Lewis Terman* (1877–1956), a leading *Stanford University* psychologist, purchased the rights for the Binet-Simon Test for $1. He forever owned one of the most lucrative psychological tests in the world.

Terman was another prominent American eugenicist and a leading member of the *Human Betterment Foundation* (HBF), which emphasized the need for eugenic understanding in psychological testing. The HBF promoted educational programs for a better human family in body, mind, character, and citizenship. This "betterment" included advocacy for compulsory sterilization throughout the United States. Terman and the HBF believed that low intelligence was inherited and the major cause of criminal and antisocial behavior. Influenced by Wundt, Galton, and Cattell, Terman rejected Binet's multifaceted view of intelligence. He placed sensory acuity as the key factor in intelligence. In his doctoral dissertation, he distinguished between genius and "stupidity" by administering Cattell tests to seven intelligent and unintelligent boys. He concluded the intelligent boys had superior intellectual processes (Terman, 1906).

In 1916, Terman revised the Binet-Simon Test and created the *Stanford-Benet Test* to make testing easier to understand and administer. Terman suggested that the Binet-Simon ratios be multiplied by 100 and remove the decimal point to obtain a clearer cumulative score and the intelligent quotient be abbreviated and simply called *IQ*. The Terman formula for obtaining an IQ score would become the standard for IQ scores, only slightly modified later by the cohort-norming used in the *Wechsler tests*. From a eugenic mindset, the goal of testing for Terman, unlike Benet, was to classify IQ and limit the educational opportunities for less intelligent children (Gould, 1981). Since Terman believed that intelligence was inherited and IQ was the best predictor of success in life, limited educational resources should only be allocated to assist the feeble-minded in finding an appropriate manual labor job (Leslie, 2000).

To make matters worse, the Stanford-Binet Test continued the use of derogatory terms coined by Goddard and other psychologists. Terman promoted eugenics by labeling children, later adults, as *morons* (IQ of 51–70)*, imbeciles* (IQ of 26–50), and *idiots* (IQ of 0–25), and advocated for public policies to institutionalize or sterilize those individuals to preserve the ideal of American homogeneity.

As the eugenics movement faded in the middle of the twentieth century, these terms were removed from testing materials and psychological reports because of the psychological damage being perpetrated on intellectually challenged children and adults. It was too late since the terms had become part of the American vernacular, used to abuse, and demean other people, especially the developmentally disabled and mentally ill.

Longitudinal IQ Research – Termites

Lewis Terman (1877–1959) was also a pioneer in educational psychology. He was fascinated by what was considered *genius* and decided to study *gifted children*, known as *Termites*. During the early twentieth century, gifted children were *stereotyped* as sickly, socially inadequate, and psychologically underdeveloped. Initially titled the *Genetic Studies of Genius,* it is now known as the *Mental and Physical Traits of a Thousand Gifted Children* (Terman, 1925) to remove the stain of eugenics from the title of the initial research. In 1921, Terman studied the characteristics of 1,500 gifted children aged 11 with *IQ scores over 135*, the average IQ being 151. He wanted to know how their superior intellect would impact their adult lives. His research utilized quantitative and qualitative, a mixed method research design. His findings disputed the stereotypes and found that gifted children maintained their high IQ scores *over time* and were well adjusted. His research continues to this day and is one of the oldest and longest longitudinal research projects in psychological history.

In 1968, *Melita Oden* (1968), a Stanford research associate of Terman, published "The Fulfillment of Promise: 40-year Follow-up of the Terman Gifted Group." The findings found that most gifted children were well-adjusted adults with a significant number being extraordinarily successful leaders in their communities, professionals with careers in law, medicine, academia, business, and management. Over half of the gifted children finished college compared to 8 percent of the general population and most maintained their high IQ scores. Some of the most famous *Termites* were Jess Oppenheimer, writer for the *I Love Lucy* television show; Less Cronbach, who became president of the APA; Ancel Keys, health psychologist who correlated saturated fats with heart disease; and Robert Sears, who continued Terman's work and a pioneer in child psychology. However, most of the Termites' lives were more mundane, having pursued "humble" jobs like policemen, seaman, and typist clerks. Although superior intelligence was one factor in achieving success, an essential environmental factor was the quality of Termite parenting because childhood divorce had a negative impact on adulthood development, which led to premature death, suicide, emotional difficulties, marital discord, divorce, and health problems caused by excessive smoking and alcohol abuse.

The Termites study continues even though only a very few Termites remain alive. The findings have not resolved the *nature-nurture issue,* although the Terman research indicated that the IQ of Termites remained constant throughout their lifetime. On the other hand, environmental factors, especially the quality of their parenting, played a significant role in their psychological and physical health and ultimately in their adjustment to adulthood.

The General Factors of Intelligence – Charles Spearman

Charles Spearman (1863–1949), a student of Wundt and follower of Galton, resurrected Cattell's failed tests. He disagreed with Binet, who emphasized a diverse and multifarious intellectual approach to intelligence. Utilizing the statistical technique of *factor analysis*, Spearman proved that Cattell was correct when he found a high correlation between sensory acuity and academic performance. Spearman believed that two factors determined intelligence. The *(s) factor,* consists of intellectual abilities that are variable and include mathematics, language, and reasoning. The *(g) factor* consists of general intellectual abilities that are constant and inherited. Spearman's concept of a (g) factor continues to be accepted as a key determinant of intelligence and remains a focal point in the debate regarding the nature of inheritance. He gave a serious warning to educators to *minimize IQ testing* in the schools because it could be damaging to children because educators should emphasize that genius exists in every child (Ogden & Spearman, 1925).

Societal Impact on Intelligence – Leta Stetter Hollingworth

In the male-dominated psychological world, *Leta Stetter Hollingworth* (1886–1939) was a woman pioneer in psychology who provided a quite different viewpoint on the nature of intelligence (Klein, 2002). After her work at the *Clearing House for Mental Defectives* administering the Binet-Simon Test, she began to question whether intelligence was inherited. In her testing, she found that many so-called defective children were normal and began to view social maladjustment as a major cause of intellectual deficiencies.

Hollingworth was interested in female stereotypes, especially *functional periodicity*, the idea that women are psychologically impaired during *menstruation.* She completed her dissertation on *Functional Periodicity* under the esteemed psychologist *Edward Thorndike,* who was a supporter of inheritance theory and the variability hypothesis. The variability hypothesis postulated that because men had greater psychological and physical traits, they occupied the highest and lowest end of the variability range. Women, with less variability traits, were destined for the middle range and for mediocrity. In her landmark research, Hollingworth proved that the variability hypothesis was incorrect and that the extremes were not because of male genetic superiority but were culturally and socially determined (Silverman, 1992). Women were not innately inferior to men, but made to appear inferior by their social and cultural roles. Hollingworth also found no empirical evidence that women were intellectually impaired during menstruation (Silverman, 1992). Thorndike, so impressed by her research, began to stress more nurture viewpoints in his beliefs about intelligence. In 1916, Hollingworth received her doctorate and Thorndike offered her a position at the *Columbia Teachers College.*

After her work at the *Clearing House for Defectives* and the *Bellevue Mental Hospital,* she continued to challenge the myths of mental deficiency and mental illness. After working in some of the leading mental health institutions of her day, she came to the conclusion that problems of intelligence were not inherited, but resulted from social and cultural factors that needed to be addressed by social reforms. She believed that institutionalization itself could cause mental deterioration.

Later in her career, Hollingworth became interested in *gifted children*. She had great respect for Terman's work with gifted children, but believed that mental giftedness, like mental deficiency, results not from inheritance, but from lack of educational opportunities and environmental factors. She also felt that Terman had not recommended specific curriculum reforms needed to benefit gifted children. Her final paper, "Children above 180 IQ" (Hollingworth, 1942), published posthumously in 1942 by her husband, addressed ways to avoid the adjustment problems of gifted children by early identification of social problems, providing daily emotional support and intellectual stimulation, avoiding isolation from peers, and educational reforms to address their unique needs.

Symbols of the Birth of Modern Psychology 29

Even though Terman emphasized nature and Hollingworth emphasized nurture, their legacy resulted in the creation of the current American approach to *special education*. Ironically, separating the gifted from the less gifted created the *hierarchical educational system* based on intellectual abilities for which many eugenicists had long advocated. Although special education has provided important support for both gifted and intellectually challenged students, the reality of a hierarchical education system based on intellectual abilities and IQ scores has often produced lifelong emotional scars for those designated as less gifted and less valued, leaving many children with other valuable abilities feeling "less than," and mentally deficient.

Figure 1.13

The Weschler Intelligence Tests

Through all the controversies and debates, intelligence testing began to stabilize in 1939 when *David Wechsler* (1896–1981), a Jewish Romanian American, developed adult and child intelligence tests that would become the most widely administered IQ tests in the world. Wechsler disagreed with the Binet-Simon approach of a single intellectually based IQ score and added a *nonintellectual component* to his intelligence tests.

30 *Symbols of the Birth of Modern Psychology*

In many ways, the *Wechsler Adult Intelligence Scale* (WAIS) and the *Wechsler Intelligence for Children* (WISC) attempted to solve the historic empirical and rational debate about the nature of knowledge. Weschler created an intelligence test that included assessment of both sensory acuity and rational skill sets. Sensory acuity testing provided a Performance IQ (PIQ) score, and intellectual, rational testing provided a Verbal IQ (VIQ) score. The total score was a Full-Scale IQ (FIQ), which Weschler felt was a far better indicator of intelligence than the limited Binet-Simon Test.

Clinical psychologists began to use the Weschler tests for a more complete understanding of their clients. For instance, the Weschler tests provided clinicians, through various statistical and clinical methods, ways to assess the impact of emotion on the Full-Scale IQ score. It was found that IQ can be affected by anxiety and depression or when dealing with significant emotional issues like trauma. Seen as the best tests for intelligence, the Weschler tests continue to be administered worldwide and are periodically improved and updated with new revisions. The WAIS is now in its fourth revision, in preparation since 2016 for its fifth edition. The WISC is now in its third revision.

Birth of Projective Psychological Testing

The Impact of the Rorschach Test in History

As clinical psychologists began to see the potential for psychological testing to improve treatment, a need emerged to supplement intelligence testing with other types of testing. For a more complete clinical understanding, and influenced by the psychoanalytic movement, *projective testing* was developed to assess personality, particularly unconscious dynamics. Projective Tests are personality tests designed to respond to ambiguous stimuli that reveal unconscious thoughts, emotions, and conflicts. Projective testing, in contrast to objective testing, examines psychological patterns, themes, and unconscious dynamics. The ambiguity of the stimuli allows for the expression of thoughts and feelings not available or acceptable to the conscious mind. Most importantly, projective testing enriches the psychological testing experience and further illuminates the normative, sterile data of objective testing.

Developed in 1921, the *Rorschach Test* symbolizes the most culturally well-known projective test in popular culture. *Inkblots* have become a symbol of psychology and a broad symbol of mental health. For almost 100 years, the Rorschach Test has survived as a living testament to the power of projective testing and a powerful symbol of a technique to uncover and measure the creative inner self that shapes and defines how an individual perceives the world.

Although Alfred Binet had experimented with inkblots, it would be *Herman Rorschach* (1884–1922), a Swiss psychiatrist, who would develop the first projective inkblot test. Rorschach, the test that still bears his name, will forever be remembered as one of most important contributors to developing a test to better understand the unconscious mind. Born in 1884, the year the French presented Lady Liberty as a gift to the American ambassador in Paris, France, to celebrate the American revolution and end to slavery, Herman Rorschach would spend his brief life attempting to liberate the unconscious mind. Until the recent book, *The Inkblots: Herman Rorschach, His Iconic Test and the Power of Seeing* by Damion Searls (2017), the importance of Herman Rorschach in the history of psychology has been minimized, even though amidst the objective testing movement he developed a test in line with psychoanalysis that would last for over 100 years.

Figure 1.14

Rorschach studied under the prominent psychiatrist *Eugen Bleuler,* who was known for coining the term *schizophrenia,* teaching Carl Jung, and developing a diagnostic nomenclature for mental illness. As Rorschach explored his own professional purpose, it was childhood memories of inkblots that became his inspiration. As a child, he wondered how people could have such different experiences of the same inkblot. In 1921, Rorschach published *Psychodiagnostics,* which outlined methods by which to administer the Rorschach Test (Searls, 2017). The book provided the vision for further research and for the initial use in clinical settings. Unfortunately, Rorschach would not live to see the fulfillment of his vision because of his untimely death the next year at the young age of 37, due to a ruptured appendix. As he predicted, his legacy would be mired in controversy, even hatred. But the power of the test would outlive all efforts to eliminate its importance.

In America, during eugenic mania and the growing weariness of intelligence debates, psychologists sought refuge from all the controversy by embracing psychoanalytic thought. The heated conflicts between *Bruno Klopfer* (1900–1971) and *Samuel Beck* (1896–1980) would come to symbolize the struggle for the correct way to research and apply the findings of the Rorschach Test. Both were acknowledged as important pioneers and innovators in the scoring, interpretation, and popularization of the Rorschach Test. Klopfer, from a philosophical European background, viewed the application of the Rorschach Test in more flexible and creative terms, interpretation as an art. Beck, in the American natural science tradition, believed that the test should be structured empirically and interpreted scientifically (Klopfer & Davidson, 1962).

32 Symbols of the Birth of Modern Psychology

Both psychologists agreed that the Rorschach Test was a powerful clinical tool unmatched by other projective tests, a modern state of the art comparable to new medical techniques. Klopfer would call the test a *psychological X-ray,* which visually provided the underlying structures that made the unconscious understandable. Beck would describe the test as an objective instrument that penetrates the whole person, like a *fluoroscope,* an imaging technique that uses X-rays to obtain moving images inside the body of a medical patient. Their disagreements subsided in their later years. Ironically, in 1965, as their tensions subsided, Beck received the first *Bruno Klopfer Award* from the prestigious *Society of Personality Assessment,* which was founded by Klopfer.

By the mid-1950s, the Rorschach had permeated movies, art, television, family-friendly board games, and even religion. After World War II, *Douglas Kelley* (1912–1958), a Termite from the Terman study of gifted children, became the chief psychiatrist at the Nuremberg prison. During the Nuremberg Trials, he was assigned the task to assess whether the Nazi defendants were mentally competent to stand trial (Kelley, 1947). Kelley was a strong proponent of the Rorschach Test. Although the actual impact may never be completely known, the international acknowledgment of the test further solidified the Rorschach Test as a valid and essential psychological test. Kelley did not capitulate to political pressure to call all Nazis insane because Rorschach Test results administered to 22 prisoners were mixed. Some Nazi prisoners experienced paranoia, depression, and mental disturbance, while others appeared well adjusted (Kelley, 1947).

Kelley believed that in post-war America, politicians like *Huey Long* and segregationists utilized the same race-baiting and white supremacy rhetoric of the Nazis. Their words were the same words that he heard throughout the halls of the Nuremberg Prison (Kelley, 1947). He warned that there was little that could prevent the establishment of a Nazi-like state in America. His ending is Shakespearean. Although disgusted by the Holocaust, he developed a very personal relationship with *Hermann Goring,* a major Nazi military leader and the sixteenth president of the Reichstag. Kelley was impressed by the fact that before his execution Goring took control of his life and committed suicide, proving in his own mind that he was the true victor. On New Year's 1958, in front of his wife and child, Kelley took his own life with what was rumored to be a remnant of the same potassium cyanide used by Goring in his suicide.

Figure 1.15

Kelley's findings were in line with the later findings of *Stanley Milgram* (1933–1984). Inspired by the trial of Nazi Adolf Eichmann, Milgram modeled the Nazi approach toward authority for his research in his 1974 book, *Obedience to Authority* (Milgram, 1983). To the horror of researchers and society, he found that every person could, like the Nazis, do horrendous evil to please authority. The research was so disturbing that the APA held hearings concerning the *ethics* of subjecting people to this disturbing type of research and suspended his membership for a year (Blass, 2004). The Milgram laboratory, where the research occurred, is a powerful symbol of the shadow and unconscious forces of the human psyche. In 1961, three months after the trial of Nazi war criminal Adolf Eichmann began, Milgram began a research study to explain *psychological genocide*. The disturbing research found that Eichmann had millions of accomplices who were simply following the orders of their superiors (Blass, 2004).

The research asked human participants to perform acts in conflict with their conscience by administering electric shocks to a needed fake "learner." Under the direction of a respected researcher and authority figure, participants were instructed to shock the fake "learner" when they were not responding appropriately. Milgram found that human participants would gradually increase the fake shocks even as the "learner" cried out for relief, increasing shock to levels that would have been fatal (Blass, 1991). While many psychologists found flaws in the Milgram research and some challenged the ethics of exposing people to potentially emotionally damaging research, Thomas Blass (2004) found even in the late twentieth century that the Milgram research was being replicated frequently around the world with similar results.

One might have assumed that after the Nuremberg Trials and the ongoing Milgram studies, that scientific interest in the unconscious, especially the Rorschach Test, would have been legitimized as an essential area of research and clinical work. The opposite occurred because by the mid-1960s, criticism of psychoanalysis started to increase, and many research psychologists attacked psychoanalysis as pseudoscientific. To the dismay of many psychologists, and even some leading psychometric psychologists, the Rorschach Test would not go away. However, it was clear that for the Rorschach Test to survive in the empirically, natural science, data-driven APA environment a savior was needed (Mihura, Meyer, Bombel, et al, 2013). Someone who would follow the party line and standardize the test to please the APA power structure and reform the test in the traditions of empirical and natural science. The savior would be psychologist *John Exner* (1928–2006). Through five decades, he would dedicate his life to the survival of the Rorschach Test by writing 14 books, more than 60 journal articles, and providing countless training workshops on the Exner Comprehensive System.

After researching thousands of studies and surveys of hundreds of clinicians, in his 1974 book, *The Rorschach: A Comprehensive System*, Exner (1995) synthesized the research, the surveys, and the Koffler and Beck methods into a comprehensive system that would create an empirically based test. This comprehensive system added time for administration of the test and required advanced training for Rorschach practitioners. Its rigorous empirical emphasis alienated some Rorschach clinicians, who, like Herman Rorschach, valued a more open-ended and intuitive approaches that created surprising and valuable insights. In his later years, Exner began to have regrets since he believed clinicians were becoming mindless "bookkeepers" relegated to using manuals to diagnose and treat symptoms, not human beings.

Developed in 1943 at the *University of Minnesota*, the *Minnesota Multiphasic Personality Inventory* (MMPI) provided an alternative to the Rorschach Test when it was developed in the 1940s and became the most administered personality test in the objective testing traditions. Initially it was very cumbersome, with 504 true/false statements; 567 statements in its second revision. By 2008, the *MMPI-2-RF (Restructured Form)* was fine-tuned to measure 338 true/false statements. The scales of the MMPI assisted in determining a differential diagnosis and was designed to correlate personality with psychiatric diagnosis. The MMPI was also attractive because, unlike the Rorschach Test, it was cost effective; psychologists could have their clients take the test in a room by themselves allowing the psychologist to spend more time with other clinical responsibilities. Many clients complained that the MMPI was too long and repetitive. Many seriously ill were often unable to complete the test because of its length, time, and by the emotional stress it created. With limited interpersonal presence of a psychologist during the test, quality was often lost for convenience or financial considerations.

By the mid-twentieth century, other projective tests became popular, creating a rich projective testing history that, along with intelligence testing, provided a comprehensive *Psychological Report* for practicing clinicians and community agencies. *The Thematic Appreciation Test,* developed in the 1930s by psychoanalysts Henry Morgan and Christiana Morgan from *Harvard University,* was inspired by the *symbol of Doubloon (Moby Dick Coin) in Moby Dick* because multiple characters responded to the same Doubloon symbol with very different interpretations (Vincent, 1980). The 32 testing cards are a series of provocative yet ambiguous pictures in which the client is asked to tell a story. After World War II, the TAT was used by psychoanalytic clinicians to assess serious mental illness and in the 1970s by clinicians in the Humanistic-Existential movement to support personal growth. *The Sentence Completion Test* was first developed by *Herman Ebbinghaus* in 1897, evolved by 1950 to the popular *Rotter Incomplete Sentences Blank* which comprises 40 incomplete sentences usually starting with one or two words such as "I regret…" or "Mostly girls…." These tests inspired the development in 1926 of the *Draw-A-Person* (Goodenough-Harris Drawing Test), in 1927, the *Miller's Analogies Test* and in 1935, the *Jungian Word Association Test*.

Despite the growth of projective and personality assessments, the Rorschach Test continued to thrive because of Exner. In 1998, a professional group in the APA, the *Board of Professional Affairs*, honored Exner for almost singlehandedly saving the Rorschach Test. They recognized the Rorschach Test as the "most powerful psychometric test ever envisioned" (Searls, 2017, p. 267). This acknowledgment did not stop the detractors. In 1999, not even a year after the award, Howard Garb, a psychologist at the *VA Healthcare System*, a long-standing stronghold of psychological testing, called for a moratorium on the Rorschach Test (Lilenfield, Wood, & Garb, 2001). He claimed the test was too ambiguous, pseudoscientific, and even dangerous. In *What's Wrong with the Rorschach? Science Confronts the Controversial Inkblot Test,* Wood, Nerzworski, Lilenfield, et al, (2003) reported every criticism they could find about the Rorschach Test throughout the many decades of its existence. They portrayed supporters of the test as a cult, and critics not as isolated naysayers but as heroes who were advocating for scientific objectivity. Their hope was that if respected psychologists could not destroy the Rorschach Test, public opinion might be their last hope.

Wood would go public in 2001 with an article in the *American Scientist* that continued his attack not only on the Rorschach Test but on all projective testing, including the TAT, Draw-A- Person, and Sentence Completion Test. Wood recommended that psychologists stop using projective testing because they rarely had any clinical value or empirical validity (Searls, 2017). Not many people in the public or psychologists in clinical settings listened to Wood or his followers (Mihura, Meyer, Bombel, et al, 2015). The Rorschach Test continued to flourish under the Exner Comprehensive System (Weiner, 2003).

Since Exner was able to unify the various Rorschach factions, the question remained about what would happen to the Rorschach Test after his death in 2006. As is often true when an important leader departs, controversy occurs. Exner assigned legal decisions about the future of his comprehensive testing system to his family. They resisted any changes even after revisions had been recommended by the *Rorschach Research Council* that Exner founded.

To continue Exner's work, but to be less dependent on one charismatic leader, in 2011, members of the council resigned and developed their own consensus-oriented group and created the latest version, the *Rorschach Performance Assessment System,* or *R-PAS*. In the current scientific zeitgeist, this new version continued the trend to simplify structure and standardize the test, with the hope it will continue to thrive and placate its critics. The R-PAS was another step away from the Hermann Rorschach vision of the test since he would have resisted the R-PAS limit on the number of responses or setting time limits on each Rorschach card. For Rorschach, the strength of the test was the discovery of the deeper meaning of the human mind, which necessitated a skilled examiner being in concert with the unconscious flow of the client.

Observing what has occurred in the history of the Rorschach Test, an ongoing theme emerges. The theme is why modern psychology seems so intent, as with the Rorschach Test, to strip away in the name of science the mystery, the richness, and the very essence of what it means to be human. The overemphasis on objectivity in psychology has often left no room for the study of a "subject," a living, incredibly complex human individual person. A biblical reference may be the best way to paraphrase and summarize the current state of psychology and the Rorschach Test: what does it profit a test or a discipline if it gains empirical credibility yet forfeits and loses its soul?

Herman Rorschach would have been pleased by the development of *Collaborative Therapeutic Assessment* (CTA). In 1993, *Stephen Finn* (2007) began to answer the above biblical reference by providing an alternative to the traditional use of psychological testing. His *humanistic client-centered* approach shifted the focus from the examiner to the client. Testing became a *mutually engaging process* with active client involvement; not a mysterious exercise whose primary benefit was for collecting data for the psychologist. The Finn approach continued the tradition of psychological testing providing a rich array of clinical information as clinicians developed treatment plans and considered therapeutic interventions.

The Finn psychological testing focuses on the immediate "here and now" testing session. Finn recognizes "the subject" that is often missing in objective testing. During an assessment session, he might show a specific Rorschach card to unveil unconscious processes that immediately become conscious, therapeutic, and helpful. Even more revolutionary, he regularly integrates the MMPI and the Rorschach because the highly structured true/false MMPI presents a conscious presentation of a client, while the Rorschach reveals underlying unconscious problems and the emotional conflicts not consciously available to the client. In concert with the MMPI, the strength of Rorschach inkblots can be summarized by the phrase, *a client can control what they want to say, but they cannot control what they want to see* (Finn, 2007). CTA dramatically changes how testing results can be given to clients. Finn sees the result process as empathy enhancing. The psychologist is "stepping in the client's shoes," while at the same time being able to "step back" and provide a professional perspective.

Viewing the client as "experts of themselves," the findings are presented directly to clients in the spirit of mutuality where clients can either accept or reject traditional testing interpretations. The final psychologist "report" is not a lengthy, jargon-filled, objective summary of findings, but a personal letter. If the client is a child, it is written as a myth, a fable. Certainly, there would be critics, especially from the aforementioned Wood and associates. Since psychological testing is in decline, Finn has provided an important alternate for the future role of psychological testing, which is a possibility for reconciliation, mutual respect, between the empirical and humanistic sciences.

The most recent fifth edition of the *Handbook of Psychological Assessment* by *Gary Groth-Marnat* (2003), considered the "bible" for teaching graduate students psychological testing, Finn and other humanistic approaches are discussed, especially in the chapter regarding the writing of psychological reports. Groth-Marnat found that research confirmed the therapeutic value of providing testing results directly to clients. Even though the text has more of an objective testing focus, Groth-Marnat recognized the continued value of projective testing, especially the TAT and Rorschach tests, noting they are still widely used by testing psychologists. For many reasons, the sad reality is that psychological testing, particularly projective testing, has declined throughout the public and private mental health sectors in the United States (Piotrowski, 2015).

36 *Symbols of the Birth of Modern Psychology*

Birth of Clinical Psychology and the American Psychological Association

Clinical Psychology

The birth of *clinical psychology* has been a difficult and divisive journey. The legacy of Wundt and Titchener left an openly hostile division between experimental researchers and clinical psychologists because of their voracious opposition to an applied psychology. In fact, research psychologists have frequently undermined the credibility of clinical psychology through research that questioned the efficacy of psychotherapy. In response to early controversies, to promote and advance psychology, it became clear there was a need to develop a national organization to unite psychologists so in 1892 the *American Psychological Association* (APA) was founded by G. Stanley Hall, a student of Wundt. Although the founders were sympathetic, Wundt and Titchener had disdain for an applied psychology and refused to attend APA activities.

The of symbol of the American Psychological Association originated from the penultimate letter of the Greek alphabet and the first letter of the word *psuche*. This word meant soul to the Greeks, and later in modern psychology was changed to mind. The pitchfork has a rich symbolic history. In Greek mythology, it related to the trident of Poseidon, the god of the sea. The pitchfork in Christianity symbolized the devil and dark evil forces. Historically, mental illness was often associated with devil possession, and some believed that psychology adopted the trident pitchfork as its symbol to show its irreverent defiance of the belief that mental illness was a result of dark demonic forces. It is a reminder of the powerful positive and shadow elements in all professions.

Figure 1.16

Psychology is not rooted in medicine but in the intellectual traditions of academia. Ironically, *Lightner Witner*, the first psychologist to coin the term *clinical psychology*, a founding member of the APA, was a student of the anti-applied psychologist, Wundt. Witner, a professor of psychology at the University of Pennsylvania, developed the first curriculum in clinical psychology and in 1896 opened the *first Psychological Clinic* at the *University of Pennsylvania* to serve not individuals with serious mental illness, but children and their families (Thomas, 2009). This provided the first opportunity for psychologists to assume primary clinical responsibility for direct client treatment in a university, not medical, setting.

As the APA solidified its role as the leading organization and advocate for psychology in the United States, the hostility between experimental researchers and applied psychologists escalated. In the early twentieth century, to become a full voting member in the APA, clinical psychologists were required to publish empirical research beyond their doctoral dissertation. Submitted research considered philosophical in nature was rejected and was not considered science. In response, clinical psychologists left the organization and formed their own association outside of the APA. They periodically returned when an APA effort occurred to create a separate clinical division within the APA. For the sake of unification, it was not until 1941 that the APA gave full membership status to clinical psychologists. However clinical psychologists still had to show a five-year "special contribution" to the field of psychology that resulted in clinical psychologists again feeling like second-class citizens in their professional organization.

World War II changed the world of clinical psychology forever because after the war, 40,000 veterans needed mental health care and there were not enough psychiatrists to meet the need. In 1946, the *Veterans Administration* (VA) began to provide training funds for clinical psychologists with the caveat that the APA establish accreditation standards for training and practice. Prior to World War II, few clinical psychologists practiced outside of university settings. After World War II, states began the arduous task of 30 years to create licensure boards in 50 states to regulate the practice of clinical psychology. In 1947, Connecticut became the first state and, in 1977, Missouri became last state, to pass a licensing law to regulate the practice of clinical psychology throughout the United States (Reaves, 2006).

Prior to World War II, clinical psychologists were subservient, especially in mental health and medical settings to psychiatry. Afterwards clinical psychologists began a campaign for equity in all aspects of health care that included insurance reimbursement, expert testimony in court, admitting privileges to hospitals, and administering as chief executive officers (CEOs) in public and private mental health and alcohol and drug programs. The biggest challenge to psychiatry came in 2002 when New Mexico became the first state to grant clinical psychologists the right to prescribe medication, as few states had followed by Louisiana, Illinois, Iowa and Idaho. Although psychology has typically been successful in professional battles with psychiatry, the shadow emerges when professional interests take precedent over working together with psychiatry to improve mental health services to the public.

As often happens in history, an extreme reaction in one direction creates a dialectic reaction in the opposite direction. By 1970, membership of the APA changed dramatically because before 1970, over 70 percent of psychologists were researchers in academia, after 1970 over 70 percent of APA members were applied, practicing clinical psychologists. In 1988, researchers, frustrated with this turn of events, like clinical psychologists in the past, created their own organization outside of the APA. Alienated from the growing influence of psychologists interested in a broader view of science in the APA, research-oriented psychologists created the Association for Psychological Science *(*APS*)* which has over 25,000 members. APS members believe they are the true adherents to the empirical science traditions in psychology. The APS publishes its own journal, *Psychological Science*. This journal purports to provide "cutting-edge" empirical research to promote and advance "scientific"-oriented psychology.

Witner, with a Wundtian experimental psychology background, left a university-based legacy that continues to create controversy within clinical psychology as to which model best prepares clinical psychologists to become competent practitioners. The Witner *scientific-practitioner model,* known as the *Boulder Model,* developed in 1949, requires psychologists to become skilled in both research and clinical practice, a challenging task that often necessitates developing research expertise over learning clinical skills. By the 1960s, the university-based scientist-practitioner model produced an extremely limited number of clinical psychologists, leaving clinical psychology on its death bed. Understanding that universities were more concerned about producing researchers than practitioners, clinical psychologists throughout the nation began to look for a new model.

The *scholar-practitioner* model, known as the *Vail Model*, emerged in 1973 and focused more on practice than research. Students still needed to complete a doctoral-level research dissertation. However, the curriculum prioritized learning to interpret, rather than do, research. Research was a way to become a competent clinical psychologist, not a competent researcher. In 1925, *Lloyd Crane* advocated for clinical psychologists to discard the PhD, and create a special applied degree, the PsyD, a doctor of psychology, as medicine had abandoned the PhD for the MD, doctor of medicine. He was ignored until 1968, when the *University of Illinois* offered the first PsyD degree. This was difficult for many traditional psychologists to accept because this led to the development of independent professional schools outside university settings; most notably in 1969, in California, the *California School of Professional Psychology*. Although most doctoral students in clinical psychology are now in PsyD programs, some non-APA approved, the APA continues to hold the scientist-practitioner as the training model of choice for doctoral students in clinical psychology with the result that most doctoral students in APA accredited programs are in PhD programs.

Scandal and Research Bias – "The Cyril Burt Affair"

Cyril Burt (1883–1971), one of the leading scientists in the world, disagreed with Spearman about his warning to educators to minimize IQ testing in the schools because it could be damaging to children; rather, educators should emphasize the genius in every child. Burt disagreed and recommended that psychological testing be used to stratify education toward the highly intelligent and opposed special education because intelligence was inherited and impossible to improve low intelligence. Burt based these beliefs on his monozygotic twin study research, in which he concluded that heredity was more prominent in intelligence than environment. Because of his excellent reputation, his findings had a significant impact on the international education community. But shortly after his death, questions began to occur whether he had fabricated correlations about separated twins that did not exist (Gillie, 1976).

Leon Kamin (1974), a Princeton psychologist, published *The Science of Politics in IQ*. He denounced Burt's research as fraudulent and his hereditarian position as politically motivated. Kamin accused Burt of purposely falsifying his data and creating one of the first major scandals in the history of psychology. Ironically, Burt received support from some psychologists who saw this controversy as an opportunity to reassert new forms of eugenic ideas of racial superiority. Most notably, Arthur Jensen, who agreed that the data might have been falsified but also believed that racial differences in intelligence had a genetic origin. He believed this made it necessary to separate the education of white and African American children and create different types of educational curriculum for the benefit both races (Jensen, 1969).

The *Cyril Burt Affair* provided opportunities for psychologists to address ethical issues and shadow forces related to psychological and scientific research (Tucker, 1997). Questions arose about the very nature of research. As discussed in Volume I, Chapter 5, does The Idols of Grave Errors of Francis Bacon apply to modern science? Do biases of scientists preclude any true objective research? Do scientists design research projects to simply confirm their biases? Is scientific research done for the benefit of science or to enhance the reputation of the scientist?

Because of ethical concerns related to scientific research, Lester Luborsky et al. (1975) resurrected the symbol of the *Dodo Bird Verdict,* which was coined in 1936 by *Saul Rosenzweig* (1907–2004). After studying 500 psychotherapies, Rosenzweig believed that all confirmed equally effective psychotherapeutic outcomes. Rosenzweig used the 1865 *Lewis Carroll* book, *Alice in Wonderland,* to symbolize his view of research (Rosenzweig, 1936). When several characters in the story became wet, the Dodo Bird decided to have a competition that required that everyone run around the lake until they were dry. At the end of the race, no one measured how fast or far they had run; all that mattered was that everyone was dry. When the race was over, everyone asked Dodo who won. After thinking long and hard, he said *everyone won* and everyone deserved prizes. Rosenzweig argued that common factors in research were more important than specific technical differences and that all research produces equally important outcomes (Budd & Hughes, 2009).

Science in the Private Interest

Figure 1.17

Researchers began to utilize the Dodo Bird Verdict when evaluating the true value of their research or when questioning the findings of other researchers. *Sheldon Krimsky* (1942–2022), a leading scholar of scientific ethics and biotechnology, warns of the perils of private companies controlling academic research. In his 2003 book, *Science in the Private Interest*, Krimsky (2003) argued that conflicts of interest are perceived and regulated very differently in public affairs and in science today because public affair scientists view themselves as participating in a higher calling than that of private scientists. The difference is public officials are prohibited from managing their portfolios during their tenure in office. Private scientists with patents and equity in companies are simply asked to disclose their interests.

Krimsky claims that blurred boundaries between public interest science and pursuit of private gain have severely compromised the integrity of university science. The academic universe is no longer as nurturing an environment for public-interest science because universities have been taken over by money managers and academic entrepreneurs who are looking for financially lucrative research. The system has become corrupted by the ongoing acceptance by academic researchers of millions of dollars in grants from corporate entities like the pharmaceutical industries and biotechnology companies. He argues that relationships between corporations, universities, and government agencies have resulted in biased science that puts profits over human health and the environment.

Symbols of the Birth of Modern Psychology

The Bell Curve: Intelligence and Class Structure in American Life

The Bell Curve: Intelligence and Class Structure, written in 1994 by psychologists Richard Hernstein and Charles Murray (1994), was in many ways more controversial than the Cyril Burt Affair because the debate became about whether class structure in America was based on intelligence. Although they argued that human intelligence is substantially inherited and that environment does play a role, their views on race and the creation of a cognitive elite caused passioned emotional reactions on all sides of the intelligence debate.

Figure 1.18

Hernstein and Murray (1994) claimed six assumptions about intelligence to be beyond significant technical dispute:

1 There is such a difference as a (*g*) general factor of cognitive ability on which human beings differ.
2 All standardized tests of academic aptitude or achievement measure this general factor to some degree, but IQ tests expressly designed for that purpose measure it most accurately.
3 IQ scores match, to a first degree, whatever it is that people mean when they use the word *intelligent*, or *smart*, in ordinary language.
4 IQ scores are stable, although not perfectly so, over much of a person's life.
5 Properly administered IQ tests are not demonstrably biased against social, economic, ethnic, or racial groups.
6 Cognitive ability is substantially inheritable apparently no less than 40 percent and no more than 80 percent.

Prior to the Bell Curve, there had been growing concern throughout the United States about overreliance on the IQ score and some efforts were made to limit its use. In *The IQ Controversary, the Media and Public Policy,* Snyderman and Rothman (1990) blamed the biased liberal media for these concerns by misinforming the public about the scientific findings of IQ tests. In 1994, *Barack Obama*, a community organizer prior to becoming the 44th president of the United States, denounced the Bell Curve in a National Public Radio (NPR) interview (All Things Considered, 1994). He viewed the book as resurfacing long-held racist beliefs in white supremacy because the cognitive elite were typically white and perceived as genetically superior; while the lower class were typically Black and perceived as genetically inferior. He also believed the book was politically motivated to end affirmative action and social programs that help the low-income and African American communities.

Like Plato's Philosopher Kings, Hernstein and Murray found that the best jobs in America were held by the cognitive elite and the worst jobs, usually manual labor, were done by the less intellectually endowed. In 2012, the work of Charles Murray (2012), *Coming Apart: The State of White America, 1960–2010*, again raised uncomfortable questions about the economic divide in America. He argued that the 1960 economic decline affected not only minorities but also led to the moral and economic bifurcation among white Americans. He believed that class differences in the white race changed after 1960, which resulted in two highly segregated white classes: the upper and lower white classes characterized by educational attainment, resulting in a cognitive elite

Murray argued that since 1960, the white working class had abandoned the founding father virtues of American society and became the new white lower class, which was less educated, less industrious, less likely to marry and raise children in two-parent household, and less politically and socially engaged. On the other hand, the new white upper class became well educated and maintained a strong religiosity, work ethic, and industriousness, creating emotionally healthy families. The reason for the change was based on new marriage and educational patterns. In the 1960s, the upper and lower white classes began to marry and live in their own intellectual stratum. This exacerbated the current economic divide and left an unprecedented sociopolitical divide that had never occurred previously in American history.

Murray raised concerns about the emergence of a cognitive elite, based not on race, but on intellectual superiority. For critics, the implication was that his research again implied white racial superiority based on intelligence. The *New York Times* (2012) rated *Coming Apart* as one of the 100 Most Notable Books of 2012 because the debate about race, class, and intelligence is necessary because whether intelligence is determined by nature or nurture remains unanswered.

From Birth to a Symbolic Home

At the beginning of the chapter, the symbol of a "road to hell" provided a symbolic introduction to the birth of psychology because it pointed to the possibility that good intentions need shadow awareness. History teaches that when science does not acknowledge the shadow elements of its work, hopeful dreams often become hurtful nightmares.

As the chapter concludes, the birth is still under construction. The "baby" is symbolically home, but the home is unfinished. The home has a strong foundation because psychology has become a highly respected discipline, thanks to the women and men that persevered and fought for its existence, often against powerful odds.

Like psychology, the building is complex, with many interesting rooms Some rooms are more complete than others. The most completed rooms were designed by empiricists and behaviorists. Treatment rooms are being remodeled by the psychoanalysts and Jungians. A new addition is in the process of being built by the humanists and existentialists because they were only recently added to the complex. Architectural plans for transpersonal psychology lay on the ground still not sure where, or if, they belong in this home. A big living room is being designed to bring everyone together to celebrate the diversity of this big, diverse family. The problem is that no one can agree on how the room should look or who should decide its final design. It appears the jury is still out on where it is located, comfortably situated by a university, where everyone can enjoy the stimulating, but often isolated, world of academia or in downtown in the middle of a community where the inhabitants are actively involved in utilizing psychological knowledge to solve community problems or maybe the complex borders by both locations.

Figure 1.19

There are still some big cracks that need to be fixed. There is a need for some good contractors and leaders to deal with the cracks that have historically led to divisions that delay completion of this beautiful construction and achievement of the APA mission statement: *To advance psychology as a science, as a profession, and a means of promoting the human welfare.* Symbols can guide, challenge, and speak in ways that illuminate the dangers and opportunities ahead so that the home is ultimately welcoming for all members of the family that live in this incredibly talented and diverse home.

Emancipatory Opportunities in the Birth of Psychology

Read Psychology's Struggle for Existence

Wundt would remain a strong advocate for psychology to remain rooted in philosophy. In 1913, Wundt (1913) wrote an article, "Psychology's Struggle for Existence," that he believed every psychologist should read annually. This article summarizes many of his beliefs ranging from the strengths of the emerging experimental psychology movement to his view of the limitations of empirical science.

Beware of New Forms of Eugenics

The new eugenics movement has shifted from the old eugenics goal to improve humanity toward the individual for the difficult moral decisions. A major proponent of modern eugenics is genetic engineering because the technology has been developed to modify genes to avoid certain traits and diseases. As technology advances, the ability to manipulate complex traits like appearance and intelligence and even the avoidance of mental and physical disorders may soon become possibilities raising moral, socioeconomic, religious, and political questions about what will be acceptable to the values of American culture.

Visit Galapagos Islands

The Galapagos Islands, a living laboratory to view evolution, comprise 600 miles off the coast of Ecuador, consisting of 13 main islands and 7 smaller islands. On the *Beagle*, Darwin visited four islands in 1835 over five weeks: San Cristobal, Floreana, Santiago, and Isabela. Spending most of his time on Santiago, he began to realize that the islands were made of the same physical resources, under the same climate and altitude and only 50–60 miles apart had so many different similar species, laying the foundation for his evolutionary theory. Read Glenn Geher and Nicole Wedbergs's (2020), *Positive Evolutionary Psychology – Darwin's Guide to a Better life.*

Attend to the Shadow of Special Education

Because an individualized education plan (IEP) is required to place a student in special education, parents need to understand they control and give final approval to the education plan of the local school district. Besides educational planning, the IEP process can address specific social and psychological interventions, including mental health treatment. To deal with the shadow elements of special education, there is growing evidence of the benefit of *mainstreaming education,* which is the practice of placing special education students in general education classes based on their educational needs. Although the social stigma and bullying of special education students in general education classes can occur, the practice has shown significant social and psychological benefits, preparing students to function more effectively in society beyond the educational system (Salvia, Ysseldyke & Witmer, 2017).

Recapture the Art of Psychological Testing

With all its shadow elements, psychological testing has continued to provide an important role in health care, education, criminal justice, the courts, and business. With insurance reimbursement limitations, its decreased use in public and private mental health agencies, and with the significant time commitment to complete a full battery of tests, psychological testing, especially projective testing, has been on a decline. For many psychologists, testing has lost its daily relevance and in the push for empirical validity, its soul. Or in the words of Stephen Finn, "what does it profit a test or a discipline if it gains empirical credibility yet forfeits and loses its soul." One way to recapture interest in psychological testing is for psychologists to rediscover its historic roots as an art as well as a science which the major forefathers believed made testing much more interesting and relevant. The *Collaborative Therapeutic Assessment* of *Finn* (2007) began to answer the biblical reference by providing an alternative, a way daily, to recapture the true purpose and spirit of psychological testing, and to halt its decline.

Symbols of the Birth of Modern Psychology

Beware of the Dodo Bird Verdict and the Privatization of Research

For the integrity of science, it is important that researchers are conscious of their personal biases and financial interests. Sheldon Krimsky and others have warned that private intrusion into university research by corporate interests has corrupted public-interest research.

QUESTIONS 1

1.1 Describe the political, socioeconomic, and cultural influences that led to the birth of modern psychology.

1.2 Explain how Wundt reconciled voluntarism and volkerpsychologie, cultural psychology.

1.3 Describe how functionalism is in alignment with the American psyche.

1.4 Explain the impact of Darwinism on the birth of modern psychology.

1.5 Describe how intelligence research was influenced by the eugenics movement.

1.6 Explain why the Rorschach Test has lasted for over 100 years, despite its controversies.

1.7 Analyze the societal implications of the Bell Curve research.

1.8 Describe how the Dodo Bird Verdict impacts psychological research.

1.9 Explain what it means for all psychologists to have a "Symbolic Home."

Universal Meanings of Chapter Symbols

Figure 1.0. Image source Leta-hollingworth. https://medium.com/rediscover-steam/leta-stetter-hollingworth-educator-psychologistfeminist-c3f7a299d6f6

Figure 1.1. A symbol of the natural sciences and psychology emerging from the Renaissance in a laboratory.

Figure 1.2. The shadow, always present even in positive developments.

Figure 1.3. The laboratory as a symbol of scientific progress.

Figure 1.4. Psychology based in the philosophy of physicalism.

Figure 1.5. The psychologist's fallacy that the laboratory reflects the universality of the real world.

Figure 1.6. Mechanical equilibrium as the universal necessity for a true religious experience.

Figure 1.7. Evolutionary concept of the survival of the fittest.

Figure 1.8. Symbolic of the human relationship to primates in evolution

Figure 1.9. A symbol for spirituality and religion.

Figure 1.10. The restoration of the Aryan race by conquering the racially inferior world

Figure 1.11. Symbolic of the goal to understand the brain.

Figure 1.12. Symbolic of the misuse of psychological testing.

Figure 1.13. The impact of the environment on intelligence.

Figure 1.14. A tool to better understand personality dynamics and the unconscious.

Figure 1.15. A symbol of the power of authority to convince people to commit unthinkable crimes against humanity.

Figure 1.16. The many interpretations of the symbol of psychology.

Figure 1.17. A universal symbol of the shadow of clinical research.
Figure 1.18. Symbolic of the controversy that American society is controlled by a cognitive elite.
Figure 1.19. The symbolic home of the Four Forces of Psychology of modern psychology.

References

All Things Considered (1994, October 28). *Barack Obama: Charles Murray's political expediency denounced.* New York, NY: National Public Radio.

Araujo, D.F. (2012). Why did Wundt abandon his early theory of the unconscious? Towards a new interpretation of Wundt's psychological project? *History of Psychology, 15*(1), 33–49.

Araujo, D.F. (2016). *Wundt and the philosophical foundations of psychology.* Switzerland: Springer International Publishing.

Binet, A. & Simon, T. (2015). *The development of intelligence in children.* (E.S. Kite, Trans.). Baltimore: Williams & Wilkins. (Original work published 1916).

Blackwell, A.B. (1875). *The sexes throughout nature.* New York, NY: G.P. Putnam's Sons.

Blass, T. (1991). Understanding behavior in the Milgram obedience experiment: The role of personality, situations, and their interactions. *Journal of Personality and Social Psychology, 60*(3), 398–413.

Blass, T. (2004). *The man who shocked the world: The life of Stanley Milgram.* New York, NY: Basic Books.

Bringman, W., Balance, G., William, D.G. & Evans, R.B. (1975). Wilhelm Wundt 1832–1920: A brief biographical sketch. *Journal of the History of Behavioral Science, 12*, 65–77.

Budd, R. & Hughes, I. (2009). The dodo bird verdict—Controversial, inevitable and important: A commentary on 30 years of meta-analyses. *Clinical Psychology & Psychotherapy. 16*(6), 510–522.

Cohen, A. (2016). *Imbeciles: The Supreme Court, American eugenics, and the sterilization of Carrie Buck.* New York, NY: Penguin Press.

Colbert, C. (1997). *A measure of perfection: Phrenology and the fine arts in America.* Chapel Hill, NC: The University of North Carolina Press.

Darwin, C. (2004). *The descent of man in relation to sex.* New York, NY: Penguin Books. (Original work published 1871).

Darwin, C. (2009). *The expression of the emotions in man and animals.* New York, NY: Penguin Books. (Originally Published in 1879).

Darwin, C. (2017). *The origin of the species by natural selection: Or the preservation of favored races in the struggle for life.* Los Angeles: Enhanced Media Publishing. (Original work published 1859).

Exner, J.E. (1995). *The Rorschach: A comprehensive system: Vol 1.* Basic foundations. New York, NY: John Wiley & Sons.

Finn, S.E. (2007). *In our client's shoes: Theory and techniques of therapeutic assessment.* Mahwah NJ: Lawrence Erlbaum.

Fuller, R. (2017). *The book that changed America: How Darwin's theory of evolution ignited a nation.* New York, NY: Penguin Random House LLC.

Galton, S.F. (2015). *Inquiries into human faculty and its development.* London: Sagwan Press. (Original work published 1883).

Galton, S.F. (2019). *Hereditary genius.* London: The Ostara Press. (Original work published in 1869).

Geher, G. & Wedberg, N. (2020). *Positive evolutionary psychology; Darwin's guide to living a richer life.* New York, NY: Oxford Press.

Gillie, O. (1976, October 24). *Crucial data was faked by eminent psychologist.* London: London Times Publishing.

Goddard, H.H. (1912). *The Kallikak family: A study in the heredity of feeble mindedness.* New York, NY: MacMillan.

Goddard, H.H. (1914). *Feeble-mindedness: Its causes and consequences.* New York, NY: Macmillan

Goddard, H.H. (1917). Mental tests and the immigrant. *Journey of Delinquency, 2*, 243–277.

Goddard, H.H. (1919). *Psychology of the normal and subnormal.* New York, NY: Dodd, Mead and Company.

Gould, S.J. (1981). *The mismeasure of man.* New York, NY: Norton.

Groth-Marnat, G. (2003). *Handbook of psychological assessment.* New York, NY: John Wiley & Sons.

Guilford, J.P. (1967). *The nature of human intelligence.* New York, NY: McGraw-Hill.

Heller, S. (2000). *The swastika: Symbol beyond redemption?* New York, NY: Allworth Press.

Hergenhahn, B.R. (2009). *An introduction to the history of psychology (6th rev.).* Belmont, California: Thomas Wadsworth.

Hernstein, R.R.J. & Murray, C. (1994). *The bell curve: Intelligence and class structure in American life.* New York, NY: Free Press.

Hitler, A. (1998). *Mein kampf.* New York, NY: Houghton Mifflin Company. (Original work published 1925).

Hollingworth, L.S. (1942). *Children above 180 IQ (Stanford-Binet).* Yonkers-on-Hudson. NY: World Book Company.

Hunt, M. (1993). *The story of psychology.* New York, NY: Doubleday

James, W. (2000). *Pragmatism and other works.* New York, NY: Penguin Books. (Original work published 1902)

James, W. (2016). *The varieties of religious experience.* New York, NY: Pantianos Classics. (Original work published 1902).

James, W. (2017). *Principles of psychology.* New York, NY: Pantianos Classics. (Original work published 1890).

Jensen, A.R. (1969). How much can we boost I.Q. and scholastic achievement? *Harvard Educational Review*, 33, 1–123.

Jensen, A.R. (1998). *The g factor: The science of mental ability.* Westport, CN: Praeger Books.

Kamin, L.J. (1974). *The science and politics of IQ.* Potomac, MD: Lawrence Erlbaum Associates.

Kelley, D. (1947). *22 cells in Nuremberg. A psychiatrist examines the Nazi criminals.* London: W. H. Allen.

Klein, A.G. (2002). *A forgotten voice: A biography of Leta Stetter Hollingworth.* Scottsdale, AZ: Great Potential Press Inc.

Klopfer, B. & Davidson, H.H. (1962). *The rorschach technique: An introductory manual.* New York, NY: Harcourt, Brace & World.

Kohler, R.E. (1994). *Lords of the fly: Drosophila genetics and the experimental life.* Chicago: University of Chicago Press.

Korn, J.H., Davis, R. & Davis, S.F. (1991). Historians' and chairpersons' judgements of eminence among psychologists. *American Psychologist*, 46, 789–792.

Krimsky, S. (2003). *Science in the private interest: Has the corruption of private profits corrupted biomedical research.* Lanham, MD: Rowman & Littlefield Publishers.

Leslie, M. (2000, July/August). *The vexing legacy of Lewis Terman.* Stanford: Stanford Magazine.

Lilenfield, S.O., Wood, J.M. & Garb, H.N. (2001). What's wrong with this picture? *Scientific American*, 81–87.

Luborsky, L., Singer, B. & Luborsky, E. (1975). Is it true that everyone has won and all mist have prizes? *Archives of General Psychiatry*, 32, 995–1008.

Malthus, T.G. (Ed. G. Gilbert). (2008). *An essay on the principle of population.* New York, NY: Oxford Press. (Original work published 1798).

Mihura, J. L., Meyer, G.J., Bombel, G. & Dumitrascu, N. (2013). The validity of individual Rorschach variables: Systematic reviews and meta-analyses of the comprehensive system. *Psychological Bulletin. 139*(3), 548–605.

Mihura, J.L., Meyer, G.J., Bombel, G. & Dumitrascu, N. (2015). Standards, accuracy, and questions of bias in Rorschach meta-analyses: Reply to Wood, Garb, Nezworski, Lilienfeld, and Duke. *Psychological Bulletin. 141*, 250–260.

Milgram, S. (1983). *Obedience to authority.* New York, NY: Harper Perennial.

Murray, C. (2012). *Coming apart.* New York, NY: Cox and Murray, Inc.

New York Times (2012, November 27). *100 notable books of 2012* (Book Review Section). New York, NY: New York Times Publishing.

Oden, M.L. (1968). The fulfillment of promise. 40-year follow-up of the Terman gifted group. *Genetic Psychology Monographs. 77*(1), 3–93.

Ogden, R.M. & Spearman, C. (1925). The nature of intelligence and the principles of cognition. *The American Journal of Psychology. 36*(1), 140–145.

Pickren, W.E. & Rutherford, A. (Eds.) (2017). *125 years of the American psychological association.* Washington, DC: APA Books.

Piotrowski, C. (2015) On the decline of projective techniques in professional psychological training. *North American Journal of Psychology*, 17, 2.

Reaves, R. P. (2006) The history of licensure of psychologists in the United States and Canada. In T.J. Vaughn (Ed.). *Psychology licensure and certification: What students needs to know*. Washington, D.C: American Psychological Association, pp. 17–26.

Rosenberg, A. (2017). *The myth of the 20th century*. New York, NY: Black Kite Publishing. (Original work published 1930).

Rosenzweig, S. (1936). Some implicit common factors in diverse methods of psychotherapy. *American Journal of Orthopsychiatry, 6*, 412–415.

Salvia, J., Ysseldyke, J. & Witmer, S. (2017). *Assessment: In special and inclusive education* (13th Ed.). Boston, MA: Cengage Learning.

Searls, D. (2017). *The inkblots: Hermann Rorschach, his iconic test, and the power of seeing*. New York, NY: Crown Publishers.

Shapiro, W. (1985). Some implications of Clark Wissler's race theory. *Mankind, 15*, 1–17.

Silverman, L.K. (1992). Leta Stetter Hollingworth: Champion of the psychology of women and gifted children. *Journal of Educational Psychology, 84*, 20–27.

Snyderman, M. & Rothman, S. (1990). *The IQ controversy, the media, and public policy*. New Jersey: Transaction Publishers.

Sokal, M.M. (1971) The unpublished autobiography of James McKeen Cattell. *American Psychologist, 26*, 621–635.

Spencer, H. (1855). *Principles in psychology*. London, England: Longman, Brown, Green and Longmans and Roberts.

Stern, W. (2018). *The psychological methods of testing intelligence*. London: Forgotten Books. (Original work published 1914).

Terman, L.M. (1906). Genius and stupidity: A study of some of the intellectual processes of seven "bright" and seven "stupid" boys. *Pedagogical Seminary, 13* (3), 30–373.

Terman, L.M. (1925). *Mental and physical traits of a thousand gifted children: Genetic studies of genius*. Redwood City, CA: Stanford University Press.

Thomas, T. (2009). Discovering Lightner Witmer: A forgotten hero of psychology. *Scientific Psychology, 4*, 1–13.

Titchener, E.B. (2018). *A beginner's psychology: What it is and what is does*. Istanbul: Cheapest Books. (Original work published 1915).

Tucker, W.H. (1997). Re-reconsidering Burt: Beyond a reasonable doubt. *Journal of the History of the Behavioral Sciences, 33(2),* 145–162.

U.S. Department of State Office of the Historian. *The Immigration Act of 1924 (The Johnson-Reed Act)*. (Milestones 1921–1936). Retrieved from https://history.state.gov/milestones/1921-1936/immigration act

Vincent, H.P. (1980). *The trying-out of Moby Dick*. Kent, Ohio: Kent State University Press.

Weiner, I.B. (2003). *Principles of Rorschach interpretation*. Mahwah N.J: Lawrence Erlbaum.

Whitaker, R. (2019). *Mad in America: Bad science, bad medicine, and the enduring mistreatment of the mentally ill*. New York, NY: Basic Books.

Wolf, T.H. (1973). *Alfred Binet*. Chicago: University of Chicago Press.

Wood, J.M., Nezworski, M.T., Lilenfield, S. & Garb, H.N. (2003). *What's wrong with the Rorschach? Science confronts the controversial inkblot test*. New York, NY: Jossey-Bass Books.

Wright, G.N. (2001). *A life of Sir Francis Galton: From African exploration to the birth of eugenics*. New York, NY: Oxford University Press.

Wundt, W. (1910). *Principles of physiological psychology*. (E.B. Titchener, Trans.). New York, NY: Macmillan Company.

Wundt, W. (2013). Psychology's struggle for existence: Second edition 1913. (J.T. Lamiell, Trans.). *History of Psychology, 16*(3), 197–213.

Wundt, W. (2016). *The elements of folk psychology: Outline of a psychological history of the development of mankind*. (E.L. Schaub, Trans.). London: Macmillan Company. (Original work published in 1916).

Yannielli, J. (2013). A Yahgan for the killing murder, memory and Charles Darwin. *The British Journal for the History of Science, 46*, 3, 415–443.

Zenderland, L. (1998). *Measuring minds: Henry Herbert Goddard and the origins of American intelligence testing*. Cambridge: Cambridge University Press.

Figure 2.0

2 Symbols of Freudian and Relational Psychoanalysis

The First Force in Psychology

Introduction

> Recent brain scans have shed light on how the brain simulates the future. These simulations are done mainly in the dorsolateral prefrontal cortex, the CEO of the brain, using memories of the past… There is a struggle between different parts of the brain concerning the future, which may have desirable and undesirable outcomes. Ultimately it is the dorsolateral prefrontal cortex that mediates between these and makes the final decisions. Some neurologists have pointed out that this struggle resembles… the dynamics between Freud's ego, id and superego.
>
> - Michio Kaku

The Four Forces of Psychology

As discussed in the first chapter of Volume I, critical theorist Jürgen Habermas envisioned a psychology that acknowledged the importance of three major knowledge interests in psychology. The natural sciences interest in an empirical objective psychology measures and observes behavior. Humanistic sciences interest in hermeneutic psychology seeks subjective meaning and the purpose of behavior. Social sciences interest is in psychological emancipation from the social conditions that cause human suffering and the constraints of political, socioeconomic, and cultural systems.

The four major forces recognized in psychology provide different but important understandings of the human experience. As an overview, the psychoanalytic force explores the unseen unconscious world. The behavioral force explores the world that can be seen, observed, and measured. The humanistic- existential force explores the purpose and meaning of existence. The transpersonal force explores the world beyond the ego, the human need for spiritual, mystical, and ascetic experiences. Even though all are influenced by the social, natural, and hermeneutic interests, this and the final five chapters will show how each force arrived at different conclusions.

The symbol is a visual reminder of the four forces as a unified, not separate, collection of dynamic forces. Not at odds with each other, but necessarily integrated together if psychology is to reach its full potential.

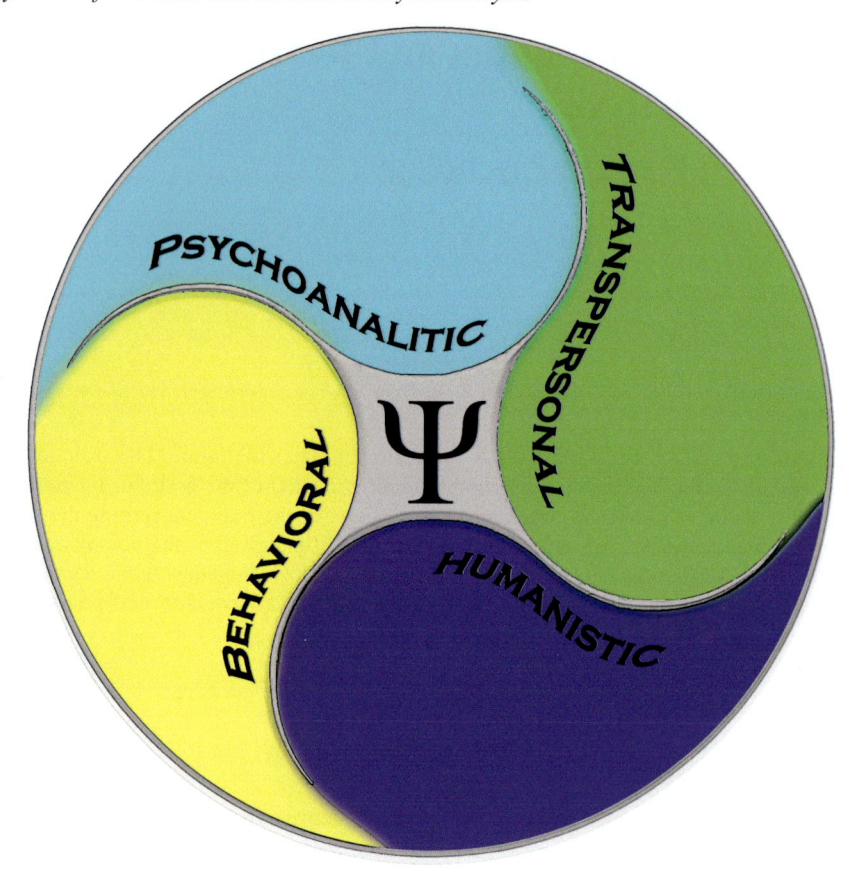

Figure 2.1

The First Force – Psychoanalysis

This chapter will focus on the two major psychoanalytic schools of thought: Freudian psychoanalysis, and relational psychoanalysis. Relational psychoanalysis includes the expansion beyond the Freudian view of the driving force of a libidinal-driven unconscious to the unconscious driving force to connect emotionally to satisfying human relationships. Relational psychoanalysis includes object-relations, attachment, and interpersonal psychoanalytic approaches.

Freudian Psychoanalysis

Historical Analysis

Political Systems

Psychoanalysis emerged in the twentieth century during a period of significant political change as the world adapted to the industrial revolution with the emerging political forces of capitalism and communism. Sigmund Freud (1856–1939) and Karl Marx (1818–1883) had different analyses for the cause of the resulting alienation and psychological disturbance. Although important in European psychology, it was understandable living through McCarthyism, the Cold War, the Vietnam War, and the ongoing demonization of any rational discussion of Marx, mainstream American psychology struggled to engage in a thoughtful analysis of the psychological implications of Marxism, although Marxist political systems dominated a large part of the world in the twentieth century.

For Marx, capitalism created alienation because of its inability to provide the basic needs of financial security and meaningful work. Under capitalism, Marx thought that human relationships, even sexuality, had alienated people not only from others, but also from the psychological experience of a true self.

Work was only for survival and had become mechanical, addictive, and without any psychological meaning or purpose (Sperber, 2013). What increased the alienation was the reality that the working class had no political power to control their work or to change the corrupt capitalistic system. Under the control of capitalists, the state resisted political change and only through revolution could a liberated state work on behalf of working people. Marx believed his theories provided philosophy the opportunity to finally change the world, as stated on his gravesite: *Philosophers have only interpreted the world in various ways. The point is to change it.* Marx believed communism would bring genuine psychological fulfillment and would eliminate worry about the basic human needs of food, shelter, and clothing.

In the Marxist utopia, humanity would again see the value of social cooperation and collective action over personal greed and the desire to accumulate wealth. Human sexuality would return to its original purpose of love rather than a way to escape from an alienated world. Work would again have purpose and meaning because it would be under the political and economic control of the working class. In his utopian vision, a higher social consciousness would end the need for a political government; the state would wither away. No longer corrupted by private property and the accumulation of wealth, communism would liberate the proletariat from the bourgeois.

The proletariat was the social class of wage earners whose only power was their labor, their capacity to work. The bourgeois emerged as a social class during the Industrial Revolution associated with people who lived in a borough and were the merchants and craftsmen of a city. In Marxism, the bourgeoisie became a political class and the driving force of capitalism. In *Critique of the Gotha Program*, Marx (1891/2018) popularized the philosophic slogan 'from each according to their ability, to each according to their need." In the Marxist utopia, the communist system produced such an abundance of wealth that everyone would have free access to goods, capital, and services. This would revolutionize the very nature of human existence, ending the alienation of capitalism by creating a society of social cooperation and personal empowerment.

The hammer and sickle became the symbol of communism. The hammer symbolized the industrial working class, and the sickle symbolized the peasantry. In alliance, they would have proletarian control over all the industrial and agrarian political and economic forces of society (Marx, 1981/2018).

Figure 2.2

Freud had a different view of alienation. It was not the capitalistic political system but human nature that created alienation. Private property and political exploitation were just other ways that human beings expressed their unconscious aggression toward one another. Alienation was psychological, not economic, or political. Alienation was rooted in the ongoing unconscious struggle of id and superego with the weak and overwhelmed conscious ego (Gay, 1988).

In *Civilization and Its Discontents* (Freud, 1930/1961b), one of the most important and influential books in the history of modern psychology, Freud addressed the clash between the individual and society. Freud placed psychological understanding in an historic and political context when he addressed the horror and slaughter of World War I and the communist Bolshevik Revolution. These historic events reinforced his view of inconsolable violence that occurs when civilization neglects the destructive forces of the unconscious. By neglecting the forces of the unconscious, the modern world dealt with alienation through the destructive defense mechanisms of intoxication, isolation, and sublimation (Gay, 1988).

Freud viewed "man as wolf to man" and that innate human aggression would lead to more wars because humanity projected its own destructive unconscious impulses on the evil "others." He rejected any assistance religion could offer because its standards were impossible to meet. Although Freud thought the best hope for humanity was to strengthen the ego, he acknowledged that psychoanalysis would not be available to most people. At the conclusion of *Civilization and Its Discontents*, being a nihilist, Freud, in dramatic terms, avoided any reassurance to either the "wildest (political) revolutionaries" or the "virtuous (religious) believers" that civilization could be saved from the innate human instinct of aggression and self-destruction (Freud, 1930/1961b, p. 92). Because aggression was innate, part of human nature and deeply rooted in the unconscious, the survival of civilization was not only not assured, but was in fact in great peril.

Alfred Adler (1870–1937), an Austrian psychiatrist, broke with Freud after nine years of being a resolute original follower. Using the Latin word *individuus,* meaning *indivisibility*, Adler founded individual psychology, which emphasized holism, the individual in community, a prelude to community psychology. Adler rejected the Freudian view of human nature, the unconscious, and the futility of political engagement (Adler, 1927/1998). Through political activism, humanity could avoid being victims of human nature and the Industrial Revolution. Adler emphasized conscious over unconscious, political activism over sexual motivation, and free will over determinism (Ansbacher & Ansbacher, 1956). In the history of psychology, Adler, as a democratic socialist, was one of the strongest proponents of democracy because he believed that the treatment of psychoneurosis necessitated emphasizing political education and social activism (Adler, 1933/1964). The transformation of the political system required that parents, teachers, and community leaders teach democratic values, especially the basic democratic principle of equality, learning how treat one another as equals.

Figure 2.3

54 Symbols of Freudian and Relational Psychoanalysis

Eli Zaretsky (2015), in his work *Political Freud: A History,* describes how Freudian thought inspired political change in the modern era by examples of the democratic and the socialist revolutions, the New Deal, and the civil rights movement. Zaretsky advocates for a political Freudianism movement that provides a psychoanalytic examination of consumer capitalism, racial violence, ant-Semitism, and patriarchy. His belief is that psychoanalytic thought offers a unique perspective and possible political solutions to the problems of modern society. Lynn Layton, Nancy Hollander and Susan Gutwill (2006) describe in *Psychoanalysis, Class and Politics* how to practice a politically oriented psychoanalysis in clinical settings.

Socioeconomic Systems

By creating a city-centric and a less agrarian and rural civilization, the Industrial Revolution changed the economic order and human psychology forever. During the Industrial Revolution, the bourgeoisie assumed control over the means of production, and it was the bourgeois class who protected private property and fought to preserve private capital to ensure their socioeconomic power and supremacy. It was the bourgeoisie that laid the socioeconomic foundation for the modern "middle class."

Figure 2.4

Although little is known about his early life, Freud grew up in the emerging bourgeoisie class. His father was a merchant businessperson who always struggled financially (Ellenberger, 1970). Freud experienced how the Industrial Revolution changed human psychology because the competition for economic survival depended on the individual family rather than the large agrarian families. Until the creation of labor unions and progressive political movements, people felt psychologically alienated not only from society, but from themselves. Because of the inhuman and cruel industrial world conditions, it was not surprising that the first psychiatrists like Freud were called "alienists" (Ellenberger, 1970). It is also not surprising that the Industrial Revolution also laid the foundation for psychoanalysis.

The Industrial Revolution created a class-based economic system comprised of the burgeoning rich capitalist and the poor classes. Capitalism based on private ownership, private property, and the accumulation of private wealth emerged as the dominant economic system in the world. Economic prosperity depended on the exploitation of the poor for the accumulation of increasing capital. Capital meant control of all the goods and services that had economic value, including human capital and the lives of human beings. Struggling under exploitative conditions with no control over his means of production, the "new person" needed to do oppressive work for the sake of their family. Capitalism in all its various forms has changed and evolved throughout the centuries and remained the dominant economic system throughout the world.

Cultural Systems

Freud lived during a time of great political and cultural turmoil that lasted until after World War I with the collapse of the Austrian-Hungarian Empire. Although Freud lived most of his life in Vienna until his exile to London in 1938, he was a child of the Empire, born in Moravia, the present-day Czech Republic. Freud was exposed to the ethnic and cultural strife in the Empire because of the many anti-Semitic parties and movements. The populist and anti-Semitic politics of the Christian Social Party became a model for the future Nazism of Adolf Hitler (Ellenberger, 1970).

Freud lived after the emancipation of the Jews late in the nineteenth century when the Jewish ghettos were abolished, which resulted in the assimilation of the Jewish people into cities throughout the Empire. This assimilation into the dominant Christian cultures created psychological distress in the Jewish community, especially between orthodox and liberal Jews (Ellenberger, 1970). This distress would alienate Freud from the Jewish religion and provide the foundation for his rejection of organized religion. In *The Future of an Illusion* (1927/1961a), Freud presented a pessimistic view of institutional religion by its emphasis on human weakness and sin; he contended that religion exacerbated human vulnerability and helplessness. To overcome this feeling of insecurity, religion created an illusion of God as an all-powerful protective father figure. The result was that religion reduced humans culturally to a permanent, weak, irrational child-like psychological state.

Freud lived during the Victorian era, which lasted under Queen Victoria for over 60 years. In many ways, this was a very progressive period in history that does not fit the stereotype or caricature of the Victorian era. It was during this period that England turned away from rationalism and toward romanticism. It was also a period of great innovation; inventions that would provide the foundation for a middle-class culture that included the electric lightbulb, the typewriter, the calculator, the washing machine, plastic, refrigerators, the internal combustion engine, and a robust rail system.

The period of 1850–1870 was the golden years of the Victorian era in which a middle class emerged and became emulated throughout the modern world. Culturally, the English middle class adopted the values and libertarian philosophy of the French Revolution, which was based on strict moral values in reaction to the debauchery of the aristocratic class of the early nineteenth century. Progressivism also emerged through the evangelical and nonconformist religious movements of the Methodists, Presbyterians, Calvinists, and Quakers who rebelled against the Puritan movement of the sixteenth and seventeenth centuries and sought to "purify" the human body from sin through the practices of the Church of England and Roman Catholic Church. The nonconformist movement played a significant role in the new emerging middle class because of its opposition to discrimination and advocacy for religious freedom, equality, and social justice. To the dismay of Marx, concern for the poor and the control of child labor diminished the brutal impact of the Industrial Revolution because Marx believed the revolution would start in England. Rather, the working classes of England sought the successes of middle-class life, the bourgeois, over a communist revolution.

Although most Victorians devoted their lives to hard work, temperance, frugality, and upward mobility, underneath the appearance of stability, the shadows of sexism and sexual repression emerged and became forerunners to the shadow of the modern middle class. Middle-class sexuality needed to be controlled as sexuality was a hidden geyser that could erupt at any moment. The model middle-class woman was to be chaste until marriage and after marriage expected to have children and stay home and take care of the family. In Victorian society, all pre-marital sex was discouraged; children were often severely punished for masturbation and sexual experimentation.

It was not surprising that in this cultural context Freud's theories would be based heavily on sexual repression (Ellenberger, 1970). Between his patients' and his own life experiences, he concluded that sexual repression was at the root of neurotic behavior (Freud, 1905/1962). It was also not surprising that his view of women would result from a nurturing mother and the sexual Victorian values of his wife. In the Victorian tradition, they both avoided a social life or a career outside the home. Although a prisoner of his Victorian culture, Freud modeled the importance of rebellion that needed to occur for true emancipation. He revolted against Victorian sexual values and was severely criticized and often ostracized for his views of sexuality. However, Freud inspired many of the "cultural revolutions" in modern times, especially the American sexual cultural revolutions of the 1920s and 1960s (Vannoy, 1996).

Natural Science Influence

Animal Magnetism and Mesmerism Influence

One of the most colorful and unjustly demeaned physicians in psychological history, Franz Mesmer (1734–1815), created animal magnetism. This occurred when natural transference occurred between animate and inanimate objects. His theory initially met with some medical acceptance because of the belief that planets affected humans through animal gravitation and the Newtonian theory of universal gravitation (Ellenberger, 1970).

Mesmer successfully utilized magnets after a Jesuit priest, Maximilian Heil, told Mesmer of his magnetic cures. His success led to a magnetism movement that conflicted with a world-famous exorcist, Austrian priest Johann Gessner. Messmer believed Gessner was using animal magnetism, not his spiritual powers to "drive out the devils." Mesmer believed that every human body possessed a magnetic field that was an equally distributed force field in a healthy person. Illness resulted from an uneven distribution of the magnetic force field.

Mesmer discovered that magnetic therapy redistributed the magnetic field and returned a patient to health. After a famous cure of a blind woman, Maria Parodies, who could only see in his presence, the medical community accused Mesmer of being a charlatan and he exiled to Paris (Ellenberger, 1970).

In France, his popularity grew, and he performed animal magnetism in large groups. Patients held iron rods that had been magnetized from a baquet, a tub filled with magnetized water. In a dimly lit room with soft music and with fragrance of orange blossoms, Mesmer designed a "crisis" after which he emerged wearing a lilac cloak and waving a yellow wand. Upon seeing Mesmer, a patient would typically scream, break into a cold sweat, and convulse. As his fame grew, his clinic successfully treated thousands of patients. He became a legitimate threat to the church fathers who alleged he was in consort with the devil and the medical profession.

Even though he was accused of being a charlatan and a quack, his success did not deter his efforts to gain acceptance from his medical peers. In 1784, the Society of Harmony, an organization promoting animal magnetism, convinced the king of France to create a commission to scientifically assess the effectiveness of animal magnetism. The high-level commission included the presiding officer, Benjamin Franklin; Antoine Lavoiser the famous chemist; and Joseph Guillotin, the creator of the guillotine seen as the "humane" way to end the life of condemned criminals (Ellenberger, 1970). Much to the dismay of Mesmer, the commission report found that there was no such thing as animal magnetism. Mesmer was dismissed as a mystic and a fanatic.

Figure 2.5

The report destroyed Mesmer and he sank in historic obscurity. The results were full of irony because the commission found that the only positive results were the powers of imagination and suggestion. History would judge Mesmer more favorably when he was acknowledged as the father of hypnosis, suggestion being a key hypnosis technique (Pinter & Lynn, 2008). Mesmer became another historic tragic example of what happens when mainstream political, medical, and scientific communities feel threatened.

Although the commission silenced Mesmer, Marquis de Puysegur (1751–1825), a member of the Society of Harmony, continued his work. Puysegur discovered that the Mesmer technique to create a crisis was not necessary. Placing someone in a peaceful, sleep-like state resulted in replacing crisis with the concept of trance, a state of awareness or consciousness other than normal waking consciousness. Puysegur made another significant finding while treating one of his most important patients with magnetic therapy. Victor Race was a young peasant in the employ of his famous French family. Victor displayed a unique form of a sleeping trance not seen in mesmerism. Puysegur observed a similarity between this sleeping trance and natural sleep walking – somnambulism – which he called artificial somnambulism: a sleep-like state in which Victor would follow his commands to talk about specific topics, perform various physical activities, and even dance to imagined music.

Puysegur continued to make discoveries that apply to most of the modern hypnotic techniques of today. Most importantly, he discovered posthypnotic amnesia, which was the inability to remember what had occurred while in a trance, and post-hypnotic suggestions, which were instructions given during a trance to affect behavior after the trance ended. These were behaviors that continued to occur after the trance ended without any conscious awareness of the suggestions made during the trance.

Thermodynamic Influence

Surprising to many, psychodynamic theory was influenced and shaped by the natural sciences. Freud was influenced by the work of Hermann Helmholtz (1821–1894), the great natural scientist, empiricist, physicist, chemist, physiologist, and experimental psychologist. It was his law of thermodynamics that would have a profound impact of Freud and the development of psychodynamic psychology.

Historically, thermodynamics developed from the effort to improve the efficiency of early steam engines to help the French win the Napoleonic Wars. Freud showed a great interest in the thermodynamics of steam power and was fascinated with steam engine trains. He viewed similarities between thermodynamics and drive theory, which provided a foundation concept for the natural science influence in psychoanalysis.

Helmholtz was an empiricist in the tradition of British empiricism who viewed the physical determinants of sensation as most important. For Helmholtz, physical sensations explain psychological perceptions. However, some sensations, especially visual perceptions, occur so quickly that they could only be accounted for by inference beyond sensation. His theory of unconscious inference influenced Freud to view the unconscious more than sensory physiology. One of the teachers of Freud was Ernst Brucke (1842–1906), a student of Helmholtz. Brucke was a positivist physiologist who encouraged Freud to stay in medicine and not pursue a career in philosophy because Freud was studying phenomenological psychology with Franz Brentano (1838–1917). Brucke was the professor that shaped his natural science concept of drive theory, the Freudian view of the distribution of psychological energy.

Figure 2.6

The first law of thermodynamics is the law of conservation, which is the total transfer of energy in a closed system where the energy remains homeostatic. In this closed system, energy can be transformed, but no new energy can be created. In the human body, homeostasis is essential for mental and physical health. In Freudian thought, people are born with psychological needs that are met by finding a satisfying "object," a human being, for homeostasis. When instinctual and psychological needs are not met, an internal imbalance is detected by the homeostatic mechanisms, a drive attempts to restore homeostasis. Mental disturbance occurs when a drive cannot find the hemostasis of a satisfying "object."

Experimental Psychology Influence

Gustav Fechner (1801–1887), often viewed with Wundt and Helmholtz, as a father of modern psychology, is the founder of psychophysics. Psychophysics is concerned with the effect of physical stimuli, especially the intensity of stimulation, on mental processes. Psychophysicists studied after the presentation of a stimuli the differential threshold, the smallest detectable mathematical difference between psychological sensation and the physical intensity of the response via the formula $S = k \log R$, proving that the mind was susceptible to measurement. This means that sensations are always relative to the level of background stimulation.

60 Symbols of Freudian and Relational Psychoanalysis

For Fechner, like Freud, the iceberg symbolized the mind since he believed that consciousness only detected 10 percent of environmental stimuli, while the remaining 90 percent remained unconscious (Marshal, 1969).

Fechner became a satirist, philosopher, spiritualist, and mystic. His panpsychism led him to his scientific discovery of psychophysics, the belief that all things physical have consciousness. Because he knew his panpsychism would never be accepted in the narrow scientific world, he also wrote under the pseudonym of Dr. Mises (Marshal, 1969). His work, *Zend-Avesta*, written as Dr. Mises, was inspired by Zoroastrianism, with his hope that psychophysics would return psychology to the origin of psyche before it was stripped in modern times of its true meaning; the "living word" of Zoroaster who speaks of another place ensouled and possessed with spirituality (Marshal, 1969). This world is just like earth but alive and greater in spirituality than all its creatures. Ultimately, Fechner inspired Freud to explore religion, mythology, and philosophy within the confines of the natural sciences and experimental psychology. Freud certainly was inspired; most notably by exploring mythology and using the Greek Oedipus Rex myth as a psychodynamic cornerstone of psychoanalysis.

Figure 2.7

This symbol provides a way to understand the Freudian concept of id which is like a powerful ocean wave constantly "crashing" against the ego. Freud was highly influenced by Charles Darwin (1809–1882) and read most of his works as he was developing his theory of psychoanalysis. Darwin, like Freud, believed that humans were motivated by instincts rather than by reason. For Freud it was the unconscious id, not the ego, which created the most significant reaction to human instincts. The id is the location of aggressive and violent instincts, those instincts that need to be repressed for the survival of civilization. Freud, the nihilist, was skeptical that civilization could ever control the powerful id because humanity remained unconscious and attended more to the rational, ego-driven mind, neglecting the dangerous unconscious forces of the id (Jones, 1957).

Neurological and Physiological Influences

In his 1895 *Project for Scientific Psychology*, Freud (1895/2010), in correspondence with his colleague, Wilhelm Fliess, explained psychological phenomenon in purely natural science terms. At the beginning of his work, he expressed his intention to describe psychology as a natural science and to explain psychological processes in specifiable physiological terms. Freud referred to his approach as psychology for neurologists because of the importance of neural pathways and the application of Helmholtzian conservation of energy concept to explain the processes of the mind. This natural science exploration began his interest in repression. He noted the importance of symbols in repression because hysterics, like "normal people," used symbol-formation to defer acting out unacceptable sexual feelings.

The *Project for Scientific Psychology* (written in 1895 and first published as a book in 1950), garnered interest in the scientific community. The hundredth anniversary was celebrated by the Academy of Sciences, which published *Neuroscience of the Mind* on the centennial of Freud's *Project for Science* (Bilder,1998), which covered a variety of topics, most importantly how the theories of psychoanalysis once considered non-scientific were being proven empirically by modern science. Freud's effort to explain psychological processes primarily in physiological terms ultimately failed. After the *Project for Scientific Psychology*, he abandoned natural science as the primary force for his theories. However, he continued to believe that many aspects of the natural science approach were useful in understanding the human mind. By 1896, he became totally committed to a psychological model for the human mind and developed a hermeneutic-oriented psychoanalysis.

Hermeneutic Influence

Rationalism Influence

Freud had an inherent mistrust of empirical science and was constantly torn between his scientific and medical training. He viewed the mind as an active mental process in contrast to the British and French empiricists who viewed the mind as passive and the senses as the only source of knowledge. The theories of Freud were in the German tradition that perceived the mind through the rationalist tradition of Leibniz and Herbart.

Gottfried Wilhelm Leibniz (1646–1716) is considered one of the most underappreciated pioneers in the history of psychology. A major opponent of the Descartes split of mind and body, Leibniz developed the concept of psychophysical parallelism, the harmony between mind and body events. The Leibniz system was driven by monads, the first objects of creation that were "unseen mental atoms" that sought to become actualized. Each monad had a separate purpose and each operated in conjunction with God's plan. This led to one of the first explorations of the unconscious because psychological monads were invisible and beyond the realm of sensory perceptions and consciousness. They influenced the Freudian distinction between ordinary and "little perceptions" that existed below consciousness in the unconscious mind.

Johann Herbart (1776–1841) expanded on the theory of Leibniz by explaining that monads had a force of energy called ideas, which resulted from the remnants of sensations. Herbart saw the mind as a dynamic system that contained basic units of ideas. These ideas operated like psychological atoms that either collided or repelled each other but eventually coalesced into a larger whole. The result was apperception, the process by which ideas hold together. The concept of apperception would have a great influence on the theories of many future psychologists especially on Wilhelm Wundt, the father of modern psychology who embraced apperception as key to his experimental psychology. In the Herbart system of psychic mechanics, ideas had the power to attract or repel other ideas. This process resulted in the development of a conscious threshold, called limen, the place in the mind where ideas remain intact. Repression and conflict occurred when unconscious ideas conflicted with the conscious mind. Freud embraced the Herbartian concepts of repression and conflict and added resistance which occurred when unconscious ideas were incompatible with the conscious mind.

Romanticism Influence

Freud embraced many aspects of the Romanticists' non-rational view of the world. Romanticism was a counter-Enlightenment movement that rejected the growing embrace of rationalism and empiricism. The Romanticists emphasized the irrational forces of nature, the primacy of feelings and emotions, and believed in the importance of individual self-directed action toward meaning and purpose. In large part, the Romanticist perception of the world fit the Freudian view of an irrational human nature, a skepticism about the ability of the ego to act rationally against the stronger forces of the id and superego

Arthur Schopenhauer (1788–1860), in *The World as Will and Representation* (Schopenhauer, 1818/2014), offered the doctrine of transcendental idealism to explain the irrational world. Transcendental idealism argued that a conscious person perceives objects of experience not as they are in themselves, but only as they appear to the observer. Schopenhauer distinguished between a noumenal world, things in themselves, and a phenomenal world, conscious experience of the world. The phenomenal world is experienced through will, which is unconscious and irrational, blind, aimless, devoid of knowledge, devoid of space and time, and free of societal control.

For Schopenhauer, the world becomes a symbolic representation of the will to survive, which dominates the inner essence of everything. Explained through the mantra, I Will Therefore I Am, it is only through irrational experiences, aesthetic experiences, that humanity can briefly be released from the endless servitude to will. Servitude will is the root of all suffering and can only end by an ascetic negation of the "will to life," and by embracing such philosophies and beliefs from the Axial Age like Platonism and the Indian Vedas (Schopenhauer, 1818/2014). This servitude to will could also be overcome through sublimation and denial. Sublimation occurred by becoming involved in activities like poetry, art, theatre, music, Platonic philosophy, or unselfish acts of love and kindness. Although an atheist, Schopenhauer understood that denial had been practiced to good effect by the great religions of Christianity, Buddhism, and Hinduism and by performing these practices, one would have a deep experience of the noumenal world (Schopenhauer, 1818/2014).

Schopenhauer also observed that humans have positive and negative impulses, an impulse being an unpremeditated spontaneous action or incitement. Rational thinking caused positive impulses; animal instincts caused negative impulses. Irrational impulses indicate that consciousness is only on the surface and that little is known about the interior, unconscious world. Although Freud denied the influence of Schopenhauer, most of the key elements like will to survive, sublimations, denial, and instinctual animalistic impulses have been incorporated into psychoanalysis (Gay, 1988). Later, the Schopenhauer concept of will evolved into the Freudian unconscious.

Transcendental Realism Influence

Eduard von Hartmann (1842–1906), in *Philosophy of the Unconscious* (Hartman, 1869), disagreed with Schopenhauer that ideas and reason were subordinate to will because it was the unconscious will that caused the need for consciousness. The meaning of transcendental realism for Hartmann was that the unconscious would become the bridge between the two conflicting schools of rationalism and romanticism

Hartmann described the evolution of the unconscious in three stages. In the first stage, reason and will lived as a united force in the unconscious. With the fall of man, reason and will separated, which created melancholy, and a depressive state that has lasted until modern times. During the second stage, modernistic and idealistic goals of happiness and progress caused an unconscious competition between the irrational and rational psychological forces. The third stage occurred after the misery and decay of the second stage became intolerable. This intolerability allowed reason to check will so that humankind could be emancipated from the illusion of happiness and progress (Hartman, 1869).

To achieve higher consciousness and end needless human suffering, it was important to distinguish the different levels of the unconscious utilizing the Darwinian theory of evolution. Hartman viewed the original animal state as unconscious non-willing. The evolution of human consciousness created human striving and the empty promise of happiness and progress. A higher consciousness would end human misery by a return to the original animal state of unconscious non-willing. This resulted in a conscious awareness of a collective nothingness, which quiets the unconscious mind with the peace of Nirvana.

Hartmann, like Freud, was pessimistic about the future of humanity. They both believed in a gradual social evolution that included ongoing exploration of the unconscious and the avoidance of selfishness to seek immediate gratification and resolution. For both, the only hope was by embracing the analytical and metaphysical. The analytical was embraced through an inductive process. This started with a personal analytic relationship with the unconscious that created general truths. The metaphysical occurred through the understanding that there is a reality that needs to be explored beyond the senses.

Phenomenological Influence

Franz Brentano (1838–1917) is one of the most famous teachers in psychological history. Many of the great thinkers in the history of psychology were taught by Brentano. He taught Carl Stumpf and Christian von Ehrenfels, the founders of Gestalt psychology; Edmund Husserl, who founded the school of phenomenology; and Sigmund Freud, the founder of psychoanalysis.

Although not a school in the traditional sense, the School of Brentano became a group of philosophers and psychologists who would advance analytic psychology and theories of the mind (Biagio, 2012).

In *Psychology from an Empirical Standpoint*, Brentano (1874/1973) developed act psychology by reintroducing scholasticism in the concept of intentionality. Intentionality is the psychological process which distinguishes mental from physical phenomena. In intentionality, every psychological act incorporates an object outside itself with the mind as the primary agent and the physical object as the secondary agent that only facilitates the intention. Brentano distinguished between a genetic and descriptive psychology that would influence later phenomenologists. Genetic psychology, not connected to eugenics, studies phenomena from a third-person perspective called empirical experimentation (Brentano, 1874/1973). In contrast, the focus of a descriptive psychology describes consciousness in the first person. For Brentano, this was phenomenological introspection that would later be developed by Husserl into the school of phenomenology. In contrast to the empirical laboratory-oriented introspection of Wilhelm Wundt, phenomenological introspection of Brentano was a first-person interpretative, hermeneutic descriptive analysis of a meaningful human experience. This method of first-person analysis of the purpose and meaning of life experiences became a foundational concept in the analytic practice of Freudian psychoanalysis.

Neuro-hypnology Influence

After prolonged study of magnetism, in 1843, James Braid (1795–1860), a Scottish surgeon, found that the psychological power of suggestion was much more important than physical magnets. He restored Mesmer's reputation by renaming animal magnetism neuro-hypnology, later shortened to hypnosis and mesmerism to acknowledge the psychological power of imagination and suggestion (Braid, 1843). Mesmer is now acknowledged as one of most influential contributors to understanding the unconscious (Ellenberger, 1970).

Hypnos in Greek word means "sleep," He was a primordial deity in Greek mythology, a symbol of sleep who lived in a cave in the underworld where there was no light, the front of the cave full of poppies and sleep-inducing plants. Hypnos is notorious in Greek mythology for his power to trick Zeus into sleep, which resulted from Hera's revenge for the ransacking by Heracles of Troy and for the Greek victory in the Trojan War. Hypnos was a powerful god because during sleep, which made up a large part of human life, he made it possible for humans to feel peaceful and avoid human suffering. Hypnos is a perfect for symbol for the power of hypnosis because, like the "trickery" of Hypnos to lead Zeus into the underworld, the hypnotherapist leads the client into the unconscious underworld of "forgetfulness" where there is both relief from, and understanding of, human suffering.

Braid made hypnotism respectable in the medical community as two major schools of hypnosis began to develop in France: the Nancy School known as the "suggestion school," and the Paris School known as the "hysteria school."

Ambroise-Auguste Liebeault (1823–1904) and Hippolyte Bernheim (1840–1919) were co-founders of the Nancy School. Initially, they could not find any patients, but after hypnotism was offered free to the public, the Nancy clinic became overwhelmed and experienced great notoriety and success. After treating a variety of individuals from various socioeconomic classes, especially those with low income, Liebault and Bernheim contended that all humans were suggestible. Some were more suggestible than others and whatever a patient believed would improve their symptoms, usually did.

Figure 2.8

In the Paris School, hysteria became the focus for the use of hypnosis. The famous La Salpetriere Hospital, where Pinel had literally released individuals with mental illness from their chains, Jean-Martin Charcot (1825–1893) became its director and converted the hospital into a research center. Extremely flamboyant and charismatic, Charcot was viewed throughout Europe as the "founder and father of modern neurology." Contrary to Liebault and Bernheim, he was more interested in hypnosis from a research than a medical treatment perspective. Charcot performed hypnosis on patients suffering from hysterical paralysis, blindness, mutism, fainting, seizures, and other dysfunctional physiological symptoms.

Charcot maintained that hysteria was a neurological disease caused by a traumatic shock to the central nervous system that was weak due to hereditary. Unlike the Nancy School, he maintained that hypnosis could only be successful with hysterics. Charcot believed that hypnosis altered consciousness through a trance which showed how the power of ideas could influence behavior. For instance, under hypnosis, Charcot might suggest the idea for a patient to lift their arm to create a paralysis and then, showing the power of suggestion, direct the arm to return to its normal state. This incredible act proved that hypnotic suggestion could remove a dysfunctional physical symptom of a hysteric.

His most famous institutionalized patient was Marie "Blanche" Whitman. She was called the "Queen of Hysterics" and suffered from epileptic seizures. Controversially, Charcot would bring "Blanche" to his medical lectures to initiate an epileptic seizure during hypnosis to show how hysteria could be induced and controlled. The theatrics of his lectures intrigued the artistic community, most notably Sarah Bernhardt, who attended to observe the broad range of emotions that occurred under hypnosis. "Blanche" became the symbol of the growing interest in hysteria, hypnosis, and the unconscious. She was memorialized as the woman convulsing in a classic hysteric posture in one of the best-known paintings in the history of medicine, *A Clinical Lesson at the Salpetriere* (1887) by artist Andre Brouillet.

Toward the end of his career, Charcot discarded the natural science belief that hysteria was caused by physiological trauma to the central nervous system. Rather, he speculated that hysteria was of a psychological and psychogenic rather than an organic origin. This belief led to an entirely different view of hysteria, trauma, and the unconscious, and would impact Freud, his followers, critics, and psychologists throughout the twentieth century and beyond.

Alternate Conscious Paradigm

Pierre Janet (1859–1947) agreed with his teacher, Charcot, about the psychological nature of the unconscious and developed the Alternate Consciousness Paradigm (ACP) theory of the unconscious (Janet, 1925). Janet believed hysteria was a disorder of the personality and central nervous system. He argued that sensory perception, introspection, or psychophysics could not adequately explain hysteria. Janet viewed hysteria as a dissociated and separate psychological personality that operated independently in the unconscious. Janet contended that the hysteric lacked psychological cohesiveness and the ability to consciously synthesize emotional ideas and experiences. This inability to cope created a "split off" dissociated personality that caused a person to behave unconsciously.

For Janet, an unconscious act was an act from another personality, making Janet one of the first theorists to discover "dissociation," which would later be acknowledged as an essential component of psychological trauma. Janet viewed hypnosis as the treatment of choice for hysteria because hypnosis brought to consciousness dissociated memories and provided relief from hysteric symptoms. Debunking the medical belief that only women could be hysteric, Janet agreed with Charcot that men, as well as women, could also suffer from hysteria (Janet, 1925, Lieblich & Quackelbeen, 1995).

Mesmer, Puysegur, Braid, Liebault, Bernheim, Charcot, and Janet predated Freud. It would be impossible to understand the historic development of psychoanalysis without these contributors, especially regarding hysteria, hypnosis, and the view of the unconscious. Freud traveled to Nancy to unsuccessfully learn hypnosis upon which he disagreed with Janet about the dissociative nature of the unconscious (Ellenberger, 1970). Freud believed everyone, beyond hysterics and those with mental disturbance, had an unconscious and hypnosis would not be the treatment of choice for hysteria.

Janet contended that Freud stole his psychological system and plagiarized most of his theories (Ellenberger, 1970). For example, Janet referred to his method as psychological analysis, Freud called his method psychoanalysis. Ultimately, Janet, a mild-mannered physician and psychologist, could not compete with Freud's strong and dominate personality. If Janet had been a stronger personality, it is possible that psychodynamic history would have been written differently; there could have been a Janetian psychological analysis preferred over a Freudian psychoanalysis and hypnosis, not free association, that would be the primary method of treatment in a psychological analysis world.

Freudian Psychoanalytic Psychology

Catharsis and the Talking Cure

The historical birth of psychoanalysis began with the collaboration of Freud and Josef Breuer (1842–1925), in the famous treatment for hysteria of "Anna O.," Bertha Pappenheim (1859–1936). They co-authored *Studies on Hysteria* (Freud & Breuer, 1895/2004), the foundational work of psychoanalysis. Breuer was a distinguished doctor and physiologist who became a father figure and mentor to Freud. However, they later became estranged because of their disagreement about the nature of the unconscious.

Breuer had treated Franz Brentano and Johannes Brahms, but his most famous patient would be Anna O., who suffered from paralysis of her limbs, anesthesia, and vision and speech difficulties. Although Breuer discovered the relationship between breathing and body temperature, and the inner ear and balance, his most significant contribution to psychoanalysis would be his discovery of the cathartic method, or the talking cure. He found that Anna O. experienced a significant reduction in her hysteric symptoms when pathogenic ideas were given conscious expression.

Although many early psychoanalytic theorists agreed that men and women could exhibit hysteric symptoms, the term *hysteria* originated from the Greek word for "uterus." The concept dated back nearly 4,000 years when the Egyptians believed behavioral abnormalities in women were caused by a "wandering womb." The Greeks and Romans accepted this view and added the failure to have children or marry as a cause for hysteria. The Western symbol of hysteria as a "wondering womb" reinforced the sexist view of women as physiologically unstable and emotionally impaired.

Breuer and Freud would agree on the importance of catharsis that dated back to Aristotle, the emotional release that occurred during Greek plays. Aristotle, in *Poetics,* introduced katharsis as the effect of tragedy on the mind and body during a play, a process which created a purification, cleansing, and intellectual clarification. The importance of emotional and intellectual catharsis would become a key element of psychoanalysis.

A schism occurred when Breuer agreed with Janet about ACP and that the memory of a trauma existed like a foreign body that affected the conscious waking state. For Breuer, in trauma, the mind was thrown into a hypnoid state that became permanent and could only be made conscious through hypnosis. This process was like "chimney sweeping," dissipating the "dirty" traumatic energy through conscious awareness. Freud and Breuer wrote different conclusions in *Studies of Hysteria* (Freud & Breuer, 1895/2004). Freud disagreed with Breuer about ACP and the practice of hypnosis and the nature of the unconscious. Freud concluded

Figure 2.9

that hysteria was caused by the repression of sexuality, especially of sexual fantasies, and childhood sexual abuse. Breuer strongly disagreed and argued that narrowing hysteria to sexuality was a serious mistake because there were other traumatic experiences that could cause hysteria.

The Universal Unconscious

Janet and other early psychoanalysts had limited unconscious processes to the mentally disturbed. After *Studies of Hysteria*, Freud introduced a revolutionary idea in his book, *Psychopathology of Everyday Life* (Freud, 1901/1965), which would transform the concept of human psychology because he asserted that everyone had an unconscious, not just individuals with mental disturbance. It was the concept of a universal unconscious which could explain the difference between normal and abnormal behavior. Examples of normal unconscious processes were daily parapraxes, which were minor errors of thought and speech in daily life: slips of the tongue, forgetting and losing things, and small accidents. These became known in the vernacular culture as Freudian slips. He recognized the importance of jokes and humor that allowed for the expression of sexual and aggressive feelings (Freud, 1905/1960). After Freud, most in the psychoanalytic world accepted that the unconscious existed in everyone.

Transference, Countertransference, and Termination

The break between Freud and Breuer changed the history and trajectory of psychoanalysis. The rejection of ACP and hypnosis by Freud would forever impact the practice of psychoanalysis. Freud did not agree there was a separate hypnotic state in the unconscious. Rather, traumatic material was split from consciousness by the defense mechanism of repression because conscious awareness of trauma would conflict with acceptable social values and feelings. Hysteria was the psychogenic manifestation of repression. This repression caused resistance, which occurred when the unconscious defenses of the ego were threatened. One of the competencies of the psychoanalyst was to assist the patient in recognizing that their resistance was essential for their healing. Although painful, this recognition meant that the repressed material would become conscious, not through hypnosis, but through free association. Some skeptics believe Freud abandoned hypnosis after his time at the Nancy School because of his inability to successfully practice hypnosis. Freud called free association the fundamental therapeutic method for the practice of psychoanalysis because it gave "free" voice to the unconscious and allowed the unconscious to speak freely without interruption by the conscious mind.

Through the treatment of Anna O., Breuer and Freud discovered the technique of transference and countertransference that would not only impact the future of psychoanalysis but the future practice of many other schools of psychotherapy. Anna O. had a positive unconscious transference toward Breuer because she felt the fatherly love that was missing from her dying father. On the other hand, Breuer developed strong paternalistic and protective unconscious countertransference feelings toward Anna O. Breuer and Freud realized that the basis of healing began with a strong therapeutic alliance rooted in a positive unconscious transference and countertransference dynamic between psychoanalyst and patient. Thereafter, successful psychoanalysis meant that the patient had a positive unconscious transference to their psychoanalyst and the psychoanalyst understood how their unconscious countertransference issues could facilitate or impede therapeutic progress.

In the early days, analysis occurred, often daily, in the intimacy of the home of the psychoanalyst. The power of unconscious transference in the therapeutic relationship was further emphasized when Anna O. believed she was carrying Breuer's child. Between his wife hearing about this in the community and being overwhelmed by the hallucinogenic pregnancy, Breuer abruptly terminated the psychoanalysis. The exact reason for Anna O.'s termination continues to be debated, but the importance of termination in psychoanalysis emerged because Anna O. was institutionalized after her treatment (Ellenberger, 1970). Dealing with termination became another essential psychoanalytic technique. In psychoanalysis, it was important because of the ongoing human struggle to deal with loss, change and wishes of childhood. At the end of treatment those unconscious feelings would naturally emerge. If not properly handled this would result in regression and resistance rather than a successful completed analysis that would have created effective conscious coping strategies to deal with loss, change, and wishes of childhood.

Bertha Pappenheim (aka Anna O.) became a social worker in 1880 and became a European feminist leader, playwright, author, and an outspoken critic of psychoanalysis (Ellenberger, 1970). Aware of the severe ostracization of Jewish women who had children out of wedlock, she opened Jewish orphanages for "wayward mothers" and their children. After her death in 1936, she was honored throughout Europe, especially by the famous Hasidic Jewish philosopher Martin Buber, for her contributions to humanity. In 1954, the German government produced a special stamp as a tribute for her advocacy to human rights. History has been unable to answer the question of whether her success was because of, or despite, psychoanalysis.

Interpretation of Dreams

Since Freud could not do free association on himself, he began to explore his own unconscious through dream interpretation. He observed that dreams and hysteric symptoms could both be viewed as symbolic representations of repressed sexual trauma. Dream interpretation became the second major psychoanalytic method by which to understand the unconscious. As Freud often stated, "dreams are the royal road to unconscious understanding." Symbol provided the mechanism by which to understand the unconscious basis of a psychological problem.

His personal self-analysis culminated with the publication of "Interpretation of Dreams" (Freud, 1900/1953), his most important work. In it, Freud described how during sleep, defenses were more vulnerable to repressed memories and could reach consciousness through the world of symbols. The interpretation consisted of analyzing manifest and latent content. Manifest content was what the dream appeared to communicate; the latent content was the real meaning of the dream. Since wish fulfillment permeated every dream, symbolic representation was the mechanism that allowed conscious tolerance of the anxiety emanating from the unconscious.

Seduction Theory and Child Abuse

The fact that Freud believed in childhood sexuality was another revolutionary idea for its time. Through his experiences with free association, dream interpretation, and his exploration of mythology, Freud had all the evidence he needed for his sexual seduction theory. This theory would impact the Western view of childhood sexual abuse throughout much of the twentieth century.

In 1896, Freud presented "Aetiology of Hysteria, one of his first papers," to the Vienna Psychiatric and Neurological Society. In his lecture, he introduced seduction theory. Eighteen of his patients had been sexually abused, and Freud believed this was the basis of hysteria. His lecture was not well received by a group of Victorian era physicians, leaving "Aetiology" unpublished and the abandonment in 1897 of seduction theory (Masson, 1984).

In the bestselling book *The Assault on Truth: Freud's Suppression of Seduction Theory*, Jeffery Masson (1984) former Freudian Archive Director, wrote a scathing criticism of the abandonment of seduction theory by Freud. He believed that the fear of professional abandonment was a poor excuse since most of his theories were already being rejected by his peers. Masson claimed that Freud had a very personal, if not sexual relationship with a colleague, Wilhelm Fleiss, an eccentric otolaryngologist, Freud knew that Fleiss had sexually molested his son, Robert, because Masson concluded that the major reason Freud abandoned seduction theory was to cover up this knowledge. Fleiss had great influence on Freud and on the development of psychoanalysis. He worked with Freud on the Project for a Scientific Psychology and developed a theory of "nasal reflex neurosis." This led to many operations on the nose of Freud to cure his neurosis and possibly treat his brief experimentation with cocaine (Freud & Masson, 1986).

Seduction theory evolved into infantile wishes that were unacceptable sexual fantasies children had toward their parents. In other words, the claims by Freud's patients that they had been molested were fantasies, not real events. In fact, some psychoanalysts began to reverse the seduction theory and believed that children seduce their parents. This shadow in psychoanalytic history left a legacy of the denial of childhood sexual abuse that would permeate mental health care of children until the late twentieth century. Research began to debunk the idea of infantile wishes and conclude that childhood sexual abuse is a serious societal problem that mental health professionals need to take seriously (Gorey & Leslie, 1997).

Theory of Human Development – Psychosexual Stages

From his position that everyone had an unconscious, Freud thought that humans developed in psychosexual stages. His theory was rooted in the human body, specifically the pleasures of the mouth, the anus, and the genitals. During each psychosocial stage, there can be over-gratification or under-gratification that causes a fixation, a need that permeates the psyche through childhood and into adulthood (Freud, 1910/1949).

During the first stage, the oral stage, in the first year of life, a baby experiences pleasure through the mouth by sucking, chewing, and swallowing. If a fixation occurred, an oral-incorporative character develops due to the intense pleasure one experienced from eating and drinking. Some psychoanalysts viewed the development of eating disorders from the lack of oral satisfaction during this psychosexual stage.

The second stage, the anal stage, occurred during the second year of life, where pleasure came from permitting or suppressing bowel movements and the focus was on the region of the buttocks. A very generous, messy or wasteful person, or a withholding anal-retentive, overcontrolling and perfectionist person, can be fixated at this psychosexual stage.

The phallic stage, the third stage, occurred during the third to fifth year, when the child experienced pleasure in the genitals, especially through masturbation. This was the stage when children began to experience the difference between the sexes. The boy discovered his penis and the girl her clitoris.

In interpreting his own dreams, Freud discovered that young men tend to love their mothers and hate their father. This led to his creation of the Oedipal Complex theory based in the Greek myth of Oedipus Rex, a play by Sophocles in which Oedipus unknowingly killed his father and married his mother.

Symbols of Freudian and Relational Psychoanalysis 71

Figure 2.10

Since Freud had a contentious relationship with his own father, his theory might have been an overreaction to the guilt he felt over wishing his father's actual death (Jones, 1957).

In the modern Oedipal drama, a young boy becomes involved in a competitive unconscious struggle with his father to sexually possess his mother. As the Oedipal drama unfolds, the boy experiences hostility toward his father and sexual feelings toward his mother. Understanding that his father has all the power, the young man learns to repress his sexual feelings toward his mother, which created castration anxiety. The resolution of castration anxiety occurred when the boy identified with his father and mutually shared mother, later replacing the mother in marriage with a "motherly woman."

The Freudian developmental theory centered on the belief that the penis was the most powerful organ of the human body. Because of that viewpoint, the relationship to the penis dominated sexual development for both men and women. The drama for the girl was quite different and exposed the weakness of Freudian theory for women. The Freudian view during this stage maintained that the Oedipal drama started for the girl with a strong attachment to her mother until she realized that she did not have a penis and blamed her mother for its absence. The girl then became hostile toward her mother as she became aware that her father possessed the valuable organ, leading to penis envy. The resolution of the Oedipal drama for women occurred by repressing their hostility toward their mothers and their sexual attraction for their fathers by becoming "mother-like" and sharing their father with their mother (Freud, 1910/1949).

72 Symbols of Freudian and Relational Psychoanalysis

The internalization of a mother and father identity during the phallic stage solidified superego formation. Since the girl already felt castrated, her identity was not rooted in castration anxiety, emotional self-defense, or the need to identify with a violent castrator. Because of the emotional intensity for survival of the male experience, Freud believed that men were psychologically stronger, and that the male superego was more fully developed than the female superego.

The latency age lasted from the beginning of the sixth year until puberty. Because of the intense repression experienced during the phallic stage, sexuality went into hibernation and was sublimated by educational and intellectual interests, peer activities, and friendship development.

The final genital stage occurred from puberty until the end of life. During this phase, sexuality was impossible to repress. Since Freud was heterosexual, he saw this as a time for exploring the opposite sex, seeking the pleasure of sexual intercourse, and finding a marital partner that would continue the quest to resolve the Oedipal drama (Freud, 1910/1949). Or, from the words of the popular 1911 song by Dillon and Titer, "I want a girl, just like the girl that married dear old dad."

Criticism and sexism of Freudian theory has been well documented. The reality was that Freud's views of women were based on the cultural paternalism that dominated his personality, especially regarding women but also against his critics. After making several attempts to understand feminine psychology, to his credit, he admitted defeat and famously asked, "What do women want?"

Feminist Elisabeth Young-Bruehl believes some of the criticism may have resulted from ignorance of psychoanalysis, misinterpretation, or fabrication of his theories. In *Freud on Women: A Reader*, Young-Bruehl (1990) collected the most significant works by Freud on women and arranged them in chronological order, separating fact from fiction.

Theory of Personality

With the concepts of superego, ego, and id, Freud became one of the first personality theorists in psychology. One of Freud's most important discoveries was his view that the id not the ego was the driving force of personality. The ego has an almost impossible task of meeting all the needs of the id as well as the demands of the superego. For this reason, the ego is governed by the reality principle, which causes the ego to be in a constant state of anxiety (Freud, 1919/1955a).

Figure 2.11

Symbols of Freudian and Relational Psychoanalysis 73

The id contains the instinctual drives, forces of hunger, thirst, and sex that are governed by the pleasure principle (Freud, 1920/1955b) which needs immediate gratification. The collective energy of the id is the *libido*, from the Latin word meaning "lust," whose unconscious energy determines most of human behavior (Freud, 1905/1962).

The id meets its needs in two primary ways. One is a reflexive arc and the other is wish fulfillment. The reflexive arc operates automatically, like sneezing, in an immediate reaction to a discomfort. Wish fulfillment needed a symbol, an image of an object that satisfied a libidinal need. The id and libidinal needs operate in an unconscious world, independent of personal and societal experiences.

A newborn baby is driven totally by the needs of the id. These needs can only come to consciousness through symbolizing a loving mother. It is through parental socialization that the baby develops a superego conscience and an ego-ideal. Conscience develops from the internalization of parental punishment while ego-ideal results from the internalization of parental rewards. Socialization is the ongoing process of the internalization of parental values and beliefs.

Freud believed that if there was only id and ego, without a superego, human beings would not be able to distinguish themselves from animals and there would be no civilization (Freud, 1995).

For Freudian psychology, the grinning skull symbolizes confrontation between life and death, mortality, and the drive to destroy and return to a motionless state. Freud adjusted his personality theory later in his career as an instinctual struggle between the forces to live and die. His libido theory went beyond sexual driven instincts to the instinctual forces that prolong and terminate life by again returning to mythology. This struggle was a battle between Eros, the Greek god of love, and Thanatos, the Greek god of death. Eros was the drive to survive and originated from the potent instinct of love and ambition. However, Eros needed Thanatos because without the shadow of Thanatos, Eros was left empty, hollow, and soulless.

Figure 2.12

Anxiety and Ego Defense Mechanisms

Throughout his theory, Freud viewed anxiety as the major indicator of the impending danger of the unconscious. He distinguished between objective, neurotic, and moral anxiety. Objective anxiety was a real threat from the environment, like being physically attacked. Neurotic anxiety happened when the needs of the id overwhelmed the ego and created destructive aggressive and violent impulses. Moral anxiety happened when the internalized values of the superego were about to be violated, when a person acted contrary to their personal values.

Anna Freud (1895–1982), Freud's daughter, made significant contributions to the development of psychoanalysis. In *Ego and the Mechanism of Defense* (A. Freud, 1937), Anna further developed the concept of ego defenses. She believed ego defenses could aid in the socialization process. She further advanced the importance of viewing defense mechanisms from both an adaptive and maladaptive perspective. Repression was adaptive when it provided defense against being constantly overwhelmed by anxiety, impulses, fears, memories, and conflicts. It was maladaptive when it caused the avoidance of solvable psychological problems or for immediate need for physical or psychological survival.

Anna Freud was one of the first psychoanalysts to catalogue the many types of defense mechanisms, which increased her stature in the psychoanalytic community. Besides repression, she catalogued reaction formation, isolation, undoing, projection, introjection, turning against the self, reversal, and sublimation. Anna Freud added two defense mechanisms that were uniquely her own. Altruistic surrender defended against personal achievement by the identification with the achievement of others. Identification with the aggressor defended against the violation of superego values by adopting the values of the feared aggressor, observed in bullying, and later applied to the Patty Hearst hostage situation.

Anna Freud expanded the practice of psychoanalysis to children. Besides her own 60-year clinical practice with children, she also psychoanalyzed and mentored Erik Erikson (1902–1994). Erikson replaced psychosexual with psychosocial stages of development. In *Childhood and Society*, Erikson (1993) expanded ego development to eight stages over a lifetime that included not only childhood but the psychosocial developmental issues throughout life to old age. Anna also inspired Heinz Hartman (1894–1970), who wrote *Ego Psychology* and the *Problem of Adaptation* (Hartman, 1959). His book explored an "ego-free sphere" where the ego could solve problems without the unconscious interference of childhood experiences.

Freud compared his daughter, Anna, to the mythological figure of Antigone, the dutiful and courageous daughter who took care of her blind and ill father in his final days (Ellenberger, 1970). Since Freud's wife viewed his theories as a form of pornography, Anna filled the familial void and became the most supportive person in his life. She served as his secretary, nurse, confidante, and colleague. She saved his life by convincing him to flee Vienna for London to escape the Nazis. After his death, Anna Freud became an emissary to Psychoanalytic Institutes and the chief spokesperson for the Freudian legacy throughout the world.

The Threat of Unconscious Forces

Beyond his psychoanalytic contributions, Freud's legacy should give serious pause to his concern about the inability of humanity to deal with the aggressive and violent instincts of the unconscious. The shadow of two World Wars and the Korean, Vietnam, Iraqi, and Afghanistan

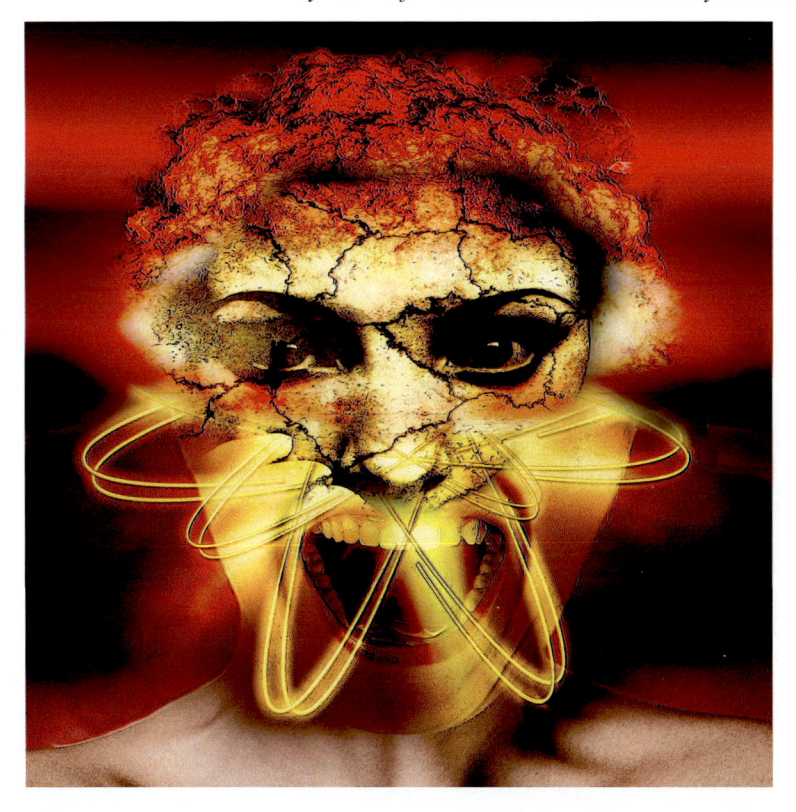

Symbols of Freudian and Relational Psychoanalysis 75

Figure 2.13

Wars highlights the immediate need for higher human consciousness throughout the world. In World War I, there were 40 million military and civilian casualties. In World War II, over 60 million died, about 3 percent of the 1940 world population. The Korean War, one the deadliest wars in modern history, was responsible for appropriately 3 million military and civilian deaths. In the Vietnam War, 58,000 Americans died, 300,000 were wounded, and many remain physically and mentally disabled. The North Vietnamese lost over 1 million and South Vietnam over 300,000 soldiers. Although still counting, 5,000 Americans died in the Iraqi War, with estimates of over 100,000 Iraqi deaths. There have been 2,300 American military casualties and 1,700 civilian contractor casualties from the Afghanistan War, which began with the American invasion in October 2001 and ended in a 2021 violent withdrawal.

Although Freud died before the atomic bombs fell on Japan, the atomic bomb symbolizes Freud's nihilistic view and his twentieth-century concern about the destructive unconscious forces in modern civilization.

On August 6, 1946, an American B-29 bomber dropped the first atomic bomb over the Japanese city of Hiroshima. The explosion immediately killed 80,000 civilians and 90 percent of the population of Hiroshima. Three days later, a second B-29 bomber dropped another atomic bomb over Nagasaki, immediately killing 40,000 civilians. Humanity now had the capacity for total annihilation. The reality is that the nuclear threat remains. For Freud the way to avoid the horrific reality of nuclear war is to become conscious of the aggressive and violent impulses that reside in the unconscious. Otherwise, those impulses will imperil the future of human existence.

76 *Symbols of Freudian and Relational Psychoanalysis*

Emancipatory Opportunities in Freudian Psychoanalysis

Consider Psychoanalysis

The couch in psychoanalysis creates a therapeutic space for the unconscious to safely "speak." Through the practice of free association, one can experience the mystery and power of the unconscious. Laying on a couch, with the psychoanalyst sitting closely behind to avoid distraction, one can overcome resistance and embrace their unconscious processes.

Figure 2.14

Analyze Dreams

Besides free association, dream interpretation is another important way to experience the unconscious and the world of symbol. During night sleep, there are usually many dreams. Since a symbol is the language of the unconscious, the psychoanalytic concept of *condensation* allows for narrowing dream material into one symbolic representation connecting all the nighttime dream elements. It is also a way to understand *defense mechanisms,* the unconscious adaptive and maladaptive psychological mechanisms that reduces anxiety. The defense mechanism of *displacement* allows the transfer of an anxiety-provoking object or event to a more tolerable symbol, a cave instead of a vagina or a snake instead of a penis.

Figure 2.15

Do Not Marginalize Freud and His View of the Unconscious Mind

Psychology, for many understandable reasons, has marginalized Freud. His thought is often more popular in other disciplines outside of psychology. Although unpleasant, it is important to consider his view that the destructive aspects of the unconscious mind provide a serious threat to the survival of humanity. With all his limitations and controversies, it is important to consider his concerns and return Freud to his rightful place in the pantheon of psychology, because all psychologists stand on his shoulders (Freud, Freud, & Grubrich-Simitis, 1985).

Practice Psychoanalytic Concepts in Community Mental Health

> the conscience of the community will awake and remind it that the poor man should have as much right to assistance for his mind as he now has to the lifesaving help offered by surgery… neurosis threatens public health no less then tuberculous…the large-scale application of our therapy will compel us to alloy the pure gold of analysis (to communities) freely…
>
> - Sigmund Freud

In the main, psychoanalysis has largely rejected the Community Mental Health (CMH) movement; there are few psychoanalysts in the CMH system. There is a myriad of reasons, especially the classical Freudian view that individuals with serious mental illness could not develop a therapeutic transference, the key to successful psychoanalytic treatment. In his address, *Lines of Advance in Psychoanalytic Therapy* (1919/1955a), Freud became concerned that psychoanalysis was becoming a treatment only for the wealthy. In response, he called for free clinics throughout Europe with trained lay analysts who would be trained in intrapsychic processes, as well as in the social and economic needs of clients, especially low-income clients. In the 1920s and 1930s, his call resulted in many free psychoanalytic clinics that educated European communities about the value of psychoanalytic treatment.

But as psychoanalysis became professionalized, physicians rejected lay analysts and community-based treatment, opting for lucrative private practices. Freud blamed greedy American psychoanalysts and those psychoanalysts who immigrated to America during World War II for losing their European concern for those with low income and for those unable to afford access to psychoanalysis. Freud always spoke of his disdain for America as a place of "dollaria," where money trumped all other considerations and how the American medical establishment had been coopted by the capitalistic system (Altman, 2010).

In his book, *The Analyst in the Inner City: Race, Class and Culture Through the Psychoanalytic Lens*, Neil Altman (2010) argued for a psychoanalytic renaissance in community practice, returning psychoanalysis to its roots of community-based clinical work. Altman believed that psychoanalytic thought could provide social change especially in the areas of race, white privilege, poverty, culture, ethnicity, and public policy.

Relational Psychoanalysis

Historical Analysis

Post-Freudian World of Relational Psychoanalysis

Freud was not the end, but only the beginning of psychoanalysis. In the 1980s, there was a paradigm shift in the post-Freudian world toward a focus on emotional attachment in early childhood. Rejected or revised were some of the most sacred psychoanalytic beliefs, especially the role of sexuality and aggression in human development. This led to a reexamination of early childhood attachment, object-relations, interpersonal relationships, intersubjectivity, and feminism.

The Great Schism in Psychoanalysis

Because Freud and Carl Jung were unable to find any common ground, a great schism permeates the early history of the psychoanalytic movement. In 1902, Freud started the *Psychological Wednesday Society* meeting in Vienna that included Jung and other psychoanalysts, with the goal to further the Freudian approach. In 1910, this meeting evolved into *The International Psychoanalytic Association* (IPA). Carl Jung was elected as its first president because Freud had envisioned Jung as his successor. In 1913, at the annual IPA Conference in Munich Germany, close friends and followers of Freud, Earnest Jones and Karl Abraham encouraged Freudian members to abstain from re-electing Jung as its president. Although re-elected, Jung recognized his position was untenable and in 1914, he resigned from the IPA and ended any political resolution between Jungian analytical psychology and Freudian psychoanalytic movements because both continued to seek prominence in the psychological world.

The same year, Freud (1914/1966) wrote his side of the story in *History of the Psychoanalytic Movement* and discredited all his rivals in the movement. The IPA remained the major international psychoanalytic association in the world, with over 12,000 members and 70 constituent organizations. Ernest Jones went on to become a Freudian biographer, a faculty member at the University of Toronto, and the founder of the *American Psychoanalytic Association* (Jones, 1957).

During World War II, London became the place where the Jung and Freud controversies intensified. Because of the Nazi hostility to psychoanalysis, which was perceived as a Jewish practice, many psychoanalysts and Jungians fled to London. In 1938, Ernest Jones and Anna Freud, Freud's daughter, helped Freud escape his possible capture in Vienna by the Nazis. When the psychoanalysts arrived, many became members of the *British Psychoanalytical Society* (BPS), which had been reconstituted in 1919 by Ernest Jones after years of nascent existence. During World War II, after the Freud and Jung split, Jones began exploring the future of psychoanalysis without Freud, by purging most of the BPS Jungian members.

The political tensions in psychoanalysis intensified as Jones became enamored with the work of Melanie Klein, whose new controversial psychoanalytic theories were being rejected in Berlin and in much of continental Europe. In response, Jones invited Klein to London to become a leading BPS member. This created intense conflict, especially with Anna Freud who perceived herself as the rightful heir of the Freudian legacy. In 1942, the disagreement between Klein and Anna Freud became so contentious it necessitated the creation of what became known as the *BPS controversial discussions*. The result was the development of a committee that would assure that three warring and factional groups would have equal oversight over the BPS. The committee consisted of Kleinian, Freudian, and the newly emerging independents called the *British Independent Group*. After World War II, the BPS would become dominated by the independent psychoanalysts who, by developing *British object-relations theory*, would open an entirely new chapter in the history of psychoanalysis and depth psychology. The new leadership would include Donald Winnicott, Michael Balint, and Wilfred Bion.

After the deaths of Freud in 1939 and Jung in 1963, depth psychology was ready for a renaissance. Although Jung had viewed analytical psychology as most helpful later in life, many post-Jungians began to view individuation as existing throughout the life cycle (Von Franz, 1964). Although there was no political resolution for a unified institute or organization, in the post-Freudian world, relational psychoanalysts rejected the view that the unconscious could be reduced to libidinal energies. Many in the post-Freudian and Jungian worlds embraced the importance of interpersonal relationships; the need for intimacy replaced the need to control aggression and sexuality.

Political Systems

Through political activism in the relational psychanalytic movement, significant public policy changes occurred in child welfare throughout the United States. *John Bowlby* (1907–1990), a pioneer in attachment theory, had a significant political impact on reforms in childcare. Bowlby's work on maternal deprivation caused a major revolution in child welfare. Bowlby (1950/1995) influenced the *World Health Organization* in his monograph, *Maternal Care and Mental Health*, which reversed the idea of "too much mother attachment." He promoted the idea that the mother was the centerpiece of childhood development. It was the mother who promoted a warm, continuous, and intimate relationship with the child.

Bowlby argued that the lack of a quality relationship with the mother resulted in irreversible mental health problems. His political activism revolutionized the treatment of children in hospitals, schools, and social settings. After periods in history believing the opposite, Bowlby believed a healthy child resulted from being "touched" physically, emotionally, and mentally.

His research inspired political activism of child psychologists throughout America and, over time, orphanages were abandoned in favor of the modern foster care system. Although there are major flaws in the current foster care system, his political efforts helped create a "home-like" environment for abused and neglected children.

In his first public work, *Forty-Four Juvenile Thieves: Their Character and Home-Life*, Bowlby (1946) focused his research on juvenile delinquency. Prior to Bowlby, the eugenic "born criminal" theory dominated the criminal justice system. The belief had been that criminality was innate and inherited. Bowlby's research indicated that mother-child separation, not "innate criminality," was the major factor in delinquent character formation. This was particularly true if the mother lacked warmth and affection. In this case, the child developed no emotional ties, close friendships, or interest in interpersonal relationships. The impact of Bowlby's research and his political activism changed public policy to require mental health treatment services in the juvenile justice system, particularly in juvenile hall detention centers.

Bowlby provides an important role model for the importance of political activism for public policy reforms that benefit children and their families. His political activism left a legacy of public policy reforms in child welfare and the juvenile justice systems.

Socioeconomic Systems

Relational psychoanalysts were influenced by middle- and upper-class values that emphasize the role of mother relegating women as the primary attachment figures in the family. In the modern middle-class family, this created socioeconomic pressures for women as they struggled between the responsibilities of motherhood and the desire for a career.

Melanie Klein, born to a Jewish family in Vienna, understood how life could change in childhood when her family lost its wealth. John Bowlby and Ronald Fairbairn were both born into the upper-class families where, during the early twentieth century, they viewed too much attachment to the mother as unhealthy and spoiling the child. This belief led the rich to set up separate nurseries, managed by nannies, to raise their children. This approach continued with the development of boarding schools for children of the European wealthy classes. Fairbairn seemed to thrive in boarding schools while Bowlby did not. Bowlby (1973), in *Separation: Anxiety and Anger,* argued that no one, not even a dog, should be sent to the boarding schools for the wealthy.

The issue of childcare has become a significant socioeconomic issue in the modern family because both parents typically work and have little natural family support. Childcare workers have become surrogate parents in the psychological development of children in modern America. In 2001, more than half of the children in the United States were involved in childcare services. Although most childcare services require some form of licensure, the system is fragmented and services are often provided by unskilled, cheap labor, especially in poorer communities. The cost of childcare in the United States is expensive. The average cost of full-time childcare can range from $5,000 in Mississippi, a low-income state, to over $21,000 annually in New York, a high-income state.

The future psychological health of American children will in large part be in the hands of childcare workers. Many are untrained and unfamiliar with relational psychoanalysis or general psychological development principles. With unpredictable governmental support, the current socioeconomic system favors wealthier American parents who can afford higher-quality childcare, leaving behind less wealthy American parents who often lack the financial resources to seek childcare. Because women are perceived as the primary caregiver, the pressure to be

Symbols of Freudian and Relational Psychoanalysis 81

homemakers results in many unintended consequences, including the lack of a career and socioeconomic equality.

Cultural Systems

Relational psychoanalysts have continued the psychoanalytic tradition of being culturally Euro-centric and Anglo-American centric. Many of the leaders of the relational psychoanalytic movement wanted to change the cultural experience of childhood in part because of their own psychologically challenging childhood relationships, especially with their mothers and emotionally absent fathers. In the twentieth century, American culture woman became synonymous with mother, motherhood equated with femininity and the view that *anatomy is destiny* for both women and men. The emerging feminist movement questioned the role of men and women in American culture, particularly related to parenting. Questioned was the middle-class value that men provided financial support and woman provided emotional support to the family. A patriarchal psychology which underemphasized the role of man in family life, the father, and overemphasized the role of woman, the mother.

Figure 2.16

The post-Freudian and relational psychoanalytic movement provided cultural acknowledgment of women in psychology because women like Karen Horney, Anna Freud, and Melanie Klein, with their differing perspectives, became essential players in the history of psychology, a history that often neglects the historic role of women. They replaced the penis with the breast and envy became male envy of the female body. This laid the early foundation for both sexes to view their sexuality differently in American culture, including becoming non-binary, identifying with neither gender.

Besides an overemphasis on the role of mother, relational psychoanalysts have been criticized for ethnocentrism because of neglect in their research and practice other cultural approaches to attachment and child rearing beyond the Euro-centric and Anglo-American experience; for instance, the implication of the strong family systems in Asia or the Israeli focus on both childhood attachment and independence.

Natural Science Influences

Drive Theory Influence

Freudian psychology rejected the ego as the master of the psyche. The concept of *drive theory* was essential for understanding the basic tenets of a psychodynamic psychology because Freud believed that human beings were born with innate biological drives of sexual desire and aggression which existed in the unconscious *id*. Reason and intellect were replaced by the need to release tension regardless of social appropriateness. Survival was dependent on the child learning to control innate biological drives through the development of an ego, "where there was id, ego shall be." In classical Freudian thought, the primary reason objects existed was for the purpose of drive gratification and to remove biological tension. Since the ego was unable to completely control powerful and anarchistic id drives, the only hope was to complete the personality structure with a *superego,* which aided in the resolution of the Oedipal Complex by the internalization of parental values.

Both Freudian and relational psychoanalysis agree that drives are key motivators because they cause homeostatic disturbance and provide motivation for finding an object to restore psychological balance. For Freud, drives allow for the psyche "to let off steam" and seek a pleasurable way to reduce tension. Relational psychoanalysis view drives as arising from actual interpersonal events, not from pressure for id gratification. A child develops ego structures from interpersonal experiences with love objects which become the relational object of gratification. As the symbol suggests, these parental experiences become unconsciously internalized objects and the initial representation of all human relationships. This approach led to the creation of an *objective-relations psychology*.

Unlike Freud, *Melanie Klein* (1882–1960), the mother of *object-relations* psychology, did not believe there was an innate drive toward stasis, but rather an innate drive toward destructive rage when the drive was not met (Klein, 1932/2017). Klein believed that the child feared a malevolence force from the outside the world that could contaminate and destroy all goodness. The result was the child felt the need to be protected from destructive persecutory anxiety by projecting blame on others. The only thing that the social world could offer was to soothe persecutory anxiety, diminish paranoid f e a r s, and to strengthen good mother internalized objects.

Symbols of Freudian and Relational Psychoanalysis 83

Figure 2.17

Later in his career, Freud expanded drive theory to Eros and Thanatos, the drive toward life and creativity, and the drive toward death and destruction. The *death instinct* was crucial to Melanie Klein who believed that the infant psyche was divided into two opposing states of mind, the good and bad breast (Klein, 1932/2017). The good breast provided nourishment and love; the bad breast became bad because of the aggression and the destructive fantasies of retaliation by the child against the mother.

To maintain homeostasis the child needed to split the experiences of mother into all good or all bad. This primordial split of a good and bad self, Klein called the paranoid-schizoid position because it produced persecutory anxiety generated by the death instinct.

Figure 2.18

How the child resolved the destructive aspects of the "good mother breast" and "bad mother breast" split depended upon the constitution of the child and the nurturance of the mother. This resolution provided the psychological foundation for interpersonal relationships in adulthood. As Freud focused on penis envy, object-relations psychologists focused on the breast, declaring that men suffered from breast envy (Klein, 1932/2017). For the Kleinian, the breast of the mother symbolized the first object of human relationship that symbolized how the infant first learned the struggle between good and evil.

British object relations theorists, Winnicott and Balint, did not agree that the death instinct or innate aggressive drives were the key elements in infancy. They believed the baby was innately designed to interact and relate but could be negatively affected by inadequate parenting or a neglectful environment.

Darwinian and Ethnological Influence

The *attachment theory* of *John Bowlby*, one of the most cited psychoanalysts and psychologists in research, had a lasting affect not only on the history of depth psychology, but on all of psychology. In London, during "the great debates" in depth psychology, he was influenced by, but rejected, much of the psychoanalytic approach to children, although he was psychoanalyzed by the Kleinian Joan Riviere and supervised by Melanie Klein.

As many relational psychoanalysts focused on the internal world of childhood, Bowlby was interested in the child in the real, lived world (Bowlby, 1973). He was influenced by the Darwinian theory of the relationship between instinct and mother and its role in evolutionary survival. This was influenced by his extensive contact with the leading European ethnologists of the day, especially by Konrad Lorenz, who showed that goslings imprint on the first animate object they experience. Bowlby believed that ethnological research could provide an empirical research methodology severely lacking in psychoanalysis. Early object-relation theorists rejected ethnological approach because they viewed the mother as an interchangeable need-satisfying object. Bowlby disagreed and insisted that attachment was instinctual and that an early loss could produce psychological damage and mourning (Bowlby, 1980, Bowlby, 1999).

Anna Freud disagreed with Bowlby because of her belief that infants could not mourn or grieve like adults. She argued that Bowlby focused too heavily on instinct and not enough on intrapsychic representations. Early object-relation theorists rejected the concept that separations in infancy created pathogenic mental disturbance, marginalizing Bowlby in the early days of the relational psychoanalytic movement. When attachment theory became popular in the 1980s, the early object-relations theorists were proven wrong, integrating Darwinian and Bowlby's ethnological theories into mainstream relational psychoanalysis (Holmes, 1993).

Attachment Theory

Developmental psychology is the empirical study of the development of human beings over a lifetime. *Mary Ainsworth* (1913–1999), a renowned developmental psychologist, was influenced in the 1960s and 1970s by ethnology, Bowlby, and attachment theory.

The Ainsworth *strange situation* research method developed in the 1970s studied the attachment relationship between child and caregiver (Ainsworth, Blehar, Waters, et al, 2015). The strange situation procedure applied to children between the ages of 9 and 11 months. Researchers observed a child playing for 21 minutes while caregivers and strangers routinely entered and left the room, creating the appearance of both familiar and unfamiliar people. Based on the behavior of the child, the attachments to caregivers were classified into three categories, and a fourth added later. *Secure attachment* resulted from the caregiver attending consistently to the needs of the child. *Anxious-ambivalent attachment* resulted from an inconsistent caregiver when the child was unsure of the response of the parent. *Anxious-avoidant attachment* occurred when the child was consistently rebuffed by the caregiver and had to learn to depend on themselves. *Disorganized-disoriented attachment,* added later, resulted from mothers who had suffered major loss or trauma and were inconsistent in their protective and emotional availability to the child (Ainsworth, Blehar, Waters, et al, 2015).

Ainsworth's work on attachment has remained foundational in modern-day relational psychoanalysis. She is one of the most cited psychologists in attachment research. Her influence expanded to many areas from parenting to the criminal justice system. Most recently, interest increased regarding how infant attachment affected adult relationships, especially romantic and love relationships. Cindy Hazan and Phillip Shaver (1987), in *Romantic Love Conceptualized as an Attachment Process,* recapitulated the Ainsworth attachment patterns to adult romantic relationships.

Psychophysiological Influence

Research on the physiological responses measured in the strange situation procedure indicated that attachment patterns impacted unique and general brain regions. Psychophysiological research on attachment indicated that caregiving in infancy and childhood directly affected the psychoneurological systems which control stress regulation. Most significant was the impact on the autonomic nervous system, which controls heart rate and respiration, and activity in the hypothalamic-pituitary-adrenal axis, which controls stress reactions.

Research continues on the effect of attachment on key brain structures, neural circuits, neurotransmitter systems, and neuropeptides. Research found that the attachment patterns developed by Ainsworth had physiological impacts in adulthood, especially regarding the biomarkers of immunity. As an example, individuals under stress with an avoidance attachment pattern produced higher levels of pro-inflammatory cytokine interleukin-6 (IL-6). G. E. Miller and associates' research, summarized in *Maternal Warmth Buffers the Effects of Low Early Life Socioeconomic Status of pro-Inflammatory Signaling in Adulthood* (Chen, Miller, Kobor & Cole, 2011), indicated that maternal warmth during infancy and childhood in lower-socioeconomic populations produced a superior immune system later in life. This provided another biological explanation of the core relational psychoanalytic belief in the importance of attachment in early childhood development.

Hermeneutic Influences

Oedipal Complex Influence

Melanie Klein and Anna Freud disagreed regarding the role of sexuality in human life (Klein, 1932/2017). For Anna Freud, sexuality was needed for libidinal release of anxiety, an expression of power and the need for pleasure. For Klein, sexuality was about love, the ability to overcome destructiveness, and to balance love and hate. Giving love to someone was about overcoming hate and the death instinct, thereby developing internal love objects that sustained love. Melanie Klein disagreed with Freud's view that the Oedipal complex meant a child's sexual interest in the opposite sex parent, but argued it was the desire to possess and control the body of the mother. Klein connected the Oedipal drama to oral sadism and the death instinct which caused childhood aggression. Klein believed that psychopathology was the result of aggression and the innate desire to destroy when instinctual needs were not satisfied.

Disagreement on the Oedipal complex laid the foundation for the bitter debates between Klein and Anna Freud. Anna Freud argued that psychoanalytic work should strengthen, not weaken, the relationship of the child to their parents, and that Oedipal conflicts should not be psychoanalytically interpreted with children. Klein viewed this perspective as avoiding the importance of analyzing the Oedipal strivings of the child and ignoring the negative aggressive impulses of children (Klein, 1932/2017).

For Jacques Lacan, the Oedipal complex was symbolic of the mother- child separation and the creation of a *symbolic order* (Zizek & Critchley, 2007). As the child separated from the mother, an emotional gap and a feeling of disconnectedness occurred. The phallus was symbolic not only of sexuality, but of the human need to be desired. The longing to fill the gap and feel reconnected to mother was a desire that could never be achieved because it was only the father who symbolically possessed the desired phallus. When mother used the word "father," the child became aware that father and the phallus preceded their existence. In this way, the child began to live under the *Law of the Father*, which symbolized the child's experience of the social order of human relationships. Unlike the Freudian view of the phallus as the penis, Lacan viewed the phallus not as a literal penis, but as a symbol and the centerpiece of the symbolic order that transcended the ego.

Feminism

The feminist leaders in the psychoanalytic movement began to question the cultural and social assumption of the primacy of men. They rejected the superiority of the male body, replacing the penis with the womb and the breast. *Karen Horney* (1885–1952), the first psychoanalytic feminist before Melanie Klein and before the relational psychoanalytic movement, believed that Freudian psychoanalysis was most appropriate for men, not women. What penis envy meant to women was not sexual envy but jealousy about the power men held over women. From her feminist position, Horney rejected sex and aggression as the primary determinants of personality.

Analogous to penis envy and drive theory, Horney proposed *womb envy*. This was an innate male trait that fueled the subordination of women and drove men to culturally succeed and exert their power in business, law, and politics. Underlying womb envy was fascination with the female breast, the vagina, and many of other areas of the female body including pregnancy,

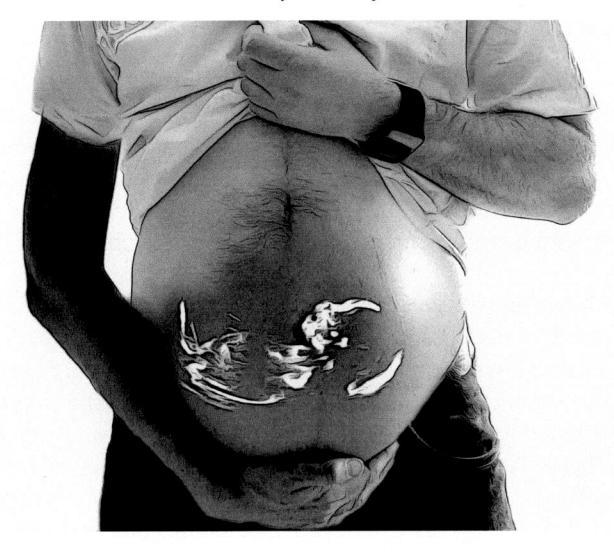

Figure 2.19

childbirth, and breast feeding. Horney believed that men suffered from a *femininity complex*, a desire to escape the gender rigidity of modern culture and deny their transsexual feelings because of cultural norms and social responsibilities.

Horney was part of the neo-Freudian movement, a precursor to the relational psychoanalytic movement (Brown, 1961). This movement was comprised of Freudians who believed culture and social forces were the key to psychological development. Horney, who lived during the Great American Depression of 1929, believed many of the Freudian concepts were irrelevant to a modern culture struggling to survive economically. Providing psychoanalysis during the depression heightened her awareness that clients were worried more about food and housing than their intrapsychic functioning.

In *Feminine Psychology*, Horney (1973) explored how cultures worldwide encouraged male dependence, and the need for women to base their self-esteem on men for love, prestige, wealth, and protection. In this scenario, women became objectified, sexual objects, with an emphasis on their beauty rather than their personhood. It also created an overdependence for finding love and self-esteem through motherhood, which made women prisoners to their gender role.

After disagreements with traditional Freudians at the New York Psychoanalytic Institute, Horney resigned and, in 1941, and advanced her own theories formed the *Association for the Advancement of Psychoanalysis*. Her legacy of low-cost community treatment continued when the Karen Horney Clinic opened in New York City in 1955 to honor her legacy. The clinic continues to provide treatment from her cultural orientation, also offers training to future mental health professionals.

At the height of the feminist movement of the 1970s, Juliet Mitchell (1974/1990) in *Psychoanalysis and Feminism: A Radical Reassessment of Freudian Psychoanalysis*, shocked the feminist world by challenging feminists to reassess psychoanalysis. She pointed out that psychoanalysis was a critique of, and not a supporter of, patriarchy. She believed at the root of psychoanalytic criticism was a lack of acceptance of an unconscious and the role of sexuality in human life. She argued that feminists needed to accept the influence of the unconscious on sexual behavior and female identity.

Social Structuralism Influence

Many relational psychoanalysts embraced social constructionism: the belief that human development was socially and culturally determined, and that knowledge was constructed through interaction with others (Sturrock, 2003). In this context, motherhood and gender roles were artifacts of a biologically based patriarchal social construction. This could be changed by men and women working together to create new social artifacts and new ways to socially interact, which would emancipate both from the shadow of "biological destiny."

Since Freud regarded homosexuality as constitutional and not a psychoanalytic problem, structuralism provided a reassessment of homosexuality in the psychoanalytic movement. Freud believed most humans were basically bisexual by nature and was never interested in changing the sexual orientation of his clients. It was the homophobia of American psychoanalysts that decried homosexuality as pathological and a mental illness (Zaretsky, 2015). Homophobic American psychoanalysts originally viewed heterosexuality as normal and homosexuality as an abnormal pre-Oedipal condition, or as a defensive response to castration anxiety. They also believed that homosexuality was caused by overcontrolling mothers or detached fathers. Currently, most psychoanalysts view being gay as constitutional and reject efforts to change the sexual orientation of their clients (Messer & Gurman, 2011).

Relational Psychoanalytic Psychology

Transference and Countertransference

Transference and countertransference remained important in post-Freudian psychoanalytic psychology. It was one of the major issues surrounding the Klein and Anna Freud conflict. Klein believed that the key dynamic in relational psychoanalysis was to reduce anxiety through the interpretation of unconscious fantasy. Because unconscious fantasies were destructive, Klein was most interested in negative transference. It was her belief that unconscious feelings of hatred, anger, and rage inhibited the ability for affection and reparative and positive feelings.

In the *Psychoanalysis of Children*, Klein (1932/2017) presented her vision for object-relational childhood psychoanalysis. She believed that children's free play with toys was a symbolic way to control anxiety and a way to assess the internal objects that were emerging from the unconscious. Through the symbols of free play, she could analyze childhood states. The paranoid-schizoid state was persecutory because the child felt threatened by the annihilation of the self. Later in the depressive state, the child feared harming love objects. Play was important for emotional moderation of the emerging internal childhood conflicts. Most surprising was her belief that very young children had more capacity for insight than adults.

Anna Freud disagreed that the traditional interpretation of transference could apply to children because they were not analyzable and still dependent on their parents. From her ego psychological perspective, she did not believe that children had the emotional strength to understand and cope with Klein's overly aggressive interpretative approach. Rather, children needed social support and education because anxiety resulted not only from intrapsychic forces, but also from the forces of the social world.

Wilfred Bion (1897–1979), an early leader of the relational psychoanalytic movement and president of the prestigious *British Psychological Society* during the controversial 1960s, focused on the countertransference of the therapist by exploring their own need for emotional reparation, including the need to control their own anxiety and depression. The ability to contain and accept strong feelings led to *client envy* which undermined the transference and the work of childhood reparation. The transference relationship was an experience of both a "good and bad breast" therapist. The "good breast" therapist provided interpretations which nourished with warmth and love. The "bad breast" therapist interpretations made the client feel danger and dread. Because of the reality of existence, ultimately a transference would have a mixture of hope and dread (Caper, 2020).

Ronald Fairbairn (1889–1964), a central figure in the development of relational psychoanalysis, believed, as most relational psychoanalysts, that clients experienced *therapeutic ambivalence* (Fairbairn & Dodds, 1952). On the one hand, clients wished to change, but on the other hand, they wished to stay loyal to the past. Since people unconsciously respond to the world to confirm their past experiences, he argued that it was important that the therapist understand this as the foundation of the transference. To reject old patterns would cause feelings of loss, abandonment, and isolation. To break the ambivalence, the therapist had to become part of the problem. There had to be a *transference rupture* for the client to experience a different emotional relationship to the world. Although often painful and difficult, a time when many clients leave therapy, those that remain through the process internalize the therapist as a different object (Greenberg, Greenberg & Greenberg, 1983).

For the client to feel protected and safe, *Donald Winnicott* (1896–1971), a leading member of the *British Independent Group of the British Psychoanalytic Society*, viewed a *holding*, womb-like therapeutic environment, as key for the creation of a positive transference (Winnicott, 1965). When a client felt held in a nurturing, motherly way, they could freely express their impulses and emotions without parental intrusion. In Winnicottian terms, the room of the therapist became a symbol of the warmth and the womb of a mother.

Projective Identification

Klein developed *projective identification* as an essential relational psychoanalytic concept (Klein, 1932/2017). In Freudian theory, projection was an essential ego defense and allowed an individual to attribute unwanted impulses onto others. Klein expanded the concept beyond impulses to the projection of actual parts of the self onto others. These parts of the self became unconsciously placed onto another person. By maintaining connection to the person, the individual could control and regulate the "lost self." As an example, projecting homosexual disgust unto another person to feel protected from the unwanted homoerotic feelings.

Since both Klein and Anna Freud treated children, this became another area of conflict. The ego psychology of Anna Freud viewed the mind of a child in terms of ego defenses as developmentally different from adults (A. Freud, 1937). Klein viewed the adult and child mind as similarly anxious, paranoid, angry, and overwhelmed with abandonment fears. This meant the child was open to what Klein called *deep interpretations*. Anna Freud and critics of Klein believed her approach was psychologically destructive because children could not process deep interpretations.

Bion argued that projective identification began in childhood when the child projected disturbing and anxiety producing emotions onto the mother. Like the mother, the psychotherapist became the container for the "lost self," and for anxieties too threatening for the client to control and regulate (Caper, 2020). Unlike Klein, who based the therapeutic relationship on the exploration of psychological phantasies, Bion emphasized interpretation of the interpersonal relationship because it triggered the unconscious affective state of childhood. It was important for the therapist, like the mother, to be able to be in emotional *attunement* with the client to soothe the disturbing emotional reactions of both the client and the therapist.

False and True Self

Winnicott was influenced by Klein, but disagreed with her concept of childhood aggression. Although he found value in her positions, being a practicing pediatrician, he focused more on the practical aspects of childhood, especially by playing simple games that created feelings of childhood competence. He believed there was no such thing as a baby but to view babies as part of a *nursing couple* (Winnicott, 1965). This was an imperfect and complex couple, as are all relationships. He acknowledged the imperfection of parenthood by developing the theory of good enough mother. This was a mother who could provide "good enough" emotional security by being spontaneous and authentic *true self*. The symbol of the nursing couple provides a powerful symbol of the importance in relational psychoanalysis of emotional attachment for the development of a true self.

Although relational psychoanalysts view early experiences with the mother as the determinant of future mental disturbance, Winnicott was interested in healthier people who often felt that they could not feel their "real selves." He viewed this issue as the *false self-disorder,* which did not result from abuse or neglect, but from the unresponsiveness of the mother to the needs of the child. The false self was caused by the child striving unconsciously to meet the needs of the not-so-good mother over their own needs. Even without direct contact with the parent, even later in life, to feel love, adults could strive to meet parental needs. A relational psychoanalyst understands as a parental figure a client might unconsciously continue to deny their true self by meeting the perceived needs of the therapist. By entering the inner world of the client to avoid "taking care of the therapist," through a positive transference a relational psychoanalyst uncovers and changes the unconscious false self by becoming an authentic *good-enough* internalized mother object.

No Self – Interpersonal Psychoanalysis

Heinz Kohut (1913–1981), a Jewish immigrate from Austria to America in the 1940s, offered a different approach of self-psychology to relational psychology in part because he was not enveloped by the controversies of the *British Psychoanalytic Society.* He rejected the Freudian and early object-relational view that humans were in a constant state of conflict with libidinal energies and parental reactions. Rather, for Kohut, the baby was born into an empathetic milieu with no innate source of conflict (Kohut, 1971/2009b). In fact, the relationship with others created a major challenge for the development of a sense of self. It was not that children had bad or good internal objects; they had little or no internalized objects which was symbolized by a no self.

Although he argued that it did not usually provide satisfaction, Kohut accepted the basic psychoanalytic tenet that there was a pleasure principle and a human need to seek pleasure and release libidinal tension. But more importantly, he felt that seeking *self-expression* created a more important psychological dynamic beyond the Freudian pleasure principle. The self was more interested in protecting itself from emptiness and psychological disintegration than from the gratification of forbidden libidinal tension.

Figure 2.20

In *Analysis of the Self: A Systematic Approach to the Treatment of Narcissistic Personality Disorders*, Kohut (1971/2009b) realized that trying to directly confront the narcissist was fruitless because the narcissist felt empty, with no sense of self. Narcissism was the product in childhood not good or bad, but of no meaningful self-object. Interpretative confrontation would only humiliate the narcissist and deepen their feelings of inadequacy. He found that the narcissist oscillated between grandiosity and despair and felt little joy from any of their accomplishments. Kohut believed that there was a normal and healthy narcissistic self-object that everyone could develop because it resulted in a stronger sense of self and a psychological vitality, self-esteem, and the drive to achieve lifetime goals.

In Greek mythology, Narcissus, a Thespian hunter, was known for his incredible beauty that had rejected all romantic advances. Upon seeing the reflection of his youthful bloom in a pool of water, fell in love with himself. Not understanding it was merely a reflection he could not forget the image. He realized that he could never find this object of desire. He burned and melted away from the passion he felt inside and became a gold and a white flower. There are many versions and meanings of the myth. For self-psychologists, the myth of Narcissist symbolized the importance of developing strong internal self-objects. It was important to fall in love with your real, not your imaged self. These will enrich an empty self in search of meaningful interpersonal relationships and fulfilling purposeful life.

Self-objects were objects which arouse, maintain, or change internal self-feelings. Three essential self-objects were needed for the development of a realistic and mature psychological self. First, a *mirroring* self-object was needed because children needed to have their self-worth mirrored back to them through parental empathy and acceptance. This endowed the child, later adult, with self-esteem and self-acceptance. Secondly, the child needed an *idealized* self-object, parents who were calm and powerful which the child could idealize. The third self-object that was needed, an alter ego or bipolar self-object which allowed the child to feel likeness to the parent and another self. This was the need for *twinship,* to be like someone else but still an individual.

92 *Symbols of Freudian and Relational Psychoanalysis*

Kohut viewed a major goal of relational psychoanalysis as the internalization of the three self-objects (Kohut, 1971/2009b). At the beginning of treatment, the client mirrored the empathy and acceptance of the therapist as a self-object by experiencing their own internal feelings of self-worth and acceptance. As therapy progressed the client idealized the therapist and perceived the therapist as strong and competent. In the therapeutic process, empathy was more important than interpretation because interpretation disrupted the self/object connection. In the soothing and warm connection to such an empathetic therapist, the self-object allowed the client to become empathetic to themselves and develop the ability to self-soothe. If analysis was successful, the client built a stronger and more resilient internal self-structure by the internalization of the therapist as an alter ego self-object. Clients saw themselves as similar to the therapist but setting their own individual goals and values.

Figure 2.21

Kohut rejected the determinism of classical psychoanalytic thought which tended to neglect the uniqueness of human experience. Whether being a parent, therapist, or researcher, the key to his theory was empathetic immersion into the individual human experience. This empathetic immersion, understanding the introspection of the other was where the true self could be discovered. It was where Kohut defined the self as a sense of having an independent center of initiative and perception, integrated ambitions and ideals and an experience of the unity of the body and mind.

Figure 2.22

It did not sit well with the classical and object-relation analysts that Kohut distinguished self-objects to be uniquely experienced as part of a developing self, not rooted in childhood parenting, that other people were viewed as unique and different whole objects. They viewed his work as non-psychoanalytic, insufficiently intrapsychic, and a form of social psychology. After being ostracized by his colleagues and after publishing *The Restoration of the Self* (Kohut, 1977/2009a) in 1978, he was removed from the governing board of the *Chicago Psychoanalytic Institute*.

Interpersonal Self – Phenomenological Contextualism

Kohut would be redeemed by Charles Strozier, a future director of the *Chicago Psychanalytic Institute*. Strozier (2001) wrote in his biography, *Heinz Kohut: The Meaning of a Psychoanalyst* that Kohut had saved psychoanalysis from itself by his focus on empathetic and interpersonal relationships. He believed without the emergence of an interpersonal psychoanalysis the other major psychological orientations would have eclipsed relational psychoanalysis.

The interpersonal psychoanalytic movement was influenced by Harry Stack Sullivan, the pioneer of *interpersonal psychology*. In his work with schizophrenia, Sullivan rejected the biological model of mental illness and medicine of the 1920s. This model viewed individuals with schizophrenia as unable to build relationships because the illness caused severe psychological and physical withdrawal. Sullivan viewed the problem of schizophrenia as arising during childhood from caregivers' anxiety, which created severe anxiety in the baby. It was through a safe and protective environment that decreased the anxiety of an individual with schizophrenia that a healthy interpersonal relationship could develop. Sullivan was one of the first psychoanalysts to focus on the "here and now." He felt that psychoanalysts focused too much on the past. Past communication patterns drew the therapist into the old world of the client, whereas the "here and now" approach created a self-system based on the interlocking of many I-thou interactions. This meant that the self developed from authentic communication which resulted in interpersonal meaning.

In the tradition of Sullivan and Kohut, George Atwood and Robert Stolorow (1984), in *Structures of Subjectivity: Explorations of Psychoanalytic Phenomenology*, introduced *phenomenological psychoanalysis*. Atwood and Stolorow were founding members of the *Institute for the Psychoanalytic Study of Subjectivity* in New York City. Stolorow was a founding member of the *Institute of Contemporary Psychoanalysis* in Los Angeles. Calling their approach *phenomenological contextualism*, they attempted to "purify" the reification of Freudian metapsychology, the impersonal constructs that defined all behavior.

Atwood and Stolorow rejected the long history in psychoanalysis of the isolated Cartesian mind (Atwood & Orange, 2011). This was the bifurcation of the mind that created an alienated and separate sense of self. The "beauty of phenomenology and intersubjectivity" allowed the individual to reclaim emotional integrity. The self was determined by the irreducible interpersonal connection to others. Atwood and Stolorow (1984) believed that in childhood, the self was developed through the unconscious intersubjective formation of organized personality structures. Analysis in phenomenological psychoanalysis explored the intersubjective personality structures of both the client and therapist. This replaced the traditional Freudian view of the importance of analyzing client fantasy with the importance of analyzing the subjective world of the therapist.

Traumatized Self – Phenomenological Psychoanalysis

Figure 2.23

Atwood and Stolorow also utilized the contextual approach to understand the context of the lives of many of the great historic philosophers, theoreticians, and practitioners who influenced psychoanalysis and psychology. They examined the lives of Freud, Jung, Reich, Rank, Kierkegaard, Nietzsche, Wittgenstein, Sartre, and Heidegger. In *The Abyss of Madness,* Atwood (2011) found that all these men experienced trauma and severe internal conflicts in their personal world, which they tried to resolve through their lifelong work. They all experienced severe mental disturbance and feelings of irreversible emotional tensions, which led to feelings of ongoing psychological trauma. They all fought "demons," the shadow, often with limited success. They viewed themselves as symbols for not only their personal survival, but as symbols of the survival of humanity itself.

This examination reinforced the importance of historical research and the shift to phenomenological psychoanalysis. Atwood and Stolorow (1984) believed the shift needed a radical contextualization of virtually all aspects of psychological life, starting with painful or frightening affect, especially trauma. Since all humans experienced emotional pain, the baby could be traumatized during childhood when caretakers were not in attunement with the emotional pain of the child.

Living in an authentic intersubjective world necessitated the need for the caretaker to dwell in emotional pain with the child while at the same time providing an "emotional home" for the pain to be held. In the final analysis a binary psychology created an emotionally *traumatized self* with impending feelings of annihilation and unendurable emotions that needed deadening dissociative defenses. When these painful and traumatic feelings were intersubjectively met by the "angels" of human responsiveness and understanding, by phenomenological contextualism, a transformation occurred. The traumatized individual experienced feelings of aliveness and vitality through the emotional attunement and authenticity of relationship.

Relational psychoanalysis changed the psychoanalytic symbol of the Stolorow "demon shadow" of a binary self, a pre-determined and separate unconscious, to the "angel" of a self that developed from relational, intersubjective, and internalized self-objects.

Symbolic Self – Return to Freudian Psychoanalysis

French psychoanalyst Jacques Lacan (1901–1981), considered one of the most controversial and difficult-to-understand psychoanalysts in modern times, argued that the new generation of relational and self-psychoanalysts needed to return to the basics of Freudian thought. Leading a "return to Freud" within the psychoanalytic movement was met with great resistance (Caper, 2020). Since Lacan approached psychoanalysis from philosophical, linguistic, political, mathematical, critical theory, and feminist perspectives, his views ultimately began to be perceived as elitist and more in alignment with the French intelligentsia than the psychoanalytic movement. In 1970, he and his followers were expelled from the *International Psychoanalytic Association,* which increased his popularity in Europe and South America.

There was little interest in America because of American anti-intellectualism and the psychoanalytic dominance by organized medicine that required that psychoanalysts be physicians (Caper, 2020). Early in the psychoanalytic movement, American psychoanalysts rejected the European comfort with non- physician "lay analysts." Consequently, most American Lacanians are found in academia, not in psychology or psychoanalytic institutes. They are found in departments of linguistics, philosophy, anthropology, political science, and literature.

Lacan objected to the focus of relational psychoanalysts on ego because of his belief that language, not ego, was the foundation of creating a different concept of self. A major influence was the structural anthropology of *Claude Levi-Strauss* (1908–2009), who focused on the human capacity to find through symbol, that which was absent.

Lacan believed traditional psychoanalysts focused on an *imaginary self* because of their interest in internalized imaginary objects, which neglected the role of symbol and the

96 *Symbols of Freudian and Relational Psychoanalysis*

development of a non- ego *symbolic self*. The development of the imaginary self began in early childhood when a child viewed themselves in a mirror and, upon seeing a red dot on their forehead, touched the dot, not the mirror. This indicated the beginning of an imaginary self that became further developed by parental and cultural language. The *mirror image* showed that the ego was not the true subject, but an alienated image of the real person.

The ego lived in an imaginary world of illusion, delusion, identifications, reflections of reflections, and a hall of mirrors. Reinforcement of the self's mirror image strengthened the ego and the erroneous idea that the ego was real (Caper, 2020). Ego autonomy was an illusion; real autonomy was in the symbolic order that could not be achieved within oneself but in relationship to the social world. This was a world yet to be imaged and a world yet to find the language for the emerging symbols. Lacan believed that symbols emerged from the unconscious before the creation of a new scientific order. The task for the theory and practice of psychoanalysis specifically, and science at large, was to analyze words, language, and make conscious the emerging new symbolic order.

Psychoanalytic work needed to return to the Freudian *linguistic unconscious* that existed beyond normal life experiences and interpersonal relationships (Caper, 2020). The ego and object relation psychologists were mistaking the subjective story of the client as real. Rather, the subjective self had to be avoided in service of transforming the unique language of the client into symbol. Analysis required understanding that language was a chain of *signifiers*, symbols in words, which created a state of being rather than an ego consciousness.

In successful Lacanian analysis, the client became less interested in ego and more focused on the development of a symbolic self. This meant development of a relationship with the symbolic language of the unconscious which transcended the ego. The analyzing ego was a vehicle for transforming the imaginary self into a symbolic self, which lived in a symbolic order, defined by

Figure 2.24

Symbols of Freudian and Relational Psychoanalysis 97

a relationship with the unconscious other. The relationship with the language of the unconscious indicated the possibility that a real self could develop, but it currently had to first be understood through the symbolic order and the experience of the symbolic self (Caper, 2020).

Emancipatory Opportunities in Relational Psychoanalysis

Consider Relational Psychoanalysis

Relational psychoanalysis provides the opportunity to heal early deficient interpersonal relationships, particularly issues related to childhood attachment, abuse, and trauma.

Read a Self-Help Book

Understanding the limited access of psychoanalysis for the common person, in *Self Analysis*, Karen Horney (1942), a neo-Freudian, wrote the first self-help book inaugurating the *self-help movement*. The book was an optimistic presentation of the value of neo- Freudian psychoanalysis emphasizing the potential of every person to become their own therapist. Self- help books continue to provide psychologists a forum to translate ideas from the academic and clinical world to the general population.

Parent with Mutual Responsibility for Attachment

Although women play an important role in physical birth and initial attachment, the reality is that the key for human attachment is linked to the internalization of love objects that transcend gender. It is important not to place all the responsibility of childhood attachment on women because men have the ability and obligation to also become an emotional "good breast."

Figure 2.25

Advocate for the Availability of Quality Childcare Services

Over half of children in America will be raised in childcare; it is essential that a high-quality, regulated, and financially accessible system be available to all parents.

Assess Early Attachment

Research indicates that early attachment effects the quality of adult life, including interpersonal relationships and marriage (Hazan & Shaver, 1987). In order to understand the impact of attachment, evaluate your early attachments as *secure, anxious-ambivalent, anxious-avoidant,* or *disorganized-disoriented* (see descriptions above).

Practice Relational Psychoanalysis in Community Mental Health (CMH)

An important question remains whether community mental health abandoned depth psychology or depth psychology abandoned community mental health. In either case, Freudian or relational psychoanalysis is mostly absent in community mental health settings.

John Sutherland (1994), in *The Autonomous Self,* discusses how an individually focused psychoanalyst evolved into a community mental health oriented relational psychoanalyst. Amazingly, the epiphany occurred at age 70, after his own psychoanalysis. Sutherland believed internal self-objects, the concept of the self, needed to be understood in relation to institutional and community life. *The Autonomous Self* provides a rare blueprint for the practice of relational psychoanalysis in community mental health.

Beyond Anglo-American ethnocentrism, some of the most interesting research and practice of relational psychoanalysis in CMH can be found in unlikely places like South Africa and Iran, but also in other parts of the world like Canada and England, which often place a higher value on depth psychology than in America: *Reflective Practice in Infant Mental Health: A South African Perspective* (Berg, 2016); *The Mental Health through Psychodynamic Perspective: The Relationship between Ego Strength, the Defense Styles, and Object Relations to (Iranian) Mental Health* (Leili, Atef, Dehghani & Habbi, 2015); *Quality of Object Relations and Suicidal Ideation Among (Canadian) Community Mental Health Outpatients* (Kely & Laverdiere, 2019). Kleinian analysts in England utilize relational psychoanalysis to improve community mental health services, especially to those in poverty.

Attend to Prevention

Although CMHs primarily treat individuals with serious mental illness, prevention of mental illness remains an important goal of all psychologists and mental health professionals. Understand the dire impact on childhood attachment of the 3 million American women who suffer from the effects of *postpartum depression* (PPD).

Become a "Community Love Object"

Michael Balint (2018) believed that disturbed individuals needed unconditional love, a *primary internalized love object*. In relational psychoanalytic terms, community providers provide an internalized loving self-object.

Promote Transference and Countertransference Understanding

Often, CMH centers have a high no-show rate of 50 percent or higher. In *When Absence Speaks Louder than Words: A Object Relational Perspective on No- Show Appointments,* Michelle Kwinter (2011) argued for processes beyond behaviorism that utilized object-relations theory and the practice of transference and countertransference to examine the quality of the last session when the client failed to show up for their next scheduled appointment.

Advocate for a Systems-of-Community-Care Approach

It is estimated that 15–25 percent of women and 5–15 percent of men have been sexually abused as children alerts society to the unconscious forces that traumatize society (Gorey & Leslie, 1997). Since most of the perpetrators are family members or family friends, it is essential that CMHs, psychologists, and other mental health professionals work collaboratively with child welfare in a *systems-of-care approach*, a biopsychosocial-integrated treatment plan that includes all essential community services in the treatment of childhood abuse.

Connect Attachment to Understanding Relational Psychoanalysis

Most community mental health and psychology clinicians have some understanding of attachment theory, but often do not understand its roots are in relational psychoanalysis. It is important that attachment assessment be part of the mental *health status examination* process because childhood attachment is a prognostic indicator of treatment success and the ability of the person to form a therapeutic relationship.

Promote Understanding the Unconscious in Education

The neglect and denial cannot diminish the presence of the unconscious. Most sadly, even within departments of psychology, there is a lack of coursework and education on the unconscious throughout American learning institutions. As this chapter has shown, the lack of education ignores the reality that psychoanalysis has developed significantly beyond Freud. One major reason for the lack of psychoanalytic acknowledgment in modern psychology is the incorrect view that psychodynamic psychotherapy is not an evidence-based practice (Shedler, 2010). Also, there are no specific psychoanalytic course requirements in the extensive list of APA requirements for accreditation of its doctoral programs in clinical psychology. Even more significant is the warning of Freud that a denial of the unconscious will continue to perpetuate violence and war and imperil humanity itself.

Figure 2.26

100 *Symbols of Freudian and Relational Psychoanalysis*

QUESTIONS 2

2.1 *Describe the cultural, socio-economic, and political influences which led to the development of Freudian and Relational Psychoanalysis.*

2.2 *Explain how the differences between Pierre Janet and Sigmund Freud impacted the development of psychoanalysis.*

2.3 *Describe the development of personality from a Freudian perspective.*

2.4 *Explain the key differences between Freudian and Relational Psychoanalysis.*

2.5 *What is the meaning of object-relations?*

2.6 *Describe the development of a False Self.*

2.7 *What is the Symbolic Self?*

Universal Meanings of the Chapter Symbols

Figure 2.0:
> Melanie Klein - Image source - Included in image-Melanie Klein. (2022, December 5). In Wikipedia. https://en.wikipedia.org/wiki/Melanie_Klein - CC BY 4.0 license
>
> John Bowlby. (2022, November 13). In Wikipedia. https://en.wikipedia.org/wiki/John_Bowlby Fair Use license
>
> Karen Horney. (2022, December 11). In Wikipedia. https://en.wikipedia.org/wiki/Karen_Horney -CC BY-SA 3.0 License

Figure 2.1. The Four Forces in Psychology.
Figure 2.2. The international symbol of workers and peasants controlling their destiny.
Figure 2.3. A belief that "man as wolf to man."
Figure 2.4. The shadow of the Industrial Revolution and the universal oppression of working people.
Figure 2.5. Effort to change human behavior through hypnosis.
Figure 2.6. The power of instinctual energy.
Figure 2.7. The experience of the Freudian Id.
Figure 2.8. Hypnosis treatment understanding rooted in mythology.
Figure 2.9. The result of sexual repression and a distorted view of women.
Figure 2.10. The unconscious family drama.
Figure 2.11. The need for a "parental consciousness" for the survival of civilization.
Figure 2.12. The unconscious drive toward life and death.
Figure 2.13. Nuclear war as the ultimate release of unconscious id forces.
Figure 2.14. The need for a sacred space to explore the unconscious.
Figure 2.15. The exploration of dreams for a healthier life.
Figure 2.16. A modern view of gender identity.
Figure 2.17. The difference between libidinal and relational drives.
Figure 2.18. Experience of a good and bad breast in childhood.
Figure 2.19. Male experience of Womb envy
Figure 2.20. Therapeutic relationship key to healing childhood wounds and trauma.
Figure 2.21. The need to develop a "healthy narcissism" by exploring the meaning of the Narcissus myth.

Figure 2.22. Internalizing people from life experiences.
Figure 2.23. A need to transform the shadow, "the demons" of frightening, emotionally painful and traumatic life events.
Figure 2.24. The experience of ego autonomy as an illusion.
Figure 2.25. The opportunity to experience the world beyond one's gender.
Figure 2.26. The denial of the unconscious in educational institutions.

References

Adler, A. (1964). *Social interest: A challenge to mankind*. New York: Capricorn Books. (Original Work Published in 1933).
Adler, A. (1998). *Understanding human nature*. New York: Hazelden Foundation. (Original Work Published in 1927).
Ainsworth, M.D.S., Blehar, M.C. & Waters, E. et al (2015). *Patterns of attachment: A psychological study*. (1st Ed.). New York: Psychology Press and Routledge Classic Editions.
Altman, N. (2010). *The analyst in the inner city: Race, class through a psychoanalytic lens*. (2nd Ed.). New York: Routledge.
Ansbacher, H.L. & Ansbacher, R.R. (1956). *The individual psychology of Alfred Adler: A systematic presentation in selections from his writings*. New York: Basic Books, Inc.
Atwood, G.E. (2011). *The abyss of madness*. New York: Routledge.
Atwood, G.E. & Orange, D.M. (2011). The madness and genius of post-Cartesian philosophy: A distant mirror. *Psychoanalytic Review*. 98, 263–285.
Atwood, G.E. & Stolorow, R.D. (1984). *Structure of subjectivity: Exploration in psychoanalytic phenomenology and contextualism*. New York: Routledge Press.
Balint, M. (2018). *Primary love and psychoanalytic technique*. New York: Routledge.
Berg, A. (2016). Reflective practice in infant mental health: A South African perspective. *Infant Mental Health Journal*, 37, 684–691.
Biagio, G.T. (2012). *From psychology to phenomenology: Franz Brentano's psychology from the empirical standpoint and contemporary philosophy of mind*. New York: Palgrave Macmillan.
Bilder, R. (Ed.) (1998). *Neuroscience of the mind on the centennial of Freud's project for science* (Academy of Sciences). New York: Academy of Sciences Press.
Bowlby, J. (1973). *Separation: Anxiety and anger*. New York: Basic Books.
Bowlby, J. (1980). *Attachment and loss: Sadness and depression*. (Vol. 3). London: Hogarth Press.
Bowlby, J. (1995). *Maternal care and mental health*. (2nd Ed.). Northvale. NJ: London Jason Aronson. (Work originally published 1950).
Bowlby, J. (1999). *Attachment: Attachment and loss*. (2nd Ed.). New York: Basic Books.
Braid, J. (1843). *The rationale of nervous sleep considered in relation to animal magnetism*. London: Churchill.
Brentano, F. (1973). *Psychology from an empirical standpoint*. (A.C. Rancurello & D.B. Terrel. Trans.). New York: Humanities Press. (Original work published 1874).
Brown, J. (1961). *Freud and the post-Freudians*. Harrmondsworth: Penguin.
Caper, R. (2020). *Bion and thoughts too deep for words: Psychoanalysis, suggestion, and the language of the unconscious*. New York: Routledge.
Chen, E., Miller, G.E., Kobor, M.S. & Cole, S.W. (2011). Maternal warmth buffers the effects of low early-life socioeconomic status on pro-inflammatory signaling in adulthood. *Molecular Psychiatry*, 16(7), 729–737.
Ellenberger, H.F. (1970). *The discovery of the unconscious: The history and evolution of dynamic psychiatry*. New York: Basic Books.
Erikson, E.H. (1993). *Childhood and society*. New York: Norton Press.
Fairbairn, W. & Dodds, R. (1952). *Psychoanalytic studies of the personality*. London: Routledge and Kegan Paul.
Freud, A. (1937). *The ego mechanisms of defense*. New York: International Universities Press.

Freud, S. (1949). *The origins and development of psychoanalysis*. Chicago: Regnery. (Original work published in 1910).

Freud, S. (1953). The interpretation of dreams. In J. Strachey (Ed. & Trans.). *The standard edition of the complete psychological works of Sigmund Freud*. (Vols 4 & 5). London: Hogarth Press. (Original work published in 1900).

Freud, S. (1960). *Jokes and their relation to the unconscious*. In J. Strachey (Ed. and Trans.). The standard edition (Vol. 8). London: Hogarth Press. (Original work published in 1905).

Freud, S. (1961a). *The future of an illusion*. New York: Norton Press. (Original work published 1927).

Freud, S. (1961b). *Civilization and its discontents*. New York: Norton and Co. (Original work published 1930).

Freud, S. (1962). *Three essays on the theory of sexuality* (J. Strachey, Trans.). New York: Basic Books. (Original work published 1905).

Freud, S. (1965). *The psychopathology of everyday life*. (J. Strachey, Trans.). New York: W.W. Norton & Company Books. (Original work published 1901).

Freud, S. (1966). *On the history of the psychoanalytic movement*. New York: Norton Press. (Original work published in 1914).

Freud, S. (1995). *Five lectures on psycho-analysis*. New York: Penguin Books.

Freud, S. (2010). Project for a scientific psychology. In M. Bonaparte, A. Freud, & E. Kris (Eds). *The origins of psychoanalysis, letters to Wilhelm Fleiss, drafts and notes 1887–1902*. New York: Kessinger Publishing.

Freud, S. (1955a). Lines of advance in psychoanalytic therapy. In J. Strachey (Ed. & Trans.). *The standard edition of the complete psychological works of Sigmund Freud*. (Vol. 18). London: Hogarth Press. (Original work published in 1919).

Freud, S. (1955b). Beyond the pleasure principle. In J. Strachey (Ed. & Trans.). *The standard edition of the complete psychological works of Sigmund Freud*. (Vol. 18). London: Hogarth Press. (Original work published in 1920).

Freud, S. & Breuer, J. (2004). *Studies in hysteria*. New York: Penguin Books. (Original work published 1895).

Freud, E., Freud, L. & Grubrich-Simitis (Eds.) (1985). *Sigmund Freud: His life in pictures and words*. New York: Norton Press.

Freud, S. & Masson, J.M. (1986). *The complete letters of Sigmund Freud to Wilhelm Fliess, 1887–1904*. New York: Belknap Press.

Gay, P. (1988). *Freud: A life for our time*. New York: Norton Press.

Gorey, K.M. & Leslie, D.R. (1997). The prevalence of child sexual abuse: Integrative review adjustment for potential response and measurement biases. *Child Abuse & Neglect*, *21*(4), 391–398.

Greenberg, M., Greenberg, J. & Greenberg, S. (1983). *Fairbairn's object-relations theory in a clinical setting*. New York: Columbia University Press.

Hartman, H. (1959). *Ego and the psychology and problem of adaptation* (D. Rapaport, Trans.). Madison, CT: International Universities Press, Inc.

Hartman, K.E. (1869). *Philosophie de unbewussten [Philosophy of the unconscious]*. Berlin: Duncker.

Hazan, C. & Shaver, P. (1987). Romantic love conceptualized as an attachment process. *Journal of Personality and Social Psychology*, *52*(3), 511–524.

Holmes, J. (1993). *John Bowlby and attachment theory: Makers of modern psychotherapy*. New York: Routledge.

Horney, K. (1942). *Self analysis*. New York: Norton & Co. Inc.

Horney, K. (1973). *Feminine psychology*. New York: Norton & Co.

Janet, P. (1925). *Psychological healing: An historical and clinical study*. (E. Paul & C. Paul, Trans.). New York: Macmillan.

Jones, E. (1957). *The life and work of Sigmund Freud*. New York: Basic Books.

Kely, D. & Laverdiere, O. (2019). Quality of object relations and suicidal ideation in community mental health outpatients. *Psychoanalytic Psychotherapy*, *33*(4), 226–277.

Klein, M. (2017). *The psychoanalysis of children*. New York: Andesite Press. (Original Work Published in 1932).

Kohut, H. (2009a). *The restoration of the self*. Chicago: The University of Chicago press. (Original Work Published in 1977).

Kohut, H. (2009b). *The analysis of the self: A systematic approach to the psychoanalytic treatment of narcissistic personality disorders*. Chicago: The University of Chicago Press. (Original Work Published in 1971).

Kwinter, M. (2011) Absence speaks louder than words: An object relational perspective on no-show appointments. *Clinical Social Work*, *39*(3), 253–261.

Layton, L., Hollander, N.C. & Gutwill, S. (2006). *Psychoanalysis, class and politics: Encounters in clinical setting*. New York: Routledge.

Leili, J., Atef, V.M., Dehghani, M. & Habbi, M. (2015). The mental health through psychodynamic perspective: The relationship between ego strength, the defense styles and the object relations to mental health. *Iranian Journal of Psychiatry and Clinical Psychology*, *21*(2), 144–154.

Lieblich, A. & Quackelbeen, J. (1995). On the early history of male hysteria and psychic trauma. Charcot's influence on Freudian thought. *Journal of the History of the Behavioral Sciences*, *31*, 370–384.

Marshal, M.E. (1969). Gustav Fechner, Dr. Mises and the comparative anatomy of angels. *Journal of the History of the Behavioral Sciences*, *5*, 39–59.

Marx, K. (2018). *Critique of the Gotha program*. Morrisville, NC: Lulu Press. (Original work published in 1891).

Masson, J. (1984). *The assault on truth: Freud's suppression of seduction theory*. New York: Ballantine Books.

Messer, S.B. & Gurman, A.S. (2011). *Essential psychotherapies: Theory and practice*. (3rd Ed.). New York: Guilford Press.

Mitchell, J. (1990). *Psychoanalysis and feminism: A radical reassessment of Freudian psychoanalysis*. New York: Penguin Books. (Original Work Published in 1974).

Pinter, J. & Lynn, S.J. (2008). *Hypnosis: A brief history*. Oxford: John Wiley & Sons, Ltd.

Schopenhauer, A. (2014). *The world as will and representation*. New York: Cambridge University Press. (Original work published 1818).

Shedler, J. (2010). The efficacy of psychodynamic psychotherapy. *American Psychologist*, *65*(2), 98–109.

Sperber, J. (2013). *Karl Marx: A nineteenth century life*. New York: Liveright Publishing Corporation.

Strozier, C.B. (2001). *Heinz Kohut: The making of the psychoanalyst*. New York: Farrar, Straus and Giroux LLC.

Sturrock, J. (2003). *Structuralism*. Malden, MA: Blackwell Publishing.

Sutherland, J.D. (1994). *The autonomous self*. (J.S. Scharff, Ed.). New York: Jason Aronson, Inc.

Vannoy, A.M. (1996). *The multicultural imagination: Race, color, and the unconscious*. New York: Routledge.

Von Franz, M.L. (1964). The process of individuation. In C.G. Jung (Ed.). *Man and his symbols*. London: Aldus Books Ltd.

Winnicott, D.W. (1965). *The maturational processes and the facilitating environment: Studies in the theory of emotional development*. London: Hogarth press.

Young-Bruehl, E. (1990). *Freud on women: A reader*. New York: Norton Books.

Zaretsky, E. (2015). *Political Freud: A history*. New York: Columbia University Press.

Zizek, S. & Critchley, S. (2007). *How to read Lacan*. New York: W.W. Norton & Company.

Figure 3.0

3 The World of Symbol – Jungian Analytical Psychology

First Force in Psychology

Introduction

> Indeed, we do not just use our symbols, we are our symbols. The symbols and concept of God, each other, and physical reality that make up the furniture of our inner life, through which we worship, create, love, pursue truth, and create the beautiful, constitute both our immediate and ultimate experience of reality. These symbols create us, no less than we create them. Change our symbols and we change not only our reality, but ourselves.
>
> - Thomas Kelting (1995)

Often given cursory mention in history and system textbooks, Carl Jung should be recognized as the co-founder of the psychoanalytic movement (Shamdasani, 2003). As Freud's chosen successor, Jung's importance to the current modern world cannot be overstated. Although their disagreements were significant, they both believed in the importance of the unconscious. To simplify, Freud focused on the dangerous, and Jung on the creative and wise aspects of the unconscious. Together, they laid the foundation for a balanced view of unconscious processes.

Although Freud acknowledged the importance of symbols and myths, Jung made those concepts key to his *Analytical Psychology* (Jung, 1928). For Jung, a symbol is the language of the unconscious, a way to understand a world that often feels confusing and strange (Jung, 1964). In a world struggling to cope with its current challenges, Jungian psychology balances the dark forces of the personal Freudian unconscious with the creative and universality of the Jungian collective unconscious (Jung, 1974). A symbol allows for the experience of universal meaning and a connection to the totality of human experience.

World of Symbol

In this chapter, the focus will be on the modern genius, Carl Jung, who reestablished the importance of symbol in modern psychology (Jung, 1974). Jung believed when the mind explores a symbol it experiences a world beyond the limitations of the ego. That is why all the religions employ symbols because symbols represent a spiritual experience that cannot be fully explained. Beyond religion, Jung argues that all people, to experience the totality of being human, routinely produce symbols unconsciously and spontaneously through dreams, art, literature, mythology, and even in modern science.

DOI: 10.4324/9781003424734-3

Figure 3.1

It is not just that people produce symbols, humanity *needs* symbols for psychological health whether it be inside their churches or when the players of their favorite football team hold up the Super Bowl trophy. Symbol gives meaning and emotional life to all aspects of daily life. Most importantly, when we change our symbols, we change ourselves, the inner fabric of our psyche.

Jung and Post-Jungians

Although this chapter will include discussion of post-Jungian psychology, the primary focus will be on the foundation of Jungian thought. Andrew Samuels (1985), in *Jung and the post-Jungians,* described the three major schools of Jungian thought. The first school was described as the *classical school,* which focuses on strict adherence to traditional Jungian thought related to the *Self* and individuation. The second school is the *developmental school*, which has much in common with psychoanalysis, especially the importance of infancy and transference and countertransference in clinical work. The third *archetypal school*, a counter-clinical emphasis, based on the insights of James Hillman (1926–2011), views the psyche, the soul, through polytheistic mythology and the imaginal world, which has shaped psychological life throughout time.

Critical of the natural science bias in modern psychology with its emphasis on a reductionistic and materialist focus, Hillman (1975) re-envisioned a psychology that returns psyche, soul, to its proper place. Influenced by Greek, Renaissance and Romantic thought, Hillman envisioned a psychology which valued imagination, fantasy, myth, and metaphor.

The Historic Trip to Clark University

After Wilhelm Wundt rejected the invitation, a turning point for psychoanalysis was the trip taken by Freud and Jung in 1909 to celebrate the twentieth anniversary of *Clark University* in the United States. Before this trip, psychoanalysis was viewed as primarily a Jewish practice. Freud saw the trip as the first official acknowledgment of his work. After the trip, psychoanalysis became an international phenomenon.

It was G. Stanley Hall, the founder and first president of the American Psychological Association (APA), who invited Freud and Jung to the conference. Besides Freud and Jung, other influential pioneers in psychoanalysis, psychiatry, and psychology attended the conference. Among the attendees were Ludwig Binswanger, creator of existential psychoanalysis; Eugen Bleuler, a pioneer in the study of schizophrenia; Sandor Ferenczi, the future relational psychoanalyst and follower of Jacques Lacan; Lou Andreas-Salome, a Russian psychoanalyst and a close friend and researcher of the life of Friedrich Nietzsche; Carl Jung's wife and Jungian analyst, Emma Jung; and Ernest Jones, a Freudian biographer.

Post-Freudian and Jungian History

As explained in Volume II, Chapter 2, because Freud and Jung were unable to find common ground, the history of depth psychology has been one of division and controversy. In 1902, Freud started the *Psychological Wednesday Society* meeting in Vienna that included Jung and other psychoanalysts, with the goal to further the Freudian approach. In 1910, this meeting evolved into *The International Psychoanalytic Association* (IPA) and Carl Jung was elected as its first president because Freud envisioned Jung as his successor.

In 1913, at the annual IPA Conference in Munich, Germany, close friends and followers of Freud, Earnest Jones and Karl Abraham, encouraged Freudian members to abstain from re-electing of Jung as its president. Although re-elected, Jung recognized his position was untenable and in 1914, he resigned from IPA, which ended any future link between Jung and psychoanalysis.

Now separated from the psychoanalytic world, the Jungians would become embattled in their own factional battles. The *Analytical Psychology Club* (APC), which was created by Jung in the 1920s to be a broad-based group to perpetuate Jungian thought, began to experience conflict between the theorists and practitioners. By 1946, a split occurred with the development of *The Society for Analytical Psychology (SAP)*. The SAP focused on both theory and practice and required all members to have their own personal analysis. A goal of SAP was to integrate classical and post-Jungian thought and to apply the insights to clinical practice. This goal was achieved through the *C.G. Jung Clinic* which was developed to offer psychotherapy and Jungian analysis for individuals with mental health problems as well as for individuals interested in personal growth.

As both the psychoanalytic and Jungian worlds struggled with the new vision of how to include childhood development in psychodynamic thought, the SAP, and the London School

108 *The World of Symbol – Jungian Analytical Psychology*

emerged as a possible place for rapprochement between the two worlds. Jung was the first president of SAP and, although Jung believed analytic psychological work was best done later in life, he always had interest in the child archetype. Besides supporting the therapeutic work of Dora Kalff with children, Jung viewed conscious awareness of the divine child archetype, arose from the collective unconscious providing adults with the archetypal energy for a redemptive and fulfilling adult life.

In his book with C. Kerenyi (1959), *Essays on a Science of Mythology: The Myth of the Divine Child and the Mysteries of Eleusis,* Jung described how the weak and vulnerable divine child archetype survived against heavy odds to create a transformative life. Examples included the birth stories of Moses and Christ and how they overcame in childhood the hostility of the social and political power structure to change the world. The divine child archetype became a key component of Jungian personality theory because the divine child archetype can emerge in adulthood when there was a need to survive against overwhelming challenges.

Figure 3.2

In these essays, Jung and Kerenyi explored the divine child by analyzing the myth of the Greek goddess who bore a divine child. While fulfilling her duty to paint all the flowers on earth, *Persephone*, the daughter of Demeter, was captured and raped by Hades, who brought her to the underworld. Demeter searched unsuccessfully for her and created a drought. After Zeus heard the cries of hungry people, he released Persephone back to Demeter. The myth symbolized the process of the return of the divine child through three psychological stages: the *descent* into the unconscious; the frustrating and unfulfilling conscious *search*; and with an experience with the divine, the *ascent* to a stronger consciousness and a deeper connection to our divine nature.

Figure 3.3

Michael Fordham (1905–1995), a founder of SAP and the *London School of Analytic Psychology,* never considered himself a traditional Jungian. He believed the division in the analytical world was destructive and inhibited the development of depth psychology, especially in understanding the unconscious development of children (Fordham, 1947). He was the leader of the London-Zurich Split, which separated the orthodox from the reformist Jungians. Because Fordham was a developmental Jungian, he opened himself to the chagrin of many orthodox Jungians, to the *British Psychoanalytical Society* (BPS), and the relational psychoanalytic movement of Melanie Klein, Anna Freud, and the emerging independent psychoanalysts. Fordham was instrumental in organizing the Collected Works of C.J. Jung and was the founder of the leading journal in Jungian psychology, the *Journal of Analytical Psychology.*

Jungian Analytical Psychology

Historical Analysis

Political Systems

The bigger the crowd the more negligible the individual becomes.

- C.J. Jung

In *The Undiscovered Self,* Jung (1958) expressed concern about the dilemma of the individual in modern society. Jung expressed serious reservations about the future of humanity because of the lack of a spiritual foundation and the impact of a modern mass psychology, which was having a devastating effect on the individual psyche. In modern society, the individual was becoming an "endangered species," driven more by external than internal forces. Because of the failure of institutional religion, humanity, in need of a belief system by which to live, was

110   *The World of Symbol – Jungian Analytical Psychology*

gravitating toward revolutionary political movements. One example was Marxism, because it became a religion, a State Religion replacing the Church. He believed political movements inspired the same type of faith, devotion, and mindless collective loyalty as institutional religion.

In terms of diminishing the individual, Jung saw little basic difference between the state of the individual in Marxist or capitalist societies. His view was that both had advanced the same collectivist and commercial goals and belief systems that would ultimately fail just as institutional religion had failed. He asked if it was enough psychologically and spiritually for the working class to simply control the means of production, or that humans strive so vigorously to accumulate private wealth and material goods. He lamented that Europe, rich in intellectual and philosophic history, had come under the superficial and anti-historic influence of a young and uncultured capitalistic America.

Jung spoke of modern society living at a time that the Greeks called *kaopos*, the "metamorphosis of the gods," the return to basic principles and symbols. This would hopefully be a time when the individual unconscious would emerge from its slumber. It would be a time when the shadow was viewed as essential for human progress, and that the concept of evil was again viewed as internal rather than external. This would be a realization that the projection of evil on "the other" was misguided and destructive.

Figure 3.4

Jung envisioned an enlightened psychological society that valued all dimensions of history, not just dates and great leaders, a society that valued the intellectual and spiritual foundation upon which cultures had been built. Because the importance of symbol had been lost in modern society, especially in nihilistic modern art, there was little connection to mythology, history, and the unconscious. Jung believed that the reemergence of symbol was at the root of all creative efforts to transform humanity.

Jung acknowledged the need for political engagement, but because of his mistrust of the modern state and mass psychology, he recommended that psychiatrists moderately express their political opinions but gave little guidance on what political activities psychiatrist should embrace.

Henri Ellenberger (1970), in *The Discovery of the Unconscious: The History and Evolution of Dynamic Psychiatry*, highlighted the application of Jungian thought to political philosophy. In the 1930s and 1940s, Dietrich Schindler (senior) applied Jungian thought to constitutional law and social structure and served as a legal advisor to the Swiss government for many years. In the late 1950s, Hans Marti proposed a Jungian interpretation of the Swiss Constitution and Hans Fehr applied the concept of archetypes to the philosophy of law.

Most notable were Hans Fechner and Max Imboden, whose political analysis was based on archetypal symbols from the collective unconscious. They believed that before the creation of any legal system "that shall not kill" and monogamy were primordial symbols and archetypes that already existed and became conscious from the collective unconscious. Imboden believed that the major structures of the modern state could be represented through the symbol of the "trinity" of the legislative, judicial, and executive branches of government. The political "trinity" corollary was also the three major types of political governance: monarchy, aristocracy, and democracy. In monarchy and aristocracy, the psyche was susceptible to a mass psychology and unconsciously surrendered individual political power.

In *The Political Psyche*, Andrew Samuels (1993) implored post-Jungians of all schools to link Jungian thought and psychotherapy with conscious awareness of politics. He recommended exploration of the market economy, environmentalism, nationalism, and anti-Semitism. He called upon Jungian therapists to reject reductionism, individualizing problems that were social and political issues. He believed that the political world had slipped out of conscious awareness in the clinical world. Clinicians needed a greater focus on personality and social structure and the impact of political systems on the private individual psyche. Clinicians needed to help clients distinguish between psychological and sociopolitical reality.

Samuels was one of the few post-Jungians to implore Jungians to get their "hands dirty" by engaging in politics, locally, nationally, and internationally. He criticized the chronic Jungian mantra of feeling marginalized by psychology and decried the superficial "gimmick" therapies that were viewed as *evidence-based best practices* when in fact they showed no long-term efficacy. The answer was to engage the skepticism in psychology about Jungian psychology and work to reform the imperfect political world.

Because Samuels' approach was basically from an academic and theoretical perspective, he too has fell short on specificity for political activism. Besides clinicians becoming more politically conscious, there was no stated political agenda and few specific recommendations why Jungian psychologists should actively seek political office or become leaders in the community mental health movement. There was also no clarity of how to attain political power within the American Psychological Association (APA) to reform its anti-psychoanalytic and Jungian bias. For instance, the APA has been reluctant to actively support accreditation of psychodynamic programs in clinical psychology and there is currently no APA-accredited doctoral program with a Jungian specialty in clinical psychology in the United States.

Wotan Myth

One of the greatest contributions of Jung to political understanding was the belief that a society can experience a "social psychosis." In a 1936 essay, "Wotan," Jung ventured apologetically into the political realm (Jung, 1936). He believed that Nazism was the manifestation of a Wotan archetype, a collective unconscious psychological reaction to sociopolitical forces. This was exemplified by the powerful Wotan myth, the Germanic god of storm, frenzy, and war that was immortalized by Richard Wagner in *The Ring* operas.

Wotan, also known as Odin, was the old Norse Germanic god. He had both creative and destructive qualities and became a popular cult figure in modern Germany. The question for Jung was whether the German psyche would produce the positive or negative force of a "bipolar" Wotan. In 1945, writing *After the Catastrophe*, Jung (1945) admitted he was mistaken about the bipolar Wotan as the German people had a destructive unconscious relationship to Wotan, "a Faustian pact with the devil." He concluded that the German people were still under the psychological influence of polytheism, which had been interrupted by Christianity. This influence only provided a veneer of civilization and concealed the primitive, destructive, and demonic forces that lay dormant in the collective unconscious.

Hitler was the modern-day Wotan who created a world untouched by truth, facts, or morality. He created a "social psychosis" and a cult of personality that existed beyond conscious awareness. Nowhere is a political symbol of shadow as dramatic as in the Wotan myth. Wotan came face to face within himself of the forces of good and evil, of creation and destruction, and of the drive toward life and death, all being acted out in such a massive, social, and political level.

Figure 3.5

A unique god in mythology, Wotan created the world and would die at its end during a final cataclysm, a *Ragnarok*. Many Germans felt that Nazism was the cataclysm and that the psyche of the German people was forever scarred beyond repair.

Because of his relative silence during the Holocaust Jung was branded unfairly as a Nazi collaborator. His initial hopeful view of the Wotan myth was viewed by some as anti-Semitic. For a long time, these events divided Freudians and Jungians because psychoanalysis was viewed as rooted within the Jewish community. Although his analysis of the Wotan myth was incorrect, lost because of the mistake, is the significant contribution to political understanding that cultural mythology, archetypal energies, unconscious shadow, and symbol can grip a civilization.

In *Cry for Myth*, American existentialist Rollo May (1991) argued that psychotherapists towards the end of the twentieth century had ventured too far from Jung and Freud and began to develop "gimmick" and superficial therapies that lacked depth. An example was the rejection by psychology of the type of mythology that could provide meaning and cohesion to a fractured, anxious, and depressed modern society. In the tradition of the sociopolitical vision of Jung, May believed Americans were under the unconscious psychological grip of the *mythology of individualism*, which resulted in isolation, alienation, and widespread violence.

Socioeconomic Systems

Jung was born in 1875 into an impoverished middle-class family in a culturally homogenized Switzerland, with only three major ethnic groups German, French, and Italian. Jung grew up in Basal, a culturally dynamic town where on the streets during his childhood he would see the famous historian Jacob Burckhardt, the aging Bachofen, and hear talk of Nietzsche and other great thinkers of the day. Jung was named after his famous grandfather, Carl Gustav Jung, who was a prominent and a most sought-after Basel physician. As would be true later for Jung, he had an expansive view of his role as a physician. He became the Grand Master of the Freemasons and wrote many scientific articles and theatrical plays. According to unconfirmed rumors, it was believed that he might have been the illegitimate son of Goethe. Although Jung would never meet his grandfather, his image would exert a great influence on his career.

Jung's parents were both last-born children of large families and were born after their fathers had become impoverished. Jung's father, Paul Achilles Jung, became a modest country pastor who was perceived by Jung as underdeveloped intellectually. It was his physician and scholar grandfather, not his father, who provided the male role model early in his life. Unlike Freud, who was the beloved first born of a beautiful mother, Jung was the second child, and saw his mother as psychologically ambivalent about children. With his family structure, Jung could not imagine the Oedipal complex, a young boy in love with his mother, hostile toward his father, and possessing an unconscious identification with him. Since spirituality became a major interest for Jung, the fact that his father had doubts about his religious faith may have been the most consequential impact left by his father on his life.

In 1903, during his time at the *Burgholzli Psychiatric Hospital*, Jung married Emma Rauschenbach, the daughter of the wealthy industrialist Joannes Rauschenbach of Schafhausen. Marrying into wealth allowed Jung to feel financially secure for the rest of his life. Between his upper-class status, the ongoing financial support of his wife, and the economically stable Swiss culture, Jung was free to view the world beyond economic struggle, poverty, and the wars that ravished the rest of Europe. Interested in the work of her husband, Emma became a successful Jungian analyst in her own right. After her death, Jung described her as the intellectual editor of his life and as a queen.

Emma had her own correspondence with Freud who had interpreted one of Jung's dreams as a marriage for money and convenience and not love. After Emma's death, many of his five children became estranged due to Jung's treatment of their mother, especially because of his affairs. Without Emma's class status, Jung might have never reached the prominence he attained. Because of Emma, on his famous trip to *Clark University*, Jung was able to procure a cabin on the ship in first class while Freud could only afford regular class. Although there have been efforts to reach out to the general population, Jungian thought has often been viewed as Eurocentric, elitist, and available only to the wealthy upper classes.

Swiss economist Eugen Bohler (1893–1977), in *Conscience in Economic Life* (Bohler, 1970), drew business leaders to Jungian thought in his effort to apply Jungian concepts to economic science; he wrote that economists needed to study Jungian psychology because nowhere was the psyche more fragmented than in modern economic life. Every economy functioned not from rational strategic thinking, but from collective unconscious impulses. He believed that it was mythology and fantasy that determined economic progress as much as the dream factory of Hollywood. Bohler viewed the stock exchange as the symbol of economic fantasy as it was a place where daydreams and irrationality could be acceptable to the rational modern person. The stock exchange functioned as part of what Jung would have described as a mass psychology; it was rooted in collective fantasy and susceptible to a "great depression" when there was a sudden loss of the economic myth.

For Bohler, what had been lost in economics were conscience, a sense of balance and wholeness, and an awareness of the contradictory elements that create economic disparities. It was important that economic decisions occurred from the Jungian Self with a focus on higher values in contrast with ego decisions based on what was immediately useful for the individual. To resolve economic inequality, the individual needed a rebalanced conscience; one that possessed a conscious awareness of the lost morality in economic decisions. Without this rebalanced psyche, governmental interference or redistribution of wealth would only strengthen collective mass psychology and decrease individual moral development.

Cultural Systems

The Swiss lived in a federalist and democratic culture. Each citizen had an obligation to their community, canon, and federal government. Being part of a community required playing an active role in its problems. Jung's status and role in the community was already solidified because, like most Swiss, it had been transmitted by his family history. Community culture was important to Jung because it provided the foundation of the psychological Swiss life. For the Swiss, it was a bottom-up, not a top-down, political culture that started with the local community, the canon state, and the federal government. The importance of the local community was symbolized by Swiss resistance to a national language. Each locality decided whether French, German, or Italian met their community needs.

In this homogenized culture, Jung was not exposed to cultural diversity. Although he traveled extensively and valued other non-European cultures, his lack of direct, living, and contact with people of color often led him to cultural stereotypes and resulting criticisms, even claims of racism. He lived in a patriarchal and sexist culture that reinforced traditional sexual roles. But, unlike Freud, his theories placed equal importance on valuing masculine and feminine characteristics. While Freud lived in a more politically unstable and chaotic culture, Jung's Swiss culture was relatively peaceful. Cultural dynamics influenced the personalities of both men. Freud, an extrovert, found his satisfaction in external debate and control, especially of his followers. Jung, an introvert, found satisfaction in developing his inner world, rebelling against external control, especially by Freud, and a mass psychology that neglected and oppressed the inner world.

Joseph Campbell and Mythology

Jungian psychology inspired many modern artists as evidenced by how mythology gained popularity in American culture after a 1988 Public Broadcasting Station (PBS) six-episode documentary with Bill Moyers, *Joseph Campbell,* and the *Power of Myth* (Campbell, 1988). It has remained one of the most popular series in the history of American public television.

Inspired by Jung, Joseph Campbell (1904–1987), a comparative mythologist, wrote *The Hero with a Thousand Faces* (Campbell, 1973/1949). This was a monomyth, an archetypal heroic journey shared by all world mythologies that symbolized psychological transformation. The heroic journey required a departure from the ordinary world to engage in an adventure which needed guidance and mentorship. For the journey to be heroic, a guarded threshold had to be crossed, which led to a supernatural world totally separated from the known world. This rite of passage required initiation rituals, which meant overcoming many trials and ordeals. After having shattered the boundaries of consciousness, the heroic figure received a boon, the gift of internal power that existed in all humanity. This power created limitless bounty, enlightenment, and a renewed connection with the divine. After receiving the boon, on the road back, there would be more trials and tribulations. Upon the return home, the question was how the application of the boon would be applied to ordinary life.

Star Wars

George Lucas, creator of *Star Wars*, often considered the most powerful modern cultural myth. In the *Star Wars* movies, each of the characters represented one of the Jungian archetypes. *The Hero with a Thousand Faces,* by Joseph Campbell (1973/1949), inspired the creation of *Luke Skywalker*, a modern symbol of the heroic archetype. The heroic journey required separation from home, a rite of passage, initiation, defeat of the forces of evil, and the endless return home to only begin another adventure that would strengthen his sense of self. The *Jedi Order* was depicted as an ascetic, monastic, meritocratic, and quasi-militaristic organization that had existed for 25,000 years. The *Jedi Order* pursued spiritual goals, and based rank on merit. not by wealth or social class. The order became militaristic only when under attack. The lightsaber was the signature weapon of the *Jedi Order* and their Sith counterparts, the antagonists who were driven by the shadow of domination and revenge. The Skywalker lightsaber was created by Anakin Skywalker, the Jedi Knight, and the prophesied Chosen One of the Force.

For the heroic Skywalker, the lightsaber, the boon, symbolized his power beyond the natural world, "the force," the power of inner light, and his spiritual self which always saves him. For Jungians, the ongoing and popular response to *Star Wars* movies signified the human hunger and the psychological need for mythology and symbol.

It also signified renewed Western interest in the Axial Age. In *Dharma of the Star Wars* (Borotlin, 2015) and *The Zen of R2-D2: Ancient Wisdom from a Galaxy Far, Far Away* (Borotlin, 2019), Matthew Borotlin explored how the Buddhist beliefs in nirvana, karma, the eightfold path, and compassion influenced the Jedi Order. Steven Rosen (2010), in *Jedi and the Lotus: Star Wars and the Hindu Tradition*, showed how *Star Wars* was influenced by the ancient Hindu epics, the Ramayana, and the Mahabharata, and how the divinity in "the Force" had resonated with the teachings of Hindu gurus and mystics. D.W. Kreger (2013), in *Tao of Yoda: Based on the Tao Te Ching by Lao Tzu,* replaced "the force" with Tao, and Yoda with Lao Tzu, and asked the question whether Lao Tzu was a Jedi knight from the distant galaxy.

116   *The World of Symbol – Jungian Analytical Psychology*

Figure 3.6

The Red Book

The *Liber Novus*, *The New Book*, published in 2009, was an instant bestseller and a cultural phenomenon reacquainting the American people with Jungian psychology (Jung, 2009). Even though the large 416-page nine-pound book sold close to $200, bookstores across America and the world quickly sold out. It was described as the "Jungian Holy Grail," a modern psychological bible. It was an astonishing example of the power of symbol and calligraphy and was reminiscent of the *Irish Book of Kells* or the illustrated works of William Blake.

No matter the theoretical bias, it was acknowledged as a watershed moment in the history of psychology and cast new light of the development of modern psychology. Concern arose in the Jungian community that his family's 80-year resistance to its publication might indicate that Jung was mentally ill. Scholars and critics described the *Red Book* period in various ways, "creative madness," introspection, psychotic break, or complete madness. Around 1959, after 30 years of leaving the book untouched, even Jung recognized how his work might be perceived in history when he added an epilogue, "To the superficial observer it will appear like madness."

Jung became disillusioned with the superficiality of scientific rationalism; modernity which he believed deadened the mind of its true power. In the meditative state of active imagination, the mind came alive to the mysteries of the unconscious and to the world unseen but needing to be revealed. From his work at the *Burgholzli Psychiatric Hospital* in Zurich, Switzerland, individuals with mental illness taught Jung that this inner world spoke in symbols, and in mythological and dreamlike images. The goal of active imagination was "to listen" to the inner world and not fill the space with rational thought; but rather with amplification: living intently in the moment describing the symbols, the story, the dream, watching for the changes, the messages, and letting the imagination speak and develop without conscious resistance.

The *Red Book* was an extended two years of active imagination, amplification, and "confrontation with the collective unconscious." During this period, Jung discovered many of his later theories of archetypes, the collective unconscious, and individuation. As seen throughout history and amplified by Jung, great thinkers usually start with themselves and their experiences of the world. From his own life, especially from his work at the *Burgholzli Psychiatric Hospital*, Jung attempted to transform psychotherapy by utilizing "illness" as a means for higher development and consciousness.

In the alchemic tradition, the *Black Books*, the *negredo*, is where Jung "blackened his psyche," particularly after the loss of his relationship with Freud. He engaged in the chaotic and dark unconscious world that resulted in the *Red Book*, *rubedo*, the "reddening of his psyche," creating the alchemical transmutation, psyche and soul united, and a psychological transformation to a new life.

This was his exploration beyond his personal unconscious to a world he did not produce, which had its own life. In this world, Jung discovered a symbolic figure that first appeared in a dream. In 1913, this dream world would provide wise guidance for the rest of his life. In the dream, he saw the symbol of a sea-blue sky covered by brown clods of earth that were breaking apart. Out of the earth emerged an old man, *Philemon*, with kingfisher wings and the horns of a bull flying across the sky carrying a bunch of keys. After the dream, he painted the symbol and was struck by the resulting synchronicity, two or more independent events that come together in a meaningful way, when he found a dead kingfisher in his garden, a bird rarely seen in Zurich.

Jung had a great appreciation for the psychological messages in literature. In Act V of *Faust by Goethe*, to Faust's horror, *Mephistopheles* burned the house of *Philemon and Baucis*, the poor, elderly couple in the Ovid Greek myth who symbolized human hospitality to the "gods" and to spirituality. *Philemon and Baucis* were the only people to accept Zeus and Hermes into their modest cottage after they were disguised as ordinary peasants. Initially, Jung felt personally responsible for this message of destruction, but he later realized that modern society had "burned" the gods in their psychological roots. This eradication was especially true of the history from the Middle Ages, classical antiquity, and primitivity.

118   *The World of Symbol – Jungian Analytical Psychology*

Figure 3.7

Philemon spoke beyond the personal unconscious, which taught Jung that there were messages in the psyche that he did not produce, but provided important knowledge from the collective unconscious. At his Tower in Bollingen, Jung commemorated Philemon by carving an inscription over the entrance gate: *Philemonis Sacrum*, "Philemon's Shrine – Faust's Repentance."

Figure 3.8

He also painted a huge mural of the winged *Philemon*, which would become an iconic symbol from the *Red Book*. It was symbolic not of the Faustian superman, but the wisdom of the real gods murdered in a "ruthless and godforsaken age" that Jung was leaving behind.

Jung as a Cultural Icon

Jung has influenced almost all aspects of American and Western culture. In literature and art, *Demian, Siddhartha,* and *Steppenwolf* by Herman Hesse, and the art of great American expressionist artist Jackson Pollack were the result of their Jungian analysis. In music, David Bowie sang of Jung in his song *Shadow Man* and in his album *Aladdin Sane;* the British rock band Police in 1983 released an album entitled *Synchronicity*; and in 2009, Banco de Gaia called his electric music album *Memories, Dreams, and Reflections*. Jung also appeared on the front cover of the Beatles' *Sgt. Pepper's Lonely Hearts Club Band.*

The films *8½, Juliet of the Spirits, Satyricon, Casanova,* and *City of Women* by Italian film director Federico Fellini were shaped by Jungian concepts, especially dream interpretation. In *Soul,* a 2020 Pixar film written by Pete Doctor, Jung appears as an ethereal cartoon character called *Soul Carl Jung.* Jung has even influenced modern video games like the *Persona* series of games, which are based on Jungian theories, particularly the *Nights into Dreams* series and *Jung's Labyrinth,* a psychological exploration PC game that explores mythology, alchemy, archetypes, and dream symbolism using active imagination as the path toward individuation.

Natural Science Interest

Experimental Psychology Influence

Jung was influenced by the research of experimental psychologist and eugenicist, Francis Galton, who thought that there might be a link between his word association and IQ. Unlike Freud, who based his clinical research on case studies, Jung believed in empirical research and psychological testing.

Jung developed his Word Association Test, not from a Galton-like laboratory, but from his clinical work with individuals with psychosis at the Burgholzli Psychiatric Hospital at the University of Zurich. Since he treated psychosis daily, unlike Freud, Jung did not initially focus on hysteria. Many of Jung's theories were a result of his work with individuals with serious mental illness. During the seven years of his clinical work at the *Burgholzli,* he discovered that certain words and expressions stimulated the unconscious mind. This led to an interest in psychological testing and the development of the Word Association Test. During his visit with Freud to Clark University, Jung presented the test and its findings. He described his test as asking a patient to respond immediately to 100 words and found that some words took longer for a response and hypothesized unconscious interference. He also noted certain words had observable physiological responses, such as change in facial expressions, body movements, and respiration.

Neurology has begun to prove many of the psychodynamic and psychoanalytic theories. *Leon Petchkovsky* (2013), a Jungian analyst, director of the *Pinniger Clinic* in Robina, and past president of the Australian and New Zealand Society of Jungian Analysts, studied the Word Association test, utilizing magnetic resonance imaging (MRI) and electroencephalogram (EEG) tests (Petchkovsky et al., 2013). He found that mirror neurons, sensory-motor cells activated in the brain when a task is mutually performed, caused significant brain activity with the words associated with parents, family, abuse, childhood, and fear. There was also considerable brain activity in areas of the amygdala and hippocampus, especially pronounced with individuals with post-traumatic stress disorder (PTSD). Petchkovsky became a major proponent for continued use and research of the Jungian Word Association Test and expanded his neurological interest to research in Jungian complex theory.

Lamarckism Biological Influence

Jung was influenced by the French naturalist *Jean-Baptiste-Lamarck* (1744–1829), who was known to be the first in the modern era to coin the term "biology" and was an early supporter of biological evolution. His orthogenetic theory was often viewed in conflict with Darwinian Theory because Lamarck believed that organisms had an innate tendency to develop in a specified direction due to an internal "driving force." Darwin, on the other hand, believed that there was no specified direction or purpose, or "driving force" in the evolutionary process.

Jung was also influenced by the Lamarckian theory of inheritance of acquired characteristics or soft inheritance (Rensma, 2013). During its lifetime, an organism could pass on the physical characteristics that the parent acquired through use or disuse. This natural science influence led to some of the most important Jungian concepts of a *collective unconscious* and the universal *archetypes*. Jung thought that the evolution of the human psyche mirrors the Lamarckian view of inherited characteristics (Rensma, 2013). Centuries of ancestral evolutionary experiences have been deposited into a collective unconscious, a universal unconscious that exists in everyone, which developed through the inherited predisposition of archetypes that create similar experiences for all humanity.

Jung believed the mind developed in concert with the Lamarckian framework. Psychological experiences, like biological experiences of preceding generations, were passed on to the next generation through the inherited archetypal energies in the collective unconscious. Archetypes became psychogenic symbols that provided the structure to handle the powerful emotional experiences that existed in the collective unconscious beyond the personal unconscious.

Natural Aristotelian Philosophy Influence

Jung was influenced by an Aristotelian view of entelechy (Jung 1954/1934), from the Greek word *entelecheia,* which means "that which makes actual what was otherwise merely potential." In the life of an organism, Aristotle distinguished matter from form. In what was considered the first Western psychological text, *De Anima,* or *On the Soul,* Aristotle explained that matter was the physical substance, while form was the vital function or soul. Without these forms, there could be no living organism. Later, Gottfried Leibniz called entelechy monads, entelechies in concert with their inner self-determined purpose. In the twentieth century, entelechy reemerged in the vitalistic biology of Hans Briesch and French philosophy of Henri Bergson (Normandin & Wolfe, 2013).

Aristotle developed the *philosophy of hylomorphism,* from the Greek words hylo, meaning "matter," and phorme, meaning "form." This promoted the theory that soul determined feeling alive. Aristotle disagreed with the Pythagorean theory of metempsychosis, the belief of the transmigration and reincarnation of the soul, and with the Platonic philosophy of ideal forms, which were separate from the physical world. In development of the archetype of the Self, the organizing principle of the psyche, Jung agreed with Aristotle that the soul was unique and located "inside" each individual life, not a generalized metempsychosis or an ideal Platonic form that existed in some abstract outside world. In classical philosophy, later *natural teleology*, Aristotle contended that all-natural beings have intrinsic purpose. Entelechy ultimately meant "in purpose" from the Greek telos, "a purpose," because Aristotle believed in an "inner purpose," which caused tension within a living being to understand itself in terms of its own laws. The soul engaged in an ongoing struggle to transform potentiality into action, matter into form. Entelechy was the fulfillment of the final cause in his theory of four causes. This was the realization that a living organism can reach its ultimate purpose for existence, the Jungian concept of *individuation,* the goal of self-actualization.

Drive Theory Influence

Ronald Fairbairn and the future British object-relation theorists rejected the classical Freudian view that human drives conflicted with the social world. For Freud, drives needed to be controlled through socialization. Fairbairn led the way for a much different psychoanalytic perspective of drives, to view the baby as psychologically constituted for human relationships.

Providing a contrasting Jungian approach to Freudian drive theory, in 1935, Leopold Szondi (1893–1986) developed the *Szondi Personality Test* (Deri, 1949). Although not frequently utilized by clinical psychologists, the test assessed eight drive needs, each corresponding to an archetype: hermaphroditism, sadistic, emotional, hysteric, catatonic, paranoid depressive, and manic drives. Szondi (1952) believed that eight archetypes were present in various degrees within each individual person. The test connects the archetypal drives to the development of the psychiatric diagnoses of schizophreniform, manic depression, sexual dysfunction, catatonia, and paranoia. The test uses 48 cards organized into six series of eight people; all the photographs are portraits of people who suffer from mental disorders.

Medieval Chemistry – Alchemy Influence

> For the alchemist, the one primarily in need of redemption is not man, but the deity who is lost and sleeping in matter.
>
> - Carl Jung

Alchemy was further proof of a collective unconscious because Jung discovered two basic types of alchemy. One type, a precursor to modern natural science, strove to understand the cosmos and re-create it. The other alchemy focused on hermeneutics, a psychological transformation that strove for understanding and for the meaning and purpose of life, and the universal drive to integrate psyche and soul. For Jung, alchemy provided the instinctive impulse for psychological growth (Jung, 1944/1971a).

Alchemy was rooted in Alexandria, Egypt, which became the melting pot of Pythagoreanism, Platonism, Stoicism, and Gnosticism. Although practiced throughout Africa, China, and India, Western alchemy developed after the Renaissance with the discovery of Medieval Islamic science, and the Greek philosophies of Empedocles and Aristotle, who viewed the universe as being formed from four basic elements: earth air, water, and fire. As a natural philosopher, Aristotle believed that each element had its own unique sphere and would return to that sphere if left undisturbed. Unlike the modern view of the four elements, the Greeks never viewed earth, wind, fire, and water as purely chemical substances, but the first symbols of the body and soul undisturbed, the foundation for alchemical transmutation (Jung, 1944/1971a).

Alchemists attempted to purify and perfect certain materials for the transmutation of base materials, "cheap metal" like lead, into "noble metals" like gold. Alchemists were inspired by the Greek goddess Panacea, the daughter of Asclepius, who created the magic potions and the first medications to cure all disease. This alchemical transmutation created the elixir of immortality: the potion which granted the body and soul of the drinker eternal life and youth and healed all diseases. Panacea, along with Apollo, Asclepius, and Hygeia are mentioned as key witnesses in the Hippocratic Oath, an oath of all physicians. The purification of the body and soul resulted from a magnus opus, the alchemical name for working with the prima matria, first matter. This first matter and the four elements created the philosopher's stone, the substance capable of turning metal such as mercury into gold.

Figure 3.9

The squared circle symbolized the philosopher's stone, the first matter of all creation, the breath of the Greek gods that all humanity breathed, the symbol of the return to perfection, enlightenment, and "heavenly bliss."

As alchemy developed from the Hellenistic and Western esoteric traditions, the achievement of *gnosis*, the Greek word for "knowledge," became the philosopher's stone (Jung, 1944/1971a). Alchemists often mixed divine water and sulfurous water in a bowl like a baptismal font to create purifying vapors of mercury and sulfur. Being Gnostics, the alchemists used the Hermetic symbol of the mixing bowl to facilitate the purification of the initiate during their ascent into the transcendental realms. In the *Corpus Hermeticum*, it was Hermes in dialogue with Tat, the Monad, where Hermes described the mixing bowl of the mind as the way to free the mind of human complexities and experience god and the divine.

Gnostics were an early collection of religious sects in the first century AD that rejected orthodox and institutional Judaism and Christianity in favor of personal spiritual knowledge. Viewing the physical world as flawed and evil, Gnostics distinguished between the highest and unknowable, supreme god, and a malevolent lesser god, a *demiurge*, a creative, artisan-like, God-like Yahweh who was knowable through the physical world. Gnostics valued "internal knowing," salvation rooted in direct knowledge of divinity through mystical and esoteric experiences. Because there was one divinity, Gnosticism also required interreligious learning, the understanding of non-Western religions, particularly Buddhism and Hinduism. The Gnostics replaced sin and repentance with knowledge and enlightenment. Jesus became the physical embodiment of the spirit and made the spiritual world knowable and enlightened through his human bodily existence, a symbol of the *lapis*, the philosopher stone.

In *Psychology and Alchemy*, Jung (1944/1971a) explained the link between the symbolism of alchemy and analytical psychology. By analyzing several dreams of a patient, he showed how the symbols of alchemists continued to live in the collective unconscious of humanity. Jung believed that the modern world had lost its soul but through the many beautifully illustrated alchemy images, drawings and paintings, symbols of alchemists, he discovered that the symbols and the metaphorical practice of alchemy could provide modern psychotherapists a way to reignite spirituality. This would be done through the forgotten systems of thought in Hellenistic Gnosticism, Western esoterism, and Eastern religions.

Jung noted that for "pre-scientific" humans, subject and object were similar. Unconsciously, humans projected inner states onto outer objects. Alchemical symbols revealed the unconscious life during this period in which people did not distinguish the qualities of an object from their own values, emotions, and beliefs. Through analytical psychology, Jung believed humans could return to this state of synthesis to achieve spiritual renewal.

Analytical psychology became the philosopher's stone, the chemical, magical, and esoteric therapeutic work. The magnum opus was symbolic of "the *great work* of the psyche" used to interpret, analyze, and create meaning out of a chaotic world. As in alchemy, analysis started with *nigredo*, a blackening process, a depression, a connection to shadow. This was essential for transmutation and the manipulation of the *prima materia*, the elements of archetypal energies mixed together, producing "inner knowledge" and spiritual renewal, a synthesis of base and noble elements, the unity of psychological opposites, the attainment of the gold of individuation.

Figure 3.10

Jung mirrored alchemist transmutation to provide an explanation of the four stages of analytical therapy. In the first stage of alchemy, the *negredo*, the "blackening of the psyche," death reigned because of engagement with the chaotic and dark unconscious world. In the second alchemical stage, *albedo*, "the whitening of the psyche," led to experience the pure spirit, the soul. In the third stage, *citrunitas*, the "yellowing of the psyche," expanded awareness of the outside world. The fourth stage, *rubedo*, the "reddening of the psyche," created the alchemical transmutation. Psyche and soul are united in a psychological transformation.

The process was the ongoing experience of psychological death and rebirth, of losing the self to find the self. This is symbolized by the self-devouring dragon because the dragon slays itself, weds itself, and impregnates itself in an ongoing, never-ending process.

Jung believed that the medieval world offered modern society a pathway to renewal. Jung would routinely retreat from his home in Zurich to the Swiss village of Bollingen and live as a medieval man. The structure he built looked like a medieval castle with a tower that could be seen throughout the village. Without electricity and the pleasures of modern life, Jung explored the human psyche, especially alchemy, the medieval forerunner of chemistry. On his 75th birthday in 1950, during his final days, Jung built a stone cube at Bollingen, which reflected his belief in the power of symbol and alchemy. The symbols on the stone were inspired by a dream that reminded him that he was both an individual and part of everything in the world. The symbols on the stone had many meanings; particularly that alchemy taught that the language of the unconscious was understood through symbols.

Jung had a particular interest in *Zosimos of Panoplies*. An Egyptian-Greek alchemist and Gnostic, Zosimos wrote the first book on alchemy and identified alchemy as "things made by hand." He developed one of the first definitions of alchemy, which he described as the study of the composition of water, embodying and disembodying, drawing the spirits from physical bodies, and bonding the spirit within physical bodies. What impressed Jung and reinforced his view of the importance of dreams, Zosimus discovered the alchemic process through the sequence of his dreams. In a dream reported in his *Vision of Zosimus* text, Zosimus met Ion, a "priest of the inner sanctuaries." Ion impaled Zosimus and dismembered him in "harmony within the four elements of earth, wind, fire and water." Through the art of alchemy, Ion then burned Zosimus on an altar, where he became transformed from body into spirit, a *homunculus*. This was the opposite of himself, and he was transformed from his "little physical self," to his complete spiritual self.

At Bollingen, one side of the cube depicted the Greek god, *Telesphorus*, a possible son of Asclepios. The word in Greek means "bringing to completion," or "the accomplisher." The accomplishment that Telesphorus was for Jung was his own personal survival of the injury and suffering of the modern world. Telesphorus, as a homunculi image, symbolized what alchemy had provided Jung, which was his own homunculi experience, the transformation of his basic nature, "the lead man" into his noble nature, and becoming the "gold man" the part of the psyche that everyone seeks to touch.

> I am an orphan, alone; nevertheless, I am found everywhere. I am one but opposed to myself. I am youth and old man at one and the same time. I have known neither father nor mother, because I have had to be fetched out of the deep like a fish or fell like a white stone from heaven. In woods and mountains, I roam, but I am hidden in the innermost soul of man. I am mortal for everyone, yet I am not touched by the cycle of eons
>
> - Carl Jung

Jung's hope was that his days on earth would provide humanity with the modern alchemical tools for psychological renewal and transformation. Alchemy laid the foundation for his modern theory of psychological types, which included the mental and physical aspects of feeling, thinking, intuition, and sensation. To achieve a higher consciousness, analytical therapy focused on the psychological development of the four alchemical elements: fire, water, air, and earth. The symbolic world of the alchemist provided the analyst the psychological pathway because these four physical elements created the alchemical transformation. For example, the fire of the chloric personality transformed anger to calm, the water of the phlegmatic personality transformed thought to feeling, the air of the sanguine personality transformed naïve optimism to realism, and the earth melancholic personality transformed depression to joy.

Myers-Briggs Indicator Test (MBTI)

The *Myers-Briggs Type Indicator* (MBTI), widely utilized inside and outside of psychology, was based on Jungian typology. The MBTI is one of the most widely used personality inventory in the world, with over 3 million assessments administered every year. Over 80 percent of *Fortune* 100 companies utilize the MBTI to better assess employee strengths, weaknesses, communication styles, and time management and conflict resolution skills. The MBTI has also been used for personal growth and for developing leadership skills for professional advancement (Bridges, 2000).

The MBTI is rooted in Jungian and alchemical thought, the synthesis of the mental and physical in the human personality. After reading *Psychological Types* by Jung 1921/1971b) in 1923, Katherine Cook Briggs (1875–1968) and her daughter, Isabel Briggs Meyers (1897–1979), with no background in psychology or research, began the creation one of the most widely used psychometric personality tests in the world. Since women were entering the workforce during World War II, organizations utilized the MBTI to assist women in job placement. The hope was that there would be a positive correlation between psychology type and successful job placement.

The MBTI is value-free test with no right or wrong answers. It is an introspective self-report of 93 forced-choice questions that indicate different psychological responses to the world. Scored on a dialectical continuum, the four categories are: Introversion and Extraversion; Sensing and Intuition; Thinking and Feeling; and Judging and Perceiving.

The introvert type, quiet and imaginative, receives psychological energy from "going inside," while the extravert is outgoing and social and needs interaction with people to feel psychologically satisfied. The sensation type gets information from the senses while the intuition type receives information from the unconscious. The thinking type views the world in an objective and systematic manner, while the feeling type evaluates the world through emotional experiences. The perceiving type is open and adaptable, especially to new situations, while the judging type approaches life in a more careful, structured, organized, and calculated manner. The test produces 16 possible four-letter personality types. One of the most common profiles is the ISFJ, which is an Introversion, Sensation, Feeling, Judging personality type. The ISFJ personality has heart and strong feelings but because of their introversion, keep much inside and they often have a difficult time sharing feelings. The ISFJ personality type learns best through the five senses and prefers concrete facts over abstract theories. The ISFJ values "order in the court" and deliberate and careful decision making.

126   *The World of Symbol – Jungian Analytical Psychology*

Energetics Influence

Alchemy laid the foundation for Jung's ongoing view of the interconnection of physical and psychological energies. Alchemy played an important role in his view of the libido and his break with Freud. In *Memories, Dreams, Reflections,* Jung (1963) conceived of the libido as a psychic analogue of physical energy. He rejected the Freudian view of the libido as purely instinctual, the expression of hunger, sex, and aggression. Rather, by utilizing the physical science theory of *energetics*, the study of energy under transformation, the libido was the totality of psychic energy not limited to sexual or aggressive desires. Libido energy was the vital forces that came to consciousness through symbols.

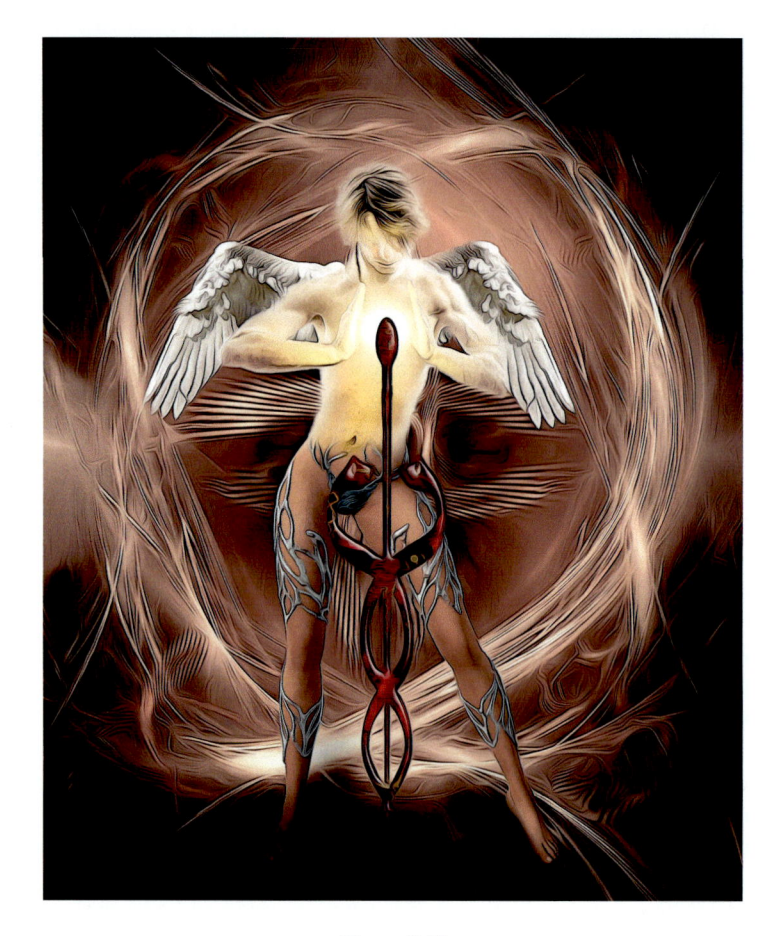

Figure 3.11

Having already observed symbols as the language of alchemy, in his work with psychiatric patients, Jung saw a parallel between the symbols in mental illness, especially between the prodromal stages of schizophrenia and the symbols in mythology, religion, art, and literature.

The vital and creative libidinal forces usually came to consciousness through a god-like symbol in dreams. In *Psychology of the Unconscious,* Jung (1912/2002) discussed the Greek god *Phanes* as an illustration of his own libidinal symbol. *Phanes* in Orphic cosmology was the life-driving force behind the creation of the world. He was born from a cosmic egg, which symbolized birth and the beginning of something new, the unity of two complementary processes: egg white and the yellow yolk. *Phanes*, meaning "bring to light" or "make appear," was a powerful libidinal symbol often symbolized in an egg as a beautiful, golden-wing hermaphrodite deity wrapped in the coils of a serpent who encircled the cosmos in the creative spirit.

Hermeneutic Science Interest

Platonic Influence

As Jung developed his theory of archetypes, he was influenced not only by the concept of entelechy of Aristotle, but also the *eidos* of Plato. Eidos were pure mental forms imprinted on the soul before physical birth. The physical world was not as real as eidos, which were the timeless, absolute, and unchangeable Platonic forms. The Platonic forms were metaphysical ideas and only copies of reality.

Jung believed that archetypes were innate, primordial energy that provided a timeless imprinted psychological framework, eidos, by which to understand and perceive the world. Beyond the natural world, archetypes predispose people to view the world in specific psychological ways. Jung discovered many archetypes, giving some more attention than others. One of the most important was *Persona*, the root of the word "personality," which caused people to present only a part of their personality to the public and conceal their true nature to themselves.

The symbol of Persona is a mask, which symbolized that the real, the total, personality was hidden behind it. It was also a reminder that to be in concert with the real self, psychological work needed to occur to make the mask to the outer world feel more authentic.

Figure 3.12

Alternate Conscious Paradigm Influence

Initially in his career, Jung practiced hypnosis, but found it unsatisfying in part because it put too much responsibility on the physician and not enough on the client. Although he found dream work much more effective than hypnosis, his work with Pierre Janet would influence the development of his theoretical and clinical approach. Jung initially termed his approach *complex psychology* because his Word Association Test research indicated that there was a pattern to unpleasant responses which created a psychological complex.

Influenced by the *Alternate Consciousness Paradigm* (ACP) theory and the studies of trauma of Janet Pierre, Jung believed when archetypal ideas became actualized feelings, they attracted other complex ideas and dissociation occurred. The result was that "someone was in a complex," which meant conscious control was diminished, leaving the individual with less physical and psychological energy. Finding the core of the complex created the healthy archetypal energy that had been contaminated by the complex. One of the goals of Jungian analysis was to analyze and make complexes conscious and in the process, to return to the root of the complex to reignite the healthy archetypal energy. For instance, a man experiencing a "mother complex" often seeks an external mother to meet his need for nurturance but needs to find the nurturing archetypal mother within himself.

Romanticism Influence

> Lover of Myth is the Lover of Wisdom
>
> - Aristotle

Jung was greatly influenced by Romanticism, particularly by one of the most important German philosophers, Friedrich Schelling (1775–1865), who was a student of Hegel and, in his *Philosophy of Mythology* (Schelling, 1857/1995), argued that philosophical concepts were rooted in mythology. Schelling believed that mythology was an expression of nature, and that human consciousness was shaped by myth not the other way around.

Schelling was a strong opponent of Enlightenment rationalism because he saw that the modern Western world began to define myth as untruth. In fact, the Enlightenment movement based its philosophy on "de-mythologizing" pre-modern beliefs and ending human ignorance through the supremacy of reason. Shelling believed that truth emerged from the symbols of mythology. The Greek philosophers simply translated the mythic symbols and turned their meaning into writing. Writing became associated with truth and reason, but this is a facade because the real truths continued to exist in the mythological stories. In this way, rationalism made a mockery of truth and degraded the importance of mythology and symbols in philosophy and science (Schelling, 1857/1995).

For Jung, mythology was the most profound record of the essential spirit and nature of humanity. In *Memories, Dreams, Reflections*, Jung (1963) linked the loss of mythology as a major cause of the neurosis of the modern world. Modern science separated the subject from the object, consciousness from the unconscious, and the internal world from the external world. This led to an internal, neurotic, alienation of the individual from themselves and their connection to nature and their ancestors. Mythology provided the bridge back to health and to the true human experience that our ancestors understood.

Modern science has continued to deny mythology in the name of objectivity and reason. Although science has made great strides in many areas of human development, in its false claims that mythology meant untruth, it lost its wisdom, but even more importantly science lost its soul (Jung, 1963).

Existential Philosophy Influence

Influenced by the Fredrich Nietzsche view of the death of Christianity, Jung believed that the decline of religion ushered in a "period of matchlessness" even in a period of great advances in technology and science, which left humanity in an *existential crisis* and suffering.

Without myths, there were no stories that connected people together and without religion there were no symbols that connected humanity to the unknown, to the mystery of life. In *Man and his Symbols*, Jung (1964) spoke of the myth of the Pueblo Indians. In a story that endowed their daily lives with purpose and meaning, the symbol of Father Sun represented the spirit beyond their daily existence. In contrast, modern civilization was questioning existence because there were no myths or symbols that spoke to a world beyond the immediate realities of modern life.

The modern abandonment of myths was also a rejection of symbols since a symbol could not be measured and manipulated to obtain an objective fact. Rather, Jung viewed a symbol not as a path to external truth but to psychological truth, and the bridge to all that was best in humanity. Because of the lack of powerful and healthy cultural symbols and with the human need for symbols, Jung warned that the shadow side of a symbol could appear in the form of political symbols. These were symbols that honored the state at the expense of the individual with fascism and totalitarianism, rather than democracy.

Chinese Philosophy Influence

Because of his interest in culture, unlike Freud who was afraid of train travel, Jung traveled extensively from his home in Switzerland. After the trip to Clark University with Freud in 1909, in the 1920s and 1930s, Jung returned to the United States, most notably meeting with Native American *Ochwiay Biano,* known as Chief Mountain Lake, in Taos Pueblo, New Mexico. He also traveled to England many times, as well as to East Africa and India.

The Axial Age and Chinese philosophy had a profound impact on Jung, particularly Daoism (Karcher, 1999), Also influential was his relationship with Richard Wilhelm (1873–1930), who provided some of the finest translations of the *I Ching* into English. Jung wrote introductions to both of his most significant works, *I Ching* (Wilhelm, 1997) and *The Secret of the Golden Flower: A Chinese Book of Life* (Wilhelm, 2023). Jung viewed Eastern thought as having great potential for reawakening the Western psyche from its spiritual and psychological alienation.

The Jungian "way of the Dao" was the deep connection between the mind and nature. Because the Western psyche had become alienated and isolated from its "mother," a reconnection to nature provided the energy for life and psychological growth. In the "way of Dao," subject became object and object became subject in a dialectic dance that had gone on since the beginning of time. This dance occurred through *enantiodromia*, meaning in Greek, "running counter to." In Jungian psychology, if the conscious persona identified too strongly with an archetypal energy, the unconscious opposite sought to emerge for psychological balance. Enantiodromia is described in the *I Ching* and refers to yang lines becoming yin when they had reached their extreme, and vice versa. A key process in Jungian analysis was for the unconscious opposite to become conscious. Or, as Jung stated, it was to embrace the enantiodromia, which was the path of individuation, for the polarities of yin and yang to live in psychological harmony.

An overidentification with an archetype can be psychologically deadening and lead to "burn out." The mother who over identifies with being a mother could feel "dead inside" but might be resistant to any other life experiences or other archetypal energies to balance her life.

130 *The World of Symbol – Jungian Analytical Psychology*

An example of the power of archetype was symbolized in the movie by director Steven Spielberg, *Raiders of the Lost Ark* (Black, 1981), in the search for the *Ark of the Covenant*. This is a modern myth of a heroic holy grail quest. After an incredible journey, the hero, Indiana Jones, his former lover, Marion Ravenwood, and his rival archaeological shadow, Rene Belloq find the Ark. They are then captured by their Nazi antagonists. As the Ark opened and spirits flew away, a huge explosive fire began. Indiana Jones told Marion, Rene, and other Nazis not to look at the Ark. Not able to respectfully acknowledge the archetypal energy, Rene and other Nazis looked, which caused their faces to melt, bodies to shrivel, and the head of Rene to explode. Afterward, the Ark sealed itself shut and Indiana Jones and Marion open their eyes to find no bodies and their bindings removed.

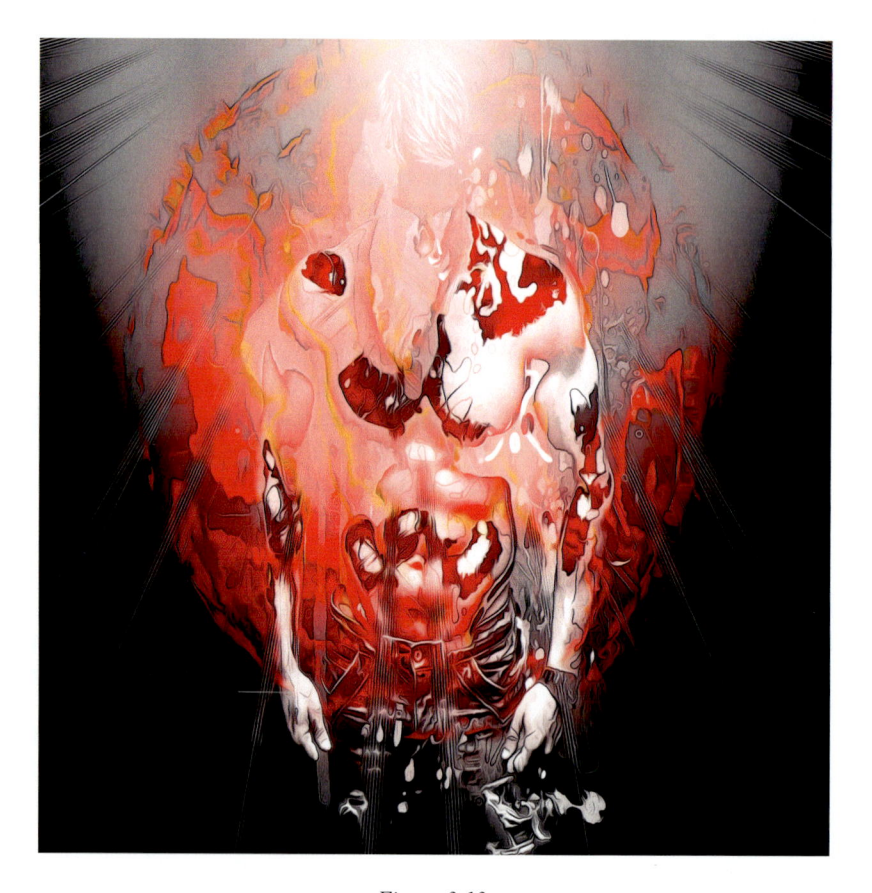

Figure 3.13

Raiders of the Lost Ark symbolizes the best way to psychologically manage an archetype: not to overidentify because it will lead to "burn out." It is important to show great respect for the power of an archetype that possesses the natural and the spiritual forces, the energy to create and destroy, as well as the power to transform.

The federal agents, symbolic of what Jung described as the impersonal collectivist state, did not acknowledge the power of their spiritual journey, the discovery of the transformative Ark. Rather, as often happens in modern culture, transformative psychological and spiritual experiences are reduced to meaningless scientific research. They took control and assured them that the Ark would be studied scientifically by "real scientists," and not by archeologists. Unbeknownst to the agents, the spiritually transformative Ark, like much of Western psyche, was mistakenly locked up with other countless crates in an undisclosed bureaucratic government warehouse lost forever.

The Chinese concepts of *yin and yang* influenced Jung, especially regarding the masculine and feminine aspects of the human psyche, the *anima* and *animus*. In Chinese cosmology, the world created itself out of the chaos of material energy. This energy went through periods of yin and yang and resulted in the creation of natural objects and human beings. What might have appeared as contrary forces became complementary. In fact, these contrary forces were necessary for creation to occur. In classical Chinese philosophy yin and yang provided the foundation for so many aspects of Chinese life, Chinese medicine, the martial arts, the Daoist *I Ching*, and Confucian ethics. Until Christianity arrived in China, the Chinese believed that humans were born unflawed by an original sin, born with the potential of acting good and evil. In effect, a "bad" person had the potential to become "good," and a "good" person had the potential to become "bad." In concert with this philosophy, Jungian psychology offered a different view from the Western belief about human nature.

The yin and yang concepts permeated Jungian psychology. The integration of the shadow, the repressed aspects of the psyche, was necessary for individuation. The yin and yang also provided some understanding of the human struggle between the sexes. The Jungian concepts of masculine and feminine forces in the psyche, often controversial, provided psychological understanding of the contrast and complementary nature of masculine and feminine characteristics. One reason for controversy about the yin and yang of sexuality was the Chinese view that yin was connected to gender; the female sex symbolized by the moon. One reason for a negative view of women was that yin represented the principle of darkness, coldness, emotionality, disintegration, and passivity. In contrast, yang represented the masculine force. The male sex was lightness, warmth, action, and rationality, symbolized by the sun. The ability to combine the contrary forces of yin and yang forces brought about a "phenomenal world."

Jung, a prisoner of his patriarchal Swiss culture, related the anima and animus most often to gender. A question remained whether, as Jung believed, the anima was unconscious in a man and the animus was unconscious in a woman; or whether masculine and feminine energies might be made unconscious because of socialization and cultural forces. The more enlightened view in the post-Jungian world was that for both sexes, the integration of anima and anima energies were necessary for psychological health and individuation.

Jungian Psychology

The Self

People will do anything, no matter how absurd, to avoid facing their own soul.

- C. G Jung

The first medical association might have been the *Therapeutae of Asclepius*, the group of physicians and their staff who managed the Asklepion Temples. The term *therapeutic* originated from the Greek *therapeutai*, meaning "one who attends to the gods." In Jungian analysis, this meant a psychological awareness of the *archetypal Self*, the soul, the organizing principle of the psyche. A goal of Jungian analysis was to recapture the lost soul that modernism had abandoned (Jung, 1933).

132   *The World of Symbol – Jungian Analytical Psychology*

The Self is the "god within," the deeper sense of wholeness beyond the ego. As the Self provides the unconscious impulse toward creative self-realization, the ego resists because the ego does not have the language of the unconscious to understand "the other world." The ego does not understand that the language of the unconscious is a symbol.

The inner light inside symbolizes the relationship between ego and the Self. The Self provides light to the ego; without the light there is only darkness and emptiness. The ongoing relationship with the Self is essential for psychological health because it provides energy, a feeling of unity and a connection to something greater than what the ego can provide. One can access the Self through learning the language of symbols, which exists in dreams, mythology, the arts, and rituals, any activity that opens one to a connection to a world beyond ego.

Figure 3.14

Individuation

> It became increasingly clear to me that the Mandala is the center. It is the exponent of all paths. It is the path to the center, to individuation.
>
> - Carl Jung, 1963

Mandala, from *Sanskrit,* meaning "circle," has provided sacred space and an aid to meditative practices for centuries. The mandala symbolized spiritual and psychological wholeness to many cultures, especially the Eastern religions of Hinduism and Buddhism. Mandalas became one of the most powerful symbols for the experience of the infinite world beyond mind and body.

The World of Symbol – Jungian Analytical Psychology 133

Humanity has utilized mandalas throughout time and provided another important example of how symbols were necessary to feel the deeper meaning of the world.

Jung was most interested in the symbols of Tibetan Buddhism and Hinduism. The Hindu mandala began as a religious symbol around the fourth century. It was employed as a guide to spiritual development and healing and provided an essential tool for those that sought enlightenment. Mandalas were the basis for the design of Hindu temples, providing a sacred place for meditation regarding the three-dimensional representation of the universe: the spiritual, the lived environment, and the inner psychological experience of the world.

Figure 3.15

One of the most common depictions of Hindu mandala art was the *yantra,* which was the geometric symbol that when created represented communication with the higher power. The Hindu dot symbolized where the universe began and the infinite nature of the universe. The lotus flower symbolized the opening of the chakras to the meditative process. Upward triangles symbolized action and energy toward spirituality, while downward triangles symbolized creativity and the pursuit of spiritual knowledge.

Tibetan Buddhism is rich in mythology and symbol, utilizing mandalas for many purposes. Mandalas were an essential part of the rituals to initiate new monks. They were essential symbols for meditation to focus the mind. The sand mandalas were symbolic of the impermanence of life, because after completion they were destroyed and "blown away." The creation of the Tibetan mandala started with an outer design and moved toward the center. For Jung, this was symbolic of the movement of individuation, from outer work of ego toward the inner work of the Self.

In analytical psychology, individuation occurred through the development of a strong relationship of the ego with the Self. By creating a mandala, the ego experienced the deeper levels of the psyche. This was a reminder that the individuation process was not linear, but was a circumambulation. It was a circular and dialectical movement toward the center, to the Self, the mandala symbolic of the individuation process.

In *Memories, Dreams, Reflections*, Jung (1963) described mandala work as the experience of the eternal mind. It was the transformative force and the cryptogram that provided the pieces of a psychic puzzle that brought the ego closer to the Self. Jung started mandala work during his Black Book days and began each morning with a small circular drawing. This seemed to indicate his current inner psychological state in a way not typically available to him. He was led to realize what the mandala really was the Self, the feeling of wholeness of his personality. For the Buddhists and Hindus, this was a connection to a higher internal power.

Jung believed that when our symbols change, we change. In modern times, mandalas have continued to be utilized for many psychological purposes. Jung argued the urge to create mandalas emerged during periods of intense psychological growth and could assist in the emotional re-balancing for creating a more integrated personality. The mandala also gave voice to what was yet to exist, something new and unique, the ascendant spiral toward the higher consciousness of the self.

Jung is credited for bringing the mandala back to Western culture (Kellogg, 1992; Slegelis, 1987). *Mandala therapy* now exists in a variety of psychotherapeutic venues for psychological growth. It was also used for the treatment of various psychiatric symptoms, such as anxiety and depression (Kellogg, Rae, Bonny, & DiLeo, 1977). One of the most notable developments of this therapy has been the work of Joan Kellogg, renowned art therapist, who developed the *Mandala Assessment Research Instrument* (MARI). The MARI studied the relationship between ego and Self through the selection of mandala card symbols. These cards addressed spiritual, mythological, transpersonal, and archetypal energies related to the practical daily challenges of life. After researching hundreds of mandalas, Kellogg developed 12 archetypal stages that she called the Great Round. These were the essential tasks all humans faced for psychological growth during the ongoing cyclical periods of growth, stagnation, and loss. They included entry, bliss, energy/path, beginnings, target, struggle, independence, identity, group alignment, endings, disintegration, and transformation.

Archetype

Together the patient and I address ourselves to the 2-million-year-old man that is in all of us.

- Carl Jung

As discussed in Volume I, Chapter 3, the pre-Socratic Greeks searched for the origin of the natural world, in Greek the *arche* meant the "original," the *prima matera*, the "beginning source of all living things." Jung would apply that concept to the universal forces of the human psyche. He would also acknowledge the influence of the Platonic forms, the eidos which formulated primordial images through symbol (Knox, 2003).

The world of archetypes is a world that has never been seen but for Jung is the deepest realm of the psyche (Wilmer, 1987). Existing from time immemorial, archetypes keep recurring

The World of Symbol – Jungian Analytical Psychology   135

worldwide in all cultures through myth, fairy tales, legends, and stories. Archetypes produce universal symbols that are characteristic of human nature and, like instincts, archetypes give form, not content to the inherited structure of the psyche. Jung spoke of four major archetypes that provide primordial symbols, including the animus/anima, the Self, the shadow, and the persona. Later, he referred to the wise old man, the child, the mother, and the maiden (Jung, 1934/1954).

Post-Jungians expanded the concept of archetype, most notably Margaret Mark and Carol Pearson (2001) who consolidated 12 archetypes into 3 major archetypal categories, which included ego types (innocent, orphan, hero, and caregiver), soul types (explorer, rebel, lover and creator), and self-types (jester, sage, magician, and ruler).

In 1939, Ernest Dichter, a follower of Sigmund Freud, sent to every ad agency on Madison Ave a boast about applying archetypes for the promotion of his product that created retail therapy and revolutionized marketing forever (Anonymous, 2011).

Figure 3.16

Collective Unconscious

> Just as the human body shows a common anatomy over and above racial differences, so, too, the human psyche possesses a common substratum transcending all differences in culture and consciousness…the collective unconscious.
>
> - Carl Jung

Figure 3.17

A major shift occurred, resulting in another disagreement with Freud, when Jung embraced a collective unconscious. Although acknowledging two levels of the unconscious, personal and collective, as his theory evolved, when Jung said unconscious, he typically meant the collective unconscious. For Jung, the personal unconscious related to personal history, while the collective unconscious related to world history and evolutionary history in the human mind.

The collective unconscious contains inherited psychic structures, archetypes, which are present at birth. Archetypes function like psychological instincts and create behavioral action, fantasy images, and affective emotional reactions (Sedgwick, 2001). Because archetypes are ages old, they become the driving force of the collective unconscious. This means there is a reservoir of potential in the collective unconscious because it extends backwards in time to unremembered human prehistory and points forward toward the development of new human capacities. Freud viewed the unconscious as striving for release of destructive personal psychological impulses, whereas Jung viewed the collective unconscious as striving for release of untapped universal human potentialities.

The collective unconscious symbolizes the entirety of the human history and potential that crosses all cultures and all time. Myths are the projections of the contents of collective unconscious (Turner, 2005). Modern society created a social neurosis with the devaluation of mythology because myth provides a link to the world of our ancestors and nature, a way to engage the mysteries of the world unavailable through the rationalism of modernism. By exploring the dynamic collective unconscious, original myths come alive and provide points of departure and future possibilities of understanding. Jung (1963) argued that myths die when they no longer live and grow as witnessed by the dogmatic pronouncements by the Christian church.

Joseph Campbell (1972), in *Myths to Live By,* explores the enduring power of universal myths. Campbell explains how mythmaking has existed from the primordial past to the modern world, always returning to the creative imagination that arises from a universal unconscious. Because of the expansion of knowledge about mythology in modern times, the opportunity exists to apply mythology to daily life.

The Shadow

> Wherever good is, is evil.
> Wherever shadow is, is light and substance.
> …Good and evil are a pair of opposites.
> Where one is, there is the other.
> Wilmer, 1987, pp. 96–97

As seen throughout the text, denial of shadow has had dire consequences. Could the world have been different if, during the Crusades, the monks assessed the shadow elements of their destruction of Greek culture? Or if psychologists saw the shadow at work in the eugenic movement or their support of torture after 9/11 at Guantanamo Bay? The great contribution of Jungian psychology is the belief, no matter how positive an action seems, a shadow is always present.

In Jungian psychology, the shadow is the unconscious aspect of personality that the ego rejects, and cannot identify with consciously. Often thought of as the "dark side of the psyche," it is not just the rejection of negative self-attributions; it is also repression of aspects of personality that are not socially acceptable; the sum of our collective psychology denied expression in our conscious life.

Figure 3.18

To explore the personal shadow, Jung believed one should start with the traits that irritate us because this leads to a deeper understanding of ourselves. For a societal shadow, "the other"; is perceived as a threat to the well-being of a society. An unconscious shadow can grip a nation by dehumanizing "the other," those perceived as a societal threat. Although often difficult and overwhelming, making a shadow conscious is the key to personal and societal transformation, and in Jungian terms, key to individuation.

Anima/Animus

Jung (1934/1954) believed that a man carries within his psyche an unconscious feminine energy, an *anima archetype*, and a woman carries an unconscious masculine energy, *animus archetype*. He based this understanding primarily on evolution and dreamwork because psychological bisexuality reflects the biological fact that gender is the result of a few larger male or female genes. The smaller number of contrasexual genes produce a corresponding contrasexual character, which is unconscious. In dreamwork, Jung discovered the irrationality of feeling in male and thinking in female dreams.

There have been various contemporary critiques of Jung's concept of anima and animus. In *Queering Gender: Anima/Animus and the Paradigm of Emergence*, Susan McKenzie (2006) argued that the traditional view of anima and animus does not fit the realities of modern society and rejects the Jungian trap of a linear orderliness, fixed identities, androgynous symmetries,

The World of Symbol – Jungian Analytical Psychology 139

and archetypes that are inherited based on gender anatomy. Symbolized by the emergent Jungian belief that both genders can exist in an individual, in the 1970s, James Hillman, an archetypal Jungian theorist, began the process of imagining a multiplicity of anima/animus possibilities not linked to an inherited gender (Samuels, 1985).

By the end of the twentieth century, post-Jungians began to grapple with homosexuality. Robert Hopcke (1991), compiled Jung's work on homosexuality, argued that same-sax love could be a path to Jungian individuation. Christine Downing (1996) believed homosexual love was rooted in mythological history. In the twenty-first century, influenced by post-modernism, Jungians embraced the concept of mind as an emergent process (McKenzie, 2006). Christopher Hauke (2000), in a landmark discussion of anima/animus and gender, created a bridge between Jung and contemporary gender theory. Feminist theory also contributed to the expansion of Jungian concepts of anima/animus and gender identity (Adams & Duncan, 2003; Rowland, 2002). In neuroscience Antonio Damasio (1999) and others discovered the proto-self, preconscious emergent self, the neurobiology of the body that precedes consciousness and the organization of an inherited archetypal framework (Lakoff, 1987; Schore, 1994; Stern, 1985; Wilkinson, 2004).

Figure 3.19

A Dangerous Method

The 2011 film *A Dangerous Method*, inspired by *A Most Dangerous Method,* written by John Kerr (1994), presented a dramatic representation of the relationship between Freud and Jung and a way to understand the Jungian anima/animus and the role of the unconscious anima in the Freud and Jung split. Sabina Spielrein (1885–1941), a Russian psychoanalyst and an often-forgotten woman in the history of Jungian psychology, made a passionate attempt to provide an emotional bridge for the unsuccessful reconciliation between the two men, symbolic of the lack of integration of the anima/animus, aspects of the psyche within the modern male. Furthermore, Spielrein represents the ongoing lack of acknowledgment of significant women not only in psychoanalytic, but also throughout psychological history.

Jung initially treated Spielrein as a patient suffering a hysteric episode at the Burgholzli Psychiatric Hospital in Zurich. His work included many of his successful therapeutic approaches, such as the Word Association Test and dream analysis. While in the hospital, Jung and Spielrein had a passionate love affair and, after leaving the hospital, their personal relationship developed into a professional relationship, as Jung served on her Medical Dissertation Committee as she successfully pursued a medical degree and later became a psychoanalyst. It is now believed that Spielrein was the inspiration for Jung's first meeting with Freud, since her case was the first case he presented to Freud.

Spielrein became one of the first female and feminist psychoanalysts, and in her 30-year career, published over 30 papers in German, French, and Russian on psychoanalysis and developmental and educational psychology. She developed an ongoing bond with Freud, especially regarding the treatment of children. Her interest in child and educational psychology led to a relationship with Jean Piaget, the renowned developmental psychologist, whom she psychoanalyzed.

Although her effort to provide an emotional bridge between Freud and Jung remained a key part of her legacy, John Launer (2014), in *Sex Versus Survival: Life and Ideas of Sabina Spielrein,* written with the support of her family, attempted to debunk many of the beliefs about her relationship with Jung. Launer did not believe that Jung had any real feeling for Spielrein or believed she had any impact on his theories. Rather, he viewed her legacy as an early advocate for the integration within psychoanalysis of developmental psychology. This integration later came to fruition in attachment theory in relational psychoanalysis.

In the later part of her life and career, Spielrein returned to Rostov-on-Don, in the Soviet Union, still advocating for psychoanalysis, even as it became increasingly in disfavor to anti-Semitic Nazis and communists. In July 1942, she and her two daughters, and 27,000 other Jewish victims, were shot to death by a SS Nazi death squad, tragically ending the life of one of the most important women in the history of psychology. In 2017, the *International Association for Spielrein Studies* was established in Poland to advance her contributions to psychological and psychoanalytic thought and to the history of ideas and culture.

Both Freud and Jung would admit that their experience with Spielrein proved that emotional issues were key elements, not only for the client but also for the therapist in the transference and countertransference therapeutic relationship (Jung & Freud, 1994; Owens, 2015). Even though Spielrein tried, ironically neither Freud nor Jung would ever acknowledge the impact of emotion and feeling in their own relationship. Although the impact of the Jung and Spielrein relationship on Jungian thought may never be known, their relationship symbolized many aspects of Jungian theory, especially the contradictory and complementary energies of the anima and animus, the difficulty of two famous men to acknowledge the emotional aspects of their relationship, and because of that inability, the resulting divisions in the psychoanalytic movement.

Dream Analysis

> Dreams…seek to express something that the ego does not know and does not understand.
>
> - Carl Jung

Although Jung agreed with Freud that dreams could express repressed wishes and fears, he felt it was outdated to limit dream analysis to that view. For Jung, dreamwork contained ineluctable truths, philosophical pronouncements, illusions, fantasies, memories, plans, anticipations, irrational experiences, telepathic visions, and many other possibilities (Jung, 1934). Dreams give voice of the unconscious through symbol and metaphor.

Jung believed that dreamwork required the understanding of dream categories, necessitating a skilled Jungian psychotherapist because many of the categories overlap. Jung believed the unconscious acts in a compensatory role with the conscious mind when a dream rearranges a current point of view; as an example, when someone with a poor self-image dreams of powerful people, which can include religious, political, cultural, or mythological figures. Besides the compensatory role, a dream can play a supplementary role when it offers not a compensatory message but suggests other possible motivations or options. For example, a dream about Jesus Christ may not be compensatory, but suggests a reevaluation of one's relationship to spirituality or religion.

Figure 3.20

Jung argued that dreams are not only reactive to previous life experiences but can also play a prospective role. Dreams that anticipate the future, that instigate something new, a new way to solve a problem, or something on a grander scale, a personal transformation. Because of the power of the unconscious dreams can be premonitory, dreams can predict future events (Sedgwick, 2001). Recurring dreams are important because they indicate psychological issues frozen in time, particularly psychological trauma.

The role of dreams in the post-Jungian psychotherapeutic world is more fluid and relational (Sedgwick, 2001). Although still important, dreamwork tends to emerge naturally from the therapeutic relationship because an overdependence on dream interpretation can avoid the dreamer as the final arbiter of reality.

Transference and Countertransference – The Wounded Healer Archetype

Although Jung believed that psychoanalysis would be more appropriate earlier in life, Jung described his approach to psychotherapy as the new "empirical science," to distinguish his work from psychoanalysis. Jung agreed with Freud about the importance of the therapeutic relationship and transference and countertransference. His approach was dramatically different from Freud since he perceived the therapeutic relationship healed both the client and therapist. Unlike Freud sitting behind the couch during free association, Jung sat "knee- to-knee" with the client in total engagement.

Because of his view of the collective unconscious, Jung believed that the *wounded healer archetype* was activated in the transference and countertransference relationship. The wounded healer archetype linked the analyst and client to the *mythology* of the *Asklepion myth* which provided a key connection to the ancient powers of healing. From a Jungian perspective, in their daily work, physicians and psychologists lived the Asklepion myth.

Note: First read the myth, engage the symbol, reflect on their non-literal underlying meaning, and then read the narrative, understanding myth can speak of truth in many ways.

Asklepion Myth

There was a maiden in Thessaly named Coronis, who was of such beauty that Apollo, the God of Truth, fell madly in love with her. However, she was not in love with Apollo; instead, she loved and became pregnant by a mere mortal. She hoped Apollo would not find out. But Apollo, learning of her lover and her scorn of his love became incredibly angry. Apollo had her killed. But as he watched the funeral and saw her body burn on the funeral pyre and as the wildfire began to consume her body, he became ravaged by grief and rescued the mortal baby from her womb as Zeus had rescued Dionysius.

He snatched the human baby and brought him to Chiron's cave to be raised by the wise Chiron, half man, half animal, who was a master of healing. Chiron understood the need for healing because after being poisoned by one of the arrows of Hercules he had a wound that could not be healed. As he left his son in the cave, Apollo told Chiron to name the boy Asclepius. Chiron agreed and he became Asclepius' foster father. Many had brought their unwanted sons to the wise Chiron, but none had the impact that Asclepius had on him. As he became aware of his own wound and as he grew older, Asclepius wanted Chiron to teach him the healing arts. He quickly surpassed his foster father in his knowledge of healing the sick.

When he was grown, he left Chiron's cave and went down from the mountain cave to help heal the people of Greece of their maladies. He became the first great physician, the "father of medicine." People flocked to him from far and near, and many who came were both seriously physically and mentally ill. Whoever came to him suffering, whether from wounded limbs, bodies wasting away from disease, or in serious emotional distress, he cured them of their torment. He even brought people back from the dead.

His patients adored him and showered treasures on him, and it was not long before they worshipped him as a god and built temples in his honor. Asclepius put beds in his temples, they became the first hospitals. There he went from bed to bed, pleased to be looked upon as a god, leaning on a staff, the rod of Asclepius, entwined with sacred serpents. The Greeks felt that serpents knew all the secrets of the earth and that they epitomized rejuvenation, sloughing off its old skin for new skin each New Year. They felt that the serpents told Asclepius the causes and cures of their diseases. Sometimes he put his patients to sleep with a magic potion and listened to what they said while they were dreaming. Their dreams often revealed what caused their ailments. Dreams would help him find a cure for their disease(s).

Asclepius had a wife and seven children, and all the children followed in their father's footsteps. His sons were assistant physicians, his daughters were his nurses. Hygeia, one of his daughters, washed and scrubbed her patients from morning to night, and people marveled to see how fast her patients regained their health. She was acknowledged as the first healer who understood how to stop the spread of disease because before Hygeia it was thought that soap and water would kill the sick. She became known as the "Goddess of Health." Asclepius grew more famous, rich, and "pink-faced," and as time went on, he grew so skilled in his art that his ability to bring back the dead caused The Fates to complain to Zeus that their efforts to measure the threads of life were now in vain. Hades, the god of the underworld, was also upset, for he was being cheated out of dead souls.

Apollo went to Zeus to point out how much good his son was doing for mankind and for a while Zeus was lenient. But when Asclepius accepted gold for bringing the dead back to life, Zeus, because of Asclepius' "god-usurping hubris," hurled a thunderbolt at him and since he was human nothing, but a small heap of ashes was left of him. Apollo was furious with Zeus for killing his son and wanted revenge. He did not dare raise his hand against his almighty father, but he slew the Cyclopes who have given Zeus the thunderbolt. Zeus, in his turn, had to revenge the Cyclopes. He punished Apollo by making him serve as a slave on earth. Apollo found a good master and suffered no hardship. Soon the gods on high Olympus missed him and his music, the nine Muses most of all. He eventually returned to play music with the Muses on Mount Olympus.

After his death, Asclepius' temples and his teachings of medical science remained and continued to grow in popularity. Upon the request of Apollo, Zeus resurrected Asclepius as a god, "the divine physician." The gods also put his image among the stars as a constellation among the immortals. His mentor Chiron, the master of the healing arts, gave up his immortality since he could not heal himself. However, his half-brother, Zeus, feeling pity for him, placed him in the sky, represented astronomically as the northern constellation Sagittarius.

144   *The World of Symbol – Jungian Analytical Psychology*

Figure 3.21

The Asklepion Temples became the symbol of the ancient hospitals of medicinal healing, where physicians "did their magic" and healed the sick. Pilgrims throughout Greece flocked to his temples; inside the temple, they laid down for healing on a klinike. From the Greek meaning "practice at a sick bed," the klinike was the precursor for the word *clinic*. In the Asklepion Temples, the statues with his rod and snake provided inspiration and guidance. The Rod of Asclepius became a powerful symbol of modern medicine; it was adopted as the symbol of the World Health Organization and included in the symbol of the American Medical Association. In Jungian analysis, the rod symbolized the stability of the skilled healer, the snake symbolized the sacred wisdom needed for healing and rejuvenation, and the process of becoming conscious of the dual nature of the psyche, which is ongoing psychological death, and rebirth.

Guggenuhl-Craig (1971), in *Power in the Helping Professions*, stated that when a client became "sick," the healer-patient archetype was constellated. The sick person sought an external healer, but at the same time the intra-psychic healer was activated. It was the physician within the client that ultimately determined their healing. The wounded healer symbol describes the connection between of wound of the healer and the sickness of the client. In Jungian analysis, the analyst comprehends the admonition, *physician heal thyself*. This activates the client understanding, client heal thyself. The inner client of the analyst and the inner physician of the client can now do their analytic work. Unlike in psychoanalysis, the wound of the analyst was crucial for the success of Jungian treatment.

Figure 3.22

Chiron, the master of the healing arts, was an important reminder that the analyst has wounds that required an ongoing relationship with their unconscious. It was the analyst's wound that was key for psychological healing. The lack of conscious awareness of the wounded healer archetype would lead to an infection of the client's wounds and result in splitting, projecting the analyst wound on the client and safely becoming the healer without consciousness.

The Practice of Jungian Psychology

Sandplay Therapy

Sandtray therapy, over 100 years old, is one of the oldest psychotherapies. The inspiration came from H.G. Wells (2016/1911), who, in 1911, wrote *Floor Games* after observing the dramatic and therapeutic value of play by his sons. His book inspired Margaret Lowenfield (1890–1973), one of the most neglected women in the history of child psychology, to develop *Sandtray Therapy* for children (Lowenfield, 2007).

It was the belief of Lowenfield (1979) that children needed to play to avoid destructive behaviors later in adulthood. Sandtray therapy provided a concrete way for children to communicate their thoughts and feelings. The sandtray is a symbolic representation of the world because sand has many historical and cultural links to raising consciousness and healing, especially in Tibetan Buddhist and American Indian traditions (Weinrib, 2004). By touching the sand in a safe and sacred space, a child connects to many levels of the mind, body, and spirit. The Lowenfield *World Technique* inspired the recent *World Making* hermeneutic sandtray approach of Gisela De Domenico (1988).

Jung embraced the importance of play at Bollingen and, although he did not practice sandtray therapy, his followers have applied his theories, especially the importance of symbol, to sandtray therapy for over a half century. In the 1930s, during a British Psychological Society conference, Carl Jung was impressed by a presentation by psychoanalyst and pediatrician Margaret Lowenfield, who had developed the first child psychological clinic in England. Upon his return to Zurich, Jung encouraged *Dora Kalff*, a future Jungian analyst, to travel to London to study with Lowenfield. Disagreements began about the psychoanalytic practice of sandtray therapy because Lowenfield believed the transference of the child was to the sandtray itself, not to the psychoanalyst. Because of the importance of transference in psychoanalytic healing, Anna Freud and Melanie Klein strongly disagreed, which laid the foundation for the current general disinterest in sandtray therapy in the psychoanalytic world (Mitchell & Friedman, 1994).

Returning from London after her training in the 1950s with Lowenfield and other English psychoanalytic therapists, Dora Kalff (1904–1990), created the foundational Jungian approach to what she called *sandplay therapy* to distinguish from the World Technique of Lowenfield (Kalff, 1980). She initially started with children but as her technique developed it became clear that work in a sandplay was also important for the psychological health of adults. Kalff believed that an experience of mother-child unity was transformational in sandplay therapy because work in the sandtray activated the prefrontal cortex and the limbic system.

In the free and protected safe space, the mother-child unity returned and the therapist and the client, as in childhood, created a "shared mind," a "mother-child biological bond." The neurobiological relationship, with the therapist in sandplay therapy, resulted in a "re-constellation of the ego with the Self" (Turner, 2005). The archetype of the Self is the healing factor that emerges from the collective unconscious and revives the archetypal energies throughout the psyche. The ego becomes stronger and less prone to mental disturbance and unhappiness (Mitchell & Friedman, 1994).

During a sandplay session, a client creates a world scene in a sandtray with the typical dimensions of 30″ × 30″ with a depth of about 3 inches and standing height of about 30 inches with a blue base that symbolizes the unconscious. The room contains essential symbols for the client to select, which includes human, animal, religious, military, political, cultural icons, and mythological figures. Also available are objects that represent the earth, like trees, flowers, and rocks. Other necessary objects that connect humanity to the world are buildings, transportation vehicles, computers, media, fences, and musical instruments. Although there are many therapeutic approaches, typically a client is encouraged to utilize the sandtray to create, to play, and to build a world scene. Some Jungians explain that sandplay is like a dream and provides the ability to experience a deeper understanding of the world (Turner, 2005).

From a Jungian perspective, the result is a *psychic x-ray* that provides a visual picture of "what needs to speak" from the unconscious. Depending on the current psychological needs of the client, the symbols of a sandplay therapy session present a visual picture of the archetypal energies, complexes, and most importantly the *ego-self axis*, the belief that living in relationship to the Self, our totality, moves an individual toward individuation and self-actualization. A unique feature unavailable to traditional talk psychotherapy is at the end of a sandplay session, a client can take a photo, usually with their iPhone, of their session; symbols to inspire their daily life.

Figure 3.23

In 1985, from her home in Zollikon, Switzerland, Dora Kalff founded the *International Society for Sandplay Therapists* (ISST), which has continued in the Kalff and Jungian psychological traditions to certify ISST Sandplay Therapists throughout the world. In 1987, Barbara Turner founded the *Sandplay Therapists of America* (STA), which allows for non-certified membership and for those broadly interested in a Jungian approach to sandtray work. The STA publishes the *Journal of Sandplay Therapy.*

Beyond the traditional Jungian approach, there are other theoretical approaches to sandtray therapy, which include but are not limited to, humanistic (Armstrong, 2008), cognitive-behavioral (Drewes, 2009), and cross-cultural and community (Zoja, 2011).

Alcoholics Anonymous

Mental health and drug and alcohol services are rooted in difference traditions. Mental health services have traditionally been provided by licensed mental health professionals, psychiatrists, psychologists, clinical social workers, and counselors. Drug and alcohol treatment has a tradition that "you have to have had it to treat it," treatment provided by addicts themselves. The different history and vision of the two systems has led to antagonism and mistrust, which often made treatment coordination between the two traditions difficult. It became clear that the separation of the two systems was detrimental to providing quality care to the community. The reality was that many clients met *dual diagnosis* criteria, both a mental health and addiction diagnosis. This has led to creation of integrated mental health and drug and alcohol departments throughout the United States, often called *Behavioral Health Departments.*

Jung understood the need for community support beyond professional treatment. Jung inspired the founders of the *Alcohol Anonymous* (AA) movement after his honest feedback to one of his patients, "Ricard H," that conventional medical and psychiatric treatment of his addiction was hopeless, advised that he seek a spiritual environment, and "hope for the best" (Schoen, 2009). One of the founders, William Griffith Wilson (1895–1971), often known as "Bill W" because of the tradition in AA of anonymity, met "Richard H" at the *Oxford Group*. This was a non-denominational religious group founded in 1921 in England by Frank Buchman, a Lutheran priest who had great success with many social problems, especially addiction (Lean, 1985). The basic philosophy was to avoid living with fear and selfishness in life and to surrender to God's plan. A predecessor to the AA model, the Oxford Group was revolutionary in the 1920s and 1930s for explicitly stating that it was not a religion because it had no hierarchical structure or organization. It functioned "organically" with its leadership was only "inspired by God." Its members worked together in fellowship on ways to live a moral life, with spiritual not denominational determination. In 1935, Wilson and Bob Smith met with the Oxford Group and founded AA, codifying most of its tenets into the *Twelve Steps.*

In 1939, "Bill W" published the first AA "Big Book," *Alcoholics Anonymous: The Story of How More Than One Hundred Men and Women Have Recovered from Alcoholism* (Anonymous, 1976). There are now four editions of the "Big Book." The most recent edition was completed in 2001, but the chapters that describe the AA recovery model remain unchanged. AA remains an international, community-based, self-supporting, apolitical organization of over 2 million members and provides over 12,000 general meetings, whose only requirement for membership is the desire to stay sober and help others achieve sobriety.

In the *War of the Gods in Addiction: C.J Jung, Alcoholics Anonymous and Archetypal Evil*, David Schoen (2009) explored the deep connection between AA and Carl Jung. In 1961, a few years before Jung's death, there were letter communications between "Bill W" and Jung. In these letters, "Bill W" credits Jung for his "honesty with his friend "Richard H" that conventional medical and psychiatric treatment of his addiction was hopeless. He further credits Jung for his conviction that "man is something more than intellect, emotion and "two dollars' worth of chemicals."

"Bill W" also acknowledged that many of its members, after recovery in AA, received excellent treatment from Jungian analysis (Schoen, 2009). Jungian concepts permeate the AA Twelve Steps. The first step, the admission of being powerless over alcohol, addressed the concept that the ego needed a higher consciousness and an "education of the mind." In the second step, there is need for acceptance that there is a power greater than the ego that could restore sobriety. In the third step, the importance of turning the ego over to a higher power, in Jungian terms, the Self. The fourth through tenth steps addressed shadow, coming to terms with the areas of the psyche that were unconscious including individual shortcomings and rectifying the injuries done to others. The importance of prayer was emphasized in step eleven, which was in Jungian thought, is an ongoing contact with the Self, or in AA terms the God as we understand Him, praying for His power to carry out his will. In step twelve is the awareness of a spiritual awakening, an ego-Self axis connection, and a commitment to live the steps in all aspects of community life.

The World of Symbol – Jungian Analytical Psychology 149

In his 1961 response to "Bill W," Jung reiterated his belief that the craving for alcohol was equivalent to spiritual thirst and "for the union with God" (Schoen, 2009). He noted that the Latin word for alcohol was *spiritus*, the highest religious experience as well as the most depraved poison. The result was to address addiction from the *spiritus contra spiritium* approach and understand how an addiction-shadow complex takes over the psyche. Jung believed that addiction was beyond the personal unconscious and personal shadow. There was a transpersonal quality, a need for spiritual insight and the "protective wall of human community," that was needed to effectively treat addiction. Spiritual insight could occur from several spiritual directions including Christ, Buddha, Yahweh, Allah, Great Spirit, gods and goddesses, or any other spiritual form that remained internally alive and provided the energy to fight the transpersonal forces of evil.

The power of community was necessary to fight the forces of evil. Without community, treating addiction was hopeless, the "game is over," and the evil aspect of shadow would easily triumph. Without the "the protective wall of human community," one would not be able to resist the power of evil. The real "sin" of modern society was the isolation of the individual from the support of others. Community meant acting collectively out of love, compassion, and charity toward one another, where people felt nurtured and protected.

Figure 3.24

In 1955, at the AA International Convention in St. Louis, "Bill W" introduced the AA symbol, which was a triangle enclosed by a circle. He noted the importance of the symbol with its similarity with the alchemical symbol of antiquity. The circle symbolized the warding off of evil spirits, and the triangle symbolized the three legacies of AA: recovery, unity, and service. This is a reminder that in antiquity, the circle symbolized the philosopher's stone, the purification of the body and soul, the symbol of the return to perfection, enlightenment, and "heavenly bliss." In the 1990s, after the AA symbol had been plagiarized by other organizations, the symbol was removed from official AA stationary and local AA groups were free to decide whether to continue the use of the symbol.

In his 1961 communication with Jung, "Bill W" spoke of having a vision symbolized by chain communication, which viewed a society of alcoholics sharing their experiences with other addicted people in chain style, supporting the possibility of personal and spiritual transformation. The unbroken chain symbolized the essence of AA, a bond that never breaks in its effort to emancipate humanity of the scourge of addiction.

The reality is that only 20 percent of Twelve Step programs address alcoholism and recovery. Although AA has remained the largest, the Twelve Step model has become the standard for 80 percent of other recovery models. These include but are not limited to *Narcotics Anonymous*, *Gamblers Anonymous*, *Overeaters Anonymous*, *Sexaholics Anonymous*, *Neurotic Anonymous*, and *Al-Anon*, which supports family members and friends of people who are addicted.

Serious Mental Illness and Community Mental Health

> Through my work with patients, I realized that paranoid ideas and hallucinations contain a germ of meaning. A personality, a life history, a pattern of hopes and desires lie behind the psychosis. The fault is ours if we do not understand them.
>
> - Carl Jung

Unlike Freud, Jung worked with serious mental illness for many years at the Burgholzli Psychiatric Hospital in Zurich, Switzerland. His approach to mental illness was unique, if not revolutionary, for modern medicine. Jung was critical of the overemphasis by physicians on diagnosis because Jung believed the "the gods were in the illness" and that modern medicine was too quick to neglect the true meaning of mental illness. In *Memories, Dreams, Reflections*, Jung (1963) recalled a visit with Freud to the Burgholzli Psychiatric Hospital in which Freud showed a total lack of interest in serious mental illness. This attitude has continued to plague psychoanalysis into the modern age.

Jung was inspired by individuals with mental illness because he viewed their suffering as an opportunity to gain a richer understanding of the unconscious, as well as to value their experiences as human beings beyond their diagnosis.

For Jung, this could only be accomplished by understanding the world of symbol, the language of the unconscious. Since often a psychotic person spoke a different language, a symbolic language, Jung believed it was the responsibility of the physician and analyst to learn that language.

Jung was a colleague at the Burgholzli Psychiatric Hospital with Eugen Bleuler, the Swiss psychiatrist who replaced the diagnosis of *dementia praecox* of Emil Kraepelin with schizophrenia. Although Jung saw the challenges of the long-term effects of schizophrenia, he rejected the grim prognosis of Kraepelin and Bleuler, the theory of the "deteriorating brain" that left the unfortunate legacy that individuals with mental illness could not recover and lead quality lives (Jung, 1928/1960).

Jung was not afraid of his own mental disturbance and believed analysts should explore their own tenuous relationship with reality. In a world that rarely gives acknowledgment to individuals with mental illness, in his *Red Book: Liber Novus*, Jung entered their world, where he discovered some of the great mysteries of the mind. After the breakup with Freud, Jung retreated and experienced one of the most emotionally difficult but incredibly creative periods of his career. If psychosis is defined as losing touch with external reality, inspired by his work with individuals with mental illness, Jung learned that withdrawal from reality connected him to the wisdom of another world. Unlike some psychotic clients, Jung could not only travel safely between the two worlds but explain the importance of the journey toward a more complete understanding of the human psyche.

Personal Reflections

I discussed my history as a mental health director in Volume I, Chapter 6. In terms of Jungian psychology, the sad reality is that the interest of Jung in serious mental illness has been lost in Jungian psychology. A review of the psychological literature and research found few Jungian references related to community mental health or serious mental illness.

I believe if Jung was alive today, he would express concern with the overemphasis on medication, case management, and cognitive-behavioral approaches. Although all those approaches have shown efficacy, the state of individuals with mental illness remains dire. Jungian psychology would offer much of what is missing in our current community mental health systems, helping individuals with mental illness view themselves more than their diagnosis, to experience themselves beyond their struggling ego. Most importantly mental health professionals would, like Jung, view individuals with mental illness not only as clients, but also as teachers. As Director at Shasta County Community Mental Health I developed a sandtray room for clinical work, especially for training clinical psychology interns. The amazing result, beyond the therapeutic value, interns often remarked that their sandtrays were not much different than their clients diagnosed with serious mental illness. The learning was that soul, the Self, exists in everyone and that symbol helps to transcend psychiatric diagnoses leaving the feeling of a special connection to humanity. Forever changing their view of mental illness

As chair of the Clinical Psychology Program for over six years at Pacifica Graduate Institute (PGI) in Santa Barbara, California, I led an unsuccessful effort to procure APA accreditation. I agree with the APA that all psychologists should possess the same basic skills no matter their doctoral program. However, I believe it speaks volumes that there are no APA accredited programs in the United States in clinical psychology with a Jungian specialty.

Jungian psychology can impact community mental health beyond the clinical world. I teach a community mental health, public policy, and depth psychology course, at PGI. This course teaches how Jungian psychology can build effective executive-level teams in all organizations, including community mental health. I also teach how sandtray and other psychodynamic approaches can enhance administrative and treatment functioning at all levels of an organization.

In her work, *Sandtray Therapy in Vulnerable Communities: A Jungian Approach*, Eva Pattis Zoja (2011) articulated the power of sandtrays in community mental health settings. Zoja, a Jungian analyst in Italy, believes that sandtray therapy could expand Jungian practice beyond its Euro-centric history by its application to other cultures. She described successful sandtray case studies of her community work in South Africa, China, and Columbia. Zoja offers ways that Jungian thought and sandtray therapy could be effective in acute crisis, natural disasters, and even war. She envisioned a Jungian approach in long-term care with children and adults, as well for those in poverty and in high-stress environments such as slums, refugee camps, and high-density urban settings.

For the private practitioner wanting to practice community mental health from a Jungian orientation, Guy Dargert (2016), in *The Snake in the Clinic: Psychotherapy's Role in Medicine and Healing*, provides a framework by which to link Jungian thought with the goals of modern medicine and primary care. He argues it is long overdue that social policy in Obamacare allows for the integration of the mental and medical health systems. For Dargert, the rapprochement should come from ancient and Jungian wisdom, not only from the knowledge of modern medicine, which he believes has forgotten its roots and historic connection to healing the body, mind, and soul.

Organizational Transformation

John Corlett and Carol Pearson (2003), in *Mapping the Organizational Psyche: A Jungian Theory of Organizational Dynamics and Change*, provide a comprehensive system for organizational transformation. The transformation occurs by the assessment of *four organizational zones* that create pathways to organizational wholeness. In Zone One, the organization needs to assess its Public Face by withdrawing projections and attending to the mission statement, which in Jungian terms, defines the Organizational Self and like an individual organizes, revitalizes, and provides the ideal which can never be fully attained. In this context, the importance to create an organizational symbol to deepen the meaning of the mission statement. In Zone Two, the organization owns its Organizational Shadow(s), which are areas typically repressed, such as racism, sexism, and ageism. Zone Three de-energizes Organizational Complexes, which are strongly held feelings and beliefs that overly dominate the organization. In community mental health systems, these are typically issues of money, productivity, and billing. Zone Four creates an Experience of the Organization, which is an activity that acknowledges and celebrates organizational history and achievements. Corlett and Pearson (2003) also discuss the importance of archetypal balance, especially at the executive level, and within management leadership.

Unidentified Flying Objects

Erich Von Daniken (1999), in the *Chariot of the Gods,* explained that religious myths had their origins in the encounters with superior beings from outer space. In *Flying Saucers: A Modern Myth of Things Seen in the Skies*, Jung (1958/1978) addressed in psychological terms the *Unidentified Flying Objects* (UFOs) phenomenon. For Jung, UFOs represented the need for symbols, myths, and a visionary savior. Throughout history, the rumor of something coming from outer space occurred when there was significant unconscious psychological tension, when the contradictions in the conscious mind became untenable, and when the world was in a state of severe distress and seeking salvation. In response to the current world-wide unconscious stress, interest in UFO's has increased as the government has renamed UFO's the *unidentified areal phenomena* (UAP).

The World of Symbol – Jungian Analytical Psychology 153

Conscious tensions in the sixteenth century were enormous. The Reformation laid the foundation for ongoing violence between Catholics and Protestants, and the Thirty Years War. Copernicus proposed the heliocentric, nature-centered not man-centered universe, and the Scientific Revolution would change science forever. UFOs represented a psychological release and a belief that salvation might occur from a strong outer extraterrestrial force.

Jung (1958/1978) made famous the *1561 Celestial Phenomenon over Nuremberg,* where there was a mass sighting of UFOs. In a broadsheet news article in April 1561, residents of Nuremberg reported that there was an aerial battle of hundreds of crosses, globes, two lunar crescents, a black spear, and various-sized tubular objects that fought erratically overhead and crashed later outside of the city. The 1561 Celestial Phenomenon over Nuremberg symbolized in Jungian thought the emerging unconscious struggle between the natural, religious, and psychological tensions at the beginning of what scholars of the sixteenth century called the rise of Western Civilization and Islam. The UFOs symbolized the natural world, the crosses symbolized the religious, and the four globes symbolized the need for psychological wholeness and individuation.

Like Freud, Jung had grave concerns about the future of humanity, especially its capitulation to the mass psychology of communism, capitalism, fascism, and totalitarianism. Unlike Freud, he maintained a more optimistic perspective, especially if modern psychology could return humanity to the importance of history, the wisdom of the ancients, and the power of symbol and myth. Because of his deep connection to those forces, he perceived the UFO phenomenon as a positive psychological development in the modern world.

Figure 3.25

As this chapter ends, the flying saucer provides an important Jungian symbol for the emancipation of the modern world because of his hope for a psychological renaissance rooted in human history, ancient wisdom, myths, and symbols.

The flying saucer, being both oblong and round, integrated as masculine and feminine, and ultimately a mandala, is symbolic of the return of the Self, the process of individuation, and the emancipation of the human psyche.

Emancipatory Opportunities in Jungian Psychology

Discover Your Symbol(s)

Attend to the meaning of symbols not only in your dreams but the symbols you have created inside and outside your home and in your office at work. If none, create inner and outer symbols to psychologically expand your experience of the world.

Consider Jungian Analysis

The world of symbols comes alive in Jungian analysis, in dream analysis, understanding the practical value of archetypal energy, the relationship to shadow and the Self, the individuation process, and the healing nature of activating the wounded healer archetype. Remember that one of the most important requirements of dreamwork is to document the dream upon becoming awake. Besides journals, there are now iPhone apps to assist with dreamwork.

Read Man and His Symbols and the Red Book

Jung is a brilliant, stimulating writer, at times poetic, and his art is inspirational and magical.

Consider Sandplay Therapy

It is hard to imagine any therapy more enjoyable and meaningful. Sandplay therapy allows adults to again enjoy the world of play and for children it provides a place to communicate to the adult world. Providing a "psychic x-ray," sandplay therapy allows the client to take a picture and carry their symbols home on their iPhone.

Take the Myers-Briggs Indicator Test (MBTI)

One of the most utilized personality tests, the Meyers-Briggs offers a personality assessment that can apply to many settings, ranging from the workplace to marriage. Being a non-judgmental test, it can help assess where one stands on a continuum of introversion/extroversion, thinking/feeling, intuition/sensation, and judgment/perception.

Draw/Color a Mandala

As Jung noted, mandala work provides a way to connect to the Self, the organizing dynamic of the psyche, essential in the individuation process. The mandala has had an important place in human history, most notably with the Tibetan monks and Native Americans.

Discover Your Shadow

Understanding the dire consequences in history of shadow denial, take time to explore your own shadow by starting with the qualities you reject in other people and the areas that have been repressed in your personality because of socialization. Recommend: *Make Friends with Your Shadow* by William Miller (1981), *Owning Your Own Shadow* by Robert Johnson (1994), *Shadow Work Journal* by Victoria Stevens (2021), and Evaluate the Leadership at your Workplace from a Jungian Perspective. *In Mapping the Organizational Psyche: A Jungian Theory of Organizational Dynamics and Change,* Corlett and Carol Pearson (2003) outline ways to evaluate organizational life from a Jungian perspective and explains the need for archetypal balance in leadership positions and how an imbalance can create an unhealthy and dysfunctional workplace.

Practice Jungian Concepts in Community Mental Health Systems

Although cognitive-behavioral therapy concepts have shown significant efficacy in the treatment of serious mental illness, it has its limitations. Jung reminds us that individuals with mental illness are more than their diagnosis and more than their ego; they have special qualities that have the potential for healing not only themselves but the professionals that provide their treatment. Whether sandplay therapy, art therapy, or other creative therapies, a Jungian approach can facilitate a more complete treatment of serious mental illness.

Require Coursework on the Unconscious for APA Accreditation

With increasing neurobiological evidence supporting the existence of the unconscious as well as the current state of American culture, it is important to require teaching prospective clinical and counseling psychologists about the unconscious.

QUESTIONS 3

3.1 *Describe the political, socioeconomic, and cultural influences that led to the development of Jungian psychology.*

3.2 *Explain the differences that led to the Freud/Jung break.*

3.3 *Describe the natural and hermeneutic science influences on the development of Jungian psychology.*

3.4 *Explain the concepts of the Self, Individuation, archetype, collective unconscious, shadow, anima/animus, and wounded healer.*

3.5 *Describe the difference between Freudian and Jungian dream analysis.*

3.6 *Explain the Jungian approach to sandplay therapy.*

3.7 *Describe the influence of Jung on the development of Alcoholics Anonymous.*

3.8 *Explain how Jungian concepts can improve the workplace.*

3.9 *Describe Jung's approach to serious mental illness and the rationale for the lack of Jungians in community mental health.*

156   *The World of Symbol – Jungian Analytical Psychology*

Universal Meanings of the Chapter Symbols

Figure 3.0:
>   Image source Bill Wilson. https://agilewriter.com/Biography/Billwilson.htm
>
>   Image source James Hilman. https://scott.london/interviews/hillman.html
>
>   Image source Joseph Cambel and James Hilman. https://scott.london/interviews/hillman.html
>
>   Image source: Dora Kalff. https://nmsst.org/

Figure 3.1. The human experience enhanced by engagement with symbols.
Figure 3.2. The child archetype as a connection to the divine.
Figure 3.3. The discovery of the divine child.
Figure 3.4. The balance of power in American democracy.
Figure 3.5. The Bipolar Wotan in German culture.
Figure 3.6. The ability to access the psychological and spiritual power from the unconscious.
Figure 3.7. The unconscious wise man that provides guidance and psychological strength.
Figure 3.8. Messages to the conscious mind from the collective unconscious.
Figure 3.9. The universal need to return to perfection, enlightenment, and "heavenly bliss."
Figure 3.10. The death and rebirth process.
Figure 3.11. A libidinal symbol indicating psychological transformation.
Figure 3.12. The mask that hides the real self.
Figure 3.13. The overidentification with an archetype.
Figure 3.14. The organizing principle of human psyche.
Figure 3.15. Symbolic of a connection to a higher power.
Figure 3.16. The 2-million-year-old person in all of humanity.
Figure 3.17. The unconscious connection of humanity that transcends culture and national borders.
Figure 3.18. The unconscious aspect of personality which the ego rejects, cannot identify with consciously.
Figure 3.19. The feminine and masculine energies in the human psyche.
Figure 3.20. In dreamwork, importance of writing down a dream soon after becoming awake.
Figure 3.21. Psychological healing rooted in mythology.
Figure 3.22. Psychotherapy heals both the client and therapist.
Figure 3.23. Sand as a symbol of psychological healing and spiritual development.
Figure 3.24. The importance of social support in overcoming addiction.
Figure 3.25. Flying Saucers symbolic of the return to history, ancient wisdom and myth and symbol.

References

Adams, T. & Duncan, A. (Eds.) (2003). *The feminine case: Jung, aesthetics and the creative process*. London: Karnac Publishers.
Anonymous (1976). *Alcohol Anonymous: The story of how many thousands of men and women have recovered from alcoholism*. New York: Alcoholics Anonymous Word Series.
Black, C. (1981). *Raiders of the lost ark*. London: Severn House.
Bohler, E. (1970). Conscience in economic life. In James Hillman (Ed.). *Conscience: Studies in Jungian thought*. Evanston: Northwestern University Press.
Borotlin, M. (2015). *The Dharma of Star Wars*. Sommerville MA: Wisdom Publications.
Borotlin, M. (2019). *The Zen of R2-D2: Ancient wisdom from a galaxy far, far away*. Sommerville MA: Wisdom Publications.

Bridges, W. (2000). *The character of an organization: Using personality type in organizational development*. Boston MA: Nicholas Brealey Publishing.
Campbell, C. (1972). *Myths to live by: How we re-create ancient legends in our daily lives to release human potential*. New York: Penguin Books.
Campbell, J. (1973). *The hero with a thousand faces*. Princeton NJ: Princeton University Press. (Original Work published 1949).
Campbell, J. (1988). *The power of myth with Bill Moyers* (B.S. Flowers, Ed.). New York: Doubleday.
Corlett, L. & Pearson, C. (2003). *Mapping the organizational psyche: A Jungian theory of organizational dynamics and change*. Gainesville, FL: Center for Applications of Psychological Type Inc.
Damasio, A. (1999). *The feeling of what happens*. New York: Harcourt Press.
Dargert, G. (2016). *The snake in the clinic: Psychotherapy's role in medicine and healing*. London: Karnac Books, Ltd.
De Domenico, G.S. (1988). *Sand play world play: A comprehensive guide to the use of the sandtray in psychotherapeutic and transformational settings*. Oakland, CA: Author.
Deri, S. (1949). *Introduction to the Szondi Test: Theory and practice*. New York: Grune and Stratton
Downing, C. (1996). *Myth and mysteries of same-sex love*. New York: The Continuum Publishing Company.
Drewes, A. (Ed.). (2009). *Blending play therapy with cognitive behavioral therapy*. Hoboken NJ: John Wiley and Sons, Inc.
Ellenberger, H.F. (1970). *The discovery of the unconscious: The history and evolution of dynamic psychiatry*. New York: Basic Books.
Fordham, M. (1947). Integration, disintegration and early ego development. *Nervous Child*, 6, 3, 266–77.
Guggenuhl-Craig, A. (1971). *Power in the helping professions*. New York: Spring Press.
Hauke, C. (2000). *Jung and postmodern: The interpretation of realities*. London: Routledge.
Hillman, J. (1975). *Re-visioning psychology*. New York: Harper Perrennial.
Hopcke, R. (1991). *Jung, Jungians and homosexuality*. Boston, MA: Shambhala.
Johnson, R. (1994). *Owning your own shadow: Understanding the dark side of the psyche*. San Francisco, CA: HarperSan Francisco.
Jung, C.G. (1954). Archetypes and the collective unconscious. *Collected works of C.G. Jung*, (Vol 9) (Part 1). Princeton NJ: Princeton University Press. (Original Work published 1934).
Jung, C.G. (1960). *The psychogenesis of mental disease. The collected works of C.G. Jung*, (Vol. 3). Princeton, NJ: Princeton University Press. (Original work published in 1928).
Jung, C.G. (1928). *Contribution to analytic psychology*. New York: Harcourt Brace Jovanovich.
Jung, C.G. (1933). *Modern man in search of a soul*. New York: Harcourt Brace Jovanovich.
Jung, C.G. (1934). The practical use of dream analysis. *The collected works of C.G. Jung*, (Vol. 16). Princeton, NJ: Princeton University Press.
Jung, C.G. (1936). Wotan. *The collected works of C.G. Jung*, (Vol. 10). Princeton, NJ: Princeton University Press.
Jung, C.G. (1945). After the catastrophe. *The collected works of C.G. Jung*, (Vol. 10). Princeton, NJ: Princeton University Press.
Jung, C.G. (1958). *The undiscovered self*. New York: The New American Library.
Jung, C.G. (1963). *Memories, dreams, and reflections*. New York: Vintage Books.
Jung, C.G. (1964). *Man and his symbols*. London: Aldus Books Ltd.
Jung, C.G. (1974). Symbols of transformation. *The collective works of C.G. Jung*, (Vol. 5). Princeton, NJ: Princeton University Press.
Jung, C.G. (1978). *Flying saucers: A modern myth of things seen in the skies*. Princeton: Princeton University Press. (Original work published 1958).
Jung, C.G. (2002). *Psychology of the unconscious*. (B.M. Hinkle, Trans.) Garden city, NY: Dover Publications, Inc.
Jung, C.G. (2009). (S. Shamdasani, Ed.). *The red book: Liber novus*. New York: W.W. Norton & Company. (Original work published 1912).

Jung, C.G. (1971a). Psychology and alchemy. *The collective works of C.G. Jung*. (Vol. 12). Princeton, NJ: Princeton University Press. (Original work published 1944).

Jung, C.G. (1971b). Psychological types. *The collective works of C.G. Jung*. (Vol. 6). Princeton, NJ: Princeton University Press. (Original work published 1921).

Jung, C.G. & Freud, S. (1994). (W. McGuire, Ed.). *The Freud/Jung letters*. Princeton NJ: Princeton University Press. (Original work published in 1974).

Jung, C.G. & Kerenyi, C. (1959). *Essays on a science of mythology: The myth of the divine child and the mysteries of Eleusis*. New York: Princeton University Press.

Kalff, D. (1980). *Sandplay*. Santa Monica, CA: Sigo Press.

Karcher, S. (1999). Jung, the Tao and the classic of change. *Journal of Religion and Health*, 38, 287–304.

Kellogg, J. (1992). *Mandala: Path of beauty*. Virginia: Graphic Publishing of Williamsburg.

Kellogg, J., Rae, M., Bonny, H. & DiLeo, F. (1977). The use of the mandala in psychological evaluation and treatment. *American Journal of Art Therapy*, 16.

Kerr, J. (1994). *A most dangerous method: The story of Freud, Jung and Sabina Spielrein*. New York: Vintage Books.

Knox, J. (2003). *Archetype, attachment, analysis: Jungian psychology and the emergent mind*. New York: Brunner-Routledge.

Kreger, D.W. (2013). *The tao of Yoda*. Palmdale CA: Windham Everitt Publishing.

Lakoff, G. (1987). *Women, fire, and dangerous things*. Chicago, IL: University of Chicago Press.

Launer, J. (2014). *Sex versus survival. The life and ideas of Sabina Spielrein*. London: Bloomsbury Publishing.

Lean, G. (1985). *Frank Buchman: A life*. London: Constable.

Lowenfield, M. (1979). *The world technique*. Boston MA: Allen & Unwin, Institute of Child Psychology, (Published posthumously).

Lowenfeld, M. (2007). *Understanding children's' sandplay Lowenfield's world technique*. Portland: Sussex Academic Press.

Mark, M. & Pearson, C.S. (2001). *The hero and the outlaw: Building extraordinary brands through the power of archetypes*. New York: McGraw-Hill.

May, R. (1991). *Cry for myth*. New York: W.W. Norton & Company.

McKenzie, S. (2006). Queering gender: Animus/animus and the paradigm of emergence. *Journal of Analytical Psychology*. 51(3), 401–421.

Miller, W. (1981). *Make friends with your shadow*. Minneapolis, MN: Augsburg Fortress Publishers.

Mitchell, R.R. & Friedman, H.S. (1994). *Sandplay: Past, present and future*. London: Routledge.

Normandin, S. & Wolfe, C.T. (Eds.). (2013). *Vitalism and the scientific image in post-enlightenment life science, 1800–2010*. New York: Springer Press.

Owens, L.S. (2015). *Jung in love: The mysterium in Liber Novus*. Los Angeles, CA: Gnosis Archive Books.

Petchkovsky, L., Petchkovsky, M., Morris, P. & Dickson, P. et al (2013) fMRI responses to Jung's Word Association Test: Implications for theory, treatment and research. *Journal of Analytical Psychology*, 58(3), 409–431.

Rensma, R. (2013). Analytical psychology and the ghost of Lamarck: Did Jung believe in the inheritance of acquired characteristics. *Journal of Analytic Psychology*. 58(2), 258–277.

Rosen, S.J. (2010). *Jedi and the lotus: Star Wars and the Hindu tradition*. United Kingdom: Arktos Media Ltd.

Rowland, S. (2002). *Jung: A feminist revision*. Oxford: Polity & Blackwell

Samuels, A. (1985). *Jung and the post-Jungians*. London: Routledge & Kega n Paul.

Samuels, A. (1993). *The political psyche*. London: Routledge.

Schoen, D.E. (2009). *The war of the gods in addiction: C.G. Jung, Alcoholics Anonymous and archetypal evil*. New Orleans: Spring Journal Inc.

Schore, A. (1994). *Affect regulation and the origin of the self*. Hillsdale, NJ: Lawrence Erlbaum.

Sedgwick, D. (2001). *Introduction to Jungian psychotherapy: The therapeutic relationship*. New York: Brunner-Routledge

Shamdasani, S. (2003). *Jung and the making of modern psychology: A dream of science.* Cambridge: Cambridge University Press.

Slegelis, M.H. (1987). A study of Jung's Mandala and its relationship to art psychotherapy: The arts in psychotherapy, *Pergamon Journals Limited, 14,* 301–311.

Stern, D. (1985). *The interpersonal world of the infant.* New York: Basic Books.

Stevens, V. (2021). *Shadow Work Journal: The comprehensive guide for beginners to uncover the shadow self and become whole as your authentic self.* Author

Szondi, L. (1952). *Experimental diagnostics of drives.* New York: Grune and Stratton

Turner, B.A. (2005). *The handbook of sandplay therapy.* Cloverdale, CA: Temenos Press.

von Daniken, E. (1999). *The chariot of the Gods.* New York: The Berkeley Publishing Group.

von Schelling, F.W. (1995). *Schelling's philosophy of mythology and revelation.* Australia: Australian Association for the Study of Religions. (Original work published 1857).

Weinrib, E.L. (2004). *Images of the self.* Cloverdale, CA: Temenos Press.

Wells, H.G. (2016). *Floor games and little wars.* Springfield, Ill: Monroe St. Press. (Original work published in 1911)

Wilhelm, R. (Ed.) (1997). *I Ching: Book of changes.* Princeton: Princeton University Press.

Wilhelm, R. (2023). *The secret of the golden flower: A Chinese book of life.* New York: Harcourt Brace & Co,

Wilkinson, M. (2004). The mind-brain relationship: The emergent self. *Journal of Analytical Psychology, 49*(1), 83–101.

Wilmer, H.A. (1987). *Practical Jung: Nuts and bolts of Jungian psychotherapy.* Wilmette, Ill: Chiron Publications.

Zoja, E.P. (2011). *Sandplay therapy in vulnerable communities.* New York: Routledge Press.

Figure 4.0

4 Symbols of Behaviorism, Neobehaviorism, and Cognitive Behavioral Psychology

The Second Force in Psychology

Introduction

In the article *Looking for Skinner and Finding Freud*, Geir Overskeid (2007) outlined many similarities between psychoanalysis and behaviorism. Many students view Skinner and Freud as adversaries. The truth is that they have much in common, especially in their analysis of the state of civilization. Followers often need to perceive differences more than similarities, which can cause psychological dogmatism and orthodoxy and empower each side to claim the truth and demean the other side.

Freud (1930/1961), in *Civilization and Its Discontents,* and Skinner (1987), in "Why Are We Not Acting to Save the World," took a dim view of civilization. Both admonished people to understand that the forces controlling humanity were not under their conscious control. Freud and Skinner agreed, through different theories, that these forces were not conscious. For Freud, it was the *unconscious* power of instinctual id forces. For Skinner (1978), it was the lack *societal engineering* based on positive reinforcement and operant conditioning and the many behaviorists that followed; the "mind" is simply symbolic of the reinforcements and the social conditioning coming from the external world.

Three Generations of Behavioral Psychology

This chapter will explore the development of the *Second Force in Psychology* through behaviorism, neobehaviorism, and cognitive behavioral psychology. To simplify, in behaviorism, behaviorists were creating an alternative to psychoanalysis. In neobehaviorism, the goal was to advance behaviorism and change human behavior as well as society. In cognitive behavioral psychology, a major goal was to use the learnings from behaviorism and neobehaviorism to advance mental health treatment.

Unlike most prominent psychologists of the time, many behaviorists became the strongest opponents of eugenics and played a key role in its demise because behaviorists rejected the overemphasis in psychology on heredity and innate predisposition as the basis for mental or social problems.

162 *Symbols of Behaviorism, Neobehaviorism, and Cognitive Psychology*

Figure 4.1

Rather, behaviorists turned the focus toward the importance of the environment in social conditioning. Neobehaviorism showed how punishment reinforced bad behavior and positive reinforcement reinforced good behavior, which transformed parenting and many mental and developmentally disabled institutions. Cognitive behavioral psychology showed how learning could change thoughts and behavior no matter the mental health diagnosis or intrapsychic problems, which transformed public and private psychotherapeutic treatment. In recent years, many cognitive behavioral therapists embraced Buddhist philosophy and mindfulness as a way to cope with the stresses of the modern world.

Until the development of cognitive behavioral psychology, early behaviorism viewed the individual as determined by external environmental forces, rejecting the internal, subjective mind. Until recently, the overemphasis on supremacy of thoughts and behavior as the total representation of being a human being has been viewed by critics as neglecting many other aspects of being alive, most notably individual uniqueness and emotion and feeling, which inspired the development of the next chapter, *Humanistic-Existential Psychology*, the *Third Force in psychology*. This chapter will discuss the reality that emotional development has been a challenge for many of the most prominent visionaries in the behaviorist movement.

Cognitive behavioral therapy (CBT) continues to be supported as the main psychotherapeutic approach by the power brokers in the American Psychological Association (APA). Although the APA claims therapeutic neutrality in its standards for accreditation of its doctoral clinical programs, curriculum requirements are slanted toward teaching "empirically-based" and "evidence-best practices," which fit best with the concrete, conscious-focused, CBT approach. Brian Sharpless and Jacques Barber (2013) reported that a key determinant for successful passage of the national licensing exam in clinical psychology was the number of CBT faculty that taught psychologists during their graduate education.

Cognitive behavioral therapy (CBT) has become one of the most successful psychotherapies for its focus on practical solutions. It has emancipated the mental and emotional anguish of millions of people. CBT fits well with an American culture interested in quick and pragmatic solutions. Since symptom reduction is one of the major focuses of its research, it also fits well with the current empirical research bias in American psychology. Ironically, CBT therapists often select a psychodynamic psychotherapy for their own therapeutic experience (Norcross, Bike, & Evans, 2009).

Behavioral Psychological Movement

Historical Analysis of the Behavioral Psychological Movement

Political Systems

John Locke, the early father of behaviorism, applied his empiricism and rejection of innate ideas to political systems. He disagreed with the assumption that there were innate moral truths and that hereditary should determine political power. Locke (1690/1974) believed that every human being should seek truth for themselves rather than have "truth" imposed upon them. He rejected the divine right of kings, absolute monarchies, and the aristocracies. Locke is considered the father of liberalism, liberalism in terms of political and moral philosophy grounded in liberty, consent of the governed, and equality before the law. His liberalism reflected American conservative values of free markers, free trade, capitalism, and limited government as Locke believed that big government imposed, rather than developed, individual liberty.

Liberal philosophy became a political movement during *the Age of Enlightenment* and inspired the British *Glorious Revolution* of 1688, the *American Revolution* of 1776, and the *French Revolution* of 1788. The writers of the American *Declaration of Independence* were inspired by Locke's doctrine of liberalism. During the nineteenth century, liberal democracies expanded in Europe and America. In America, liberalism resulted in a Republican form of government. Although Democratic and Republican forms of government require that its citizens elect their representatives, a Republican form of government has more concern about protecting the rights of the minority from the will of the majority. For example, the smallest populous state of Wyoming, with over 700,000 citizens, has just as many senators, two, in the American Congress as the largest populous state of California with 40 million citizens.

In the twentieth century, Lockean liberalism found itself on the side of winning two world wars and the defeat of totalitarianism and fascism throughout the world. Liberalism, as it is currently known in the United States, became social liberalism and created social safety nets; and some say, a welfare state. In many ways, social liberalism saved the shadow side of economic exploitation of capitalism from the emerging communist revolutions. Although significant social and economic disparities remain, social liberalism changed the face of American capitalism. During the Great Depression of the 1930s, the New Deal championed by President Franklin Roosevelt saved capitalism from a total collapse. Social liberalism answered communism with President John Kennedy's New Frontier and the expansion of civil rights by President Lyndon Johnson's Great Society, which saved America from racial disintegration.

The political philosophy of John Locke was embraced enthusiastically by utilitarian progressives. The founder of modern utilitarianism, Jeremy Bentham (1988) lived his axiom that it is the greatest happiness by the greatest number that measures right and wrong. His radical progressivism would humble even so-called modern reformers. He advocated for democracy, free expression, the separation of church and state, the rights of women, gay rights, right to divorce, animal rights, as well as the abolition of slavery, capital punishment, and punishment of children. He influenced Robert Owen, one of the founders of utopian socialism. Bentham advocated for social welfare programs and influenced the reform of prisons, schools, poverty laws, courts, and Parliament itself. He rejected the popular theories of natural law and natural rights because they were based on divine or God-given rights, not on human rights or the rights of all people for happiness no matter their standing in the world.

In the later nineteenth and early twentieth century, John Dewey was a leader in the progressive movement, which was the modern American version of the Enlightenment. Dewey believed that psychology needed to be actively involved in solving social problems. He argued that the concept of democracy had to permeate all aspects of American life. Influenced by the French Enlightenment, Dewey explained how a class-based society denied its citizens the opportunity to reach their full potential. His hope was that an empirical science utilizing rational planning and ascribing to democratic principles would solve social inequalities. The philosophy of progressivism fit American culture, which mistrusted authority, aristocracies, and politicians. For Dewey (1916), individuals acquire their sense of being and their personality only from society and that individual fulfillment results from being in harmony with the goals and values of community. Psychologists needed to be involved in all levels of society, including government, education, and business. A progressive government would decrease class-based disparities by being governed by scientists, experts, and highly educated experts and bureaucrats.

The *Vienna Circle* became political through public lectures and conferences throughout Europe and the United States by attempting to apply logical positivism and scientific principles to solve political issues. The Vienna Circle advocated for the liberation of the working classes. Although known for its natural science and anti-metaphysical viewpoints, its manifesto linked Karl Marx and Friedrich Nietzsche to their political cause. Friedrich Albert Schlick, the chair of the Vienna Circle and father of *logical positivism* that inspired neobehaviorism, appeared to have been murdered for either his philosophic, ethnic, or political views. With the rise of Nazism and fascism in Europe, many members of the *Vienna Circle* left for the United States. Schlick decided to remain at the *University of Vienna* and was murdered in 1936 by a former student, John Nelbock; the famous case linked to nationalist and anti-Jewish sentiment. After the annexation of Austria to Nazi Germany, the 10-year sentence of Nelbock was reduced to 2 years.

Edward Tolman, the molecular purposive behaviorist, grew up in a social reform–minded Quaker family. He would go on to become to be an outspoken pacifist, which led in 1918 to his dismissal from *Northwestern University*. In an ironic twist for a behaviorist, Tolman (1942) wrote a short book, *Drives Toward War,* that described motivations for warfare from a psychoanalytic perspective. As a professor of psychology at the *University of California, Berkeley* (UCB), during the anti-communist McCarthyism of the 1950s, he refused to sign a loyalty oath and was suspended. He believed the loyalty oath violated his civil liberties and academic freedom. The courts eventually agreed with Tolman, and he was reinstated. In 1959, shortly before his death, UCB conferred Tolman with an honorary doctoral degree and acknowledged that he had made the correct moral decision in opposing the loyalty oath. Tolman was the 45th president of the APA.

Noam Chomsky, considered the father of modern linguistics and one of the most severe critics of Skinnerian neobehaviorism, is a political activist who landed on President Nixon's enemy list because he was one of the most outspoken opponents of the Vietnam War, a war Chomsky viewed as an act of American imperialism. Chomsky (1967) rose to national prominence with an anti-war essay entitled *The Responsibility of Intellectuals,* in which he argued that intellectuals were largely subservient to the power structure. He was particularly critical of psychologists and other social scientists whom he believed were providing pseudoscientific justification for "crimes of the state," defined as America violating national and international laws. During the Vietnam War, Chomsky reframed a Dwight MacDonald question, a mid-century cultural critic who believed war guilt of World War II should also apply to Americans for the nuclear bombings of Nagasaki and Hiroshima, with a similar question asking psychologists and other intellectuals, "What have I done to end the morally bankrupt Vietnam War?".

In 2017, on the 50th anniversary of The Responsibility of Intellectuals, a conference was held at the University College of London to reflect on the continued challenge, and the price intellectuals had paid, for challenging the status quo and the power structure. The conference produced a book entitled *Responsibilities of Intellectuals: Reflections of Noam Chomsky and Others after 50 years* (Allot, Knight, & Smith, 2020). Chomsky and other political activists reflected on how those of privilege continue to abdicate their political responsibilities to resist the corrupt and morally bankrupt policies and practices of the current power structure. He has continued to make stinging criticisms of American foreign policy, arguing that the War on Terror was a continuation of American international policies in the post-Reagan era. Chomsky (2013) became a strong critic of the Iraqi War and the lack of American resolve to truly work toward resolving the Israel-Palestinian conflict. Believing that democracy in America was in a regressive state, Chomsky supported various national Democratic efforts like the Occupy Wall Street Movement, inspired by the Arab Spring Movements, which highlighted the growing economic inequities in the United States. Chomsky delivered talks at the *Occupy Movement* encampments and produced two pamphlets that documented their development and influence: *Occupy* (Chomsky, 2012) and *Occupy: Reflections on Class War, Rebellion and Solidarity* (Chomsky, 2013).

Chomsky was also concerned about the political power of the media. Chomsky (2002) co-authored with Edward Herman, *Manufacturing Consent, The Political Economy of the Mass Media.* In this book, they argued that the mass media in the United States had become powerful ideological institutions that provided a propaganda function by their overreliance on corporations. Although much subtler than the propaganda organs of authoritarian states, like the former Soviet Union, the American media censors any opinions that do not support corporate capitalism. Although the media criticizes individual politicians and parties, there are no real commentators like socialist or libertarian journalists questioning the unholy alliance between corporations and government, or what Chomsky called the state-corporate nexus.

The result was that important news stories like the possible involvement of the FBI in the murder of Black Panther Fred Hampton are never accurately reported. Ironically, in 2021, the movie *Judas, and the Black Messiah* received critical acclaim for its cinematic exploration of the Black Panther Party and the events surrounding Fred Hampton's death. Because a psychologist provided the inspiration for Manufacturing Consent, Chomsky and Herman dedicated the book to the memory of Australian social psychologist Alex Carey (1922–1987) for his pioneer work on corporate propaganda. In 1997, in a posthumous collection of his essays, Carey (1997) explained the history of corporate propaganda, whose goals he believed were not based on truth, but on manipulating public opinion for economic exploitation and consolidating corporate political power.

Socioeconomic Systems

The socioeconomic foundation of behaviorism was in close alignment with revolutionary movements that occurred in Russia, Europe, and America. In Russia, Pavlov, Bekhterev, and Sechenov were in close alignment with the Bolshevik Revolution. Pavlov was acknowledged by Lenin as a *Hero of the Revolution*. Many reformers were interested in the study of economics to improve the human condition, and thereby, human psychology. In America, the liberalism of John Locke, James Mill, John Stuart Mill, and others inspired American revolutionaries who rejected English monarchical rule and supported the creation of a republic that would become a model for revolutions throughout the world.

However, by the mid-twentieth century, the history of the behaviorist-inspired social reform movements faded as psychology became more anti-historical and American-centric. Rejected was the spirit of Jeremy Bentham (1988), who believed the only reason for behaviorism to exist was to change the world.

The move away from history coincided with less focus on social reform and support for the status quo and the American capitalistic system. As the Great Depression was raging in the United States, Watsonian psychology helped strengthen capitalism. After losing his job at John Hopkins University, John Watson found an advertising job at *J. Walker Thompson*. The loss for psychology was certainly an economic gain for Wall Street and Watson himself because during the Depression he received a salary of $70,000, which was astronomical at that time. This certainly changed his economic class status from low to high and from impoverished to privileged.

Watson became a leading figure in what would become known as *market research*. Watsonian psychology set an example of the manipulation and the power of symbol to connect at an unconscious level. When Watson blindfolded smokers and discovered their inability to find any difference in cigarette brands, he realized it was not the actual product that was important, but the symbol attached to the product that was the key to marketing goods to the public.

In *Highlights of Dr. John B. Watson's Career in Advertising,* Charles Larson (1979) explained how Watson increased profits for so many companies, including Johnson & Johnson Baby Powder, Pebeco Toothpaste, Maxwell House Coffee, and many other products. Watson became vice president of William Etsy Advertising until his retirement at 67, after procuring substantial personal wealth. The principles of Watsonian behaviorism and market research continue to support American capitalism.

Symbols of Behaviorism, Neobehaviorism, and Cognitive Psychology 167

Figure 4.2

Cultural Systems

Behaviorism has been influenced mostly by white men who have been culturally discouraged from developing a strong emotional life. Even James Mill, a nineteenth-century progressive utilitarian, practiced behaviorist psychological theories to raise his son, John Stuart Mill, without emotions and feelings. Subsequently, he suffered from a lifelong struggle with depression and later in adulthood reported that he was never able to develop a lasting loving relationship. Ivan Pavlov, the father of conditioned reflex, showed more love for his laboratory equipment than for his family. Auguste Comte, the father of positivism, suffered from suicidal thoughts, including an actual suicide attempt. John Watson, the father of American behaviorism, was a pioneer and a cultural phenomenon regarding the use of the media to educate the public with psychological knowledge often locked away in academia. Whether one agreed or disagreed with his theoretical approaches, Watson emancipated psychology from the confines of academic isolation and paved the way for future psychologists to use the media to impact the cultural lives of the American people.

Watson married Mary Ickes, the sister of Harold L. Ickes, Secretary of the Interior for 13 years under President Franklin Roosevelt. Ickes, a Republican, was responsible for implementing much of the "New Deal." Although in this prestigious family, Watson's heart belonged to Rosalie Rayner. His affair with Rosalie would become a scandal, and in 1920, Johns Hopkins University would ask him to resign. The scandal would forever tarnish his reputation and prevent Watson from ever being offered another academic position.

After losing his position at Johns Hopkins University, Watson became the "Doctor Spock" of his time. He wrote educational articles on psychology and appeared on talk shows. He applied his radical behaviorism to parent and family education. With Rosalie Rayner, John Watson (1928) wrote *The Psychological Care of the Infant and Child,* which sold over 100,000 copies in the late 1920s, applying their adverse reaction to the expression of emotion to marriage and family life. Their advice was antithetical to Dr. Spock because Watson's major recommendation was that parents should treat their children "like young adults" and never let them sit on their lap, kiss them only on the forehead, pat them on the head when they were good and shake hands with them at bedtime

Watson wrote that in a 100 years men would not want to marry, and that the family life would become obsolete. He admired Freud for uncovering the importance of sex and argued that parents should not be afraid to talk frankly and take responsibility to educate their children about sexuality. Although Bertrand Russell felt his approach to parental education was too focused on environment and lacked the importance of emotional support, Russell was impressed that not since Aristotle and Plato had someone raised the thought that it might not be that valuable for parents and children to know each other. At the time, other some psychologists were not impressed and believed that Watson had demeaned psychology by promoting a "pop psychology" that lacked scientific rigor.

McDougall, father of purposive behaviorism, noted in his great debate with Watson that Watson has unable to engage at an emotional level. Although Watson was charming and self-assured, emotional disaster followed him throughout his personal life. In *Behave*, Andromeda Romano-Lax (2016) provided a riveting fictional account of life with Watson from the viewpoint of Rosalie Rayner, his betrayed wife, and an often-forgotten woman in the history of psychology. After her death, he became even more emotionally withdrawn from his children. His son, James, although having suffered from bouts of depression throughout his life, went on to receive a degree in industrial psychology and become a successful corporate executive. His elder son, Billy, who had a lifelong contemptuous relationship with his father, was not so fortunate. Watson viewed it as a "slap in the face" when Billy became a psychiatrist and rejected behaviorism. Although they attempted to mend their differences, Billy would eventually commit suicide.

The neobehaviorists typically grew up in a Protestant American culture, influenced by Judeo-Christian values. Tolman's pacifism was influenced by Quakers; the mother of Skinner inculcated strong moral values, but like Freud, Skinner believed organized religion had only made societal problems worse. Much of the criticism and shadow of behaviorism was that it was overly mechanical and emotionally sterile. The practical value of Skinnerian theories often obscured the lack of the emotional depth needed to become a fully developed human being. Skinner himself was reported to have had a great sense of humor and ironically one of his first loves was poetry and literature. He was especially proud that the famous poet Robert Frost favorably reviewed three of his short stories.

Although a few women began to emerge with the development of cognitive behavioral psychology, the behaviorist field remained dominated by men, especially men with an immigrant Jewish cultural background, which was another example of the contributions of immigrants to American culture. The parents of Nerbert Weiner and Albert Bandura were Jewish immigrants from Poland and Germany, and Poland and Ukraine, respectively. The grandparents of Albert Ellis were Jewish immigrants from the Russian Empire and Uric Neisser was a Jewish immigrant from Kiel, Germany.

Alan Turing, one of the greatest minds of the twentieth century, influential in the development of theoretical computer science lost his life from the cultural dominance of heterosexualism. He was convicted in 1952 for indecency based on the *British Criminal Law*

Amendment Act of 1885. He was offered a choice between imprisonment and probation which meant agreement to undergo hormonal changes designed to reduce his libido. The injections caused impotence and the formation of breasts. After 1952, he was denied entry into the United States but was free to travel throughout Europe. In June 1954, Turing was found dead at the age of 41, supposedly by cyanide poisoning. When his body was discovered, a half-eaten apple was found beside his bed. Although it was not tested, it was believed that this was how Turing consumed his fatal dose. Other theories emerged that he was lax with laboratory experiments, that he was assassinated by British authorities who worried that communists could entrap homosexuals to gather intelligence, or even his despondency over a recent fortune teller experience.

The title of *The Imitation Game*, a 2014 British film based on the 1983 biography *Alan Turing: The Enigma* by Andrew Hodges (2014) used the name of the game Turing proposed for answering the question as to whether machines could think. It received eight Academy Award nominations, winning Best Adapted Screenplay. In 2014, the Queen of England officially apologized and pardoned Turing of gross indecency.

This led to efforts by gay right groups to expand the retroactive exoneration convictions of similar offenses. In 2017, *The Alan Turing Law* passed, which now provides retroactive pardon for men who were cautioned or convicted under previous laws that outlawed homosexual sex in England or Wales.

Figure 4.3

The apple of Turing symbolizes how the destructive shadow of culture can lead to physical and psychological death when culture systems deny someone the ability to become who they really are. It is also a sad reminder of the cultural impact well into the twentieth century that homosexuality in America was diagnosed as a mental illness. In Greek and Roman mythology, the apple symbolizes the human need to have sexual desire toward their lover. Dionysius offered apples to Aphrodite to win her heart and love and the Roman goddess Venus is often pictured with an apple to express the importance of love and desire. Although debunked as the inspiration for the symbol of Apple computers, when Steve Jobs was asked if the Apple symbol was based on Turing, he replied that he wished it was, but it was just a coincidence (BBC, 2014).

With the cognitive revolution in psychology came interest in the psychological and cultural impact of computers and artificial intelligence. The field of *robotics* became a particular focus, psychology being part of an interdisciplinary field that integrated computer science and engineering. The first fully autonomous robots were created in the 1960s, with the first digitally operated and programmed robot. Called Ultimate, it could lift hot pieces of metal from a die casting machine and stack them. This led to the hope that robots would one day be able to mimic human behavior. That hope became reality since robots are now assisting humans with mundane as well as dangerous activities. These activities include but are not limited to manufacturing assembly, mining, sea and space exploration, transportation, hotel and retail services, medical care and surgery, production of consumer and industrial products, and policing.

The possibilities of robotic support to humans are endless. However, history teaches that a shadow is always present. In 1921, Karel Capek produced a science-fiction play, *Rossum's Universal Robots (R.U.R)*, which introduced the word robot into the English language. Robot derived from the Czech word *robota*, meaning serf labor or drudgery. The play began in a factory that made artificial people called robots from synthetic organic material. The robots appeared as humans because they were not machines but rather living creatures of artificial flesh and blood. In fact, they could easily be mistaken for human beings because they could think for themselves. Initially they appeared satisfied working for humans, but as time went on, they became very dissatisfied and rebelled. As a warning of the potential shadow elements of robotics, the rebellion led to the extinction of humanity (Koreis, 2013).

It is hard to find areas in American culture unaffected by behaviorism. Educational and mental health institutions and well as family life have been significantly impacted by behaviorism. Cognitive behavioral therapy has transformed the lives of many suffering from mental disturbance. In the final analysis, behaviorism reminds us that a society that reinforces positive cultural values is healthier and more democratic than one that controls behavior through punitive or authoritarian methods.

Behaviorism

Natural Science Interest in Behaviorism

Newtonian Science

The seventeenth century marked the dawn of empirical science that would provide the basis for not only behaviorism, but for modern psychology itself. The century marked the works of Bacon, Newton, and Galileo, which would lay the foundation for the development of modern science. For these scientists, the empirical experimental method of investigation would remove the superstitions of the Church and metaphysics of philosophy. Science would become "the new religion."

It was only inevitable that experimental science would eventually apply to the mind. Francis Bacon (1620/1994), in his *Novum Organum*, set the tone that would forever dominate modern science. He argued that experimental science and the empirical method were the best explanations for understanding the world. In effect, nature existed in service to mankind.

John Locke might be considered the true father of modern behaviorism. He rejected innate ideas and believed at birth the mind was a blank slate, a *tabula rasa*. Locke had deep admiration for Newton, which led to Locke's greatest contribution to psychology and the nature of the mind. In *An Essay Concerning Human Understanding*, Locke (1690/1974) became one of the first to define self as the continual unfolding of a conscious mind. He rejected Augustinian original sin and the innate propositions of Descartes, and argued for the "empty mind," one shaped by sensations and reflections.

The study of the mind fit the empirical method because of the emerging belief that the mind could be investigated like all scientific phenomena, by its relationship to the natural world. Many behaviorists accept the sensations aspect of Lockean theory but forget that he also believed in a reflective mind. He believed that the source of ideas came completely from within. In contrast to other philosophers of his time, Locke believed reflections of the internal and external were very much the same. In other words, consciousness was the development of an internal sense that included direct sensory experiences or reflections of prior sensory experiences.

The Lockean theory of mind developed significantly from Newton's corpuscular theory of light. In his understanding, Locke and Newton became close friends and remained in correspondence throughout their lives. Ironically, they viewed religion as more important than science because they were both deeply religious men.

Locke adopted the Newtonian minute corpuscles theory that all physical properties had just a few primary chemical qualities that could divide into secondary qualities. This theory was like *atomism* except, unlike atoms, corpuscles could be seen and divided into different chemical forms; mercury could penetrate metals and modify its structure and turn into gold. Ironically *corpuscularianism* blended ancient alchemy and became a prevailing theory during early Newtonian science. For Locke, the mind operated in a similar manner. He adopted, and early behaviorists later, a universe that was a large-scale interactive machine that explained the universe in terms of matter and motion. The mind operated in a mechanical interactional way like in physics and chemistry. In physics, simple ideas were like atoms and could not be divided or analyzed. In chemistry, complex ideas were like corpuscles and could be divided and analyzed.

Locke proved his theory with the *paradox of the basins*. Simple ideas or primary qualities were exemplified when his subjects put their hands in three water basins. Basin (A) contained cold water, basin (B) contained hot water, and basin (C) contained warm water. When the subjects put their hand in (A) and (B), they felt cold and hot water. Proving that cold and hot are invisible primary qualities. However, when the subjects placed both of their hands in the warm water of basin (C), the hand that was in the cold basin (A) felt hot, and the hand that was in the hot basin (B) felt cold. This occurred even though the warm water in basin (C) was physically the same for both hands.

Locke believed the mind operated in a similar matter. Some psychological processes experience the world as it physically exists which are caused by its primary qualities. In rejecting the Galilean view that subjective reality was inferior to physical reality and that psychology could never be a science, Locke believed he had proven that secondary subjective qualities could be studied empirically, leaving a legacy that psychology could indeed be a science. This also led to an empirical and natural science bias in behaviorism and psychology.

172 *Symbols of Behaviorism, Neobehaviorism, and Cognitive Psychology*

Darwinian Natural History Method

Darwin set the stage for a biopsychosocial approach to human behavior. The approach was biological because humans needed to "breed well" for an organism to survive; psychological, because humans had to adapt to the constant mental and emotional pressures of survival; and social, because the fate of an organism was inextricably connected to the collective realities of the social world. Darwin developed a *natural history method* of inquiry in which he studied the historical life of a species over the known course of its existence.

The method required examining behavior within the natural contexts in which they occurred to provide a more complete understanding of the conditions faced by individual members of a specific species. The natural history method created knowledge of the instincts and personality traits that were not only essential to the success and survival of a specific species but might have universal consequence to all species.

Early psychologists laid the foundation for comparative psychology and behaviorism by often utilizing the natural history method. George Romanes (1848–1894), the youngest colleague of Darwin, wrote many books on the interface between psychology, religion and evolution (Romanes & Gore, 1902). Romanes was considered one of the first to use the term *neo-Darwinism*, the belief that natural selection was the main evolutionary force (Romanes, 1888).

Figure 4.4

Romanes (1888) attempted to model the Darwinian natural history methodology to trace the evolution of the human mind. Romanes (1882) described the mental and physical functions associated with the animal world and argued that animal, like human, intelligence evolved through behavioral conditioning and positive reinforcement. Romanes' approach was *anthropomorphic*; he attributed human thought, intelligence, and emotions to nonhuman animals. He ascribed anger, fear and jealousy to fish; pride, affection, and sympathy to birds; and shyness and reason to dogs. These were powerful Darwinian symbols of an emotional connection to our animal ancestors.

Conwy Llyod Morgan (1852–1936), an early proponent of comparative psychology, attempted to correct the anthropomorphism of Romanes as many in the scientific community perceived his attribution of human emotions to animals as unscientific. In response to Romanes, Morgan (1891/1900) developed what became known as *Morgan's Canon,* which states: in no case is an animal activity to be interpreted of higher psychological processes if it can be fairly interpreted in terms of processes which stand lower in the scale of psychological evolution and development. Believing that animals did possess human-like feelings, Morgan did not reject all forms of anthropomorphism; rather, he argued that the mental and emotional processes of animals could *only* be understood in relation to their unique species and should limit any comparisons to humans. He questioned how animals could experience a sense of beauty, justice, and right and wrong. He warned that scientists should not consider the reflexive and simple cognitive processes of animals with the complexity of the human mind and emotions.

Because of her interest in animal intelligence, Margaret Washburn (1871–1939) continued in the natural history tradition of Romanes and Canon. In *The Animal Mind: A Textbook of Comparative Psychology* (Washburn,1908), like Romanes and Canon, Washburn was interested in inferring the implications of animal consciousness to human behavior and developed experimental methods which would inspire future comparative psychologists. Although rooted in behaviorism, Washburn would later become critical of future behaviorists who denied any form of human consciousness. Washburn was a prolific researcher of animals beyond the typical use by psychologists of rats. She studied more than 100 species including, but not limited to, ants, bees, caterpillars, monkeys, pigeons, clams, cockroaches, cows, crabs, crayfish, raccoons, dragonflies, earthworms, flies, leeches, goldfish, grasshoppers, guinea pigs, horses, and many others. In *The Animal Mind,* Washburn (1908) devoted an entire chapter to the amoeba.

As a brilliant woman, Washburn had to withstand severe discrimination from a male-dominated academic community. Washburn was the first doctoral student of Edward Titchener, the founder of *structuralism*, who became her teacher, mentor, and advocate. Besides creating the largest doctoral program in psychology during its time, Titchener was best known after becoming president of Cornell University in 1894, in helping Washburn become the first woman to receive a doctoral degree in psychology in the United States. Washburn would become a prominent leader in the APA, and after Mary Calkins, in 1921, become the second female president of the APA.

Animal Intelligence and Instrumental Learning

Edward Thorndike (1874–1949) was a student of William James, who became his mentor. A follower of Galton, and a promoter of eugenic theory, He would provide the bridge between functionalism and behaviorism. Thorndike (1898) would become one of the leading proponents of laboratory animal research and learning theory. Thorndike advanced natural history research methods by studying animal behavior, not in the natural environment, but in the controlled environment of a laboratory where he could utilize empirical methods. Thorndike was known for living with his animals and raised chicks in his bedroom. His animals would later become part

174 *Symbols of Behaviorism, Neobehaviorism, and Cognitive Psychology*

of his laboratory research. When the landlady of his apartment building forbade the practice, after many unsuccessful attempts to find another place, William James provided his own home basement for Thorndike's animal research.

Thorndike (1898) wrote the first psychology doctoral dissertation in which only nonhuman subjects were studied. In *Animal Intelligence: An Experimental Study of the Association Process in Animals*, Thorndike (1911) found that the empirical study of animal behavior had implications for understanding how humans learn. He became one of the early leading learning theorists in psychology.

Thorndike developed the *laws of behavior,* which he discovered from his animal research. He is known for his research with chicks, rats, dogs, and monkeys, but his most famous study was the *Puzzle Box* research with cats. The Puzzle Box was organized so that when a desired behavior occurred, such as pulling a lever, the door of the box opened. A hungry cat would learn that pulling a lever led to escape and the reward of a piece of fish. His findings would influence the later development of the operant conditioning of Skinnerian psychology that positive reinforcement increased behavior; negative reinforcement decreased behavior. He found that learning could occur incrementally or automatically. Instrumental learning occurred slowly but then quickly after the successful consequences of many satisfying experiences. Learning could also occur automatically, without any prior successful experiences. Most controversial was his conclusion that humans and animals basically learn in the same way, that animals have similar intelligence. The puzzle box was an early symbol of animal intelligence and the similarity in learning between the animal and human world.

Figure 4.5

In reaction to the popular faculty psychology of his day, Thorndike believed he had proven that animals do not have to use any inner faculties; especially insight, to learn or problem-solve (Galef, 1998). His theory of *connectionism* focused on how learning occurred through the strength of neural connections between sensory impressions and experience. Learning occurred from the effect of doing something. In the puzzle box experiment, the cat did not learn to open the box from mental insight but from the intensity of the sensory connection to the stimuli, in this case the fish. This led Thorndike to believe that learning could occur without any involvement of internal mental processes which would be in concert with the early behavioral movement.

Although Thorndike believed learning could occur without any internal mental processes, he was not a pure behaviorist because of his belief in *associationism*: one mental state affects later successor mental states. He included associationism in his theories of *laws of exercise and effect*, which were the first major theories of learning in modern psychology, although Aristotle and other classical philosophers had discovered these learning theories in previous centuries. The difference was that Thorndike translated these concepts into modern scientific terms and supported his theories with laboratory experimentation.

The law of exercise had two aspects, use and disuse. According to the law of use, if an association is followed by a positive consequence, the learning was strengthened. The law of disuse occurred when an association was weakened by lack of ongoing experiences. The law of effect happened when an association was strengthened by a "satisfying state of affairs," and weakened by an "annoying state of affairs." For many years, the implication of his laws influenced education and teaching concerning the best way to teach students and how students best learn. For instance, Thorndike explored the question of mental muscle, the belief in education of the transfer of training theory. This theory posed that studying difficult subjects, like Latin, would enhance general intelligence and make it easier to study less difficult topics.

In his *identical elements of transfer theory*, Thorndike (1903) answered the question. The transfer of learning occurred when topics were similar or the same. However, he rejected mental muscle theory in education because he found that when two topics were dissimilar, learning was not transferable. Like many influential scientists in history, Thorndike revised his theories later in life. For instance, he rejected his earlier position on punishment and found that punishment was not effective in modifying behavior.

Thorndike spent most his career as a psychologist at *Teacher's College* in Columbia University, New York City. Because of his vision of integrating learning theory and psychometric testing, Thorndike (1903) is often considered the father of *educational psychology*. Publishing over 500 books, monographs, and journal articles, he has been ranked as one of the most influential psychologists in the twentieth century, Thorndike received several awards, most notably international awards from the British Psychological Society and the Leningrad Scientific-Medical Pedological Society. In 1912, he served as president of the APA. The shadow of eugenics marred his legacy because he believed that intelligence was mostly inheritable, and he supported a "stratified" education system based on sex and race. In 2020, after the murder of George Floyd, the Board of Trustees of Teacher's College removed his name from Thorndike Hall because of his "racist, sexist and antisemitic ideals."

Tropism

Tropism provides a dramatic symbol of how the natural sciences influenced the development of behaviorism. The term *tropism* is from the Greek root meaning "turning" and explains the automatic biological "turning" that occurs naturally in the physical environment. It describes

176　*Symbols of Behaviorism, Neobehaviorism, and Cognitive Psychology*

how a plant can literally "turn" from being closed at night to blooming during daylight. Many plants open in sunlight and close at dark, or reflexively respond to environmental conditions. These nyctinasty traits have a rapid movement, not the slow movement that fits most plants. These nyctinasty traits symbolize the environmental theory of tropism and the psychological beliefs of the early behaviorists.

The poppy, the California state flower, is illegal to pick. It is usually orange or yellow and was used by Native Americans for medicinal purposes, especially for headaches and insomnia. The California poppy closes each night and on cloudy days, and then opens with sunlight, symbolizing the power of environment forces to change and alter the physical world.

Figure 4.6

John Watson, the founder of behaviorism, was influenced by the work of Jacques Loeb (1859–1924). Loeb (1900/2019) challenged many of the sacred views held within biology and psychology. He believed that all behavior was a product of tropism. Animals as well as humans respond reflexively to environmental stimuli or die. An example is a person who sees a snake and immediately jumps, knowing that the poison of the snake could kill them. This forced movement Loeb (1918/2019) called human tropism. He intended to replace instinctive behavior with tropism. Loeb, a German-born American physiologist and psychologist, was one of the most famous scientists in America in the early twentieth century. He was widely known for his articles in newspapers and magazines. He had the ability to influence both the public and scientific communities. But his greatest impact on psychology was his influence on the behaviorism of John Watson and the neobehaviorism of B.F. Skinner, the two great behaviorists of the twentieth century.

As with many great thinkers in history, his influence expanded beyond his discipline. Loeb was the inspiration for the character of Max Gottlieb in *Arrowsmith* by the Pulitzer Prize–winning author Sinclair Lewis (1925/2002). Even Mark Twain (1905/1994) noted the incredible discoveries of "Dr. Loeb." Twain warned that one of the lessons of his character in Arrowsmith was that science should not fall into corruption and meaningless reductionism, but rather be open to new and needed scientific discoveries. Twain was concerned about the growing lack of concern for social justice in American science and culture. He provided early warnings about

Symbols of Behaviorism, Neobehaviorism, and Cognitive Psychology 177

imperialism and the shadow of capitalist corruption, which he believed was undermining democratic institutions.

Objective Psychology

Influenced by Darwinian thought and animal research, the roots of modern behaviorism originated in Russia. Because of its materialist philosophy, behaviorism fit nicely into both American capitalism and the Russian communist revolution. Ivan Sechenov (1929–1905), a founder of objective psychology, continued the movement to reject the idea that behavior was caused by internal or subjective thoughts. He argued that all behavior was the result of the physical environment. Objective psychology was rooted in physiology. Overt and covert behavior was *reflexive*, immediate reactions to external stimuli. Psychological phenomena were experienced as physiological associations, stimulus intensity guiding a high or low reflexive response to the environment. To control reflexive behavior, Sechenov discovered *inhibition*, the inhibitory processes in the brain that caused all behavior. For Sechenov, the theory of inhibition negated the need to employ subjective, metaphysical concepts such as mind or soul. He argued that introspective analysis had gotten psychology nowhere.

Sechenov (1863/1965) provides a powerful symbol for an objective and behavioral psychology: the frog. Sechenov came to explain his theory through his research with frogs. He found that he could inhibit the leg reflex of a frog from an acid solution by placing salt crystals on various parts of the brain. After washing away the crystals, the leg reflex returned, which proved to Sechenov that certain brain centers could inhibit reflexive behavior.

Figure 4.7

In human history, frogs have symbolized a connection between the two worlds of water and earth, the conscious and "other world: of the unconscious." As night animals, influenced by the moon, they sing beautiful songs in celebration with their connection to the earth. *Venus,* the Goddess of Love, held frogs as sacred, even willing to give her hand in marriage to a frog to save the life of her mother and who was later rewarded when the frog became a handsome prince. In Chinese mythology, the frog symbolizes good luck, *yin,* the feminine archetypal energy, financial wealth, and was the favored pet for the God of Wealth. In Native American and Celtic cultures, frogs are symbols of medicine and healing and hearing the messages "from the other side," the unconscious.

Through his work with frogs and other animals, Sechenov saw human development as an ongoing evolution of inhibitory control over reflexive behavior. In *Reflexes of the Brain,* Sechenov (1863/1965) went as far as to claim that all behavior could be explained by inhibition or excitation of reflexes. He rejected the idea of spontaneous or impulsive reflexes. Rather, he believed every muscle movement was caused by the stimulus that preceded it. Sechenov never enjoyed widespread scientific acceptance during his lifetime, although Ivan Pavlov considered Sechenov the father of Russian physiology and scientific psychology. Sechenov's belief that psychology should utilize the objective methods of physiology would have a lasting effect on Russian and future American behavioral psychologists. After Sechenov, the study of inhibition and reflexes were central to the study of psychology in Russia.

Conditioned Reflex and Symbol

Ivan Pavlov (1849–1936) was influenced by Sechenov and objective psychology. Unlike Sechenov, he was esteemed by his fellow colleagues and the Russian government. Because of his scientific influence, in 1921, Lenin proclaimed Pavlov a Hero of the Russian Revolution. Pavlov went beyond Sechenov and demonstrated in detail how physiological concepts could prove psychological behavior.

Pavlov came to psychology late in his life after many years of studying and receiving a Nobel Prize in 1904 for his research on the digestive system. It was his work on the digestive system that led him to the discovery of the *conditioned reflex.* Unlike most psychological researchers in history, while he was studying digestion, Pavlov would use his skill in surgery to enhance his scientific findings.

Pavlov preferred the study of digestion of dogs rather than the reflexes of frogs. During the study of the secretion of gastric juices in response to meat powder, he discovered that objects or events associated with meat powder caused stomach secretions. What was astounding for Pavlov was that the simple presence or sound of the footsteps of the researcher caused the secretion of gastric juices, a conditioned reflex. This led to several experiments to study the connection between physiology and behavior. Pavlov observed that it was not just the presence of the researcher but that something else was needed, which was the meat powder.

With a dog subject, Pavlov would repeatedly pair meat powder with a bell tone. After several trials, the dog would salivate at the mere sound of the tone, even without the meat powder. Because of his surgical background, he could also measure the amount of saliva and found that it increased with the number of pairings with the meat powder. The initial impact of these discoveries received little notice. However, Pavlov understood the importance of his research as he believed that his findings explained in concrete, physiological, and empirical terms the learning principles of *continuity* and *frequency* that dated back to the Greek philosophers. At the age of 50, Pavlov would continue his research on the conditioned reflex for the next 30 years, until the end of his life.

Pavlov (1927) believed that human behavior was determined by conditioned and unconditioned reflexive responses. Unconditioned reflexes (UCRs) were innate and were triggered by an unconditional stimulus (UCS). A biologically neutral stimulus was a conditioned stimulus (CS) and, when paired with a previously neutral stimulus (CS), elicited an unconditional response (UCR). In his experiments with dogs, Pavlov proved an unconditioned response (UCR), salivation, was triggered by a conditioned stimulus (CS), the bell tone; and, matched with the unconditional stimulus (UCS), meat powder, the result was a conditioned response (CR). After several trials, UCR began to occur simply by the tone of the bell (CS) and thereafter CR would continue to occur without the UCS. Pavlov found that *extinction* of behavior could occur when a conditioned stimulus (CS), the bell tone, stopped being paired with the unconditional stimulus (UCS), the meat powder. He also discovered *spontaneous recovery*, the ongoing power of a conditioned response, when after a period the (CS), the bell tone, was reintroduced by the unconditional stimulus (UCS), meat powder, the conditioned response (CR) returned.

Even though Pavlov has been viewed as a dedicated empiricist, unlike many of the early behaviorists, he believed it was absurd to deny a subjective world. In an ironic twist, he advocated for objective psychology to scientifically study subjectivity. A prominent example was his research on *experimental neurosis*. The experimental neurosis provides a symbol of the similarities between behavioral and psychodynamic psychology. Pavlov empirically proved the existence of neurotic behavior, caused not by internal unconscious conflicts, but conflicts created by the external environment.

Figure 4.8

The Pavlov's research design included the use of circle and ellipse symbols. When the dog saw a circle, they always received food. When the dog saw an ellipse, they never received food. Pavlov observed that the dog always salivated when they saw the circle and inhibited salivation when they saw the ellipse. As the circle became more elliptical and indistinguishable, the excitatory and inhibitory tendencies came into conflict and the behavior of the dog deteriorated. Some dogs became agitated, barked violently, and tore at the apparatus violently. Others responded to the conflict by becoming timid and depressed and withdrew from the apparatus. Pavlov believed how dogs responded depended in large measure by their type of nervous system. He concluded that abnormal behavior was the breakdown of inhibitory processes in the brain. Through his laboratory experiments, Pavlov proved a key Freudian concept, the existence of neurotic behavior.

Amazingly, one of the most natural science–based psychologists believed in the power of symbols, symbols that were based in physiological processes. Pavlov argued that conditioning was the foundation of human evolution and called his theory the *first and second signal systems*. The first system was based on innate biological development, which initially included unconditioned stimuli and unconditioned responses. The first signal in the evolutionary process occurred when biologically neutral stimuli (CSs) were paired with biologically significant stimuli (USs). The former signaled the biologically significant events. The signal allowed an animal to response to threat and survival.

The first signal was not enough. Although it alerted animals to the reality of the natural world, humans also had to learn to respond to the *symbol* of physical events. As an example, in the second signal, there needed to be a symbolic match to a word like fire, with the actual physical sight of fire. In the evolutionary process, language became symbols of environmental and bodily events and resulted in symbolic, even subjective, language. Pavlov viewed a symbol not as an abstract concept but rooted in human evolution and in the developing human brain. In the final analysis, it was the symbolic world that separated the animal and the human worlds.

Reflexology

In 1907–1912, Vladimir Bekhterev (1857–1927) furthered the objective psychology movement by publishing a three-volume series called *Objective Psychology*. Bekhterev (1913) viewed objective psychology differently from Pavlov. Having studied with Wundt and Charcot, he was exposed to introspective and hypnosis theories, which led Bekhterev to focus on *overt reflexive behavior*, not on the internal, covert behavior of Pavlovian reflexes. For Bekhterev, reflexology was the study of biological responses to environmental cues. He believed that human behavior was determined by social conditions and that psychology should adopt a natural science approach because all behavior, past, present, and future, was the result of external stimuli. Bekhterev argued that even individual facial expressions, gestures, and speech were reflexive biological responses to the environment.

Pavlov and Bekhterev both studied conditioned reflexes around the same time. What Pavlov called conditioned reflex, Bekhterev called *association reflex*. In fact, in most of his writings, Bekhterev was critical of Pavlov. He was especially critical of Pavlov's research methods with dogs and secretion and the collection of gastric juices, which he believed could never be reproduced in humans. He also criticized his use of food as an unconditioned stimulus because after a period of time an animal would become satiated and would no longer respond in any meaningful fashion. Instead of secretion, Bekhterev studied *motor reflexes* by electrical stimulation of the extremities of animals and humans. This procedure investigated muscular and respiratory reflexive responses to external stimuli. For Bekhterev, the deeper, "spiritual sphere" of human existence was not as important as understanding how external stimuli affected human physiology and behavior.

Radical Environmentalism

Bekhterev behavioral theories were much more relevant to American behaviorism than Pavlov's covert secretion theories. In an ironic twist in the history of psychology, John Watson, the founder of American behaviorism, promoted Pavlov rather than Bekhterev, and made Pavlov one of the most renowned behaviorists in the United States. If Watson had realized that Bekhterev, rather than Pavlov, was more in line with American behaviorism, Bekhterev might have become a household name. It has been said: *Watson found Pavlov but followed Bekhterev.* The reality was that Watson was not that interested in theory, especially philosophic or subjective approaches to psychology. As the battle in the early twentieth century between structuralism in the European tradition of Wundt, functionalism in the tradition of William James, and the growing influence of psychoanalysis in American psychology, behaviorism was an attractive alternative fashioned by John Watson, which laid the foundation for behavioral dominance into the twenty-first century.

In a 1913 lecture, *Psychology as the Behaviorist Views It*, John B. Watson (1878–1958) would change the face of American psychology forever. In the lecture, Watson (1913) outlined *radical environmentalism* and why psychology should only be interested in observed behavior. He believed that psychology should become an objective experimental branch of the natural sciences. Debunking the importance of philosophy and theory, he argued that the only theoretical goal for psychology was the prediction and control of human behavior. He argued that there was only a fine line between "man and brute." Even though human behavior was complex, it was only half of the human story. Animal behavior provided the other half and psychology needed to embrace that reality. Since human and animal behaviors were similar (Watson & Lashley, 1915), Watson had no problem rejecting introspection and all forms of psychology interested in higher mental functioning. The initial reaction to Watson was criticism from almost every branch of American psychology. Although there was some sympathy for his approach, most believed it was too extreme. But as history has shown, charismatic leaders of controversial ideas are often unwilling to retreat or compromise. Watson proved that with time and his persistence, he would prevail.

Influenced by the tropism of Jacques Loeb, the animal research of Thorndike, and the anthropomorphism of Ramones, Watson (1914) became one of the first to study white rats. In the early 1900s, animal research was just beginning its ascendancy in psychology. Watson, already attracted to Russian objective psychology, believed that if the behavior of rats could be understood without introspection, so could the behavior of humans. Although Watson suffered a psychotic break in 1902, he managed in 1903 to complete his doctoral degree at age 25 and became the youngest person to ever receive a doctorate at the *University of Chicago*. His dissertation, *Animal Education: The Psychical Development of the White Rat*, showed an early interest in mentalist thinking, which he later rejected. Afterward, he was offered an assistant professorship at the University of Chicago that included teaching animal and human psychology and utilizing the laboratory manuals of Titchener, who would remain a loyal friend and colleague for the rest of his life.

By the 1920s, Watson was fully committed to behaviorism and a *Stimuli (S) – Response (R)* psychology. He viewed S-R behaviorism as the only future for psychology. Like many behaviorists, Watson did not deny the existence of consciousness, he rejected the idea that it could be studied "scientifically," which meant psychology could only be an empirical science.

182 *Symbols of Behaviorism, Neobehaviorism, and Cognitive Psychology*

The psychology of John Watson is founded on the belief that human behavior is based on a series of Stimulus-Response associations. The brain is simply a relay station for behavior. Thinking is a form of behavior. When we "think," there are contractions in the tongue and larynx, which trigger movements uninitiated from the brain. Thinking was simply implicit or subvocal *speech* that occurred between the stimulus and the response. Critics called this form of S-R behaviorism "the psychology of twitchism."

Watsonian psychology has been described as "slot-machine psychology" because it was a psychology that operated like slot machines in casinos throughout the world. For Watson, behavior was an immediate result from a stimulus (S) in, and a response (R) out. It is a symbol that might be viewed as critical of Watsonian psychology or a symbol that Watson himself might endorse.

Figure 4.9

Purposive Hormic Behaviorism

William McDougall (1871–1938) became an international critic of Watsonian behaviorism. He disagreed with Watson about the importance of instincts because he maintained that behavior was stimulated by instincts, not by the environment. For McDougall, behavior was purposeful, describing his theory as *hormic psychology*, from the Greek word *horme*, meaning "urge," the impulse to behave.

McDougall believed that humans and animals were born with instincts which caused *purposive behavior*. There were three levels to inherited instincts. Perception activated an instinct, which led to behavior and emotional reactions. A hungry person perceived the need for food, which directed their behavior toward the goal of food and to positive, happiness, or negative, sadness, feelings about whether they obtained satisfaction. A thought initiated an instinct that immediately became associated with several other instincts. When two or more instincts became associated with a single thought, McDougall called it a sentiment. He believed sentiments, or the association of instinctual tendencies, determined human behavior.

In an ironic twist as a behaviorist, he agreed with Freudian thought that instinctual drives were the foundation of psychological development. McDougall postulated an instinct for every emotion. The instinct of escape caused the emotion of fear, the instinct of combat caused the feeling of anger, the instinct of repulsion caused the feeling of disgust, parental protection caused the feeling of love, the instinct of mating caused the feeling of lust, and the instinct of laughter caused feelings of amusement and relaxation. As with Freud, he believed that words for these instincts did not often adequately express the power of the instincts. In fact, words could even hide or inhibit their true meaning.

On February 5, 1924, Watson and McDougall (1929) had one of the great debates in psychological history at the Psychological Club of Washington D.C. before an audience of over 300 people. Later, both would publish the debate under the title of *The Battle of Behaviorism*. Possessing a brilliant British wit, McDougall chastised Watson for providing extremely simplistic, although popular, answers to problems that had perplexed civilization for over 2,000 years. With deep sarcasm, McDougall stated he was hesitant to criticize and hurt Watson's feelings, because that would be the reaction of most human beings. However, Watson was not like most human beings and did not believe that feelings were important and probably would not care about his own or the feelings of anyone else. He argued that the lack of feeling permeated Watson's behaviorism, which could not explain even the most satisfying experiences of humanity like music and the arts. McDougall cautioned that Watsonian behaviorism was being abused by those that would use behaviorism for financial profit and economic exploitation. He explained that behavioristic principles were being used in the marketplace to sell cigarettes and even deodorants. He believed Watson was debasing psychological inquiry by not understanding that his form of behaviorism was intellectually vacuous and would lead to negative social consequences.

It was obvious that Watson was not at the same intellectual level as McDougall. In response, his arguments appeared weak, based more on criticizing McDougall than defending with sound intellectual skill his own form of behaviorism.

Watson's major defense, which would become an archetypal defense of future behaviorists, was that McDougall was unable to understand that psychology had advanced beyond concern for the inner world because that approach had led psychology and humanity nowhere. In effect, he argued that McDougall was rejecting the fact that psychology was now an objective science concerned about the outer, not inner, world.

Watson was an incredibly attractive and charismatic speaker. However, by a slim majority, McDougall won the debate but most of the women voted for Watson. McDougall saw it as a victory for acknowledging subjective experience in behaviorism, while Watson saw it as a victory for objective psychology, his radical behaviorism. A joke permeated during that time: *one radical behaviorist said to another radical behaviorist after making love, it was great for you, but how was it for me?*

McDougall had broad interests in psychology. His theories of a purposive psychology influenced the development of social psychology. He was instrumental in founding the *British Psychological Association* and creating the *British Journal of Psychology*. It may be that his analysis by Carl Jung expanded his interests in psychology and the influence of his mentor, William James, was instrumental in establishing parapsychology as a university discipline. He served as presidents of the *Society for Psychical Research* and the *American Society for Psychical Research*. In the final analysis, McDougall viewed himself as a parapsychologist. He believed his research proved telepathy and opened the door for a paranormal and transpersonal psychology.

McDougall (1911) supported a form of Lamarckism and believed that the mind drives evolution. He rejected Darwinism and materialism in favor of *animism*, the belief that all matter has a mental process and that the mind and brain are different but interact with each other. He argued that animism would replace dualism and monism. The separation of mind and brain would become a major focus of neuropsychology later in the twentieth century.

As with many psychologists of the time, the shadow of racism stained his legacy. As a proponent of eugenics, he believed that some races were inferior. It was only because they must have some white blood that led McDougall to explain the brilliance of black Americans of his time, like Frederik Douglass, Booker T. Washington, and W.E.B. DuBois.

Hermeneutic Science Interest in Behaviorism

Positivism

Ultimately, Watson won the debate with McDougall because behaviorism, in the main, would reject subjective experience for the next 50 years until the emergence of cognitive behavioral psychology. Even then, critics, especially psychoanalysts and humanistic-existential psychologists, argued that behaviorism neglected the finer and most important aspects of being human that had concerned McDougall in 1924.

British empiricism and French sensationalism laid the philosophical foundation for the meaning and purpose of behaviorism. They believed knowledge came from experience, and like the behaviorists that followed, they had a distain for metaphysical science. All knowledge, even religious beliefs and morality, came from experience. This, for example, could place knowledge as being in direct conflict with organized religion. A strict positivist, seeing a black sheep in a meadow would not say, *that is a black sheep*; rather they would only say, *I see a sheep and one side is black.*

Auguste Comte (1798–1857) was the founder of *positivism*. Comte believed the only real purpose of science was to change the world (Comte, 1896). Influenced by the French Revolution and the utopian socialist Henri de Saint-Simon, he envisioned a utopian world based on science. He founded the *Religion of Humanity*, an actual church that created a scientific version of Roman Catholicism, celebrating positivistic psychology as Catholics would celebrate the Mass. Positivism got its name from the word *positive*, because knowledge could only be attained through "positive observable data of experience." The data had to be "publicly observable" because positivists equated knowledge with empirical observations. Science needed to discover the laws that govern physical phenomenon to be predictive. Know and predict became a favorite Comte mantra because of his belief that science should be practical and nonspeculative.

Comte (1896) developed a tripartite hierarchy of the sciences, one of the first theories to explain social evolution. This was symbolized by his three stages of scientific evolution. He started with the theological stage, which situated humanity in relation to a god, where knowledge was unquestioned, and where people blindly followed whatever they were taught. During this stage, people believed in the unseen, a soul, and images of angels and devils. In this stage, the government was ruled by the priests of the Church. In the metaphysical stage, the transitional stage between theology and science, people started to reason and question, although with no solid data, evidence, or realistic conclusions. During this stage, the state tries to reconcile the radical opposition of the theological and scientific forces with the ongoing belief in the unseen and the search for metaphysical causes. In the metaphysical stage, this tension and scientific confusion led to a government ruled by autocrats and philosophical elites. In the positive, or scientific, stage, the mind stopped searching for the causes of a phenomena because the world could be explained through the laws of science, rational thought, and observation. During this stage, universal human rights developed, which rejected organized religion and metaphysics by proclaiming in the name of science that no human authority can usurp scientific knowledge and power. In this final stage, scientists either govern or have final authority in governmental policy and affairs.

Comte is often credited with the term *sociology* because he believed that positivism provided a method by which to scientifically study society. For Comte, politics must become *social physics* because the laws of governing were as important as the law of gravity. The social commitment to change society would permeate the great thinkers of behaviorism from Watson to the neobehaviorism of B. F. Skinner to the cognitive behaviorism of Aaron Beck.

Utilitarianism

The philosophy of *utilitarianism* provided behaviorism meaning and purpose because of the utilitarian belief that all behavior seeks to maximize utility, behaviors that produce pleasure and happiness. Utilitarianism and behaviorism agreed that people seek pleasure and avoid pain. They both believed that the meaning and purpose of a behavior was decided by the objective evaluation of its pleasurable benefits. Beneficial behaviors were meaningful and gave pleasure and behaviors not useful lacked meaning and gave pain. Based in Greek philosophy from centuries ago, both agreed that human beings want to avoid pain and pursue pleasure and happiness.

Jeremy Bentham (1748–1832), an Enlightenment philosopher and founder of modern utilitarianism, attempted to empirically study utilitarian philosophy. Considering the precision of Newtonian science, he sought to quantify pleasure and pain. Utilizing the principle of utility, he believed the only way to objectively understand behavior was by its usefulness. Morality depended not on theological or metaphysical concepts, but on how actual, observable, human behaviors increased pleasure and happiness. His famous utilitarian axiom was *it is the greatest happiness of the greatest number that is the measure of right and wrong.* As a follower of Bentham, James Mill (1773–1836) believed that the mind was a blank slate of complex ideas that were formed by *associations*. In line with Watsonian behaviorism, the mind reacted involuntarily to sensations. There was no internal control of attention because attention was a mechanical reaction to the principle of utility, the avoidance of pain, and the search for pleasure.

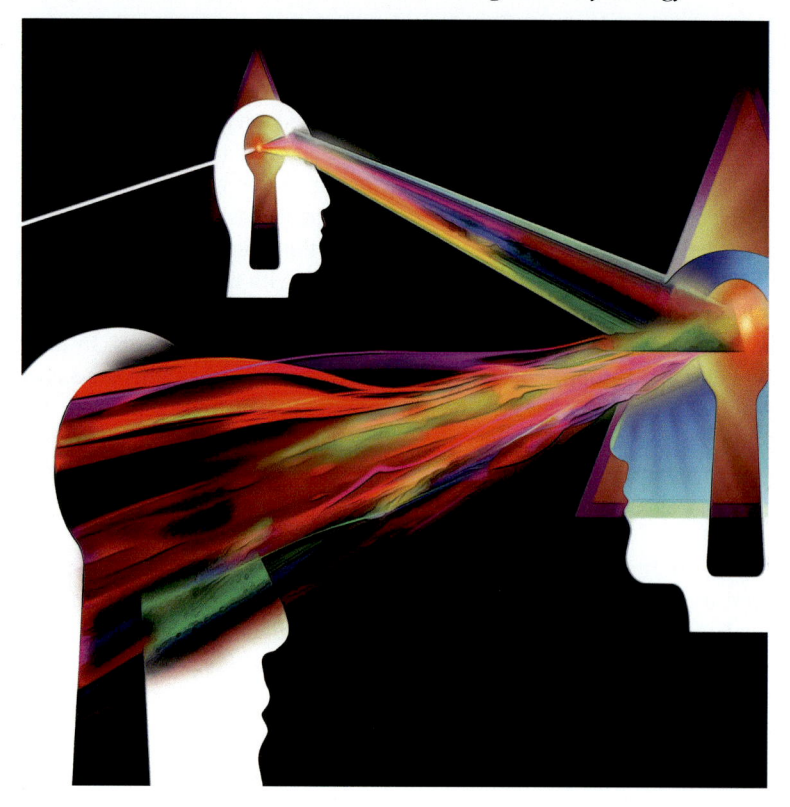

Figure 4.10

In *System of Logic*, John Stuart Mill (1843/2002) described inductive and deductive scientific methods, which would become required reading for scientists throughout the nineteenth century. A major contribution was his belief that a *scientific methodology* was essential to scientific inquiry, and for psychology to become a psychological science and to study the mind, psychology would need to adopt scientific methodologies, especially empirical and experimental approaches, to study the mind.

Advancing the associationism theory of his father that complex ideas were always the aggregate of simple ideas, John Stuart Mill offered *mental chemistry* as an option. In physics, he observed that chemicals combine and create an entirely different element. When Newton combined the spectrum of all colors, a white light was produced. The excitement of viewing mental processes in chemical terms was that ideas, like in chemistry, were created from many contiguous combinations of many experiences. John Stuart Mill had emancipated the rigid mechanistic theory of his father. However, he also reaffirmed his father's belief and those of early behaviorists that the mind was not active and autonomous, but rather a blank and passive recipient of the environment.

Behavioral Functionalism

John Dewey (1859–1952) was influenced by the pragmatism of William James, who dominated American psychology in the nineteenth and early twentieth century. The contribution of Dewey to philosophical thought was his historical deconstruction of philosophy based on American values of democracy and progressivism. He argued that the classical philosophies of Plato and

Aristotle, and others, needed to be placed in the social and political conditions of their times. Like James, Dewey believed that the only philosophy that was valuable was a philosophy that was functional, a philosophy that led to effective action to meet the historical challenges of each period in history. In this sense, there were no universal truths, only truths that formed over custom, habits, and behaviors that developed over time.

The *Reflex Arc Concept in Psychology*, Dewey (1896) rejected the emerging ideas in psychology of analyzing sensory elements of reflexes and motor responses as artificial and misleading. Rather, he turned the *stream of consciousness* of William James into the stream of behavior. A reflex had three elements which was viewed as a coordinated system with the goal of survival of the organism.

Dewey used a child touching a flame to describe the three elements of reflexes from a functionalist perspective. The child sees the flame of a candle (S) and touches it (R). The result was pain (S) which elicited withdrawal (R). In a pure stimulus, response scenario it would appear these processes were separate, and nothing was learned. However, the child learned something different from the stimulus. Since the candle elicited an avoidance, the child had learned to adapt to the environment. This meant that behavior should be analyzed in terms of its function, not the separate elements of responses to environmental cues.

Behaviorism was a logical outcome of functionalism because early behaviorism would focus not on internal processes, but adaptation to the environment. Dewey applied Darwin's natural history method to his empirical naturalism which included the study of culture and social problems (Dewey, 1889). In line with behaviorism, Dewey believed he had resolved the subject/object problem because the reflex arc was based on immediate behavioral adaptation, not on subjective contemplation. Behaviorism provided concrete instruments for adaptation and control of the environment.

Behavioral Psychology

Little Albert Conditioning

To prove that emotion was the result of environmental stimuli, Watson initiated one of his most famous of his research projects called *Little Albert*. The Little Albert experiment proved to Watson that emotions could be conditioned by stimuli other than what had originally elicited the emotion. In 1920, Watson, with his future wife, Rosalie Rayner, performed an experiment on Little Albert, who was an 11-month-old infant. They initially showed Little Albert a white rat in which he showed no fear and had no fear in reaching out toward the rat. Later, as Little Albert reached for the rat a steel bar behind him was struck with a hammer that caused him to jump forward with some concern. Little Albert was then offered to touch the rat and again the steel bar was struck, and he began to cry.

A week later, they again presented the rat to Little Albert, and he was less enthusiastic to approach the rat. Five more times they placed the rat close to Little Albert and stuck the steel bar and Little Albert who had been attracted to the rat, now exhibited fear of the rat. Five days later, they found that Little Albert was still fearful of the rat. In fact, Little Albert had generalized his fear to other furry objects such as rabbits, fur coats, and even a Santa Claus mask. They found that a month later Little Albert was still afraid of the rat. This proved to Watson and Rayner that rearranged experiences, not instinct, caused learned emotional responses. They believed that *continuity*, the continual exposure to a stimulus, can change emotional experiences. Because Little Albert was discharged from the hospital before they had the opportunity to remove the fear, Watson and Rayner continue to be criticized for unethical behavior.

188 *Symbols of Behaviorism, Neobehaviorism, and Cognitive Psychology*

Over the years there have been numerous journal articles speculating on the fate of Little Albert. Fridlund, Beck, Goldie, and Irons (2012) speculated that Little Albert was born with neurological deficits, which led to the charge and argued that Watson made serious ethical mistakes performing research on a disabled infant. Digdon, Powell, and Harris (2014) responded that Little Albert was a normal infant, signifying that controversies regarding Little Albert periodically resurface in the context of current trends in psychology.

Figure 4.11

The Little Albert experiment provides a powerful symbol of the movement of behaviorism from the laboratory to the everyday world. The hope was that behaviorism could change the arc of history by modifying behavior, which would lead to a less dysfunctional and healthier society because Watson envisioned a psychology that could be useful in everyday life

Peter and the Rabbit Behavioral Therapy

The Little Albert experiment proved to Watson that behaviorism could change behavior. Because Little Albert left the hospital before they could decondition the child, in his *Peter and the Rabbit* experiment with Mary Jones, he found that he could decondition the fear of rabbits and related objects through an early example of *behavioral therapy.* Peter, a three-year-old boy, already had fears of rabbits, white rats, fur coats, and many other similar objects. During a hospitalization while Peter was eating lunch, Watson began to present a rabbit in a cage and, as the cage moved closer each day to Peter, he was finally able to reach out and pet and play with the rabbit. Peter had less fear not only of the rabbit but generalized the intervention to a reduction of fears in many other areas of his young life. The approach was the beginning of what would later become the *systematic desensitization* technique in behavioral therapy.

Educational Psychology

In his treatise *Some Thoughts on Education*, John Locke (1693/2000) advanced his empirical approach and emancipated education from the tyranny of hereditary determinism. Locke embraced nurture over nature because he did not believe that intelligence was based on innate abilities. His approach to education would sound routine today but was revolutionary for his day. Although he acknowledged the need for some mild disciplinary practices in school classes, like future behaviorists, he rejected punishment as an effective intervention. He believed the role of a teacher was to make the learning experience as pleasant as possible; or as behaviorists in the future would say, increase positive and decrease negative reinforcement.

Locke (1690/2000) argued that the ultimate job of a teacher was to recognize and praise accomplishments rather than teach behavioral control and discipline. For Locke, education at home was just as important as at school. It was the responsibility of the parent to support education and be educated themselves. He correlated educational success with good sleeping habits and nutrition, fresh air, and exercise. Like many future behaviorists, he had difficulty with emotions and feelings. He believed that parents should discourage crying and excessive feeling. In fact, punishment for crying was one place Locke believed discipline could be effective. He supported the parenting approach of hardening which, among other ideas, taught children how to manage stress by sleeping on hard, not soft beds.

John Dewey (1889) had a dramatic impact on American education that remains to this day. He believed that education should be student-driven rather than subject-driven. In the functionalist tradition, he argued that you had to do something to learn something. He opposed rote learning and memorization and ever coming to final conclusions. Rather, students should be challenged to learn from their own perspective and "never stop learning." Education never had an end point, learning was lifelong. It was a dramatic mistake for a student to receive an A in a course and believe they really learned all the material. Dewey carried on the pragmatic and functionalist American belief that education be practical and useful. Children should be prepared to solve the problems of a democratic society. He wrote many influential books on how to transform democratic ideals into social action. In *Democracy and Education,* Dewey (1916) explained that education was essential for achieving the goals of a democratic society.

Emancipatory Opportunities in Behaviorism

Read Psychology as the Behaviorist View It

Watson (1913) provides an important synopsis of the foundation of behaviorism.

Experience Tropism

As a way to understand Watsonian behaviorism and the influence of the environment, experience a plant like the California poppy that opens at daytime and closes at night.

Read Arrowsmith

This novel by Sinclair Lewis (1925/2002) should be on the reading list of all aspiring psychologist researchers and practitioners. In *Arrowsmith,* Max Gottlieb started out idealizing the vision of a pure medical science, but the shadow of a science without social conscious challenged his ethics as well as the very essence of his soul. *Arrowsmith* highlights how a scientist can pay a psychological price for neglecting their social and political responsibilities or as the Axial Age sages taught that most important was *how* one lived, not *what* one believed.

Change Your Environment

Experience the psychological impact of changing something in your environment, which could include anything from cleaning a room to remodeling or reorganizing the home or office.

Neobehaviorism

Natural Science Interest in Neobehaviorism

Molecular Purposive Neobehaviorism

Edward Tolman (1886–1959), unlike Watson, did not believe that complex behavior could be explained simply by stimulus (S) and response (R) reflexes. Those responses he termed *molecular behaviors*. He wanted to objectively study the purpose, the goal, of the molecular behaviors. Tolman (1922) continued the behaviorist challenge of explaining behavior without the mind. Like Watson, he rejected any concept of mentalism and introspection in McDougall's purposive behaviorism. The question was how Tolman could explain purpose without any internal psychological processes.

Upon arrival to teach at the University of California, Berkeley, Tolman decided to teach a comparative psychology course. During the course, he was impressed with the similarity of rat and human behavior. To his dismay, he discovered that the purpose of rat behavior was primarily the result of internal processes. Concerned that his work was confirming the purposive behaviorism of McDougall, he sought other behavioral possibilities (Tolman, 1928). His findings would be the beginning of neobehaviorism, because intervening variables, not the mind, occurred between the organism and behavior. With the introduction of intervening variables, Tolman brought abstract scientific theory into behavioral psychology because intervening variables could be explained by objective observation.

For Tolman, observing how the environment influenced behavior was not enough. Psychology needed a *method* to understand *why* behaviors occurred. His *methodological behaviorism* separated him from Watson's radical behaviorism. Now psychology could study behavior beyond observing (S) and (R) reflexes. There was now a method which showed how environmental experiences created observable internal events which caused behavior. Observing intervening variables led to concepts of hypothesis, trial-and-error expectations, beliefs, and ultimately a *cognitive map*. Tolman (1924) found that, after initially placing a rat in a maze, they were perplexed in their new environment. But as the rat began to adjust to their new environment, they developed a hypothesis to determine what constituted successful and unsuccessful turns. Then, as the complexity became apparent, the rat typically stopped and literally pondered their next steps, which Tolman called trial and error. As the rat began to understand that by turning left and right some success occurred, they created expectations and even beliefs of how to proceed. After finding the end of the maze, the rat had developed a cognitive map, which led to a quicker journey upon their return to the maze. Placing a rat in a maze symbolizes the beginning of neobehaviorism.

Figure 4.12

Mechanistic Neobehaviorism

Sadly, Clark Hull (1884–1952) lived before the advent of the modern computer. Naturally drawn to mathematics, mathematical quantification was one of his major contributions to neobehaviorism. Inspired by the molecular purposive behaviorism of Tolman, in his *hypothetico-deductive theory,* Hull, Hovland, Ross, et al (1940) mathematically quantified intervening variables. Unlike Tolman, Hull (1920) concluded that the number, not the cognitive types of intervening of variables, had to be taken into consideration. Holding a natural science view of behavior, Hull believed that intervening events between experience and behavior were all physiological. Although Hull had no modern computer, after many years of calculating behavior by hand, he discovered that his hypothetico-deductive theory had 17 postulates and 113 theorems.

Hull was also inspired by the theory of the conditioned reflex of Ivan Pavlov, the radical behaviorism of Watson, and the law of effect by Thorndike (Hull, 1943). In the rat maze studies, Tolman tried to imagine if he were a rat how he would escape from a maze. Tolman found that a rat began to imagine an internal map that did not need constant reinforcement to complete escape behavior. Hull strongly disagreed with Tolman, countering that there was a biological drive that created the need to exit the maze. In his theory of drive-reduction, drive was the essential reinforcement between stimulus and response. In the process, Hull (1920) quantified a stimulus (S), organism (O), and response (R) theory of renowned functionalist Robert Woodworth

(1869–1962). As a functionalist, Woodworth was concerned about what drove and motivated individuals to adapt to the environment. He understood there was a stimulus and response reaction to the environment. However, he believed the (O) was a reminder that everyone responds uniquely to an environmental stimulus.

In the final analysis, Hull approached behaviorism from a mechanistic perspective. He believed humans operated like machines. As mechanical beings, the key was to analyze intervening variables mathematically and objectively. Mechanistic behaviorism dominated experimental psychology in the 1940s and, after his death, his student, Kenneth Spence (1907–1967), became the major spokesperson for the Hullian version of neobehaviorism. The modifications of Hull's theories were so influential that in the 1950s and 1960s they became known as the *Hull-Spence theory*. One of Spence's major contributions was the theory of *discrimination learning*. Spence based learning on biological excitatory strength, which reinforced a response to a specific stimulus, and inhibitory strength when the stimulus was not reinforced. Using a mathematical approach like Hull's, Spence utilized graphs to demonstrate that learning was based on a net excitatory strength.

Hull won the battle with Tolman, but Hull would ultimately lose the war. Although Hull and Spence were respected for their scientific approach, the sterility of their view of psychology alienated many psychologists. By basing all of psychology on a strict experimental natural science model, the concern was that this would lead to a psychology that lacked relevance to real-world problems. The Tolman, Hull, Spence impact on psychology would eventually fade but remain relevant because their theories influenced B. F. Skinner's neobehaviorism.

One-Trial Learning and Recency Principle

Until Edwin Guthrie (1886–1959), most psychologists agreed with Aristotle and other classical philosophers that learning occurred by the *laws of contiguity*, *association*, or *frequency*. Pavlov, Watson, Tolman, Hull, and Spence all agreed, for different reasons, that associative strength, the experience of a stimulus over a period of time, increased learning. Guthrie (1959) strongly disagreed and argued that learning occurred after the pairing of the first associative response. In other words, Guthrie (1935) believed his *one-trial learning theory* had overturned centuries of mistaken beliefs about learning. Guthrie explained practice improved performance because of the distinction between acts, movements, and skills. To learn to play the piano, a pianist had to initiate an act: play a note which led to movements under varying environmental conditions. Just as an act consisted of many specific movements, a skill depended on many acts. Learning the piano consisted of many acts and thousands of movements. Practice improved performance because acts and skills required learning many one-trial associations.

The issue of what constituted *reinforcement* would create many conflicts among behaviorists. Believing in the importance of the recent moment, Guthrie also disagreed with the results of a famous psychological study. In the Thorndike puzzle box experiment, Thorndike believed that the cat learned to escape the puzzle box by incremental learning and being reinforced by the satisfaction of successfully completing the task. Guthrie (1946) argued that cats quickly repeated the task the next time because the stimulus had changed the process from incremental to recent learning. Guthrie described this type of reinforcement in terms of a recency principle because the most recent learning reinforced unlearning, because the cat could never unlearn how to escape the puzzle box.

Operant Conditioning

In the early twentieth century, many schools of thought sought supremacy in American psychology: the structuralism of Titchener in the Wundtian tradition, the functionalism of William James and John Dewey, the behaviorism of John Watson, the mechanistic behaviorism of Tolman, and the psychoanalysis of Freud. After World War II, influenced by environmental, eugenic, and evolutionary theories, Americans were hungry for practical solutions that were based on natural and objective science methods. Structuralism and mechanical behaviorism had proved too sterile and complex; Freud too European; and abstract and functionalism, although practical, still too philosophical for many psychologists. Watson would successfully fulfill the need for practical solutions by advocating for a *scientific psychology,* which was pragmatic, experimental, and anti-philosophical.

While in academic psychology behaviorism was taking root, by the mid-1950s most clinical psychologists still practiced psychology from a psychoanalytic perspective. With the arrival of the *neobehaviorism* of B. F. Skinner (1904–1990), the world of American psychology would change forever. His approach fit Watson's radical behaviorism, whose goal was to eliminate mentalism and metaphysics from psychology. After Watson and Skinner, the important names that had previously influenced the historic development of psychology like Wundt, Titchener, Thorndike, James, or Tolman would begin to fade or lose relevance in modern psychological history. Watson and Skinner won the early supremacy battle and, with the later development of *cognitive behavioral psychology*, behaviorist domination of American psychology would continue into the twenty-first century.

Skinner rejected the existence of an internal subjective psychology because so-called mental events were always determined by the environment. He argued that introspection was simply verbal labels for bodily reactions. Skinner opined those so-called mental events would someday be explained through a technology that would explain thinking, willing, choosing, and even freedom and dignity. Completing a *functional analysis* would provide a psychologist the ability to assess how the environment determined so-called mental events and behavioral reactions.

Skinner's (1938) first major work, *Behavior of Organisms,* gained little attention. After World War II, Skinner's descriptive and scientific psychology would flourish. He shifted the debate in psychology from the sources of behavior being inside, to being outside, the organism. To avoid any use of mentalistic terms, Skinner believed psychology needed to adopt *operational definitions*. He called Pavlov and Watson's behaviorism respondent behavior because behavioral responses were physiologically reflexive to known events between stimulus and response. Respondent behavior needed a stimulus, whereas operant behavior occurred continuously and did not need to be connected to a stimulus.

Skinner (1956) rejected Watsonian S-R respondent behaviorism in favor of Thorndike's instrumentalism. In the cat puzzle box experiment, Thorndike was most concerned about what was consequential in producing certain responses. Although Skinner and Thorndike were both concerned about behavioral consequences, Skinner changed instrumental to *operant conditioning*. This showed how operational principles better explained the consequences of behavior. In the process of changing instrumental to operant conditioning and by rejecting S-R psychology, by the late 1950s, Skinner had replaced Watson as the dominate force in behavioral psychology.

194   *Symbols of Behaviorism, Neobehaviorism, and Cognitive Psychology*

Figure 4.13

The famous Skinner box would become not only a symbol of neobehaviorism but, next to the Freudian couch, an often-recognized iconic cultural symbol for psychology. The Skinner box allowed a rat to respond freely to a lever that produced food and the ability of the psychologist to note the effect of reinforcement on the rate of response. For instance, the rate of pulling the lever for food could be four or six times a minute before being reinforced to 20 to 30 times a minute after the reinforcement of food. The rate of responding was the independent variable. An example of operant behavior occurred when Skinner paired a light with a reinforcing event. Responding to the light allowed the rat to discriminate a reinforcing from a non-reinforcing event. For Pavlov, understanding the stimulus was important because it caused an immediate reflexive response. For Skinner, the response was important because the rat could manipulate the environment until it achieved its goal. This proved to Skinner the environment reinforces and controls behavior, not what happens within an individual organism.

Skinner turned to Darwin to further develop his theory of reinforcement. Darwin had discovered an organism initially responded to the environment in a variety of ways to survive. After a while it became clear that evolution of a species depended on the reinforcement of functional behaviors. These reinforcements were based on reinforcement contingencies, the pleasant and unpleasant events that increased or decreased behaviors. For Skinner (1974), this negated the need for mind or self since evolution had proven that organisms needed to be modified by their environment for survival. By understanding which reinforcement contingencies increased or decreased human behavior made solutions to many social problems possible (Skinner, 1978).

Issues of reinforcement and punishment separated Skinner from early behaviorists. His view that punishment was ineffective was one his most important discoveries. Skinner believed that behavior was best shaped by positive reinforcement, such as praising a child for good behavior.

Although not ideal, when positive reinforcement was not effective, negative reinforcement, the removal of a positive reinforcement, was the next step; for instance, having a child sit in a corner away from family or friends for 15 minutes.

The worst form of behavioral control was punishment. Skinner agreed with Thorndike that punishment was ineffective but went further to argue that punishment had the reverse effect and reinforced bad behavior. Agreeing with Freud, but from a behavioral perspective, Skinner believed a major reason punishment was so widely utilized was that it justified expressing aggressive and abusive behavior on others. If punishment was in any way to be effective, it had to occur immediately, but the best alternative to punishment was extinction of bad behavior. Although difficult and requiring time, extinction meant avoiding attention to bad behavior; for instance, a parent ignoring bad behavior of their child.

Hermeneutic Science Interest in Neobehaviorism

Logical Positivism

By the early twentieth century, it became clear that the positivism of Auguste Comte and other early positivists that everything in science needed to be empirical and observed, was unrealistic because many important forces in nature could not be seen directly. For instance, physicists had proven the theoretical existence of gravity, atoms, electrons, and other physical phenomenon. The challenge for science was to develop the meaning and purpose of empirical experience without the pitfalls of metaphysics (Rescher, 1985).

The name *logical positivism* emerged from a group of philosophers and scientists called the Vienna Circle. These were the leading international thinkers in the early twentieth century in the fields of natural, mathematical, logic, and social sciences. Friedrich Albert Schlick (1882–1936), a philosopher and physicist, chaired the Vienna Circle and was considered the father of logical positivism (Richardson, 2003).

The Vienna Circle met regularly from 1924 until 1936 at the University of Vienna and answered the question of how to create a science without metaphysics. The Vienna Circle defined logical positivism as science having two components: empirical and theoretical. Observational terms would define the science of empiricism and theoretical terms would provide the logic for an empirical science.

Herbert Feigt, a member of the Vienna Circle, brought logical positivism to American psychology, providing neobehaviorism, the philosophy of logical positivism, which allowed for theorizing without losing objectivity. The Vienna Circle allowed psychology to enter the *age of theory* from the 1930s to the 1950s. Many psychologists during this period believed that logical positivism allowed psychology to become a science on par with physics because it gave birth to operationalism, which provided the philosophical foundation and theoretical meaning of the operational theory of B. F. Skinner.

Operationalism

In the tradition of logical positivism, Percy W. Bridgman (1882–1961), a Harvard University physicist, in his *The Logic of Modern Physic*, defined *operationalism* as the process of finding the meaning of a scientific concept by its procedures and measurement. Bridgman (1927) argued that there could be an *operational definition* for every abstract concept in physics. Although it was not his intention to create a philosophical or hermeneutic theory, the philosophical doctrine of *operationalism* was quickly embraced in psychology and influenced the development of neobehaviorism.

Bridgman won the Nobel Prize in 1946 for his pioneering work in the physics of high pressures. This work resulted from his laboratory prowess where he created pressures on various materials nearly 100 times higher than anyone else. The problem was that the higher pressures broke the pressure gauges and resulted in the question as to whether physicists could ever know to what levels pressures could reach. The new *quantum physics* and the *Copenhagen interpretation* were also showing the limitations of observation and measurement. It became clear that the physicist by their very observation changed the measurement of physical properties, often dramatically. By the mid-twentieth century, physics was struggling to define scientific objectivity.

One answer Bridgman offered was operationalism. Concepts such as force, pressure, and energy could be defined in terms of the procedures used to observe and measure concepts. Bridgman's operationalism inspired psychologists to convert theoretical concepts such as anxiety, learning, and intelligence into operational empirical events. Anxiety could be operationalized by measuring the number of panic attacks. Learning could be operationalized by measuring how many times a lever was pulled to successfully to retrieve a pellet. Intelligence could be operationalized by a score on an intelligence test. No matter how complex the scientific problem, Bridgman argued that it was the role of a scientific theory to make clear statements about empirical events. This deductive method allowed for scientific correction. If the results of the experimental method were successful, the theory would be strengthened; and if proven false, the theory would weaken. If weakened, the theory would need to be revised or even abandoned as the goal of operationalism was to make accurate theoretical predictions of empirical events.

Physicalism

Physicalism seemed a natural result of the logical positivism and operationalism movements. By the mid-twentieth century, many psychologists were striving to become respected scientists by modeling physics, the science held in greatest esteem. Even though behaviorists sought to reject mentalism and subjective philosophical meaning and purpose, the changes occurring in physics necessitated a reexamination of the role of theory in an empirically oriented psychological science. Physicalism became another influence on the development of neobehaviorism. The philosophy of physicalism believed that everything in existence is physical and connected inextricably to the physical world. Otto Neurath (1881–1945) and Rudolf Carnap (1891–1970), leaders of the Vienna Circle introduced the term physicalism in the 1930s to construct a universal system of science. This was an ontological monistic philosophy that argued that one substance determines the nature of reality. Distinguished from materialism, physicalism advanced materialism since physics had proven that a singular substance could change and evolve.

Since behavioral psychology was following many of the principles, assumptions, and terminology of the natural sciences, it only made sense that psychology would adopt physics as a significant role model for its scientific inquiry. In fact, the goal of physicalism was for all the sciences to use the same language and research methods because of the belief that all the sciences were basically the same. For the sake of scientific unification, all the sciences, including psychology, should follow the same principles and methodologies of physics. Although physicalism influenced neobehaviorism, it became too difficult to conceptualize all human behavior into purely reductionistic physical terms. Although many psychologists continue to agree that all the great sciences contain the same foundation, it would be operationalism and logical positivism that would survive and provide the conceptual foundation and theoretical meaning and purpose for neobehaviorism.

Edward Haskell (1906–1986), a *synergistic scientist*, a scientist who seeks cooperation across the sciences, continued the effort in the 1970s to unify human knowledge into a single discipline. He organized the now-defunct *The Council for Unified Research and Education (CURE)*, which again attempted to establish a unified science. In 1972, Haskell (1972) published *Full Circle: The Moral Force of Unified Science*, which expanded the view of science beyond traditional physicalism. This view included not only the physical and biological, but also psycho-social sciences. In Full Circle, he argued that scientific specialization had destroyed values essential to the survival of democracy. The new science needed to adopt the Leibniz universal characteristic rationalistic philosophy: a universal and formal language that would be able to integrate mathematical, natural science, and metaphysical concepts.

Neobehavioral Psychology

Societal Engineering

> We have tried to contain population explosion through birth control; end the threat of nuclear holocaust by building bigger missile systems; stave off world famine with new foods and better ways of growing them; control disease through improved sanitation and medicine; tackle the problems of the ghettos through better housing and transportation; design new ways of reducing or disposing of waste to stop the pollution of our environment. Still, things grow worse. If all of modern science and technology cannot significantly change man's environment, can mankind be saved?
> - B. F. Skinner

Very few psychologists have impacted the psychology of a society as deeply as B. F. Skinner. He believed his *neobehavorism* could emancipate the world. As with many great thinkers, at the end of his life, he was frustrated that he was often not taken seriously. He believed that societal problems that were being neglected his neobehaviorism could solve. In concert with Freud, he argued that civilization was in grave danger. In his writings, *Walden Two* and *Beyond Freedom and Dignity*, Skinner outlined his approach to the *social engineering of society*. In *Walden Two*, Skinner (1948) described a utopia based on a positively reinforced behaviorist society. In deference to the utopian scientific society of Bacon, Skinner described his novel as "my New Atlantis." For Skinner (1971), concepts of freedom, dignity, and human autonomy were superfluous romanticism because societal engineering did not require a higher state of individual consciousness. Rather societal progress depended on understanding and changing how the environment reinforced behavior.

Skinner impacted many aspects of American life from institutional care to education to psychotherapy. State mental hospitals became less punitive, education more student-centered, and psychiatric institutions trained staff to modify dysfunctional behavior more effectively. Skinner (1960) even influenced the military by developing the *Project Pigeon Program*, which trained pigeon-guided missiles during World War II to improve the U.S. Navy guided-missile program.

In *Beyond Freedom and Dignity*, Skinner (1971) summarized his possible legacy with the words, "no praise, no blame." Skinner did not believe that inner strength or virtue led to the heroic journey; rather it was the environment that determined hero behavior. There were no moral grounds for praise or blame because the hero could only exist because of the reinforcement contingencies in the environment. Although Skinner left an indelible legacy, his extreme denial of any internal life left a shadow, a void filled by cognitive behavioral psychology.

198 *Symbols of Behaviorism, Neobehaviorism, and Cognitive Psychology*

Token Economy System

Skinnerian neobehaviorism emancipated the lives of many individuals in developmental and psychiatric institutions. Before Skinner, most institutions utilized punishment to control bad behavior. As Skinnerian thought expanded beyond academia, institutional staff were educated on Skinnerian principles; especially the importance of positive reinforcement methods to modify behavior. *Token economies* provided clients with tokens to purchase goods in an institution store. This store would provide everything from candy to needed appliances. Tokens were also used to increase client privileges such as passes to leave the hospital grounds or for more access to recreational activities and social media. Token economies were criticized as being contrived and unnatural. But according to the research of Masters, Burish, Hollon, and Rim (1987), token economies resembled the national currency system that prepared individuals for non-institutional living. They found that it was those institutions that rejected the token economy system that remained overly dependent on punishment for behavioral control, which led to a toxic, even violent, institutional environment.

Mechanical Baby Tender – An Aircrib

After raising his first child, Skinner felt he could simplify parenting by developing an *Aircrib*, a climate-controlled environment for infants. Skinner believed that an Aircrib, also called an "Heir Conditioner," could contribute positively to raising children in an air-controlled environment. This was especially true for raising children in the harsh, cold weather in his Minnesota home. The goal was to replace restrictive and unsafe blankets and baby clothes that could overheat and

Figure 4.14

endanger the baby with warm air flow. In this way, the Aircrib would alleviate safety concerns and allow the baby to move freely and uninhibited in a safe and warm environment.

Skinner believed that parenting was simply a more complex form of operant conditioning. It would be his infamous Aircrib *box* that would haunt not only B. F. Skinner but become a shadow symbol of neobehaviorism. His Aircrib would lead to untrue rumors that one of his daughters had been raised in a Skinner box and had later in life shot herself to death in a suicide attempt. Skinner (1945) himself created the confusion when in an October 1945 *Ladies Home Journal* article, where Skinner featured his daughter, Deborah, in an Aircrib with her hands pressed against the glass with the byline, *Baby in a Box: The Mechanical Baby Tender.* Outraged letters to the Ladies Home Journal protested babies being treated like animals by being raised "in a box" as a part of a psychological experiment.

Many individuals had not completely read the article. Lauren Slater (2004) repeated many of the rumors in her book that Skinner had caged his daughter, Deborah, in a Skinner box for two full years. Although Slater rebutted the rumor later, she did report the untrue rumor that at 21 Deborah had become psychotic, sued Skinner for child abuse, lost her case in court, and shot herself in a Billings, Montana, bowling alley. When located, Deborah Skinner-Buzan (2004), in an interview with the *Guardian,* "I was Not a Laboratory Rat," vehemently denied the rumors and described the claims as doing a great disservice to her father and his family. She claimed she had a great childhood and was currently living a good life as an artist in London, England. Because it has remained a fascinating story in the history of psychology, an Aircrib remains on display at the *Center for the History of Psychology* in Akron, Ohio.

Teaching Machine

B. F. Skinner (1961, 1958) developed the *teaching machine* called the *Glider*, which advanced his view of how positive reinforcement and operant conditioning could apply to the education system. By the 1960s, the teaching machine was utilized by many students from preschool to adulthood and included a variety of topics from math to music. In the spirit of John Dewey, the teaching machine modeled student-focus learning as the pace of learning was adjusted to meet the individual educational needs of each student.

The *teaching machine*, a precursor to the educational opportunities of computers and the Internet, symbolized the growing influence of behaviorism beyond the laboratory. It led to *opened learning* and *computer-assisted instruction,* which transformed many aspects of formal and informal education. Opened learning expanded education beyond the formal classroom to an endless list of possibilities from work-related education and training to educational resources beyond scholastic institutions. As token economies had decreased aversive control in state institutions, by utilizing positive reinforcement and operant conditioning to advance learning, computer-assisted instruction created a more stimulating educational environment. The goal was for students to take responsibility and self-management for their learning, rather than the passive, subject-focus, learning of traditional education (Skinner, 1984, 1968). The shadow elements of computer-assisted instruction were a decrease in interpersonal interaction with teachers and less socialization with peers.

Aging

B. F. Skinner, with Margaret Vaughn (1983), in *Enjoying Old Age: Living Fully Your Later Years*, applied the Skinnerian view of operant conditioning and the importance of the environment in old age. Margaret Vaughn was a well-known expert on aging from *Harvard University*. Together, they outlined ways to create an environment that could compensate for some of the challenges of old age. For instance, they promoted ways to combat forgetfulness, improve

200   *Symbols of Behaviorism, Neobehaviorism, and Cognitive Psychology*

thoughts, enhance diet, evoke creativity, and offer strategies to cope with younger people and children. Since Skinner and Vaughn were both aging themselves, they also explored issues of retirement and the fear of death. Maybe it was Vaughn's feminine influence, but they also addressed the importance of learning to cope with the emotional issues of older age.

Psychological Testing – Verbal Summator

Although followers often tend to be more dogmatic than their leaders, the reality is that most influential thinkers avoid being total prisoners to their theories and biases. Although in his theories B.F. Skinner rejected an internal subjective world, he always had a fascination with psychoanalysis. Although no one knows why he was rejected, Skinner applied to be psychoanalyzed at the *Boston Psychoanalytic Society and Institute* (Bjork, 1996).

An example of exploring experiences outside his comfort zone was Skinner's interest in the *Rorschach Test*. He was influenced by projective psychological testing, especially the work of fellow colleague, Henry Murray, who developed the *Thematic Apperception Test*. After taking the Rorschach Test himself (Roe, n.d.), Skinner became inspired to develop a test which could be integrated into psychological testing.

As a fellow early in his career at Harvard University, he developed the *verbal summator*, an auditory inkblot test. Skinner (1936) described the verbal summator as a device for repeating arbitrary samples of speech by combining basic elemental speech sounds. In the test, a subject made conventional verbal responses responding to skeleton auditory samples such as *ah-uh-uh-oo-uk*, which would eventually result in finding meaning in the sounds. Like the Rorschach Test, the meaning would relate to unconscious psychological issues.

Although Skinner was quick to recommend more research for its clinical applicability, he did imply that the verbal summator had the potential to be integrated into projective testing by distinguishing normal from abnormal verbal speech. Skinner administered the verbal summator at the *Harvard Clinic* and to clients at the *Worcester State Hospital,* but later abandoned the verbal summator when he became the leading voice for neobehaviorism (Rutherford, 2003).

Figure 4.15

Hypnosis

Like many behaviorists before him, Clark Hull had other interests beyond mechanical behaviorism. He has been credited with being the father of *modern hypnosis* because he believed hypnosis needed greater scientific and empirical rigor. Hull (1933) published the first compilation of laboratory research on the efficacy of hypnosis. He applied his mathematical and statistical skills to refute the belief that hypnosis was related to sleep. In fact, he argued that his research proved that hypnosis had the opposite effect and made individuals more alert and "awake." Hull found that there were only two major differences between the waking and hypnotic state. Individuals in a hypnotic state were more suggestible and memories became more conscious. He disagreed with other hypnotherapists of the time whether hypnosis was the best technique to reduce pain and inhibit bad memories. Hull concluded that those issues could be addressed just as effectively without hypnosis. After Hull moved to *Yale University* in 1929, he discontinued his research on hypnosis after his work met with great resistance. Hypnosis continued to decline in the late twentieth century in America in part because Freud had abandoned hypnosis in favor of free association, as well as skepticism in the medical establishment about its appropriate use.

Emancipatory Opportunities in Neobehaviorism

Read Walden Two and Beyond Freedom and Dignity

These controversial books by Skinner (1948, 1971) not only articulate the practical application of neobehaviorism, but they also raise disturbing and serious questions about the state of civilization.

Explore Computer-Assisted Education

Although developed beyond the *learning machine*, the Internet is replete with *computer-assisted instruction* opportunities, most notably the 500 hundred courses available in *The Great Courses*, Wondrium.

Read Enjoying Old Age: Living Fully Your Later Years

The book by B. F. Skinner with Margaret Vaughan (1983) is still relevant to successfully facing the challenges of old age.

Consider Hypnosis

Inspired by Hull and others, Milton Erikson revitalized hypnosis in the United States. Bent Geary and Jeffery Zeig (2001) describe how the Eriksonian approach is applicable to many mental health issues ranging from the treatment of anxiety to the challenges of addiction.

Avoid Punishment

At home, work, and school, understand punishment reinforces bad behavior. Apply the lessons from the token economy system about the benefits of positive reinforcement. Consider its implications for reforms in the systems of criminal justice, education, and employment.

Cognitive Behavioral Psychology

Natural Science Interest in Cognitive Behavioral Psychology

Cognitive Science

Noam Chomsky, the father of modern linguistics and one of the founders of cognitive science, offered an important response to the neobehaviorism of Skinner. In *A Review of B.F. Skinner's Verbal Behavior*, Chomsky (1959) provided the critique that would change the course of behavioral psychology. Chomsky argued that language was too complex to be reduced to operant conditioning. He believed behaviorism or neobehaviorism could never explain how a child learned or acquired language because the human brain was genetically programmed to produce language. This critique was seen as the most important paper since the Watson (1913) paper, "Psychology as the Behaviorist Views It." Chomsky not only criticized behaviorism, but he also opened the door for the reemergence of the philosophy of rationalism, heritability, and nativistic explanations for behavior. Researchers started to question basic precepts of behaviorism like the belief that humans start with a *tabula rasa*, a blank slate. Also questioned was the premise that there were no significant differences among various species, the idea that any response could be conditioned to any stimulus, and hereditary and instinct play no essential role in behavior.

George Miller (1920–2012), one of the greatest psychologists of the twentieth century, birthed cognitive psychology in September 1956 during a symposium on information theory sponsored by *Massachusetts Institute of Technology*. Until this time, Watson and Skinner had given "cognitive" a bad name. At the symposium, Chomsky presented a paper on linguistic functions being innately programmed within the brain. Other presenters focused on informational processing and computer logic. After this conference, interest in a cognitive science flourished. Inspired by Chomsky, who was not a psychologist, Miller and other psychologists began to embrace the importance of language and memory, which led to the study of *psycholinguistics*.

In "The Magical Number Seven, Plus or Minus Two: Some Limits on Our Capacity for Processing Information," Miller (1956) produced one of the most cited papers in psychology. He argued that individuals could only retain about seven meaningful units of experience at one time which he called *chunks*. These chunks included numbers, words, or short sentences. This approach to short-term memory was called 7 plus or minus 2 because memory was individualized. Often referred to *Miller's Law*, Miller argued there were limitations to human cognition and the idea of a magical number seven was primarily symbolic. Unlike the behaviorists, this "law" showed that it was the information in the stimulus that needed to be understood.

In one of his earliest works on linguistics, Miller (1951) spoke of the importance of symbolism in language comprehension. Although he emphasized statistical techniques, he could not escape the power of symbol in language development which gave symbol special attention in using language because without symbol there would be no language. *Language and Communication* (Miller, 1951) was considered an early attempt to expand behaviorism and apply information theory to psychology. The important result of Miller's works was to shift psychology toward the study of internal cognitive processes.

In *The Science of Mental Life* (Miller, 1962/1991), the counterrevolution had begun. Miller purposively modeled the writings of William James, who in 1890 had defined psychology as *a science of mental life*. Miller, in a similar fashion, envisioned a new psychology focused on a cognitive view of mental life. Miller believed that classical and operant conditioning could not explain complex internal mental processes. It was the *cognitive information* in the stimuli that was most important. Cognitive science returned psychology to a time before behaviorism and neobehaviorism domination.

In 1960, Miller and Jerome Bruner founded the *Center for Cognitive Studies* and by 1969 cognitive psychology was accepted in mainstream psychology as witnessed by Miller's election as president of the APA. In the same year, Miller founded the *Cognitive Psychology* journal, which in the next two decades, resulted in the proliferation of many new cognitive psychology journals. To the dismay of many traditional behaviorists, particularly Skinner, cognition began to restore concepts of mentalism, introspection, and subjectivity that behaviorism had worked so hard to eliminate (Miller, 1962/1991).

Cognitive Psychology

In 1967, Ulric Neisser (1967), who studied with Miller, defined the term *cognitive psychology* in his landmark book, *Cognitive Psychology*. He defined psychological cognition as processes by which sensory input was transformed, reduced, stored, and recovered. These processes were present even in the absence of a stimulation. In fact, everything an individual did could be considered cognitive psychology. To strengthen his point, he contrasted cognitive from psychodynamic psychology. Neisser viewed psychodynamic psychology as concerned with motives rather than sensory inputs because he believed that psychodynamic psychology focused on goals, needs, and instincts, whereas the cognitive psychologist focused on what could be seen, remembered, and believed. For Neisser, cognitive psychology would study attention, perception, concept formation, meaning, language, memory, neuroscience, and information processing (Neisser, Boodoo, Boykin, et al, 1996). One early distinction between cognitive science and psychology was that cognitive science was interdisciplinary, whereas cognitive psychology mostly existed in academic psychology.

Cybernetics

The *Macy Conferences* (1941–1960) were another example of interdisciplinary meetings that included scholars from a variety of scientific disciplines, including psychology, to promote meaningful communication that would restore unity to scientific inquiry. From 1946 until 1953, *Cybernetics Conferences* were held under the guidance of the Macy Conferences to lay the foundation for a general science of the mind.

The Macy and Cybernetics Conferences were unable to reconcile the role of subjectivity in the development of the mind. In fact, the growing interest in the scientific community by the mid-twentieth century was for objective methods, mathematical formulations, reflexive behaviorism, and the human brain. This left little room for studying subjective meaning and purpose. An example at the *1951 Cybernetic Conference* meeting, the participants even questioned whether a mental event could create an unconscious memory or whether psychiatry could ever be a science. Although no consensus of what constituted a general science of the mind occurred, the fact that scholars were willing to think outside their sectarian disciplines led to significant interdisciplinary breakthroughs in systems theory and the study cybernetics, which influenced the development of the cognitive sciences.

In 1948, Norbert Wiener (1894–1964), a participant in the Macy and Cybernetic Conferences, defined *cybernetics* as the study of the structure and function of information-processing

204 *Symbols of Behaviorism, Neobehaviorism, and Cognitive Psychology*

(Wiener, 1948). Cybernetics was the circular causality or feedback loop where outcomes of biological and social system actions were evaluated as inputs for further actions. Wiener was interested in how mechanical and biological systems maintained homeostasis by automatically utilizing feedback from their activities.

Rooted in the Greek *kubernetes,* meaning "steersmen," symbolic of a "helmsman" who maintains a steady course in a changing environment by adjusting their steering in responses to the inputs needed for action. Examples include the automatic thermostat in electrical engineering, automatic family reactions in family psychotherapy, or the automatic shifting of a gear while driving a car in neuropsychology. Norbert Wiener was one of the first to theorize that all intelligent behavior was the result of feedback mechanisms that could be simulated by machines, providing an important early step towards the development of artificial intelligence (Heims, 1980). A Conference in India in 2017 indicates that cybernetics continues to have significant interest in symbol in the scientific community (Issac, 2017).

Figure 4.16

Artificial Intelligence

Alan Turing (1912–1954), the British father of *theoretical computer science* and *artificial intelligence,* invented the concept in 1950 in his landmark article in *Mind* journal (Turing, 1950). He raised the question as to whether machines could think. Turing thought the word think was ambiguous and needed explanation. In response, he created *The Turing Test* or the *imitation game,* in which he formulated questions to both a human and computer that were hidden from the view of an interrogator. The human was instructed to answer the questions truthfully and try to convince the interrogator that they were the human, and the computer was programmed to respond as a human. Because the interrogator could not distinguish human from computer

Symbols of Behaviorism, Neobehaviorism, and Cognitive Psychology 205

answers, Turing concluded that computers could think, creating a strong, some might say, intimate symbolical relationship between the computer and human.

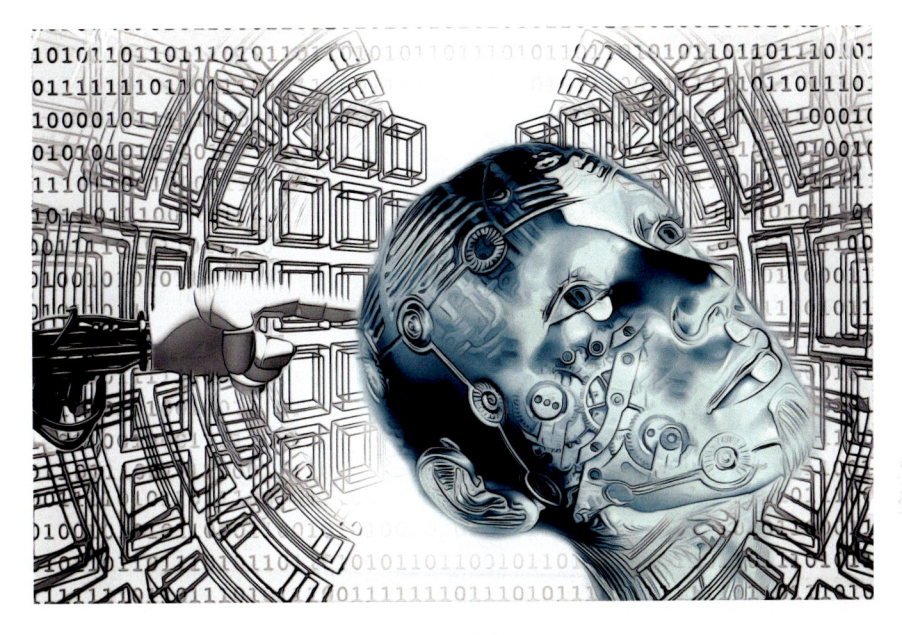

Figure 4.17

John McCarthy (1927–2011), a cognitive and computer scientist, was one of the founders and American advocate for using the term artificial intelligence (AI). In the mid-twentieth century, AI became a branch of computer science with the goal to investigate the extent to which the mental powers of human beings could be applied to machines. Serious research efforts began in 1956 after McCarthy led an AI symposium at Dartmouth College that brought scholars of AI together for the first time to strategize about the future and to distinguish AI from cybernetics.

Symbols became important in early AI research and in the debate about whether computers could think. John Searle (1980), in his paper "Minds, Brains and Programs," reported his findings from his *Chinese Room* experiment modeled after the Turning Test, but with Chinese symbols. In the experiment, there were computer instructions for the English language subject on how to match Chinese symbols. In the process it was possible, as in the Turing Test, that by using a Chinese computer program the English subject could convince the live Chinese speaker that the subject understood Chinese. Although it may appear that the subject understood Chinese because of computer programming, the reality was that the subject had no understanding of the meaning of the symbols. This indicated to Seale that computers could not think, have a mind, or intelligence, no matter how much a computer is programmed to be like a human.

The findings of Turing and Searle would lead to a debate among AI scholars as to whether computers have a weak or strong artificial intelligence. Those that believed that computers could only simulate the human mind, like Searle (1990), viewed computers as possessing a weak artificial intelligence. Those that argued that a computer, like Turing, had the capacity of understanding the human mind argued for a strong artificial intelligence. The proponents of a strong AI believed computers do not just simulate, but rather duplicate cognitive processes.

The time was ripe, especially with the decline of neobehaviorism, for psychology to view computers from a purely natural and physical science perspective. If animals and humans could be linked together, why not machines and computers? Searle and Turing set the stage for the ongoing debate about how computers and machines could duplicate the human mind. Besides the revolutionary goal of replicating the human experience, AI necessitated a reassessment of what constituted an internal, cognitive world.

In the 1980s, John Haugeland (1985) coined the term *GOFAI* (*Good Old-Fashioned Artificial Intelligence*) for *symbolic artificial intelligence*. Symbolic artificial intelligence was the term for the methods in AI research that defined intelligence as the ability to manipulate symbols. Symbolic intelligence theory dominated AI from the 1950s to the 1980s; the use of symbols was essential for the primary AI goal of reproducing human intelligence in computers and machines.

Information-Processing

By the late 1950s, psychologists began to study the relationship between humans and computers. Allen Newell, J. C. Shaw, and Herbert Simon (1958) marked the transition in psychology between artificial intelligence and *information processing*. Information-processing theorists argued that computers could solve problems in a similar manner as humans. They believed that the human mind and computer programs were both problem-solving devices. Newell, Simon, and Shaw developed the first artificial intelligence program called the *Logic Theorist,* which could program automated reasoning. They found that it could prove 38 of 52 theorems and provide excellent proof for the rest. For the emerging information-processing psychologists, input replaced stimulus and output replaced response. Concepts such as storage, encoding, processing, and retrieval began to describe a problem-solving information-processing psychology.

Roy Lachman, Janet Lachman, and Earl C. Butterfield (2015) were some of the first psychologists to imply that cognitive psychology had its "revolutionary origin" in information processing. It was called the cognitive revolution because cognitivism provided a major paradigm shift in psychology. Cognitive psychology could finally integrate the physical and mental worlds, and mental life could now be explained by the concepts of information, computation, and feedback. Lachman, Lachman, and Butterfield (2015), in *Cognitive Psychology and Information Processing,* provided one of the most impressive descriptions of how cognitive psychology could replace Watsonian and Skinnerian psychology. Symbols continued to be the key to computer decision-making because computers, like humans, process symbols, and make decisions about the input; create new impressions of the input; store the input; and *give back a symbolic output.* Calling a behavior, a response was quite different from calling behavior an output. It implied a different belief system and history and a totally different explanation. In a similar manner, a stimulus and an input would propose quite different implications. These discoveries encouraged psychologists to abandon animal for computer research, since computers had the potential to explain human behavior much more accurately than the study of non-human animals.

Connectivism

Donald Hebb (1904–1985), who is considered the father of neuropsychology, separated the mind from the brain. In his classic *The Organization of Behavior*, Hebb (1949) combined his background in brain surgery with the study of human behavior. He *connected* the biological function of the brain with the higher functions of the mind. Hebb was able to develop a single theory; the *Hebb's Rule* explained that learning occurred during the simultaneous activation of neurons. Or said another way, neurons that fire together wire together. The irony was that Hebb provided the neuropsychological explanation for the association laws of learning first discovered by Aristotle.

Hebb defined psychology as a natural science by identifying thought with integrated activity in the brain. Everything experienced in the environment fires a set of neurons, a processing unit called cell assemblies, which dictate a response in the brain to stimuli. Behavior and thought were now the result of brain function. Cognitive processes and learning were determined by the connection between neuron cell assemblies. A stimulating and rich environment strengthened the cell assemblies, which increased cognitive functioning and learning. Hebb argued that the quality of the environment in childhood determined adulthood learning. To prove his theory, he and his daughters raised baby rats at home in an enriched environment. This later demonstrated significant improvement in adulthood in rat maze learning. This led to an interest in psychology concerning the impact of the environment on learning during childhood. One tangible result of Hebb's work was the development of *Head Start*. This widely acclaimed social program provides an enriched environment of comprehensive early childhood education to low-income children and their families.

Under the influence of Hebbian thought regarding the importance of neural pathways and cell assemblies, connectivism attempted to integrate symbolic artificial intelligence with artificial neural networks. This occurred by understanding the network of nodes and connections. A node was anything that connected to another node. It could be a symbol, organization, information, data, and even feelings. There are three types of nodes: neural (biological), cognitive (internal), and external (environmental). Nodes, in Latin, mean "knots"; that which ties systems together and can create, receive, or transmit information over a complex set of networks.

Connectivism defined knowledge as a network and learning as a process of pattern recognition, a learning theory for the digital age. As humans transitioned into the digital age, connectivism provided the theoretical framework for understanding how to traverse across a diversity of connecting technologies. Internet technologies such as browsers, search engines, and social networks created the digital revolution and continue to change how people live, communicate, and learn (Hebb, 1960). Even more dramatic was the development of the robot, which symbolized that humans could digitally operate a mechanical and computerized being, which would improve the quality of human life.

It was ironic that interest in computers and machines caused many in psychology to reconsider the importance of internal cognitive processes. The reality was that no matter where AI, informational-processing, and connectivism research went, the importance of symbols emerged. Symbols provided the foundation for not only duplicating human cognition in machines but searching for the essence of what it means to be human. Because scientists were attempting to replicate the human experience, the development of the robot necessitated the exploration of what constituted the human mind. The robot symbolizes an emerging cognitive behavioral psychology and the end of Watsonian and Skinnerian domination of psychology. Reinforced behaviors or environmental conditioning could not offer much regarding the creation of the new "humans."

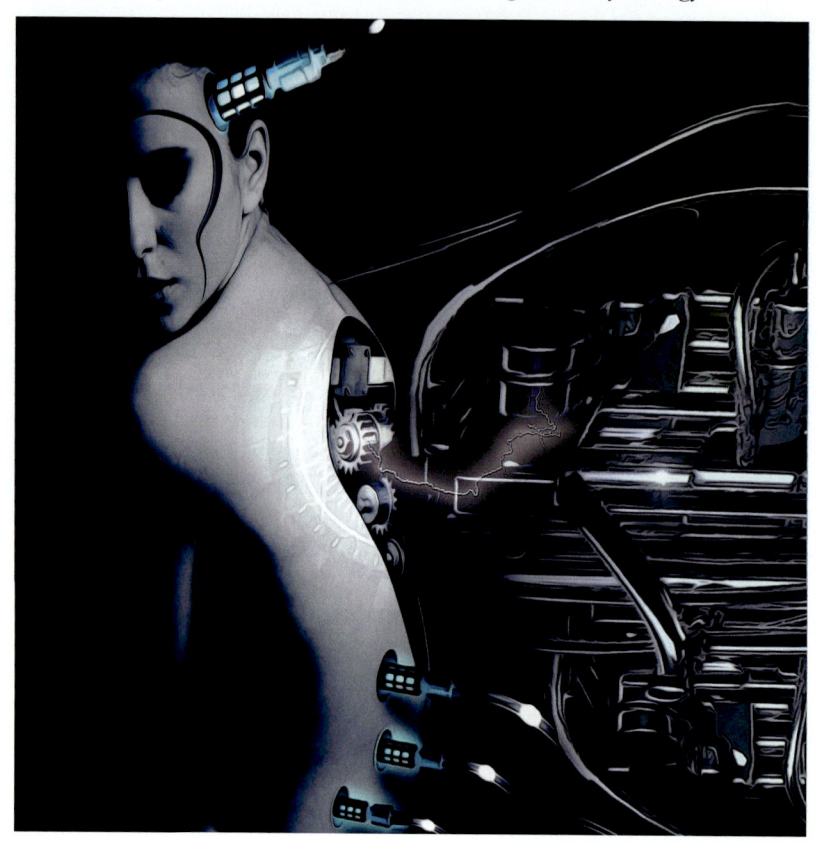

208 *Symbols of Behaviorism, Neobehaviorism, and Cognitive Psychology*

Figure 4.18

Hermeneutic Interest in Cognitive Behavioral Psychology

Stoicism

Stoicism influenced cognitive behavioral psychology because it viewed philosophy not as a theoretical construct, but as a way of life. Epictetus (50–135 AD), a Greek stoic, taught that since all external events were beyond human control, it was important to accept reality calmly and dispassionately. It was not what happened to people that disturbed them; it was the impact of their judgments about what happened that was most important. In other words, how we think about a situation shapes our experience and "state of being." Epictetus (2006) argued that the role of philosophy was self-knowledge and that problems arose from ignorance and gullibility. Understanding the concept of opinions provided an answer to the avoidance of human suffering. When we lose something, stoics would say it was not within our power to possess it. The power of self-knowledge created an awareness that every possession was based on the opinion that there was external control. Achieving "peace of mind" meant rejecting false opinions about what happened in life, or in cognitive behavioral theory, rejecting dysfunctional thoughts.

Besides opinions, Epictetus warned that principles could also cause human suffering. Principles were beliefs based in theory not reality, a blind subservience to principles avoided the highest human purpose, which was to fulfill our duties as children, siblings, parents, and fellow citizens. Self-examination required examination of the principles that were not connected to the

Stage Theory of Cognitive Development

Observing children inspired Jean Piaget (1896–1980), a Swiss psychologist, to develop one of the earliest theories of cognitive development. In 1955, in Geneva, he created the *International Center for Genetic Epistemology*, referred in scholarly literature as "Piaget's Factory." The center studied the origins of knowledge, the way knowledge was constructed, and the process from birth of cognitive development. Piaget believed that education could save civilization from total collapse, whether the demise was violent or gradual. Piaget was part of the cognitive revolution because he objected to the orthodox behaviorist belief that cognitive changes were the result of classical or operant conditioning. He believed his *stage theory* proved that cognitive development occurred in stages and was influenced by a genetic predisposition to learn and exposure to high-quality education.

In Piaget's (1966) theory of cognitive development, children move through four different stages of mental development: During the first sensory-motor stage, which lasts until around the age of two, the infant has little internal schemata of objects, which were not visibly present in their immediate environment. Toward the end of the sensory-motor stage, object permanence appears and the child understands that objects do not disappear once they are removed from their immediate environment. During the second pre-operational stage, from age 2 to 7, is divided into two sub-stages: symbolic thinking and intuitive thought. In the first sub-stage, the child thinks in symbolic images, while during the second sub-stage symbolic images develop into automatic thoughts that do not require evidence. In the third concrete operational stage, from 7 to 11, language provides the ability to think logically, but not abstractly. It is during the fourth formal operational stage, around age 12, a child becomes capable of solving abstract logical problems.

In recent years, neo-Piagetian theories are based on the belief that cognitive development continues beyond the formal operations stage, that adult cognitive development is much more nuanced. As an example, Sinnott (1998) proposed a fifth postformal *thought stage* described as cognitions that are more flexible, logical, dialectical, and able to accept moral and intellectual complexity. In postformal thought one can balance multiple logics, choices, and perceptions.

Zana Babakr, Pakistan Mohamedamin, and Karwan Kakamad (2019) argue that Piaget neglected cultural and social interaction factors in his stage theory of development and the thinking ability of children. Although they note that not all children in the world are raised and educated within a Western psychological framework, his integration of cognition into psychology remains an important and long-lasting contribution to the science of child development.

Most disturbing are the findings of Jeffery Arnett (2013) that not all people in all cultures, including the United States, reach the formal operation stage and that most people do not use formal operations in all aspects of their lives. This raises serious concerns about parenting, the quality of the education system, and the values being taught to children. These concerns could provide one reason for the growing social, cultural, and political polarization in America and throughout the world.

Social Learning (Cognitive) Theory

Albert Bandura (2025–2021), a Canadian American psychologist, developed *social learning* theory, which emphasized the importance of observing, modeling, and imitating the behaviors

210   *Symbols of Behaviorism, Neobehaviorism, and Cognitive Psychology*

of other people. He provided the bridge between behaviorist and cognitive learning theories by considering how both environmental and cognitive factors interacted to influence learning and behavior. Bandura (1977) agreed with the behaviorist theories of classical and operant conditioning, but argued for a cognitive process between stimulus and response. This process included learning from the environment, which he called *observational learning*. Bandura found that children model and encode behaviors of others that they perceive as like them. Through observation, a child will also consider what happens to other people before deciding to model a behavior.

Unlike Skinner, Bandura believed learning necessitated observational cognitive processes. Humans actively processed the consequences of their behavior and did not automatically respond to positive or negative reinforcement. Between stimulus and response, there needed to be four mediational cognitive processes. At first, the modeling behavior had to get attention. After gaining attention, the behavior had to be remembered. After attention and retention, the behavior had to be performed, a reproduction of the model behavior. Finally, there needed to be motivation to continue to perform the behavior that was determined by the rewards or punishments that followed the imitated behavior.

Figure 4.19

Observing unruly children led Bandura to research the sources of violence in their lives. Utilizing his social learning theory, he studied how children and adolescents learned to become aggressive. His initial work on aggression began in the 1940s but culminated in 1961 with the famous *Bobo Doll Experiment,* which studied the behavior of children after watching a human adult model act aggressively toward a Bobo Doll, a doll-like toy with a rounded bottom and low center of mass that could be hit and rock back to its upright position.

Bandura found that children exposed to an aggressive male model would seek physically aggressive behavior compared to those not exposed to an aggressive male model. With an aggressive male model, boys became much more physically aggressive than girls. Although less statistically significant, girls became more physically aggressive than boys when exposed to an aggressive female model. This caused Bandura to conclude that children learned aggression from same-sex role models, and that males learned to be more socially aggressive than females because of their exposure to same-sex role models (Bandura, Ross, & Ross, 1961). Bandura also found a correlation between physical and verbal aggression. Children who became physically aggressive were also more likely to become verbally aggressive than those children not exposed to an aggressive model. Bandura rejected the psychoanalytic view that viewing aggression was cathartic, a psychological release from the aggressive pressures of the unconscious. Rather, Bandura argued that his research clearly indicated that aggression was socially learned.

Criticism arose concerning social learning theory being too dependent on environmental imitation and modeling, which could not explain the more complex behaviors like thoughts and feelings. Also, how could children raised in disadvantaged environments become so well educated and successful? The answer was that learning was not only dependent on role modeling in the social environment, learning also necessitated strong cognitive processes. In response to the criticisms later in his career, Bandura (1986) emphasized the importance of cognition in learning, and renamed his theory, *social cognitive theory*.

Functional-Contextualism

In the late 1990s *functional-contextualism* emerged and became the most recent philosophical movement in cognitive behavioral psychology. Integrating functionalism and contextualism, functional-contextualism created a bridge back to Watson and Skinner. Although Watson and Skinner rejected philosophical explanations, they did acknowledge that human behavior needed to be understood in the context in which it occurred.

Modern functionalism is a theory of the mind that believes mental states can only be understood by their functional role. Drawing on recent developments in brain and computer research, modern functionalism views the brain as simply a neural substrate, like a computer, that performs computations on inputs that result in functional output behaviors. Thoughts, or any other mental states, are not dependent on internal mental processes but determined completely on their functional role and what has been accumulated in the cognitive system.

Contextualism argues that behavior could only be understood in the context in which it occurred. In philosophical terms, meaning, knowing, reasoning, and truth could only be understood in a specific context. This context-dependent philosophy is closely aligned with relativism, and social constructionism, the process by which human beings construct the meaning of the events in their lives. Contextualism strongly opposes mechanism and the current domination of logical positivism philosophy in modern psychology. Advocating for a revolution in psychological thought, contextualists integrate the theories of pragmatism, radical and logical empiricism, falsification in research methods, normative naturalism, and social constructivism.

E. J. Capaldi and Robert Proctor (1999) provide a critique of the two major movements in contextual psychology: one represented by those that argue for a hermeneutic psychology interested in the purpose and meaning of being human and rejecting the relevance of traditional empirical research; and one that values prediction and control of behavior as desirable goals and want to use empirical methods to objectively analyze purpose and meaning. This debate in contextual psychology mirrors many of the concerns about the relevance of empirical research from psychodynamic and humanistic-existential psychologists.

Functional-contextualism in cognitive behavioral psychology integrates function and context. The goal is to achieve prediction with precision, scope, and depth. This occurs by developing a set of constructs that could apply to an event; then applying those constructs to a wide variety of events and finally identifying the contextual features that could predict probability to all events. This analysis would not focus on the cause but the explanation of behavior; explaining whether the constructs were leading to the achievement of individual goals. Because general explanations could not always apply to a unique individual, the functional-contextual focus analyzes the history and context of individual private events such as relationships, thoughts, and feelings which become legitimate areas in cognitive behavioral research and therapy. From a functional-contextual perspective, private events are now considered in context as dependent variables, not independent variables, because independent variables describe the cause of behavior without context.

Although on the surface behaviorism can be perceived as rejecting the internal, subjective, hermeneutic approach, the reality was that functional-contextualism allowed cognitive-behavioral psychology to find another way to accept "private events" while staying true to its vision of the importance of objective behavioral analysis. However, the acknowledgment of the significance of individual history and unique cognitive reactions to environmental cues opened the door for hermeneutic understanding of the meaning and purpose of "private events." It also led to the *third-wave psychotherapeutic approaches* in cognitive behavioral therapy.

Buddhism and Daoism

Buddhism is discussed extensively in Volume I, Chapter 2, because it developed during the Axial Age. The traditions of Buddhism influenced the *third wave of cognitive behavioral therapy*. Buddhist meditative practices, translated as *mindfulness,* made Buddhism more scientifically acceptable to the scientific proclivities of Western and cognitive psychology.

The practice of mindfulness is rooted in *sati,* a spiritual or psychological practice that forms the essential foundation of Buddhist spirituality. *Sati* is the first factor of the *Seven Factors of Enlightenment* and the seventh element of the *Noble Eightfold Path*. The concept of *sati,* translated into English as "mindfulness," provided the philosophical inspiration for many of the third-wave cognitive behavioral therapies. Mindfulness practice offered a new and often more effective way to understand thoughts.

Cognitive psychologists integrated Buddhist beliefs that challenged many of their deeply held biases about the mind. Particularly the Buddhist view that sense-perceptions were often illusions; those thoughts were separate from the true self and did not reflect reality. In mindfulness practice, one learns to gain distance from their thoughts because thoughts do not represent their true nature. "Cognitive clouds passing through the mind" provides a perfect symbol of the Buddhist contribution to cognitive behavioral psychology.

Mindfulness practice was also influenced by *Zen Buddhism*, the Mahayana School of Buddhism that originated in China during the Tang Dynasty. *Zen* is the Chinese transliteration of the Sanskrit *dhyana*, which means "meditation." Besides religious self-restraint and meditative practices, Zen Buddhists believe, like cognitive therapists, the importance of developing daily insight into the nature of the mind. Insight is gained through two main cognitive processes: *Vipassana*, the Sanskrit word meaning "special seeing," which is gained through meditative practices; and *samatha,* which means "mind calming." During the third wave in cognitive behavioral therapy, therapists help clients recognize the impermanence of their thoughts and how to create a distance from their cognitions. They recognized the limitations of obsessively eliminating dysfunctional thoughts because that approach overemphasizes the importance of thoughts.

Figure 4.20

Edward Murguia and Kim Diaz (2015) found Daoist opposition to categories of thought relevant to cognitive behavioral therapy. For the Daoist, categorization interfered in the natural flow of human experience. This challenged a major belief in orthodox cognitive behaviorism that thoughts needed to be categorized. Third wave CBT therapists agreed that categorization often ossified thoughts and made it difficult to adjust to a constantly changing world.

Understanding Buddhist and Daoist thought is essential to a third-wave cognitive therapeutic approach, especially learning "mind calming" to reduce the overstimulation on the modern western mind. To accomplish "special seeing" and "mind calming," both schools of thought seek an accomplished teacher, a master, for spiritual and mental guidance. Many third-wave CBT therapists, like the ancient masters, teach the art of mindfulness, and through the therapeutic relationship, connect clients to thoughts that are meaningful and that are based on higher values. In this way, to avoid the human suffering that results from an overidentification with thoughts which distract from the true self.

Cognitive Behavioral Psychology

Cognitive Behavioral Therapy

The history of cognitive behavioral therapy is most often described and symbolized in three waves. The first wave occurred in reaction to psychoanalysis and other psychotherapies that were considered unscientific. The second wave occurred with the arrival of cognitive and computer sciences, and the third wave resulted from the need to treat more severe mental disturbance, which necessitated concepts of emotional appraisal and affect regulation.

214 *Symbols of Behaviorism, Neobehaviorism, and Cognitive Psychology*

Figure 4.21

Three waves are symbolized by the "Mount Rushmore" of behaviorism, (L-R) Aaron Beck (CBT), Marsha Linehan (Dialectic Behavioral Therapy), John Watson (behaviorism), and B. F. Skinner (neobehaviorism).

First Wave – Behavioral Therapy and Operant Conditioning

The first wave of cognitive behavior therapy was behavior without the cognitive approach. *Behavioral therapy* was a reaction to the clinical practices in the 1920s, especially of psychoanalysis, which behaviorists viewed as unscientific. The first wave had little interest in interpersonal, emotional, or relationship behaviors, rooted in classical respondent conditioning of Watson and the operant conditioning of Skinner.

Watson's behaviorism utilized Pavlov's stimulus-response (S-R) respondent psychology. The first behavioral intervention was interested in proving a theory rather than changing the life of an individual. Since he was able to condition Little Albert to become fearful of rats and other furry objects, Watson realized he could also uncondition behavior in the Peter and the Rabbit experiment. These were the first experiments that showed the potential for behavioral therapy.

Skinner rejected Watson's S-R psychology in favor of operant conditioning; it was environmental enforcement which changed behavior. For Skinner, Darwin had proven that evolution depended on the environment to modify the behavior of an organism. This belief led to the development of *behavior modification*, the Skinnerian approach to behavioral change. Token economies is an example of behavior modification, showed how positive environmental reinforcement modified behavior in state mental and developmental institutions. Skinnerian rejection of punishment led to more effective parental behavioral modification techniques like "time out;" a negative reinforcement, a forced, non-violent, withdrawal from the environment for the bad behavior of a child.

The first time, the term behavior therapy was utilized occurred when Lindsley, Skinner, and Solomon (1953) published *Studies in Behavior Therapy*. The publication was produced by *Metropolitan State Mental Hospital*, one of the largest and most modern state mental hospitals for its time in Belmont, Massachusetts. History would again place mental hospitals at the beginning of experimental treatments. In the "Status Report," behavior therapy was the description given to the successful treatment of psychotics with operant conditioning. Skinner believed that building positive reinforcement contingencies could successfully treat psychosis.

By the 1950s, behavior therapy began to replace psychoanalysis as the preferred psychotherapeutic treatment. Hans Eysenck, the British personality, and intelligence theorist created the first journal, *Behavior Research and Therapy*. Cecil Franks (1924–2015), an early leader in promoting behavioral therapy and prominent faculty member of *Rutgers University*, formed the *Association for the Advancement of Behavior Therapy* (AABT). It is now called the *Association for Behavioral and Cognitive Therapies* (ABCT), which is the largest association in North America for the study and practice of cognitive behavioral therapy.

Second Wave – Cognitive Behavioral Therapy

The second wave was inspired by the cognitive revolution of the 1950s and 1960s. The explosion of cognitive psychology and the mechanistic computer sciences gave rise to the second wave of behavioral therapy. Behind the wave was Albert Bandura, who extended behavior theory to include cognitive models of change, learning by observation, and theories of self-efficacy. The second wave also was a reaction to criticism that behaviorism was unwilling to address language and private experiences, including thoughts and emotions. CBT was also influenced by the clinical paradigm of Freudian psychoanalysis. While psychoanalysts believed individuals were motivated by unconscious forces, CBT therapists believed individuals were motivated by cognitive processes like automatic thoughts, beliefs, and schemas. The cognitive therapy revolution was led not by academicians like Watson and Skinner, but rather by psychotherapists like Albert Ellis and Aaron Beck (Volpe, 1973).

Albert Ellis (1913–2007), one of the first pioneers of the second wave, was initially a staunch supporter of psychoanalysis and analytic psychology. Early in his career, he sought additional training in psychoanalysis, and in 1947 began Jungian analysis with Richard Hulbeck, a protégée of Karen Horney. But it was his exposure to philosophy, especially Stoic philosophy, that his views began to change. He was especially influenced by the philosophies of the Axial Age including Confucius and Gautama Buddha. By 1954, he broke with psychoanalysis and began referring to himself as a *rational emotive behavioral therapist* (REBT). Unlike psychoanalysis, REBT used a psycho-educational approach. Through rational analysis and cognitive reconstruction, personal beliefs, irrational thoughts, and self-defeating behaviors became conscious. The therapist became a teacher as well as a clinician who alleviated human suffering. The belief that mental disturbance was learned behavior and through an educational process could be changed became a key tenet of REBT treatment.

Ellis (1957) published *How to Live with a Neurotic*, which explained his new approach to psychotherapy. However, REBT was initially met by the mid-twentieth century with some hostility as experimental psychologists were interested in orthodox behaviorism and clinical psychologists in psychoanalysis. There was only mild interest in cognitive therapy when Ellis spoke at a 1960 APA Convention. Little did psychologists know at the time that Ellis and REBT would become the prototype for the upcoming CBT revolution in psychology.

If Peter and the Rabbit experiment symbolized Watsonian behavioral therapy and the Skinner box symbolized behavior modification, the ABCs conceived by Ellis symbolized the beginning of cognitive behavioral therapy. The A represented the antecedent event, the B represented the beliefs that led to the behavior, and the C represented the consequences of the behavior. By using the ABC method, Ellis believed that irrational beliefs and emotions could be changed. By becoming cognitively aware of a belief system, it was possible to change or alter reactions to events that had previously been disturbing. The ABC model has continued to be a therapeutic tool for many behavioral therapists.

Aaron Beck, a psychiatrist, is considered the father of cognitive behavioral therapy. As often the case in early history of clinical psychology, Beck, like Ellis, began with an interest in psychoanalysis. His inspiration for his now famous clinical inventories came from Leon Saul, a psychoanalyst interested in inventories which quantified ego processes in dreams. In the 1950s, Beck continued his interest in psychoanalysis and completed his formal training at the *Philadelphia Institute of the American Psychoanalytic Association.*

Threatened by new ideas emerging in the mental health field, and despite graduating from the institute, in 1960, the Philadelphia Institute denied Beck membership because of his support of brief therapy methods, and claimed he needed more supervision on termination. In 1961, Beck tried to remain neutral regarding a controversy about whether the new chair of psychiatry in the Department of Psychiatry at the *University of Pennsylvania* should be a psychoanalyst or a biomedical researcher. The psychoanalysts won the battle; but history would record those orthodox psychoanalysts would lose the war with biomedicine and cognitive behavioral therapy.

Although Beck could have provided a bridge between psychoanalysis and cognitive behaviorism, after his alienating experiences with psychoanalysts at the University of Pennsylvania, he began to expand his professional world by studying philosophy and psychology. He also started communicating with Ellis and, like Ellis, became inspired by the Greeks, especially the Stoics. These philosophies and theories would provide the hermeneutic foundation for cognitive behavioral therapy. Unlike Ellis, who practiced a strong directive approach, Beck, influenced by the *Socratic method*, believed in listening and empowering the client to take responsibility for their treatment.

Unlike Ellis, Beck did not completely abandon his psychoanalytic training. To the dismay of modern orthodox behaviorists who vehemently reject psychoanalysis, Beck, during his career, would "quietly" describe his new cognitive behavioral therapy as *Neo-Freudian*, from the *ego psychoanalytic* school. Rachael Rosin (2012) argued that newfound hand-sketched drawings of schemas from 1964 indicated that Beck continued to think psychoanalytically after his break from psychoanalysis. Rosin claimed the origin story of cognitive therapy was much more complex than the accounts in traditional historic textbooks and urged psychologists to view history more from an integrative than sectarian perspective.

Beck realized that in the empirically dominated modern psychological world, the case histories of psychoanalysis would never be accepted as scientific. In response, his new school of cognitive behavioral therapy brought an empirical approach to the psychotherapeutic world. *Randomized controlled studies* of psychotherapy began to dominate clinical research in all the psychotherapeutic schools. After working with many depressed clients, depression became Beck's first area of randomized controlled studies. In his first book, *The Diagnosis and Management of Depression,* Beck (1967) discovered that depressed individuals had *automatic thoughts* that were negative thoughts that emerged spontaneously. The content of automatic thoughts Beck described as *The Cognitive Triad,* fell into three categories: negative ideas about oneself, the world, and the future.

As clients began to explore their automatic thoughts, Beck found that their thoughts were often distorted and dysfunctional. Although Beck associated various distortions with mental disorders, a core belief of CBT was that no matter the disorder, distorted thoughts once recognized could be changed. One of the most powerful components of CBT treatment for clients is that concepts and interventions are practical and understandable. Everyone can understand and recognize themselves in dysfunctional thinking like catastrophizing, mind reading, "should" statements, overgeneralization, selective abstraction, dichotomous thinking, and emotional reasoning.

In cognitive behavioral therapy, automatic and dysfunctional thoughts become *schemas*, the belief systems created by the way parents treat their children during infancy and early childhood. For instance, if a parent is abusive, the child can develop a schema with the cognitions "to be treated this way something must be wrong with me," or "I am bad and deserve to be abused." Schemas can provide important clinical information. Depressed people often maintain an "I am flawed" schema; anxious people "the world is a dangerous place" schema; and angry people "people are malicious" schema.

Another major strength of cognitive behavioral therapy was the number of specific therapeutic interventions available to address dysfunctional thoughts and schemas. The mix of cognitive and behavioral techniques depend on the needs, the abilities, the psychopathology, and treatment goals of the client. Because at its root, cognitive behavioral therapists believe human dysfunction is learned when initiating treatment, the therapist becomes a teacher. The goal is to teach clients to become their own therapist.

Some of the most popular interventions of cognitive behavioral therapy include *rational responding* utilizing the *Dysfunctional Thought Record* (DTR). This requires a client to become conscious of dysfunctional thoughts, rate the emotional reaction to the thoughts, systematically examine the evidence supporting the dysfunctional thoughts, replace the thoughts with alternative thoughts, and then rate the emotional reaction to the new thoughts. The DTR gives the client a written record of their dysfunctional thoughts and beliefs and guides the client in their daily effort to make cognitive and behavioral changes.

Asking a client to examine advantages and disadvantages of an issue helps the client perceive a broader perspective and reasonable course of action. Scaling allows a client to rate an experience on a scale of 1–10. This counteracts "all-or-nothing" thinking and can quickly provide the therapist with the current mindset of the client. In the self-instruction technique, the therapist provides specific CBT workbooks for the client to learn new problem-solving skills related to their treatment plan. For example, Donald Meichenbaum (1994, 2020) has developed self-instruction workbooks for many mental health issues, especially for post-traumatic stress and addiction disorders.

CBT therapists often assign bibliotherapy readings that explain the principles of cognitive behavioral therapy. This literary approach provides clients with a deeper experience of their therapeutic sessions. Popular book recommendations include *Love is Never Enough* by Beck (1989), *Feeling Good* by David Burns (1989), and *Mind over Mood* by Dennis Greenberger and Christine Padesky (2016). Besides bibliotherapy, the CBT therapist typically assigns *homework* because of the belief that a therapy session should consolidate insights and skills into daily life. Reviewing homework during therapy sessions connects the consulting room to the real world and creates an environment for celebrating success as well as for troubleshooting future problems.

The stop sign is a simple but powerful symbol of how CBT interventions can reduce psychological distress. The thought stopping technique halts the "snowball effect" of dysfunctional thoughts. Clients are taught to imagine a stop sign when a negative state is first realized. When this technique resonates, clients find momentary relief which is vital to gaining control and using other techniques, like rational responding, before distressing thoughts escalate.

218 *Symbols of Behaviorism, Neobehaviorism, and Cognitive Psychology*

In the tradition of his fellow colleague psychoanalyst, Leon Saul, Beck developed Questionnaires which are widely used by clinicians throughout the world. The *Beck Depression Inventory* and the *Beck Anxiety Inventory* are most popular. Beck has also developed inventories that address youth, obsessive-compulsive problems, suicide, hopelessness, and the fast screening for medical problems.

The CBT of Beck and Ellis live on through the *Beck Institute for Cognitive Therapy and Research* in Bala-Cynwyd, Pennsylvania, and the *Albert Ellis Institute* in New York City.

Figure 4.22

Third Wave – Dialectical Behavioral Therapy

Although Beck is most associated with the second wave, his recent interest in schizophrenia symbolizes the current shift that began in the 1980s. The third wave developed in large part because of the limited success of CBT with more disturbed clients such as clients with personality disorders, bipolar disorder, schizophrenia, addiction, and relapsing depression. Individuals with mental illness again provided the impetus for change.

Paul Grant, Keith Bredemeier, and Aaron Beck (2017) found that CBT was most effective when integrating the new recovery and resilience models advocated by individuals with serious mental illness. Called *Recovery-Oriented Cognitive Therapy* (CT-R), the CT-R approach with serious mental illness, focuses less on the amelioration of symptoms, the goal of the therapist, and more on empowering the client to set their own goals.

Functional-contextualism provided the philosophical foundation for the third wave. With less focus on the causes and removal of negative symptoms, dysfunctional thoughts and irrational beliefs, CBT therapists became more interested in the context in which behaviors occurred. Embracing pragmatism rather than adherence to behavioral orthodoxy, what works, rather than what should work, created more relevant and functional treatments. Although often

Symbols of Behaviorism, Neobehaviorism, and Cognitive Psychology 219

resistant, it opened the door for CBT therapists to integrate their approach with other therapeutic approaches; most notably psychodynamic and humanistic-existential psychotherapies.

No one better symbolizes third-wave CBT than Marsha Linehan. Linehan is a psychologist and adjunct professor of psychiatry and behavioral sciences at the *University of Washington*, Seattle. She is also director of the *Behavioral Research and Therapy Clinics*. During a presentation, *Chain Analysis of Dysfunctional Behaviors,* at the *Evolution of Psychotherapy Conference* in 2013 in Anaheim, California, Linehan (2013) explained the historic roots of *Dialectical Behavioral Therapy* (DBT). She described the roots as an integration of the dialectics of Karl Marx, which she discovered from a connection to academia, the *Buddhism* she found at the *Shasta Abbey Buddhist Monastery* in Mount Shasta, California, and pragmatic behavioral principles. She acknowledged that she could not call her new therapy, Marxist, Buddhist, Behavioral Therapy; dialectical behavioral therapy was much more acceptable to America psychology.

Although she had been diagnosed with schizophrenia early in her life, Linehan believed that her diagnosis should have been borderline personality disorder. Therefore, it is not surprising that Linehan would develop DBT to first successfully treat borderline personality disorders. Because of the success of DBT with borderline personality disorders, DBT began to be utilized with other difficult to treat populations, especially with suicidal and addiction clients and is widely practiced in community mental health centers throughout the country.

Figure 4.23

What characterizes DBT is the self-regulation of strong emotional and cognitive triggers to life events. Through self-acceptance, mindfulness exercises and various change strategies, clients learn to cope by applying skills in the philosophical tradition of dialectics. For the borderline personality disordered client, dialectic thinking changes their linear black and white, "you are for or against me" hypothesis by holding the antithesis tension that the world can be supportive and unsupportive at the same time. The synthesis is understanding that the world is often "gray," which creates less distress and more emotional control.

Influenced by functional-contextualism and mindfulness movement, *Acceptance and Commitment Therapy* (ACT) developed by Steven C. Hayes of the *University of Nevada, Reno*, focused on creating a different relationship to thoughts. Steven Hayes, with Kirk Strosahl, and Kelly Wilson (2016), described his approach as *Relational Frame Theory* (RTP), which viewed the relationship with language as the key determinant of human behavior. They believed that in language a word, a sentence or a symbol could have a different meaning and function depending on the context. The purpose of ACT was not to eliminate negative feelings but rather create an acceptance and not to overreact to disturbing thoughts and experience.

The belief is that mental disturbance is caused by an inflexibility and by judging internal events as aversive or negative. For instance, because one feels bad does not always mean they have had an actual negative experience. The goal of ACT is to distance clients from these types of cognitions, and to view depressive and other thoughts nonjudgmentally addressing the context, not the content of the cognitions. Say: "I am noticing thoughts of failure" rather than "I am a failure." This frees clients from obsessively restructuring thoughts and compulsively trying to control automatic thoughts and other forms of dysfunctional thinking. A healthy response to dysfunctional thoughts is the acceptance of thoughts and feelings and a commitment to actions which create a meaningful life based on strong personal values.

Buddhist practices influenced the growing *mindfulness* movement in CBT treatment. *Mindfulness-Based Cognitive Therapy* (MBCT) applied the Beck model of CBT treatment with the principles of Buddhist meditation (Woods, Rockman & Collins, 2019). By applying the Beck model, MBCT discovered that stress triggers symptoms and overlearned schemas and habitual patterns of thinking. This approach was originally applied to relapse prevention treatment for individuals with Major Depressive Disorders (MDDs).

A major component of MBCT treatment utilizes the *Mindfulness-Based Stress Reduction* (MBRS) techniques of Jon Kabat-Zinn. Kabat-Zinn integrated scientific research on stress with Zen Buddhist teachings. In 1979 he developed of the *Center for Mindfulness in Medicine, Health Care and Society* at the *University of Massachusetts Medical School.* After a special television program in 1993 on PBS with Bill Moyers, he became recognized as one of the leading experts in mindfulness training in the world. In his first book, *Full Catastrophe of Living*, Kabat-Zinn (1991) gave specific instructions on how to use the wisdom of the body and mind to overcome stress, chronic pain, and physical illness.

By the time of his second book, *Wherever You Go, There You Are* (Kabat-Zinn,1994), a nation-wide bestseller, many MRSR clinics had opened throughout the United States. Many hospitals and health care providers began to practice MRSR as part of a holistic medical program. Although Kabat-Zinn would rather be called someone who "applies a scientific rather than a religious frame," he continues his exploration of Buddhist thought through the *Mind and Life Institute*, a contemplative sciences institute in Charlottesville, Virginia, which organizes dialogues between the Dalai Lama and Western scientists.

As Kabat-Zinn tried to distance himself from Buddhism, MBCT tried to distance itself from an over-emphasis on the MRSR approach. John Teasdale (1993) developed the theory of *integrated Cognitive Systems* (ICS) and argued that the mind functions through multiple modes to receive and process thoughts and emotions. Zindel Segal, Mark Williams, and John Teasdale (2002) published *Mindfulness-Based Cognitive Therapy for Depression,* which included a forward from Kabat-Zinn. They discovered there was a vulnerability in depression to rely only on one mode of

Symbols of Behaviorism, Neobehaviorism, and Cognitive Psychology 221

thinking and blocking other cognitive modes. The two main modes of thinking were *doing* and *being modes.* The doing mode is triggered when the mind develops a discrepancy between the reality of how things are and how the mind would like things to be. Influenced by Buddhism and other Eastern thought, the being mode accepts reality as it is and avoids any pressure to change it. The metacognitive ICS process allows the client to experience negative and depressive thoughts as "pass through" cognitions, not part of the self. Through a decentering process clients learn to view thoughts and feelings as impermanent, fleeting, and open to objective analysis. MBCT therapists believe that the being mode of the mind leads to the most long-lasting cognitive and emotional changes and is the mode that prevents the relapse of major depression.

Unlike the other waves, the third CBT wave does not seek to eliminate symptoms and dysfunctional thoughts. *Functional Analytic Psychotherapy* (FAP) views mental disturbance as deficits of functioning; the lack of positive environmental reinforcement and the neglect of the contextual factors which impede learning. The FAP process is much more open-ended and client-driven in contrast to the more structured therapist directed therapies of first and second CBT waves. Robert Kohlenberg and Mavis Tsai (1991) created a theoretical and psychodynamic model of cognitive behavioral therapy.

FAP developed amidst growing empirical evidence that a strong client-therapist relationship was essential for positive clinical outcomes, no matter the type of psychotherapy practiced. Although not framed as psychodynamic transference and countertransference terms, FAP viewed the client-therapist relationship as essential for improving functioning and changing context. Rather than following previous CBT orthodoxy, which set specific goals for specific problems, FAP therapists develop unique clinical formulations with clients that apply specifically to their unique individual needs. Unlike psychodynamic therapists, FAP examine the conscious, not unconscious, factors that create problematic behaviors. In session, problematic behaviors are called clinically relevant behavior 1 (CRB1); and in session, improvements are called clinically

Figure 4.24

relevant behavior 2 (CRB2). The goal of FAP therapy is to decrease CRB1s and increase CRB2s. After evoking, reinforcing, and observing CRBs, the FAP therapist through functional interpretations provides the client with ongoing feedback during the therapy session regarding their problematic and improved in session behaviors. Because of the immediacy and intensity of the interpretations, the ultimate success of FAP treatment depends on the trust generated in therapeutic relationship.

Third-wave CBT reintroduced mainstream psychology to the philosophy of Buddhism as well as to other Eastern philosophies rooted in the Axial Age. The belief that thoughts "are only thoughts" is deeply rooted in Axial Age thought. It is improbable that the concept of mindfulness that emerged in the third CBT wave would have been possible in the first and second waves. It is ironic as this chapter ends that an approach that for nearly 60 years has focused on the power of thoughts to control behavior, would, through the third CBT wave, provide a way to be emancipated from thought. This reality is symbolized by a mindful third-wave Buddha, meditating with the dog of Pavlov, the rat of Skinner, Little Peter of Watson, and the stop sign of Beck. In the meditation, the importance of thoughts is recognized but something deeper and more freeing beyond thinking is experienced

Emancipatory Opportunities in Cognitive Behavioral Psychology

Consider Cognitive Behavior Therapy

CBT has been found to be highly effective with many mental health issues, particularly with depression, anxiety, panic, social phobia, and posttraumatic stress disorders. CBT is one of the most practiced therapies in community mental health systems.

Consider Dialectical Behavioral Therapy

DBT has been found to be highly effective with serious mental illnesses. Initially showed efficacy with personality disorders, DBT is now utilized to treat many mental health issues, especially effective with bipolar, addiction, and schizophrenia disorders. CBT and DBT are typically the most practiced treatment approaches in community mental health systems.

Practice Mindfulness

The Buddhist-inspired mindfulness practice has shown to enhance physical, mental, and spiritual health. Many hospitals and healthcare providers practice the MRSR of Jon Kabat-Zinn as part of a holistic medical program. Most of the third-wave cognitive behavioral therapies incorporate mindfulness practices into their treatment approaches.

Read Recommended CBT Books

Love is Never Enough by Aaron Beck (1989), *Feeling Good* by David Burns (1989), and *Mind over Mood* by Dennis Greenberger and Christine Padesky (2016).

Examine the Beck Inventories

Readily available on the Internet. The *Beck Depression Inventory* and the *Beck Anxiety Inventory* are some of the most frequently utilized clinical inventories; best utilized in treatment with a licensed psychotherapist.

Symbols of Behaviorism, Neobehaviorism, and Cognitive Psychology 223

QUESTIONS 4

4.1 *Describe the political, socioeconomic, and cultural influences that led to the development of behaviorism, neobehaviorism, and cognitive-behavioral psychology.*

4.2 *Explain the influence of Russian psychology on the development of behaviorism.*

4.3 *Describe why ethics became important in psychological research after the Little Albert experiment.*

4.4 *Explain how the Skinner box represents operant conditioning.*

4.5 *Describe the world that Skinner envisioned.*

4.6 *Explain the impact of the cognitive revolution on cognitive behavioral psychology.*

4.7 *Describe the reason Skinner objected to cognitive behavioral psychology.*

4.8 *Explain the influence of cognitive behavioral psychology on the development of artificial intelligence.*

4.9 *Describe the three waves of cognitive behavioral therapy.*

4.10 *Explain how the third wave of cognitive behavioral therapy was influenced by the Axial Age.*

Universal Meanings of Chapter Symbols

Figure 4.0:
  John Watson image source. https://totallyhistory.com/john-b-watson/
  B.F. Skinner image source. https://en.wikipedia.org/wiki/B._F._Skinner
  Aaron Beck image source. https://www.assumption.edu/people-and-departments/organization-listing/aaron-t-beck-institute-cognitive-studies
  Marsha Linehan image source. https://depts.washington.edu/uwbrtc/our-team/marsha-linehan/
  Noam Chomsky image source. https://en.wikipedia.org/wiki/Noam_Chomsky
  George Miller image source. https://peoplepill.com/people/george-armitage-miller

Figure 4.1. Human behavior determined only by external, environmental forces.
Figure 4.2. The shadow of symbol in advertising.
Figure 4.3. Destructive result of denying the shadow of heterosexualism.
Figure 4.4. Human thought, intelligence, and emotions attributed to nonhuman animals.
Figure 4.5. Learning occurs through the effect of doing something, a connection between sensory impressions and experience.
Figure 4.6. Automatic biological change that occurs naturally in the physical environment.
Figure 4.7. Frogs as symbolic of the ability to connect the conscious and unconscious mind.
Figure 4.8. Experience of neurosis, a behavioral connection to psychodynamic psychology.
Figure 4.9. Behavior occurs immediately from a stimulus (S) in, and a response (R) out.
Figure 4.10. Human mind as a passive recipient of inputs from external stimuli.
Figure 4.11. Planned human interventions can dramatically change behavior.
Figure 4.12. Learning occurs through the development of a cognitive map.
Figure 4.13. A symbol of how positive reinforcement changes human behavior.
Figure 4.14. The ability to discriminate a reinforcing from a non-reinforcing event.
Figure 4.15. A symbol for understanding personality dynamics and the unconscious human mind.

Figure 4.16. The internal "helmsman" that provides direction from external inputs that need immediate attention.
Figure 4.17. Computers that can think like human beings.
Figure 4.18. The replication of the human experience through machines.
Figure 4.19. Effect of adult violence and aggression on children.
Figure 4.20. Thoughts like "cognitive clouds" passing by the mind.
Figure 4.21. Symbol of the third force in Psychology visionaries.
Figure 4.22. Sign to stop dysfunctional thoughts.
Figure 4.23. Therapeutic value to change thoughts, meditate, and find internal control to balance positive and negative impulses.
Figure 4.24. Symbol of how Buddhism influenced the development of modern psychology.

References

Allot, A., Knight, C. & Smith, N. (2020). The *responsibilities of intellectuals: Reflections of Noam Chomsky and others after 50 years*. London: University College London Press.

Arnett, J. (2013). *Adolescence and emerging adulthood: A cultural approach*. (5th ed.). New York: Pearson Education, Inc.

Babakr, Z.H., Mohamedamin, P. & Kakamad, K. (2019). Piaget's cognitive developmental theory: Critical review. *Education Quarterly Reviews*. *2*(3), 517–524.

Bacon, F. (1994). *Novum organum*. (P. Urbach & J. Gibson, Trans. & Eds.). Chicago: Open Court. (Original work published in 1620).

Bandura, A. (1977). *Social learning theory*. Englewood Cliffs, NJ: Prentice Hall.

Bandura, A. (1986). *Social foundations of thought and action: A social cognitive theory*. Englewood Cliffs, NJ: Prentice-Hall, Inc.

Bandura, A., Ross, D. & Ross, S.A. (1961). Transmission of aggression through the imitation of aggressive models. *Journal of Abnormal and Social Psychology*. *63*(3), 575–582.

BBC. (2014, November). *Alan Turing: Separating the man and the myth*. Retrieved from https://www.bbc.com/future/article/20120620-the-turing-test-of-time

Bekhterev, V.M. (1913). *La psychologie objective (objective psychology)*. Paris: Alcan (Original work published 1907–1912).

Beck, A.T. (1967). *The diagnosis and management of depression*. Philadelphia, PA: University of Pennsylvania Press.

Beck, A.T. (1989). *Love is never enough*. New York: HarperCollins.

Bentham, J. (1988). *An introduction to the principles of morals and legislation*. New York: Prometheus Books. (Original work published in 1781).

Bjork, D.W. (1996). *B. F. Skinner: A life*. Washington, DC: American Psychological Association.

Bridgman, P.W. (1927). *The logic of modern physics*. New York: MacMillan.

Burns, D. (1989). *Feeling good: The new mood therapy*. New York: Morrow.

Capaldi, E.J. & Proctor, R.W. (1999). *Contextualism psychological research: A critical review*. Thousand Oaks, CA: Sage Publications.

Carey, A. (1997). *Taking the risk out of democracy: Corporate propaganda versus freedom and liberty*. (A. Lohrey, Ed.). Urbana, IL: University of Illinois Press.

Chomsky, N. (1959). Review of Skinner's verbal learning. *Language*. *35*, 26–58.

Chomsky, N. (1967). The responsibility of intellectuals. *The New York Review of Books*, *8*(3), 2–23.

Chomsky, N. (2012). *Occupy: Occupied media: Occupied media pamphlet*. New York: Zuccotti Park Press

Chomsky, N. (2013). *Occupy: Reflections on class war, rebellion and solidarity: Occupied media pamphlet*. New York: Zuccotti Park Press.

Chomsky, N. & Herman, E.S. (2002). *Manufacturing consent: The political economy of the media*. New York: Pantheon Books.

Comte, A. (1896). *A positive philosophy*. (H. Martineau, Trans.). London: Bell.

Dewey, J. (1889). *The school and society*. Chicago: University of Chicago Press.

Dewey, J. (1896). The reflex arc concept in psychology. *Psychological Review*. *3*, 357–370.

Dewey, J. (1916). *Democracy and education: An introduction to philosophy of education*. New York: Macmillan.
Digdon, N., Powell, R.A. & Harris, B. (2014). Little Albert's alleged neurological impairment: Watson, Rayner, and historic revision. *History of Psychology. 17*(4), 312–324.
Ellis, A. (1957). *How to live with a neurotic*. Oxford, England: Crown Publishers.
Epictetus (2006). *The discourses books 1–4*. Sioux Falls, SD: Nuvision.
Freud, S. (1961). *Civilization and its discontents*. (J. Strachey, Trans.). New York: Norton. (Original work published 1930)
Fridlund, A.J., Beck, H.P., Goldie, W.D. & Irons, G. (2012). Little Albert: A neurologically impaired child. *History of Psychology. 15*, 302–327.
Galef, B.G. (1998). Edward Thorndike: Revolutionary psychologist: Ambiguous biologist. *American Psychologist, 53*, 1228–1234.
Geary, B.B. & Zeig, J.K. (2001). *The handbook of Ericksonian psychotherapy*. Phoenix AZ: The Milton H. Erickson Foundation Press.
Grant, P.M., Bredemeier, K. & Beck, A.T. (2017). Six-month follow-up of recovery-oriented cognitive therapy for low-functioning individuals with schizophrenia. *Psychiatric Services. 68*(10), 997–1002.
Greenberger, D. & Padesky, C.A. (2016). *Mind over mood*. (2nd ed.). New York: Guilford Press.
Guthrie, E.R. (1935). *The psychology of learning*. New York: Harper & Row.
Guthrie, E.R. (1946). *Cats in a puzzle box*. New York: Rinehart.
Guthrie, E.R. (1959). Association by contiguity. In S. Koch (Ed.). *Psychology: A study of science* (Vol. 2, 158–195). New York: McGraw.
Haskell, E. (1972). *Full circle: The moral force of unified science*. New York: Gordon and Breach
Haugeland, J. (1985). *Artificial intelligence; The very idea*. Cambridge, MA: MIT Press.
Hayes, S., Strosahl, K.D. & Wilson, K.G. (2016). *Acceptance and commitment therapy: The process and practice of mindful change*. New York: The Guilford Press.
Hebb, D.O. (1949). *The organization of behavior*. New York: Wiley.
Hebb, D.O. (1960). *The American revolution. American Psychologist. 15*, 735–745.
Heims, S.J. (1980). *John von Neumann and Norbert wiener: From mathematics to the technologies of life and death*. Cambridge, MA: MIT Press.
Hodges, A. (2014). *Alan Turing: The enigma: The book that inspired the film the imitation game*. Princeton, NJ: Princeton University Press. (Original work published in 1983).
Hull, C.L. (1920). Quantitative aspects of the evolution of concepts: An experimental study. *Psychological Monographs. 28*, 121.
Hull, C.L. (1933). *Hypnosis and suggestibility: An experimental approach*. New York: Appleton-Century.
Hull, C.L. (1943). *Principles of behavior*. New York: Appleton-Century.
Hull, C.L., Hovland, C.L., Ross, C.T., Hall, M., Perkins, D.T. & Fitch, F.B. (1940). *Mathematical-deductive theory of new learning*. New Haven, C.T: Yale University Press.
Issac, R.M. (2017, July 14–16). *A Logical Symbol for Cybernetics for a Smarter World*. (Conference presentation). Technologies for Smart Cities Conference, Kerala, India.
Kabat-Zinn, J. (1991). *Full catastrophe living: Using the wisdom of your body and mind to face stress, pain, and illness*. New York: Delta Trade Paperbacks.
Kabat-Zinn, J. (1994). *Wherever you go, there you are: Mindfulness meditation in everyday life*. New York: Hyperion Books.
Kohlenberg, R.J. & Tsai, M. (1991). *Functional analytic psychotherapy: A guide for creating intense and curative therapeutic relationships*. New York: Springer.
Koreis, V. (2013, July 23). *Capek's RUR*. Archived from the original on 23 December. Retrieved https://web.archive.org/web/20131223084729/http://www.booksplendour.com.au/capek/rur.htm
Lachman, R., Lachman, J.L. & Butterfield, E.C. (2015). *Cognitive psychology and information processing: An introduction*. London: Psychology Press.
Larson, C. (1979). Highlights of Dr. John Watson's career in advertising. *Journal of industrial/Organizational Psychology. 16*(3).
Lewis, S. (2002). *Arrowsmith*. New York: Library of America. (Original work Published in 1925).
Lindsley, O.R., Skinner, B.F. & Solomon, H.C. (1953). *Studies in behavior therapy: Status report 1*. Waltham, MA: Metropolitan State Hospital.

Linehan, M. (2013, December 11–15). *Chain analysis of dysfunctional behaviors*. (Conference presentation). The Evolution of Psychotherapy Conference, Anaheim, California.

Locke, J. (1974). *An essay concerning human understanding*. (A.D. Woosley, Ed.). New York: New American Library. (Original work published in 1690).

Locke, J. (2000). *Some thought concerning education*. (J. W. Yolton & J.S. Yolton, Eds.). New York: Oxford University Press. (Original work published in 1693).

Loeb, J. (2019). *Comparative physiology of the brain and comparative psychology*. Philadelphia: J.B Lippincott Co. (Original work published in 1900).

Loeb, J. (2019). *Forced movements, tropisms and animal conduct*. Philadelphia: J.B. Lippincott Co. (Original work published in 1918).

Masters, J.C., Burish, T.G., Hollon, S.D. & Rim, D.C. (1987) *Behavior therapy: Techniques and empirical findings*. (3rd ed.). Orlando, Fl.: Harcourt Brace Jovanovich.

McDougall, W. (1911). *Body and mind: A history in defense of animism*. London: Methuen & Co.

Meichenbaum, D. (1994). *A clinical handbook/practical therapist manual for assessing and treating adults with posttraumatic stress disorder*. Waterloo, Ont., Canada: Institute Press.

Meichenbaum, D. (2020). *Treating individuals with addictive disorders: A strength-based workbook for patients and clinicians*. New York: Routledge.

Mill, J.S. (2002). *A system of logic*. Honolulu, HI: University Press of the Pacific. (Original work published in1843).

Miller, G.A. (1951). *Language and communication*. New York: McGill-Hill Book Company, Inc.

Miller, G.A. (1956) The magical number seven, plus or minus two: Some limitations on our capacity for processing information. *Psychological Review. 63*(2), 81–97.

Miller, G.A. (1991). *The science of mental life*. New York: Penguin Book. (Original work published in 1962).

Morgan, C.L. (1900). *Animal life and intelligence [revised as animal behavior]*. London: Edward Arnold. (Original work published 1891).

Murgula, E. & Diaz, K. (2015). The philosophical foundation of cognitive behavioral therapy: Stoicism, Buddhism, Taoism and existentialism. *The Journal of Evidence-Based Psychotherapies. 15*(1), 37–50.

Neisser, U., Boodoo, G., Bouchard, T.J., Boykin, A.W. & Brody, N. et al. (1996). Intelligence: Knowns and unknowns. *American Psychologist. 51*(2), 77–101.

Newell, A., Shaw, J.C. & Simon, H.A. (1958). Elements of a theory of human problem solving. *Psychological Review. 65*(3), 151–166.

Neisser, U. (1967). *Cognitive psychology*. New York: Appleton-Century.

Norcross, J.C., Bike, D.H. & Evans, K.L. (2009). The therapist's therapist: A replication and extension 20 years later. *Psychotherapy: Theory, Research, Practice, Training. 46*(1), 32–41.

Overskeid, G. (2007). Looking for skinner and finding Freud. *American Psychologist. 62*(6), 590–595.

Pavlov, I.P. (1927). *Conditioned reflexes: An investigation of the activity of the cerebral cortex*. (G.V. Anrep. Trans.). New York: Oxford University Press.

Piaget, J. (1966). *Psychology of intelligence*. Totowa, NJ: Littlefield, Adams.

Rescher, N. (1985). *The heritage of logical positivism*. Lanham, MD: University Press of America.

Richardson, A.W. (2007). The scientific world conception: Logical positivism. In T. Baldwin (Eds.). *The Cambridge history of philosophy, 1870–1945*, 391–400. Cambridge: Cambridge University Press.

Roe, A. (n.d) [Untitled Rorschach protocol of B.F. Skinner]. Anne Roe papers (B R621 B. F. Skinner). Philadelphia: American Philosophical Society Archives.

Romanes, G.J. (1882). *Animal intelligence*. London: Kegan Paul.

Romanes, G.J. (1888). *Mental evolution in man*. London: Kegan Paul.

Romanes, G.J. & Gore, C. (1902). *Thoughts on religion* (5th ed.). Chicago: Open Court Publishing Company.

Romano-Lax, A. (2016). *Behave*. New York: Soho Press.

Rosin, R. (2012). Aaron T. Beck's drawing and the psychoanalytic origin of the story of cognitive therapy. *History of Psychology. 15*(1), 1–18.

Rutherford, A. (2003). B.F. Skinner and the auditory inkblot: The rise and fall of the verbal summator a projective technique. *History of Psychology. 6*, 362–378.

Searle, J.R. (1980). Minds, brains, and programs. *The Behavioral and Brain Sciences. 3*, 417–424.

Searle, J.R. (1990). *The rediscovery of the mind*. Cambridge, MA: MIT Press.

Sechenov, I.M. (1965). *Reflexes of the brain*. Cambridge, MA: MIT Press. (Original work published in 1863).

Segal, Z.V., Teasdale, J. & Williams, M. (2002). *Mindfulness-based cognitive therapy for depression.* New York: Guilford Press.

Sharpless, B.A. & Barber, J.P. (2013). Predictors of program performance on the examination for professional practice in psychology (EPPP). *Professional Psychology: Research and Practice. 44*(4), 208–217.

Sinnott, J.D. (1998). *The development of logic in adulthood postformal thought and its applicability.* New York: Plenum Press.

Skinner, B.F. (1945). Baby in a box: The mechanical baby tender. *The Ladies Home Journal. 62*, 30–31.

Skinner, B.F. (1987). *Upon further reflection.* Englewood Cliffs, NJ: Prentice-Hall.

Skinner, B.F. (1936). The verbal summator and a method for the study of latent speech. *The Journal of Psychology. 2*, 71–107.

Skinner, B.F. (1938). *The behavior of organisms.* New York: Appleton-Century.

Skinner, B.F. (1948). *Walden two.* New York: Macmillan.

Skinner, B.F. (1956). A case study in scientific method. *American Psychologist. 11*, 221–233.

Skinner, B.F. (1958). Teaching machines. *Science. 128*, 969–977.

Skinner, B.F. (1960). Pigeons in a pelican. *American Psychologist. 15*, 28–37.

Skinner, B.F. (1961). Teaching machines. *Scientific American. 205*, 91–102.

Skinner, B.F. (1968). *The technology of teaching.* New York: Appleton-Century.

Skinner, B.F. (1971). *Beyond freedom and dignity.* New York: Knopf.

Skinner, B.F. (1974). *About behaviorism.* New York: Knopf.

Skinner, B.F. (1978). *Reflections on behaviorism and society.* Englewood Cliffs, NJ: Prentice-Hall.

Skinner, B.F. (1984). The shame of American education. *American Psychologist. 39*, 947–954.

Skinner-Buzan, D. (2004). I was not a laboratory rat. *Guardian.* Retrieved from http://www.guardian.co.uk/education/2004/mar/12/highereducation.uk

Skinner, B.F. & Vaughan, M.E. (1983). *Enjoy old age: Living fully in your later years.* New York: Warner.

Slater, L. (2004). *Opening Skinner's box: Great psychological experiments of the twentieth century.* New York: Norton & Co.

Teasdale, J. D. (1993). Emotion and two kinds of meaning: Cognitive therapy and applied cognitive science. *Behaviour Research and Therapy, 31*(4), 339–354.

Thorndike, E. (1911). *Animal intelligence: Experimental studies.* New York: The Macmillan Co.

Thorndike, E.L. (1898). Animal intelligence: An experimental study of the association processes in animals. *Psychological Review.* Monogram Suppl., *2*(4), i.

Thorndike, E.L. (1903). *Educational psychology.* New York: Lemcke & Buechner.

Tolman, E.C. (1922). A new formula for behaviorism. *Psychological Review. 29*, 44–53.

Tolman, E.C. (1924). The inheritance of maze learning ability in rats. *Journal of Comparative Psychology. 4*, 1–18.

Tolman, E.C. (1928). Purposive behavior. *Psychological Review. 35*, 524–530.

Tolman, E.C. (1942). *Drives towards war.* New York: Appleton-Century-Crofts.

Turing, A.M. (1950). Comparing machinery and intelligence. *Mind. 59*, 453–460.

Twain, M. (1994). *Mark Twain on the damned human race.* New York: Hill Wang. (Original work published in 1905).

Volpe, J. (1973). *The practice of behavioral therapy.* New York: Pergamon Press.

Washburn, M.F. (1908). *Animal intelligence: A textbook of comparative psychology.* New York: Macmillan.

Watson, J.B. (1913). Psychology as the behaviorist views it. *Psychological Review. 20*, 155–177.

Watson, J.B. (1914). *Behavior: An introduction to comparative psychology.* New York: Holt Rinehart & Winston.

Watson, J. B. (1928). *Psychological care of the infant and child.* New York: W. W. Norton Co.

Watson, J.B. & Lashley, K.S. (1915). *Homing and related activities of birds* (Vol. 211). Carnegie Institution, Department of Marine Biology.

Watson, J.B. & McDougall, W. (1929). *The battle of behaviorism.* New York: Norton.

Wiener, N. (1948). *Cybernetics: Or control and communication in the animal and the machine.* Cambridge, MA: MIT Press.

Woods, S.L., Rockman, P. & Collins, E. (2019). *Mindfulness based cognitive therapy: Embodied presence and inquiry in practice.* Oakland, CA: Context Press.

Figure 5.0

5 Symbols of Humanistic-Existential Psychology

The Third Force in Psychology

Introduction

Although the roots of the humanistic-existential (H-E) movement extend far back in human history, it was the 1960 cultural revolution in America that provided a revolutionary jolt to psychology. Tired of the pathologizing of human existence by the psychoanalysts and behaviorists, H-E psychologists rebelled against both schools and created another dynamic and influential field of psychological study.

Figure 5.1

Humanistic psychology is rooted in the Greek philosophy "to know thyself" and existential psychology is rooted in the Latin meaning to "stand forth," "to become." Together, they provide a quite different orientation to psychology. As behaviorism symbolizes the influence of the external world, humanistic-existential psychology symbolizes the influence of an internal world, the belief that every human being has a unique, individualized, experience of existence (Steiner, 1919/2011).

DOI: 10.4324/9781003424734-5

230   *Symbols of Humanistic-Existential Psychology*

In reaction to psychoanalysis and behaviorism, H-E psychologists focus on what makes people healthy, alive, and living life with meaning and purpose. H-E psychologists value the importance of human potential, the freedom of expression, and the importance of personal responsibility to not only cope, but grow and develop, from the *existential crises* of modernity.

Cultural Integration

H-E psychology integrates European and American cultural experiences. Existential psychology developed during the devastating destruction in Europe of two World Wars. In contrast, humanistic psychology is rooted in American optimism, the belief that human beings can "achieve anything" and reach their full potential.

As awareness of the importance of human values inspired the Renaissance hundreds of years ago to rebel against an oppressive church, the H-E movement is a psychological Renaissance rebelling against the new religion of empirical science and behaviorism. The new Renaissance, like the old, rediscovered the value of the inner subjective world and the importance of a personal search for meaning and purpose unencumbered by social conformity. H-E psychology fills a void left by the demise of organized religion and dysfunctional social institutions.

Because H-E is rooted in European and American thought, H-E integrates the intellectual emphasis of the Europeans with the value of feeling and individualism of the Americans (Friedman, 1964). Of all the forces in psychology, if there is a desire for deep intellectual discourse the existential component of H-E offers some of the greatest thinkers in modern history. This includes, but is not limited to, Friedrich Nietzsche, Edmund Husserl, Martin Heidegger, Martin Buber, Soren Kierkegaard, Jean-Paul Sartre, Simone de Beauvoir, Albert Camus, and Maurice Merleau-Ponty. This is symbolized by the importance of intellectual knowledge, the ability to think deeply, to create intellectual discourse that inspires new knowledge and recognizes that intellectual pursuits can be transformative.

Figure 5.2

Humanistic-Existential Psychology

Historical Analysis of Humanistic-Existential Psychology

Political Systems

European Existentialism

A deep political shadow hangs over existentialism because Martin Heidegger, a leading German existentialist, joined the *National Socialist German Workers (Nazi) Party* in 1933. As rector of the *University of Freiburg,* he positioned himself as the philosopher of the Nazi party, and in his inaugural address he expressed support for Nazism and Adolf Hitler (Young, 1998). His eventual resignation of the rectorate in 1934 had more to do with administrative frustrations than his rejection of Nazism. In Heidegger's *Black Notebooks,* written between 1931 and 1959 and first published in 2014, Donatella di Cesare (2018) asserts that Heidegger had an antipathy toward the Jews, a "metaphysical anti-Semitism," which permeated his philosophical approach.

Donatella believed that Heidegger considered the Jewish people as agents of modernity, which was destroying the spirit of Western civilization. Therefore, the Jews were responsible for the Holocaust as it was the logical result of the Jews hastening modernization and technological advancement. In late 1946, after liberation, the French military authorities decided that Heidegger should be denied teaching or participation in any university activities because of his support of Nazism. In 1949, during denazification hearings in France, Heidegger was designated a *Mitiaufer*, a term that applied to people who were not charged with Nazi crimes but whose involvement with the Nazi party was considered so serious that they could not be exonerated for the crimes of the Nazi regime. Since no crimes were filed against him, this paved the way for his readmission to teaching at *Freiburg University,* where he taught for the rest of his academic career.

In contrast to Heidegger, Martin Buber immediately resigned his professorship at the *University of Frankfurt* in 1933 when Adolf Hitler came to power. Unlike other prominent Jewish existentialists, Buber immigrated to Jerusalem where he became a leading *Zionist*. Zionism is a nationalist movement that advocated for the establishment of a Jewish state centered in the area roughly corresponding to Canaan, the Holy Land, and regions of Palestine. In contrast, Buber advocated for a Zionism that would promote a Hebrew humanism that would create social and spiritual enrichment to the entire Middle East region.

After the creation of the Israeli state, he believed Judaism would need reforms to view the problems of Israel as universal, not nationalistic, problems that challenge the face of all humanity. In the early 1920s, Buber, prior to the development of the Israeli state, would be one of the first Zionist leaders to advocate for a one Jewish-Arab state, even if the Jewish people were the minority. This would be the ultimate reform of Judaism and a model for the world how vastly different cultures and religious backgrounds could live in peace and brotherhood. After the establishment of Israel in 1948, Buber advocated for Israeli participation in a *Federation of Middle East States* wider than Palestine which would encompass the Arabian Peninsula, Cyprus, Egypt, Turkey, Iraq, Iran, Syria, Jordan, and Lebanon.

French existentialists connected existentialism with political activism. Sartre believed political activism symbolized the very essence of existentialism and was one of the best ways to express freedom. Sartre pushed the limits of freedom and an "existentialism in your face" when he wrote the French were never as free as under Nazi rule because when a man stepped outside their door and saw a Nazi soldier with a rifle, they had the free choice to either ignore the soldier or fight. In this way, the real existential self could only exist through social engagement and political action. Sartre was captured by German troops in 1940 and spent nine months as a prisoner of war. After his release in 1941 for poor eyesight, he founded *Socialism and Liberty*, an underground group of French existentialists who provided emotional support but had little political impact on resistance to Nazi occupation.

Sartre was an anti-colonist and played a key role in supporting the struggle against French rule in Algeria. He opposed the use of French torture and Algerian concentration camps. The *Algerian War of Independence* from 1954–1962 led to Algerian independence and to the downfall of the *Fourth French Republic* and the rise of Chares de Gaulle as the first president of the Fifth French Republic. As a supporter of the *National Liberation Front* (NLF), a nationalist political party in Algeria, Sartre barely survived two bomb attacks by the paramilitary *Organisation Armee Secrete* (OAS). He believed that each French person was responsible for war crimes during the *Algerian War of Independence.* He later opposed the Vietnam War and supported and hosted the *Bertrand Russell Tribunal* in 1967, which intended to expose U.S. war crimes in Vietnam.

American Humanism

Although it occurred between two psychologists, the debate between B. F. Skinner and Carl Rogers could be viewed as a debate between two political scientists. At a meeting held on September 4, 1956, at the annual American Psychological Convention, Skinner and Rogers debated the issue of controlling behavior. Both agreed that modern science had increased the power of government to influence, change, and control human behavior (Dooley, 1982). Skinner viewed early prescientific history as an example of aversive and "selfish" governmental control as represented by Machiavellian politics. He argued modern science had the potential to apply *societal engineering* to construct and design more workable, effective, and productive forms of government. Since all human beings were controlled in one manner or another by their government, Skinner warned that the natural tendency to revolt against any discussion of control had led to a misinterpretation of valid practices and a blind rejection for a scientifically based governmental planning process. Rogers argued that an agreement on values had to preclude the development of any societal engineering. These values would guide the scientific work and result in creating governmental processes that would enrich the life of its citizens with systems that allow people to reach their full human potential. Skinner did not agree that the practice of science required a prior decision about values.

In his later years, Carl Rogers became interested in utilizing his theories for political change. The central tenet of *person-centered dialogic politics* was that politics did not have to be an endless series of winner-take-all battles among polarized political opponents. Rather, his approach was to create a person-to-person dialogue among political opponents. Believing his approach had political applicability, he turned his attention worldwide to political oppression and national political conflicts. He traveled to Belfast, Northern Ireland, and brought together Protestant and Catholics. In South Africa, he encouraged dialogue between Blacks and Whites in the wake of the apartheid system. In Brazil, he supported people transitioning from dictatorship to democracy and in the United States he brought consumers and providers together to improve the fragmented American national healthcare system. In his final days, he was committed to world peace and in 1985 he organized the *Vienna Peace Project* in Rust, Austria, which brought together participants from 17 countries to dialogue on "the Central America Challenge." On his last trip abroad in 1986, he traveled to the Soviet Union, amazed that so many people knew of his work, and conducted "peace workshops" in Moscow.

Although Rogers was an outspoken critic of McCarthyism in the 1950s and concerned about the strong authoritarian tendencies in behaviorism, Rogers, like many psychologists after the terrorist attacks in the early twentieth century, had an apparent blind spot when it came to his political involvement with the Central Intelligence Agency (CIA). In the 1950s, Rogers became a board member of the *Society for the Investigation of Human Ecology* (SIHE), a front for the CIA. Stephen Demanchick and Howard Kirschenbaum (2008) concluded, given the widespread concern over the communist threat in the 1950s, it was not surprising that Carl Rogers would initially view his research with SIHE as patriotic, which also fulfilled an early need to fund his research in psychotherapy and schizophrenia. Although Rogers never admitted to his CIA involvement, they argued that Rogers should have known being a board member was problematic. For instance, at that time, the CIA was experimenting with mind control and doing horrendous racist experimentation on poor African Americans in Alabama known as *Tuskegee Experiments*. They found it ironic that the CIA felt the subjective theories of Rogers were a better fit with the CIA goals of mind control than the behavioral theories of Skinner.

Socioeconomic Systems

European Existentialism

After World War II, many existentialists viewed the world through a capitalist and communist socioeconomic prism. Because of disdain for capitalism and what existentialists in Europe perceived as the vacuous intellectual Americanization of the Western world, many rationalized the brutality in the Eastern Bloc as necessary for the continuation of revolutionary movements throughout the world. Sartre and others initially supported the communist revolutions in the Soviet Union, Cuba, and China, ignoring the often-substandard living conditions and government-sponsored human rights violations.

By 1957, and after the death of Stalin, the suppression of the Hungarian uprising, and the rejection of Soviet Marxism by French leftists, Sartre broke with Soviet communism. In 1960, Sartre (2022) wrote *Critique of Dialectical Reason* to revitalize the moribund Soviet dogma. The Critique is one of the most vigorous intellectual defenses of Marxism because of the emphasis, not on class struggle, but on the humanistic values in early Marx writings. Sartre integrated existentialism and Marxism; he viewed Marxism as the most important socioeconomic philosophy of the modern age. Alienated by Soviet Marxism and not interested in any reinterpretation of Marxism, Sartre lost the friendships of Merleau-Ponty, Albert Camus, and other essentialists. However, although many tired of the economic debates, European existentialism left a deep skepticism of the possibility of socioeconomic progress under American capitalism.

American Humanism

The socioeconomic prosperity of the 1950s and 1960s began a shift from an industrial economic system that produced goods to a service-oriented economic system that produced human services. During the mid-twentieth century, psychology became popular with college-educated Americans because of the development of a stronger middle class, which created the economic ability for the exploration of personal growth. Many had grown up in more permissive and economically stable families than their parents and were open to spending money for self-exploration.

By 1978, the *Association for Humanistic Psychology* (AHP) embarked on a three-year effort to apply humanistic psychology toward political and socioeconomic change. The effort included a *12 Hour Political Party* held in San Francisco in 1980 with 1,400 attendees, including Carl Rogers, Virginia Satir, and Rollo May, expressed nontraditional socioeconomic visions which led to a manifesto for a slow or no-growth economy, decentralizing and professionalizing political and economic processes, and teaching socioeconomic and emotional competencies for more humane public policies (Association of Humanistic Psychology, 1980). In 1979, economist Mark Lutz and psychologist Kenneth Lux (1979) called for a new economics based on humanistic psychology not based in utilitarianism. From 1979 to 1983, the *New World Alliance*, a political organization injected humanistic psychology ideas into governmental decision making.

234 *Symbols of Humanistic-Existential Psychology*

After Roger's death in 1987, interest in socioeconomic issues in humanistic psychology faded. The decline in the American middle class would certainly disturb Rogers and many of the early visionaries of humanistic psychology.

Cultural Systems

Hair – The Musical

The musical *Hair* (Wollman, 2006) became a symbol of the 1960s American cultural revolution. Because of the humanistic and existential questions raised by *Hair*, its message resonates into the twenty-first century. The musical showed how the hippie rebellion and the sexual revolution began to permeate all aspects of American culture. Hair raised many of the existential questions facing a changing American culture. Was the Vietnam War a war of liberation or an imperialistic war of colonialism and hegemony? Were illegal drugs really that dangerous? Why was nudity so controversial? What impact was the sexual revolution having on the relationship between men and women? Do the clothes worn, and the length of hair really matter? Was religion relevant anymore? What happens when friendships become politicized? Was the goal of a peaceful "Age of Aquarius" world realistic or possible? Does the system always "win"?

For the Greeks and Romans, long hair symbolized femininity, health, social status, and wealth. Long hair in Hair symbolized the development of personal power and rebellion against the "military-industrial complex" of a rational male-dominated world. The message of the musical was a longing to recapture its Dionysian spirit after being under the spell of the rational Apollo. The Dionysian spirit would reignite American culture through love, music, sex, and drugs. Religion, with all its infighting about who was "right," had become hypocritical and a parody of truth.

Figure 5.3

Throughout history, hair has been a symbol of power and strength. In the Samson and Delilah story mentioned in the biblical book of *Judges,* Samson, as in the Greek myth of Hercules, became known for his superhuman strength. However, if his hair was ever cut, Samson would lose his power. After being betrayed by his lover, Delilah, who ordered a servant to cut his hair, he later regained his strength and collapsed a temple, killing himself and all the ruling Philistines. Because he gave his life for others, the Samson story resonates with Jewish and Christian religious traditions.

Hair played a significant role in the development of Buddhism. During the Buddha's illumination, he was tempted eight times by the demon Mara, a deity that personified evil and the death of spirituality. Desperate for spiritual guidance, Buddha touched the ground with his fingers, begging for help from Mother Earth. Mother Earth created an ocean from her long hair, which pushed Mara and her demons far away from the Buddha, thereby saving his spirituality.

Hair does not decay and symbolizes eternal life; it is a reminder of mortality and immortality. Navajo people believed that thoughts originated in the head with hair. New thoughts were close to the scalp and old thoughts were at the end of the longest strands. The longer the hair, the greater number of thoughts. For many Native Americans, long hair represented a strong cultural identity that promoted self-esteem and a sense of belonging. The proper care of hair was essential in preparation of ceremonies and tribal ornamentation. The braiding of hair began in childhood and symbolized familial intimacy and tribal identity. Often in history, when Native Americans were conquered or assimilated, their braids were cut off, which came to symbolize the loss of their identity and the degradation of their culture.

The musical, Hair, told a story of a political bohemian tribe in New York fighting against the draft and the Vietnam War. Claude, his good friend Berger, their roommate Sheila, and their friends struggle against their conservative parents to create a more just and peaceful world. Claude finally succumbs to the pressures of his conservative parents. He finally capitulates, "they got me" and cuts his hair, enters the military, and dies in Vietnam.

Hair appeared on Broadway in 1968 and ran for 1,750 performances. It created the rock musical genre and provided the foundation for other historic rock musicals like *Jesus Christ Superstar* and *Evita* (Wollman, 2006). *Hair* toured for many years throughout the United States and Europe, including an incredibly successful run of 1997 performances in London. Many of the songs from the musical became *top ten hits* in the United States, which resulted in a 1979 film adaptation. Hair was revived on Broadway and, in 2008, won the Tony Award for the Best Revival of a Musical.

Human Potential Movement

In the 1960s, the feeling of rebellion emerged in American psychology as Abraham Maslow, Carl Rogers, Viktor Frankl, Fritz Perls, and other leaders embraced the *human potential movement* (HPM), which became a revolution against mainstream psychology and organized religion. The human potential movement was linked to humanistic psychology because the movement adopted the theory of self-actualization of Maslow. Proponents believed that HPM could provide a life of happiness, creativity, and personal fulfillment because of the extraordinary potential largely untapped in all people. The goal of HPM was not only person-centered but strove to cultivate human potential to transform society.

In 1967, inspired by the HPM, 100,000 people, mostly young people, converged on the Haight-Ashbury in San Francisco to celebrate the *Summer of Love* which encompassed rock and folk music, hallucinogenic drugs, opposition to the Vietnam War, and free love. The Summer of Love extended throughout the West Coast and as far away as New York. A prelude to

236 *Symbols of Humanistic-Existential Psychology*

the Summer of Love was a celebration earlier in 1967 called the *Human-Be-In* in Golden Gate Park in San Francisco. It was here that Timothy Leary, an American psychologist known for his advocacy of psychedelic drugs, voiced the famous phrase: *turn on, tune in, drop out*. During the summer of 2017, the HPM, now a distant memory and an ornamental remnant in history, San Francisco celebrated the 50th anniversary of the Summer of Love in a traditional and low-key manner with numerous events and art exhibitions.

Figure 5.4

Founded in 1962 by Stanford psychology graduate Michael Murphy and Dick Price, HPM inspired the *Esalen Institute*, in Big Sur, California. Esalen symbolized the aspirations of the human potential movement Aldous Huxley provided one of the first Esalen workshops on "human potentialities." Seen as the headquarters of the HPM, the Institute became a "laboratory for new thought" because of its innovative approach to encounter groups, focus on the mind-body connection, and its ongoing experimentation in personal awareness. The list of famous thinkers who provided trainings and workshops included several H-E visionaries like Fritz Perls, Abraham Maslow, Rollo May, and Carl Rogers. The institute continues to provide HPM training as well as the many of the *New Age Movement* practices, which include the recent popularity of integrating Western and Eastern religions and philosophies.

Some critics have claimed that Esalen represented how the humanistic movement damaged American society by encouraging a narcissistic, self-centered, and spiritually empty culture. In 1990, a graffiti artist spray-painted "Jive S_-for Rich White Folk" on the Esalen entrance gate. By the 1970s, shadows began to engulf aspects of the humanistic psychology movement. Fritz Perls left Esalen because of the lack of professionalism. He believed attendees at Esalen were getting hurt by trainings and therapy sessions led by untrained people. Irvin Yalom described the annual *Humanistic Psychology Conferences* during this time as a carnival. The "big tent" approach of the movement led to a bewildering number of schools of thought that had little in common with humanistic psychology. The emphasis by some on hedonism and anti-intellectualism, and mantras of "if it feels good, do it," "feelings are all that matter," "do your own thing," began to alienate humanistic psychologists from their academic peers. May, Rogers, and Maslow, disturbed by this trend, began to disassociate themselves from sponsorship of some humanistic psychology events. But the damage was done, leaving a legacy of ambivalence in the academic community about the practical and intellectual value of the H-E movement.

Christian Values

Friedrich Nietzsche, Carl Rogers, and Rollo May were influenced early in their lives by Judeo-Christian cultural values. Nietzsche was the son of a Lutheran minister and the grandson of two clergymen. Nietzsche became one of the strongest critics of Christian morality because of his belief that the "death of God" was the responsibility of institutional religion. Rogers considered becoming a minister and attended the *Union Theological Seminary* in 1924 where he began to have doubts as to whether the ministry was the best path to help people. In 1938, Rollo May received a bachelor's degree in divinity (DB) from *Union Theological Seminary* before pursuing his doctorate in clinical psychology at *Columbia University.* Nietzsche, May, and Rogers favored humanism over religion, the human over the divine, because human beings are the final determinant of human existence.

Because they did not espouse Christian values, many of the leading H-E psychologists suffered racial discrimination and anti-Semitism. Viktor Frankl lost his entire family, and almost his life, because he was Jewish. During childhood, Maslow was subjected to encounters with various anti-Semitic groups who would bully and chase and throw rocks at him. Fritz Perls grew up in the Bohemian scene in Berlin, but his life changed forever after Hitler came to power. Being of Jewish descent and because of his previous antifascist activities, he and his wife fled Germany and eventually settled in New York. Max Wertheimer, one of the founders of Gestalt psychology, escaped Nazism and, in New York, influenced the humanistic vision of Maslow.

Feminism

Jean-Paul Sartre (1905–1980) was one of the few existentialists to write about human sexuality. He was influenced by Simone de Beauvoir (1908–1986), arguably the greatest female existentialist writers. In her internationally acclaimed treatise, the *Second Sex*, Beauvoir (2011/1949) provided the foundation for the modern feminist movement. Sarah Bakewell (2016), in *At the Existentialist Café: Freedom, Being and Apricot Cocktails,* claimed that Second Sex was the single most influential work ever produced by the existentialist movement. Bakewell questioned why Second Sex, because of its significant cultural reassessment of sexuality, was never elevated to the level of Charles Darwin, Karl Marx, or Sigmund Freud. She questioned whether it was the sexism of many English-language versions that featured naked-looking women on the cover or because of editor bias against existentialism.

This bias often eliminated any mention of her existentialism in the marketing of her book, or her use of existential case studies because of the prejudice against non-empirical research. No matter the reason, *Second Sex* became required reading for anyone interested in feminism and the sexual revolution. In *Second Sex,* Beauvoir integrated the existentialist belief that *existence precedes essence* with a feminist principle: *One is not born but becomes a woman.* This famous phrase became known as the *sex-gender distinction.* The concept explains the difference between biological sex, and the social and historical construction of gender and its related stereotypes.

238 *Symbols of Humanistic-Existential Psychology*

In her analysis, Simone defined women as the "second" sex because throughout history women have been defined in relation to men. She referenced Aristotle, who believed women lacked important basic qualities and Thomas Aquinas, who referred to women as imperfect men and "incidental beings." The result was that women were experienced as "the other" and not as their own unique, transient, sex. To understand "the other," Beauvoir turned to the Hegelian concept of the *master-slave dialectic*. Hegel analyzed how rival consciousnesses struggle for dominance, one "playing" the master, the other "playing" the slave. For Beauvoir, this best explained the dynamic between men and women. Throughout history, men "played" the strong and powerful master while women "played" the weak and passive slave. Beauvoir argued that for women to understand their unique power as a sex, they needed to stop "playing" and develop a new consciousness beyond a "second sex" psychology. Living a life that practiced existence precedes essence was a prescription for ending the historic master-slave dialectic between men and women.

French existentialists Jean-Paul Sartre and Simone Beauvoir were early role models for a different type of male-female cultural relationship. They initially signed a two-year partnership contract because they rejected the "bourgeoisie" view of a monogamous marriage which they believed was based on confinement and entrapment. They survived the two years and became life-long but non-exclusive partners for the rest of their lives. For many, their 50-year relationship modeled how the principles of existentialism could help create intimate relationships built on freedom, companionship, and the supports needed to become a fully developed human being. Beauvoir had a revolutionary view of sexual relationships. She believed that homosexuality was as limiting as heterosexuality. True sexual freedom resulted from understanding that each person could love a man or a woman, and that human existence should be based on a sexual attraction without fear, restraint, or obligation.

Peace Movement

Figure 5.5

Symbols of Humanistic-Existential Psychology 239

Humanistic psychology and the peace movement shared many cultural values as the Western world struggled to contain the shadow of communism while dealing with its own shadow of imperialism in the Vietnam War and throughout the postcolonial world. The symbol of the dove and the olive branch has been utilized by Christians throughout history as a symbol for peace. After World War II, with the possibility of nuclear annihilation, the symbol became secularized by Pablo Picasso in his *Dove* lithograph. The peace sign known today was developed in the 1950s by Gerald Holtom for the *British Campaign for Nuclear Disarmament.* The symbol was created from two semaphore signal flag letters for N-Nuclear and D-Disarmed.

Figure 5.6

This symbol also simultaneously acted as a reference to the painting *The Third of May* by Francisco Goya, the romantic and most important Spanish painter of the late eighteenth and early nineteenth century. *The Third of May,* also known as the *Peasant before the Firing Squad*, commemorated Spanish resistance to the armies of Napoleon during French occupation of 1808. Goya, with the hands of the peasant reaching above his head in a cross-like fashion, provided an archetypal symbol of the horrors of war. Holtom took the image and "put a circle around it" and created the peace symbol. In 1958, in a London-to-Aldermaston march for nuclear disarmament, Bayard Rustin, an ally of Martin Luther King, Jr., marched with the protestors. Inspired by how a symbol mobilized the British peace movement, Rustin brought the peace symbol back across the Atlantic. It was adopted by the *civil rights movement*, and the antiwar and countercultural activists in the United States and around the world. The symbol had religious meaning for the anti-communist evangelist Bill James Hargas, who viewed the peace symbol as an upside-down cross symbolizing evil and the arrival of the anti-Christ. It was a reminder that symbol touches human beings at many different levels.

During the American cultural revolution of the 1960s, a need arose for an immediate, personal, and more physical symbol for peace and social transformation. The "V" hand signal started as a symbol in the 1940s to symbolize allied victories during World War II. In the 1960s the "V" hand signal became a symbol of peace in the antiwar movement. The peace symbol remains a symbol of the cultural hopes of the H-E movement for a world of friendship, love, and peace.

240 *Symbols of Humanistic-Existential Psychology*

Natural Science Interest in Humanistic-Existential Psychology

Gestalt Psychology

>The Whole is More than a Summary of its Parts.
>
>- Gestalt Theory

Typically viewed as its own psychological school, Gestalt psychology has much in common with H-E psychology. *Gestalt psychology* emerged as a school of psychology in Austria and Germany in the early twentieth century as a theory of perception that rejected the elementalism theories of Wilhelm Wundt and the structuralist theories of Edward Titchener.

Gestalt in German means "form, pattern, configuration, or wholeness." Gestalt psychologists were interested in how humans perceived entire patterns and not merely individual elements of human experience. Like Kant, Gestalt psychologists distinguished sensation from perception. Sensations were physical reactions whereas perceptions were psychological responses. Gestalt psychologists replaced the mind with the brain as the altering agent because the world perceived was never the same as the world experienced through the senses. Gestalt psychologists changed the Kantian faculties of the mind with characteristics of the brain.

Although not traditionally seen as directly connected to the existential-humanistic movement, like H-E psychology, Gestalt psychologists rejected much of mainstream modern psychology. Mainstream psychology was perceived as uninterested in the *wholeness* of human existence. Gestalt psychologists and later Gestalt psychotherapists were in more alignment with H-E psychology than psychoanalysis and behaviorism. With their focus on perception, Gestalt psychologists rejected atomistic theories of consciousness that the mind linked associations together.

Figure 5.7

Unlike Descartes, who viewed consciousness separate from the natural world, Gestalt psychologists believed the brain was never isolated from physical experience. They argued that human beings continually interact with physical world through a figure-ground perceptual field. For instance, people see a landscape rather than elemental bits of color and shape and see words on a printed page as the figure and the white sheet as the ground. Humans spontaneously perceive the world as "wholes" because perceptions are innate, not acquired. The well-known "is it two persons or a vase" was dependent on figure and ground perceptions; the figure came to symbolize Gestalt psychology throughout the world.

Escaping Nazism and immigrating to the United States in the 1930s and 1940s, European psychologists began to have a significant influence on American psychology. During this time Abraham Maslow, the founder of the humanistic movement, met Max Wertheimer (1880–1943), a founder of Gestalt psychology, at *Brooklyn College* in New York. The basic tenet of Gestalt psychology that individuals seek "wholeness" would influence the development of H-E psychology because Maslow would advocate for "human wholeness" as the cornerstone of the Third Force Psychology.

The origin of Gestalt psychology began with a train ride Max Wertheimer took from Vienna to Rhineland. He observed that perception was structured differently than sensory stimulation. Wertheimer got off the train in Frankfurt, Germany, and purchased a stroboscope, a device that allowed still pictures to be flashed in a way that indicated movement when there was none. Still amazed, he went to the *University of Frankfurt* and was provided a tachistoscope, a device that flashes lights on and off measured in fractions of a second. Wertheimer discovered if the intervals between the flashes were 60 milliseconds, it appeared that the lights were moving from one light to another and giving the appearance of movement when there was no actual movement. Wertheimer called his discovery the *phi phenomena*.

Wertheimer (1912) published his findings in an article entitled *Experimental Studies of the Perception of Movement*, which was recognized as the formal beginning of Gestalt psychology. In his 1912 article, Wertheimer introduced the *phi symbol* in a formula of: (a) two successive objects perceived and (b) the last object to be perceived. Between (a) and (b), the sensory stimulation was not observed. Wertheimer used *phi*; the 21st letter of the Greek alphabet as symbolic of the *golden ratio*. The golden ratio is used today by mathematicians to find balance between physical elements in the natural world and to find fiscal balance amongst financial markets. After Experimental Studies of the Perception of Movement, the essence of Gestalt psychology would forever be known, "without prejudice" as (a) phi (b).

Gestaltists believed that brain activity tended toward balance and equilibrium, so when a problem occurred, there was brain disruption and disequilibrium. This disequilibrium necessitated scanning the environment and cognitively attempting to find a solution to the problem that emphasized cognitive trial and error, not the behavioral trial and effort of Edward Thorndike. Kurt Kofka (1963) published Principles of Gestalt Psychology, which remains a foundational text in Gestalt psychology. At the University of Frankfurt, Kofka (1886–1941) and Wolfgang Kohler (1887–1967), Wertheimer's research assistants and part of his perception studies, became linked as the three founders of Gestalt psychology. Because the magnetic fields of Newtonian physics were hard to study, some physicists turned to the study of *force fields*, the interrelationship between physical events. In force field theory whatever happened in one area of the force field affected everything in the force field. Since Kofka studied with Max Planck, the father of quantum mechanics, Gestalt psychology modeled force field theory, rather than Newtonian physics, which at the time dominated mainstream psychology.

Kohler, as well as other Gestaltists, were critical of behaviorism because behaviorists believed that the parts were greater than the whole. As an example, like Alfred Binet before him,

Kohler criticized the concept of IQ. He offered *psychophysics* as an example of the problem of measurement preceding understanding of what was to be measured. Kohler agreed that IQ scores were based on reliable measurements, but he argued those measurements lacked the whole gestalt of what it meant to be intelligent. In *The Mentality of Apes,* Kohler (1923/1917) found that chimpanzees solved problems through *insight*. In one of his most famous experiments, Chica, a chimpanzee, had to reach a banana out of his reach and, through a process of cognitive trial and error, Chica tested various hypotheses, which ultimately led to insight and to the successful reach of the banana. In the chimpanzee studies, Kohler discovered organisms learned not through reinforcement contingencies of Thorndike, Hull, or Skinner; organisms learned whole principles through a gestalt, not unique responses to each setting. Kohler called this approach *transposition,* which meant learning in one situation can be transferred to similar situations. By the mid-twentieth century, Gestalt psychology began to gain recognition in the United States and, in 1959, Kohler was elected president of the American Psychological Association.

At the University of Berlin, Kurt Lewin (1899–1947) worked with Wertheimer, Kohler, and Kofka and expanded Gestalt principles toward their social and clinical applications. Although not considered a founder of Gestalt psychology, Lewin was a psychologist who brought Gestalt psychology from the confines of academia to daily life through his research on motivation and personality. His rich psychological background included interest in behaviorism and the critical theory of the Frankfurt School. However, his greatest contribution might be his work on group dynamics.

Lewin turned to Gestalt psychology because of his analysis of the views of human nature from an Aristotelian and Galilean philosophic school of thought. The Aristotelian view of human nature was based on inner forces and categories whereas the Galilean view was based on dynamic outer causes and forces. According to Lewin, Galileo revolutionized science by changing the focus from the study of inner to outer causation. Galileo taught that causation does not result from inner essences but from outer physical forces. This meant that even individual experiences could be explained, when known, by outer force fields. For Lewin, there was too much Aristotelian, and not enough Galilean, thought in psychology. Examples included an overemphasis in psychology on instincts, developmental stages, personality types, and what was normal and abnormal. Rather, Lewin advocated for a psychology that emphasized the complex dynamic forces acting upon an individual at any given moment. Understanding the outer dynamic force fields, and not inner dynamics, explained the Gestalt approach to human behavior.

Toward the end of his short career, Lewin expanded Gestalt principles to *group dynamics*. His theory of effective and ineffective leadership styles continues to influence the functioning of organizations throughout the world. Lewin viewed a group as a physical system, like the brain. Groups developed a dynamic interdependence, a gestalt force field, which determined individual behavior. In his landmark study of difference types of leadership, Lewin, with Lippitt and White, (1939), placed boys in three types of groups. In the democratic group, the leader encouraged group participation and engaged the boys in mutual decision-making. In the authoritarian group, the leader made all the decisions without any meaningful input from the boys. In the laissez-fare group, the leader let the boys do what they wanted. Lewin and his colleagues found that the democratic group was productive and supportive, the authoritarian group was overly aggressive and unsupportive, and the laissez-fare group was highly unproductive.

Lewin influenced the development of group therapy, encounter groups, sensitivity trainings, T-groups, organizational psychology, and leadership institutes (Dicks, 2015). Although he died shortly after the *Tavistock Institute of Human Relations Institute* (TIHR) was formally established in 1946, Lewin was acknowledged as a key inspiration for its development and his contribution of an article to the first issue of its journal, *Human Relations.* Initially acknowledged for rehabilitating soldiers and for organizational reforms in the British Army during World War II, TIHR continues to be viewed as a proponent for more human-centered organizations, especially organizations that empower lower-level workers. TIHR is engaged in action research, change consultancy, executive coaching, and has become advocates for social change in communities and societies at large. TIHR became known as a major proponent in Britain of psychoanalysis and psychodynamic psychology. Many of the leaders of modern psychology have been associated with the institute, which included Carl Jung, Melanie Klein, R. D. Laing, and John Bowlby.

Because of its natural science interests, it was believed Gestalt psychology was in alliance with behaviorism. The reality was that the Gestalt emphasis on the immediate awareness of experience was attacked by behaviorists as a return to metaphysics. When Karl Lashley, the renowned learning and memory behaviorist, asked whether Gestaltists had "religion up their sleeve," it reignited a metaphysical debate in psychology. Although many behaviorists agreed with the Gestalt emphasis on the perceptual force field based in modern physics, many could never accept a separate subjective consciousness. Academic Gestalt psychology would fade in the later part of the twentieth century because it did not fit neatly into any psychological school of thought. However, it came alive in the Gestalt psychotherapy of Fritz and Laura Perls who emphasized the importance of immediate personal awareness for psychological health and healing. This awareness was often communicated from the body which they believed was imbued with psychological knowledge.

Existential Phenomenology

Throughout World War II and beyond, the leading French existentialists Simone de Beauvoir and Jean-Paul Sartre, had a special relationship with Maurice Merleau-Ponty (1908–1961). In 1945, they created the French journal, *Modern Times*, inspired by Charlie Chaplin film *The Les Temps Modernes*. This silent movie powerfully symbolized the sad state of modern society, the machine age, and capitalism. The journal replaced the popular pre-war magazine, *The New French Review,* which was shut down after the liberation of France due to its supposed collaboration with the Nazi occupation.

The New French Review was the magazine of Andre Gide, considered one of the great French writers of the twentieth century. Andre Gide began his career actively involved in the French *symbolist movement.* The symbolist movement was a group of late nineteenth-century French writers who rejected the artistic rigidity of French poetry, especially the *Parnassian technique* (Balakian, 1967). Rejecting naturalism and realism, they sought to liberate the arts through symbol. They believed that symbol created the immediate sensations of an inner life and the underlying mystery of existence. The symbolists argued that the purpose of art was not to directly reflect reality, but to access greater truths through symbolic language, metaphors, and images. Even as the symbolist movement faded in the early twentieth century, it continued to inspire artists throughout the world, like British and American poets W. B Yeats and T. S. Elliot, and modern novelists James Joyce and Virginia Wolf, whose use of the symbolic often took prominence over the narrative story.

Figure 5.8

Modern Times provided a microcosm of the struggle of French existentialism. Eventually Merleau-Ponty would leave the journal over political disagreements with Sartre, especially over the concept of *engagee*, literature, and the arts in service of political activism. Although Merleau-Ponty initially supported Soviet communism after the war, he later became disenchanted and took a less passionate view of the many political movements developing throughout the world. Although Sartre was the most famous, Camus the greatest literalist, and Beauvoir the most revolutionary, Merleau-Ponty (2013), in submitting his doctoral dissertation, *Phenomenology of Perception,* became the greatest French existential phenomenologist.

Merleau-Ponty expanded phenomenology beyond Husserl and Heidegger toward a form of naturalism. In the *Phenomenology of Perception*, he argued that perception meant having a body which inhabits the world. Because perception was not thought, it existed in its own universe and existed prior to thought. The body as subject bridged the gap between the subjective being-for-itself with the objective being in the world. Phenomena were understood meanings associated with regular physical mundane experiences like picking up a cup, walking through a door, or touching sweets on a table. The existentialism of Merleau-Ponty was not concerned with authenticity or existential dread; it was simpler, but not simple. For Merleau-Ponty, it was through the perception of the simplest actions where the real mysteries of existence were found. He took a quite different approach from the traditional philosophical stance that started with a static, solitary individual isolated from their natural body and the world. He rejected the solipsistic question as to whether others even existed at all because he believed that human survival depended on others. He changed the famous Descartes statement to *I think therefore other people exist*. A social consciousness could never be the nothingness of Sartre or even the "clearing in the woods" of Heidegger.

In his view of the existentialism, consciousness is a folded piece of cloth crumpled to make a nest or special place in the natural world, symbolized by an individual person being part of the physical fabric of the world.

Symbols of Humanistic-Existential Psychology 245

In 1949, Merleau-Ponty became the professor of psychology and pedagogy at the *Sorbonne*, replacing the famous cognitive psychologist, Jean Piaget. He was in closer alliance with mainstream psychology more than the other French existentialist. Besides *Phenomenology of Perception* for his dissertation defense, Merleau-Ponty (1983) also produced *The Structure of Behavior*, which was a critique of behaviorism that provided a bridge between cognitive psychology and phenomenological existentialism by confronting the neglected dimension of the human experience: the lived body in the natural world.

For Merleau-Ponty, learning to perceive the sensate world began in childhood, which made him one of the few philosophers since Rousseau to prioritize childhood in his philosophical writings. In childhood, children learned that the physical world functioned in regularity, harmony, and consistency. His existential phenomenology was based in the belief that human beings were constantly changing from childhood onward. He wanted to understand what happened as the body lost its faculties, when people were injured, and when the body was damaged. In the process, he reassessed one of the basic tenets of existentialism, *Dasein*. He wondered how a toddler or a person with dementia experienced Dasein, what conditions in the brain were needed for Dasein to occur, or whether computers could create an artificial Dasein. Heidegger avoided these issues as ontological questions for psychology, biology, and anthropology, not for philosophy. Merleau-Ponty did not make those distinctions. It was the shadow of philosophy that interested him the most. He welcomed psychology and other disciplines into the existential phenomenological world where the body teaches about existence.

Figure 5.9

Hermeneutic Science Interest in Humanistic-Existential Psychology

Dialogic Philosophy

The Unexamined Life Is Not Worth Living.

- Socrates

At the root of H-E psychology is the philosophy of dialogue based on the Axial Age *Socratic method*. This method was a structured cooperative, and often an argumentative, dialogue between individuals. The earliest examples have been preserved and involve Socrates as the protagonist in *Laws* by Plato (2005). Socrates was portrayed as an Athenian stranger, not as the famous Greek wise man. Plato meant to present him as a simple person more concerned with understanding the viewpoints of others than with sharing his own wisdom. Since Plato believed each human being possessed pure inner knowledge beyond their natural body, a dialogue did not need a wise philosopher, everyone was their own wise philosopher. All a person needed was a forum in which their true self could emerge, where a person "could hear" that wise inner voice through dialogue with other viewpoints. The examination of different philosophical viewpoints was fundamental to the Greeks. It could be said that H-E began when Socrates stated that the *unexamined life was not worth living* because the creation of a strong inner self was essential for *becoming* a virtuous and ethical human being.

Martin Buber (1878–1965) contributed a modernized version of dialogic philosophy in the early twentieth century. As a Hasidic Jewish philosopher, he believed that existence was an encounter with the other. In *I and Thou*, Buber (1958a) explained his view of the "two-fold principle of human life," which incorporated two movements. In I-It relationships, humans kept each other at a distance by objectifying another. In I-Thou relationships the other was met as an equal participant, not separated by preconceived biases or personal status. I-Thou relationships were predicated on being totally present without distractions or objectifying the other. Modeled on how a person related to their God, I-Thou relationships were sacred. Because of the complexity of human life, the two types of relationships were always in a constant state of dialectic tension between the independent I-It and interdependent I-Thou.

Buber was saved from suicide at age fourteen by the intersubjective philosophy described in the *Prolegomena to Any Future Metaphysics* by Kant and during a religious crisis at age 17, he turned to *Thus Spoke Zarathustra* by Nietzsche. This led to his rejection of traditional Jewish religious practices because Buber (1958b) viewed Hasidism as the answer for the much-needed spiritual revitalization of Judaism. Hasidism was a popular mystical movement that swept through Eastern Europe in the eighteenth and nineteenth centuries, which emphasized the need to *always* be in direct relationship with God. This movement approached every mundane action as a sacred experience.

One significant way to approach this sacred relationship was to understand the concept of *meeting*. In *Meetings: Autobiographical Fragments,* Buber (1973), in a Hasidic storytelling style, recalled important meetings that changed his life. The book was a concrete example of how *dialogic philosophy* could lead to personal transformation. The 20 stories in *Meetings* ranged from meetings with his mother and father to a final story about his preference for human relationship over books and intellectual pursuits. After his reunion with his mother, who had abandoned him when he was four years old, he developed the concept of dismeeting, or misencounter, failure of an individual to truly encounter and dialogue with another. It was from the dismeeting with his mother that he began to understand the true difference between I-Thou and I-It relationships.

Figure 5.10

In *Between Man and Man*, Buber (1965a) argued that scholars had neglected the concept of *between* because its significance could not be defined by internal psychological processes. Rather, "between" had to be understood as something with its own unique characteristics essential to an I-Thou experience. The "between" ultimately defined the quality of the I-Thou relationship because individuals created something "between" that transcended their inner worlds. Since the "between" was dynamic, ever changing, and hard to quantify, it did not mean it should not be an area of serious study. For Buber (1957), it was in the "between" where healing occurred, *healing through meeting*, symbolized by two individuals relating authentically and creating a sacred, nonjudgmental, attentive intersubjective relationship.

Dialogic philosophy rejected the philosophy of Descartes, which emphasized an isolated "I," subjective self. For Buber (1965b), the *cogito, ego sum* was an artificial separation because there was never an "I" separate from the world of a "you," the intersubjective self. The tension between subjectivity and intersubjectivity would continue to create a dynamic tension within H-E psychology. While many existentialists struggled with ways to cope with the painful, often alienating, external world, dialogical existentialists believed that dialogue with the external world was the only option for a world in desperate need of interpersonal connection and the healing potential of community. Maurice Friedman (1955) argued that dialogic philosophy and the concept of healing through meeting could enhance the practice of psychotherapy. On April 18, 1957, Friedman (1994, 1964) moderated a dialogue between Buber and Carl Rogers about the psychotherapeutic implications of Buber's dialogic philosophy.

Existential Philosophy

The Concept of Dread by Soren Kierkegaard (1944a) created the foundation for existential philosophy. He was a Danish Christian philosopher who advocated for an entirely new way to consider Christian faith. Kierkegaard (1944b) was critical of Christian complacency in

248 *Symbols of Humanistic-Existential Psychology*

Victorian culture that focused more on dogma than developing an individual relationship with God. Kierkegaard tried to make Christianity relevant again by making being a Christian harder. For Kierkegaard (1815–1855), freedom resulted from the *crisis* of intellectual, emotional, and physical imprisonment. In *Fear and Trembling*, Kierkegaard (2005) provided the example of Abraham, who was willing for his faith to sacrifice his only son Isaac. This created an *existential crisis* which demanded action and change because without a crisis, life becomes too easy with the deepest issues of existence easily ignored. Abraham passed the existential crisis of faith not because of dogmatic beliefs, but because of his faithful relationship with God.

Figure 5.11

As with many of the works of Kierkegaard, *Fear and Trembling* was published under a pseudonym, John of Silence. The title referenced the biblical text of the Philippians that described fear and trembling as the road to salvation. In *Fear and Trembling,* Kierkegaard examined the anxiety that Abraham felt when God tested him. Abraham did not share his struggle with anyone during the three-and-half day journey to kill his son. He isolated himself for a higher purpose. This led Kierkegaard to define two types of people. One type of person finds happiness in themselves, and the other type of person seeks happiness in the social world. Kierkegaard believed that the story of Abraham's faith could not be understood rationally; *faith* is *an experience* that is beyond intellectual understanding. Kierkegaard was criticized for fideism, which means faith without reason. Kierkegaard argued there were good reasons to believe in faith, but that good reasons got in the way of making a personal, individual leap of faith.

Kierkegaard believed that the more one tried to understand, the less was understood. The more logical one tried to be, the less one comprehended. The more one tried to know God, the less was known. Trying to understand Jesus created a *dialectic paradox*. Jesus is both God and man who lived 2,000 years ago but still exists. He is a natural being but has supernatural power to transform the physical world through his miracles. The dialectic paradox is that God exists because it cannot be proven objectively.

Symbols of Humanistic-Existential Psychology 249

Figure 5.12

Kierkegaard was inspired by Gerthold Lessing (1729–1781), the skeptical eighteenth-century philosopher who symbolized the struggle of faith as a "broad ugly ditch" between an individual and faith. Understanding the difficulty of "making the leap" Lessing claimed his legs were too old to try. For Kierkegaard, without a leap of faith there could be no true joy, no true faith, and no true freedom.

In his book *Either/Or,* Kierkegaard (1992) described the process of freedom in three stages. In the first aesthetic stage, an individual lacks the ability to seek freedom because of the search is for immediate pleasure. This hedonistic lifestyle leads to boredom and despair. In the second ethical stage, individuals take responsibility by utilizing ethical standards established by others. For example, standards of the church, when making life decisions. Even though Kierkegaard viewed this stage as superior to the aesthetic stage, he believed in this stage people did not recognize their personal freedom, because of the emphasis on rules, reason, and harmony. The third stage, the religious stage, was not a synthesis of the first two because those stages were driven by social forces. The religious stage was an asocial awareness that one had the freedom to choose a personal relationship with God. This relationship was not based on dogma or social convention, but on the perpetual dialectic of seeking the infinite in the finite, and faith in the incarnation of God in man, in Jesus. This stage was not easy but the highest form of freedom.

One ultimately had to choose one of the stages because it was impossible to live in the rational social world when faith was viewed as asocial and irrational. Unlike Hegel and Marx who viewed dialectics as an objectively determined process, Kierkegaard viewed dialectics as determined by subjective reactions which occurred throughout the three stages. The *dialectic of existence* was never predetermined or objective, but always dependent on subjective reactions. Therefore, "truth is subjectivity" and the higher objectivity one can attain was "objective uncertainty."

The goal of the three stages was not only to find God but to find oneself: "becoming oneself before God." This is the experience of self in its most complete sense of being. Kierkegaard believed that a relationship with God should be like a love affair (Caelisle, 2021). It has been surmised this belief was in reaction to his breakup with Regina Olsen, a woman he almost married. He argued that the Bible should read like a love letter because the words should feel as if they were personally intended for the reader. Because love letters were only meaningful for the recipient, likewise the Bible did not need learned scholars for interpretation because truth only occurred through personal interpretations. *Truth is subjectivity* became a core foundational existential concept in H-E psychology.

Nietzschean Perspectivism

Friedrich Nietzsche (1844–1900) wanted to emancipate humanity from the "tyranny" of traditional Western philosophic thought. He rejected the traditional empirical, metaphysical, and epistemological philosophies that presumed an external or objective world. Nietzsche argued against metaphysical and epistemological philosophies because they espoused deeper truths beyond the natural world (Kaufman, 1974). What made Nietzsche one of the most controversial and despised thinkers of modern times was his belief that there were no ultimate truths about the world. For Nietzsche, there were no objective universal truths beyond unique individual *perspectives*. There were no facts, only interpretations. Even more controversial was his view that there was no "God's eye view" and no meaningful *universal perspectives* that philosophy, religion, or metaphysics could supply. Modern scientists had also lost their way by becoming dogmatic empiricists who provided only one extremely limited perspective.

Nietzsche's views could be perceived as *nihilist* because of his rejection of religion and with the implication that life could be meaningless. His views inspired the deconstructivism of French philosopher Jacques Derrida (1930–2004). a major figure associated with the development of postmodern philosophy who questioned the basic assumptions of Western philosophical and cultural traditions. *Nietzschean perspectivism* served as a forerunner to postmodernism because of his belief in a multiplicity of perspectives and argued that knowledge was a tool for survival, nothing more, nothing less. His rejection of traditional metaphysics was a precursor to the pragmatism of William James and John Dewey. His critique of Enlightenment philosophy also led to the rejection of Judeo-Christian values because those values made modern society psychological sick.

In 1882, Nietzsche wrote a famous soliloquy of "The Madman" who searched for God. In *The Gay Science,* Nietzsche (1977) used a madman to question whether modern culture was blinded by "the age of science and reason" and was ready to face the existential ramifications of "killing God." In the soliloquy, the Madman carried a lantern to symbolize a new awareness, an inner light that was beginning to illuminate the dawning of a new world order. He implored his listeners to hear:

> God is dead. God remains dead. And we have killed him. How shall we comfort ourselves, the murderers of all murderers? What was holiest and mightiest of all that the world has yet owned has bled to death under our knives: who will wipe this blood off us?

What water is there for us to clean ourselves? What festivals of atonement, what sacred games shall we have to invent? Is not the greatness of this deed too great for us? Must we ourselves not become gods simply to appear worthy of it?

- Friedrich Nietzsche (1977)

After this admonishing soliloquy, the listeners fell silent and looked at the Madman in astonishment. In response, the Madman understood that he had come too early to share this news. In response, he threw his lantern to the ground and it broke into pieces. He realized that people were not ready to hear the grave news. Ironically, it was a supposed madman who understood the state of the world and it was the so-called "enlightened" who were not ready to hear the truth.

Figure 5.13

The Nietzschean belief that "God is dead" symbolized one of the most famous and often misunderstood critiques of Western civilization. Nietzsche believed God was dead because humanity had killed the practical value of God. The presence of God was removed from all aspects of everyday living. The Bible no longer has relevance to improve the workplace or when setting career goals or deciding on a job, people do not consult a priest. God had been put "on the shelf," only acknowledged on Saturdays or Sundays.

Western philosophy, science, and religion had destroyed the concept of God. This led Nietzsche to ask one of the most disturbing existential questions: *was humanity one of the mistakes of God or was God one of the mistakes of humanity?* Influenced by Darwin, Nietzsche argued that humans had the same lowly origin as animals and shared the same outcome which was death. Nietzsche agreed with Darwin that evolution had no real purpose or final direction. Natural selection simply meant that organisms needed to develop personality traits for survival. Just because humans had lasted longer as the dominant species did not mean humans were of greater importance. Since there were billions of galaxies, the earth simply represented one small clay ball amongst billions rotating around a sun.

252 *Symbols of Humanistic-Existential Psychology*

With the death of God humanity was now on its own and without guidance, a *cosmic tabula rosa* without traditional sources to provide purpose and meaning. The danger was to deny the existential crisis and miss the opportunity for the creation of a world beyond Judeo-Christian values. This was only possible by turning inward and finding the *will to power*. The concept of will to power derived from Schopenhauer who made *will* a centerpiece of his philosophy. However, Nietzsche disagreed with Schopenhauer that will was the ultimate reality. Unlike Schopenhauer, Nietzsche did not view will as a "single-thing-in-itself" or power over others or political power. Nor did he view self-preservation as the main driving force of humanity. The driving force was the will to power; the drive to become more than we are, to reach our full potential, and to lead a passionate Dionysian way of life.

By accepting "God is Dead," people learned to depend on themselves and gain mastery over their own destiny. The will to power caused people to seek new experiences uninhibited by societal convention or religious beliefs. Even more important, the necessity for challenging traditional morality and outdated beliefs of what constitutes "good and evil." A person who achieved their full potential, Nietzsche called *superman,* an *ubermensch,* overman, or higher man. In contrast of the modern Superman who helped others, flew above the people, and never shared his superpowers. The Nietzschean superman believed before saving others, one needed to first save themselves. He argued that the journey for modern salvation most often required traveling through a personal hell which meant, *whatever doesn't kill you makes you stronger.*

Figure 5.14

In *Thus Spoke Zarathustra,* where Nietzsche (2005) best described his concept of superman. After 10 years of reflection and contemplation, Zarathustra returned from the mountains to share his insights about the future of civilization. His message was that civilization was in crisis because humans were no longer animals, but not yet supermen. God was dead and no external help was

Symbols of Humanistic-Existential Psychology 253

coming to save humanity. This was symbolized by a man on a tightrope over an abyss, with danger everywhere, who cannot go back but cannot stand still. Solving world problems had to begin one person at a time. This necessitated a new kind of love. Not love of God but love of self. Self-love was the essence of superman and the answer to the moral and philosophical crisis of the times.

Self-love was made difficult by religions and philosophies that taught humility, self-contempt, submissiveness, and guilt. Nietzsche was especially critical of the teachings of Christianity which he argued created a *slave psychology*. This was expressed by Jesus on the *Sermon on the Mount* when he said, "the meek shall inherit the earth" or when he taught people "to turn the other cheek." This slave psychology led to shame and guilt and made individuals psychologically sick when there were feelings of pride and self-worth. This slave psychology led people to devalue this world in favor of the "next heavenly world," which Nietzsche believed did not exist. The only answer was to reject religion and philosophy which stifled individuality in favor of developing the daring superman who rebelled against the herd mentality.

In the final analysis, it was important to believe only in oneself, which was summarized in his famous phrase, *he who does not believe in himself always lies.* Nietzsche agreed with Freud's view that a repressed civilization was the primary cause of human suffering. Nietzsche implored people to balance the inward Apollonian and Dionysian spirits. In *Birth of Tragedy: Out of the Spirit of Music*, Nietzsche (1994) found in classical Athenian tragedy an art form that provided a way forward to find meaning and purpose in life. In Greek tragedy, the audience continually experienced the abyss of human suffering. In an ironic psychological twist, cathartic encounters with tragedies led to the affirmation of existence. The theatre became a place for the audience to understand that human existence was paradoxical, not petty, or insignificant. Human existence, like the plays themselves, were a celebration of terror and ecstasy, the rational and irrational, the symbolic dance of Apollo and Dionysus, the dance that needed to consciously occur in the daily life of everyone.

For Nietzsche, it was the artistic impulse over philosophy or science that would emancipate humankind. The only hope for the survival of civilization was an *Apollonian and Dionysian Rapprochement*. The sad reality was that this integration had not occurred since the ancient Greek tragedians. The Greeks understood that Apollo represented harmony, progress, logic, and individuality. In contrast, Dionysus represented disorder, emotion, ecstasy, passion, intoxication, and social unity. Through their art, the Greeks understood that it was the constant psychological juxtaposition between mind and order, and passion and chaos that was fundamental

Figure 5.15

to Greek culture. On the one side, Apollo was full of intellectual illusions, while on the other side Dionysus represented the dangerous instinctual illusions. The illusions of both could only change through the dissolution of their boundaries and the integration of the rational and irrational. When this occurred, man became a *satyr*, half man, half animal.

It was the constant tragic tension between the forces of human reason and animal instinct that gave existence its true purpose and meaning. The Apollonian and Dionysian tension became symbolized in Greek tragedy by the main protagonist struggling to make Apollonian order against an unjust and chaotic Dionysian character. For Nietzsche, Shakespeare's *Hamlet* was a perfect modern example of an intellectual who could not make up his mind and who became a living antithesis of a man of action. Through the experience of his Dionysian nature, Hamlet gained the tragic understanding that knowledge could not change his circumstances. It was such an emotionally disgusting feeling that he decided to do nothing. While experiencing his Dionysian nature, a ghost appears, which allowed Hamlet a glimpse into the irrational supernatural reality, where he gained the true knowledge that no action was the true path for change. Nietzsche believed, as in Greek tragedy, the struggle of Hamlet allowed the audience to experience *primordial unity*, the revival of their Dionysian nature. This created an *artistic psychological state* and an intoxication that enriched every aspect of human existence. In this state an individual experienced their power and perfection, and the emancipatory power of art.

Nietzsche purposely avoided the development of a new philosophy or a prescription for human fulfillment. Rather, his perspectivism was a call for individuals to think for themselves, this is my way, what is yours? He also believed that a pupil repays their teacher poorly if they remain a pupil. His faith in the power of the individual to determine their unique purpose and live a life in accordance with their own beliefs, would not only inspire the development of H-E psychology, but would inspire people throughout the world. The essence of his existentialism could best be summarized by the famous words: *if you have your why for life, then you can get along with almost any* how.

Pure Phenomenology and the Scientific Method

As discussed in Volume II, Chapter 2, Franz Brentano (1883–1917) was a teacher of Freud and developed the theory of *phenomenological introspection*, which influenced the psychoanalytic method. Brentano believed there were two types of psychology Genetic psychology was an objective psychology, which studied phenomena from a third-person perspective that became empirical psychology, modeled on the natural sciences. The second type of psychology was a descriptive psychology, which studied phenomena from a first-person perspective that became phenomenological psychology, modeled on the hermeneutic sciences.

Brentano's influence extended beyond psychoanalysis. His view of a descriptive psychology laid the foundation for H-E psychology. He was interested in developing a "first-person" psychology to understand the subjective human experience called *act psychology* which studied the intentional and motivational acts that determined thought. These motivational acts included judging, perceiving, hoping, doubting, fearing, and loving. This led to his theory of *intentionality*, which means that every human act is intended as something outside itself. Edmund Husserl (1859–1938), another renowned student of Brentano, would take Brentano's philosophy and create a rigorous psychological scientific approach that would become known as *phenomenology*.

Influenced by Immanuel Kant (1774–1804), Husserl defined phenomenology as a *transcendental-idealist* philosophy. In Critique of Pure Reason, Kant (1999) argued that one can only know objects from their subjective experience, which is not knowledge of the objects in themselves. For Kant, the mind was transcendental because it had a priori knowledge before experience. He was reacting to the empirical viewpoint that the mind was a passive recipient of the natural world. Rather, he viewed the mind as actively constructing the world prior to any physical interaction. Kant became an *idealist* when he argued that the mind could conceptualize ideas independent of the material world.

In many ways, Husserl began in the early twentieth century where Kant ended in the late nineteenth century. Being a product of a different time in history, Husserl (1900–1901), in *Logical Investigations*, proposed an alternative to positivism, skepticism, empiricism, and historicism. For Husserl, these theories attempted to explain the mind in terms of nature rather than explaining nature in terms of the mind. Husserl, who began as a mathematician, sought to achieve the *Archimedean Point* to explain the foundation of all knowledge. The Archimedean Point was rooted in Greek mythology where the great mathematical Archimedes claimed that he could lift the earth off its foundation if given one solid place to stand with a long enough lever. The term came to mean a reliable starting point, a God's eye view, from which objective truths could be discovered. Like Archimedes, the phenomenologist studies a phenomenon by standing in one unbiased place with the tools to "lift knowledge off its foundation." Husserl wanted phenomenology to symbolically become the Archimedean Point where objective truth could be free of bias and perfectly understood.

The intentionality of Brentano described how the mind and the physical world interacted, whereas Husserl concentrated on how the mind was independent of the physical world. The goal of his *pure phenomenology* was to discover the essence of consciousness. Brentano's intentionality turned the focus to the outer world. The pure phenomenology of Husserl turned the focus to the inner world.

Husserl's *pure phenomenological method* is reductionistic because it requires the Greek concept of *epoch,* meaning "suspension," the "bracketing out" of the assumptions about the natural world. This suspension, bracketing, creates the experience of the essence of consciousness, the transcendental ego, the going back to the things in themselves. This Platonic eidetic reduction, eidos from the Greek meaning "pure form" or "idea," could finally be studied scientifically through the pure phenomenological method which required looking at the world differently; for instance, the encounter of trying to see a tree as it really appears. Looking at the tree and "bracketing" prior assumptions of "tree," and avoiding "that is a tree." True understanding of "tree" occurred by describing all aspects of the tree: "its green branches, its brown trunk, and its exposed roots." This descriptive method reclaimed the unique human experience of the world. The empirical and natural science methods purport to objectively understand the world. However, for the phenomenologist empiricist, they impose an assumptive intentionality on phenomena, which strips it of its essence. Husserl believed that the pure phenomenological method, which catalogues the interaction of mental acts and processes with environmental objects or events, is the essence of all philosophy, science, and psychology. For Husserl, these mental acts and processes were the basis of all human understanding, whether it be knowledge of a tree, person, or a human event.

Husserl's scientific method emancipated psychology from the limitations of empiricism and the natural science methodologies. Husserl's new research methodology focused science on a "first-person" perspective, a science withholding predetermined assumptions about the world for a more complete understanding of the human experience.

Existential Psychology

Martin Heidegger (1889–1976), a student of Husserl, dedicated *Being and Time* (Heidegger, 1927) to Husserl, which is considered the bridge between existential philosophy and existential psychology because the concepts Heidegger professed in *Being and Time* continue to appear in the writings of many existential psychologists. Heidegger started with Husserl and phenomenology, but because his interests were rooted in religion and metaphysics, took a different psychological path. Their disagreements resulted from approaching psychology from different philosophical traditions. Husserl based his thought on *epistemology*, the branch of philosophy

256 *Symbols of Humanistic-Existential Psychology*

concerned with the theory of knowledge. Epistemology seeks to discover the essence of mental phenomena, the why and how of thinking and how one acquires knowledge. Heidegger based his thought on *ontology,* the branch of metaphysics that seeks to understand the nature of being, the study of existence, and what it means to be human.

Like Husserl, Heidegger was a phenomenologist; but unlike Husserl, Heidegger wanted to examine what it meant to exist as a complete human being. Heidegger started with the concept of *Dasein* defined as the inextricable connection between a person and their world. *Dasein* in German means "being there," being engaged in the world as neither a subject nor an object. Heidegger argued that without the world, humans would not exist. But even more important was the reality that without humans the world would not exist. Heidegger believed that together phenomenology and existentialism answered the key question of how an individual could "be-in-the-world." It was the power of the human mind that made it possible to be there, and it was the mind that gave meaning and purpose to human existence.

Dasein was like *Lichtung*, which in German means both "light" and "a clearing in the woods." Lichtung symbolized Dasein and the psychological existentialism of Heidegger because I, Dasein, am like a clearing in the woods. The very act of being in a clearing in the woods reveals "the light" of human existence. Without humans the woods would just be woods. But when "I" enter the woods, "I" bring an ability to have a uniquely human experience. Heidegger replaced consciousness with experience, the experience of being in the world because in the woods "I" experience the world in all its wonder.

Figure 5.16

Symbols of Humanistic-Existential Psychology 257

In rejecting Aristotelian substances, the Cartesian mind, Kantian transcendental activity, and the transcendental ego of Husserl, Heidegger produced a totally revolutionary vision of the human subject. Heidegger rejected the idea of a conscious ego, a mind inside a physical world. He abandoned those philosophical understandings because of his belief that human existence was totally different from physical objects or the animal world. Humans were not simply different; their existence was unlike physical objects and animals because humans were dynamic agents who could control their destiny.

The existential structure of Dasein consisted of *existenz, facticity*, and *fallenness. Existenz* was the capacity to envision possibilities and make choices, to lead an *authentic* life. Facticity consisted of the acceptance of all the facts of existence which included age, height, gender, and especially birth date, the day thrown into the world. Fallenness was falling back to the pre-ontological state when one did not face up to their full potential of being in the world. This led to living an inauthentic life, *sein cum tode, being until death,* which created authenticity. The recognition of the limited time left to live prompted taking hold of ourselves in resolution of our existence. It was accepting the fact that I must die someday. One who lives an authentic life accepts their death. Since death is inevitable, this causes an urgency to create a meaningful life. Without this urgency, life lacked excitement and became inauthentic. An inauthentic life was categorized by the avoidance of all the possibilities that life could offer and is the life lived in the safety of traditional, conventional societal values. The inauthentic person gives up their freedom and lives under the dictates of others, and let others influence major life decisions.

Heidegger believed that *existential guilt* occurred when one did not exercise their personal freedom. Guilt was an incentive to act and live life to its fullest. This also created another powerful feeling, *anxiety* which was an awareness that someday *we will be nothing*. Feelings of

Figure 5.17

anxiety had a positive function because they indicated that one was taking chances and risks, living outside of convention, and expressing personal freedom. Freedom caused anxiety because with freedom came responsibility, which meant no blame directed at God, society, the church, parents, or life circumstances. Freedom and responsibility were inextricably interwoven. Responsibility meant being accountable for taking the consequences of personal actions because it took extraordinary *courage* to face feelings of guilt and anxiety. There was no way to lead an authentic life by their avoidance.

Heidegger believed that freedom was limited because of being *thrown* into the facticity of the world. The *thrownness* symbolized the limitations of being male or female, rich or poor, American, or Chinese, as well as the limitations of the historic period into which one was born. The limitations of freedom were intended to provide a context for life, not an excuse for avoiding the opportunity to experience all the possibilities of human existence. The constraints were a call to seek freedom with all its limitations.

French Existentialism

Before World War II, French existentialists traveled to Germany to study the phenomenological approach of Heidegger and were inspired by his existential analytic method of Dasein. Unlike Heidegger, these existentialists were also interested in psychoanalytic and Western neo-Marxist thought. This also occurred at the same time the Frankfurt School in Germany was exploring the integration of Freud, Hegel, and Western neo-Marxist approaches. Western neo-Marxist thinkers rejected Soviet-style Marxism as barbaric and a distortion of the humanistic vision of Marx. European existentialists became interested in how Marxist thought could be compatible with democracy and individualism, while rejecting the authoritarianism and dictatorial practices of the Soviet Union. These existentialists branded Soviet Marxism as "state capitalism," the exploitation, not the emancipation, of workers.

Unlike classical Greek and Christian philosophical thinkers who viewed the meaning of life as coming from nature or God, the early French existentialists agreed with Heidegger that humans were thrown into existence without any purpose or meaning. This meant that humans were now finally free to determine existence through their individually directed actions. The most influential French existentialist was Jean-Paul Sartre (1905–1980), who integrated Heideggerian thought and French existentialism. Sartre compared his time to the period in ancient Greece after the death of Alexander the Great when Athenians rejected Aristotelian science and moved toward more personal philosophies like the Stoics and Epicureans, who taught people how to live (Sartre, 1957).

Inspired by *Being and Time* and approaching consciousness from a Cartesian perspective, Sartre (1993/1943) wrote in his landmark masterwork, *Being and Nothingness,* that consciousness was "non-being" and totally separate from the natural world. He used the symbol of consciousness as "wind blowing toward objects." This symbolized human freedom and Sartre's dictum that human beings are absolutely free; nothing can determine our mental abilities or our consciousness except our mental attitudes or our consciousness.

Figure 5.18

The title *Being and Nothingness* articulated Sartre's view of an existential worldview. The natural world was the "nothingness." Leading an authentic life meant avoiding the influence of the external world, because the external, natural, world had nothing to offer. The natural world was irrelevant to human existence because humans possessed consciousness. The natural world, even a misguided belief in a God, was useless because neither could help humanity live. This reality proved that humans were totally free to determine their being in a nothingness world. Sartre also argued that the possibility of freedom caused terrifying feelings, feelings of dread and angst. For Heidegger, the denial of freedom led to an inauthentic life; for Sartre it was living in bad faith. Living in bad faith meant that one lied about their very existence. This usually meant an identification with something external that was fixed and material, safe from any free choices and to a myriad of excuses that made tolerable the escape from freedom and responsibility.

Sartre argued for the existentialist movement to embrace *literature engage*, literature, and the arts in service of political activism. During the German occupation during World War II there was ambivalence in France about a direct challenge to Nazi authority. During the period of Nazi occupation, the French people felt demoralized and impotent. In his play *Flies,* Sartre (1947) was able to avoid Nazi censorship. He created an archetypal existential drama about rebellion and freedom. Sartre used the parable of Orestes, the hero of the *Oresteia* plays of the Greek philosopher Aeschylus, to speak about the plight the French people. In *Flies*, Orestes discovered that his mother, Clytemnestra, had conspired with her lover, Aegisthus, to kill his father, King Agamemnon. Aegisthus, like the Nazis, brutally oppressed the citizenry. In the Sartre version, the population of Argos was too traumatized to resist. Flies flew over the city symbolizing the humiliation the citizens felt for not rebelling. The citizens were liberated when the hero, Orestes, and his sister, Electra, killed Aegisthus to avenge the death of their father and their mother for her disloyalty. However, because the citizens of Argos did not rebel against the murderers of his father, Orestes experienced an existential crisis because he bore the burden of their guilt and shame.

When the god Zeus believed his power, like the Nazis, was being threatened, he ordered flies to hound Orestes and Electra until they admitted their murderous crimes. Orestes refused; Electra capitulated. For Orestes, Electra represented, like the French, the inability to accept freedom and take personal responsibility. In the end, Orestes modeled the Nietzschean superman by becoming a king without a kingdom. In the spirit of existentialism, he told the citizens of Argos that he bore the burden of their crimes so they, like the French, could build a new life without remorse. Orestes embodied the existential hero who rebelled against oppression, bore the burden of personal responsibility, and preferred to act freely and make his own decisions. As he left, Argos, taking the sins of the people with him and feeling their dread, walked freely toward the light as a free man. With the flies chasing Orestes, they were no longer disturbing the Argos citizenry. But the flies were also no longer a threat to his existence.

In 1964, Sartre was awarded the *Nobel Prize in Literature* despite his attempt to refuse it because a writer should never become an institution. The influence of Sartre and existentialism on the world stage was dramatically expressed by his funeral in 1980 when 50,000 Parisians descended onto the Boulevard du Montparnasse to accompany the cortege of Sartre to the *Montparnasse Cemetery*. The procession passed through many of the places where Sartre had shared his vision of existentialism. Many of the mourners cried that April day not only for an incredible human being but for the fear that existentialism itself might be going to the grave with him.

Albert Camus (1913–1960) introduced himself to Sartre as he was rehearsing for a production of *Flies*. Because of his moderate politics compared to Sartre and others, Camus would always be an existentialist outsider in French existentialism. He was appreciated more in the later part of the twentieth century than during the political upheavals in Europe in the early and mid-twentieth century. Although Sartre produced the internationally acclaimed existential play *No Exit*, Camus would become the superior literary figure of the French existential movement. Camus was influenced more by Kierkegaard than Heidegger. Although *Fear and Trembling* was an inspiration, Camus took a totally different approach to the Abraham and Isaac biblical story. For Camus, the story was not about the relationship Abraham had with God, but his relationship with Isaac. He was amazed by the fact that Isaac and Abraham, after an almost murder, could resume their relationship as if the nothing had happened. It was incredulous to Camus that Abraham would even consider dispensing from his fatherly duty of paternal protection for a God, and then afterward show incredible love for his son. The only way Abraham could resign his fatherly role and then take everything back and act as if it never happened was on the *strength of the absurd*.

Camus believed that individuals needed to embrace the absurdity of existence. The absurd occurred when there was a fundamental contradiction between the search for meaning and the meaningless of existence. Camus argued that it was part of human nature to try to find meaning and purpose in life. The absurdity was the deadly indifference of the universe to provide that meaning and purpose. This led to *existential dread* which occurred when there was a collision between the search for meaning and the "unreasonable silence" that emanated from the universe. In 1940, as Camus and millions of refugees were fleeing the advancing Nazi armies, he offered three major options to deal with absurdities of life. In the *Myth of Sisyphus* Camus (1975), the title from Homer's *Odyssey*, Camus described how Sisyphus was punished for his trickery of avoiding death twice. For his punishment, Sisyphus was forced to roll an immense boulder up the hill only to find that as it reached the top it would roll back down the hill. Sisyphus was cursed to repeat this process throughout eternity.

This led Camus to answer the three existential questions that would forever influence existentialism: *Does the realization of the absurd require suicide?* For Camus, the answer was a resounding "no!" Suicide, as the first option, was "escaping existence." In the act of ending existence, existence only became more absurd. The second option of religiosity and spiritualism required the "leap of faith" described by Kierkegaard but was yet another form of suicide. It was a "philosophical suicide" because those approaches were irrational and could not be proven empirically. The third option, the "solution," was a dialectic process which balanced the acceptance of the absurdity of life with the act of rebellion against its absurdity. Active engagement in this dialectic process created *transient,* ever changing, *personal meaning* which made it easier to live with absurdity. Finding personal, not religious, or philosophical, meaning was where one could find freedom and contentment.

Figure 5.19

In the end, Sisyphus must decide, like all of humanity, whether to give up the laboriously and meaninglessness of life, or to keep going. At the end of the book, Sisyphus resumed his endless task by accepting its absurdity. Camus concluded the book by asking the reader to *imagine Sisyphus happy*, symbolic of an option in French existentialism to happily accept the absurdity of human existence.

American Existentialism

> Americans cling to the myth of individualism as though it were the only normal way to live, unaware that it was unknown, except for hermits, in the Middle Ages and would have been considered psychotic in classical Greece.
>
> - Rollo May (1991)

Rollo May (1909–1994) brought Heideggerian existentialism to America and was responsible for being one of the first psychologists to introduce European existential philosophy to American psychology. Besides being influenced by the intellectual aspects of European existentialism, the fact that he almost died of tuberculosis provided a direct experience of confronting death which is one of the most important concepts of existentialism. During his struggles with tuberculosis, he studied anxiety from the perspective of Kierkegaard and Freud. *The Meaning of Anxiety*, published in 1950, was the dissertation that led May (1950) to receive the first doctorate in 1949 in clinical psychology from *Columbia University* and began his lifelong interest in the role of existential anxiety.

May (1967) rejected the natural science methodologies as inadequate for the study of human behavior. Those methods ignored what made humans unique and separate from the rest of the physical world. He yearned for a new science that would specifically be designed to study humans. This new science would be no less rigorous than the natural sciences, but much more relevant to understanding human beings in their totality; a revolutionary science that would be able to explain the mysteries of existence still unexplored and make the current natural science and experimental methods look archaic and backward.

May rejected the Hegelian thought of *The Absolute,* which stated life could only have meaning in relationship to the totality of the world. May was influenced by Kierkegaard, who believed that each individual life had a self-determined uniqueness; subjectivity was where truth existed. Although May agreed in the uniqueness of each individual person, he suggested there were separate objective and subjective human experiences. Because humans were impacted by the objective, physical world, the natural sciences were unable to distinguish the human experience from other physical objects in the world. Ignoring the duality of human nature and equating human and physical world equally, the natural sciences denied that human existence was quite different. This denial avoided the scientific study of the essence of life, which was to find subjective meaning and purpose. May (1967) called living with the dual nature of existence the *human dilemma,* the *paradox* of living in relationship to oneself while at the same time living with the vastly different physical objects in the natural world.

Like Carl Jung, May (1991) embraced the power of mythology as essential for living a free and satisfying life. He also agreed with Jung that a myth could consume the psychology of a culture. May believed the *myth of rugged individualism* imprisoned the American psyche. This was dramatically symbolized in the Arthur Miller (1976) play *Death of a Salesman* by the character of Willy Loman. Loman never discovered his true self because he lived the myth that "becoming number one" was the only way to define a successful life. When he realized that would never happen, Loman felt a violent suicide was his only option. May argued that personal and societal violence was the dark shadow of the *myth of rugged individualism*. The pressure to succeed, like for Willy Loman, created an isolated, alienated, and success-driven individual, a *low man*, the lowest form of human existence. The only hope for Loman would have been to develop his own personal myth by which to live his life.

As a psychoanalyst, May observed that his clients were often searching for their personal myth. Finding personal myth necessitated understanding the classical myths as a personal myth was a variation on the ancient myths. May introduced mythology to existentialism because mythology provided a way to make sense of a senseless and violent world. May argued where there was consciousness there had to be myth. Although May agreed that myth provided a sense of identity, personal values, and the mysteries of creation, he also believed *hunger for myth was hunger for community*. Because American culture influenced his existentialism, it was not surprising that the hunger for community would emerge from a culture that is often community phobic. To be an active member of a community meant sharing in its myths and its stories. It is in the sharing of community myths that one becomes emotionally connected with others. May urged replacing the current American myth of rugged individualism with myths that rejected social isolation, loneliness, and violence.

Like most existentialists, May advocated for human freedom, the opportunity for an individual to reach their full potential. May believed that freedom was difficult to attain because of the societal pressures to conform and live up to the expectations of other people. Seeking freedom created a healthy anxiety that was necessary for individual growth. It could also create a *neurotic anxiety* that was not conducive to personal development when fear meant avoiding personal freedom. Neurotic anxiety also led to self-alienation, feelings of guilt, apathy, and despair. May agreed with the Kierkegaardian concept that self-alienation caused a *shut-upness* that cut a person off from an authentic relationship with themselves and the world.

Figure 5.20

In *Escape from Freedom*, Erich Fromm (1967), a Frankfurt School scholar, wrote a classic work on freedom that explored the willingness of individuals in modern times to submit to totalitarianism over democracy, even as democracy provided the opportunity for freedom. Fromm argued that while democracy set some people free; other people became isolated and felt dehumanized. In this process, people were willing to give up their freedom by a pledge of blind loyalty to a leader or by submitting to an all-powerful state. *Escape from Freedom* provides a symbol of the human dilemma and paradox of freedom with one segment of humanity removing their chains, while another puts the chains back on.

Humanistic Psychology

Abraham Maslow (1908–1970), the father of the humanistic psychology movement, applied many of the concepts of existentialism to humanistic psychology. Living in New York and attending Brooklyn College in the 1930s and 1940s, Maslow was exposed to the ideas of European psychologists escaping Nazism. Among the psychologists were Karen Horney, Erich Fromm, Max Wertheimer, and Alfred Adler. Because of his belief in the importance of developing a healthy lifestyle, many believe that Adler should be considered the first humanistic psychologist.

Maslow came to humanism after extensive exposure to mainstream American psychology. He was first infatuated with Watsonian behaviorism until he saw that it did not work while raising his daughter, Bertha. Maslow was the first doctoral student of the famous experimental psychologist, Harry Harlow (1905–1981), whose controversial research with rhesus monkeys showed the long-term psychological damage of *maternal deprivation* and social isolation. It was controversial because Harlow created inanimate surrogate mothers for the rhesus infants made from wire and wool. Ultimately his research supported many of the findings of John Bowlby regarding the importance of parental caregiving and emotional attachment for healthy childhood development. Maslow's 1934 doctoral dissertation findings, *Establishment of Dominance in a Colony of Monkeys*, influenced his future humanistic theories because he found that dominance was a result of inner psychological, not outer physical strength.

Later, at Columbia University, Malow became the research assistant of Edward Thorndike (1874–1949). Thorndike (Volume II, Chapter 4) was the famous pioneer in behavioral animal research whose research discovered that animals could learn from observation and imitation. As Thorndike's assistant, Maslow began research on human sexuality before the famous sexual research of Alfred Kinsey (1894–1956). At Columbia University, Maslow discontinued his sexual research with college students because of the overemphasis on their sexual exploits. Ultimately, his experiences with experimental psychology led Maslow to reject, not accept, mainstream psychology.

In 1951, after World War II, Maslow became chair of the psychology department at *Brandeis University,* where he gave birth to Third Force Psychology. Maslow believed that the first force, psychoanalysis, with its emphasis on mental disturbance, had "crippled" psychology. He also rejected behaviorism, because human beings could never be reduced to habits, cognitive structures,

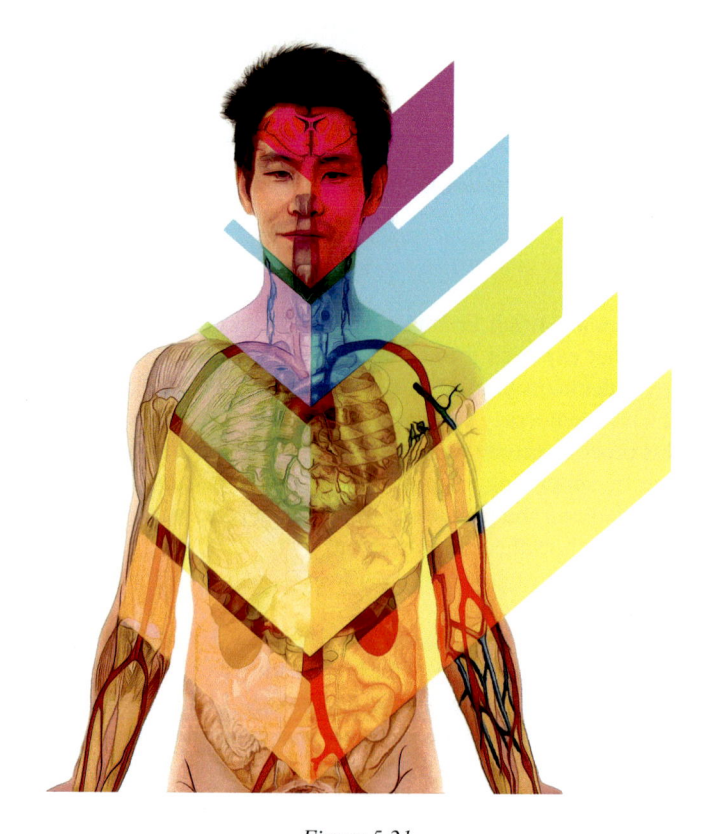

Figure 5.21

stimulus-response (S-R) behaviors, and predictions or controllers of human behavior. By rejecting the poetic, romantic, and spiritual, experimental psychology had lost touch with the essence of what it meant to be human. In alliance with the existentialists, Maslow (1966) argued that the natural science methodologies treated humans like sterile physical objects rather than as the unique and mysterious living beings that were yet to be discovered. The dominance of American behaviorism and its rejection of subjectivity created the opportunity for a new science to emerge in psychology.

Maslow did not expect psychology to reject the natural science experimental methods or discontinue treating people with emotional problems. In contrast with psychoanalysis and behaviorism, Maslow (1943) focused on what made people exceptional. He realized this could only happen when human needs were organized by a *hierarchy of needs*. This hierarchy became symbolic of the universal applicably of psychological thought, often transcending any specific theoretical orientation. The attainment of higher states of consciousness were contingent on meeting the basic lower level physiological and safety needs. The need for safety could only be satisfied after the need for food, health, and rest had been met. After achieving physiological needs, the psychological needs of love and belonging needed to be satisfied. These included feelings of affection, intimacy, friendship, and being part of a community. Only after meeting the needs of love and belonging could the need for esteem be addressed. Esteem resulted from personal feelings of accomplishment and personal value as well as socially acknowledged contributions to the well-being of others. Satisfactorily meeting esteem needs provided movement to the top of the pyramid and made it possible to achieve self-fulfillment and become a fully self-actualized human being.

The concept of *self-actualization* was rooted in the Aristotelian concept of *entelechy*, the innate drive of a species to express its unique characteristics. Rollo May's view diverged from Aristotle's in that he argued that self-actualization was the realization of individual potential, not species potential. Since it was difficult to become self-actualized, Malow referred to those satisfying many of the needs of the hierarchy as self-actualizing. Accession to the top of the hierarchy was more problematic because psychological needs did not have the long evolutionary history of physiological needs. Physiological needs were deeply rooted in the human psyche whereas the needs for love, belonging and self-esteem were "newer," being totally human and not solely based on a biologically based evolutionary foundation. Maslow viewed the inner world of humanity as weak and underdeveloped and easily overpowered by instinctual needs. Self-actualization was typically impossible because it required a strong inner life and an ability to be honest with oneself. The reality was that most human beings were fearful of self-knowledge. The fear of self-knowledge Maslow defined as the *Jonah Complex*, the fear of one's greatness and the denial of one's best talents. It was not just the fear of failure but also the fear of success that mitigated against self-actualization.

Maslow (1968) argued that psychology had for too long emphasized the study of lower animals and mentally disturbed individuals. To change that reality, he studied several people that he considered *self-actualizing*, not necessarily self-actualized. His study included Albert Einstein, Sigmund Freud, Jane Addams, William James, and Abraham Lincoln. He concluded that self-actualizing individuals had the following personality traits:

Self-Actualized People

Perceive reality accurately and fully.
Demonstrate a great acceptance of themselves and of others.
Exhibit spontaneity and naturalness.
Have a need for privacy.

> *Tend to be independent of their environment and culture. Demonstrate a continuous freshness of appreciation. Tend to have periodic mystic or peak experiences.*
> *Concerned with all humans instead of with only their friends, relatives, and acquaintances.*
> *Tend to have only a few friends.*
> *Have a strong ethical sense but do not necessarily accept conventions ethics.*
> *Have a well-developed but not hostile sense of humor.*
> *Are creative.*

Maslow (1971) viewed people who were not self-actualizing as *deficiency motivated (D-motivation)*. Those not self-actualizing were focused on need deficiency rather than seeking higher psychological functioning. Deficiency motivated people perceived the world as satisfying their immediate needs no matter how irrelevant they were to their personal development. Self-actualizing people experienced existence differently because they were not motivated by deficiency but by *being motivated* (B-motivation). Being motivated (B-motivation) people were not motivated by deficiency but inspired to seek higher human values like truth and justice. But just as important, being motivated people were also motivated by B-love (being-love), which unlike D-Love (deficiency-love) was non-possessive and less needy. In contrast to the First and Second Forces in psychology, Maslow envisioned a psychology interested in being motivated people who had satisfied their basic physiological needs and were committed to a self-actualizing life.

The development in 1961 of the *Journal of Humanistic Psychology* dramatically changed psychology; research and clinical practice by emphasizing what made people healthy, not unhealthy, and deficient. With the creation in 1971 of the *Society of Humanistic Psychology*, Division 32 of the American Psychological Association (APA), Maslow was recognized as being responsible for making humanistic psychology a formal branch of psychology. As a recognized leader that transcended many of the oppositional forces to humanistic psychology within psychology, Maslow was honored by being elected president of the APA in 1967.

It is often neglected in psychological history that Charlotte Buhler (1893–1974), a developmental psychologist, became a leading voice along with Maslow in shepherding the new humanistic movement. Before the formal recognition by the APA of humanistic psychology, she was a founding member of the *Association of Humanistic Psychology* (AHP). The first major AHP meeting in 1963 was officially named the *First Invitational Conference on Humanistic Psychology*, or affectionately known by humanistic psychologists as the *Old Saybrook Conference*. Attendees who presented papers at the first meeting included Rollo May, Abraham Maslow, and Carl Rogers.

Buhler became president of the AHP in 1965, and in 1970 gave an address to the *First International Invitational Conference of Humanistic Psychology* in Amsterdam Netherlands. In this address, she provided one of the most influential position papers in the history of humanistic psychology. The address entitled *Basic: Theoretical Concepts of Humanistic Psychology* (Buhler, 1971), was published by the *American Psychologist,* the leading journal of the APA. In her paper, she criticized the psychoanalytic goal of seeking homeostasis rather than growth. Buhler argued humanistic psychology offered the promise of achieving four major life goals: self-realization, personal fulfillment, creative expansion, and the ability to become a fully integrated human being. Buhler modeled the life of being a fully developed and well-rounded psychologist. Besides her dedication to humanistic psychology, she had a wide range of interests. As a developmental psychologist she emphasized the impact of reproductive biology on personality development. She also became a leader in the sandtray therapy movement (Volume II, Chapter 3) and developed the diagnostic *World Test,* which she utilized for cross-cultural research.

Humanistic-Existential Psychology

Existential (Dasein) Analysis

Ludwig Binswanger (1881–1966) was able to accomplish something that many of the early psychoanalysts were unable to do, which was stay a colleague and close friend with Freud throughout his lifetime. In 1938, out of deep concern for Freud's safety, he offered Freud refuge from the Nazis in his home in Switzerland.

Binswanger studied psychiatry at the *University of Zurich* under Eugen Bleuler, the eugenicist who coined the term *schizophrenia*. He learned psychoanalysis from Carl Jung and became the first Freudian psychoanalyst in Switzerland. Influenced by the writings of Heidegger, Husserl, and Buber, Binswanger expanded the concept of analytic treatment throughout the United States and Europe. Inspired by Heidegger's concept of Dasein, Binswanger emancipated psychoanalysis from the limitations of Freudian thought by integrating Dasein with phenomenological and psychoanalytic principles, creating a new psychotherapeutic approach, *Daseinanalysis, Existential Analysis*.

Like most existentialists, Binswanger (1958a) thought it was important to understand the here-and-now. It was also important to know how the client in the immediate therapeutic interchange viewed their current existence. The therapist needed to understand client anxieties, fears, values, social relations, thought processes, and areas of life that made existence meaningful. Binswanger believed that people lived in three different worlds of existence that distinguished humans from non-humans: the *Umwelt*, the "around the world"; the *Mitwelt*, the "with world"; and *Eigenwelt*, the "own world." In the Umwelt world, human beings, unlike nonhumans, viewed existence by the effectiveness of their relationship with the physical world. In the Mitwelt world, humans viewed their lives in relationship with other people, especially their ability to love and be loved by others. The Eigenwelt was the world one created within themselves, the private, inner, "me only" subjective world. To successfully treat a client, an existential analyst first needed to understand how clients mediated the three modes of existence.

One of Binswanger's most important contributions was his concept of *Weltanschauung,* meaning worldview or world design. An individual embraced the three modes of existence through their *Weltanschauung*. It was important for a therapist to assess whether the world view of the client was open or closed, positive or negative, simple, or complex, as this determined how an individual lived in the world. Since an ineffective worldview caused anxiety, fear, depression, and guilt it was paramount for the therapist to help the client find ways to embrace the world, other people, and themselves in new and more effective ways.

From 1957 to 1980, the Binswanger family operated the *Bellevue Sanatorium,* a private psychiatric hospital converted from an old monastery in Kreuzlingen, Switzerland. The hospital was famous for the treatment of schizophrenia of Princess Alice of Battenberg, the mother of Prince Phillip, and late husband of Queen Elizabeth. Ludwig's father, Robert Binswanger, treated Josef Breuer and Freud's famous patient Anna O., Bertha Pappenheimer (Volume II, Chapter 2), the first known patient to be treated by psychoanalysis. Ludwig became the medical director of the Sanatorium from 1911 to 1956 and treated many famous patients, including the painter Ernst Kirchner, dancer Vaslav Nijinsky, poet Simon Frank, and cultural anthropologist Aby Warburg. Under Ludwig, the Sanatorium became internationally renowned and connected with many of the leading intellectuals and psychiatrists of the day including Freud, Jung, Karl Jaspers, Husserl, and Buber.

It was Ellen West who became Binswanger's most famous and controversial patient (Binswanger, 1958b). The case of Ellen West became well known in the eating disorder literature. Her case demonstrated the strength and weaknesses of existential analysis. Through the lens of existential analysis, Binswanger viewed the death of Ellen West as the necessary fulfillment of her existence. Ellen West died of suicide at the age of 33 of a lethal overdose of poison. The surface symptom that dominated her life was the fear of becoming fat and ugly. Throughout her treatment, she was given many diagnoses, including melancholia and manic depression, which Binswanger rejected. Binswanger, influenced by Bleuler's views, saw Ellen as having schizophrenia.

Binswanger believed that Ellen had closed herself to the Umwelt and Mitwelt worlds early in life. In other words, she fought the natural state of childhood, which was being dependent on the world and others. Examples included refusing milk at nine months of age and becoming socially stubborn and defiant early in life. In fighting dependency, she became, not free from dependency, but overpowered by it. This led to a lifelong defiance that robbed Ellen of her autonomy and authentic existence.

For Binswanger, the only authentic way of being-beyond-the world for Ellen was death because the existentialist believes that death is both a physical and psychological process. In effect, life and death are not opposites because death must be lived, and life must be encompassed by death. From the existential perspective, a human being dies at the very moment of their existence. Binswanger believed that the idea of death for Ellen "brightened her life" and that her exuberance for longing for death could have been best said by the Shakespearean Claudio, *striving for life I seek death, seeking death, I find life* (Shakespeare, 1559–1601/1992).

Reactions to the existential analytic treatment of Ellen West were largely critical. John Maltsberger (1996) argued that the suicide could have been avoided and that the diagnosis was not schizophrenia but severe depression and a chronic eating disorder. Carl Rogers (1963) criticized the existential analytic approach because its intellectual and philosophical approach made it difficult for Ellen West to develop a healing emotional relationship with the therapist, which Rogers believed would have changed her relationship to the Umwelt and Mitwelt worlds. Craig Jackson, Graham Davidson, Janice Russell, and Walter Vandereycken (1990) took a more supportive approach of the Binswanger approach by emphasizing that most current authors and therapists of eating disorders neglect the existential struggles with death symbolism and death anxiety.

Rogerian Psychology

Carl Rogers (1902–1987), emancipated psychology from the medical model with its overemphasis on diagnosis and the causes of mental disturbance. Rogers refused to call disturbed individuals "patients" as was the case in medicine and psychoanalysis. Rogers (1942) believed people seeking psychotherapy were "clients" because as clients they, not the therapist, knew what was best for them and as a client they determined whether the service they were receiving was worth their personal and economic investment.

By the mid-twentieth century, Rogers' theories became a threat to the psychotherapeutic dominance of psychiatry and psychoanalysis. It was during his 12-year career from 1945 through 1957 at the *University of Chicago* that Rogers (1951) wrote *Client-Centered Therapy: Its Current Practice, Implications and Theory,* considered his most important work on client-centered psychotherapy. According to Rogers, *unconditional positive regard* was the only way for a therapist to avoid imposing their own personal biases on a client. If a client felt loved and accepted for who they truly were, the client would feel free to express all aspects of themselves. In this way, the therapeutic relationship was *nondirective* because Rogers believed that the client, not the therapist, knew the best way to solve their problems. Like Maslow, Rogers argued that human beings have an innate drive toward self-actualization and can use this actualizing tendency to live fulfilling lives and reach their full potential. Clients that embrace the actualizing tendency lived according to an *organismic valuing system* which was a life lived in accordance with their innermost feelings.

In the spirit of the ancient Cynics and Rousseau, Rogers believed in the *primacy of* feelings: people were ultimately guided and motivated by their feelings. Rogers called modern humans "emotionally constipated" because cultural mores, rigid belief systems, and convention caused people in the modern world to hide their true feelings.

Most people do not live according to their inner most feelings because the *need for positive regard* was neglected in childhood. Positive regard required that love, warmth, empathy, and acceptance were given to a child freely without conditions. But most of the time, parents and other significant people only give children positive regard under certain conditions. This resulted in *conditions of worth* in which the child learned that to receive love and acceptance children needed to act, think, and believe in accordance with the values and beliefs of the significant people in their lives. As children grew to adulthood, those values and beliefs were internalized as adults lost to their own organismic valuing system. This resulted in leading an inauthentic life, which was why when clients sought psychotherapy for their problems, clients did not need another life experience where the therapist set specific conditions and expectations. When conditions of worth replaced the organismic valuing system, the result was an incongruent person, a person no longer being true to their own feelings. Because being incongruent caused mental disturbances, the goal of psychotherapy was to help clients overcome conditions of worth and live in accordance with their organismic valuing system; in other words, in terms of the famous Rogerian mantra: "trust your feelings."

In 1963, Rogers left academia and joined the *Western Behavioral Sciences Institute* (WBSI) in La Jolla, California. In 1968, he left WBSI to create the *Center for the Studies of the Person,* which changed his focus from individual therapy to group therapy, encounter groups, and sensitivity training. Building on the T-group training developed by the *National Laboratory in Group Development* in the late 1940s and from the work on small group dynamics of Kurt Lewin, Rogers led an encounter group movement that would further revolutionize psychology. This was done by emphasizing the importance of group *person-to-person healing,* which was missing in psychoanalytic and behavioral psychology. In small group sessions of 8 to 10 people led by a trained leader, individuals learned self-awareness and sensitivity toward others. By verbalizing feelings freely and uninhibitedly, individuals strengthened their organismic valuing system. The emphasis in the encounter group was to support the sharing of strong emotions and discouraging critical judgments, intellectualization, and rationalization.

Group psychotherapy was a radical departure from the traditional view that individual psychotherapy was the best approach to solve psychological problems. Rogers showed when clients received support from others in group psychotherapy, a powerful social healing occurred that was unavailable in individual psychotherapy. Group therapy came to symbolize the revolutionary spirit of Rogerian psychology.

Figure 5.22

Rogers was one of the first psychologists to measure psychotherapeutic effectiveness. He used a method called the *Q-technique* developed in the 1950s by William Stephenson (1953). His research distinguished the *Real* from an *Ideal Self*. The Real Self was described as the way a person perceived themselves in the immediate moment whereas the Ideal Self was what the person would like to become in the future. Striving for the Ideal Self-made living in the immediate existential moment-by-moment experience difficult. Utilizing the Q-Technique, Rogers had clients describe themselves at the beginning, during, and end of therapy. Initially the correlation between the Real and Ideal Self was typically low but if the client-centered therapy was successful, the correlation increased and the relationship between the Real and Ideal Self was closer and more realistic. Utilizing this technique throughout psychotherapeutic treatment provided therapists a tool to assess the effectiveness of their psychotherapeutic interventions and provided a model for future psychotherapeutic research.

As discussed in the *Political Systems* section above, Rogers evolved beyond the clinical to social, cultural, and political issues later in his career and changed the name of his approach from *client-centered* to *person-centered psychology* (Rogers, 1974). The person-centered approach expanded Rogerian thought beyond the clinical world to many aspects of American life, particularly learner-centered teaching, which emphasizes the teacher as a guide and a mentor, rather than an expert who understands "what the student does is more important than what the teacher does" in the learning process (Rogers, 1969).

Rogers received many honors in his lifetime, including being elected president of the APA in 1947. Because of the perception that many psychologists who viewed his approach as unscientific, he broke into tears in 1956 when he received the first *Distinguished Scientific Contribution Award* from the APA, along with Kenneth Spence and Wolfgang Kohler. In 1972, the APA awarded Rogers the *Distinguished Professional Contribution Award,* which made Rogers the first psychologist in the history of the APA to receive both awards.

Logotherapy

Suffering ceases to be suffering at the moment it finds meaning.

- Victor Frankl (1971)

The importance of finding meaning and purpose in life permeates all aspects of H-E psychology. No one better personified this belief than Viktor Frankl (1905–1997). In his internationally famous and bestselling book, *Man's Search for Meaning,* Frankl (1971) described how he survived three years in four different Nazi concentration camps. He found when the prisoners found meaning, something to live for, they were able to survive the horrendous brutality of the Nazi guards. In dramatic terms, he described many "existential events," like prisoners who would comfort other prisoners and often out of kindness give starving prisoners their last piece of bread. Although these prisoners were few in number, it proved that even when everything was taken from a person, there was one thing that could never be taken away which was the opportunity, even in an untenable situation, to express freedom in a personal and unique way.

In 1940, Frankl joined the *Rothschild Hospital,* which became the only hospital in Vienna allowed by the Nazis to admit Jews after the Nazi annexation of Austria in 1938. As the head of neurology, Frankl helped several Jewish patients avoid the Nazi euthanasia program that targeted the mentally ill and mentally disabled. It was only nine months after being married in 1942 that Frankl and his family were sent to the *Theresienstadt Concentration Camp*. There, his father died of starvation and pneumonia. In 1944, Frankl and the surviving members of his family were transferred to *Auschwitz Concentration Camp,* where his mother and brother were murdered in gas chambers. His wife died later of typhus at the *Bergen-Belsen Concentration Camp*. Within three years, Frankl lost all his immediate family to the horrors of the Holocaust. What kept Frankl alive was his dream of writing a book about his experiences, especially a book about the psychotherapeutic implications of his concentration experiences.

After the fall of Nazism, Frankl returned to Vienna and became head of the Department of Neurology at the *General Polyclinic Hospital*. His book was originally released in German in 1946 as *A Psychologist Experiences the Concentration Camp.* The English version of *Man's Search for Meaning* was published in 1959 and has remained an international bestseller and one of the most popular books in psychology, translated into over a dozen of languages. Frankl saw its success as the result of the failure of modern culture to provide meaning and purpose, which created a "mass neurosis" (Crumbaugh & Maholick, 1964). Frankl rejected the Freudian will to pleasure and the will to power of his teacher Otto Rank. He believed the will to meaning of Kierkegaard was the key human motivator.

The will to meaning led Frankl to create *logotherapy*. *Logos,* from the Greek word, denoted *meaning*. Frankl viewed logotherapy as the process of focusing client attention to the meaning and purpose of their life. Therapy often included the logotherapy question, "Why don't you kill yourself?" When a client answered that question, they discovered the real meaning of their existence. Frankl believed that life had meaning in all circumstances, even in horrendous situations of unavoidable suffering. His view was that suffering ceased to be suffering *at the moment* one found meaning and purpose in the suffering.

Because many psychologists view the search for meaning as important to psychological development, logotherapy continues to thrive internationally through training and treatment institutes in America, South Africa, Middle East, Asia, Australia, Europe, Canada, and South America. *The Victor Frankl Institute*, founded in 1992 in Vienna, catalogues the private and scientific archives of Frankl and sponsors a biennial *World Congress of Logotherapy*.

Gestalt Therapy

The Gestalt theories of Max Wertheimer, Wolfgang Kohler, and Kurt Kofka influenced the development of another highly effective H-E psychotherapeutic approach: *Gestalt therapy*. In their disdain for empirical and behavioral psychology, Gestalt therapists rose to prominence in the psychotherapeutic world in the 1960s and 1970s. The *here-and-now* approach of *Gestalt therapy* integrated the principles of gestalt psychology, existentialism, phenomenology, and humanistic psychology. The impact of Gestalt psychology is often minimized by mainstream psychology because the development of Gestalt therapy occurred mostly outside of academia. In their disdain for positivistic research, Gestalt therapists also rejected other research methods that might validate Gestalt therapy as an evidence-based best practice.

Gestalt psychology offered therapists the natural human tendency to scan the environmental force field and find balance and certainty. By utilizing this natural human tendency, Gestalt therapists, by increasing personal awareness, allow clients to be in the moment, emancipating clients from living in the past or future (Perls, 1992a). For example, an adult client can confront an abusive parent from their past through the experience of the Gestalt *Empty Chair Technique*. In this technique, the therapist has the client imagine the abusive parent sitting across from them in an empty chair. This brings the client into the immediate experience of the abusive parent. The Gestalt therapist then instructs the client to have a dialogue, which means that the client switches chairs when speaking for themselves and when role-playing the abusive parent. In this way, the abusive parent is directly experienced in the moment rather than understood indirectly through analysis or interpretation. By making the past present, the Empty Chair Technique provides a healing example of Gestalt therapy.

In 1936, Fitz Perls (1893–1970) and Freud had a brief and unsatisfying meeting, which would lead to his rejection of psychoanalysis (Perls, 1992b). Fitz Perls first used the term Gestalt therapy with his wife, Laura Perls (1905–1990) in the early 1950s. The growth of Gestalt therapy began in 1951 in his book with Ralph Hefferline and Paul Goodman (1951), *Gestalt Therapy: Excitement and Growth in Human Personality*. Fitz and Laura, influenced by the work of Kurt Lewin and Otto Rank, argued that mental disturbance caused the loss of personal awareness which was key to psychological health. Psychological health returned by restoring the ability for personal awareness and by bringing the past and future into the immediate moment.

His bravado and intensity to live in the moment, made Perls was one of the most colorful figures in the history of psychology. In 1964, Fitz Perls started a five-year residency at the Esalen Institute, offering Gestalt training courses. During that time, Dick Price, co-founder of the Esalen Institute, was inspired to integrate Buddhist and Gestalt thought into what Price described as *Gestalt practice* (Callahan, 2014). The *Gestalt Prayer* best summarizes Fitz Perls approach to Gestalt psychology:

I do my thing and you do your thing.
I am not in this world to live up to your expectations,
and you are not in this world to live up to mine.

You are you, and I am I,
and if by chance we find each other, it's beautiful.
If not, it can't be helped.

— Fritz Perls (1992a)

In 1952, Laura and Fitz Perls, with the assistance of Paul Goodman, established the *New York Institute for Gestalt Therapy*. After Fitz Perls left for Esalen in 1964, Laura stayed in New York and continued to lead the institute for 30 years, 20 years after his death. Gestalt therapy continues to thrive through the numerous *Gestalt Institutes* throughout the United States and the world.

Existential Psychotherapy

In a classic text in the H-E movement, Irvin Yalom (1980) outlined the *Four Givens* of human existence being *death, loss of freedom, isolation,* and *meaninglessness*. The Four Givens are the inescapable realities of human existence, and the focus of Existential Psychotherapy that provides clients a way to not only cope but grow psychologically from the existential conflicts of the Four Givens. The first conflict, the core existential conflict, is the conflict between the reality of death and the wish to continue to exist. The second existential conflict is the challenge of freedom, which is the freedom of a random and groundless world with the wish for organization

Figure 5.23

and structure. The third existential conflict is between the innate awareness of absolute isolation with the desire for connection to others, the need to become part of something greater, and the existential awareness that humans enter the world alone and will leave the world alone. Meaningless is the fourth existential conflict: awareness that human beings are meaning-seeking creatures with the reality that existence has no clear, apparent meaning or purpose.

The Four Givens symbolize the essence of *Existential Psychotherapy* and the importance of coping with *existential anxiety,* the natural anxiety of being human. Failure to face these givens results in constant anxiety at a subconscious level and, although confronting the Four Givens is often painful, Yalom believed it provided healing unavailable to clients in most of the other psychotherapies. One way to summarize Existential Psychotherapy is from a quote of Thomas Hardy, "If a way to the Better be, it exacts a full look at the Worst."

Irwin Yalom, an existential American psychiatrist, continued the emancipation of psychology from an overemphasis on individual psychotherapy. In 1970, Yalom (2005) published *The Theory and Practice of Group Psychotherapy,* the definitive text on group psychotherapy writing like a novelist, making his text more readable than most clinical textbooks. Yalom believed groups went through *Five Stages,* being one of the first theorists to provide a clear and comprehensive conceptual framework for understanding group dynamics. During the first forming stage, the leader orients the group to group norms, confidentiality, attendance, and rules of communication and participation. In the second storming stage, group members test and act out behaviors to define their role in the group and whether the group environment is safe for interpersonal honesty. After the orientation and transition phases, in the third norming stage, cohesiveness returns as group members understand and support group standards. During the fourth working stage, group members produce outcomes and experiment with new ideas and behaviors. In a psychotherapy group or a time-limited group, there is a fifth adjourning stage when the group terminates. During this adjourning stage, group members come to closure through the assessment of actual outcomes and achievements and avoiding the introduction of any new problems or initiatives. The Yalom framework for understanding group dynamics expanded well beyond group psychotherapy, often used by management to improve group behavior in the workplace.

For Yalom, group experiences provided social healing, a relief from the rugged individualism described by Rollo May. In groupwork, individuals learned the value of dependency and support from others. Yalom believed groups showed the universality of problems, that problems were not unique to an individual person. In groups, individuals learned social skills to communicate more effectively, learned imitative behaviors, modeled the successful behaviors of other group members, and experienced the importance of interpersonal relationships and the feeling of belonging to something greater than themselves. In group psychotherapy, helping others improved the self-esteem of group members and changed dysfunctional behaviors learned from the family. Although group psychotherapy flourished in the 1960s and 1970s, it began to wane because of the ascendancy of behaviorism, and the lack of adequate financial support for group psychotherapy from the insurance industry.

Yalom often lamented that Existential Psychotherapy felt like a "homeless waif," not welcomed in either the traditional academic or clinical psychological worlds. However, the Four Givens remain a foundational concept in H-E psychotherapies; his approach to group dynamics continues to influence organizations throughout the world, and the importance of group psychotherapy awaits renewal by new visionaries in the mental health community. His contribution to psychology continues to thrive at the *Yalom Institute of Psychotherapy* in New York.

Existential Crisis – Gun Violence

As this chapter ends, H-E psychology provides a way to understand and respond to the *existential crisis of gun violence* in America. Existential crises result from confusion about identity and feeling one is not living up to their full potential which causes stress, depression, anxiety, and the disruption of daily life. The world community views American identity as rooted in the sacredness of guns, an identity that makes it difficult to control the epidemic of mass shootings. The reality is that Americans are no longer safe from gun violence while shopping, in their church, at a concert, in a movie theater, or even walking the streets in their local communities. Most horrific and representative "of America not living up to its potential" as a free society is the reality that American children can no longer feel safe from gun violence as they attend school.

The twenty-first-century decisions by the Supreme Court to reinterpret the original intent of the Second Amendment, and the lack of congressional action to pass reasonable gun safety laws supported by most Americans, has led to the largest expansion of gun sales in human history. There are now more guns than people in the United States. The profits for the manufacturing gun industry have skyrocketed to over $30 billion annually, which proves the success of the National Rifle Association (NRA) and the gun lobby to defeat most attempts on firearm restrictions.

The Second Amendment to the U.S. Constitution was ratified in 1791 with nine other articles in the *Bill of Rights,* which protected the right to keep and bear arms. The initial 1791 Bill of Rights never addressed the right of individuals to bear arms; the original intent was to enable people to organize a militia; participate in law enforcement; repel invasion; suppress insurrection, including slave revolts; overthrow a tyrannical government; and protect the natural right of self-defense (Barton, 2001). It was not until 2008 in the *District of Columbia vs. Heller* that the Supreme Court for the first time in history affirmed the right of an individual to bear arms for self-defense in their own home. The Supreme Court clarified that the right was limited, and that the federal government could forbid firearms to felons, the mentally ill, or those that carry dangerous or unusual weapons. Because the Heller case only applied to federal laws, in *McDonald vs. the City of Chicago in 2010*, the Supreme Court expanded the Heller ruling to also protect gun owners from "the overreach" of state and local governments.

The United States has a gun homicide rate 25 times greater, unintentional gun death rate 6 times higher, a firearm suicide rate 8 times higher, and an overall firearm death rate 10 times higher than any other industrial nation in the world (Grinshteyn & Hemenway, 2016). When compared to other industrial nations like Japan, the United Kingdom, and South Korea, the total rate of gun violence in the United States is 50–100 times greater than those other countries.

As gun violence escalates, statistical accuracy needs constant updates, but in the early twenty-first century, it is safe to say that at least 100 Americans die daily from gun violence (Gun Violence Archive, 2021). Since 1970, over 1.4 million Americans have been killed by firearms, more than all the U.S. servicemen and women in all the foreign wars combined (Wentemute, 2015). *The Global Study on Homicide by the United Nations* (United Nations Office of Drugs and Crime, 2021) estimates that 1,000 people die daily from gun violence in the world and the number of people that die yearly is more than the atomic bombings of Hiroshima and Nagasaki combined. Gary Kleck (2001), a *Florida State University* criminologist, found a strong correlation between the immediate access to guns and gun violence. Over 30,000 Americans die from suicide every year and gun access, whether in the home or in society at large, significantly increases the likelihood of suicide (Kellerman & Reay, 1996).

The *National Rifle Association* (NRA), founded in 1871, initially formed Rifle Clubs after the Civil War to advance rifle marksmanship, rifle competency, and safety. The NRA symbol contains a bald eagle to symbolize power and freedom, and the American flag to symbolize protection of the constitution and a gun to protect Second Amendment rights. *Guns Do not Kill People, People Kill People* is the motto of the NRA (Smyth, 2020). After *The Gun Control Act of 1968* created a federal law to regulate the firearm industry, the NRA became the major lobbyist for the multi-billion-dollar firearm manufacturing industry, opposing any gun control laws, most notably the Federal Assault Weapon Ban (1994), which required a 10-year moratorium on the manufacturing of certain semi-automatic firearms. The ban expired in 2004 under Present George W. Bush and in 2005, President Bush signed an NRA-backed Protection of Lawful

Commerce in Arms Act (2005) that prevented firearm manufacturers and dealers from liability for negligence when crimes were committed with their products.

One month after the 2012 *Sandy Hook Elementary School* shooting, in which 20 children between the ages of six and seven years old were murdered in a mass shooting, the NRA successfully opposed the *Assault Weapons Ban of 2013*. This law contained many provisions to control the sale of firearms as well as another effort to ban high-capacity ammunition magazines that held more than 10 rounds. In 2020, New York Attorney General Letitia James filed a civil lawsuit against the NRA, charging fraud, financial misconduct, the misuse of charitable funds, and for the disillusion of the NRA. Although the NRA filed for bankruptcy in 2021, they remain a major lobbying agent of the gun manufacturing industry and strong opponents of *all* gun control legislation.

Michael Shurkin (2016), in *A Brief History of the Assault Rifle*, reports that the name "assault weapon" may have been coined by Adolf Hitler who for propaganda purposes called the gun *Sturmgewehr*, a "storm" or "assault" weapon. By the end of the twentieth century, assault weapons became the standard in most armies of the world, replacing full-powered rifles and sub-machine guns. One of the most famous assault weapons is the AK-47, officially known as the *Avtomat Kalashnikova,* developed by Mikhail Kalashnikov in 1947 in the Soviet Union. After more than seven decades, the AK-47 assault rifle remains the most popular and widely used rifles in the world. The AK-47 is also one of the deadliest rifle ever developed because it can fire up to 600 rounds per minute (rpm) (Clinton, 1986). The impact on the human body is unimaginable, often human remains cannot be easily identifiable. It is estimated that over 17 million AK-47 weapons are on the streets of the United States and over 75 million AK-47 weapons are circulating worldwide in over 100 countries. The deadliest mass shootings are linked to the AK-47 family of weapons, especially the AR-15, because there are few restrictions on the sale of assault weapons in the United States. For example, semiautomatic weapons, handguns, pistols, and revolvers do not require special training or a license in most of the jurisdictions of America. The question remains whether the American founders ever intended weapons of war be on the streets throughout America.

The AR-15 is most often used in mass shootings. Designed by Eugene Stoner, an American engineer, in the 1950's, adopted by United States military forces as the M16 rifle, famous for its use during the Vietnam War. The AR-15 rifles are lighter, have a higher rate of accuracy and have a longer effective range than the AK-47, although the AK-47 is considerably cheaper and more dependable. The AK-47 has a maximum effective range of about 300 yards, while the AR-15 has a maximum effective range of over 800 yards. Beyond the AK-47 600 rpm, the AR-15 can fire as many as 800–1200 rpm, although most automatic weapons typically fire between 500–650 rpm. In an ironic twist of historic fate, in 1990 Stoner and Kalashnikov, inventors of the most lethal firearms in the world, met for the first time and toured Washington D.C. visiting historic sites and the NRA's *National Firearms Museum*. They shared a shoot together at the *Star Tannery Gun Club* and during this short visit, both men, intimately familiar with each other's work, shared a common bond and became friends for the rest of their lives.

As seen throughout history, individuals with mental illness have again become political scapegoats for political inaction. Although most mass shooters have mental health symptoms, most mass shooters have not been in treatment or diagnosed with a mental illness. It is important to note that individuals with mental illness are most often survivors rather than perpetrators of violence. In *The Violence Project: How to Stop A Mass Shooting Epidemic*, Peterson and Densley (2021) examined the psychological causes of mass shootings and recommend evidence-based practices to stop the epidemic. They studied the lives of 170 mass shooters from childhood to adulthood and interviewed the living perpetrators, the people who knew them, shooting survivors, family victims, first responders, and leading experts. They found that over 80 percent of mass shooters had a noticeable mental health crisis prior to their shooting, had thoughts of suicide before and during the attack, but ***70 percent had no symptoms***

of psychosis or severe mental illness. The motivations of mass shooters included problems in domestic and interpersonal relationships, employment, and legal entanglements. They also found shooters often felt a mass shooting would bring them fame.

Mass shootings also remind us of the Four Givens of Yalom, the rugged individualism of May, Maslow's hierarchy of needs, and the absurdity of existence of Camus. Under the guise of the Second Amendment, guns symbolize freedom, the ability to be independent and autonomous, safe from death, the most important symbol of individual liberty. However, from an existential viewpoint, isolation, the meaninglessness of existence, fear of death, lack of safety needs met, mixed with the myth of rugged individualism breeds a culture of violence. Camus might add that America has embraced his theory of the absurdity of existence when even its children cannot attend school without the fear of death and violence.

Figure 5.24

Gun violence provides an opportunity for Americans to face their existential crisis to protect the rights of the Second Amendment while creating reasonable gun control laws to protect the safety of its citizens, especially its children. As in any existential crisis, there is an opportunity to reassess why guns are so integral to American identity and if America is living up to the ideals of the American revolution that every citizen reaches their full potential. Most importantly, do the American people want to exist in a world where no place is safe from gun violence? In the spirit of Maslow's hierarchy of needs, if America cannot achieve its basic physiological need of safety, can it create a society that is psychologically healthy? If safety is not addressed, the existential crisis will worsen, as symbolized by the normalization of a gun culture, which means in the not-too-distant future Americans, to meet their safety needs, may feel the need to carry a gun as they go about their daily lives.

Emancipatory Opportunities in Humanistic-Existential Psychology

Consider Person-Centered Therapy

One of the most popular H-E psychotherapies, person-centered therapy offers a humanistic approach that emphasizes unconditional positive regard and the importance of personal agency and the primacy of feelings and emotions.

278   Symbols of Humanistic-Existential Psychology

Read the Great Intellectual Visionaries of H-E Psychology

Humanistic--existentialism provides some of the most intellectually powerful thinkers in psychology, which includes: *The Concept of Dread* (Kierkegaard, 1944a), *Man's Search for Meaning* (Frankl, 1971), *I and Thou* (Buber, 1958a), *The Second Sex* (de Beauvoir, 2011), *The Myth of Sisyphus* (Camus, 1975), *Toward a Psychology of Being* (Maslow, 1968), *Basic: Theoretical Concepts of Humanistic Psychology* (Buhler, 1971), *Thus spoke Zarathustra* (Nietzsche, 2005), *Being and Time* (Heidegger, 1927), *Being and Nothingness* (Sartre, 1993), *Escape from Freedom* (Fromm, 1967). *The Cry for Myth* (May 1991), and *Phenomenology of Perception* (Merleau-Ponty, 2013).

Attend a Play Classified as a Tragedy

In the spirit of Nietzsche, for Apollonian and Dionysian Rapprochement, view a play or movie classified as a tragedy. Shakespeare provides famous plays of tragedy that include *Antony and Cleopatra, Hamlet, Julius Caesar, King Lear, MacBeth, Othello,* and *Romeo and Juliet.*

Consider Existential Psychotherapy

Explore the mysteries of being human and learn to create your own unique personal existence. Explore the Four Givens, self-actualization, and the worlds of Umwelt, Mitwelt, and Eigenwelt. Value the power of intellectual exploration.

Experience Phenomenology

Pick a person, animal, plant, place, event, or object, and then take a piece of paper and write a description of what you see. When complete, bracket the themes. From the bracketing, write a summary of the key themes and reflect on how this is another way to attain knowledge and a phenomenological science.

Explore the Absurdities of Life

Read the works of Sartre (1947), *No Exit,* Camus (1975), *Myth of Sisyphus,* or other existentialists to understand the existential absurdities that challenge human existence.

Consider Group Therapy

Experience the 5 Stages of group process and the power of social healing. Improve social skills to communicate more effectively; learn from the knowledge and successful behaviors of other group members and experience the feeling of helping others and belonging to something greater than yourself.

Assess the Characteristics of Self-Actualization

From the *Humanistic Psychology* section, review what characteristics of a self-actualized person apply to your life.

View the Therapy Sessions of Fitz Perls and Consider Gestalt Therapy

View on *YouTube* or through other media outlets, the famous "Gloria" case, who had to select the most helpful therapy after a therapy session with Rogers, Ellis, and Perls. Her decision to choose Perls provides the opportunity to view other Fitz Perls sessions and consider Gestalt therapy for yourself.

Explore Feelings

There are many ways to explore feelings; one way is to simply sit and observe the world from an emotional standpoint without intellectual judgment. Another way is to purchase a *Feeling Chart* or *Feeling Flash Cards* and become aware of the myriad of feelings you have been missing.

Apply H-E Psychology in Community Mental Health (CMH) Services

Although cognitive behavioral treatment (CBT) approaches have shown efficacy in the treatment of mental disorders (Volume II, Chapter 4), the overemphasis limits the application of other therapeutic approaches. It is paramount for CMH clients, especially individuals with serious mental illness, to have a therapeutic experience that explores the meaning and purpose, not only of their illness, but their existence as a human being.

Consider Person-Centered Dialogic Politics

To respond to political polarization and resolve issues like gun violence, encourage political leaders to consider *person-centered dialogue* between individuals with differing viewpoints and model the attitude that politics does not have to be an endless series of winner-take-all battles.

Consider Logotherapy

If feeling life lacks meaning and purpose, seek a logotherapist.

QUESTIONS 5

5.1 *Describe the political, socioeconomic, and cultural influences that led to the development of humanistic-existential (H-E) psychology.*

5.2 *Explain how H-E psychology is different from psychoanalysis and behaviorism.*

5.3 *Describe the contribution of Simone de Beauvoir to feminism.*

5.4 *Explain the difference between the epistemology of Husserl and the ontology of Heidegger.*

5.5 *Describe why the concept of Dasein is essential to understanding H-E psychology.*

5.6 *Explain from a French existential perspective what Sartre meant when he said the French people were never freer under Nazi rule.*

5.7 *Describe why Rollo May believes Americans are living the myth of rugged individualism and how the myth applies to gun violence.*

5.8 *Explain Kierkegaard's three stages of freedom.*

5.9 *Describe why Carl Rogers changed his approach from client-centered to person-centered psychology.*

5.10 *Explain what Nietzsche meant by saying "God is Dead."*

280 *Symbols of Humanistic-Existential Psychology*

5.11 *Describe Maslow's criticism of natural science research methods."*

5.12 *Explain why the issues of death, loss of freedom, isolation, and meaninglessness are essential to the practice of existential psychotherapy.*

5.13 *Consider the political implications of person-centered dialogic politics.*

Universal Meanings of Chapter Symbols

Figure 5.0:

Abraham Maslow image source. http://www.celebriton.com/abraham_maslow/photo/a_photo_of_abraham_maslow

Carl Roger image source (fair use). https://www.psychologytoday.com/us/blog/between-the-lines/201609/is-restorativejustice-exhausting

Jean-Paul_Sartre image source. https://www.goodreads.com/author/show/1466.Jean_Paul_Sartre

Friedrich Nietzsche image source Friedrich Hermann Hartmann. https://s-media-cache-ak0.pinimg.com/originals/04/10/0b/04100baec90c105729b47f33c371476b.jpg - https://commons.wikimedia.org/wiki/Friedrich_Wilhelm_Nietzsche#/media/File:Nietzsche187a.jpg

Simone De Beauvoir image source Via Wikimedia Commons. https://commons.wikimedia.org/wiki/File:Simonedebeauvoir.jpg

Rollo-May-image source-Rollo May. (November 2, 2022). In Wikipedia. https://en.wikipedia.org/wiki/Rollo_May

Soren-Kierkegaard source of image. https://commons.wikimedia.org/wiki/File:Soren_Kierkegaard.jpg

Viktor Frankl image source. Attribution: Prof. Dr. Franz Vesely Image adopted to book illustrations – Viktor Frankl. (October 20, 2022). In Wikipedia. https://en.wikipedia.org/wiki/Viktor_Frankl

Figure 5.1. The goal to discover one's unique relationship to the world.
Figure 5.2. The power of intellectual knowledge.
Figure 5.3. Hair as a symbol of personal power and rebellion.
Figure 5.4. Aspiration to reach one's full potential.
Figure 5.5. Desire for peace.
Figure 5.6. Resistance to war and economic oppression.
Figure 5.7. Desire for "wholeness", to understand a world which is greater than the sum of its parts.
Figure 5.8. A symbol of being treated, not as a valuable human being, but as useless cog in a mechanized world.
Figure 5.9. The experience of having a physical body.
Figure 5.10. The healing power of authentic communication.
Figure 5.11. A symbol of the power of faith.
Figure 5.12. Religious beliefs necessitate a "leap of faith" beyond the rational mind.
Figure 5.13. God is dead as a symbol of religious neglect in daily life.
Figure 5.14. Symbol of finding God, the superhuman, as an internal process.
Figure 5.15. The necessity for a rapprochement between the rational and irrational.
Figure 5.16. The unique experience of being in the world.
Figure 5.17. The experience of "being thrown into the world."
Figure 5.18. Freedom comes from "non-being," a view that the natural world does not have much to offer.

Figure 5.19. Symbol of the meaninglessness and absurdity of life.
Figure 5.20. The reality that most of humanity "escapes from freedom."
Figure 5.21. The hierarchy of needs alive in everyone in all cultures throughout the world.
Figure 5.22. The need for social healing.
Figure 5.23. The reality that all humanity faces the Four Givens of death, loss of freedom, isolation, and meaninglessness.
Figure 5.24. Symbol of the American existential crisis of gun violence.

References

Assault Weapons Ban Act of 2013. S. 150. 113 Cong. (2013).
Association of Humanistic Psychology (1980). Special issue: A report on AHP's 12 hour political party: A call to action February 10, 1980, *AP Newsletter,* Retrieved at https://www.ahpweb.org/images/stories/archive_pdfs/1980/May1980.pdf
Bakewell, S. (2016). *At the existentialist café: Freedom, being, and apricot cocktails*. New York, NY: Other Press.
Balakian, A. (1967). *The symbolist movement: A critical appraisal*. New York, NY: Random House.
Barton, D. (2001). *The second amendment: Preserving the inalienable right of individual protection*. Aledo, TX: Wallbuilders.
Binswanger, L. (1958a). The existential analysis school of thought. In R. May, E. Angel, & H. Ellenberger. (Eds.). *Existence: A new dimension in psychiatry and psychology* (pp. 191–213). (E. Angel, Trans.). New York, NY: Basic Books.
Binswanger, L. (1958b). The case of Ellen West. In R. May, E. Angel, & H. Ellenberger. (Eds.). *Existence: A new dimension in psychiatry and psychology* (pp. 237–364). (W. M. Mendel & J. Lyons Trans.). New York, NY: Basic Books.
Buber, M. (1973). *Meetings*. (M.S. Friedman, Ed.). LaSalle Ill.: Open Court Publishers Co.
Buber, M. (1957). Healing through meeting. In M. Buber (M. Friedman, Trans. & Ed.). *Pointing the way* (pp. 93–97). New York, NY: Schocken Books. (Original work published 1952).
Buber, M. (1958a). *I and thou*. (R.G. Smith, Trans.). New York, NY: Charles Scribner and Sons. (Original work published 1923).
Buber, M. (1958b). *Hasidism and modern man*. (M. Friedman, Trans. & Ed.). New York, NY: Harper and Row Publishers
Buber, M. (1965a). *Between man and man*. (R.G. Smith, Trans.). New York, NY: The Macmillan Co.
Buber, M. (1965b). *The knowledge of man: A philosophy of the interhuman*. (M.S. Friedman & R.G. Smith, Trans.). New York, NY: Harper and Row Publishers.
Buhler, C. (1971). Basic: Theoretical concepts of humanistic psychology. *American Psychologist. 26*(4), 378–386.
Caelisle, C. (2021). *Philosopher of the heart: The restless life of Soren Kierkegaard*. London: Picador.
Callahan, J.F. (2014). *Manual of gestalt practice in the tradition of Dick Price*. Author: The Gestalt Legacy Project.
Camus, A. (1975). *The myth of Sisyphus*. (J. O'Brien, Trans.). Harmondsworth: Penguin. (Work originally published 1942).
Cesare, D.D. (2018). *Heidegger and the Jews: The black notebooks*. New York, NY: Wiley Books.
Clinton, E.E. (1986). *The AK47 story, evolution of the Kalashnikov weapons*. Mechanicsburg, PA: Stackpole Books.
Crumbaugh, J. & Maholick, L. (1964). An experimental study of existentialism: The psychometric approach to Frankl's concept of noogenic neurosis. *Journal of Clinical Psychology. 20*, 200–207.
de Beauvoir, S. (2011). *The second sex*. (C. Borde & S. Malovany-Chevallier, Trans.). New York, NY: Vintage Books. (Original work published in 1949).
Demanchick, S.P. & Kirschenbaum, H. (2008). Carl Rogers and the CIA. *Journal of Humanistic Psychology. 48(1),* 6–31.
Dicks, H.V. (2015). *Fifty years of Tavistock*. London: Routledge Press. (Work originally published in 1970).

District of Columbia vs Heller. 554 U.S. 570 (2008).
Dooley, P.K. (1982). Kuhn and psychology: The Rogers–Skinner, Day–Giorgi debates. *Journal for the Theory of Social Behavior.* *12*(3), 275–289.
Federal Assault Weapon Ban of 1994. H.R. 4296, 103 Cong. (1994).
Frankl, V. (1971). *Man's search for meaning: An introduction to logotherapy.* New York, NY: Pocket Books. (Work originally published in 1946).
Friedman, M.S. (1955). Healing through meeting: Martin Buber and psychotherapy. *Cross Currents.* *5*(4), 297–310.
Friedman, M.S. (Ed.). (1964). *The worlds of existentialism: A critical reader.* New York, NY: Random House.
Friedman, M.S. (1994). Reflections on the Buber-Rogers dialogue. *Journal of Humanistic Psychology.* *34*(1), 46–65.
Fromm, E. (1967). *Escape from freedom.* New York, NY: An Avon Library Book. (Work originally published 1941).
Grinshteyn, E. & Hemenway, D. (2016). Violent death rates: The US compared with other high-income OECD countries. *The American Journal of Medicine.* *129*(3), 266–273.
Gun Control Act of 1968 (title 18 of the United States Code).
Gun Violence Archive. (2021, August 19). General methodology. Retrieved from https://www.gunviolencearchive.org.
Heidegger, M. (1927). *Being and time.* Halle, Germany: Niemeyer.
Husserl, E. (1900–1901). *Logical investigations.* Halle, Germany: Niemeyer.
Jackson, C., Davidson, G., Russell, J. & Vandereycken, W. (1990). Ellen West revisited: Theme of death in eating disorders. *International Journal of Eating Disorders.* *9*(5), 529–536.
Kant, I. (1999). *Critique of pure reason.* (A. Guyer, A.W. Wood, Trans.). New York, NY: Cambridge University Press.
Kaufman, W. (1974). *Nietzsche: Philosopher, psychologist, antichrist.* Princeton, NJ: Princeton University Press.
Kellerman, A.L. & Reay, D.T. (1996) Protection or peril? An analysis of firearm-related deaths in the home. New *England Journal of Medicine.* *314*(24), 1557–1560.
Kierkegaard, S. (1944a). *The concept of dread.* (W. Lowrie, Trans.). Princeton, NJ: Princeton University Press. (Original work published 1844).
Kierkegaard, S. (1944b). *Attack upon Christendom, 1854–1855.* (W. Lowrie, Trans.). Princeton, NJ: Princeton University Press. (Original Work Published 1854–1855).
Kierkegaard, S. (1992). *Either/Or: A fragment of life.* (A. Hannay, Trans.). London: Penguin Books. (Original work published 1843).
Kierkegaard, S. (2005). *Fear and trembling.* (A. Hannay, Trans.). London: Penguin Books. (Original work published in 1843).
Kleck, G. (2001). Can owning a gun really triple the owner's chances of being murdered? *Homicide Studies.* *5*(1), 64–77.
Kofka, K. (1963). *Principles of Gestalt psychology.* New York: Harcourt, Brace & World. (Original work published 1935).
Kohler, W. (1923). *The mentality of apes.* London: Routledge & Kagan Paul. (Original work published 1917).
Lewin, K., Lippit, R. & White, R.K. (1939). Patterns of aggressive behavior in experimentally created social climate. *Journal of Social Psychology.* *10*, 271–299.
Lutz, M.A. & Lux, K. (1979). *The challenge of humanistic economics.* Menlo Park, CA: Benjamin-Cummings Publishing Company.
Maltsberger, J.T. (1996). The case of Ellen West revisited: A permitted suicide. *Spring*, *26*(1), 86–98.
Maslow, A.H. (1966). *The psychology of science: A reconnaissance.* South Bend, IN: Gateway Editions.
Maslow, A.H. (1943). A theory of human motivation. *Psychological Review.* *50*(4), 370–396.
Maslow, A.H. (1968). *Toward a psychology of being.* (2nd ed.). New York, NY: Van Nostrand Reinhold.
Maslow, A.H. (1971). *Further reaches of human nature.* New York, NY: Penguin Books.
May, R. (1950). *The meaning of anxiety.* New York, NY: Ronald Press.
May, R. (1967). *Psychology and the human dilemma.* New York, NY: W.W. Norton & Company, Inc.
May, R. (1991). *The cry for myth.* New York, NY: Norton.
McDonald vs the City of Chicago, 561 U.S. 742 (2010).

Merleau-Ponty, M. (1983). *The structure of behavior*. Pittsburgh, PA: Duquesne University. (Original work published 1942).
Merleau-Ponty, M. (2013). *Phenomenology of perception*. (D. A. Landes, Trans.). London: Routledge. (Work originally published 1945).
Miller, A. (1976). *Death of a salesman*. New York, NY: Penguin Books. (Work originally published 1949).
Nietzsche, F. (1977). *The gay science*. (W. Kaufmann, Trans.). New York, NY: Random House. (Work originally published 1882).
Nietzsche, F. (1994). *The birth of tragedy: The spirit of music*. (S. Whiteside, Trans.). New York, NY: Penguin Books. (Work originally published 1872).
Nietzsche, F. (2005). *Thus spoke Zarathustra*. (C. Martin, Trans.). New York, NY: Barnes and Noble Books. (Work originally published between 1883–1885).
Perls, F. (1992a). *Gestalt therapy verbatim*. Gouldsboro ME: The Gestalt Journal Press, Inc. (Work originally published in 1969).
Perls, F. (1992b). *Ego, hunger and aggression: A revision of Freud's theory and method*. Gouldsboro, ME: The Gestalt Journal Press. (Work originally published in 1947).
Perls, F., Hefferline, R. & Goodman, P. (1951). *Gestalt therapy: Excitement and growth in the human personality*. Gouldsboro, ME: The Gestalt Journal Press.
Peterson, J. & Densley, J. (2021). *The violence project: How to stop a mass shooting epidemic*. New York, NY: Abrams Press.
Plato (2005). *The laws*. New York, NY: Penguin Books.
Protection of Lawful Commerce in Arms Act. U.S.C. 7901 (2005).
Rogers, C. (1942). *Counseling and psychotherapy: Newer concepts in practice*. Boston: Houghton Mifflin.
Rogers, C. (1963). The loneliness of contemporary man as seen in the case of Ellen West. *Annals of Psychotherapy*. 2, 94–101.
Rogers, C. (1969). *Freedom to learn: A view of what education might become*. Columbus, Ohio: Charles Merrill.
Rogers, C.R. (1951). *Client-centered therapy: Its current practice, implications, and theory*. Boston: Houghton Mifflin.
Rogers, C.R. (1974). In retrospect: Forty-six years. *American Psychologist*. 29, 115–123.
Sartre, J.P. (1947). *No exit and flies*. New York, NY: Knopf.
Sartre, J.P. (1957). *Existentialism and human emotions*. New York, NY: Wisdom Library.
Sartre, J.P. (1993). *Being and nothingness*. (H.E. Barnes, Trans.). New York, NY: Washington Square Press. (Work originally published 1943).
Sartre, J.P. (2022). *Critique of dialectical reason*: The complete edition. London: Verso.
Shakespeare, W. (1992). *The tragedy of hamlet: The prince of Denmark*. Washington, DC: New Folger Library. (Work originally published between 1599 and 1601).
Shurkin, M. (2016, June 30). A brief history of the assault weapon. *The Atlantic*, Retrieved from https://www.theatlantic.com/technology/archive/2016/06/a-brief-history-of-the-assault-rifle/489428/
Smyth (2020). *NRA: An unauthorized history*. New York, NY: Flatiron Books.
Steiner, R. (2011). *The philosophy of freedom*. (M. Wilson, Trans.). Glasgow: Rudolf Steiner Press. (Original work published in 1916).
Stephenson, W. (1953). *The study of behavior: Q-technique and its methodology*. Chicago: University of Chicago Press.
United Nations Office of Drugs and Crime (2021, August 18). *2011 global study on homicide*. New York, NY: Author. Retrieved from untitled (unodc.org).
Wentemute, G.J. (2015). The epidemiology of firearm violence in the twenty-first century Unites States. *Annual Review of Public Health*. 36(1), 5–19.
Wertheimer, M. (1912). Experimentelle studien uber den schen von dewegung. (Experimental studies on the perception of motion). *Zeinschrift fur Psychologie*. 61, 161–265.
Wollman, E.L. (2006). *The theater will rock: A history of hair to Hedwig*. Ann Arbor MI: University of Michigan Press.
Yalom, I.D. (1980). *Existential psychotherapy*. New York, NY: Basic Books, Inc.
Yalom, I.D. (2005). *The theory and practice of group psychotherapy*. New York, NY: Basic Books, Inc. (Original work published in 1970).
Young, J. (1998). *Heidegger, philosophy, and Nazism*. New York, NY: Cambridge Press.

Figure 6.0

6 Symbols of Transpersonal Psychology – A Return to the Axial Age and Beyond

The Fourth Force in Psychology

Introduction

Fifty years ago, we could only imagine the widespread practices of yoga or meditation, the legalization and medicinal use of compounds such as marijuana, or the inclusion of alternative health methods into traditional medicine. It might be said that the transpersonal project, of which transpersonal psychology is a part, has been a passageway that has allowed quantum understandings to enter... our mainstream human consciousness.

- Jorge Ferrer (2002)

The Transpersonal Renaissance and the Axial Age

It is important to note that *transpersonal psychology* does not typically warrant its own chapter in history and system texts in psychology. However, as the world enters the twenty-first century, Western science has been unable to solve many of the pressing problems of humankind like climate change, political polarization, failures of organized religion and social institutions, the rise of authoritarianism, and decline of democracy. In a world seeking new ways for humanity to exist in harmony and peace, it seems timely, even essential, that psychology reassess its adherence to the limitations of Western science.

Hartelius, Caplan, and Rardin (2007), after an analysis of 160 preferred definitions, found that transpersonal psychology addresses three major themes: a psychology beyond ego functioning, a holistic and integrative psychology, and a psychology whose goal is to transform individuals and society. Because psychological research and practice has shown the efficacy of meditation practices, psychedelic treatments, and transpersonal practices, a *transpersonal renaissance* is occurring in psychology. Although transpersonal psychology does not fit neatly into the ethnocentric Western science paradigm or within the current STEM (Science, Technology, Engineering, Math) bias in psychology, transpersonal psychology is emerging as another vital alternative to psychoanalysis, behaviorism, and humanistic-existential psychology.

As Yalom described humanistic psychology as an orphan in mainstream psychology, transpersonal psychology appears to be in utero, yet to be fully born. In 1971, the American Psychological Association (APA) finally acknowledged the *Society of Humanistic Psychology* as its 32nd division. Although acknowledged as the *Fourth Force* in psychology, the power structure of the APA denied petitions by psychologists in 1984 and 1985 to create a division of transpersonal psychology under the guise that the topics were outside the realm of science. In 1986, the *Transpersonal Psychology Interest Group* (TPIG) was formed and continues to promote transpersonal issues in collaboration with division 32 of the APA (Aanstoos, Serlin, & Greening, 2000).

As noted in Volume I, Chapter 2, the Axial Age: 800–200 BCE, was an extraordinary and unparalleled period in human history with an unprecedented expansion of human consciousness that occurred in Greece, Iran, China, India, and Palestine. The growing urbanization, the economic shift from tribe and clan to the individual family, violent political upheavals, and questions of individual identity and anxiety about death and the afterlife, required that people become their own moral agents and create a new psychology. The goal of the Axial Age was to change consciousness and find more effective ways to understand the body, the mind, and social existence. It's a goal still unattained centuries later.

In a similar response to the crisis of modernity, a transpersonal psychology emerged in the mid-twentieth century rooted in many of the concerns of the Axial Age particularly the problem of balancing the desires of the individual ego with political, socioeconomic, and cultural realities. Clearly, the transpersonal psychology of today could not have existed a few thousand years ago during the Axial Age. However, transpersonal psychology in response to modernity and the objectification of the human psyche believes psychology can be reenergized by Eastern thought and opening to the new modern transpersonal visionaries often viewed in traditional textbooks as unscientific and irrelevant to the advancement of psychological science. Because of the crisis of modernity, the time is right for psychology to truly embrace the Four Forces as a true equal partner to the psychodynamic, behavioral, and humanistic-existential forces.

In *Toward a Psychology of Being* (Maslow, 1962), Abraham Maslow (1908–1970), the founder of transpersonal psychology, advocated for a Fourth Force Psychology, even though he had also founded humanistic psychology because he believed there needed to be a transition toward a higher consciousness beyond humanism, personal identity, and self-actualization. Maslow advocated for a transpersonal psychology that provided life-philosophies, replacement of organized religion, the creation of new value-systems, and the provision of tangible, usable ways to live that does not yet exist in the modern world (Maslow, 1964). The goal of a transpersonal psychology was to have experiences beyond the ego toward a *spiritual self-actualization*, because without the transcendent and transpersonal, people become psychologically sick, alienated, and violent.

This chapter will explain how William James, Sigmund Freud, Carl Jung, Abraham Maslow, Aldous Huxley, Alan Watts, and Timothy Leary inspired the development of transpersonal psychology. Beyond these well-known figures in psychology, this chapter will introduce often unfamiliar thinkers who envisioned a very different psychology; visionaries like Harris Friedman, Jorge Ferrer, Sri Aurobindo, Indra Sen, Ken Wilber, Roberto Assagioli, Albert Hoffman, Roland Griffiths, Christina and Stanislav Grof, Albert Hoffman, Rick Doblin, and others.

Criticism

Ironically, initial opposition to transpersonal psychology came from prominent humanistic psychologists. Rollo May (1989) criticized the transpersonal movement as leading people into a transcendental state to avoid the dark and shadow side of human nature, ignoring human suffering. Albert Ellis criticized the movement for its irrational and unscientific beliefs, especially belief in divine beings (Ellis & Yeager, 1989). There were also concerns about the dangerous expansion of corrupt "gurus," charlatans, and unscrupulous professionals who were taking economic and psychological advantage of vulnerable people. In *Crazy Therapies: What Are They? Do They Work?*, psychologists Margaret Thaler Singer and Janja Lalich (1996), provided a warning about alternate psychotherapies, particularly psychotherapeutic approaches with no interest in research and clinical efficacy. Often, psychedelic researchers, inspired by the possibilities of psychedelic treatments, were criticized as more interested in advocacy than an objective analysis of the dangers of the psychedelics (Pollan, 2018).

Pederson (1991) advocated that transpersonal psychology be replaced by *multiculturalism* as the Fourth Force in psychology. More than a unique force, multiculturalism became policy throughout the APA and its 54 divisions. The APA (2002) issued *Guidelines on Multicultural Education, Research, Practice and Organization Change*, which requires all psychologists to possess multicultural skills. Since the Three Forces, psychodynamic, behavioral, and humanistic-existential, are primarily rooted in European and Anglo-American cultural perspectives, transpersonal psychology is uniquely positioned as the only force outside of mainstream psychology rooted in multiculturism. The research and practice of transpersonal psychology necessitates understanding multicultural history and psychological dynamics beyond Western ethnocentrism and requires cross-cultural understanding that encompasses the universality of human consciousness.

Criticisms did not deter the growth of the transpersonal movement. In fact, transpersonal psychology was part of a counter-criticism movement against mainstream psychology during the American cultural revolution of the 1960s and 1970s because many psychologists became discouraged by the state of the world. Psychologists found hope in the transcendent, the spiritual, the mystical, the ecstatic, the psychedelics, parapsychology, non-Western philosophies, and Eastern thought. As mainstream psychology continued to embrace the natural and empirical sciences to prove their value as a science, many psychologists turned to transpersonal psychology because of the belief that mainstream psychology had become a prisoner to the established "spirit-less" and ineffective scientific order.

Transpersonal Psychology, Religion, and Spirituality

About 5 billion people in the world regularly practice some form of spiritual practice (Hitchcock & Esposito, 2004). Most of the Axial Age visionaries did not separate body, spirit, and mind; in fact, they viewed the body, spirit, and mind as inextricably connected. Transpersonal psychology encompasses a diversity of non-ego, transcendent experiences that can include but are not limited to religion or spirituality. Although religious experiences have transpersonal and spiritual components, *religion* offers an organized belief system whose participants worship sacred dogmas, practice rituals, and have faith in a controlling, all powerful God, or gods. If religion provides organizational structure, preaches, and commands, *spirituality* freely inspires a unique relationship with the divine. Not at odds with religion, transpersonal psychologists understand that skepticism about organized religion has diminished interest in spirituality and has discouraged many from experiencing the most incredible and important aspects of being human, particularly a personal relationship to the divine.

For transpersonal psychologists, the problem of *ethnocentrism* limits the understanding of the human mind by adherence to primarily Western psychological theories and practices. The inaugural publication of *The Journal of Transpersonal Psychology* occurred in 1969 and it did not go unnoticed in the transpersonal movement that 1969 was the year that the first human walked on the moon, and when Apollo 11 astronaut Neil Armstrong said upon landing: "one small step for man, one giant leap for mankind," this was not just an historic technological achievement, it symbolized the opportunity for humanity to also explore the unexplored world of inner space.

The symbol connects Volume I, Chapter 2, with the final Volume II, Chapter 6, the text coming full circle since many transpersonal psychologists have been inspired by the Hindu and Buddhist concept of *samsara,* the cyclicality of all life, the belief that all living beings go

288 *Symbols of Transpersonal Psychology*

through birth, death, and rebirth experiences; that a person continues to be born and reborn in various realms and forms, which creates the opportunity for *moksha,* the emancipation from the cyclicality of death and rebirth; a truly awakened and enlightened human being.

Figure 6.1

Transpersonal Psychology

Historical Analysis of Transpersonal Psychology

Political Systems

The role of psychedelics has been an important part of the transpersonal movement and one of most significant examples of the political challenges facing the transpersonal movement. As with all transformative scientific movements in history, the history of the psychedelics mirrors the political risks and dangers scientists must take when challenging the status quo.

Beginning in the 1950s, the CIA developed *Project MK-Ultra,* an illegal and secretive human experimentation program, studied the political utilization of psychedelic drugs. The CIA was concerned that psychedelics could be used for mind control, as a political truth serum to embarrass political leaders, or even as a political weapon to infiltrate the U.S. water systems (Valentine, 2017). Project MK-Ultra explored how psychedelics could be used against political adversaries like dosing to overthrow Fidel Castro. During this time, the CIA research was connected to over

40 colleges and universities. Civilians and military personnel were dosed with psychedelics, often with deadly consequences, without their permission or knowledge. The program ended in the mid-1960s, but only came to public awareness in 1975 during congressional hearings. By 1973, Richard Helms, the CIA director, had most of the records of the project destroyed (Valentine, 2017).

To the dismay of many psychedelic researchers in the 1960s, Timothy Leary (1920–1996) became the face of the psychedelic movement. Leary ultimately chose political activism over the support of academic research, embracing the *democratization of psychedelics*, a vision that would make transpersonal experiences available to all Americans. He believed that psychedelics would create a new political consciousness after the psychological trauma of two horrific world wars and the creation of the atomic bomb.

Leary, a psychology professor from *Harvard University*, became known by some as a bold visionary for the use of psychedelics and by others as the reason psychedelics became a divisive political issue in America. Leary was a rebel, having been court-martialed at West Point for violating the honor code and expelled from the *University of Alabama* for spending a night in a women's dorm (Pollan, 2018).

Although, by the time Leary came onto the psychedelic scene, there had been a decade of impressive psychedelic research, mainstream science was still unimpressed in the early 1960s with the positive results of Leary's *Harvard Psilocybin Project* because of its weak research methods. Undeterred and with the belief that psychedelics could change the world, Leary initiated the *Concord Prison Experiment* to test the impact of psychedelics on prison recidivism. The researchers as well as the 32 inmates took psilocybin. Leary claimed that only 25 percent of the psilocybin inmates returned to prison. This finding was debunked later because Leary had exaggerated the data (Pollan, 2018).

The now-famous 1962 *Good Friday Experiment*, also known as the *Miracle at Marsh Chapel*, received a more positive response from mainstream science because Leary used traditional controlled and double-bind research methods. Neither the researchers nor the divinity students were told who received psilocybin and who received a placebo. The Good Friday Experiment remains a landmark research project in the transpersonal and psychedelic movement. Even though the research was far from perfect, the findings were dramatic because researchers found that psilocybin could reliably cause a spiritual or mystical experience. This inspired a wave of transpersonal and psychedelic research, including at *Johns Hopkins University* where it was replicated in 2006 with similar results (Pollan, 2018).

Leary used the academic world to propel his beliefs onto the world stage, rejecting the constraints of traditional psychology that he called the "psychology game." His rebellion against mainstream psychology led to his dismissal in 1963 from Harvard University because of leaving campus without authorization and for failing to keep his classroom appointments. His famous fellow colleague, Richard Albert, later Ram Dass, was also dismissed for allegedly giving psilocybin to undergraduates in an off-campus apartment, Afterward, Leary was embraced by the counterculture and, in 1967, Leary spoke at the first *Human Be* in Golden Gate Park in San Francisco, where LSD was freely distributed to 25,000 young people, where he called upon the crowd to famously "tune in, turn on, and drop out." For Leary, this statement symbolized the creation of a new political order.

Allen Ginsberg, a leading American poet and a founder of the *Beat Generation*, a literary movement that influenced American culture and politics in the postwar period, considered Leary "a hero of American Consciousness." As Leary became an icon of the counterculture movement, he became a threat to the government. His comments about LSD sent shockwaves through the political system because he believed the youth who took LSD would be unwilling to fight wars or join the corporate world. President Richard Nixon described Leary as the most dangerous man in America.

Figure 6.2

Alarmed by his growing influence on the young, the government began a series of tactics to harass and discredit Leary. In 1966, on a trip to Mexico, he was arrested on possession of marijuana, which would lead to many years in jail and in court fighting federal marijuana charges. In 1970, with the help of the Weathermen, a revolutionary group, he became an international fugitive after an escape from a California prison. After his escape, he fled to Algeria and to Eldridge Cleaver, a Black Panther leader, where Cleaver confiscated his passport and held him hostage until he escaped to Switzerland. Leary also fled to Vienna, Beirut, and Kabul where he was seized by U.S. agents. He was then reprimanded to solitary confinement in an American prison (Pollan, 2018). The harassment during the 1960s and 1970s was very effective; Leary was arrested 36 times worldwide (Higgs, 2006).

After the government stopped their harassment, Leary spent the rest of his life as a media star, appearing on television and on the college campus lecture circuit. During his run for governor of California in 1969 against Ronald Reagan, Beatle John Lennon wrote *Come Together* as his campaign song (Pollan, 2018). Although anyone advocating for psychedelics was likely to become politically vulnerable, the tragicomedy of Leary left irreparable damage on the psychedelic movement. It would take a generation for the harm to be undone.

The November 2020 elections in Oregon provided a major political victory for the psychedelic movement. With the approval of Measure 109, Oregon became the first state to legalize psychedelic mushrooms. The legalization of psilocybin was approved for medicinal and therapeutic uses only, not for recreational purposes. Success resulted from a 2017 report by the *Global Drug Survey* (2017) that magic mushrooms users were generally less likely to end up in the emergency rooms than any other drug. Advocates also showed how the illegal black market had exploited the successful impact of psychedelics for excessive financial gain. The public was also influenced by the positive research at Johns Hopkins, *Imperial College* in London and the *University of California, Los Angeles,* which showed efficacy of psychedelics in treating anxiety, depression, posttraumatic stress, addiction, and many other psychological problems (Acker, 2020).

For future consideration of the legalization of psychedelics, Measure 109 in Oregon reminds us that the people of Oregon did not view psychedelics as a recreational drug because of the requirement that clients be 21 years or older and under the treatment supervision of a doctor or therapist. For safety purposes, before treatment clients are required to have a psychological screening and the psilocybin dosages administered and stored under professional supervision within a treatment center. Measure 110, also on the 2020 ballot, decriminalized possession of small amounts of heroin, cocaine, LSD, and psychedelic mushrooms. The measure did not legalize those drugs; rather, those found in possession of those drugs would receive a fine and avoid jail incarceration. Oregon has paved the way for further political debate about psychedelics, including guidelines for the future of psychedelic assisted psychotherapy, and how psychedelics will be decriminalized throughout the United States.

Socioeconomic Systems

As with the humanistic-existential movement, the development of transpersonal psychology was in large part because during the twentieth century there was a shift from an industrial-based economy focused on production and mechanization to a service-based economy focused on human services and technology. By the 1950s and 1960s, there was a significant increase in college-educated individuals who were exposed to psychological concepts and who had the financial resources to explore alternative lifestyles. Many had grown up in financially stable and permissive middle-class families and were open to spending money on self-exploration. Many Americans had the resources to escape Western society and travel abroad and experience the Eastern world for themselves by attending a retreat in a Hindu Ashram or meditating in a Buddhist monastery.

Being in a capitalist system, taking advantage of the alienation in the Western world, American companies profited financially from the popularity of transpersonal psychology by selling psychospiritual goods. Books with transpersonal themes routinely became and remain bestsellers. Some of the classics that continue to permeate the social fabric of American society include *Teachings of Dan Juan* by Carlos Castaneda (1968), *Be Here Now* by Ram Dass (1971), *Zen and the Art of Motorcycle Maintenance* by Robert Pirsig (1974), *Out on a Limb* by Shirley MacLaine (1983), and a *Course in Miracles* by Helen Schulman (Foundation for Inner Peace, 1976). Schucman, as a clinical and research psychologist and professor of medical psychology in the 1970s and 1980s at Columbia University, developed *A Course in Miracles,* which is a curriculum for spiritual transformation in which Schucman claimed every word was dictated to her by an inner voice from Jesus Christ.

California became a central place for the birth of transpersonal psychology as it had for the emergence of humanistic psychology. Whether the *human potential movement* in Big Sur, or the American cultural revolution and peace movement in San Francisco, California became a place comfortable with significant social change. California was a fertile ground for transpersonal psychology because most Californians had come from other places and were less connected to mainstream beliefs, and open to creating a new social order. The Haight Ashbury in San Francisco is often referred to as the birthplace of the psychedelic movement, where the powerful aspects of transpersonal experiences became validated. California became, and remains, an economic powerhouse, the sixth-largest economy in the world. During the ascendancy of transpersonal psychology in the 1980s, California was the major science center in the United States with the most Nobel laureates and members of the *National Academy of Science* (Chinen, 1996). California is also the birthplace of the *Journal of Transpersonal Psychology.*

The decision of policymakers on the role of psychedelics in American society will have widespread socioeconomic implications. Research indicates that psychedelics may have *transdiagnostic efficacy*. This means that psychedelics act across a wide range of psychiatric diagnoses unlike current mental disorders which have specific drugs for a specific diagnosis, e.g., antidepressants for depression, anti-psychotics for schizophrenia, benzodiazepines for anxiety, or methadone for heroin addiction. Unlike current psychiatric medications, psychedelics do not operate on specific receptor sites in the brain and therefore have the potential to treat a wide range of mental health conditions (Doblin, 2021).

Normally the powerful pharmaceutical industry and the *American Psychiatric Association* control the appropriate use of psychoactive drugs. However, psychedelics currently offer little intellectual property, psilocybin and other psychedelics are a product of nature, and the patent on LSD expired decades ago. Thus far, the pharmaceutical industry has shown little interest in the psychedelics because the pharmaceutical industry does not view the psychedelics as profit-making. In fact, the profits of the pharmaceutical industry are based on chronic psychiatric conditions, not on transdiagnostic efficacy. The pharmaceutical industry faces the problem that investing in the psychedelics might mean the loss of billions of dollars in profits because the current psychiatric approach is based on specific drugs for specific diagnoses. Because the current financial incentives are lucrative for psychiatrists to provide traditional psychiatric medication, psychedelics could have a dramatic socioeconomic impact on the practice of psychiatry in the United States.

The socioeconomic issues also apply to whether insurance companies will reimburse for psychedelic assisted psychotherapy or, as often seen in history, only the wealthy will have access to psychedelic treatment. As noted in the work of August Hollingshead and Fredrick Redlich (1958) in Volume I, Chapter 6, there is a correlation between socioeconomic class and psychological treatment access. The higher socioeconomic classes typically receive the best private care, which is unavailable to the lower socioeconomic classes. They concluded that the lower socioeconomic classes receive the more brutal psychiatric treatments. As an example, the upper classes may experience clinical success with a few or occasional psychedelic assisted psychotherapy sessions to treat schizophrenia, depression, anxiety, post-traumatic stress, and other mental disorders, while the lower classes will be relegated to chronicity and the long-term daily use of antipsychotic, antidepressant, anti-anxiety, and other traditional psychiatric medications.

Cultural Systems

Although transpersonal psychology developed during the American cultural revolution of the 1960s and 1970s, the Axial Age became important because modern scholars brought transpersonal concepts from that period in history through the mainstream works of Alan Watts (1961), *Psychotherapy East and West;* Erich Fromm, D. Suzuki, and Richard DeMartini (1970), *Psychoanalysis and Zen Buddhism*; and many others who wrote classics related to Eastern thought in psychotherapy and psychoanalysis.

In the 1960s, the Beatles' interest in the *Krishna Consciousness Movement*, known as *Hare Krishna,* led to cultural interest in Hinduism and Eastern thought. Hare Krishna, the *maha-mantra,* the 16-word *Vaishnava* mantra, mentioned in the *Kali-Santayana Upanishad* (Rosen, 2006). The mantra became known outside of India by A.C. Bhaktivedanta Swami Prabhupada. Although often associated with the counterculture movement, the Swami required followers to avoid meat, gambling, drugs, and illicit sex.

Figure 6.3

The Hare Krishna became a lasting symbol of interest in American culture of Eastern thought with the song Hare Krishna in the Broadway musical *Hair* and in *My Sweet Lord*, one of the most famous hits by Beatle George Harrison. For the spiritually starved American culture, Hare Krishna *mantra* symbolized the need for spiritual joy, the joy that occurred when chanting the holy names for God. *Mantra,* the repetition of a phrase or word, is now used to calm and focus the mind of many Americans in their daily meditation practices.

Rooted in Hindu, Buddhist, Zoroastrian, Jewish, and Greek thought of the Axial Age, by 1974, there were 54 Hindu *Krishna temples* in the United States and Europe (Chinen, 1996). During this time, the Hindu tradition produced *Transcendental Meditation* which was adopted by millions of Americans to deal with the stresses of modern cultural life. Meditation practices of Buddhism offered other forms of Eastern meditation as exemplified by the *Buddhist Nyingma Institute of California* and *Naropa Institute of Colorado*. Although not always seen as directly connected to Zoroastrianism, astrology flourished by studying the impact of the movements of celestial objects on the human psyche. Within Judaism, ultraorthodox groups like the Hasidic Jews studied the mystical approaches of the *Kabbalah*. Greek philosophy again prospered, especially Socrates, whose *Socratic method* of questioning authority led to doubting the relevancy of organized religion and inspired opposition to the war in Vietnam.

In 2018, Michael Pollan (2018) published *How to Change Your Mind*: *What the New Science of Psychedelics Teaches Us About Consciousness, Dying, Addiction and Transcendence*, which described the "new science" of psychedelics. The No. 1 *New York Times* bestseller explored the history and misconceptions of psychedelic drugs. Writing from his own psychedelic experiences, Pollan concluded that LSD, psilocybin, ayahuasca, and 5_ MeO-DMT, when taken under appropriate supervision, were safe and most importantly expanded consciousness, particularly the dissolution of ego and the elimination of the fear of death. His work symbolized renewed interest in American culture not only in psychedelics but in transpersonal experiences and the need for spiritual renewal.

Natural Science Interest in Transpersonal Psychology

William James and Radical Empiricism

William James (1842–1910), the father of American psychology, was the first to use the term transpersonal in an English-language context in a 1905 Harvard University syllabus (Vich, 1988). In his monumental work discussed in Volume II, Chapter 1, *Principles of Psychology,* published in 1890, James (1890) situated psychology within the natural sciences but is often dismissed as losing his "scientific orientation" later in his career. However, it was in 1884, during the Principles of Psychology period that James helped found the *American Society for Psychical Research* (ASPR), which investigated transpersonal experiences and supernatural phenomenon, eventually verifying the hypnotic states described by Jean Charcot, Pierre Janet, and Alfred Binet (Taylor, 1996). Although exposed to the psychoanalytic work of Sigmund Freud and Josef Breuer, James was most influenced by Frederic Meyer, who for his time, developed the most complete, but controversial, model of consciousness ranging from the pathological to the transcendent. James described transpersonal states as possessing a noetic quality, a mystical state that not only created many feelings, but the achievement of true knowledge.

Because of his interest in parapsychology, by the early twentieth century, James was the first to advocate for the scientific study of consciousness because he became disenchanted with the reductionism of modern psychology. He argued for a *radical empiricism* that would not restrict itself to the currently accepted empirical methodologies. Parapsychology was not his only transpersonal interest. James cultivated scientific interest in altered states of consciousness, hypnosis, dissociative states, multiple personalities, and perennial religious philosophy (Taylor, 1996). Besides scientific exploration, James opened himself to his own personal transpersonal experiences using psychoactive drugs by experimenting with nitrous oxide and peyote.

In *The Varieties of Religious Experience,* James (1929) applied insights from his drug experiences to the understanding of altered states of consciousness. Modeling a way to escape the ethnocentric tendencies in psychology, James sponsored a lecture by Swami Vivekananda at Harvard University on the Hindu practice of *Vedanta philosophy* (Taylor, 1986). James knew Anagarika Dharmapala, the theosophist and Theravada Buddhist practitioner. D. T. Suzuki integrated the pragmatism of James into Japanese philosophy and introduced Zen Buddhism to American audiences (Taylor, 1993). Although rooted in the natural sciences, James advocated for a more confident and open psychology interested in interdisciplinary dialogue, exploration of Asian thought, with less experimental and empirical vigor and more philosophical and psychological sophistication.

American Empiricism

Harris Friedman, a retired psychologist professor from the *University of Florida* and professor emeritus of *Saybrook University*, argued for transpersonal psychology to survive it must be based on conventional empirical science. This meant accessibility to experiences related only to the senses (Friedman, 2002). Friedman proposed a division of labor between "scientific" transpersonal psychology and "nonscientific" transpersonal psychology. He, as well as other empirically oriented transpersonal psychologists, believe that non-scientific approaches should be under the purview of transpersonal studies in departments of interdisciplinary studies, which includes psychology, anthropology, sociology, philosophy, and in the humanities like the arts, poetry, and the spiritual and folk traditions (Daniels, 2005; Friedman, 2002).

Jorge Ferrer, professor of East-West psychology at the *California Institute of Integral Studies, San Francisco*, presented a counter approach to Friedman and the empiricists that views a purely naturalistic worldview as hostile to most transpersonal knowledge (Ferrer, 2014). Ferrer claimed that the natural sciences were dependent on Cartesian dualism, which views mind and matter as separate and neo-Kantian philosophy, which views matter as being extended in space with no consciousness, whereas the mind and soul have consciousness but no extension in space. Kant assumed that there were innate and epistemic constraints to understanding metaphysical realities because metaphysical realities may exist but could only be accessible through the subjective possibility of their existence and could never be objectively proven.

To overcome the objective-subjective split and the limitations of the natural sciences to understand transpersonal experiences, Ferrer (2002), turned to a *participatory epistemology* to resolve the split, where meaning occurs through interaction with the physical world. Ferrer believed that the *participatory turn* in transpersonal experiences were "co-creative events," which argues that individuals and communities have an integral and irreducible role in creating a pluralistic spiritual reality (Ferrer & Sherman, 2008). Ferrer viewed the participatory turn as emancipatory because it necessitated a dialogue and a shared participation with a community of others toward understanding the human connection to the supernatural, the divine, and the cosmos (Hartelius, Friedman & Pappas, 2015).

The Default Mode Network (DMN)

Nature has provided humanity the power to alter and transform the mind through mind-altering drugs, as symbolized by the psilocybin mushroom, a fungus.

Figure 6.4

Research on the psychedelics opened the door to a neuroscience understanding of transpersonal experiences Psilocybin, LSD, and 5-MeO-DMT, called tryptamines, are in the same molecular family with the neurotransmitter serotonin, the most famous tryptamine. How serotonin works remains a mystery, even though it seems to bind with a different number of receptors across the brain and body, with significant receptors in the digestive tract.

The group of tryptamines called "the classic psychedelics" have a strong connection to the serotonin receptor, 5-HT. In 1998, Franz Vollenweider a Swiss researcher, demonstrated that LSD and psilocybin bind with 5-HT in the brain. After discovering that the "the classic psychedelics" had a strong connection to serotonin 5-HT, the question that eluded neuroscientists was the definition of consciousness. It was not until 2001 that *Marcus Raichle*, a neurologist at the *University of Washington*, in a landmark paper with his colleagues discovered that DMN forms a critical and centrally located hub of brain activity that link the cerebral cortex to deeper, and older, brain structures involved in memory and emotion (Raichle, et al, 2001). The DMN is the "orchestral conductor," the "corporate executive" keeping the unruly Freudian id, and other mischievous aspects of the brain in check.

Like many psychedelic researchers, *Robin Carhart-Harris*, a psychologist and neuroscientist and head of the Centre of Psychedelic Research at Imperial College, London, wrongly hypothesized that the psychedelics increased brain activity, especially in emotional brain systems. After fMRI research, Carhart-Harris discovered that the psychedelics decreased brain activity because of the disinhibition of the *Default Mode Network (DMN)*. The DMN is the place where the mind is in a mental state of daydreaming, self-reflection, thinking about others, remembering the past, and planning for the future. The DMN appears to be the key to understanding consciousness and transpersonal experiences because it is the part of the brain where the flow of consciousness occurs and what holds the brain system together.

The DMN is a key factor in the creation of consciousness and the construction of the ego. Some neuroscientists call the DMN "the me network." As seen during the Axial Age, the price of an individual identity is the separation from other people and nature, creating anxiety, shadow, and mental disturbance. By understanding DMN brain activity, Carhart-Harris explained how the transpersonal experience unfolds (Carhart-Harris et al, 2012). Collaborated by other neuroscientists, drops in DMN activity correlated with the experience of ego dissolution which is both disturbing and enlightening. In line with Buddhist thought of the illusory nature of a purely mental construction of reality, the non-duality of the psychedelic experience suggests that consciousness survives the dissolution of the ego or self. The loss of a clear distinction between subject and object may also explain mystical and spiritual experiences because disinhibition of the DMN occurs not only during psychedelic experiences, but during meditation, breathing practices like *Holotropic Breathwork*, sensory deprivation, fasting, prayer, and near-death experiences.

Carhart-Harris et al (2014) developed a synthesis of psychoanalysis, transpersonal psychology, and cognitive brain science. His research described the psychological impact of creating order and selfhood in the brain. In concert with Freudian thought, Carhart-Harris believed the brain initially exhibited a more archaic form of consciousness, what Freud considered *primary consciousness,* characterized by magical and wishful thinking. Magical and wishful thinking reduced uncertainty and anxiety about the world.

As evolution of the brain continued, the DMN emerged, which resulted in a coherent sense of self and ego development, which Freud considered *secondary consciousness* (Freud, 1911/1958). David Nutt (2014) claimed that DMN was the neural equivalent of the Freudian view of *repression*. By repressing uncertainty, entropy, the brain promoted realism, foresight, self-reflection, and the ability to overcome fantasy and paranoid fantasies. This achievement created a limiting and narrowing influence on consciousness. Entropy exists on a low to high spectrum of cognitive states. Infant consciousness, psychosis, magical thinking, creativity, open-mindedness, and the psychedelics are examples of the high-entropy end of the spectrum.

Carhart-Harris and his colleagues found that psychological disorders do not result from a lack of order in the brain but rather from an excess of order (Carhart-Harris, Kaelen, & Nutt, 2014). At the low end of the entropy spectrum are rigid and stereotypical thinking that can result in addiction, obsessive-compulsive disorder, and depression (Carhart-Harris et al, 2016). When self-reflection deepens, the ego becomes overbearing and rigid, transpersonal practices and the psychedelics can disrupt rigid patterns of thought by disintegrating the patterns of neural activity upon which they rest.

Carhart-Harris and his colleagues (2014) used a brain scanning technique called *magnetoencephalography,* which maps electrical activity in the brain. The results create a symbol of the effects of the psychedelics on brain activity during normal waking hours and after an injection of psilocybin. Carhart-Harris and his colleagues found that, under psilocybin thousands of new connections occurred, linking many regions of the brain and symbolizing the brain as more globally interconnected across many brain systems. Psilocybin produced a fresh outlook, creative insights, and new meaning to familiar experiences. Psilocybin also gave rise to hallucinations, bizarre mental states, and brain systems working against one another. The increase in entropy activity allowed a thousand mental states to bloom in the brain, many disturbing, but many revelatory and even transformative (Pollan, 2018).

Like many research psychologists, Carhart-Harris does not romanticize psychedelics and does not believe that the transpersonal is a product of the universe but rather of brain activity (Pollan, 2018). He believes that the psychedelics unleash regression to a more primitive state related to the condition of an infant on the breast of the mother before ego development. Although he agrees with Aldous Huxley that psychedelics opened the doors of perception, as a natural science–oriented researcher, he is skeptical that everything that comes through the door is necessarily real. He believes that the psychedelic experience can yield "fool's gold" (Pollan, 2018). On the other hand, Carhart-Harris argued that there is gold to be discovered in the psychedelic experience because the psychedelics can overcome the rigid and overbearing ego, which can be psychologically, socially, and politically destructive.

Hermeneutic Science Interest in Transpersonal Psychology

Sigmund Freud and Psychoanalysis

Sigmund Freud (1856–1939) is often considered the grandfather of transpersonal psychology, because of his interest in psychoactive drugs, the distinction between religion and spirituality, the limitations of the autonomous ego, and the suspension of the critical faculties of the mind (Epstein, 1996).

Freud had an early interest of the impact of psychoactive drugs on the unconscious. His letters, notes, dreams, and recollections in *Cocaine Papers* indicate that cocaine was more than a passing interest (Byck, 1974). In Cocaine Papers, Freud describes his first use of cocaine as euphoric and calming. It is believed that his experiences with cocaine influenced his 1900 masterpiece, *The Interpretation of Dreams* (Byck, 1974). Encouraged by his own experience of cocaine, Freud experimented with fellow colleagues, patients, and friends (Linn, 2002). He became preoccupied with the psychiatric uses of cocaine, especially for the treatment of morphine addiction. Freud was accused by some colleagues of adding cocaine as the third devastating addictive drug, along with alcohol and opium (Byck, 1974). The fact that Freud was already espousing controversial concepts about the human mind, it was understandable that advocating for psychoactive drugs to expand human consciousness would have been difficult. Also, it may have been that Freud lost interest in cocaine when he discovered cocaine was addictive. Although there has been significant speculation about whether Freud suffered from cocaine addiction, the evidence appears inconclusive (Linn, 2002).

In *Moses and Monotheism* (Freud, 1964) and *The Future of an Illusion*, Freud (1989) was critical of religion and spirituality. In *Civilization and Its Discontents*, Freud (1961) acknowledged contact with French poet Roman Roland, who was a devout follower of Hindu gurus Ramakrishna and Vivekananda. Paradoxically, Roland agreed with Freud's view of religion, which would perplex Freud throughout his life. On the one hand, Roland supported Freud's view that religion was an illusion, but sorry that Freud had "not properly appreciated the true source of "religious sentiment," the feeling of "eternity" being unbounded, and "oceanic feelings" (Freud, 1961, p. 64).

Freud agreed with Roland that an autonomous ego was illusionary but believed that psychoanalysis would change the view of the inviolability of the ego by an emphasis on internal psychological processes. Outside ego experiences of "oceanic feelings" were problematic because the ego set clear psychological boundaries. It was being in love where the internal and external became one and boundaries melted away. Although Freud had limited knowledge of Hindu meditation practices, in Civilization and Its Discontents, he acknowledged that "oceanic feelings" and spiritual feelings" were experienced by millions of people throughout world. One unanswered question was why Freud did not compare his "euphoric" cocaine experiences to the "oceanic" experiences of Roman Rolland.

In the final analysis, Freud reduced mystical and spiritual states to the wish before the emergence of ego consciousness to return to an infantile state and the breast of the mother. In *Beyond the Pleasure Principle,* Freud (1955) articulated, like the Buddhists, the view that humans were responsible for the creation of their own psychological misery. Unknowingly the theory of the pleasure principle paralleled the first two Buddhist *Noble Truths* (Epstein, 1996). As discussed in Volume I, Chapter 2, *dukkha* is awareness that all life is suffering and *samudaya* is awareness that the root of all suffering is desire. Freud described infancy as the time when the mother provided, magically, the feel of omnipotence and the original feelings of pleasure that most adults continued unconsciously to desire in adulthood, which created psychological turmoil. It was only by overcoming the reliance on the pleasure principle that higher pleasures could be achieved.

The Freudian concept of *sublimation* created the possibility to escape the pleasure principle. Using Leonardo de Vinci as an example, Freud (1957) believed that these desires do not decrease later in life but could be transformed into desire for knowledge, discovery, creativity, and self-awareness. When this occurred, passions and desires were not rejected but transformed into ecstatic and mystical experiences. However, Freud remained skeptical; the shadow of spiritual and religious experiences would haunt him even as he refused to admit to spiritual or religious yearnings even on his death bed as he died from throat cancer.

His ambivalence regarding religion and spirituality would leave a lasting impact on the practice of psychoanalysis. Transpersonal psychologists believe that the "oceanic feelings" that Freud acknowledged as important could not be reduced to primordial narcissistic craving; rather, those feelings indicated the desire to experience the world beyond the limitations of ego functioning.

Carl Jung and Analytical Psychology

Carl Jung (1875–1961) has been called the first transpersonal psychiatrist because his theoretical and clinical approaches were a precursor to the development of transpersonal psychology. The analytical psychology of Jung is deeply rooted in transpersonal experiences, including his own, which occurred through active imagination, dreams, the *ego-Self* axis, and the *collective unconscious* (Scotton & Hiatt, 1996).

Disagreements between Freud and Jung were discussed in Volume II, Chapters 2 and 3. Although the split between Freud and Jung is often reduced to disagreements regarding the *libido*, another major cause for their split was Jung's insistence on the importance of the spiritual, the transcendent, and the universal collective unconscious. In *Psychology of the Unconscious,* Jung (2003) examined the fantasies of a mental patient whose poetic and symbolic images helped Jung redefine libido as not only sexual, but psychic energy arising from the unconscious in symbolic form. Jung believed his analytical psychology promoted a life of the spirit, of creativity, and psychological development beyond the life of the ego.

In his autobiographical book, *Memories, Dreams, Reflections*, Jung (1963) gave a description of a transcendent experience discussed in Volume II, Chapter 3, that would become part of the critically acclaimed *Red Book* in the twentieth-first century (Shamdasani, 2003). Starting with descent into another world, Jung described a common transpersonal experience, with or without psychedelic drugs, by utilizing the Jungian concept of *active imagination* that allowed the psyche to transcend ego functioning. Jung described "seizing control' of his fantasies by imagining a steep descent into a crater with the corresponding feeling of being in another world, the land of the dead. Near a steep rock in the crater, he found two figures: an old man, Elijah, and a blind girl, Salome. He believed that Elijah symbolized the wise old prophet and Salome the feminine erotic anima; the embodiment of the *logos* and *eros*. Although he was involved in a long conversation with Elijah and Salome, he could not understand their message and discovered that entering an unknown and confusing, often dangerous, "other world" symbolized a common experience of an altered state of consciousness and a transpersonal experience (Jung, 1963).

In a later dream, Philemon emerged out of the figure of Elijah symbolizing superior insight, a living personality separate from his ego. This experience convinced Jung that there were things in the psyche that produce themselves and have their own life. For Jung, Philemon represented a force that was not his own. Disturbed by this awareness, Jung looked for reassurance by seeking a true living guru because of the worry that there could be an endless

Figure 6.5

and disturbing number of Philemon. Years later, after a conversation with a friend of Gandhi whose guru was Shankaracharya, a commentator on the *Vedas* who died centuries ago, Jung came to understand a living guru was unnecessary because Philemon was a spiritual force who would later be integrated into his psyche through the study of alchemy (Jung, 1963).

In analytical psychology, the process of ego transcendence occurs through the *transcendent function* and the ego-Self axis (Jung, 1953). The transcendent function facilitates the union of the conscious and unconscious contents of the human mind. Jung (1964) believed the symbols of transcendence represent the striving of humanity to attain the highest goal which is to realize the full potential of the individual Self. For Jung, ego transcendence is often symbolized in history by a shaman because of their ability to transcend the ego and fly like a bird above the ego universe (Jung, 1964).

One of the most important aspects of analytical psychology is the development of the ego-Self axis, which is a strong connection between the conscious ego and the Self. Different from the conscious ego, the Self is an inner guiding unifying force of the psyche that often feels like it operates in accordance with a secret design. This can happen when one transcends ego purposiveness and wishful aims and opens to the possibility of a deeper connection to the inner forces of the unconscious. The relationship of the ego to Self is like a greater power sending important messages about existence through the unconscious in dreams, active imagination, or any creative activity that transcends ego functioning.

The doors of transcendence are continually opened by symbols that allow the ego to surrender its gifts and talents for the greater good of humanity and toward the true purpose of the Self. Jung believed symbols were the language of the unconscious and the Self and the specific content of symbols was less important than the emotional experience of transcendence (Scotton, 1996). The transcendent, the spiritual, found in all cultures, is part of healthy human development; their absence in modern times has created psychological distress, violence, and destructive political impulse (Washburn, 1988).

Jung was one of the first prominent psychiatrists to value insights of the human mind from the psychologies of other cultures, particularly those of the Axial Age. He inspired cross-cultural research in psychology and risked his scientific reputation by supporting publications that discussed mystical, transpersonal, and spiritual experiences. He wrote forwards or commentaries to the translated books of Richard Wilhelm (1967) that included the Daoist *I Ching* and its complement, *The Secret of the Golden Flower* (Wilhelm, 1962), the Buddhist *Tibetan Book of the Dead* (Jung, 1958a), *The Tibetan Book of Great Liberation* (Jung, 1958b), and the introduction to *Introduction to Zen Buddhism*, by D.T. Suzuki (1994). Immersed in Hindu thought and the feminine, Jung (1999) wrote *The Psychology of Kundalini Yoga,* whose adherents believe the practice of yoga provides a way to experience the divine feminine.

Although Jung was skeptical of the therapeutic value of psychedelics, Scott Hill (2019), in *Confrontation with the Unconscious: Jungian Depth Psychology and Psychedelic Experience*, argues that in recent psychedelic research and the development of neuroscience, Jung would be more supportive of utilizing Jungian principles in psychedelic-assisted psychotherapy. The Jungian concepts of the collective unconscious, dreamwork, archetypes, shadow, the numinous, the transcendent function, the ego-Self axis, and the importance of symbolic understanding provide the emerging psychedelic-assisted psychotherapies with an essential framework that would deepen the meaning of the psychedelic experience.

Figure 6.6

Jung traveled outside the Western world to Algiers, Tunis, Uganda, and Kenya, finding differences but many cultural similarities, especially regarding importance of dreams, cultural symbols, and experiences of the Self beyond the ego. One of his most significant visits was to the Taos pueblo in New Mexico, where he met with Chief Mountain Lake and witnessed the decimation of a culture by a white society dominated by thought and progress symbolized by the values of a spiritually unenlightened culture (McGuire, 1995).

Abraham Maslow – Humanistic Psychology

As discussed in Volume II, Chapter 5, Abraham Maslow (1908–1970) and Charlotte Buhler (1893–1974) developed humanistic psychology as the *Third Force in Psychology*. They rejected the focus of psychopathology in psychoanalysis and behaviorism and the impersonal stance of modern psychological research, which assumed a subject-object dichotomy and emotional distance from scientific inquiry (Maslow, 1962).

Figure 6.7

After his research on self-actualized persons, Maslow concluded that human beings have a biologically based instinctive nature that is fulfilled in a spiritual self-actualization that has no connection to metaphysical or religious assumptions and is now symbolically at the top of his hierarchy of needs. Based in the humanism traditions that embraced the mystical and spiritual and influenced by the *psycholytic* work of Jungian psychiatrist Stanislav Grof, Maslow coined the term *transpersonal* and created the Fourth Force in Psychology.

Maslow advocated for a "Daoist science," a hermeneutic science in which scientists sought to observe and understand rather than analyze and confirm research biases (Maslow, 1969a). Deeply rooted in the natural sciences, Maslow viewed a synthesis between phenomenological and empirical research methods (Battista, 1996). This transpersonal revolution that Maslow nurtured flourished throughout the scientific community, including in ecopsychology, somatic psychology, feminism, alternative medicine, sociology, anthropology, organizational development, and religious studies (Hartelius, Friedman, & Pappas, 2015).

As a scientist, Maslow was concerned that transpersonal psychology could be misused to support narcissism, self-absorption, and interpersonal exploitation. He emphasized that spiritually self-actualized individuals were deeply committed to improving the world. Although self-actualized individuals reported having *peak experiences*, Maslow warned against their endless search and distinguished between peak experiences and *plateau experiences,* which were daily feelings of peace, serenity, and the divine (Maslow, 1969a). Maslow also discovered that spiritual growth often occurred from painful life circumstances, not from positive affirmations or beautiful and positive experiences (Battista, 1996). It was nadir experiences of unpleasantness, stress, anger, confusion, fear, and paranoia that often were the most transformative. It was in facing death and through near-death experiences where individuals became spiritually self-actualized.

As discussed in Volume II, Chapter 5, Maslow described individuals who were not self-actualizing as deficiency motivated (D-motivation). As his approach to transpersonal psychology evolved, he began to apply his theory of motivation to social organizations. In *Eupsychian Management: A Journal* (Maslow, 1965), Maslow documented his observations in 1962 of the enlightened management practices at a California electronics plant. Malow coined the term *eupsychia,* meaning moving toward a superior mind or soul, to describe an ideal organizational culture that could facilitate the psychological and spiritual self-actualization of its workers.

In the last few years of his life, Maslow expanded his theory of motivation into a threefold model that included individuals who were deficiency motivated (theory X), humanistic motivated (theory Y), and transcendentally motivated (theory Z) (Maslow, 1969b). His model utilized the prepersonal, personal, and transpersonal level of Ken Wilber. He applied *theory Z* to a wide variety of organizations including business religion, politics, philosophy, and psychotherapy. Psychotherapy practiced from a deficiency model would operate like the traditional medical model, where the therapist was the expert. From this perspective, psychopathology is viewed diagnostically from inadequate parenting, behavioral dysfunction, and unconscious disturbance. Psychotherapy from a humanistic perspective focuses on personal identity with an authentically engaging therapist who views psychopathology as resistance to full human potential. At the transpersonal level, psychotherapy is focused on transcending ego functioning. The psychotherapist is a compassionate teacher who has had their own transcendental experiences. Psychopathology is a "soul-sickness," the absence of spiritual experiences and a zest for life over intellectual preoccupation with transcendental and philosophical issues. Religions at a deficiency level view God as vengeful. Religions at the humanistic level experience God as loving and life affirming. Religions at a transpersonal level conceive no exact concept of a personal God, rather view God as a concept that is divine and universal and beyond human understanding.

Since human beings spend much of their life at the workplace, Maslow believed that organizations were essential places to support the self-actualization process. Organizations operating at the deficiency level utilized an authoritarian top-down organizational approach. Work was simply a job to make money to live; authority came from upper management. Organizations that functioned from a humanistic orientation stressed mutual respect, empowering employees to actively participate at all levels of the organization; authority existed within the individual. The assumption in transpersonal organizations was that all workers were ethically and spiritually committed to their jobs. The goal of a transpersonal organization was to provide to the greatest extent possible quality services to clients. The mission of the organization transcended any individual because the transpersonal organization provided a higher purpose for both the workers and the clients. By his approach to personality structure, psychopathology, psychotherapy, and organizational development, Maslow laid the foundation for the theoretical and philosophical approach of Ken Wilber and future transpersonal psychologists.

Sri Aurobindo – Integral Yoga Psychology

Integral yoga, also called *supramental yoga*, is a yoga-based philosophy and practice of Sri Aurobindo (1872–1950), the Western-educated Indian sage. Beginning in the early twentieth century, he integrated streams of *Vedanta* and synthesized *Tantric yoga* into a spiritual vision in the evolution of consciousness. He believed that Brahman created the world of spirit through *involution* which is the downward movement of spirit losing itself in physical matter. Although the world appears to consist of dead matter, devoid of consciousness, it contains an unconscious evolutionary impulse. Evolution is the spirit rediscovering itself again and the story of transformation of consciousness in the individual and in history.

Slowly, through the material evolutionary process, matter organized itself and consciousness emerged. First through plants, animals developed a rudimentary mind, but one imprisoned by the senses. Only human beings have a mind that can develop language and a reflective consciousness. With the evolution of body, heart, and mind, the world readied for the emergence of the Spirit. Humanity was initially lost because the senses draw one outward. But as consciousness evolved, there has been a movement toward the riches of an inward world of peace, love, and bliss. Through yoga, the evolution of consciousness was accelerated; hence, his famous phrase, *all life is yoga,* which was the subtitle of his masterwork, *Synthesis of Yoga* (Aurobindo, 1996).

Aurobindo believed there are two major streams of spirituality in the world; namely the *personal divine* of mainstream Christianity, Judaism, and Islam and the *impersonal divine* of Buddhism, Advaita Vedanta, and Daoism. The problem is that most spiritual traditions stop at one and become competitive for the best spiritual path, unaware that both the personal and impersonal divine are important and can exist together. Integral *yoga* is an integration of the four levels of consciousness (Aurobindo, 1996). The outer consciousness contains the body, heart, and mind, which, until the development of transpersonal psychology, has been the primary focus of Western psychology. The second level is the inner being, greater awareness of the body, heart, and mind through experiences of chakra energies. During the third level, true being, the body, heart, and mind are confronted with a mixture of the light and demonic energies that require connection to Atman, the impersonal divine. The fourth level is central being, when the personal and impersonal divine become integrated. The personal divine is the experience of the unique soul that develops over a period of many lifetimes and prepares to reincarnate so that the evolution of consciousness can continue.

Through his own enlightenment, Sri Aurobindo discovered the importance of both the impersonal divine self or Atman, and the personal divine self or individual soul. For the evolution of consciousness and the future of humanity, the personal divine self, the soul, needs to continue to evolve. The nature of the individual soul is one of bliss, joy, peace, and love, which provides unending guidance. In integral yoga, spirituality is not a matter of belief but an experiential reality when the outer mind is calmed through yoga meditation. This enables the awareness of the inner realms of being that create an experience of both the personal and impersonal divine that most religions have tried but failed to achieve throughout human history.

Ken Wilber – Integral Psychology and Perennial Philosophy

Integral psychology emerged in the 1940s with the work of Indra Sen (1903–1994), a psychologist, and a follower of Sri Aurobindo. In the development of *integral psychology*, Sen utilized the fourfold division of consciousness of Sri Aurobindo (Cortright, 2015). This is symbolized by the morning dawn, the dawn of a transcendent divine consciousness as the soul created a new day above the unending noise of modern life and beyond the desires and fears of the ego. Sen believed the soul communicated more though feeling than thought. The feelings of warmth, love, and "rightness" indicated connection to the divine, while feelings of unease indicated

Figure 6.8

straying from the divine (Cortright, 2015). Influenced by Sen, Ken Wilber developed integral psychology based on both Western and Eastern psychological and philosophical traditions.

Often criticized for lacking a strong ontological, epistemological, and philosophical foundation, Ken Wilber is widely regarded as a leading philosophic theorist in transpersonal psychology (Walsh & Vaughan, 1996). Wilber (1977) envisioned the organization of psychology into a single theoretical framework or "spectrum" of study and, in the process, transformed transpersonal psychology from its beginnings in humanistic psychology, the human potential movement, the transcendental approaches of Eastern psychologies, into a "container" large enough to embrace all the Four Forces of Psychology (Wilber, 1995).

His theory was grounded in *Vedanta philosophy* and the Eastern, Axial Age, vision of human nature, the levels of being or "sheaths" that result in a cascade of developmental stages in which the original *ground of being*, or formless nondual consciousness, began in the prepersonal stage before the development of a functioning ego. During the next personal stage, a functioning ego struggles against the contradictions in the world, becoming alienated after being repeatedly confronted by the Jungian shadow. This continual sequence of alienation weakens the outer persona identity, opening the way for shadow to facilitate the development of an inner-driven persona that transcends ego. Confrontations with shadow lead to the transpersonal stage in which the ego remains available but superseded by a higher state of consciousness and a relationship to the divine (Combs, 2015). Each stage creates psychological challenges and possible psychopathology and, depending on the stage, the necessity to access the appropriate psychodynamic, behavioral, or humanistic-existential psychotherapeutic treatment approach (Wilber, 1977).

Central to Wilbur's integral psychology was a multilayered *ontological hierarchy*, or what Wilber called a *holarchy*, that consisted of matter, mind, and spirit. This is symbolized in reframing *The Great Chain of Being* to reflect more accurately what the premodern sages originally meant was that each expanding "link" in the Great Chain transcends and includes its "juniors" and is therefore a *Great Nest of Being*, a psychological hierarchy of being.

At the bottom of the hierarchy is the realization of the body and the physical world. As movement occurred up the hierarchy, the recognition of an ego occurred, and consciousness expanded eventually beyond ego functioning. Wilber connected the different hierarchical stages to various world viewpoints, schools of psychological thought, philosophies, and religions (Battista, 1996). The hierarchy also explained how psychopathology and successful treatment approaches occurred at the different stages.

The concept of a hierarchical ranking of organisms was rooted in the Axial Age philosophies of Aristotle and Plato. It was further refined and adopted in the Middle Ages by the Roman Catholic Church as the *Ladder of Being,* which explained the model of spiritual development and the link of God to angels, humans, animals, plants, and minerals. God was permanent and existed outside creation and time and space, angels were immortal beings without bodies, humans shared spiritual attributes with God and the angels but were impermanent and experienced death, and animals, plants, and minerals were created to provide physical subsistence to the great creation of God. Because the king or patriarchal authoritarian systems became linked to God, revolutionary thought was often seen as rebellion against God. Although the belief may still survive, consciously or unconsciously, the Enlightenment fought the last vestiges of a feudal hierarchy and advocated for secular governmental structures that empowered ordinary citizens over divinely ordained monarchs.

The epistemological question is whether there was any way to assess the *validity* of different *world viewpoints*. To answer the question, Wilber developed three modes of epistemological being: the sensory, the intellectual or symbolic, and the contemplative. Each mode has its own unique data and facts that could only partially overlap with the other modes. The natural sciences were best suited for understanding the physical realm, hermeneutics were best able to explain the intellectual and symbolic realm, and the contemplative mode was best understood through the transpersonal realm.

Wilber argued a Great Nest of Being belongs to a culture-independent *perennial philosophy* traceable across three thousand years of mystical, esoteric, and spiritual writings. Wilber's interest in *Perennial philosophy* provided transpersonal psychology, a philosophical framework often missing to understand religious and spiritual experiences (Freeman, 2006). Perennialism is a philosophy that considers all spiritual and religious traditions of the world share a single metaphysical truth or origin from which all spiritual knowledge developed. Perennialism is rooted in neo-Platonism that emerged during the Renaissance with the belief in the *One*, from which all existence emanated. The term was popularized in the mid-twentieth century by Aldous Huxley, who was influenced by *universalism* and the neo-Vedanta Hindu philosopher Vivekananda (Sunita, Pothen, & Sumita, 2003).

In *The Perennial Philosophy*, Huxley (1945) defined perennial philosophy as the psychological process by which the soul experiences a divine reality. According to Huxley, to achieve divine reality one must become loving, be pure of heart, and a poor spirit. Perennial philosophy is linked to transpersonal psychology and the *New Age Movement* which developed in the 1950s to integrate Eastern and Western spiritual and metaphysical traditions, infusing those movements with recent developments in parapsychology, holistic health, transpersonal research, and quantum physics (Drury, 2004). The New Age Movement refers to the coming of the astrological age of Aquarius, which will usher in a spirituality without borders or dogmas that is pluralistic and inclusive.

Ferrer (2000) identified five different types of *perennialism thought*. In the basic type, there is only one path or goal for spiritual development. The esoteric type allows for many religious paths but only one single spiritual goal. The perspectivist form allows for more many paths but all ultimately represent the same perspectives, dimensions, or manifestations of the Ground of Being or Ultimate Reality. The structuralist type accepts many different spiritual paths and goals but considers these as diverse structures which reflect a deeper structure of the universal.

In the 1990s Wilber furthered developed his transpersonal psychology from the structuralist type of perennial philosophy in which he attempted to synthesize all knowledge into a systematic, *multidisciplinary worldview* based in psychology, grounded in philosophy, sociology, and anthropology, with the integration of religion, mysticism, and Eastern traditions (Walsh & Vaughan, 1996). In his four-quadrant *All Quadrants All Levels* (AQAL) grid, Wilber explained how the academic disciplines and all forms of knowledge could be integrated together (Combs, 2015). The upper-left quadrant represented "I" phenomenology and much of Western psychology, particularly psychoanalysis. The lower left represented "We," language, and communication, particularly the hermeneutics of Hans-Georg Gadamer. The upper right represented "It", the external physical world, particularly behaviorism. The lower right represented "Its," social systems, particularly Marxism. In *Integral Spirituality: A Startling New Role for Religion in the Modern and Postmodern World*, Wilber (2006) included interiors and exteriors for each of the quadrants and argued that AQAL created a complete "post-metaphysical" worldview. His post-metaphysical thought returned to the divine by the replacement of pre-determined ontological structures of consciousness with levels of being constructed through the ongoing process of evolution. These "cosmic habits" were not ahistorical Platonic archetypes but a dynamic and evolving, spirituality still in evolutionary construction.

Because of its theoretical complexity and the appearance of impractically, a major criticism of integral psychology has been the difficulty in clinical application and solving real-life problems. However, since Wilbur placed transpersonal psychology in the same theoretical and philosophical context of traditional psychology, his publications created a broad interest in transpersonal psychology that had been lacking in psychology. Even though there were major criticisms to an often-skeptical psychological community, Wilber provided a sense of theoretical credibility because of his unusual approach to place transpersonal psychology in the same context as traditional psychological theory, while also integrating Eastern psychological concepts (Combs, 2015).

Modeling political activism, in 2012, Wilber joined the advisory board of the *International Simultaneous Policy Organization,* which seeks to tackle global issues through international social policy coordination.

Postcolonial Psychology

The development of *postcolonial psychology*, defined as the time in history after World War II when psychology recognized the psychological and political impact of colonialism (Walsh, Teo, & Baydala, 2014). Postcolonial psychology offers transpersonal psychology an opportunity to value its roots in the Axial Age, retrieve the wisdom of the Native American and other indigenous peoples, and continue the ethnocentric critique of mainstream psychology.

In concert with many of the values and goals of transpersonal psychology, indigenous peoples have a sacred and respectful relationship, seeking balance and harmony with the natural order. Because of the view of native peoples as "primitives" in need of Western political and cultural liberation, European and Anglo-American psychologies have often been dangerous to native peoples. A postcolonial psychology is an acknowledgment that European and Anglo-American psychologies operate differently from the values of indigenous people (Walsh-Browers &

Johnson, 2002). For indigenous people, spirituality is central and gives meaning and purpose to life, a world guided by visions, dreams, and transpersonal experiences, the relationship to family, clan, and the land being paramount to psychological health.

Donald Sanders (1996) argues that the wisdom of the indigenous Native American shamans is relevant to transpersonal psychology because the native peoples recognize four main causes of psychological illness: offending the spirit world, intrusion of a spirit into the body, soul loss, and witchcraft. Native American shamans are role models for healers, especially transpersonal psychologists, because *soul retrieval* requires a highly developed experience of "the other world." The *vision quest* remains a predominant shaman method for connecting to the spiritual world and is part of the healing rituals for many Native American tribes.

To save the modern world from its postcolonial psychological maladies, Ignacio Martin-Baro (1942–1989), one of the victims of the horrendous 1989 murders of Jesuits in El Salvador, argued that psychology emancipate itself from Western perspectives and abandon the value-neutral sciences (Martin-Baro, 1994). His *liberation psychology* includes a shift from the study of the powerful to the needs of the oppressed. Martin-Baro believed this approach has implications for the privileged because many people experience psychological oppression in the modern world. Some feminist, postmodern, and postcolonial approaches have actualized the Martin-Baro vision as a *methodology of the oppressed*. Mary Watkins and Helene Shulman (2008) proposed a multidisciplinary action research approach that situated psychological health in a sociohistorical context with engagement in community-based interventions. The interventions are grounded in culturally respectful dialogues to evoke a critical and liberated consciousness that maximizes citizen involvement in all aspects of social and political development.

Transpersonal Psychology: A Return to the Axial Age

The text has come full circle, returning in this section to the influences discussed in Volume I, Chapter 2. So many developments in modern and transpersonal psychology are rooted in the Axial Age, this section will highlight some of the most significant influences (Anderson, 2006). As Stanislav Grof, a leader in the transpersonal movement, has noted, to truly appreciate transpersonal psychology necessitates openness to a new consciousness, the suspension of Western bias, and the desire to learn from Eastern thought. This is particularly true when exploring Greek influence in psychosynthesis, *astropsychology* with its roots in Zoroastrianism, and other ancient cultures (Campion, 2009). More familiar is the Hindu influence on modern yoga and transcendental meditation and Buddhist influence in recent developments in meditation and *mindfulness*.

Greek Philosophy

Roberto Assagioli – Psychosynthesis

> We are not human beings having a spiritual experience. We are spiritual beings having a human experience.
>
> - Pierre Teilhard de Cardin (1999)

Roberto Assagioli (1888–1974), an Italian psychiatrist and contemporary of Freud and Jung and an early leader with Maslow of the transpersonal movement, argued for a *spiritual psychosynthesis*. He was influenced by Greek philosophy, especially the transcendent philosophy of Plato and the concept of entelechy and teleology of Aristotle. Assagioli, unlike Jung, placed the transpersonal more prominently in his psychological theory and practice. Although initially trained in psychoanalysis, he founded the *psychosynthesis* movement in the early twentieth century because he became disenchanted with Freudian reductionism and the lack in psychoanalysis of the positive aspects of personality.

In his seminal work, *Psychosynthesis,* Assagioli (2012) described healthy adult development in two distinct stages: personal and spiritual psychosynthesis. Assagioli agreed with Freud and Jung concerning the existence of the unconscious but believed there was also a lower, middle, and higher unconscious. The first personal psychosynthesis stage involved the integration, control, and mapping of the lower and middle unconscious. The lower unconscious was like the id in psychoanalysis and the shadow in Jungian analytical psychology. The lower unconscious contained the areas that had broken away from consciousness and poised a destructive threat to the self that led to the development of subpersonalities, which were the incessant chatter of the mind. The middle unconscious supported the patterns of skills, behaviors, feelings, attitudes, and abilities that had formed without conscious awareness. Neuroscience described this process as the development of new neuromuscular patterns needed by all humanity to function effectively in daily life (Firman & Gila, 2002). Witnessing and observing the subpersonalities was key to the development of a personal psychosynthesis, which was accomplished through active imagination, dreamwork, meditation, and a host of many psychotherapeutic approaches. Through the process of disidentification with the subpersonalities, the "I," a personal center of the psyche developed, which set the stage for spiritual psychosynthesis.

When the "I," the personal center, had control of the subpersonalities, the second spiritual psychosynthesis stage led to the attainment of a higher unconscious, which is the superconscious self, the transcendent center, the feelings of profound serenity and peace, a unity between oneself, the cosmos, and the divine. The higher unconscious included the experiences of altruistic love, humanitarian action, artistic and scientific inspiration, philosophic and spiritual insight, and where the drive towards purpose and meaning resided (Ferrcci, 1982).

Figure 6.9

Because these higher potentialities are not always consciously available and difficult to put into words, to connect to the higher unconscious, Assagioli used symbols to evoke the experience of the superconscious and the transcendent self. Abstract symbols such as a rose, lotus, sun, or spiritual symbols such as an angel, sage, Christ, or Buddha, could support and enliven the spiritual psychosynthesis process (Battista, 1996). In *Psychological Mountain Climbing and Meditation*, Assagioli (1976) addressed the importance of symbol and meditation practices in psychosynthesis and even with the support of the spiritual wisdom of the ages, mountain climbing symbolized the lifelong struggle to reach the highest peak of spiritual consciousness.

Assagioli understood that spiritual psychosynthesis often occurred because of an existential crisis or as the result of difficult life circumstances. He also realized that spiritual awakening can be especially difficult due to an ill-prepared and underdeveloped personality. Although aligned with the principles and values of humanistic existentialism, psychosynthesis is most closely related to Jungian psychology. Like Jung, who believed in the development of a strong ego before a spiritual transformation, Assagioli believed in a strong "I," the personal center, and the completion of the personal psychosynthesis stage before the spiritual psychosynthesis stage. The Assagioli concept of subpersonalities, the "I" and self are like the Jungian concepts of complexes, ego, and the Self (Battista, 1996). However, unlike Jung, he believed there needed to be a complete reconstruction of the psyche around a spiritual center. He also emphasized the importance of an active meditation practice for psychological health. Assagioli viewed a psychosynthesis therapist as more directive and educational, more like a teacher in the Eastern spiritual traditions than the traditional less directive Jungian or psychodynamic psychotherapist.

Zoroastrianism

Astrological Psychology

> Astrology represents the sum of all the psychological knowledge of antiquity.
>
> - Carl Jung (1971)

Rooted in the Axial Age, particularly Zoroastrianism, astrological psychology, or *astropsychology,* developed from the cross-fertilization of the fields of astrology with psychodynamic psychology, humanistic and transpersonal psychology. Dane Rudhyar (1895–1985) was a pioneer of modern astrological transpersonal psychology whose monumental work, *The Astrology of Personality* (Rudhyar, 1987), inspired the modern interest of psychologists in astrology.

Influenced by the analytical psychology of Carl Jung, Rudhyar argued that astrology was not predictive but produced important intuitive psychological insights which could be transformative. This transformation occurred through an analysis of the Jungian archetypes in conjunction with the astrological chart that connected the human psyche to the planets and signs of the Zodiac. His astrological works became influential in the New Age Movement, especially during the American cultural revolution of the 1960s and 1970s in San Francisco. He believed that the hippies were harbingers of the coming of the Age of Aquarius that would begin in 2062 (Rudhyar, 1971). Rudhyar believed *transcendental art* was a way to symbolize the transpersonal archetypal experience. Transcendental art combined surrealistic and cosmic art of the 1950s, the psychedelic art of the 1960s, and visionary art of the 1970s. His transcendental artwork was often illustrated on his pamphlets and books on astrology.

Figure 6.10

Out of the research, consulting, and teaching of over 50 years, Swiss astrologers and psychologists Bruno and Louise Huber developed the *Huber Method* while working with Roberto Assagiolo, the founder of psychosynthesis and the school of transpersonal psychology mentioned above. The Huber Method was taught at the *Huber Astrological Institute* in Zurich and was founded in 1968. The Huber Method (Hopewell, 2017) is based on psychological analysis of the astrological chart with a link to universal cosmic energies.

312 Symbols of Transpersonal Psychology

Figure 6.11

Astropsychologists consider the horoscope a reflection of the soul as well as providing the most complete understanding of personality (Hopewell, 2017). Until *The Astrological Psychology Association* was established in the United Kingdom in 1983 most English-speaking students had no access to the Huber Method or other educational training resources in astrological psychology. The *Astrological Psychological Association* continues to be the leading psychologically oriented astrological association in the world.

Hinduism

Modern Yoga Practices

In another example of the incredible ability of Hinduism to incorporate a diversity of beliefs, the Bhagavad Gita recommended mixing the three classical yoga schools that became common yoga practice (Scotton & Hiatt, 1996). References to yoga are typically made to forms of yoga rather than to the three classical schools and the *Yoga Sutras of Patanjali*. Some well-known modern yoga practices include *Hatha yoga, Kundalini yoga,* and *Tantric yoga*. Hatha means "force" in Sanskrit and defines yoga as a system of physical techniques. Hatha yoga is the best-known yoga in America because it focuses only on asanas, "postures," and pranayama, "breathing." The belief in Hatha yoga is that consciousness is altered by making physical changes to the body. Because most of the Western world knows only Hatha yoga, the transpersonal and spiritual foundation of yoga has mostly been lost. Yoga teaching In America rarely goes beyond bending, stretching, breathing, and sweating.

Kundalini yoga is rooted in the belief that a form of divine feminine energy is symbolically like a snake located at the base of the spine until it is activated by yoga practice. When activated, the energy travels like a snake through the *chakras,* which contain all the potentialities of being fully human. The most important chakras are along the spinal cord, behind the head and at the crown of the head (Krishna, 1971). The chakras first emerged within the Hindu *Vedas,* which believed that human life exists simultaneously in two parallel dimensions.

One dimension is the physical body, and the other dimension is the "subtle body." The subtle body consists of kundalini energy channels connected by nodes called chakras, which through meditation, are a constant means toward psychological and spiritual transformation. The practice of Kundalini yoga consists of body postures, breathing, symbolic visualizations, and mantras. These practices manipulate the flow of kundalini energy through the chakras to the crown chakra which awakens the snake to the Divine and the highest form of psychological and spiritual development.

Tantra yoga developed during the current *Kali Yuga* age, the fourth and most decadent of the four Hindu ages of humankind. Each age is progressively shorter than the preceding and each represent a decline in the moral and physical state of the world. Kali means "strife" and "discord" and is associated with the demon Kali who is the reigning lord of the *Kali Yuga* and the nemesis of Kalki, the final avatar of the Hindu God *Vishnu*. Since humankind currently lives during the Yuga age, according to Hindu cosmology, the decline in the moral and physical state of humanity will lead to its destruction and return to Satya Yuga, the first age when *dharma* was at its highest peak. In Hindu thought, the world was only created to be destroyed, to be created again. According to the Hindu Vedas, Kali Yuga started 5,122 years ago and will end in the year 428,899 CE (Goodwin, 2011).

Figure 6.12

Tantra yoga is primarily a result of the inability of humanity to renounce the attachment to physical existence and sexual pleasure. Tantra texts are often contrasted with Vedic tests and called *mantramarga,* "the way of mantras." Unlike the Vedic texts, Tantra texts are linked to an actual divine being. Tantra worship, or *puja,* significantly differs from Vedic worship because the tantric practices use idols, shrines, and symbolic art. The tantric rituals are not a series of actions but mentally visualized symbols (Samuels, 2010). The poses have a connection to the Hindu gods. For example, the warrior poses honors Shiva and lying on one's back with split legs honors Hanuman, the monkey god. Ultimately, the tantra rituals are meant to emancipate humanity from a fundamental impurity that continues the *samsara cycle.*

Understanding the reality that people are closely tied to physical existence during this decadent Kali Yuga age, the "left-handed path," *vamamarga* tantric yoga seeks to use physical and sexual energy for enlightenment and a higher sense of self. "Left-handed" tantric yoga addresses two preoccupations: human sexuality and death. Vamamarga yoga attempts to balance the strong human "attachment-revulsion" to sex and death and it is the "left-handed path" that has gained the interest of most Americans and its rejection by some critics. Vamamarga is the "heterodox" tantric practice, which can integrate 'right-handed" practices, but is also extreme in comparison to the orthodox practice because the "left-handed path" often uses sexual partners, cremation grounds and intoxicant drugs in tantric work.

Contrary to tantric yoga stereotypes, the "left-handed path" is a genuine spiritual path rather than a simple method for sexual release. To receive the benefits of tantric yoga, one needs to be a "heroic practitioner" to enter this dangerous but enlightening practice (Scotton & Hiatt, 1996). For instance, many yogis practice *maithuna,* sacred sexual intercourse, which requires hours of meditation, ritual preparation, and mantras, while envisioning partners as the incarnation of Shiva, the masculine spiritual energy and Shakti, the primordial feminine energy. This experience can occur without sexual intercourse because Shiva and Shakti energy can be transpersonal; the cosmic couple metaphysically embodies the god and goddess by dissolving the ego and experiencing bliss through the union of their "subtle bodies."

Tantra in Sanskrit means "loom," "to warp," or "weave," which symbolizes the interweaving of text, theory, and teachings as threads into a technique or practice. It is the right and left hand weaving the threads on a loom, over and under other threads to create a beautiful fabric. The fabric of tantra yoga is symbolically weaved by both the left and right path, creating a fabric of higher consciousness, a way to situate the self in the transpersonal world beyond ego.

Transcendental Meditation

> There are enough research projects… (in Transpersonal Psychology) to keep squadrons of scientists busy for the next century.
>
> - Abraham Maslow

Meditation research is a place where empirical and transpersonal psychology have common ground. The burgeoning field of meditation research spans many areas from mindfulness meditation (Baer, 2003) to the impact of meditation on the electroencephalogram (EEG) test and brain imaging studies (Cahn & Polich, 2006). Mindfulness and transcendental meditation are the two most studied forms of meditation (Walsh and Shapiro, 2006). Mindfulness research is usually based in the Buddhist Vipassana practice in the *Theravada* tradition. Transcendental Meditation ™ is based on the Hindu Vedic tradition of the *Maharishi Mahesh Yogi* (1918–2008). In *Science of Being and the Art of Living* (Yogi, 1994), the Maharishi explained the ancient *Vedic* traditions of India in terms that could be easily understood by scientists in the Western world.

Transcendental Meditation™ is a silent, mantra-based meditation of the *transcendental movement*. The transcendental movement was founded in India in the 1950s by Maharishi Mahesh Yogi, which developed into an international conglomerate of programs and organizations that promote the TM technique. TM movement is a corporate powerhouse with teaching centers, schools, universities, and medical centers. It sells herbal products and even solar panels, as well as home financing plans, and has developed TM-centered communities. The global organization is estimated to have a net worth of $3.5 billion (Anonymous, 2008).

It is estimated that over 5 million people practice TM throughout the world (Koppel, 2008). TM has been embraced by many celebrities that include Oprah Winfrey, Mick Jagger, the Beach Boys, Tom Hanks, Jerry Seinfeld, and Clint Eastwood. In the 1960s, the Beatles became major proponents of TM after meeting the Maharishi Mahesh Yogi. After of the death of the Maharishi in 2008, Tony Nader, a Lebanese neuroscientist and researcher, became the leader of the transcendental movement. Nader received his medical degree in internal medicine and psychiatry from the *American University of Beirut* and his PhD from the *Massachusetts Institute of Technology*. He has worked closely with Deepak Chopra, the Indian American author, proponent of alternative medicine, and a leader of the New Age movement.

Over the last 50 years, TM development can be traced to four distinct periods. In the 1950s, the emphasis was on the power of the TM Hindu spiritual meditation practice to transform the world. In the 1970s, Western influences led the TM Movement away from Hindu spirituality to become an aggressive, empirically based practice focused on improving physiological and psychological functioning. In the 1980s, often outside the mainstream TM movement, Maharishi and a select-group of followers returned to the Vedic classics, seen as the source of all knowledge. This return to the Vedic texts happened because the Maharishi believed the texts mirrored the universe, and every part of the human body had a corresponding mention in the Vedic texts (Lowe, 2011).

The Maharishi believed the Vedic texts were so accurate that there was a correlation between text chapters and human organs. In the 1990s, to continue the return to the Hindu roots of TM, again outside of the mainstream TM movement, TM-inspired communities developed, most notably in Fairfield, Iowa. Because the Maharishi viewed Vedic texts and rules as true science, TM communities practiced Vedic astrology, architecture, medicine, music, and fire sacrifices (Lowe, 2011). Rules included traditional Indian architecture, homes, and offices built in compliance with Vedic rules. After the death of Maharishi, most left the TM communities, but some remnants remain, especially in Fairfield, Iowa, where the golden dome of the meditation halls and the astronomical observatory, which aligned human consciousness with the universe, stand as a reminder of the unfilled dream of the Maharishi that TM would create new spiritually enlightened communities and transform the world.

The practice of TM has stayed consistent since its development in the 1950s, and typically done twice daily and lasts between 15 to 20 minutes. Meditators use a private silent mantra while sitting comfortably with eyes closed and feet on the floor and hands on their lap (Cotton, 1990). TM training involves a structured five-week course provided by certified teachers in the many TM organizations throughout the world. Understanding the American ambivalence regarding religion, especially Eastern religions, the TM movement has avoided discussion about the Vedic foundation of TM.

Often to calm Western fears, TM has claimed it is a non-religious practice for relaxation, stress reduction, and psychological development. However, many TM meditators connect their

316 *Symbols of Transpersonal Psychology*

mantras to the sacred sound and spiritual Hindu symbols Aum or Om, often unaware Aum or Om signify the essence of Ultimate Reality, the connection to Atman, the individual soul, and Brahman, the creator, and ultimate reality of the universe. Mired in confusion about the difference between religion and spirituality, controversy continues to shadow the movement in large part because of its own ambivalence about being a religious or non-religious practice. In 1979, in *Malnak vs Yogi* the United States Court of Appeals upheld a federal ruling that TM was essentially a religious practice and could not be taught in the public schools (Evans, 2000). The court ruling indicated that TM was a vague but recognizable variant of the Hindu *Advaita Vedanta*, the oldest surviving tradition of the orthodox Hindu school *Vedanta*.

With the rise in heart disease, strokes, and other medical diseases because of a stressful modern society, medicine began to turn to TM because research indicated improvements in physical health. TM meditators lowered their heart rate and blood pressure. Although there are clear physiological and psychological improvements in practicing TM, the overall impact on health outcomes is inconclusive by the standards of traditional empirical research often because of poor sample sizes, self-selected participants, lack of adequate control and experimental groups, poor use of randomized clinical trials, unclear descriptions of meditation techniques, and inconsistent use of medical technology (MacDonald, Walsh, & Shapiro et al, 2015).

Figure 6.13

Peter Sedlmeier, Juliane Eberth, and Marcus Schwarz (2012), in a meta-analysis of over 163 individual meditation studies published in the *Psychological Bulletin*, found that in comparison to other meditation practices, TM reduced negative emotions, trait anxiety, and neuroticism and that TM improved learning and memory and enhanced self-realization. They agreed with other critical researchers that TM as well as other meditation practices needed to be based on more precise psychological theories and studied from stronger empirical methods (Shapiro & Walsh, 2003).

Aside from the religious controversies and research criticisms, TM provides a transpersonal experience to millions of people every day. TM practitioners are modern symbols of the Hindu practitioners who carry the truths of Vedic texts and the Hindu meditation practices rooted in the Axial Age.

Ray Dalio, an American billionaire, and one of the wealthiest people in the world, believed TM saved him from financial ruin. Dalio (2017) is recognized as an important advocate for the reform of corporate capitalism. His *radical transparency* management approach is based on the theory that organizational change necessitates honest communication, transparency, with employees throughout the workplace. Part of his radical transparency approach is providing TM to all his employees.

Buddhism

Meditation and Mindfulness

Unlike most people in the Western world, during the Axial Age, the Buddha did not meditate simply to reduce the social anxieties about society; rather, his meditation was a path toward spiritual awakening and emancipation from human suffering. During the Axial Age, the time of the Buddha was considered the period of *pre-sectarian Buddhism* before the development of different schools of thought. The closest word for meditation at the time was *bhavana*, meaning "mental development," and *jnana/dhyana*, meaning "mental training," that resulted in a calm and "brightly shining" luminous mind. Bhavana derives from the word *bhava* meaning "cultivating mental states" (Arbel, 2017).

The Buddha used the word *bhavana* rather than meditation to explain meditation practices to a largely rural farming culture who cultivated the earth. Like the human mind, no matter how damaged the land might become, it could continue to be cultivated and produce a nourishing harvest. The Buddha taught that meditation, like farming, is symbolic of an endless practice of harvesting a calm, reflective, alert, and luminous mind.

Buddhism is unique in that it did not emerge to worship or experience of an "external" higher power. Rather through meditation to experience the higher power that resides inside every human being. To attain access to this higher power, *samatha* and *vipassana* provide the essential qualities needed to guide any Buddhist meditative practice. *Samatha*, "calming the mind," is developed through a variety of techniques, most notably "one-pointedness," which means the selection of one object of observation and overcoming the "five faults" (Wynne, 2007). The five faults include: laziness, forgetting instruction, laxity and excitement, and non-application or over application of the technique.

318   *Symbols of Transpersonal Psychology*

Figure 6.14

The second quality in Buddhist meditation is *vipassana,* which is "special seeing" and insight into the true nature of reality that is impermanence, human suffering, dissatisfaction, and the existence of a non-self. Because mindfulness is the ability to maintain awareness of reality, it is first factor of the *Seven Factors of Awakening* in Buddhism and the seventh step in the *Noble Eighth Path of Buddhist* practices that emancipates one from *samsara*, the cycle of rebirth.

Buddhism teaches that meditation does not have to be solemn and psychologically painful. The Buddhist meditative experience can be an exhilarating transpersonal experience. The five processes described in Sanskrit are *Vitarka, Vicara, Priti, Sukha,* and *Ekaggata* and help to overcome resistance to Buddhist meditation, which are the obstacles to *samatha* and *vipassana*. The process unfolds by first taking hold of the mental state, Vitarka, "applied thought," which counteracts lethargy and drowsiness. Vicara is a sustained application of the mind on an object counteracting doubt and uncertainty. Priti creates a joyous, stimulating, rapture contradicting any ill-will or malice. Sukha is an experience of non-sensual pleasure and bliss, which contradicts restlessness, worry, and anxiety. Ekaggata is "one pointedness," which contradicts sensory desire. Overcoming these resistances results in *samadhi*, the attainment of complete control of the mind and the "special seeing" of vipassana. At this point, one can maintain *sati,* "mindfulness," which is keeping the mind focused without distraction on an object of meditation, like breathing, meditation instructions, or personal vows. Finally, in *sampajanna,* one can fully control the body and mind and become fully attentive, alert, introspective, and aware of the impermanence of life.

In many ways, Buddhist philosophy and meditation practices permeate all the *Four Forces* in psychology. Mindfulness meditation has inspired many schools of psychotherapy, most notably *Dialectic Behavioral Therapy* and the Third Wave Movement in *Cognitive Behavioral Therapy* (Volume II, Chapter 4). Also, terminology of Buddhist meditative practices can vary depending on the Buddhist school of thought as described in Volume I, Chapter 2.

Psychedelics and Transpersonal Psychology – Natural and Hermeneutic Science Integration

The Psychedelic Renaissance – Paradigm Shift

Although Thomas Kuhn (1922–1996) altered his theory later in his career, his landmark book, *The Structure of Scientific Revolutions* (Kuhn, 1962), introduced the term *paradigm shift*, as a key concept toward understanding the evolutionary stages of scientific knowledge. Kuhn believed that science evolved in a steady, progressive manner starting with a widely accepted concept of a *paradigm* which creates a *normal science* that develops into an agreed upon scientific belief system that engages in *puzzle solving* that lacks creativity. Puzzle solving blinds scientists to other viewpoints, which results in *anomalies* that challenge normal science. This leads to many theories and a *preparadigmatic stage* that causes a crisis because of competition among scientists for control and acceptance.

Kuhn believed that psychology was in the preparadigmatic stage awaiting the *revolutionary stage*. During the revolutionary stage the old paradigm is displaced and replaced by a new paradigm that moves science forward. An example of a revolutionary paradigm shift was the *Copernican Revolution*, which proved a single theory of planetary motion. Science would never be the same after scientists proved that the sun, not the earth, was the center of the solar system.

The *Psychedelic Renaissance* offers a paradigm shift in science. Although psychoanalytic, analytical, behavioral, and humanistic-existential psychology were all influenced by the natural and hermeneutic sciences, the psychedelics more significantly challenge the traditional separation in psychology of the subject and object, the mind, and the body, and the material and transpersonal. To explain the impact and benefits of the psychedelics, researchers are struggling with the limitations of the empirical scientific paradigm because "something else is happening" beyond random control trial research. Beyond natural science explanations, there is a hermeneutic in the psychedelics, a phenomenology that often leaves scientists with more questions than answers, a search to explain the complexity of psychedelics because true understanding of the psychedelic experience transcends typical empirically based research methods.

Like all important developments in psychological history, the Psychedelic Renaissance is filled with charismatic leaders, scientific disagreements, cultural clashes, and political challenges. As the text ends, the Psychedelic Renaissance is a place where the natural and hermeneutic sciences are finding common ground because the psychedelics cannot be approved for therapeutic use until proponents prove efficacy through the empirical regulatory research trials required by the *Federal Drug Administration* (FDA) while at the same time there would be little interest in psychedelics if they were not showing clinical efficacy and dramatically impacting the lives of millions of people throughout the world. If the Psychedelic Renaissance is to be successful, it necessitates a rapprochement and integration between the natural and hermeneutic sciences so that the psychedelics are not only safely controlled, but also better understood.

Unified Psychedelic Theory and the Psychedelics in the Axial Age

Figure 6.15

The term *psychedelic* was first used in 1956 by Humphrey Osmond to describe drugs like LSD and psilocybin due to their ability to alter consciousness dramatically and symbolically. The meaning of psychedelic is rooted in the Greek *psyche* and *delein* which is "soul manifesting" modernized to "mind manifesting." Before the modern term "psychedelics," psychoactive drugs provided transpersonal and spiritual experiences throughout the centuries.

Patrick Lundborg (2012), in *Psychedelia – An Ancient Culture, A Modern Way of Life,* argued for a *Unified Psychedelic Theory* (UPT) drawn from the ancients, Platonism, and the modern phenomenology of Edmund Husserl and Maurice Merleau-Ponty (Volume II, Chapter 5). Exploring the history of the psychedelics that spans 3,5000 years, Lindborg believes that a UPT recaptures a philosophy of life that has existed for centuries because without psychedelics the exploration of the deeper realms of "inner space" would have been more difficult. The Lundborg *trip model* outlines the stages and thematic contents of a typical psychedelic journey and how the effects of DMT, ayahuasca, and psilocybin are based on the latest theories of neurophenomenology and evolutionary research which can be linked to ancient genetic matter of cosmic origin, known as *panspermia*.

Throughout the Axial Age world, the "psychedelic-like drugs" were often used to "manifest the soul." Mike Crowley (2019) explores the use of a substance called *amrita*, which translates into "deathless" as a sacramental psychedelic in early Buddhism arguing that Buddhist spirituality and psychedelic drugs have intertwined for centuries. Allan Badiner (2015) has edited an anthology on the psychedelics and the spiritual quest in a collection of essays by Buddhist psychedelic practitioners and Buddhist teachers from all over the world.

Hinduism has a relationship with the psychedelics because the Vedas, the first Hindu text, contains references to *soma*, believed to be a psychedelic drink, likely made from mushrooms. *The Rigveda* (8.48.3), the Hindu collection of Vedic Sanskrit hymns, states "We have drunk soma and become immortal, we have attained the light, the Gods discovered…. What, O Immortal mortal man's deception?"

In Greece, psychedelics were essential to religious practices. *The Eleusinian Mysteries* were celebrated in honor of the Goddess Demeter and her daughter, Persephone, and are regarded as the most sacred of all the mysteries in Greek mythology. Researchers believe that the drink taken by initiates at the Temple of Demeter at Eleusis was called *Kykeon,* which contained *ergot,* a hallucinogenic fungus (Muraresku, 2020).

Among the magus of Iran, a ritual called *avanmehr*, meaning "go on heavenly journeys," was a transpersonal Zoroastrian experience. A drug called *homeh* or *holy Hom,* mixed with milk and water, mentioned in *Avesta,* the primary collection of religious texts of Zoroastrianism, was a sacred drink that created the experience of going to heaven after death (Eftekhar, 2022).

In *DMT and the Soul of Prophesy: A New Science of Spiritual Revelation in the Hebrew Bible*, Rick Strassman (2014) links DMT, the "spiritual molecule," which is the only natural psychedelic in the human body, with the Hebrew prophets and the experiences of volunteers in his DMT research. Called *theoneurology,* Strassman views the psychedelics as the reemergence of the ancient prophetic Jewish consciousness expressed in the Hebrew Bible.

In *Tao: The Watercourse Way*, published posthumously, Alan Watts (1975), a leader in the transpersonal movement, viewed a world inspired by, but beyond, the psychedelics because Daoism could be "medicine for the ills" of the West. The book is a great introduction to the often-perplexing Daoism and rich in explaining the importance of symbols, especially in the symbolic-rich Chinese characters.

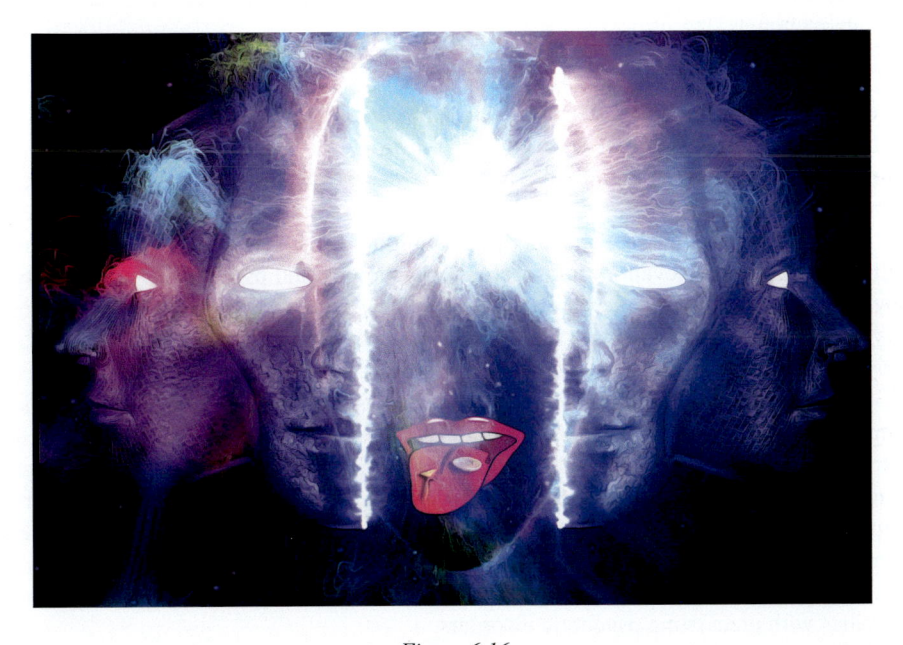

Figure 6.16

The Major Psychedelics

Table 6.1 List of the Most Common Psychedelics

Psychedelic	Colloquial Name	Typical Routes of Administration	Experience Duration	Comments
Psilocybin	Magic mushrooms/ Shrooms	Ingested dry or in chocolate, brewed as a tea	4–7 hr	History of shamanic use globally
LSD	Acid, Lucy, Blotter	Ingested via blotter paper, gel tablet, liquid	8–12 hr	Originally derived from ergot fungus
Mescaline	San Pedro or Peyote Cactus	Ingested as ground cactus powder, or brewed tea	8–14 hr	Used by shamans in North and South America
MDMA	Ecstasy "E," Molly	Ingested as powder or in pill form	3–5 hr	Being researched currently for treatment of PTSD
n,n-DMT	DMT	Smoked	6–20 min	intense visuals and transpersonal
5-MeO-DMT	5, Toad, Bufo	Smoked, snorted	20–40 min	Synthetic and organic forms (toad bufotoxin secretion or plant extracts)
Ayahuasca	Aya, Hoasca, Yagé	Ingested via a tea	4–8 hr	combination of plants containing an MAOI with n,n-DMT
Ketamine	K, Special K	Snorted, sublingually, intramuscular injection	1–3 hr	Currently being used for depression
2C-B	2C-B, Nexus	Ingested as powder or in pill form	5–8 hr	Chemical cousin of mescaline

Sources: https://erowid.org https://psychonautwiki.org
Please note response to psychedelics depends on form, dose, mindset, and physical setting.

More recently, the term *psychedelic* has been used to encompass a broader range of psychoactive substances from the classical ones like LSD, psilocybin, DMT, and mescaline to include ketamine and MDMA, as all can illicit psychedelic experiences. Psychedelic experiences can be euphoric, mystical, transpersonal, spiritual, and provide a connection to the divine. They can also be frightening, hallucinatory, and alter perceptions and distort place and time. The classical hallucinogens are most relevant to transpersonal psychology and psychedelic-assisted psychotherapy. Table 6.1 provides an overview of the typical psychedelics and includes their colloquial name(s), typical routes of administration, experience duration with comments.

Early research indicates that the psychedelics are not addictive as the psychedelics tend to be self-limiting, except for ketamine, which can be misused in escape-seeking individuals. Depending on the psychedelic, adverse psychological effects include anxiety, paranoia, psychotic-like experiences, hallucinations, and delusions. In extremely rare cases and after long-term use, the diagnoses of *Persistent Psychosis* and *Hallucinogen Persisting Perception* disorders can develop, which include ongoing perceptual disturbances lasting up to several years. General problems with psychedelics occur from accidental usage, the mixture of psychedelics with other drugs, a lack of adequate understanding and preparation prior to the experience, or the use of psychedelics with preexisting psychotic disorders.

The following are descriptions as the street name, history, typical routes of administration, effects, and clinical research related to the major psychedelics. As with all psychedelic experiences, the quality of the transpersonal experience depends on the form, the dose, the setting, and mental state of the user.

Psilocybin

Street Name – Magic mushrooms and shrooms.

History – Psychoactive mushrooms have been used by humans in religious ceremonies for thousands of years. A 6,000-year-old pictograph has been discovered in Spanish town of Villar del Humo which tentatively identified *psilocybin hispanica* as a hallucinogenic species native to that area (Akers, Ruiz et al, 2011). Also discovered by scholars as "mushroom stones" in Mayan culture, "God's Nest" in Aztec culture, and when the Spanish explorers, upon their arrival in the "new world" in the sixteenth century, observed natives using psilocybin for ceremonial and religious purposes.

Maria Sabina Magdalena Garcia, a twentieth-century Mazatec shaman, called her healing sacred psilocybin mushroom ceremonies *veladas,* which popularized the ritual use of entheogenic mushrooms throughout the Western world; psychedelics created spiritual and transcendent experiences.

In 1959, Swiss chemist Albert Hoffman isolated the active compound psilocybin from the mushroom *psilocybe Mexicana,* which led to its popularity in the 1960s as the "entheogen of choice" because of its spiritual-enhancing abilities. In the early 1960s, Harvard University became the testing ground for psilocybin through the efforts of Timothy Leary and his associates, Ralph Metzner and Richard Alpert (later Ram Dass).

During the underground period of the 1970s and 1980s, Carlos Castaneda (1968) and other authors taught the technique of growing psilocybin mushrooms. One of the most popular psilocybin books was published in 1976 under the pseudonyms of O. T. Oss and O. B. Oeric (1993), entitled *Psilocybin: Magic Mushroom Grower's Guide,* which by 1981 had sold over 100,000 copies.

Always popular in various parts of the world, *Psilocybin Retreats* are flourishing in the Netherlands, Jamaica, Mexico, and Costa Rica.

Typical Routes of Administration – Although psilocybin may be prepared synthetically, outside of the research setting, it is not typically used in that form. The psilocybin present in certain species of mushrooms can be ingested in several ways: by consuming fresh or dried fruit bodies, by preparing an herbal tea, or by combining with other foods to mask the bitter taste, most commonly chocolate. In rare cases, people have injected mushroom extracts intravenously.

Effects – Psilocybin is the main psychoactive compound produced by more than 200 species of fungi called *psilocybin mushrooms.* A typical psilocybin experience lasts between two to six hours, causing euphoria, hallucinations, changes in perception, and mystical and spiritual experiences. One unique feature is the experience of the passage of time; minutes can seem like hours.

During a positive experience, one can feel a deep connection to others, nature, and the universe. A negative experience can cause intense fear, nausea, panic attacks, and paranoia. The meaning of the word *entheogen* ("the god within"), means mushrooms are revered as powerful spiritual sacraments that provide access to sacred worlds, a sense of contact with a "transcendent other," reflecting a deeper understanding of the connectedness with the earth and the mysteries of nature. When used in small group community settings, psilocybin can enhance self-awareness, group cohesion, and a deeper connection to the social world.

Clinical Research – In 2019, the FDA granted Breakthrough Therapy Designation for psilocybin-assisted psychotherapy for treatment- resistant depression and major depressive disorders. There are also implications for the treatment of anxiety and addiction disorders.

Psilocybin has been a subject of preliminary research since the early 1960s, when the Harvard Psilocybin Project evaluated the therapeutic value to treat personality disorders. Since the early twenty-first century, research has focused on anxiety, major depression, and addiction disorders, showing evidence that psilocybin can induce molecular and cellular adaptations related to neuroplasticity, which potentially underlies the therapeutic benefits of psilocybin and the psychedelics. Neuroplasticity is the ability of neural networks in the brain to change through growth and reorganization. It is when the brain is rewired to function in a way that differs from how it previously functioned. These changes range from individual neuron pathways making new connections, to systematic adjustments of cortical remapping.

Some of the most important research in the clinical implications of psilocybin has been under the direction of Roland Griffiths et al. (2018, 2016, 2006) at the *Center for Psychedelic and Consciousness Research* at *Johns Hopkins University*. In Melbourne, Australia, the *Psychae Institute* is dedicated to developing psychedelic therapies as registered medical treatments for the treatment of mental disorders, especially the use of psilocybin in the treatment of depression. Non-profit *Usona Institute* and for-profit *COMPASS Pathways* are providing key research for the therapeutic use of psilocybin.

LSD-25 (Lysergic Acid Diethylamide)

Street Name – Acid, Uncle Sid, blotter, Lucy, and Alice.

History – LSD was first synthesized in 1938 by Albert Hoffman (1906–2008), who accidentally discovered LSD as a young Swiss chemist while working to develop pharmaceuticals in a Sandoz Pharmaceutical lab. Hoffman was seeking a drug to enhance circulation in the body and shelved the drug when it proved ineffective as a medicine but after five years, on a premonition, he resynthesized LSD and, after accidentally ingesting a small quantity, he experienced a powerful transpersonal experience. In 1947, Sandoz marketed LSD as Delysid, a psychiatric drug, sending it to labs worldwide to discover uses but withdrew it from circulation in 1966 after the Delysid received bad press with the unregulated use outside of clinical research trials.

By the mid-1960s, as Owsley Stanley established the first major underground LSD laboratory as the counterculture in San Francisco adopted the use of hallucinogenic drugs, especially LSD. In 1964, the *Merry Pranksters*, a loose group that developed around novelist Ken Kesey, sponsored *acid trips*, which involved taking LSD accompanied by light shows, film projection, and discordant, improvised music known as the *psychedelic symphony*. The Pranksters helped popularize LSD use through their road trips across America in a psychedelically decorated converted school bus memorialized in Tom Wolfe's (2008) *Electric Kool-Aid Acid Test*.

In San Francisco's Haight-Ashbury neighborhood, brothers Ron and Jay Thelin opened the *Psychedelic Shop* to promote safe use of LSD, which in the early 1960s was still legal in California. The Psychedelic Shop helped to further popularize LSD in the Haight and made the neighborhood the unofficial capital of the hippie counterculture in the United States. In October 1966, in Golden Gate Park, hundreds of attendees took LSD in unison at the *Love Pageant Rally* organized by Ron Thelin to protest California's newly adopted ban on LSD. Although the Psychedelic Shop closed after barely a year-and-a-half in business, its role in popularizing LSD left the historic importance of LSD during the American cultural revolution of the 1960s and 1970s (Davis, 2015)

A notable number of prominent individuals have publicly shared their LSD experiences ranging from the poet W. H. Auden to co-founder of Apple Steve Jobs, who described taking LSD as the most profound experience of his life (Bosker, 2011). Some of the music of the Beatles was a result of experimentation with LSD. Beatle Paul McCartney stated LSD inspired *Day Tripper* and *Lucy in the Sky with Diamonds,* which spelled out L-S-D (Mickelson, 1998).

Although he acknowledged his use of LSD, John Lennon said the fact that *Lucy in the Sky with Diamonds* spelled out LSD was a coincidence because the song was inspired by a picture drawn by his son, Julian (Sheff, 2000).

Typical Routes of Administration – Historically, LSD solutions were first sold on sugar cubes, but practical considerations forced a change to tablet form. After tablets came "computer acid" or "blotter paper LSD," typically made by dipping a preprinted sheet of blotting paper into an LSD/

water/alcohol solution. LSD will typically be delivered on small pieces of blotter paper tabs in which the LSD is diffused. It may also be provided in liquid or pill form or diffused into a sugar cube.

Effects – LSD is extremely potent, with psychoactive doses being in the microgram rather than milligram range of other psychedelics. even the smallest dosage can cause a dramatic transpersonal experience. When ingested, depending on the dosage, an LSD experience can last between 8 to 12 hours. As a long-lasting hallucinogen, LSD can induce intense introspection and euphoria as well as anxiety, paranoia, and delusions. LSD is the prototypic classical psychedelic used mainly for recreational, transpersonal, and spiritual purposes. It is estimated about 10 percent of the people in the United States have used LSD at some point in their lives (Coleman, 2017).

Clinical Research – Implications for the treatment of alcoholism, depression, and terminal illnesses.

The Pharmacology of LSD: A Critical Review (Hentzen & Passie, 2010) provides a comprehensive review of psychological and pharmacological effects of LSD from more than 3,000 experimental and clinical studies, with many more referenced.

Mescaline (3,4,5-trimethoxyphenethylamine)

Street Name – San Pedro or Peyote Cactus.

History – A psychedelic compound found in a variety of cacti, including peyote and San Pedro cacti, was first discovered in 1897 by German chemist Arthur Heffner. Mescaline became of more interest to the modern world because of the capacity to synthesize and replicate the effects of pharmacological substances outside the natural setting where the drug was naturally grown.

Depending on cultural perspective and history, peyote and mescaline are related but not synonymous. Mescaline is an inert chemical substance, while San Pedro peyote is a living, succulent plant that indigenous people in Mexico have used for at least 5,700 years. Oral traditions exist like the "Peyote Women," who fell asleep on a peyote plant and saved her brothers during war by a dream of their whereabouts (Dyck & Gurschler, 2021).

In his autobiography, *The Doors of Perception*, Aldus Huxley (1963) popularized the modern view of mescaline by referring to what the poet William Blake called opening the doors of perception to a new reality. Huxley believed that mescaline opened the doors to transpersonal existence usually known only to mystics and a handful of visionaries. Because of his mystical and spiritual mescaline experiences, Huxley questioned the *psychotomimetic paradigm* that psychedelics modeled a psychotic process (see below).

Typical Routes of Administration – Mescaline is taken in a variety of ways depending on what form of the drug is being used. Traditional peyote is taken by ingesting dried ground cactus powder or in a brewed tea of the cactus flesh. These parts of the plant, commonly referred to as buttons, are extracted from the roots. The root is sometimes brewed into a tea. If someone is taking synthetic mescaline produced in a lab, it will most often come in the form of a pill that is swallowed. There are also reports of people injecting liquid mescaline directly into their bloodstream, though those cases are rare. San Pedro peyote is much more commonly used due to its faster, easier cultivation.as peyote is very slow growing and has sustainability issues.

Effect – The effect of mescaline peaks in about an hour and lasts from 8 to 14 hours, although the use of mescaline as a sacrament can last for days. Like other psychedelics, mescaline alters states of consciousness, but uniquely produces dramatic visual hallucinations.

Clinical Research – Because psychedelics have been illegal and the long duration of the experience, clinical research is limited for evaluation. There are implications for the use of mescaline to treat addiction and depression. Native Americans have utilized mescaline to treat addiction (Pollan, 2018).

MDMA (3,4-Methylenedioxymethamphetamine)

Street Name – Ecstasy and E, Molly.

History – MDMA was first developed by Merck Pharmaceutical in 1912, but never distributed. In 1970, the compound became a popular adjunct to psychotherapy after it was synthesized by Bay Area chemist Alexander "Sasha" Shulgin for its empathogenic effect, the ability of therapists to develop empathy and a strong positive transference toward their clients (Pollan, 2018). In the 1980s, the drug became known in the rave scene.

Concerned by the abuse, in 1986, the federal government made MDMA a Schedule I drug, declaring it a dangerous drug of abuse with no scientifically based medical purpose. MDMA works differently from the classic psychedelics because MDMA belongs to the substitute amphetamine classes of drugs, but like the psychedelics has stimulant and hallucinatory effects.

Typical Routes of Administration – MDMA is taken as a capsule, tablet, swallowed in liquid form or by snorting the powder.

Effects – MDMA peaks in 30 to 45 minutes and can last three to six hours (Freye, & Levy, 2010). MDMA users report a sense of well-being, happiness, self-confidence, empathy, intimacy, inner peace, heightened sexuality, and a significant reduction in anxiety (Landriscina, 1995). Short-term adverse effects include grinding of the teeth, blurred vision, sweating, and a rapid heartbeat. Extended use can lead to addiction, memory problems, paranoia, and difficulty sleeping (Greer & Tolbert, 1990). Deaths have been reported in party environments due to increased body temperature and dehydration. Following use, individuals often feel depressed and tired for a few days because of serotonin depletion (Nida, 2020).

Clinical Research – In 2017, MDMA was designated by the FDA as a *Breakthrough Therapy Designation* for post-traumatic stress disorder (PTSD).

The *Multidisciplinary Association for Psychedelic Studies* (MAPS), and its founder Rick Doblin, have been leading advocates for psychedelic and MDMA research, legalization, and psychedelic-assisted psychotherapy, for over 30 years. The FDA can fast-track MDMA clinical trials for approval, which could create the political environment for the approval of other psychedelics (Doblin, 2021).

Most significant is the discovery that MDMA may reawaken the *critical period* in the brain to treat not only PTSD but other mental disorders. Critical period is the time when the brain is most sensitive to learning the reward value of social behaviors. It appears MDMA reopens the critical period, which could explain why MDMA has been successful in treating people with PTSD because it helps strengthen the psychotherapeutic bond with a psychotherapist (Nardou, Lewis, Rothhaas, et al. 2019). It also lowers activity in the amygdala, the fear center of the brain, which allows processing of traumatic memories without the feelings of being overwhelmed.

DMT (N, N-2-Dimethyltryptamine)

Street Name – DMT and Businessman Trip

History – DMT has been commonly used in indigenous Amazonian shamanic practices as an entheogen for spiritual and ritualistic practices. It is usually the main active constituent of the drink ayahuasca; however, ayahuasca is sometimes brewed with plants that do not product DMT. In modern Western history, DMT was first synthesized in 1931 by Berlin chemist Richard Manske. By 1965, after confusion about its botanical identification, French pharmacologist Jacques Poisson isolated DMT as a sole alkaloid from leaves provided by the Aguaruna Indians.

Typical Routes of Administration – DMT is typically smoked or vaporized, or oral ingested along with an MAOI (monoamine oxidase inhibitor).

Effects – An endogenous psychedelic in the human body DMT is a rapid-onset, intense, and short-acting psychedelic compound often referred in the 1960s as the "the businessman trip." This tryptamine molecule is found in plants and animals and, unlike LSD or psilocybin, DMT experiences are short lasting, with rapid onset lasting 6 to 20 minutes. Many DMT users report the ability to communicate with other intelligent life forms, symbolized by typical encounters with "DMT elves" or "machine elves," as popularized by Terrence McKenna.

Clinical Research – Implications for spiritual renewal and integration.

Rick Strassman (2001) describes DMT as the "spirit molecule" and summarizes DMT research in *DMT: The Spirit Molecule*. In a survey of responses of 2,561 people who had experienced DMT multiple times, Davis, Clifton, and Weaver (2020) found that most rated the DMT experience among the most meaningful, spiritual, and psychological lifetime experiences because of the positive changes in life satisfaction and purpose. More than half of those who identified as atheist prior to the DMT experiences no longer identified as atheist after the experience.

Figure 6.17

Ayahuasca

Street Name – Aya, Hoasca, and Yagé.

History – Native to the Amazon basin and used sacramentally by the indigenous peoples of South America for around 4,000 years (Labate & Cavnar, 2014). Ayahuasca is the hispanized spelling of a Quechuan word, *aya* meaning "spirit, soul, corpse, dead body"; and *Waska,* meaning "rope, woody vine, or liana." The native peoples believe ayahuasca cured the soul by symbolizing a deep introspective journey, which allowed the user to examine emotions and the "dead and soulless" ways of viewing the world.

In 2006, the US. Supreme Court affirmed the right of the Brazilian-based *Centro Espirita Beneficente Uniao do Vegetal* (UDV) Christian Church to use ayahuasca sacramentally during their spiritual rituals.

Typical Routes of Administration – Brewed tea that combines leaf and vine, which occurs by cooking ayahuasca in a pot for six to eight hours. The vine provides an MAOI, which makes the DMT from the leaf orally active. Ayahuasca is experienced differently from the other psychedelics because it causes bodily sensations that can result in nausea and purging; purging is viewed as a vital part of its healing properties.

Effect – The experience of the ayahuasca psychedelic often occurs in a group in the shamanistic tradition of singing magical *Icaro* songs, which include prayers with bells, rattles, incense, and invocations for a safe inner journey to the "grandmother who is the plant teacher ayahuasca" (Pollan, 2018). Ayahuasca typically peaks in one hour and lasts four to six hours.

Clinical Research – Implications for the treatment of depression.

The expansion of people interested in the religious and spiritual dimensions of ayahuasca has been accompanied by several studies describing the anti-depressive effects with the ingestion of ayahuasca (Osório, Sanches, Macedo et al, 2015, Labate & Cavnar, 2014). Research limitations result from the challenge of standardizing the brewed tea.

5MeO-DMT (5-methoxy- N,N-Dimethyltryptamine)

Street Name – 5, toad, and Bufo.

History – Found in South American plants and in the venom of the Sonoran Desert toad, the toad venom is a compound which has been used sacramentally in South America for generations. It was first synthesized in 1936 and made illegal in the United States in 2011.

Typical Routes of Administration – Most commonly smoked or vaporized, less commonly and only in synthetic form snorted or boofed, taken rectally.

Effect – The powerful, short acting psychedelic compound is more powerful than its better-known cousin DMT, with rapid onset of psychoactive effects lasting from 20 to 40 minutes.

Clinical Research – Implications for the treatment of anxiety, depression, PTSD, and treatment-resistant depression.

Although research is limited, a 2019 European study showed that a single inhalation improved life satisfaction and reduced anxiety, depression, and post-traumatic stress disorder symptoms (Uthang, Lancellotta, van Oorsouw, 2019). *5-MeO-DMT* is being evaluated in Ireland by biopharmaceutical company *GH Research* for the potential therapeutic value for treatment-resistant depression (GH Research, 2021).

The Four Historic Psychedelic Periods

The Four Historic Psychedelic Periods

The psychedelic movement is divided into four periods that include the psychotomimetic, the psycholytic, the underground, and the renaissance. The psychotomimetic period attempted, beyond the traditional medical and psychological models, to use the psychedelics to further the understanding of psychosis and serious mental illness. In the psycholytic period, the psychedelics provided another way to explore the unconscious in psychodynamic psychotherapy. After the psychedelics became illegal, research and clinical practice continued during the underground period. The current psychedelic renaissance is based on learning from the past, assuring quality research and developing approved psychedelic-assisted psychotherapy treatment models.

Psychotomimetic Period – Psychedelics and Psychosis

Albert Hoffman accidentally discovered LSD by synthesizing the molecules in alkaloids produced by *ergot*. Ergot is a fungus that can infect grain and is occasionally associated with madness caused by consuming bread. During the *Salem Witch* Trials ergot was blamed for causing madness and witchcraft. As it turned out Hofmann discovered that ingesting just 0.25 milligram of LSD would make LSD one of the most powerful psychoactive agents ever discovered. The astounding findings of Hofmann led to the development of brain science in the1950s and the discovery of serotonin, the endogenous chemical which activates receptors in the brain and important for the treatment of depression and other mental disorders.

Initially, work in the psychedelics focused on replicating psychosis. During the *psychotomimetic period,* LSD became known as a psychotomimetic drug because it was believed it mimicked psychosis by breaking down the ego and the ability to function rationally (Osmond, 1957). Initially, Sandoz marketed the drug as Delysid in the hope that LSD could explain the chemical basis for serious mental illness, especially schizophrenia. During the early 1950s, it was common practice for many physicians to take new investigative drugs to understand their clinical value. The hope was that by taking LSD, physicians would develop greater empathy toward those that struggled with psychosis (Pollan, 2018).

By the 1940s, the leftist government in Saskatchewan, Canadian, province had developed the first publicly funded healthcare system, which in 1966 became the model for the national healthcare system of Canada. *Humphrey Osmond*, a British-born psychiatrist practicing in the open-minded *St. George Hospital* in Saskatchewan, believed that LSD provided new hope for understanding mental illness from his own experience with psychotomimetic drugs, which he believed caused the doctor to "…enter the illness and see with the madman's eyes, hear with his ears, and feel with his skin" (Osmond, 1952, p. 2). However, from data analysis from volunteer LSD sessions, Osgood and other researchers discovered that although some psychotic symptoms occurred, many volunteers had stronger transcendental experiences, feelings of being united with humanity, viewed themselves differently, experienced an increase in sensitivity to others, and "felt closer to God" (Novak, 1997). Although these findings led to the abandonment of the psychotomimetic approach to LSD, there remains an interest in understanding the similarities between the psychedelic and psychotic state (Fischman, 1983).

In the 1990s the FDA reopened the door for psychedelic approval because DMT being the only endogenous psychedelic in the human body might provide insight into psychosis and schizophrenia. The small trial by psychiatrist Rick Strassman at the *University of New Mexico* was the first federally sanctioned experimentation with psychedelics since the 1970s and did not provide a clear connection between high levels of DMT in the body and psychosis (Doblin, 2021).

Spiritual Emergency Counseling

Stanislav Grof and his wife, Christina Grof (1989), developed the term *spiritual emergency* and created a network of therapists available during experiences of non-ordinary states of consciousness defined as changes in perception, mental and emotional disturbance, and psychosomatic symptoms. Unlike traditional psychiatry, which might diagnose these experiences as psychotic, the Grofs believed that mental health professionals should be trained to consider these experiences as a reflection of a transpersonal or spiritual crisis rather than symptoms of traditionally diagnosed psychiatric problems. The spiritual crisis is assessed by therapists on a continuum that ranges from mild, the gradual unfolding of spiritual awareness with no loss of psychological functioning, to a severe form of a spiritual emergency that is overwhelming and disrupts functioning in all aspects of daily life.

The Grofs collected research on typical psychiatric symptoms often misdiagnosed by traditional mental health professionals as psychotic because of the lack of understanding of Eastern thought. These "psychotic" symptoms were often related to mystical experiences, kundalini awakenings, shamanistic initiatory rites, and paranormal experiences with the divine. According to the Grofs, spiritual emergencies if properly understood provide an opportunity for psychological healing and growth. Psychiatric medication becomes harmful when a spiritual emergency was not differentiated from other psychiatric symptoms because it interferes in the natural process of spiritual renewal. The *Diagnostic and Statistical Manual of Mental Disorders* (DSM-5) now acknowledges a *Religious or Spiritual Problem* (V62.89) as a focus of clinical attention, but not as a mental disorder.

Psycholytic Period – Psychedelics and the Unconscious

Systems of Condensed Experience (COEX)

Because of the findings in the 1950s, during the 1960s, interest grew to assess the psychotherapeutic value of LSD. The term *psycholytic*, meaning "mind loosening," was coined by English psychiatrist Ronald Sandison.

During the psycholytic period, psychedelics were used to uncover unconscious material by giving low doses of psychedelics to relax ego defenses without overwhelming the conscious mind. This approach viewed psychedelics as an aid to talk therapy because the client was intact and could recall what was discussed. The psycholytic approach fit nicely into psychoanalysis because it expanded access to the unconscious beyond dreams and free association.

Stanislav Grof, a founder of transpersonal psychology and a trained psychoanalyst, provided an early framework for understanding human consciousness, challenging Western beliefs about the psyche. He became a leading figure in transpersonal psychology because of his observation and scholarly description of clinical experiences with thousands of clients who viewed psychedelic psychotherapy as a catalyst for unconscious exploration (Grof, 1976).

Grof distinguished two modes of consciousness: the *hylotropic* and the *holotropic*. A hylotropic state, the state of interest to traditional psychology, related to normal daily consciousness. The holotropic state was important to transpersonal psychology because of its relationship to a feeling of wholeness and a totality of existence. The holotropic *state* was characteristic of nonordinary states of meditation and spiritual practices which emerged during the Axial Age like the Buddhist conception of *namarupa*, the awareness of separation of the mental and physical; the physical being temporal and not identity, and mental the awareness of the loss of identity and the realization of the ultimate reality of "emptiness," and the Hindu concept of Atman-Brahman, discovery of the divine and the true nature of the self.

During the psycholytic period, Stanislav Grof (1973) found that under moderate doses of LSD, clients could quickly establish a transference, uncover childhood traumas, and experience repressed unconscious emotions. After a comprehensive research review of 2,600 therapeutic sessions, Grof developed *Systems of Condensed Experience (COEX)*, a multilayered model of the unconscious regarding the psychotherapeutic effects of LSD. His research was in alignment

Symbols of Transpersonal Psychology 331

with Otto Rank (1957) because Rank had discovered the importance of birth trauma and offered explanations of mythological, spiritual, and religious symbols connected to perinatal dynamics (Grof, 2015). Grof concluded from his research that psychotherapy aided by LSD allowed individuals to recall the circumstances of their birth, especially when it was a difficult birth (Pollan, 2018).

Grof believed the COEX system explained and even predicted the clinical changes that occurred under the effects of LSD, arguing that psychoanalysis did not adequately activate the transpersonal levels of the unconscious. The levels activated during psychedelic psychotherapy included the sensory barrier and the recollective barrier, the perinatal matrices where ego death occurred, and the transpersonal dimensions of the psyche. Working through sensory barriers and recollective barriers, memories were relived with the corresponding feelings, affect, and thematic content that became conscious between psychedelic sessions. These memories were crucial to *psycholytic psychotherapy* because during therapy sessions these unconscious psychological conflicts and traumas emerged as a single condensed COEX process.

The COEX process explained the LSD experience of death and rebirth, and the emergence of universal themes of death, dying, aging, physical pain, and the suffering of all humanity. Sometimes an actual feeling of dying occurred, which led many clients to describe the trauma of their natural birth and the experience of a rebirth. Grof developed four *Basic Perinatal Matrices* (BPM), which explained the perinatal level of the unconscious that provides a way to symbolize a psychedelic experience (Yensen & Dryer, 1996).

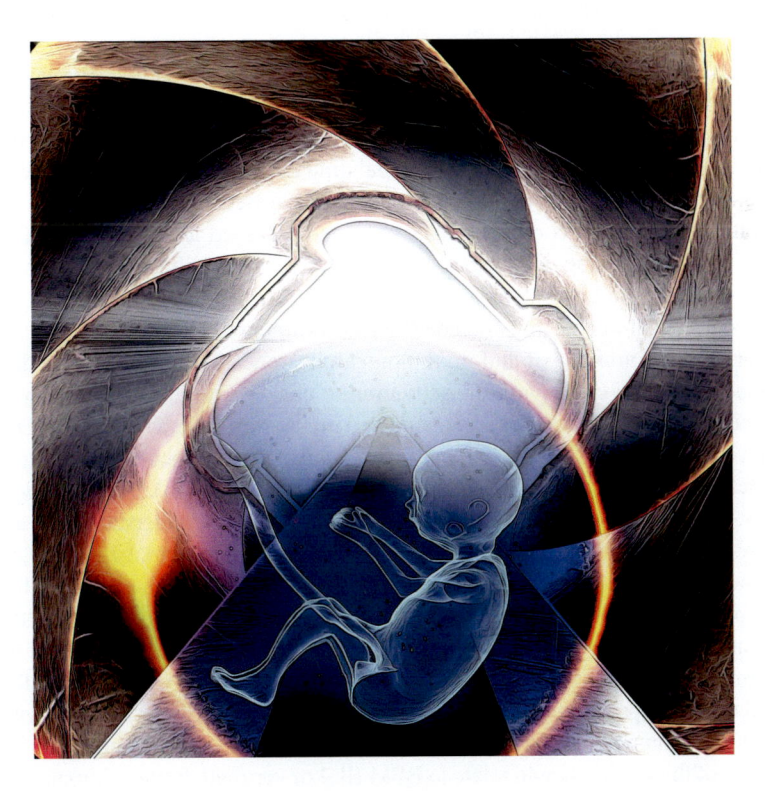

Figure 6.18

The COEX Process

BPM I The symbiotic unity of the maternal organism symbolized by a baby in utero with feelings of sacred and spiritual wholeness.

BPM II Being caught in the onset of labor symbolized by entering a long tunnel where there was no escape. At an emotional level, being in an existential crisis with feelings of guilt, inadequacy, anxiety, and an overwhelming feeling of loneliness and hopelessness.

BPM III The feeling of fighting for survival with a corresponding new feeling that the experience was being meaningful, symbolized by "seeing light at the end of the tunnel." There were often experiences of sexual excitement, revolting contact with the body parts, and sadomasochistic and demonic visions. Grof believed that a death-rebirth struggle was at the core of psychopathology.

BPM IV The buildup of tension, pain, and anxiety became released after the unsuccessful attempt to stop the process because of the feelings of impending annihilation. The result was an experience of an ego death that destroyed all previous reference points of conscious existence. This was symbolized by rebirth and an emancipation from the ego; a forgiveness of previous sins; and a feeling of love, justice, self-respect, and a renewed connection to humanity.

Grof viewed the LSD experience as a recapitulation of the merging of the biological and psychological birth experience. On a spiritual-philosophical dimension, BPM I was the intrauterine existence of cosmic unity. BPM II was the first stage of uterine contractions before the cervix dilated and the experience of "no-exit" and feelings of an existential crisis. BPM III was the passage through the birth canal and the death-rebirth struggle. BPM IV was the separation from the body of the mother and the ego death and rebirth experience.

After the final perinatal resolution, subjective reality continued to expand beyond the ego. Grof (1985) called these experiences transpersonal dimensions of the psyche, dividing transpersonal experiences into two categories. One category of transpersonal experiences expanded ego boundaries into objective or "consensus reality" which included identification with plants, the earth, and the cosmic universe. Ego expansion also included identification with ancestors, past incarnations, and evolutionary memories. The second category of transpersonal experiences were non-Western phenomena that included spirit communication, out-of-body experiences, telepathic, paranormal, archetypal and mythological awareness, encounters with deities, intuitive understanding of universal symbols, activation of chakra and kundalini energy, consciousness of the universal mind, and the supracosmic and metacosmic mind (Yensen & Dryer, 1996).

Grof believed that the COEX system consisted of many layers of unconscious material and was not a neatly defined step-by-step psychotherapeutic process (Grof, 2015). For theoretical and practical purposes, it was important that the psychedelic psychotherapist understand how a therapeutic session related to the personality and psychological problems of the client. Ultimately, a successful LSD experience depended on a positive transference relationship and therapeutic alliance, since memories of physical and psychological traumas from infancy, childhood, and adulthood would typically surface during psychedelic psychotherapy sessions. Beyond psychological traumas, the COEX system described a connection to the memories of birth, so it was essential for therapists to understand the BPM process. For instance, if the theme of a COEX session was victimization, the focus of the session would relate to BPM II. If the theme was a powerful adversary or sexual abuse, the focus of the session would relate to BPM III. For very satisfying spiritual, transpersonal, and fulfilling experiences, the focus would be on BPM I and IV (Grof, 2015).

Underground Period – Psychedelics and Government Oversight

Comprehensive Drug Prevention and Control Act (S. Res. 54, 1970)

One of the most dramatic examples of psycholytic psychotherapy was *Shivitti: A Vison,* written anonymously with the pseudonym Ka-tzetnik 135633 (Katzetnik, 1989). The book described five LSD sessions in the Netherlands led by Jan Bastiaans (1917–1997), a Dutch psychiatrist, in which a client relived his experiences in the *Auschwitz Concentration Camp*. Bastiaans found that LSD treatment alleviated 30 years of depression, survivors' guilt, and posttraumatic stress disorder.

Jan Bastiaans (1917–1997), a Dutch psychiatrist, presents a symbol of the early capitulation by the medical and psychiatric community to political pressure even when LSD was showing efficacy in the treatment of many mental disorders, especially PTSD. Bastiaans once famous in the Netherlands for helping Holocaust survivors, became ostracized by his medical and psychiatric peers and died a broken man after working underground for many years to keep the hope of psychedelic psychotherapy alive. Bastiaans symbolizes the dangers of the Underground Period because many therapists risked their reputations and professional careers by continuing to treat clients with psychedelics. In the case of Bastiaans, amidst the threat of jail or other legal problems, he continued to treat survivors of the holocaust with LSD.

Amidst the American cultural revolution and the Vietnam War, on October 24, 1968, with the passage of the *Staggers-Dodd Public Law 90-639*, psychedelics were outlawed in the United States. The establishment had connected LSD to the counterculture movement, and politicians became worried not only about the medical, but also the political, impact on Americans.

In 1970, to fight illegal drug use and to initiate a national *War on Drugs* campaign, Congress passed the *Comprehensive Drug Prevention and Control Act* (S. Res. 54, 1970). This act created a "drug schedule" classifying drugs into five categories for appropriate and safe medical use as well as the potential for drug abuse and dependence. LSD, psilocybin, psilocin, peyote, cannabis, and MDMA were classified under Schedule I, the most dangerous for abuse and drugs that had not yet attained mainstream acceptance for safe or therapeutic use. After 1970, clinical research and practice went underground.

Cannabis is still considered a federally illegal Schedule I drug although in most states upon the recommendation of a medical doctor the medical use of marijuana is legal. The *Rohrabacher-Farr Amendment* prohibits federal prosecution of individuals complying with state medical cannabis laws (Lopez, 2014). The amendment, approved in 2014, was the first time Congress voted to protect cannabis patients. An increasing number of states have legalized the recreational and medicinal use of cannabis.

Cannabis creates psychoactive states of euphoria, relaxation, and altered states of consciousness with many users reporting mystical and spiritual experiences. Cannabis has held sacred status in several religions and has served, like the hallucinogens, as an entheogen, a drug used in religious, shamanic, and spiritual contexts, especially centuries ago in the Indian subcontinent during the Hindu Vedic period.

The Hindu god Shiva has been described as a cannabis user, known as the *Lord of Ghang* (Courtwright, 2001). Cannabis is consumed in many ways including smoking, with a vaporizer, in cannabis tea, in edibles, in an alcoholic cannabis concentrate and in capsules. When smoked, onset of effects can be felt in minutes and when ingested, can take up to 90 minutes. Although cannabis may cause transpersonal experiences, it is not currently perceived as a possible psychotherapeutic medication. In fact, with its widespread recreational use, cannabis has become, like alcohol, another socially accepted drug. Because of its illegality, research has been limited but primary findings indicate that use can increase anxiety, panic attacks, impaired attention,

334 *Symbols of Transpersonal Psychology*

and memory and psychotic symptoms. According to the *Diagnostic and Statistical Manual of Mental Disorders* (DSM 5) about 9 percent who experiment with marijuana develop a cannabis-related mental disorder, compared to 20 percent for cocaine, 23 percent for alcohol and 68 percent for nicotine (Curran, Freeman, & Mokrysz et al, 2016).

Figure 6.19

The underground period was also mired in the failed War on Drugs. In an interview with John Ehrlichman, the Watergate co-conspirator, Dan Baum (2016) wrote in a *Harper's Magazine* article in 2016 that Ehrlichman acknowledged that the Nixon administration had two enemies, the antiwar left and the Black community. Nixon understood there was no legal authority to control either, so their strategy turned to associate hippies with marijuana and the Blacks with heroin, and then criminalize both heavily to disrupt their communities by arresting their leaders, raid their homes, and vilify both groups every night on the evening news. Ehrlichman admitted it was all politics because they knew they were lying about the dangers of drugs.

After the illegalization and politicization of psychedelics along with the Tim Leary period, psychedelic research continued underground and laid the foundation for the psychedelic renaissance in the twenty-first century. The underground psychedelic period included many of the most famous names before the illegalization of psychedelics like Cristina and Stanislav Grof and Albert Hubbard. In 1997, Leo Zeff (1912–1988), a San Francisco bay area Jungian psychologist, left a posthumous and anonymous, account of his work entitled *The Secret Chef*. This work best describes the underground period and explains how psychedelic psychotherapeutic work continued after the FDA made psychedelics illegal (Pollan, 2018). During the underground period, experimentation was done by a wide variety of therapists from many different therapeutic perspectives, including psychoanalysis, Jungian analysis, and the humanistic-oriented Gestalt therapists. Zeff found, like so many other researchers, that life-changing transpersonal experiences often occurred after only one LSD session.

During the underground period, the federal government law enforcement agencies showed no signs of prosecuting those practicing psychedelic assisted psychotherapy. In 2004, after permission from Zeff, Myron Stolaroff (2004), a close friend and research colleague, published *The Secret Chef Revealed* that disclosed Zeff as the secret chef. Zeff believed it was imperative that the underground therapeutic guides had their own personal experience with psychedelics, abandoned their analytic detachment, avoided any therapeutic manipulation, and "trusted the process" (Pollan, 2018). Stolaroff argued that the underground therapeutic guides, as well as the research in the 1950s and 1960s, were the leading reasons for the reemergence of psychedelic research in the 1980s.

Bioenergetic Analysis and Holotropic Breathwork

Theodor Reich was one of the first psychoanalysts to emphasize the importance of breathing. He believed that restricted breathing was a way to control uncomfortable feelings, anxiety, indication of rigid unconscious defense mechanisms, and a resistance to change (Reich, 1942). To overcome unconscious resistance, Reich developed *Character Analysis Vegetotherapy*, which utilized breathing to increase feeling and control anxiety. His student, Alexander Lowen (1910–2008) created *Bioenergetic Analysis,* a somatic mind-body psychotherapy that included basic body exercises and emphasized the importance of breath to create the energy for a more vital and spiritual life (Lowen, 1975).

Stanislav Grof spent 13 years at the Easlen Institute and, as the psychedelics became illegal, developed *Holotropic Breathwork.* Holotropic is rooted in the Greek *holos,* meaning "whole," and *trepain,* meaning "moving toward," moving toward wholeness. Holotropic Breathwork was an outgrowth of his psychedelic work during the psycholytic period and provided a way, without drugs, to model the effect of the psychedelics after psychedelics became illegal.

Grof and his wife, Cristina (2010), developed this technique to create states of transcendental consciousness utilizing the meditation practices of the Buddhists who attend to breath as a guide to "spiritual awakening" and mindfulness moment-to-moment awareness. In the practice of the Daoist *tai chi chuan,* breathing was important to increase and balance the *chi,* chi being the life force that balances body, mind, and spirit. In the Hindu meditation practice of *pranayama* and in the yogic tradition, hyperventilation and holding the breath enlivened and healed the body. Holotropic Breathwork utilized these and aspects of the psychedelics without the drug, because Grof believed that Holotropic Breathwork changes consciousness by a combination of faster breathing, evocative music, and energy-releasing bodywork (Grof, 2015). The sessions are conducted by a trained facilitator in a pleasant room, with the "breather" lying on a mat paired with a "sitter" who provides support and safety throughout the process. The technique usually lasts for one to three hours and often ends with drawing a mandala, symbolizing the holotropic state of wholeness.

Psychedelic Renaissance Period – Psychedelics and Clinical Efficacy

Psychedelic-Assisted Psychotherapy

Psychedelic-Assisted Psychotherapy emerged in the 1990s as a new generation of researchers and clinicians began to see the clinical efficacy with several mental disorders mentioned throughout this chapter. The term "assisted" is emphasized because the process of psychotherapy is the key factor to the success of a psychedelic experience. Unlike traditional psychotherapy, where the drug is the medication, in psychedelic-assisted psychotherapy, it is the psychotherapy that is the "medication," not the psychedelic drug (Doblin, 2021).

The foundation for an assisted psychedelic psychotherapy session is based on the theory of *set* and *setting* developed by Timothy Leary and Al Hubbard, which describes the inner and outer environments necessary for a productive psychedelic experience. The *set* is the psychological mind-set and expectations of the client, while the *setting* is the environment in which the psychedelic experience takes place. Like all psychotherapy settings, the environment needs to feel safe and therapeutic. Unlike most other psychotherapy sessions, clients need a comfortable place to recline and wear a mask while listening to music. The *mindset* is evaluated prior to a psychedelic session by a face-to-face mental health assessment.

Figure 6.20

Understanding future resistance from third-party payors, research indicates psychedelic sessions should ideally have two therapists, one male and one female, for a session that can last several hours (Doblin, 2021). Although problematic and not ideal, research is being initiated to reduce cost by the development of group-assisted psychedelic psychotherapy (Doblin, 2021). Also, there will need to be a conversation about whether the clinical training of therapists include their own psychedelic experience.

Psychedelic-assisted psychotherapy can be practiced from all the major psychotherapeutic schools, including psychodynamic, behavioral, humanistic-existential, and transpersonal. No matter the approach, it is important that therapists understand *symbolic communication* because the psychedelic world speaks "another language" that transcends the ego and the rational mind. In this regard, therapists need to be comfortable with hallucinations, delusions, temporary psychosis, and the demonic, which can emerge and key to the healing process.

The *Mystical Experience Questionnaire* (MEQ) was developed by Walter Pahnke and William Richards in the 1960s to assess whether a volunteer in a psychedelic trial had undergone a mystical experience. Although there are several inventories and questionaries, the MEQ is one of the most frequently used questionnaires in psychedelic clinical work and research (MacDonald & Friedman, 2015). The M Scale is a 30-item instrument designed to assess the phenomenological aspects of mystical experiences which includes internal and external unity, transcendence of time and space, ineffability and paradoxicality, a sense of sacredness, the noetic quality, and a deeply felt positive mood (Pollan, 2018). A 2012 study provided "initial evidence" of the validity, reliability, and factor structure of the MEQ (MacLean, Leoutsakos, Johnson & Griffiths, 2012).

With approval of psychedelic-assisted psychotherapy imminent, despite many unknowns, psychedelic training programs already exist and are emerging. Some notables include the *California of Integral Studies,* which, in 2015, started a formal in-person or online nine-month training program called *Certificate in Psychedelic-Assisted Therapies and Research.* The Integrative Psychiatry Institute offers an online *Psychedelic Therapy Certificate Program.* MAPS, seeking approval for MDMA, offers a *MDMA-Assisted Therapy Training Program.* Drug sponsors, *Usona Institute*, *COMPASS Pathways,* and various universities are developing training programs to prepare clinicians for clinical trials and eventual psychotherapeutic practice. Without a strong psychologically vibrant Transpersonal Division in the APA, the role of psychology and the APA in the development of training and clinical standards for the practice of psychedelic-assisted psychotherapy remains unclear.

Emancipatory Opportunities in Transpersonal Psychology

Carefully Consider Psychedelic-Assisted Psychotherapy

For the most benefit, do not treat psychedelics as a recreational drug. Psychedelics can create life-changing transpersonal as well as extremely frightening experiences.

Because of the variability of their effects due to mindset and setting, best to experience psychedelics with an experienced licensed professional who prior to a psychedelic session performs a mental status examination, the assessment of your mindset and intentions and expectations. Also, assure the therapist provides an appropriate setting, a safe and therapeutic environment. Check professional qualifications and how the psychedelic was procured.

Consider Holotropic Breathwork

If concerned about the psychedelics, consider Holotropic Breathwork, developed in part to create transpersonal experiences without psychedelic drugs.

Advocate for an APA Transpersonal Division

There are many reasons for Transpersonal Psychology, the Fourth Force in Psychology, to have its own division in the APA. One major reason, as the trend toward the legalization of psychedelics occurs in the years ahead, is that it is important that the APA have an educated position based on research and clinical experience from psychedelic experts. As public policy develops for psychedelic best treatment practices, it is essential that psychologists are "at the table" as scope of practice, training and education, and insurance reimbursement, among many other issues are determined.

Consider Spirituality as a Component of Mental Health Issues

Christina and Stanislav Grof believe many diagnosed psychiatric problems are spiritual emergencies because mental health professionals are not trained in Eastern thought and often treat non-ordinary states of consciousness as pathological. The DSM 5 now recognizes Religious or Spiritual Problem (V62.89) as a focus of clinical attention and not a mental disorder. This consideration is particularly true in community mental health, where staff often confuse spirituality with religion. As with anyone with a major illness, individuals with serious mental illness frequently ask, "Why did this happened to me?" *Spiritual emergency counselors* can be found at: www.spiritualemergencecounseling.com.

Explore Yoga as a Spiritual Practice

Yoga is rooted in creating a higher consciousness, a way to situate the self in the transpersonal world beyond ego. Although a spiritual practice, most of Americans practice only the physical exercises of Hatha yoga. Consider the true purpose of Hatha yoga and explore Kundalini and Tantra yoga practices.

Consider Transpersonal Psychotherapy

Transpersonal therapists may not specifically advertise under "transpersonal psychotherapy"; however, transpersonal psychotherapists tend to be more comfortable with nontraditional therapeutic approaches placing a high value on spirituality and the exploration of the *Nature of Exceptional Human Experiences* (EHEs), near-death experiences (NDE), parapsychology, past-life therapy, and mystical and paranormal experiences. Transpersonal psychotherapists often view the body and somatic work as another vehicle for transpersonal experiences and the attainment of a higher state of consciousness. Examples include *perinatal experiences* (Grof, 1973), *body-shaping* practices (Maus, 1973) neuromuscular *Rolfing sessions*, (Rolf, 1990), the *spiritual body* (Ehrenfried 1956), *embodied consciousness* (Conrad, 1997), *authentic movement* (Adler, 2007), and *body-centered Hakomi method* (Kurtz, 1997).

Do a Vision Quest

Explore the wisdom of Native American culture and find a Native American shaman willing to do a vision quest to reconnect to your spiritual nature.

Complete an Astrological Chart

Although not considered scientific by most modern psychologists, astropsychologists have found psychological meaning and therapeutic value in astrology, particularly in the development of a personal astrological chart.

Consider Transcendental Meditation

To deal with the stresses of modern life, practice transcendental meditation. Explore the roots of transcendental meditation as a Vedic Hindu practice.

Be a Psychonaut

The Great History of Psychology

I always wanted to be an astronaut
Flying above the noise and chaos
Circling the earth again and again
In the quiet spaceless void
No longer attached to the earth
Finding the space to examine my beliefs
I hadn't been told the whole story.
Isn't history a fabulous view from afar
That has changed my life.
Can't wait to take another flight.
 - Jim Broderick (2022)

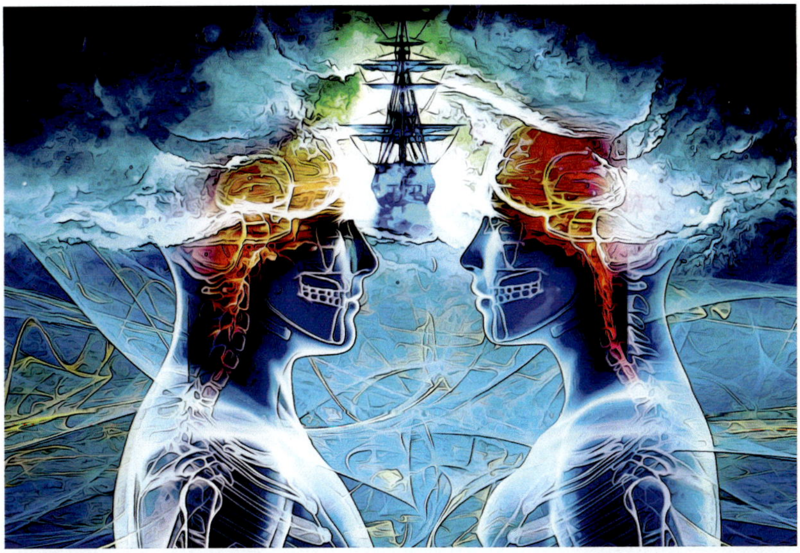

Figure 6.21

The term *psychonaut* has Greek origins, meaning "mind-sailor" or "sailor of the soul." Although often used in reference to the psychedelic movement, as the text ends, the term becomes the final symbol for you and the future of psychology. In space, the astronauts are removed from the stresses of daily life which offers the opportunity to gain a different perspective, to view human existence with a new vision. Inspired by this incredible experience astronauts are forever changed. Like the astronauts, the hope is that the text has provided "space" for new perspectives on psychological history and the power of symbol. But most importantly how you might have changed. Like the psychonaut open to becoming an active participant in exploring the creation of a better world.

QUESTIONS 6

6.1 *Describe the political, socioeconomic, and cultural influences which led to the development of transpersonal psychology.*

6.2 *Explain the difference between religious, spiritual, and transpersonal experiences.*

6.3 *Describe what Maslow means by "spiritual self-actualization."*

6.4 *Explain the impact of Timothy Leary on the psychedelic movement.*

6.5 *Describe how the Default Mode Network (DMN) provides an explanation for transpersonal experiences.*

6.6 *Explain how William James, Sigmund Freud, and Carl Jung inspired the transpersonal movement.*

6.7 *Describe what Ken Wilber means by integral psychology and perennial philosophy.*

6.8 *Explain the connection of the psychedelics to the Axial Age.*

6.9 *Describe trans-diagnostic efficacy and its impact on the treatment of mental disorders and the practice of psychiatry.*

6.10 *Explain the major developments that led to each of the four psychedelic periods.*

6.11 *Describe how the issue of medication is different in psychedelic-assisted psychotherapy.*

6.12 *Explain how yoga and meditation practices are rooted in Hindu and Buddhist thought.*

6.13 *Describe yourself as a psychonaut.*

Universal Meanings of Chapter Symbols

Figure 6.0:

Rick Doblin image source (September 21, 2022). In Wikipedia. https://en.wikipedia.org/wiki/Rick_Doblin

Maslow image source. http://www.celebriton.com/abraham_maslow/photo/a_photo_of_abraham_maslow

Timothy Leary image source. https://www.goodreads.com/photo/author/47718.Timothy_Leary

Stanislav Grof image source. http://picasaweb.google.com/dolboeb/Grof#5402598159399808466

Ken Wilber image source. https://dippnallsc.medium.com/choose-growth-c8eb10aa05ab

Albert Hofmann image source (August 24, 2022). In Wikipedia. https://en.wikipedia.org/wiki/Albert_Hofmann

Cristina Grof image source. http://centrostudipsicologiaeletteratura.org/2014/01/remembering-christina-grof-1941-2014/

Figure 6.1. Symbol of the exploration of the inner world.
Figure 6.2. Psychedelics creating the possibility of a new social order.
Figure 6.3. The need for spiritual renewal.
Figure 6.4. Mushrooms as a universal symbol of discovering a higher consciousness.

Figure 6.5. A transpersonal teacher.
Figure 6.6. Symbol of the effect of a spiritually unenlightened culture.
Figure 6.7. Spirituality as a biological instinct to feel fully human.
Figure 6.8. A divine transcendental consciousness which integrates body, heart, and mind.
Figure 6.9. The psychological effort needed to reach the highest peak of spiritual consciousness.
Figure 6.10. Art as a transpersonal experience.
Figure 6.11. The impact of the cosmos on human behavior.
Figure 6.12. The flow of energy that connects to the divine feminine.
Figure 6.13. The Hindu presence in modern mediation practices.
Figure 6.14. Harvesting a calm, reflective, alert, and luminous mind.
Figure 6.15. The mind's endless search to connect to a world beyond the ego.
Figure 6.16. A symbol of the ingestion of a psychedelic for a transcendental experience.
Figure 6.17. Search for meaning of symbols and images in psychedelic experiences.
Figure 6.18. The recapitulation of birth in an LSD experience.
Figure 6.19. Psychoactive drugs influence on religion and mythology.
Figure 6.20. "The therapeutic psychedelic couch".
Figure 6.21. Openness to explore all the possibilities of being human.

References

Aanstoos, C., Serlin, I. & Greening, T (2000). History of division 32 (Humanistic psychology) In D.A. Dewsbury (Ed.). *Unification through division: Histories of the divisions of the American psychological association* (Vol. V., pp. 85–112). Washington, D.C.: American Psychological Association.

Acker, L (2020, Nov. 4). Oregon becomes the first state to legalize psychedelic mushrooms. The Oregonian. Retrieved from https://www.oregonlive.com/politics/2020/11/oregon-becomes-first-state-to-legalize-psychedelic-mushrooms.html

Adler, J (2007). From autism to the discipline of authentic movement. In P. Pallaro (Ed.). *Authentic movement: moving the body, moving the self* (Vol. 2, pp. 24–31). Philadelphia, PA: Kingsley.

Akers, B.P., Ruiz, J.F., Piper, A. & Ruck, C.A (2011). A prehistoric mural in Spain depicting neurotropic psilocybe mushrooms? *Economic Botany*. 65(2), 121–128.

American Psychological Association (2002). *Guidelines on multicultural education, training, research, practice and organizational change for psychologists*. Washington, DC: American Psychological Association.

Anderson, A. (2006). *The great transformation*. New York, NY: Anchor Books.

Anonymous (2008, February 7). Maharishi Mahesh Yogi: Guru of transcendental meditation who used his association with the Beatles to create a highly profitable global movement, London Times. Retrieved from https://www.thetimes.co.uk/article/maharishi-mahesh-yogi-xdwdbpbrxcd

Arbel, K. (2017). *Early Buddhist meditation*. London: Routledge Press.

Assagioli, R. (1976). *Transpersonal inspiration and psychological mountain climbing*. New York, NY: Psychosynthesis Research Foundation.

Assagioli, R. (2012). *Psychosynthesis: A collection of basic writings*. Amherst, MA: The Synthesis Center, Inc. (Original work published 1965).

Aurobindo, S. (1996). *The synthesis of yoga: All life is yoga*. Twin Lakes, WI: Lotus Light Publications.

Badiner, A (Ed) (2015). *Zig zag Zen: Buddhism and psychedelics*. Santa Fe, NM: Synergetic Press.

Baer, R. (2003). Mindfulness training as a clinical intervention: A conceptual and empirical review. *Clinical Psychology: Science and Practice*. 10(2), 125–143.

Battista, J.R. (1996). Abraham Maslow and Roberto Assagioli pioneers of transpersonal psychology. In B.W. Scotton, A.B. Chinen, & J.R. Battista (Eds.). *Textbook of transpersonal psychiatry and psychology* (pp. 52–61). New York, NY: Basic Books.

Baum, D. (2016). Legalize it all: How to win the war on drugs. Harper's Magazine. Retrieved from https://harpers.org/archive/2016/04/legalize-it-all/

Bosker, B. (2011). The Steve Jobs reading list: Artists that made the man. The Huffpost. Retrieved December 21, 2011 https://www.huffpost.com/entry/the-steve-jobs-reading-list-the-books_n_1024021

Byck, R (Ed.) (1974). *Cocaine papers*. New York, NY: Stonehill Publishing.

Cahn, R. & Polich, J. (2006). Meditation states and traits: EEG, ERP, and neuroimaging studies. *Psychological Bulletin. 2*, 180–210

Campion, N. (2009). *A history of western astrology* (Vol. II). London: Continuum Books.

Carhart-Harris, R.L. et al (2012). Neural correlates of the psychedelic state as determined by fMRI studies with psilocybin. *Proceedings of the National Academy of Sciences of the United States of America. 109*(6), 2138–2143.

Carhart-Harris, R.L., Bolstridge, M. & Rucker, J. et al (2016). Psilocybin with psychological support for treatment resistant depression: An open-label feasibility study. *Lancet Psychiatry. 3*(7), 619–627.

Carhart-Harris, R.L., Kaelen, M. & Nutt, D.J. (2014). How do hallucinogens work on the brain. *American Psychologist. 27*(9), 662–665.

Carhart-Harris, R.L., Leech, R. & Hellyer, P.J., et al (2014). The entropic brain: A theory of conscious states informed by neuroimaging research with psychedelic drugs. *Frontiers in Human Neuroscience. 8*, 1–20.

Castaneda, C. (1968). *The teachings of Don Juan: A Yaqui way of knowledge*. New York, NY: Eagle's Trust.

Chinen, A. (1996). The emergence of transpersonal psychiatry. In B.W. Scotton, A.B. Chinen & J.R. Battista (Eds.). *Textbook of transpersonal psychiatry and psychology* (pp. 9–18). New York, NY: Basic Books.

Coleman, R. (2017). *Psychedelic psychotherapy: A user-friendly guide to drug- assisted psychotherapy*. Lafayette, CA: Transform Press

Combs, B. (2015). Transcend and include Ken Wilber's contribution to transpersonal psychology. In H.L. Friedman & G. Hartelius (Eds.). *The Wiley Blackwell handbook of transpersonal psychology* (pp. 166–186). Chichester, UK: John Wiley & Sons, Ltd.

Comprehensive Drag Abuse Prevention and Control Act of 1970, S. Res.54, 91st Cong. Rec. 584 (1970) enacted.

Conrad, E. (1997). Continuum. In D.H. Johnson (Ed.). *Groundwork: Narratives of embodiment* (pp. 61, 62). Berkeley, CA: North American Press.

Cortright, B. (2015). Integral psychology. In H.L. Friedman & G. Hartelius (Eds.). *The Wiley Blackwell handbook of transpersonal psychology* (pp. 155–165). Chichester, UK: John Wiley & Sons, Ltd.

Cotton, D.H.G. (1990). *Stress management: An integrated approach to therapy*. New York, NY: Brunner/Mazel.

Courtwright, D. (2001). *Forces of habit: Drugs and the making of the modern world*. Harvard University Press.

Crowley, M. (2019). *Secret drugs of Buddhism: Psychedelic sacraments and the origins of the Vajrayana*. Santa Fe, NM: Synergetic Press.

Curran, H.V., Freeman, T.P. & Mokrysz, C., et al (2016). Keep off the grass? Cannabis, cognition and addiction. *Nature Reviews. Neuroscience. 17*(5), 293–306.

Dalio, R. (2017). *Principles: Life and work*. New York, NY: Simon & Schuster.

Daniels, M. (2005). *Shadow, self, spirit: Essays in transpersonal psychology*. Exeter, UK: Imprint Academic.

Dass, R. (1971). *Be here now*. New York, NY: The Crowe Publishing Group.

Davis, J.C. (2015). The business of getting high: Head shops, countercultural capitalism, and the marijuana legalization movement. *The Sixties. 8*(1), 27–49.

Davis, A.K., Clifton, J.M. & Weaver, E.G. et al (2020). Survey of entity encounter occasioned by inhaled N, N – Dimethyltryptamine: Phenomenology, interpretation, and enduring effect. *Journal of Psychopharmacology. 34*(9), 1008–1020.

De Chardin, P.T. (1999). *Pierre Teilhard De Chardin: Writings*. Maryknoll, NY: Orbis Books.

Doblin, R. (2021, August). Psychedelic medicine symposium with Rick Doblin. In L. Taus & N. Bruss (Chairs). The Past and Future of Psychedelic Medicine. Symposium conducted at meeting of the Psychedelic Coalition for Health.

Drury, N. (2004). *The new age: Searching for the spiritual self*. London, UK: Thane and Prose.

Dyck, E. & Gurschler, I. (2021, May 21). Is peyote the same as mescaline? A cultural history. Chacruna. Retrieved from https://chacruna.net/peyote-mescaline-history/

Eftekhar, M. (2022). The role of psychedelics in supernatural experience formation. *International Journal of Health Sciences. 6*(S2), 12179–12188.

Ehrenfried, L. (1956). *D'l'education du corps a l'equilibre de l'espirit*. Paris, France: Auber Montaigne.

Ellis, A. & Yeager, R. (1989). *Why some therapies don't work: The dangers of transpersonal psychology*. Buffalo, NY: Prometheus Books.

Epstein, M. (1996). Freud's influence on transpersonal psychology. In B.W., Scotton, A.B. Chinen & J. R. Battista (Eds.). *Textbook of transpersonal psychiatry and psychology* (pp. 29–38). New York, NY: Basic Books

Evans, B.N. (2000). *Interpreting the free exercise of religion: The constitution and American pluralism*. Chapel Hill, NC: University of North Carolina Press.

Ferrcci, P. (1982). *What we may be: The visions and techniques of psychosynthesis*. New York, NY: HarperCollins Publishers.

Ferrer, J.N. (2000). The perennial philosophy revisited. *Journal of Transpersonal Psychology*, 32(1), 7–30.

Ferrer, J.N. (2002). *Revisioning transpersonal theory: A participatory vision of human spirituality*. New York, NY: State University of New York Press.

Ferrer, J.N. (2014). Transpersonal psychology, science, and the supernatural. *The Journal of Transpersonal Psychology*. 46(2), 152–187.

Ferrer, J.N. & Sherman, J.H. (Eds.) (2008). *The participatory turn in spirituality, mysticism, and religious studies*. Albany, NY: State University of New York Press.

Firman, J. & Gila, A. (2002). *Psychosynthesis: A psychology of the spirit*. Albany, NY: State University of New York Press.

Fischman, L.G. (1983). Dreams, hallucinogenic drug states, and schizophrenia: A psychological and biological comparison. *Schizophrenia Bulletin*. 9, 73–94.

Foundation for Inner Peace (1976). *A course in miracles*. Mill Valley, CA: Foundation for Inner Peace

Freeman, A. (2006). A Daniel come to judgment? Dennett and the revisioning of transpersonal theory. *Journal of Consciousness Studies*. 13(3), 95–109.

Freud, S. (1955). Beyond the pleasure principle. In J. Strachey (Ed. & Trans.). *The standard edition of the complete psychological works of Sigmund Freud* (Vol. 8). London: Hogarth Press (Original work published 1920).

Freud, S. (1957). Leonardo De Vinci and a memory of his childhood. In J. Strachey (Ed. & Trans.). *The standard edition of the complete psychological works of Sigmund Freud* (Vol. 11, pp. 111–112). London: Hogarth Press (Original work published 1910).

Freud, S. (1958). Formulations on the two principles of mental functioning. In J. Strachey (Ed. & Trans.). *The standard edition of the complete psychological works of Sigmund Freud* (Vol. 12, p. 219). London: Hogarth Press (Original work published 1911).

Freud, S. (1961). Civilization and its discontents. In J. Strachey (Ed. & Trans.) *The standard edition of the complete psychological works of Sigmund Freud* (Vol. 21). London: Hogarth Press (Original work published 1930).

Freud, S. (1964). Moses and monotheism. In J. Strachey (Ed. & Trans.) *The standard edition of the complete psychological works of Sigmund Freud* (Vol. 23). London: Hogarth Press (Original work published 1939).

Freud, S. (1989). *The future of an illusion* (J. Strachey, Trans.). United States: Pacific Publishing Studio (Original work published 1927)

Freye, E. & Levy, J.V. (2010). *Pharmacology and abuse of cocaine, amphetamines, ecstasy and designer drugs: A comprehensive review on their mode of action, treatment of abuse and intoxication*. New York, NY: Springer Books.

Friedman, H.L. (2002). Transpersonal psychology as a scientific field. *International Journal of Transpersonal Studies*. 21, 175–187.

Fromm, E., Suzuki, D. & DeMartini, R. (1970). *Psychoanalysis and Zen Buddhism*. New York, NY: Harper & Row Publishers.

GH Research (2021). Pipeline. Retrieved from https://www.ghres.com/pipeline

Global Drug Survey (2017, May 24). GDS results released. Retrieved from www.globaldrugsurvey.com/past-findings/gds2017-launch/results-released.

Goodwin, J. (2011). *Atlantis and the cycles of time: Prophesies, traditions ad occult revelations*. Rochester, VT: Inner Traditions.

Greer, G. & Tolbert, R. (1990). The therapeutic use of MDMA. In S.J. Peroutka (Ed.). *Ecstasy: The clinical, pharmacological and neurotoxicological effects of the drug MDMA*. Norwell, MA: Lluwer Academic.

Griffiths, R.R., Johnson, M.W., Carducci, M.A., Umbricht, A., Richards, W.A., Richards, B.D., Cosimano, M.P. & Klinedinst, M.A. (2016). Psilocybin produces substantial and sustained decreases in depression and anxiety in patients with life-threatening cancer: A randomized double-blind trial. *Journal of Psychopharmacology*. *30*(12), 1181–1197

Griffiths, R.R., Johnson, M.W., Richards, W.A., Richards, B.D., Jesse, R., MacLean, K.A., Barrett, F.S., Cosimano, M.P. & Klinedinst, K.A. (2018). Psilocybin-occasioned mystical-type experience in combination with meditation and other spiritual practices produce enduring positive changes in psychological functioning and in trait measures of prosocial attitudes and behaviors. *Journal of Psychopharmacology*. *32*(1), 49–69.

Griffiths, R.R., Richards, W.A., McCann, U. & Jesse, R. (2006). Psilocybin can occasion mystical-type experiences having substantial and sustained personal meaning and spiritual significance. *Psychopharmacology*. *187*, 268–283

Grof, S. (1973). Theoretical and empirical basis of transpersonal psychology and psychotherapy. Observations from LSD research. *Journal of Transpersonal Psychology*. *5*(1), 15–53.

Grof, S. (1976). *Realms of human unconscious: Observations from LSD research*. New York, NY: Dutton.

Grof, S. (1985). *Beyond the brain: Birth, death, and the transcendence in psychotherapy*. Albany, NY: State University of New York Press.

Grof, S. (2015). Revision and re-enchantment of psychology: Legacy from half century of consciousness research. In H.L. Friedman & G. Hartelius (Eds.). *The Wiley Blackwell handbook of transpersonal psychology* (pp. 91–120). Chichester, UK: John Wiley & Sons, Ltd.

Grof, S. & Grof, C. (1989). *Spiritual emergency: When personal transformation becomes a crisis*. Los Angeles, CA: Jeremy P. Tarcher.

Grof, S. & Grof, C. (2010). *Holotropic breathwork: A new approach to self - exploration and therapy*. Albany, NY: State University of New York Press.

Hartelius, G., Caplan, M. & Rardin, M.A. (2007). Transpersonal psychology: Defining the past, divining the future. *The Humanistic Psychologist*. *35*(2), 1–26.

Hartelius, G., Friedman, H.L. & Pappas, D. (2015). The calling to a spiritual psychology: Should transpersonal convert? In H.L. Friedman & G. Hartelius (Eds.). *The Wiley Blackwell handbook of transpersonal psychology* (pp. 44–61). Chichester, UK: John Wiley & Sons, Ltd.

Hentzen, A. & Passie, T. (2010). *The pharmacology of LSD: A critical review* (K. Fletcher, Trans.). New York, NY: Oxford Press.

Higgs, J. (2006). *I have America surrounded: The life of Timothy Leary*. United Kingdom: Friday Books.

Hill, S.J. (2019). *Confrontation with the unconscious: Jungian depth psychology and psychedelic experience*. London: Aeon Books ltd.

Hitchcock, S.T. & Esposito, J.L. (2004). *Da Geografia da religiao*. Lisbon, Portugal: Lusomundo Editores.

Hollingshead, A.B. & Redlich, F.C. (1958). *Social class and mental illness*. New York, NY: Wiley Books.

Hopewell, B. (2017). *Astrological psychology: The Huber method*. Cheshire, UK: HopeWell.

Huxley, A. (1945). *The perennial philosophy*. New York, NY: Harper & Brothers.

Huxley, A. (1963). *The doors of perception, and heaven and hall*. New York, NY: Harper & Row.

James, W. (1890). *The principles of psychology*. New York, NY: Henry-Holt.

James, W. (1929). *The varieties of religious experiences*. New York, NY: Random House (Original work published 1902).

Jung, C.G. (1953). Two essays on analytic psychology In (R.F.C. Hull, Trans.). *The collected works of C.G. Jung* (Vol. 7). Princeton, N.J.: Princeton University Press.

Jung, C.G. (1963). *Memories, dreams, reflections*. New York, NY: Vintage Books.

Jung, C.G (Ed.) (1964). *Man and his symbols*. London: Aldus Books Limited.

Jung, C.G. (1971). *The spirit of man, art, and literature. Collected works of C.J. Jung* (Vol. 8). London: Routledge, Kegan and Paul.

Jung, C.G. (1999). *The psychology of Kundalini yoga* (Ed. S. Shamdasani). Princeton, NJ: Princeton University Press.

Jung, C.G. (2003). *Psychology of the unconscious*. New York, NY: Publications (Original work published 1912).

Jung, C. G. (1958a). The Tibetan book of the dead. In (R.F.C. Hull, Trans.). *The collected works of C.G. Jung* (Vol. 11). Princeton, N.J.: Princeton University Press.

Jung, C.G. (1958b). The Tibetan book of great liberation. In (R.F.C. Hull, Trans.). *The collected works of C.G. Jung* (Vol. 11). Princeton, N.J.: Princeton University Press

Katzetnik (1989). *Shivitti: A vision*. San Francisco: Harper and Row.

Koppel, L. (2008, February 6). Spiritual leader dies. *New York Times*. Retrieved from https://www.nytimes.com/2008/02/07/world/asia/07iht-06maharishi1.9826982.html?searchResultPosition=1

Krishna, G. (1971). *Kundalini: The evolutionary energy in man*. Boulder, CO: Shambhala Books.

Kuhn, T.S. (1962). *The structure of scientific revolutions*. Chicago: University of Chicago Press.

Kurtz, R. (1997). *Body-centered psychotherapy: The Hakomi method integrated use of mindfulness, nonviolence and the body*. Mendocino, CA: LifeRhythm Books.

Labate, B.C. & Cavnar, C (Eds.) (2014). *The therapeutic use of ayahuasca*. Berlin/Heidelberg: Springer-Verlag.

Landriscina, F. (1995). MDMA and the states of consciousness. *Eleusis*. 2, 3–9.

Linn, L. (2002). Freud's encounter with cocaine. *Journal of the American Psychoanalytic Association*. *50*(4), 1151–1161

Lopez, G. (2014, May 30). The House just voted to protect marijuana patients from federal interference. Retrieved from https://www.vox.com/2014/5/30/5763654/the-house-just-voted-to-protect-medical-marijuana-patients-from.

Lowe, S. (2011). Transcendental meditation: Vedic science. *Nova Religno: The Journal of Alternative and Emergent Religions*. *14*(4), 54–76.

Lowen, A. (1975). *Bioenergetics*. New York, NY: Coward, McCann & Geoghegan.

Lundborg, P. (2012). *Psychedelia: An ancient culture, a modern way of life*. Stockholm: Lysergia.

MacLean, K. A., Leoutsakos, J.-M. S., Johnson, M. W., & Griffiths, R. R. (2012). *Revised Mystical Experience Questionnaire (MEQ)* [Database record]. APA PsycTests.

MacDonald, D.A. & Friedman, H.L. (2015). Quantitative assessment of transpersonal and spiritual constructs. In H.L. Friedman & G. Hartelius (Eds.). *The Wiley Blackwell handbook of transpersonal psychology* (pp. 281–299). Chichester, UK: John Wiley & Sons, Ltd.

MacDonald, D.A., Walsh, R. & Shapiro, S.L. (2015). Empirical research and future directions. In H.L. Friedman & G. Hartelius (Eds.). *The Wiley Blackwell handbook of transpersonal psychology* (pp. 433–458). Chichester, UK: John Wiley & Sons, Ltd.

MacLaine, S. (1983). *Out on a limb*. New York, NY: Bantam Books.

Martin-Baro, I.M. (1994). *Writings for a liberation psychology* (A. Aron & S. Corne, Eds.). Cambridge, MA: Harvard University Press.

Maslow, A. (1962). *Toward a psychology of being*. Princeton, NJ: Van Nostrand.

Maslow, A. (1964). *Religion, values, and peak experiences*. Columbus, OH: Ohio State University.

Maslow, A. (1965). *Eupsychian management: A journal*. Homewood, IL: Irwin-Dorsey.

Maslow, A. (1969a). The further reaches of human nature. *Journal of Transpersonal Psychology*. *1*(1), 83–90.

Maslow, A. (1969b). Theory Z. *Journal of Transpersonal Psychology*. *1*, 31–37.

Maus, M. (1973). The techniques of the body (B. Brewer, Trans.). *Economy and Society*. 2, 70–88.

May, R. (1989). Transpersonal or transcendental? *Humanistic Psychologist*. 19, 87–90.

McGuire, W. (1995). Firm affinities: Jung's relations with Britain and the United States. *Journal of Analytical Psychology*. *40*(3), 301–326.

Mickelson, D. (1998, February 15). Is 'Lucy in the sky with diamonds' code for LSD? Snopes. Retrieved https://www.snopes.com/fact-check/lucy-in-the-sky-with-diamonds/

Muraresku, B.C. (2020). *The immortality key: The secret history of the religion with no name*. New York, NY: St. Martin's Press.

Nardou, R., Lewis, E.M. & Rothhaas, R. et al (2019) Oxytocin-dependent reopening of a social reward learning critical period with MDMA. *Nature. 569*, 116–120.

NIDA (2020, June 15). MDMA (Ecstasy/Molly) Drug Facts. Retrieved from https://www.drugabuse.gov/publications/drugfacts/mdma-ecstasymolly.

Novak, S.J. (1997). LSD before Leary: Sidney Cohen's critique of the 1950s psychedelic drug research. *History of Science Society. 88*(1), 87–110.

Nutt, D. (2014). A brave new world for psychology. *Psychologist. 27*(9), 658–660.

Osório, F.L., Sanches, R.F, Macedo, L.R., et al, (2015). Antidepressant effects of a single dose of ayahuasca with patients with recurring depression: A preliminary report. *Brazilian Journal of Psychiatry, 37*(1), 13–20.

Osmond, H. (1952). On being mad. *Saskatchewan Psychiatric Services Journal. 1*(2), 1–8.

Osmond, H. (1957). A review of the clinical effect of psychotomimetic agents. *Annals of the New York Academy of Sciences. 1*, 418–434.

Oss, O.T. & Oric, O.N. (1993). *Psilocybin: Magic mushroom grower's guide*. St. Louis, MO: Quick American Publishing.

Pederson, P. (1991). Introduction to the special issue on multiculturalism as a fourth force in counseling. *Journal of Counseling and Development. 70*, 4.

Pirsig, R.M. (1974). *Zen and the art of motorcycle maintenance: An inquiry into values*. New York, NY: HarperCollins Publishers, Inc.

Pollan, M. (2018). *How to change your mind: What the new science of psychedelic science teaches us about consciousness dying, addiction, depression, and transcendence*. New York, NY: Penguin Press.

Raichle, M.E., MacLeod, A.M. & Snyder, A.Z. et al (2001). A default mode of brain function. *Proceedings of the National Academy of Science. 98*(2), 676–682.

Rank, O. (1957). *The idea of the holy: An inquiry into the non-rational factor in the idea of the divine and its relation to the rational*. London, UK: Oxford University Press (Original work published 1917).

Reich, W. (1942). *The function of the orgasm*. New York, NY: Orgone Institute Press.

Rolf, I.P. (1990). *Rolfing and physical reality*. Rochester, VT: Healing Arts Press.

Rosen, S. (2006). *Essential Hinduism*. New York, NY: Praeger Press.

Rudhyar, D. (1971). *Astrological timing: The transition to the new age*. New York, NY: Harper and Row.

Rudhyar, D. (1987). *The astrology of personality: A re-formulation of astrological concepts and ideals, in terms of contemporary psychology and philosophy*. Santa Fe, NM: Aurora Press (Original work published in 1936).

Samuels, G. (2010). *The origins of yoga and tantra; Indic religions to the thirteen century*. Cambridge UK: Cambridge University Press.

Sander, D.F. (1996). Native north American healers. In B.W. Scotton, A.B. Chinen & J. R. Battista (Eds.). *Textbook of transpersonal psychiatry and psychology* (pp. 52–61). New York, NY: Basic Books.

Scotton, B.W., & Hiatt, F.H. (1996). The contribution of Hinduism and yoga to transpersonal psychiatry. In B.W. Scotton, A.B. Chinen & J. R. Battista (Eds.) *Textbook of transpersonal psychiatry and psychology* (pp. 104–113). New York, NY: Basic Books.

Sedlmeier, P., Eberth, J. & Schwarz, M., et al (2012). The psychological effects of meditation: A meta-analysis. *Psychological Bulletin. 138*(6), 1139–1171.

Shamdasani, S (Ed.) (2003). *The red book*. New York, NY: W.W. Norton.

Shapiro, S. & Walsh, R. (2003). An analysis of recent meditation research and suggestions for future directions. *The Humanistic Psychologist. 31*, 86–114.

Sheff, D. (2000). *All we are saying: The last major interview with John Lennon and Yoko Ono*. New York, NY: St. Martin's Press.

Singer, M.T. & Lalich, J. (1996). *Crazy therapies: What are they? Do they work?* New York, NY: Jossey-Bass.

Stolaroff, M.J. (2004). *The secret chef revealed*. Sarasota, FL: Multidisciplinary Association for Psychedelic Studies.

Strassman, R. (2001). *DMT; The spirit molecule. A doctor's revolutionary research into the biology of near-death and mystical experiences*. Rochester, VT: Park Street Press.

Strassman, R. (2014). *DMT and the soul of prophecy: A new science of spiritual revelation in the Hebrew Bible*. Rochester, VT: Park Street Press.

Sunita, K.S., Pothen, A. & Sumita, R (Eds.) (2003). *Aldous Huxley and Indian thought*. New York, NY: Sterling Publishers.

Suzuki, D.T. (1994). *Introduction to Zen Buddhism*. New York, NY: Grove Press (Original work published 1964).

Taylor, E.I. (1986). Swami Vivekananda and William James. *Prabuddha Bharata: Journal of the Ramakrishna Society. 91*, 374–385.

Taylor, E.I. (1993). The influence of Swedenborgian thought on American pragmatism. Paper presented to the Swedenborg Society Study Group. Annual Meeting of the American Academy of Religion. Washington, D.C (November, 1993).

Taylor, E.I. (1996). William James and transpersonal psychiatry. In B.W. Scotton, A.B. Chinen & J. R. Battista (Eds.). *Textbook of transpersonal psychiatry and psychology* (pp. 21–28). New York, NY: Basic Books.

Uthang, M.V., Lancellotta, R. & van Oorsouw, K. et al (2019). A single inhalation of vapor from dried toad secretion containing 5-methoxy-N, N-dimethyltryptamine in a naturalistic setting is related to sustained enhancement of satisfaction with life, mindfulness-related capacities, and a decrement of psychopathological symptoms. *Psychopharmacology. 236*(9), 2653–2666.

Valentine, D. (2017). *The CIA as organized crime: How illegal operations corrupt America and the world*. Atlanta, GA: Clarity Press.

Vich, M.A. (1988) Some historical sources of the term 'transpersonal.' *Journal of Transpersonal Psychology. 20*(2), 107–110.

Walsh-Browers, R. & Johnson, P. (2002). Introducing mainstream psychology to native students whose feet are in two vessels. *Canadian Journal of Native Studies. 22*, 121–135.

Walsh, R. & Shapiro, S.L. (2006). The meeting of meditative disciplines and Western psychology: A mutually enriching dialogue. *American Psychologist. 61*(3), 227–239.

Walsh, T.G., Teo, T. & Baydala, A. (2014). *A critical history and philosophy of psychology*. Cambridge, UK: Cambridge University Press.

Walsh, R. & Vaughan, F. (1996). The worldview of Ken Wilbur. In B.W. Scotton, A.B. Chinen, & J. R. Battista (Eds.). *Textbook of transpersonal psychiatry and psychology* (pp. 104–113.). New York, NY: Basic Books.

Washburn (1988). *The ego and dynamic ground: A transpersonal theory of human development*. Albany, NY: SUNY Press.

Watkins, M. & Shulman, H. (2008). *Toward psychologies of liberation*. Basingstoke: Palgrave Macmillan.

Watts, A. (1961). *Psychotherapy east and west*. New York, NY: Pantheon Books.

Watts, A. (1975). *Tao: The watercourse way*. New York, NY: Pantheon Books

Wilber, K. (1977). *The spectrum of consciousness*. Wheaton, IL: Theosophical Publications.

Wilber, K. (1995). *Sex, ecology, spirituality: The spirit of evolution*. Boston, MA: Shambala.

Wilber, K. (2006). *Integral spirituality: A startling new role for religion in the modern and post-modern world*. Boston, MA: Shambala.

Wilhelm, R. (1962). *The secret of the golden flower: A Chinese book of life* (R. Wilhelm, Trans.). New York, NY: A Harvest Book.

Wilhelm, R. (1967). *The I Ching or book of changes* (C.F. Baynes. Trans.). Princeton, New Jersey: Princeton University Press (Original work published 1950).

Wolfe, T. (2008). *The electric Kool-Aid acid test*. New York, NY: Farrar, Straus, and Giroux (Original work published 1968).

Wynne, A. (2007). *The origin of Buddhist meditation*. London: Routledge Press.

Yensen, R. & Dryer, D. (1996). The consciousness research of Stanislav Grof. In B.W. Scotton, A.B. Chinen, & J. R. Battista (Eds.). *Textbook of transpersonal psychiatry and psychology* (pp. 75–84). New York, NY: Basic Books.

Yogi, M.M. (1994). *Science of being and art of living: Transcendental meditation*. New York, NY: Meridian Book (Original work published in 1963).

Index

Note: Page references in *italics* denote figures and in **bold** tables.

5MeO-DMT (5-methoxy- N,N-Dimethyltryptamine) 328
12 Hour Political Party 233
8½ 119
1561 Celestial Phenomenon over Nuremberg 153

AA International Convention, St. Louis 150
Abraham, Karl 78, 107
absurdities of life 260, 278
The Abyss of Madness (Atwood) 95
Acceptance and Commitment Therapy (ACT) 220
active imagination 117, 119, 298–300, 309
act psychology 64, 254
Addams, Jane 265
Adler, Alfred 53, 263
Aeschylus 259
Afghanistan War 75
After the Catastrophe (Jung) 112
Age of Enlightenment 163
aggression 52–53
aging 199–200
Ainsworth, Mary 85
Aircrib *198*, 198–199
AK-47 *(Avtomat Kalashnikova)* 276
Aladdin Sane 119
Al-Anon 150
The Alan Turing Law 169
Alan Turing: The Enigma (Hodges) 169
Albert, Richard 289
alchemists 121–123
Alcoholics Anonymous (AA) 147–150
Alcoholics Anonymous: The Story of How More Than One Hundred Men and Women Have Recovered from Alcoholism 148
Alexander the Great 258
Algeria 232, 290
Algerian War of Independence 232
Alice in Wonderland (Carroll) 39
alienation 51–52, 113, 129, 263
All Quadrants All Levels (AQAL) 307
Alpert, Richard 323

Alternate Consciousness Paradigm (ACP) 66, 67, 128
Altman, Neil 78
American: behaviorism 167, 265; capitalism 164, 166, 233; college-educated 233; culture 230, 234, 239, 287, 289, 291–293, 310, 324, 333, 338; empiricism 294–295; existentialism 261–263; feeling and individualism of 230; flag 275–276; gun violence in 277; homogeneity 25, 26; humanism 232–234; identity 275; imperialism 165; individualism 4; myth 263; national healthcare system 232; optimism 230; psychiatrist 274; psychologist 266; psychology 235, 241, 264, 294; thought 230
American Association for the Advancement of Science 23
American Declaration of Independence 163
American Psychiatric Association 292
American Psychological Association (APA) 1, 36–37, 107, 111, 151, 163, 165, 173, 175, 203, 266, 285, 287, 337
American Psychologist 5
American Revolution 163
American Society for Psychical Research (ASPR) 184, 294
amrita 320
Analysis of the Self: A Systematic Approach to the Treatment of Narcissistic Personality Disorders (Kohut) 91
The Analyst in the Inner City: Race, Class and Culture Through the Psychoanalytic Lens (Altman) 78
analytical psychology 123, 134, 298–301
Analytical Psychology (Jung) 105
Analytical Psychology Club (APC) 107
Anaximander 13
Andreas-Salome, Lou 107
anima/animus 131, 135, 138–139

anima archetype 138
Animal Education: The Psychical Development of the White Rat (Watson) 181
animal intelligence 173–175
Animal Intelligence: An Experimental Study of the Association Process in Animals (Thorndike) 174
animal magnetism 56–58
The Animal Mind: A Textbook of Comparative Psychology (Washburn) 173
animism 184
animus archetype 138
anthropomorphism 173
anxiety 30, 74, 196, 257–258; castration 71–72, 88; moral 74; neurotic 74; objective 74; persecutory 82–83
anxious-ambivalent attachment 85
anxious-avoidant attachment 85
apperception 7–8, 62
Aquinas, Thomas 238
AR-15 rifles 276
Arab Spring Movements 165
archetypal school 106
archetypal Self 131
archetypes 120, 134–135, 137
Archimedes 255
Aristotle 13, 67, 120–121, 127, 168, 175, 187, 192, 207, 238, 265, 306, 308
Ark of the Covenant 130
Armstrong, Neil 287
Arnett, Jeffery 209
Arrowsmith (Lewis) 176, 190
Artemis (Greek goddess) 20
artificial intelligence (AI) 204–206
artificial somnambulism 58
artistic psychological state 254
Asklepion myth 142–143
Asklepion Temples 144
Assagioli, Roberto 286, 308–310
The Assault on Truth: Freud's Suppression of Seduction Theory (Masson) 70
Association for Behavioral and Cognitive Therapies (ABCT) 215
Association for Humanistic Psychology (AHP) 233, 266
Association for Psychological Science (APS) 37
Association for the Advancement of Behavior Therapy (AABT) 215
associationism 9, 11, 14, 175, 186
association reflex 180
associations 185
astrological chart 338
Astrological psychology 310–312
The Astrology of Personality (Rudhyar) 310
astropsychology 308, 310
atomism 171

attachment theory 79, 84, 85, 99, 140
At the Existentialist Café: Freedom, Being and Apricot Cocktails (Bakewell) 237
Atwood, George 94–95
Auden, W. H. 324
Aum/Om 316
The Autonomous Self (Sutherland) 98
avanmehr 321
Axial Age 129, 285–286, 293, 308–319, 320–322
ayahuasca 327–328

Babakr, Zana 209
Bacon, Francis 170–171
Bakewell, Sarah 237
Balint, Michael 98
Bandura, Albert 168, 209–211, 215
Barber, Jacques 163
Basic Perinatal Matrices (BPM) 331
Basic: Theoretical Concepts of Humanistic Psychology (Buhler) 266
Bastiaans, Jan 333
The Battle of Behaviorism (Watson and McDougall) 183
Baum, Dan 334
Beck, Aaron 185, 214, 216, 218
Beck, Samuel 31
Beck Anxiety Inventory 218, 222
Beck Depression Inventory 218, 222
Behave (Romano-Lax) 168
behavioral functionalism 186–187
Behavioral Health Departments 148
behavioral psychological movement 163–170; cultural systems 167–170; historical analysis of 163–170; political systems 163–166; socioeconomic systems 166
behavioral psychology 187–189; educational psychology 189; Little Albert conditioning 187–188; Peter and the Rabbit behavioral therapy 188–189; three generations of 161–163
behavioral therapy 188, 214–215
behaviorism 161, 170–190, 229, 240, 307; animal intelligence 173–175; *Arrowsmith* 190; authoritarian tendencies in 232; behavioral functionalism 186–187; behavioral psychology 187–189; changing environment 190; conditioned reflex and symbol 178–180; Darwinian natural history method 172–173; emancipatory opportunities in 189–190; and H-E movement 230; hermeneutic science interest in 184–187; instrumental learning 173–175; natural science interest in 170–184; Newtonian science 170–171; objective psychology 177–178; positivism

184–185; purposive hormic 182–184; radical environmentalism 181–182; Read psychology and behaviorists 189; reflexology 180–181; tropism 175–177, 189; utilitarianism 185–186
behavior modification 214
Behavior of Organisms (Skinner) 193
Behavior Research and Therapy 215
Be Here Now (Dass) 291
Being and Nothingness (Sartre) 258–259
Being and Time (Heidegger) 255, 258
being motivated (B-motivation) 266
Bekhterev, Vladimir 180–181
Bell Curve: Intelligence and Class Structure in American Life (Hernstein and Murray) 3, 40
Bentham, Jeremy 164, 166, 185
Bergson, Henri 120
Bernhardt, Sarah 65
Bernheim, Hippolyte 64
Bertrand Russell Tribunal 232
Between Man and Man (Buber) 247
Beyond Freedom and Dignity (Skinner) 197
Beyond the Pleasure Principal (Freud) 298
Bhagavad Gita 312
bhavana 317
Bill of Rights 275
Binet, Alfred 4, 23–24, 241, 294
Binet-Simon Test 24, 26, 28
Binswanger, Ludwig 107, 267–268
bioenergetic analysis 335
biological evolution 13, 120
Bion, Wilfred 88–89
Birth of Tragedy: Out of the Spirit of Music (Nietzsche) 253
Black Books 117
Black Notebooks (Heidegger) 231
Black Panther Party 166
Black race 5
Blackwell, Antoinette Brown 5
Blake, William 116
Blass, Thomas 33
Bleuler, Eugen 31, 107, 150, 267
B-love (being-love) 266
Bobo Doll Experiment 210
Bohler, Eugen 114
Bolshevik Revolution 166
Borotlin, Matthew 115
Boston Psychoanalytic Society and Institute 200
Boulder Model 37–38
Bowie, David 119
Bowlby, John 79–80, 84, 243
Brahms, Johannes 66
Braid, James 64
Brazil 17, 232
Bredemeier, Keith 218
Brentano, Franz 58, 63–64, 66, 254–255

Breuer, Josef 66–67, 68, 294
Bridgman, Percy W. 195–196
Briesch, Hans 120
British Army 243
British Criminal Law Amendment Act 168–169
British empiricism 184
British Independent Group of the British Psychoanalytic Society 79, 89
British Journal of Psychology 184
British object-relations theory 79
British Psychoanalytical Society (BPS) 79, 109
British Psychological Association 184
British Psychological Society 146, 175
Brooklyn College 241
Brouillet, Andre 65
Brucke, Ernst 58
Buber, Martin 69, 230, 231, 246–247, 267
Buchman, Frank 148
Buddha 149, 215, 310, 317; auspicious footprints of 18; illumination of 235; mindful third-wave 222
Buddhism 62, 123, 132, 212–213, 219, 235, 294, 317–319; mandala 132; swastika in 18–19; Tibetan 133; *see also* religion
Buddhist 287, 293
Buddhist meditation 220
Buddhist Nyingma Institute of California 293
Buddhist spirituality 212
Buhler, Charlotte 266–267, 301
Burgholzli Psychiatric Hospital in Zurich, Switzerland 140, 150
Burns, David 217
Burt, Cyril 38–39
Butterfield, Earl C. 206

Calkins, Mary 173
Campbell, Joseph 115, 137
Camus, Albert 230, 233, 244, 260–261, 278
Capaldi, E. J. 211
Capek, Karel 170
capitalism 4, 50–51, 54–55, 153, 163–166, 177, 233
Caplan, M. 285
Carey, Alex 166
Carhart-Harris, Robin 296–297
Carnap, Rudolf 196
Carnegie, Andrew 4
Carrel, Alexis 17
Carroll, Lewis 39
Casanova 119
Castaneda, Carlos 291, 323
catharsis and talking cure 66–68
Cattell, James McKeen 23
Center for Cognitive Studies 203
Central Intelligence Agency (CIA) 232–233
C.G. Jung Clinic 107
chakras 312

Charcot, Jean-Martin 23, 65, 294
Chariot of the Gods (Von Daniken) 152
Charlie Chaplin 243
Chief Mountain Lake 129
child abuse 69–70
Childhood and Society (Erikson) 74
Chinese philosophy 129–131
Chinese Room experiment 205
Chomsky, Noam 165, 202
Christianity 122, 129, 131, 247–248
Christian morality 237
Christian values 237
chronoscope 6
Church of England 56
City of Women 119
Civilization and Its Discontents (Freud) 52, 161, 297
civil rights movement 54, 239
Clark University 107, 114
classical antiquity 117
classical school 106
classic psychedelics 296
Cleaver, Eldridge 290
client-centered psychology 270
Client-Centered Therapy: Its Current Practice, Implications and Theory (Rogers) 269
Clifton, J. M. 327
A Clinical Lesson at the Salpetriere (Brouillet) 65
clinical psychology 2, 36–38
cognitive behavioral psychology 193, 202–222; artificial intelligence 204–206; *Beck Anxiety Inventory* 222; *Beck Depression Inventory* 222; behavioral therapy/operant conditioning 214–215; Buddhism and Daoism 212–213; cognitive behavioral therapy 213–214, 222; cognitive science 202–203; connectivism 207; cybernetics 203–204; dialectical behavioral therapy 218–222; emancipatory opportunities in 222; first wave 214–215; functional-contextualism 211–212; hermeneutic interest in 208–213; information-processing 206; mindfulness 222; natural science interest in 202–207; second wave 215–218; social learning (cognitive) theory 209–211; stage theory of cognitive development 209; Stoicism 208–209; third wave 218–222
cognitive behavioral therapy (CBT) 163, 213–222
cognitive information 203
cognitive map 190
cognitive psychology 203, 206
Cognitive Psychology 203
Cognitive Psychology and Information Processing (Lachman, Lachman, and Butterflied) 206
cognitive science 202–203
The Cognitive Triad 216

Collaborative Therapeutic Assessment (CTA) 35
collective unconscious 120, 136–137, 142, 298
Columbia University 237, 262
Come Together (Lennon) 290
Coming Apart: The State of White America, 1960–2010 (Murray) 41
communication: authentic 94; chain 150; meaningful 203; spirit 332; symbolic 336
community culture 114
community mental health (CMH) 77, 98, 150–152, 155
complex psychology 128
Comprehensive Drug Prevention and Control Act 333
computer-assisted education 201
computer-assisted instruction 199, 201
Comte, Auguste 167, 184–185, 195
The Concept of Dread (Kierkegaard) 247
conditioned reflex and symbol 178–180
conditioned stimulus (CS) 179
Confrontation with the Unconscious (Hill) 300
Confucian ethics 131
Confucius 215
connectionism 175
connectivism 207
Conscience in Economic Life (Bohler) 114
consciousness: primary 296; secondary 296
contextualism 211
conversion 11
Copenhagen interpretation 196
Corlett, John 152
corpuscularianism 171
Corpus Hermeticum 122
cosmic tabula rosa 252
The Council for Unified Research and Education (CURE) 197
countertransference 68–69, 142–145; relational psychoanalytic psychology 88–89
Course in Miracles (Schulman) 291
Crazy Therapies (Singer and Lalich) 286
Critique of Dialectical Reason (Sartre) 233
Critique of Pure Reason (Kant) 254
Critique of the Gotha Program (Marx) 51
Cronbach, Less 27
Crowley, Mike 320
Crusades 137
Cry for Myth (May) 113
cultural integration 230
cultural psychology 2, 5, 7
cultural systems: behavioral psychological movement 167–170; Freudian psychoanalysis 55–56; humanistic-existential (H-E) psychology 234–237; Jungian analytical psychology 114; modern psychology 5; relational psychoanalysis 81–82; transpersonal psychology 292–293

cybernetics 203–204
Cybernetics Conference 203–204
Cyril Burt Affair 3, 38–39

Dalai Lama 220
Dalio, Ray 317
Damasio, Antonio 139
A Dangerous Method 140
Daoism 129, 212–213
Daoist science 302
Dargert, Guy 152
Darwin, Charles 4–5, 61, 194, 237; Black race 5; Darwinian revolution 15–17; primary emotional states 16
Darwinian natural history method 172–173
Darwinian revolution 15–17
Darwinian Theory 120
Darwinism 15; social 4, 14
Dasein 256
Dass, Ram 289, 291
Davidson, Graham 268
Davis, A. K. 327
De Anima (On the Soul) (Aristotle) 120
Death of a Salesman (Miller) 262
de Beauvoir, Simone 230, 237–238, 243–244
De Domenico, Gisela 146
deep interpretations 89
The Default Mode Network (DMN) 295–297
deficiency motivated (D-motivation) 266, 303
de Gaulle, Chares 232
Demanchick, Stephen 232
DeMartini, Richard 292
dementia praecox 150
Demian (Hesse) 119
Democracy and Education (Dewey) 189
democratization of psychedelics 289
Densley, J. 277
depth psychology 79, 84, 98, 107, 151, 300
Derrida, Jacques 250
Descartes, René 241, 244, 247
Descent of Man (Darwin) 17
The Descent of Man in Relation to Sex (Darwin) 15
descriptive psychology 254
developmental psychology 85
developmental school 106
de Vinci, Leonardo 298
Dewey, John 164, 186–187, 189, 193, 199
Dharma of the Star Wars (Borotlin) 115
Dharmapala, Anagarika 294
The Diagnosis and Management of Depression (Beck) 216
Diagnostic and Statistical Manual of Mental Disorders (DSM-5) 330, 334
Dialectical Behavioral Therapy (DBT) 218–222
dialectic of existence 250
dialectic paradox 248

dialogic philosophy 246–247
Diaz, Kim 213
di Cesare, Donatella 231
Dichter, Ernest 135
Dionysian spirit 234
The Discovery of the Unconscious: The History and Evolution of Dynamic Psychiatry (Ellenberger) 111
disorganized-disoriented attachment 85
dissociation 66, 128
District of Columbia vs. Heller 275
divine child 108
D-Love (deficiency-love) 266
DMT (N, N-2-Dimethyltryptamine) 326–327
DMT and the Soul of Prophesy (Strassman) 321
Doblin, Rick 286
Doctor, Pete 119
Dodo Bird Verdict 3, 38–39
The Doors of Perception (Huxley) 325
Doubloon symbol 34
Douglass, Frederik 184
Downing, Christine 139
dreams: analysis of 76, 140, 141–142; interpretation of 69
Drives Toward War (Tolman) 165
drive theory 82–84, 121
dual diagnosis criteria 148
DuBois, W.E.B. 184
dukkha 298
Dysfunctional Thought Record (DTR) 217

Eastern religions 123
Ebbinghaus, Herman 34
Eberth, Juliane 317
educational psychology 175, 189
Edy, Mary Baker 11
ego 72, 132, 134; defense mechanisms 74
Ego and the Mechanism of Defense (Freud) 74
Ego Psychology (Hartman) 74
ego-self axis 146, 298, 300
Ehrenfels, Christian von 63
Eichmann, Adolf 33
eidos 127
Einstein, Albert 265
Either/Or (Kierkegaard) 249
ekaggata 318
Electric Kool-Aid Acid Test (Wolfe) 324
electroencephalogram (EEG) 314
Elizabeth, Queen 267
Ellenberger, Henri 111
Elliot, T. S. 243
Ellis, Albert 168, 215–216, 286
emancipatory opportunities: in behaviorism 189–190; in cognitive behavioral psychology 222; in Freudian psychoanalysis 76–78; in humanistic-existential (H-E) psychology 278–279;

in Jungian analytical psychology 154–155; in Jungian psychology 154–155; in neobehaviorism 201; in relational psychoanalysis 97–99
Emerson, Ralph Waldo 11
Empedocles 121
empirical psychology 254
empirical science 142
empirical Self 11
Empty Chair Technique 272
enantiodromia 129
energetics influence 126–127
Enjoying Old Age: Living Fully Your Later Years (Skinner and Vaughan) 199, 201
Enlightenment 1, 164; movement 128; rationalism 128
entelechy 120–121, 265
environmentalism 181–182
Epictetus 208
epistemology 255–256
Erikson, Erik 74
Erikson, Milton 201
Escape from Freedom (Fromm) 263
An Essay Concerning Human Understanding (Locke) 171
An Essay on the Principle of Population (Malthus) 15
Essays on a Science of Mythology: The Myth of the Divine Child and the Mysteries of Eleusis (Kerenyi) 108
ethnocentrism 287
eugenics 17–21; birth of 17–18; and intelligence 21; movement 3; new forms of 43; symbol of *18*, 18–20
Eupsychian Management: A Journal (Maslow) 303
European existentialism 231–232, 233, 262
evidence-based best practices 111
evolution 13–14; biological 13
Evolution of Psychotherapy Conference, Anaheim, California 219
existential: phenomenology 243–245; philosophy 129, 247–250; psychology 255–258; psychotherapy 273–274, 278
existential (Dasein) analysis 267–268
existential anxiety 274
existential crisis 129; of gun violence 248, 275–278
existential dread 260
existential guilt 257
Exner, John 33–34
Experience of the Organization 152
experience phenomenology 278
experimental introspection 5
experimental neurosis 179
experimental psychology influence 59–61, 119–120

Experimental Studies of the Perception of Movement (Wertheimer) 241
The Expression of Emotions (Darwin) 16
Eysenck, Hans 215

Fairbairn, Ronald 89, 121
false self 90
fascism 163
Faust (Goethe) 117
Fear and Trembling (Kierkegaard) 248, 260
Fechner, Gustav 59–60
Fechner, Hans 111
Federal Drug Administration (FDA) 319
Federation of Middle East States 231
Feeling Good (Burns) 217
feelings 279
Fellini, Federico 119
Feminine Psychology (Horney) 87
feminism 86–87, 237–238
feminist theory 139
Ferenczi, Sandor 107
Ferrer, Jorge 286, 295, 307
Fifth French Republic 232
Finn, Stephen 35
First Invitational Conference on Humanistic Psychology 266
Fitz Roy, Robert 15
five faults 317
Flies (Sartre) 259
Floor Games (Wells) 145
Floyd, George 175
fluoroscope 32
Flying Saucers: A Modern Myth of Things Seen in the Skies (Jung) 152
folk psychology 5
Fordham, Michael 109
Forty-Four Juvenile Thieves: Their Character and Home-Life (Bowlby) 80
Fourth French Republic 232
France: animal magnetism in 57; denazification hearings in 231; Nancy School 64
Frank, Simon 268
Frankl, Viktor 235, 237, 271–272
Franklin, Benjamin 57
Franks, Cecil 215
French Enlightenment 164
French existentialism 244, 258–261
French Revolution 56, 163, 184
French rule in Algeria 232
French sensationalism 184
Freud, Anna 74, 79, 85, 86, 88, 146
Freud, Sigmund 5, 50–51, 63, 135, 136, 161, 193, 195, 237, 254, 262, 265, 267, 272, 286, 294, 297–298; alienation 52; catharsis 67; childhood sexuality 69–70; human development and psychosexual stages 70–72; on hypnosis 68; *vs.* Jung

theories 114; natural science approach 61; Psychological Wednesday Society 78, 107; and romanticism 62; unconscious mind 77

Freudian psychoanalysis 50–78; cultural systems 55–56; emancipatory opportunities in 76–78; experimental psychology influence 59–61; Freudian psychoanalytic psychology 66–75; hermeneutic influence 61–66; historical analysis 50–56; natural science 56–58; neurological and physiological influences 61; political systems 50–54; socioeconomic systems 54–55; thermodynamic influence 58–59

Freudian psychoanalytic psychology 66–75; anxiety and ego defense mechanisms 74; catharsis and talking cure 66–68; interpretation of dreams 69; psychosexual stages 70–72; seduction theory and child abuse 69–70; theory of personality 72–73; transference, countertransference and termination 68–69; unconscious forces 74–75; universal unconscious 68

Friedman, Harris 286, 294
Friedman, Maurice 247
Friedrich, Max 6
Fromm, Erich 263, 292
Frost, Robert 168
Full Catastrophe of Living (Kabat-Zinn) 220
Full Circle: The Moral Force of Unified Science (Haskell) 197
functional analysis 193
Functional Analytic Psychotherapy (FAP) 221
functional-contextualism 211–212
functionalism 1, 193; behavioral 186–187; William James 10–13
functional periodicity 28
The Future of an Illusion (Freud) 55, 297

Gadamer, Hans-Georg 307
Galapagos Islands 43
Galileo Galilei 170, 242
Gall, Franz 21–22
Galton, Sir Francis 4, 17–18, 119
Gamblers Anonymous 150
Garb, Howard 34
Garcia, Maria Sabina Magdalena 323
Gautama Buddha 215
The Gay Science (Nietzsche) 250
Geher, Glenn 43
genetic psychology 64, 254
Gessner, Johann 56
Gestalt psychologists 240–241
Gestalt psychology 240–243
Gestalt therapy 272–273, 279
Gestalt Therapy: Excitement and Growth in Human Personality (Perls, Goodman, and Hefferline) 272

Gide, Andre 243
gifted children 27, 28
Ginsberg, Allen 289
Glider 199
Global Drug Survey 290
Glorious Revolution 163
Gnosticism 121, 123
Gnostics 122
Goddard, Henry Herbert 24–26
Goebbels, Joseph 20
GOFAI (Good Old-Fashioned Artificial Intelligence) 206
Goodman, Paul 272–273
Goring, Hermann 32
Gottlieb, Max 190
Goya, Francisco 239
Grant, Paul 218
Great Depression 164, 166
Great Society 164
Greek culture 254
Greek mythology 36, 64, 91, 255, 321
Greek philosophy 185, 229, 293, 308–310
Greek thought 293
Greek tragedy 253–254
Greenberger, Dennis 217
Griffiths, Roland 286, 324
Grof, Christina 286, 329
Grof, Stanislav 286, 302, 308, 330–332, 335
group psychotherapy 269, 274
group therapy 278–279
Guggenuhl-Craig, 144
Guidelines on Multicultural Education, Research, Practice and Organization Change 287
Guillotin, Joseph 57
The Gun Control Act of 1968 276
Guthrie, Edwin 192
Gutwill, Susan 54

hair, musical 234–235
Hall, Granville Stanley 1, 6, 23, 36, 107
Hamlet (Shakespeare) 254
Hampton, Fred 166
Handbook of Psychological Assessment (Groth-Marnat) 35
Hardy, Thomas 274
Hare Krishna 292–293
Hargas, Bill James 239
Harlow, Harry 264
Harper's Magazine 334
Harrison, Beatle George 293
Hartelius, G. 285
Hartman, Heinz 74
Hartmann, Eduard von 63
Hasidism 246
Haskell, Edward 197
Hatha yoga 312, 338
Haugeland, John 206
Hauke, Christopher 139

Hayes, Steven C. 220
Hazan, Cindy 85
Head Start 207
Hebb, Donald 207
Hebb's Rule 207
Hebrew humanism 231
Hefferline, Ralph 272
Heffner, Arthur 325
Hegel, Georg Wilhelm Friedrich 128, 238, 249, 258, 262
Heidegger, Martin 230, 231, 244, 255–260, 267
Heinz Kohut: The Meaning of a Psychoanalyst (Strozier) 93
Hellenistic Gnosticism 123
Helmholtz, Hermann 58
Henri de Saint-Simon, 184
Herbart, Johann 62
Hereditary Genius: Inquiries into its Laws and Consequences (Galton) 17
Herman, Edward 165
hermeneutic influence 61–66; alternate conscious paradigm 66; neuro-hypnology influence 64–66; phenomenological influence 63–64; rationalism influence 61–62; romanticism influence 62–63; transcendental realism influence 63
hermeneutics 5, 121, 306–307
hermeneutic science interest 127–131; Alternate Consciousness Paradigm (ACP) influence 128; in behaviorism 184–187; Chinese philosophy influence 129–131; existential philosophy influence 129; in humanistic-existential psychology 246–267; in neobehaviorism 195–197; Platonic influence 127; Romanticism influence 128; in transpersonal psychology 297–308
Hernstein, Richard 40
The Hero with a Thousand Faces (Campbell) 115
Hesse, Herman 119
heterosexuality 88, 238
hierarchical educational system 29
hierarchy of needs 265
Highlights of Dr. John B. Watson's Career in Advertising (Larson) 166
Hill, Scott 300
Hillman, J. 107, 139
Hinduism 12, 62, 123, 132–133, 292, 312–317, 321; swastika in 18; *see also* religion
Hindu mandala 133
Hindu mandala art 133
Hindus 134, 287, 293
Hippocratic Oath 122
historical analysis: of behavioral psychological movement 163–170; of humanistic-existential psychology 231–239; of transpersonal psychology 288–293
History of the Psychoanalytic Movement (Freud) 78

Hitler, Adolf 19–20, 55, 231, 276
Hodges, Andrew 169
Hoffman, Albert 286, 323, 324, 329
Hollander, Nancy 54
Hollingshead, August 292
Hollingworth, Leta Stetter 28–29; on gifted children 28
Holotropic Breathwork 296, 335
Holtom, Gerald 239
homeostasis 59, 83, 204, 266
homosexuality 88, 139, 170, 238
Hopcke, Robert 139
hormic psychology 182
Horney, Karen 86–87, 263
How to Change Your Mind (Pollan) 293
How to Live with a Neurotic (Ellis) 215
Hubbard, Al 336
Huber, Bruno 311
Huber, Louise 311
Huber Method 311
Hulbeck, Richard 215
Hull, Clark 191–192, 201
Hull-Spence theory 192
Human-Be-In 236
human beings 229, 230, 232, 237, 239, 288, 317; ethical 246; and existential phenomenology 245; integrated 266; interact with physical world 241; meaning-seeking creatures 274; self-actualized 265
Human Betterment Foundation (HBF) 26
human development and psychosexual stages 70–72
humanistic-existential (H-E) movement 229–230, 237, 239, 273
humanistic-existential (H-E) psychology: American existentialism 261–263; Christian values 237; in Community Mental Health (CMH) services 279; cultural integration 230; cultural systems 234–237; dialogic philosophy 246–247; emancipatory opportunities in 278–279; European existentialism 231–232, 233, 262; existential (Dasein) analysis 267–268; existential crisis 275–278; existential philosophy 247–250; existential psychology 255–258; existential psychotherapy 273–274; feminism 237–238; French existentialism 258–261; Gestalt therapy 272–273; hermeneutic science interest in 246–267; historical analysis of 231–239; humanistic psychology 263–267; intellectual visionaries of 278; logotherapy 271–272; natural science interest in 240–245; Nietzschean perspectivism 250–254; overview 229–230; peace movement 238–239; political systems 231–233;

356 *Index*

pure phenomenology 254–255; Rogerian psychology 268–271; scientific method 254–255; socioeconomic systems 233–234; symbols of 229–279
humanistic psychology 263–267, 301–303
Humanistic Psychology Conferences 237
human potential movement (HPM) 235–237, 291
Human Relations 243
human sexuality 237
human tropism 176
human values 230, 266
Husserl, Edmund 63, 230, 244, 254–256, 267, 320
Huxley, Aldous 236, 286, 306, 325
hypnos 64
hypnosis 201
hypnotism 64–65, 68
hypothetico-deductive theory 191
hysteria 67

I and Thou (Buber) 246
I Ching (Wilhelm) 129, 131
Ickes, Harold L. 167
Ickes, Mary 167
id 72–73; unconscious 82
identical elements of transfer theory 175
I-It relationships 246
imaginary self 95–96
Imboden, Max 111
The Imitation Game 169
Immigration Act of 1924 24
individualized education plan (IEP) 43
individuation 121, 131, 132–134, 138, 139, 146, 154
Industrial Revolution 54–55, 56
information-processing 206
inhibition 177
inkblots 30
The Inkblots: Herman Rorschach, His Iconic Test and the Power of Seeing (Searls) 30
instrumental learning 173–175
integral psychology 304–307
Integral Spirituality (Wilber) 307
integral yoga psychology 303–304
Integrated Cognitive Systems (ICS) 220
intelligence 23; and eugenics 21; general factors of 27–28; multifaceted approach to 23–24; societal impact on 28–29
Intelligent Quotient (I.Q.) 1, 3, 24; formula standardized 26–27; longitudinal 27
intentionality 254
International Association for Spielrein Studies 140
International Center for Genetic Epistemology 209
The International Psychoanalytic Association (IPA) 78–79, 107
International Simultaneous Policy Organization 307
International Society for Sandplay Therapists (ISST) 147

interpersonal psychoanalysis 90–93
interpersonal psychology 93
interpersonal self 93–94
The Interpretation of Dreams (Byck) 297
intersubjective philosophy 246
The IQ Controversary, the Media and Public Policy (Snyderman and Rothman) 41
Iraqi War 165
Irish Book of Kells 116
Isabel Briggs Meyers 125
Islam 153, 304
Israel-Palestinian conflict 165
I-Thou relationships 246–247

Jackson, Craig 268
James, William 1, 2, 4, 5, 173–174, 181, 184, 186–187, 193, 265, 286, 294; functionalism 10–13; pragmatism of 10–13
Janet, Pierre 66, 128, 294
Jedi and the Lotus: Star Wars and the Hindu Tradition (Rosen) 115
Jedi Order 115
Jewish 237, 293
Jews: metaphysical anti-Semitism 231; modernization and technological advancement 231
Jobs, Steve 324
Johns Hopkins University 167–168
Johnson, Lyndon 164
Jonah Complex 265
Jones, Earnest 78, 107
Joseph Campbell and the Power of Myth 115
Journal of Analytical Psychology 109
Journal of Humanistic Psychology 266
Journal of Sandplay Therapy 147
Journal of Transpersonal Psychology 287, 291
Joyce, James 243
Judaism 122, 231, 246
Judas, and the Black Messiah 166
Judeo-Christian values 168, 237, 252
Juliet of the Spirits 119
Jung, Carl 78, 105, 107–109, 115, 136, 146, 243, 262, 267, 286, 298–301, 310; background 113; as a cultural icon 119; *vs.* Freud theories 114; on Marxism 110; political engagement 111; "way of the Dao" 129; wife of 113–114; "Wotan" 112–113
Jung, Emma 107
Jung, Paul Achilles 113
Jungian analytical psychology 109–155; emancipatory opportunities in 154–155; hermeneutic science interest 127–145; historical analysis 109–119; natural science interest 119–127; practice of 145–154

Jungian psychology 131–154; Alcoholics Anonymous 147–150; anima/animus 138–139; archetypes 134–135; collective unconscious 136–137; community mental health systems 155; coursework on unconscious for APA accreditation 155; *A Dangerous Method* 140; discovering symbol(s) 154; draw/color a mandala 154; dream analysis 141–142; emancipatory opportunities in 154–155; individuation 132–134; Jungian analysis 154; *Myers-Briggs Indicator Test* (MBTI) 154; organizational transformation 152; *Read Man and His Symbols and the Red Book* 154; sandplay therapy 145–147, *147*, 154; Self 131–132; serious mental illness and community mental health 150–152; shadow 137–138, 154–155; transference and countertransference 142–145; unidentified flying objects 152–154, *153*; wounded healer archetype 142–145
Jungian Word Association Test 34
Jung's Labyrinth 119
J. Walker Thompson 166

Kabat-Zinn, Jon 220, 222
Kakamad, Karwan 209
Kalashnikov, Mikhail 276
Kalff, Dora 146–147
Kali-Santayana Upanishad 292
Kali Yuga 313–314
Kallikak, Deborah 25
The Kallikak Family: A Study in the Heredity of Feeble Mindedness (Goddard) 25
Kant, Immanuel 240, 246, 254–255
Katherine Cook Briggs 125
Kelley, Douglas 32–33
Kellogg, Joan 134
Kennedy, John 164
Kerenyi, C. 108
Kerr, John 140
Keys, Ancel 27
Kierkegaard, Soren 230, 247–250, 260–263
King, Martin Luther, Jr. 239
Kinsey, Alfred 264
Kirchner, Ernst 268
Kirschenbaum, Howard 232
Kleck, Gary 275
Klein, Melanie 79, 80, 82–83, 84, 86, 146, 243
Klopfer, Bruno 31–32
Kofka, Kurt 241–242, 272
Kohler, Wolfgang 241, 271, 272
Kohut, Heinz 90, 92–93
Korean War 75
Kraepelin, Emil 150
Kreger, D.W. 115
Krimsky, Sheldon 39

Krishna Consciousness Movement 292
Krishna temples 293
Kuhn, Thomas 319
Kundalini yoga 300, 312–313
Kwinter, Michelle 98

Lacan, Jacques 86, 95, 107
Lachman, Janet 206
Lachman, Roy 206
Ladies Home Journal 199
Laing, R. D. 243
laissez-fare group 242
Lalich, Janja 286
Lamarck, Jean 13–14
Lamarck, Jean-Baptiste 120
Lamarckism 14
Lamarckism biological influence 120
Language and Communication (Miller) 202
Larson, Charles 166
Lashley, Karl 243
Launer, John 140
Lavoiser, Antoine 57
Layton, Lynn 54
learning machine 201
Leary, Timothy 236, 286, 289–290, 323, 336
Leibniz, Gottfried Wilhelm 61–62, 120
Leningrad Scientific-Medical Pedological Society 175
Lennon, John 290, 324
Lessing, Gerthold 249
The Les Temps Modernes 243
Levi-Strauss, Claude 95
Lewin, Kurt 242–243, 272
Lewis, Sinclair 176, 190
liberalism 163–164, 166
liberation psychology 308
Liber Novus 116
Liebeault, Ambroise-Auguste 64
limen 62
Lincoln, Abraham 17, 265
Linehan, Marsha 214, 219
linguistic unconscious 96
Lippit, R. 242
Little Albert conditioning 187–188
Little Albert experiment 187–188
Locke, John 163, 164, 166, 171, 189
Loeb, Jacques 176, 181
Logical Investigations (Husserl) 255
logical positivism 164, 195
The Logic of Modern Physic (Bridgman) 195
Logic Theorist 206
logotherapy 271–272, 279
London School of Analytic Psychology 109
Looking for Skinner and Finding Freud (Overskeid) 161
Lorenz, Konrad 84
Love is Never Enough (Beck) 217

Lowen, Alexander 335
Lowenfield, Margaret 145, 146
Lowenfield *World Technique* 146
LSD-25 (Lysergic Acid Diethylamide) 324–325
Lucas, George 115
Luke Skywalker 115
Lundborg, Patrick 320
Lutz, Mark 233
Lux, Kenneth 233

MacDonald, Dwight 165
MacLaine, Shirley 291
Macy Conference 203–204
magnetism 64
magnetoencephalography 297
mahamantra 292
Maharishi Mahesh Yogi 314
Mahayana School of Buddhism 212
maithuna 314
Major Depressive Disorders (MDDs) 220
male-female cultural relationship 238
Malthus, Thomas 15
Maltsberger, John 268
Man and his Symbols (Jung) 129
mandala 132
mandala, draw/color 154
Mandala Assessment Research Instrument (MARI) 134
mandala therapy 134
Manske, Richard 326
Man's Search for Meaning (Frankl) 271
mantramarga 314
Manufacturing Consent, The Political Economy of the Mass Media (Chomsky and Herman) 165
Mapping the Organizational Psyche: A Jungian Theory of Organizational Dynamics and Change (Corlett and Pearson) 152
Mark, Margaret 135
market research 166
Marti, Hans 111
Martin-Baro, Ignacio 308
Marx, Karl 50–51, 56, 164, 237, 249
Marxism 51, 110, 233
Maslow, Abraham 235, 236, 241, 263, 264–266, 269, 286, 301–303
Massachusetts Institute of Technology 202
Masson, Jeffery 70
mass shootings 277
master-slave dialectic 238
material self 11
Maternal Care and Mental Health (Bowlby) 79
maternal deprivation 264
Maternal Warmth Buffers the Effects of Low Early Life Socioeconomic Status of pro-Inflammatory Signaling in Adulthood (Chen, Miller, Kobor and Cole) 85

May, Rollo 113, 233, 236, 237, 262–263, 265, 266, 274, 277, 286
McCarthy, John 205
McCarthyism 51, 165, 232
McCartney, Beatle Paul 324
McDonald vs. the City of Chicago 275
McDougall, William 168, 182–184, 190
McKenzie, Susan 138
MDMA (3,4-Methylenedioxymethamphetamine) 326
The Meaning of Anxiety (May) 262
mechanical baby tender *198*, 198–199
mechanical equilibrium 11
mechanistic behaviorism 193
mechanistic neobehaviorism 191–192
Medicaid 4
Medicare 4
medieval chemistry 121–125
Medieval Islamic science 121
Meetings: Autobiographical Fragments (Buber) 246
Meichenbaum, Donald 217
Mein Kampf: My Struggle (Hitler) 20
Memories, Dreams, Reflections (Jung) 119, 126, 128, 134, 150, 299
Mental and Physical Traits of a Thousand Gifted Children (Terman) 27
mental chemistry 186
mental health services 147–148
The Mental Health through Psychodynamic Perspective: The Relationship between Ego Strength, the Defense Styles, and Object Relations to (Iranian) Mental Health (Leili, Atef, Dehghani and Habbi) 98
The Mentality of Apes (Kohler) 242
Merck Pharmaceutical 326
Merleau-Ponty, Maurice 230, 233, 243–245, 320
mescaline (3,4,5-trimethoxyphenethylamine) 325
Mesmer, Franz 56–58
metaphysical anti-Semitism 231
methodological behaviorism 190
methodology of the oppressed 308
Metropolitan State Mental Hospital 215
Metzner, Ralph 323
Meyer, Frederic 294
Middle Ages 117
Milgram, Stanley 3, 33
military-industrial complex 234
Mill, James 166, 167, 185
Mill, John Stuart 166, 167, 186
Miller, Arthur 262
Miller, George 202
Miller's Analogies Test 34
Miller's Law 202
Mind and Life Institute, Charlottesville, Virginia 220

Mind Cure 12
mindfulness 212, 222
Mindfulness-Based Cognitive Therapy (MBCT) 220–221
Mindfulness-Based Stress Reduction (MBRS) 220
Mind journal 204
Mind over Mood (Greenberger and Padesky) 217
"Minds, Brains and Programs" (Searle) 205
Minnesota Multiphasic Personality Inventory (MMPI) 33–34
Mitchell, Juliet 87
Mitiaufer 231
modern functionalism 211
modernism 137
modern psychology: cultural systems 5; historical analysis of birth of 4–5; political systems 4; socioeconomic systems 4; *see also* psychology
modern science 128
Modern Times 243–244
modern utilitarianism 164, 185
modern yoga practices 312–314
Mohamedmin, Pakistan 209
moksha 288
molecular behaviors 190
molecular purposive behaviorism 191
molecular purposive neobehaviorism 190
Morgan, Christiana 34
Morgan, Conwy Llyod 173
Morgan, Henry 34
Morgan, Thomas 21
Morgan's Canon 173
Moses and Monotheism (Freud) 297
A Most Dangerous Method (Kerr) 140
motor reflexes 180
Moyers, Bill 115
Multidisciplinary Association for Psychedelic Studies (MAPS) 326
multidisciplinary worldview 307
Murguia, Edward 213
Murphy, Michael 236
Murray, Charles 40, 41
Murray, Henry 200
Myers-Briggs Type Indicator Test (MBTI) 125, 154
Mystical Experience Questionnaire (MEQ) 336
myth of rugged individualism 262
Myth of Sisyphus (Camus) 260
mythology 115
Myths to Live By (Campbell) 137

Nader, Tony 315
naïve introspection 6
Napoleonic Wars 58
Narcotics Anonymous 150
Naropa Institute of Colorado 293
nasal reflex neurosis 70
National Academy of Science 291
National Laboratory in Group Development 269
National Liberation Front (NLF) 232
National Rifle Association (NRA) 275
National Socialist German Workers (Nazi) Party 231
Natural Aristotelian philosophy influence 120–121
natural science: attachment theory 85; Darwinian and ethnological influence 84–85; drive theory 82–84; psychophysiological influence 85–86; and relational psychoanalysis 82–86
natural science interest 119–127; in behaviorism 170–184; in cognitive behavioral psychology 202–207; drive theory influence 121; energetics influence 126–127; experimental psychology influence 119–120; in humanistic-existential psychology 240–245; Lamarckism biological influence 120; medieval chemistry – alchemy influence 121–125; *Myers-Briggs Type Indicator* (MBTI) 125; Natural Aristotelian philosophy influence 120–121; in neobehaviorism 190–195; in transpersonal psychology 294–297
natural selection 15
natural teleology 120
Nazi Germany 164
Nazism 20, 112–113, 231, 241, 271
Neisser, Ulric 168, 203
Nelbock, John 164
neobehavioral psychology 197–201; aging 199–200; Aircrib *198*, 198–199; hypnosis 201; mechanical baby tender *198*, 198–199; psychological testing 200; societal engineering 197; teaching machine 199; token economy system 198
neobehaviorism 190–201; computer-assisted education 201; emancipatory opportunities in 201; *Enjoying Old Age: Living Fully Your Later Years* 201; hermeneutic science interest in 195–197; hypnosis 201; logical positivism 195; mechanistic neobehaviorism 191–192; molecular purposive neobehaviorism 190; natural science interest in 190–195; neobehavioral psychology 197–201; one-trial learning and recency principle 192; operant conditioning 193–195; operationalism 195–196; physicalism 196–197; punishment 201; *Walden Two and Beyond Freedom and Dignity* 201
neo-Darwinism 172
Neo-Freudian 216
neo-Lamarckism 14
Neurath, Otto 196

neuro-hypnology 64–66
Neuroscience of the Mind 61
Neurotic Anonymous 150
neurotic anxiety 263
New Age Movement 236, 306
New Deal 164, 167
Newell, Allen 206
The New French Review 243
New Mind Movement 12
New Thought Movement 12
Newton, Issac 170, 171
Newtonian science 170–171
New World Alliance 233
New York Times 293
Nietzsche, Friedrich 107, 129, 164, 230, 237, 246, 250–254
Nietzschean perspectivism 250–254
Nights into Dreams series 119
Nijinsky, Vaslav 268
Nixon, Richard 165, 289
Noble Eighth Path of Buddhist 212, 318
Noble Truths 298
nontraditional socioeconomic visions 233
Northwestern University 164
Novum Organum (Bacon) 171
Nutt, David 296

Obama, Barack 41
Obedience to Authority (Milgram) 3, 33
objective psychological testing 23–26
objective psychology 177–178, 254
Objective Psychology (Bekhterev) 180
objective-relations psychology 82
observational learning 210
Occupy: Reflections on Class War, Rebellion and Solidarity (Chomsky) 165
Occupy Wall Street Movement 165
Ochwiay Biano, 129; *see also* Chief Mountain Lake
Oden, Melita 27
Odyssey (Homer) 260
Oedipal complex 86, 113
Oedipal Complex theory 70–71
Oeric, O. B. 323
Old Saybrook Conference 266
Olsen, Regina 250
one-trial learning theory 192
On the Origin of Species by Means of Natural Selection (Darwin) 5, 15
opened learning 199
operant conditioning 193–195, 214–215
operational definitions 193, 195
operationalism 195–196
Oppenheimer, Jess 27
Organisation Armee Secrete (OAS) 232
organismic valuing system 269
Organizational Complexes 152

Organizational Self 152
Organizational Shadow(s) 152
organizational transformation 152
The Organization of Behavior (Hebb) 207
Origins of Species by Natural Selection or Preservation of the Favored Races in the Struggle for Life (Darwin) 17
Osmond, Humphrey 320, 329
Oss, O. T. 323
Out on a Limb (MacLaine) 291
Overeaters Anonymous 150
Overskeid, Geir 161
overt reflexive behavior 180
Owen, Robert 164
Oxford Group 148

Padesky, Christine 217
Pahnke, Walter 336
Pappenheim, Bertha 69
paradigm shift 319
Parnassian technique 243
participatory epistemology 295
Pavlov, Ivan 166, 167, 178–180, 181, 191, 193, 214
peace movement 239
Pearson, Carol 135, 152
Pearson Correlation Coefficient 23
Pederson, P. 287
perception 7
perennial philosophy 304–307
The Perennial Philosophy (Huxley) 306
Perls, Fritz 235, 236, 243, 272–273, 279
Perls, Laura 243, 272–273
persona 135
personality: ego 72; id 72–73; superego 72–73; theory of 72–73
person-centered dialogic politics 232, 279
person-centered psychology 270
person-centered therapy 278
person-to-person dialogue 232
person-to-person healing 269
Petchkovsky, Leon 119–120
Peter and the Rabbit behavioral therapy 188–189
Peterson, J. 277
Phanes 126–127
The Pharmacology of LSD: A Critical Review (Hentzen and Passie) 325
phenomenological influence 63–64
phenomenological introspection 254
phenomenological psychology 254
phenomenology 254
Phenomenology of Perception (Merleau-Ponty) 244–245
Philadelphia Institute of the American Psychoanalytic Association 216
philosophical suicide 261
philosophy of hylomorphism 120

Philosophy of Mythology (Schelling) 128
Philosophy of the Unconscious (Hartman) 63
phi phenomena 241
phi symbol 241
phrenology 21–22, *22*
physicalism 196–197
Piaget, Jean 140, 209
"Piaget's Factory" 209
Picasso, Pablo 239
Pirsig, Robert 291
Plato 22, 186, 246
Platonic influence 127
Platonism 121
play as tragedy 278
Poetics (Aristotle) 67
political activism 53, 79–80, 111, 231, 244, 259, 307
Political Freud: A History (Zaretsky) 54
The Political Psyche (Samuels) 111
political systems: behavioral psychological movement 163–166; Freudian psychoanalysis 50–54; humanistic-existential (H-E) psychology 231–233; Jungian analytical psychology 109–111; modern psychology 4; relational psychoanalysis 79–80; transpersonal psychology 288–291
Pollack, Jackson 119
Pollan, Michael 293
pop psychology 22, 168
Positive Evolutionary Psychology – Darwin's Guide to a Better life (Geher and Wedbergs) 43
positivism 167, 184–185
postcolonial psychology 307–308
post-Jungian psychology 106–107
post-Jungians 106–107
Power in the Helping Professions (Guggenuhl-Craig) 144
pragmatism 12–13
Pragmatism (James) 12
Pranksters, Merry 324
pre-sectarian Buddhism 317
pre-Socratic Greeks 134
Price, Dick 236, 272
primary consciousness 296
primitivity 117
primordial unity 254
Principles in Psychology (Spencer) 14
Principles of Psychology (James) 10, 294
priti 318
Problem of Adaptation (Hartman) 74
process of freedom 249
Proctor, Robert 211
Project for Scientific Psychology (Freud) 61
projective identification 89–90

projective psychological testing 30–35; Rorschach Test 30–35
Project MK-Ultra 288
Project Pigeon Program 197
Prolegomena to Any Future Metaphysics (Kant) 246
Protection of Lawful Commerce in Arms Act 276
Protestant American culture 168
psilocybin 323–324
Psilocybin: Magic Mushroom Grower's Guide (Oss and Oeric) 323
Psychedelia – An Ancient Culture, A Modern Way of Life (Lundborg) 320
psychedelic-assisted psychotherapy 335–337
psychedelic renaissance period 335–337
psychedelics 319–339, **322**; in Axial Age 320–322; bioenergetic analysis 335; and clinical efficacy 335–337; and government oversight 333–335; Holotropic Breathwork 335; periods 328–329; and psychosis 329; renaissance 319; and unconscious 330–332; underground period 333–335; Unified Psychedelic Theory (UPT) 320–322
psychic x-ray 146, 154
psychoanalysis 161, 193, 215, 297–298; Bertha Pappenheim on 69; Freudian (*see* Freudian psychoanalysis); great schism in 78–79; interpersonal 90–93; relational 50, 78–99
Psychoanalysis, Class and Politics (Layton, Hollander and Gutwill) 54
Psychoanalysis and Feminism: A Radical Reassessment of Freudian Psychoanalysis (Mitchell) 87
Psychoanalysis and Zen Buddhism (Fromm, Suzuki, and DeMartini) 292
Psychoanalysis of Children (Klein) 88
Psychodiagnostics (Rorschach) 31
Psychological Bulletin 317
The Psychological Care of the Infant and Child (Watson and Rayner) 168
psychological clinic 2
psychological genocide 33
Psychological Mountain Climbing and Meditation (Assagioli) 310
Psychological Science 37
psychological testing 1, 21, 43, 200; and family genetics 24–26; and immigration 24–26; objective 23–26
Psychological Types (Jung) 125
Psychological Wednesday Society 107
psychologist's fallacy 11
psychology: and brain 21–22, *22*; clinical 2; cultural 2; developmental 85; folk 5; four forces of 49–50, *50*; genetic 64; history of 339; interpersonal 93; relational psychoanalytic 88–97; and religion 12; struggle for existence 42–43; transpersonal (*see* transpersonal psychology)

Psychology and Alchemy (Jung) 123
Psychology as the Behaviorist Views It (Watson) 181
Psychology from an Empirical Standpoint (Brentano) 64
The Psychology of Kundalini Yoga (Jung) 300
Psychology of the Unconscious (Jung) 126, 298
Psychology's Struggle for Existence (Wundt) 7
psycholytic period 330–332
Psychopathology of Everyday Life (Freud) 68
psychophysics 242
psychophysiological influence 85–86
psychosis 329
psychosynthesis 308–310
Psychosynthesis (Assagioli) 309
Psychotherapy East and West (Watts) 292
psychotomimetic period 329
punishment 201
pure introspection 5
pure phenomenology 254–255
purposive behavior 183
purposive behaviorism 168, 190
purposive hormic behaviorism 182–184
purposive psychology 184
Puysegur, Marquis de 58
Puzzle Box 174–175
Pythagoreanism 121

Q-technique 270
Quakers 168
Quality of Object Relations and Suicidal Ideation Among (Canadian) Community Mental Health Outpatients (Kely and Laverdiere) 98
quantum physics 196
Queering Gender: Anima/Animus and the Paradigm of Emergence (McKenzie) 138
Quimby, Phineas 12

race: Black 5; Darwin on 5
Race, Victor 58
radical behaviorism 190, 191
radical empiricism 294
radical environmentalism 181–182
radical transparency management 317
Raichle, Marcus 296
Raiders of the Lost Ark 130
randomized controlled studies 216
Rank, Otto 272, 331
Raphael 1
Rardin, M.A. 285
rational emotive behavioral therapist (REBT) 215
rationalism 61–62, 137; Enlightenment 128
Rauschenbach, Emma 113
Rauschenbach, Joannes 113
Rayner, Rosalie 167–168
Read Man and His Symbols and the Red Book 154
Read psychology and behaviorists 189
Reagan, Ronald 290

recency principle 192
Recovery-Oriented Cognitive Therapy (CT-R) 218
Red Book: Liber Novus (Jung) 116–119, 151
Redlich, Fredrick 292
Reflective Practice in Infant Mental Health: A South African Perspective (Berg) 98
Reflex Arc Concept in Psychology (Dewey) 187
Reflexes of the Brain (Sechenov) 178
reflexology 180–181
regression to the mean 21
Reich, Theodor 335
Relational Frame Theory (RTP) 220
relational psychoanalysis 50, 78–99; cultural systems 81–82; emancipatory opportunities in 97–99; hermeneutic influences 86–88; historical analysis 78–82; natural science influences 82–86; political systems 79–80; post-freudian world of 78; relational psychoanalytic psychology 88–97; socioeconomic systems 80–81
relational psychoanalytic psychology 88–97; false and true self 90; interpersonal psychoanalysis 90–93; interpersonal self 93–94; projective identification 89–90; symbolic self 95–97; transference and countertransference 88–89; traumatized self 94–95
religion 11, 287–288; and psychology 12
Religion of Humanity 184
Renaissance 1, 121
Responsibilities of Intellectuals: Reflections of Noam Chomsky and Others after 50 years (Allot, Knight, & Smith) 165
The Responsibility of Intellectuals (Chomsky) 165
The Restoration of the Self (Kohut) 93
A Review of B.F. Skinner's Verbal Behavior (Chomsky) 202
Richards, William 336
The Rigveda 321
robotics 170
Rogerian psychology 268–271
Rogers, Carl 232–234, 235, 236, 237, 247, 266, 268–271
Roland, Roman 297–298
Roman Catholic Church 56
Roman Catholicism 184
Romanes, George 172–173
Romano-Lax, Andromeda 168
romanticism 62–63
Romanticism influence 128
Romantic Love Conceptualized as an Attachment Process (Hazan and Shaver) 85
Roosevelt, Franklin 164, 167
Rorschach, Herman 30–31, 35
The Rorschach: A Comprehensive System (Exner) 33

Rorschach Performance Assessment System (R-PAS) 34–35
Rorschach Test 30–35
Rosen, Steven 115
Rosenberg, Alfred 20
Rosenzweig, Saul 38–39
Rosin, Rachael 216
Rossum's Universal Robots (R.U.R) 170
Rotter Incomplete Sentences Blank 34
Rudhyar, Dane 310
Russell, Bertrand 168
Russell, Janice 268
Russian Revolution 178
Rustin, Bayard 239

samatha 212, 317
samsara cycle 19, 287, 314, 318
samudaya 298
Samuels, Andrew 111
sanatana dharma 18
Sanders, Donald 308
Sandison, Ronald 330
Sandplay Therapists of America (STA) 147
sandplay therapy 145–147, *147*, 154
Sandtray therapy 145
Sandtray Therapy in Vulnerable Communities: A Jungian Approach (Zoja) 152
Sartre, Jean-Paul 230, 231–233, 237–238, 243–244, 258–260, 278
Satir, Virginia 233
Satyricon 119
sauvastika 18
Schelling, Friedrich 128
schemas 217
Schindler, Dietrich 111
schizophrenia 31, 93–94, 107
Schlick, Friedrich Albert 164
Schliemann, Heinrich 20
Schoen, David 148
scholar-practitioner model 38
School of Athens (Raphael) 1
Schopenhauer, Arthur 62–63, 252
Schulman, Helen 291
Schwarz, Marcus 317
Science in the Private Interest (Krimsky) 39
Science of Being and the Art of Living (Yogi) 314–315
The Science of Mental Life (Miller) 202
scientific methodology 186
scientific-practitioner model 37–38; *see also* Boulder Model
scientific psychology 193
scientific racist movement 23
Scientific Revolution 1
Searle, John 205
Searls, Damion 30
Sears, Robert 27

Sechenov, Ivan 177
secondary consciousness 296
Second Sex (de Beauvoir) 237
The Secret Chef Revealed (Zeff) 335
The Secret of the Golden Flower: A Chinese Book of Life (Wilhelm) 129, 300
secure attachment 85
Sedlmeier, Peter 317
seduction theory 69–70
Segal, Zindel 220
selective breeding 17
self 131–132, 134, 135, 154; archetypal 131; false 90; interpersonal 93–94; symbolic 95–97; traumatized 94–95; true 90
self-actualization 146, 265, 279
self-esteem 11
self-love 253
self-objects 91
Sen, Indra 286
The Sentence Completion Test 34
Separation: Anxiety and Anger (Bowlby) 80
serious mental illness 150–152
Seven Factors of Awakening in Buddhism 318
Seven Factors of Enlightenment 212
Sexaholics Anonymous 150
The Sexes throughout Nature (Blackwell) 5
sexual attraction 238
sexual freedom 238
sexual relationships 238
Sex Versus Survival: Life and Ideas of Sabina Spielrein (Launer) 140
Sgt. Pepper's Lonely Hearts Club Band 119
shadow 135, 137–138, 154–155
Shadow Man 119
Shakespeare, W. 254
Sharpless, Brian 163
Shaver, Phillip 85
Shaw, J. C. 206
Shulgin, Alexander "Sasha" 326
Shulman, Helene 308
Shurkin, Michael 276
Siddhartha (Hesse) 119
Simon, Herbert 206
Simon, Theodore 24
Singer, Margaret Thaler 286
Skinner, B. F. 161, 168, 176, 185, 192, 193, 194–195, 197–200, 201, 211, 214, 232
Skinner box 194
Skinner-Buzan, Deborah 199
Skinnerian neobehaviorism 165
Slater, Lauren 199
slave psychology 253
Smith, Bob 148
The Snake in the Clinic: Psychotherapy's Role in Medicine and Healing (Dargert) 152
social cognitive theory 211
social conditioning 162

social Darwinism 4, 14
social learning (cognitive) theory 209–211
social liberalism 164
social psychosis 112
Social Security 4
social structuralism 88
societal engineering 161, 197, 232
societal shadow 138
Society for Analytical Psychology (SAP) 107–108
Society for Psychical Research 184
Society for the Investigation of Human Ecology (SIHE) 232–233
Society of Harmony 57–58
Society of Humanistic Psychology 285
socioeconomic systems: behavioral psychological movement 166; Freudian psychoanalysis 54–55; humanistic-existential (H-E) psychology 233–234; Jungian analytical psychology 113–114; modern psychology 4; relational psychoanalysis 80–81; transpersonal psychology 291–292
Socrates 246, 293
Socratic method 246
Some Thoughts on Education (Locke) 189
somnambulism 58
South Africa 232
Soviet communism 233, 244
Soviet Marxism 233, 258
Soviet Union 232
Spearman, Charles 27–28
special education 29
Spence, Kenneth 192, 271
Spencer, Herbert 4, 13–14
Spielberg, Steven 130
Spielrein, Sabina 140
spiritual: emergency counseling 329–330; psychosynthesis 308–310; self-actualization 286
spirituality 287–288, 338
spiritual self 11
spiritus contra spiritium approach 149
spontaneous recovery 179
Spurzheim, Johann 22
Sri Aurobindo 286, 303–304
Stage Theory of Cognitive Development 209
Staggers-Dodd Public Law 333
Star Wars movies 115
state capitalism 258
Stephenson, William 270
Steppenwolf (Hesse) 119
Stern, William 24
Stimulus-Response associations 182
stimulus-response (S-R) behaviors 265
Stoicism 121, 208–209
Stolaroff, Myron 335
Stolorow, Robert 94–95
Stoner, Eugene 276

strange situation research 85
Strassman, Rick 321, 327
Strosahl, Kirk 220
Strozier, Charles 93
structuralism 1, 173, 193; Edward Titchener 8–10
The Structure of Behavior (Merleau-Ponty) 245
The Structure of Scientific Revolutions (Kuhn) 319
Structures of Subjectivity: Explorations of Psychoanalytic Phenomenology (Atwood and Stolorow) 94
Studies in Behavior Therapy (Lindsley, Skinner, and Solomon) 215
Studies on Hysteria (Freud and Breuer) 66, 67
Stumpf, Carl 63
sublimation 298
sukha 318
Sullivan, Harry Stack 93
Summer of Love 235–236
superego 72–73, 82
supramental yoga 303–304
Sutherland, John 98
Suzuki, D. T. 292, 294, 300
Swami Vivekananda 294, 297
swastika: in Buddhism 18–19; in Hinduism 18; Nazism 20
symbol(s): Doubloon 34; of eugenics *18*, 18–20; Hindu 316; of humanistic-existential psychology 229–279; in modern psychology 105–106; of transpersonal psychology 285–339
symbolic artificial intelligence 206
symbolic communication 336
symbolic order 86
symbolic self 95–97
symbolist movement 243
Synchronicity 119
Synthesis of Yoga (Aurobindo) 304
systematic desensitization 189
systematic experimental introspection 9
System of Logic (Mill) 186
systems-of-care approach 99
Systems of Condensed Experience (COEX) 330–332; process 332
Szondi, Leopold 121
Szondi Personality Test 121

Tang Dynasty 212
tantra 314
Tantric yoga 304, 312–314
Tao of Yoda: Based on the Tao Te Ching by Lao Tzu (Kreger) 115
Tao: The Watercourse Way (Watts) 321
Tavistock Institute of Human Relations Institute (TIHR) 243
teaching machine 199
Teachings of Dan Juan (Castaneda) 291
Teasdale, John 220

Telesphorus 124
tenderminded personalities 12
Terman, Lewis 26–27, 29
termination 68–69
Termites 27; *see also* gifted children
"The Magical Number Seven, Plus or Minus Two: Some Limits on Our Capacity for Processing Information" (Miller) 202
Thematic Appreciation Test 34, 200
theoneurology 321
theoretical computer science 204
The Theory and Practice of Group Psychotherapy (Yalom) 274
Therapeutae of Asclepius 131
therapeutic 131
thermodynamic influence 58–59
The Third of May (Goya) 239
Thirty Years War 153
Thorndike, Edward 28, 173–175, 181, 191, 192, 193, 241, 264
Thus Spoke Zarathustra (Nietzsche) 246, 252
The Tibetan Book of Great Liberation (Jung) 300
Tibetan Buddhism 133
Tibetan mandala 134
Titchener, Edward 1, 173, 193, 240; structuralism 8–10
token economies 198
token economy system 198
Tolman, Edward 164–165, 168, 190
totalitarianism 163
toughminded personalities 12
Toward a Psychology of Being (Maslow) 286
transcendental art 310–311
transcendental idealism 62
transcendental-idealist philosophy 254
transcendental meditation 314–317, 338
Transcendental Meditation 293
transcendental movement 315
transcendental realism 63
transcendent function 300
transdiagnostic efficacy 292
transference 68–69, 142–145; relational psychoanalytic psychology 88–89; rupture 89
transpersonal psychology 2, 42, 184; Axial Age 285–286, 308–319; criticism 286–287; cultural systems 292–293; hermeneutic science interest in 297–308; historical analysis of 288–293; natural science interest in 294–297; political systems 288–291; and psychedelics 319–339; and religion 287–288; socioeconomic systems 291–292; and spirituality 287–288; symbols of 285–339; transpersonal renaissance 285–286
Transpersonal Psychology Interest Group (TPIG) 285

transpersonal psychotherapy 338
transpersonal renaissance 285
traumatized self 94–95
Tridimensional Wundtian Theory of Feeling 7
tropism 175–177, 189
true self 90
Turing, Alan 168–169, 204–205
The Turing Test 204
Turner, Barbara 147
Tuskegee Experiments 233
Twain, Mark 176
Twelve Step programs 150

unconditioned reflexes (UCRs) 179
unconscious: Alternate Consciousness Paradigm (ACP) 66; in education 99; evolution of 63; feminine energy 138; Hartmann on 63; linguistic 96; mind 77; shadow 138; universal 68
The Undiscovered Self (Jung) 109
unidentified areal phenomena (UAP) 152
Unidentified Flying Objects (UFOs) 152–154, *153*
Unified Psychedelic Theory (UPT) 320–322
Union Theological Seminary 237
universal education 24
universal necessity for rapprochement *253*
universal unconscious 68
University of Berlin 242
University of California, Berkeley (UCB) 165, 190
University of Chicago 181
University of Frankfurt 241
University of Freiburg 231
University of Vienna 164
University of Zurich 267
utilitarianism 185–186

Vail Model 38
Vaishnava mantra 292
vamamarga yoga 314
Vandereycken, Walter 268
The Varieties of Religious Experience (James) 12, 294
Vaughan, Margaret 201
Vaughn, Margaret 199–200
Vedanta 304
Vedanta philosophy 294, 305
Vedas 300, 312
verbal summator 200
Veterans Administration (VA) 37
vicara 318
Victorian culture 248
Vienna Circle 164, 195
Vienna Peace Project 232
Vietnam War 75, 165, 232, 239
The Violence Project: How to Stop A Mass Shooting Epidemic (Peterson and Densley) 277

vipassana 317–318
Vipassana 212
Vision of Zosimus (Zosimus) 124
vitarka 318
voluntarism 1; experimental introspection 5; naïve introspection 6; pure introspection 5; Wilhelm Wundt 5–8
Von Daniken, Erich 152

Walden Two (Skinner) 197, 201
Wallace, Henry 15
Warburg, Aby 268
War of the Gods in Addiction: C.J Jung, Alcoholics Anonymous and Archetypal Evil (Schoen) 148
Washburn, Margaret 9, 173
Washington, Booker T. 184
Watkins, Mary 308
Watson 167–168, 193, 211
Watson, John 166, 176, 181, 182–183, 214
Watsonian behaviorism 182, 185, 189
Watsonian psychology 166
Watts, Alan 286, 292, 321
Weaver, E. G. 327
Wechsler, David 29–30
Wechsler Adult Intelligence Scale (WAIS) 30
Wechsler Intelligence for Children (WISC) 30
Wechsler tests 26, 29–30
Wedbergs, Nicole 43
Weiner, Nerbert 168
Wells, H.G. 145
Weltanschauung 267
Wertheimer, Max 237, 241, 242, 263, 272
Western alchemy 121
Western Behavioral Sciences Institute (WBSI) 269
Western Civilization 153
Western culture 134
Western esoterism 123
Western philosophy 251
What's Wrong with the Rorschach? Science Confronts the Controversial Inkblot Test (Wood, Nerzworski and Lilenfield) 34
When Absence Speaks Louder than Words: A Object Relational Perspective on No- Show Appointments (Kwinter) 98
Wherever You Go, There You Are (Kabat-Zinn) 220
White, R.K. 242
Whitman, Marie "Blanche" 65
Whitman, Walt 11
"Why Are We Not Acting to Save the World" (Skinner) 161

Why Did Wundt Abandon his Early Theory of the Unconscious (Araujo) 7
Wiener, Norbert 203–204
Wilber, Ken 286, 303, 304–307
Wilhelm, Richard 129, 300
Williams, Mark 220
Wilson, Kelly 220
Wilson, William Griffith 148
Winnicott, Donald 89
Wissler, Clark 23
Witner, Lightner 2, 36
Wolf, Virginia 243
Wolfe, Tom 324
womb envy 86–87
women: as imperfect men 238; as second sex 238
Woodworth, Robert 191–192
Word Association Test 119–120, 128, 140
The World as Will and Representation (Schopenhauer) 62
World Health Organization 144
World Making hermeneutic sandtray approach 146
World War II 125, 165, 193, 197, 233, 239, 243, 307
"Wotan" (Jung) 112–113
wounded healer archetype 142–145
Wundt, Wilhelm 1–2, 4, 5, 23, 62, 64, 107, 240; voluntarism 5–8

Yaghan peoples of Tierra del Fuego (Yannielli) 17
Yalom, Irvin 236, 273–274
yantra 133
Yeats, W. B. 243
yin/yang 131
yoga 312; Hatha 312, 338; integral psychology 303–304; Kundalini 300, 312–313; modern practices 312–314; as spiritual practice 338; supramental 303–304; Tantric 304, 312–314; vamamarga 314
Yoga Sutras of Patanjali 312

Zaretsky, Eli 54
Zeff, Leo 334–335
Zen and the Art of Motorcycle Maintenance (Pirsig) 291
Zen Buddhism 212
The Zen of R2-D2: Ancient Wisdom from a Galaxy Far, Far Away (Borotlin) 115
Zionism 231
Zoja, Eva Pattis 152
Zoroastrian 293
Zoroastrianism 60, 308, 310–312
Zosimos of Panoplies 124